BRASS BIBLIOGRAPHY

BRASS BIBLIOGRAPHY

SOURCES ON THE HISTORY, LITERATURE, PEDAGOGY
PERFORMANCE, AND ACOUSTICS OF
BRASS INSTRUMENTS

Mark J. Fasman

INDIANA UNIVERSITY PRESS

BLOOMINGTON AND INDIANAPOLIS

Manufactured in the United States of America

Library of Congress Cataloging-in-Publication Data

Fasman, Mark J.
    Brass bibliography : sources on the history, literature, pedagogy,
performance, and acoustics of brass instruments / Mark J. Fasman.
        p.   cm.
    Includes index,
    ISBN 0-253-32130-1   '000057112
    1. Brass instruments—Bibliography.   I. Title.
ML128.W5F3   1990
016.7889—dc20   89-45198
                                                                 CIP
                                                                 MN

        1 2 3 4 5   94 93 92 91 90

It is written that, to achieve a measure of immortality, one should plant a tree, have a child, and write a book. It is to my dear wife, Alice, an exceptional woman with whom it has been my great joy to complete each of these three goals, that I lovingly dedicate this book.

BRASS BIBLIOGRAPHY

Errata

In entries 1585-1591, on p. 115, the author's name should read Smithers, Don L. It is also cited incorrectly on pp. 288 and 399.

CONTENTS

Part IV: ACOUSTICS AND CONSTRUCTION

ACKNOWLEDGMENTS

A project such as this would not be possible without the significant contributions of many persons. Perhaps most important is Charles Gorham, chair of the Brass Department at Indiana University. His was the initial idea for a project of this kind and his many suggestions helped me to organize and develop this bibliography. Additionally, I am thankful for the support given me by the other members of my doctoral committee: Keith Brown, Philip Farkas, and Harvey Phillips.

I received helpful ideas about the design and implementation of the computer programs necessary to generate this bibliography from many quarters. However, without the expert advice and guidance of Leonard Shapiro, currently chair of Computer Sciences at Portland (Oregon) State University, this project could never have been completed as efficiently or as quickly. Dr. Shapiro provided invaluable assistance in all levels of computer usage, from recommending hardware configurations and commercial software packages to suggesting software design compatible with my own bibliographic concept to actual assistance with writing and debugging the programs.

Friends and family members encouraged me to continue with this large undertaking and offered important substantive suggestions as well as moral support. Among them are Larry Fisher, Joel Charon, and Kathryn Talalay.

Finally, I am grateful to my parents, Jack and LaVerne Fasman, who taught me the value of books and the importance of perseverence, and who provided me with models of excellence and dedication.

PREFACE

When Charles Gorham suggested that a comprehensive bibliography of sources related to brass instruments might be a worthwhile topic for a doctoral document, my first response was to agree. Eleven years later, two years after the completion of that document, I still agree.

The scholarly study of brass instruments is a relatively new endeavor. With increased interest in historical and scientific research has come a demand for both sources to study and reference works which identify those sources. The establishment of the four professional brass societies (Tubists Universal Brotherhood Association, International Horn Society, International Trombone Association, and International Trumpet Guild) has been a primary stimulus for research, and the respective societies' journals have provided a forum for the presentation of that research. These publications, in conjuction with other journals devoted to brass instruments (including *Brass Quarterly, Brass Bulletin—International Brass Chronicle, Sounding Brass & the Conductor*) and coupled with the dramatic growth of graduate programs specializing in brass research and performance, have resulted in the production of a vast body of data, opinions, and resources.

Specialized bibliographies are regularly published as appendices to research papers or as articles in periodicals. Other major reference works, such as *RILM Abstracts* and *Music Index*, include references to brass instruments within their otherwise global music listings. However, neither format provides a single-volume compilation of all brass references. In particular, most of these bibliographies are date-specific, that is, they list citations for a particular month, year, or group of years.

A classified bibliography begins to address the issue of management of this enormous body of information. Most important among the classified bibliographies is the series published by Mary Rasmussen in *Brass Quarterly*. This monumental reference work is a mainly unannotated listing of available resources grouped in ten-year divisions (with several single-year compilations after 1960.) Unfortunately, the project terminated in 1962. Since that time, researchers have had to rely on other major reference works (such as *Music Index*, *RILM*, *Dissertation Abstracts*, and *New York Public Library Catalog* to identify potentially useful sources.

The present bibliography is primarily an extension of the Rasmussen compilations. A few entries date from the late eighteenth century, but mainly the period covered is 1820 to 1988. My criteria for listing a work are:

1. It is a prose writing in book, journal, or dissertation form (but I have intentionally not included reviews and most regular feature articles).

2. It appears in one or more of the following sources: Rasmussen bibliographies

as published in *Brass Quarterly; Music Index*, 1962–January, 1988; *RILM Abstracts*, 1967–1975; *Catalog of the New York Public Library Music Collection*; Adkins and Dickinson, *Doctoral Dissertations in Musicology* (1984); *T.U.B.A. Journal; T.U.B.A. Newsletter; The Horn Call; Journal of the International Trombone Association; Journal of the International Trumpet Guild*.

3. It is written in English, German, French or Italian.

The Rasmussen bibliographies and *Music Index* served as models for the classification system. The four general categoraies—Reference and Research Materials; History and Music Literature; Pedagogy, Study and Technique; and Acoustics and Construction—are further subdivided into specific areas. It soon became clear that the focus of publication had changed over the years and that the classification system should reflect new area of research. For example, the frequency of writings under the heading "Brass Bands" dropped significantly after 1970. Conversely, the number of articles on medical and dental topics did not merit a separate heading until approximately 1970. Some other headings which were added after the initial model was established are: "Performer and Composer Lists and Directories," "Research Techniques," "Jazz/Popular Styles," "Careers/Career Development," "Selecting and Purchasing Equipment," and "Mutes/Accessories."

Every attempt has been made to assure accuracy and comprehensiveness. However, given the fact that there are over 6,000 citations, most of which were gleaned from other reference works, it is inevitable that some inaccuracy exists. I would be most grateful to receive corrections, additions, and comments on format. I apologize to those whose publications have been ommitted or mis-cited.

The availability of published research has always been of critical importance to scholars and performers. But now, with the explosion of information in all areas of brass research, the primary problem is rapidly becoming identification of appropriate sources for study. It is my hope that this bliography will alleviate that problem.

PART I

REFERENCE AND RESEARCH MATERIALS

Bibliographies

1 Agrell, Jeffrey. "Index to periodical articles on the horn: additions and corrections." *The Horn Call* 9, no. 2 (Apr. 1979): 58–64.

2 Agrell, Jeffrey. "An indexed bibliography of periodical articles (Part I)." *The Horn Call* 6, no. 2 (1976): 51–55.

3 Agrell, Jeffrey. "An indexed bibliography of periodical articles on the horn (Part II)." *The Horn Call* 7, no. 1 (Nov. 1976): 45–50.

4 Agrell, Jeffrey. "Indexed bibliography of articles (Part III)." *The Horn Call* 7, no. 2 (May 1977): 49–56.

5 Agrell, Jeffrey. "A tentative bibliography of masters' theses and doctoral dissertations." *The Horn Call* 8, no. 1 (Nov. 1977): 44–47.

6 Arling, H. J. "Trombone chamber music: an annotated bibliography." *Music Educators Journal* 66 (Sept. 1979): 88.

7 Arling, H. J. *Trombone chamber music: an annotated bibliography.* Nashville: Brass Press, 1978.

8 Arling, H. J. *Trombone chamber music: an annotated bibliography.* Enlarged 2nd edition. Nashville: Brass Press, 1983.

Baird, Frank W. "A history and annotated bibliography of tutors for trumpet and cornet." *Dissertation Abstracts* 44 (Dec. 1983): 1719A.

Bell. "A bibliographic survey of the horn in chamber music, 1950–1830." *The Horn Call* 17, no. 2 (Apr. 1987): 37–44.

Bradley, Mary E. "The establishment of performance practice for the horn." *The Horn Call* 7, no. 1 (Nov. 1976): 29–31.

9 "Brass dissertations." *Journal of the International Trombone Association* 8 (1980): 12.

Brüchle, Bernhard. *Horn-Bibliographie, I-II.* Wilhelmshaven: Heinrichshofen, 1970.

10 Brüchle, Bernhard, and D. Lienhard. *Horn bibliographie, Band III: Ergänzungen zu den Ausgaben von 1970 und 1975.* Wilhelmshaven: Heinrichshofen, 1983.

11 Bryant, Steven, comp. "*T.U.B.A. Journal* index, volumes VII-VIII." *T.U.B.A. Journal* 9, no. 1 (Summer 1981): 45+.

12 Buckner, J. F. "A touch of brass." *Journal of Church Music* 18 (Feb. 1976): 11–13.

Decker, C. F. "Trumpet research: a selective bibliography." *The Instrumentalist* 27 (May 1973): 56+.

Dudgeon, R. T. "A handbook for the cornetto." *Journal of the International Trumpet Guild* 1 (1976): 30–34.

13 Fasman, Mark J. "A selected bibliography of literature related to brass instruments." D.Mus. diss., Indiana University, 1988.

14 Faulkner, Maurice. "Trumpet and French horn [1982–83 publications]." *The Instrumentalist* 38 (Dec. 1983): 42+.

15 Faust, Randall E. "An index of reviews of music and books printed in *The Horn Call*, volumes I-XI." *The Horn Call* 13, no. 1 (Oct. 1982): 93–97.

Fitzgerald, Bernard. "Research studies in brass." *The Instrumentalist* 3 (Nov.-Dec. 1948): 15.

16 Gates, C. R. "A selective annotated bibliography of articles published in English concerning history, development, and use of soprano brass instruments in the nineteenth century." *Journal of the International Trumpet Guild* 11, no. 2 (1986): 30–33.

17 Glover, S. L. "A list of brass dissertations 1976–1977." *Journal of the International Trumpet Guild* 2 (1977): 48. Reprinted in *Newsletter of the International Trombone Association* 5, no. 2 (1977): 5.

18 Glover, S. L. "A list of brass dissertations since 1972." *Journal of the International Trumpet Guild* 1 (1976): 36–38.

19 Hill, Douglas. "Self development and the performance of music." *The Horn Call* 18, no. 2 (Apr. 1988): 45.

Hill, J. "Performance practices of the 16th, 17th, and 18th centuries: a few practical references for the trombonist [includes select discography and bibliography]." *Journal of the International Trombone Association* 9 (1981): 20–23.

20 Hills, Ernie M., Jr. "Medicine and dentistry for brass players: a selected survey of recent research in the journal literature." *Journal of the International Trombone Association* 15, no. 4 (Fall 1987): 32–37.

21 "Index to *The Horn Call*, volumes I-X." *The Horn Call* 10, no. 2 (Apr. 1980): 96–104.

22 "Index to *The Horn Call*, volume XI." *The Horn Call* 11, no. 2 (1981): 93–94.

23 "Index to *The Horn Call*, volume XIII." *The Horn Call* 13, no. 2 (Apr. 1983): 79.

24 "Index to *The Horn Call*, volume XV." *The Horn Call* 15, no. 2 (Apr. 1985): 92.

25 Jenkins, R. M. "An annotated bibliography of periodical articles related to the bass trombone." *Journal of the International Trombone Association* 11, no. 4 (1983): 7–12.

26 Kohlenberg, R. "Preliminary results of a survey of trombone related research." *Journal of the International Trombone Association* 15, no. 2 (1987): 18–19.

Lewy, Rudolf. "Trombone basso." *Journal of the International Trombone Association* 5 (1977): 10–22.

27 Lindahl, Charles E. "Music periodicals: woodwinds and brass." *Notes—Music Library Association* 32, no. 3 (Mar. 1976): 558–566.

Mathie, Gordon W. "Trumpet transposition: One teacher's approach." *Brass and Percussion* 2, no. 4 (1974): 18–19 +. Includes bibliography.

28 Palmatier, T. H. "A partially annotated bibliography of tuba-related articles from Jan. 1950 to Sept. 1975." *NACWPI Journal* 25, no. 4 (1977): 37–41.

29 Popiel, Peter. "Thirty years of periodical articles concerning the baritone horn and euphonium: a compilation indexed by author." *T.U.B.A. Journal* 10,

no. 3 (Winter 1983): 6–7.

30 Rasmussen, Mary. "Brass bibliography: 1820–1829, and Addenda, 1830–1839." *Brass Quarterly* 7, no. 4 (1964): 194–197.

31 Rasmussen, Mary. "Brass bibliography: 1830–1839." *Brass Quarterly* 7, no. 3 (1964): 133–136.

32 Rasmussen, Mary. "Brass bibliography: 1840–1849." *Brass Quarterly* 7, no. 2 (1963): 78–81.

33 Rasmussen, Mary. "Brass bibliography: 1850–1859." *Brass Quarterly* 6, no. 4 (1964): 187–189.

34 Rasmussen, Mary. "Brass bibliography: 1860–1869." *Brass Quarterly* 5, no. 4 (1962): 17–22.

35 Rasmussen, Mary. "Brass bibliography: 1870–1879." *Brass Quarterly* 5 (1962): 114–116.

36 Rasmussen, Mary. "Brass bibliography: 1880–1889." *Brass Quarterly* 5 (1961): 34–36.

37 Rasmussen, Mary. "Brass bibliography: 1890–1899." *Brass Quarterly* 4 (1961): 168–172.

38 Rasmussen, Mary. "Brass bibliography: 1900–1905." *Brass Quarterly* 4 (1961): 129–132.

39 Rasmussen, Mary. "Brass bibliography: 1906–1910, and addenda, 1911–1955." *Brass Quarterly* 4 (1960): 90–94.

40 Rasmussen, Mary. "Brass bibliography: 1911–1915, and addenda, 1916–1955." *Brass Quarterly* 3 (1960): 166–170.

41 Rasmussen, Mary. "Brass bibliography: 1916–1920, and addenda, 1921–1955." *Brass Quarterly* 3 (1960): 114–116.

42 Rasmussen, Mary. "Brass bibliography: 1921–1925, and addenda, 1926–1955." *Brass Quarterly* 3 (1959): 67–72.

43 Rasmussen, Mary. "Brass bibliography: 1926–1930, and addenda, 1931–1955." *Brass Quarterly* 2 (1959): 158–166.

44 Rasmussen, Mary. "Brass bibliography: 1931–1935." *Brass Quarterly* 2 (1959): 117–125.

45 Rasmussen, Mary. "Brass bibliography: 1936–1940, and addenda, 1941–1955." *Brass Quarterly* 2 (1958): 63–77.

46 Rasmussen, Mary. "Brass bibliography: 1941–1945, and addenda, 1946–1955." *Brass Quarterly* 1 (1958): 232–239.

47 Rasmussen, Mary. "Brass bibliography: 1946–1950, and addenda, 1951–1955." *Brass Quarterly* 1 (1958): 168–181.

48 Rasmussen, Mary. "Brass bibliography: 1951–1955." *Brass Quarterly* 1 (1957): 93–102.

49 Rasmussen, Mary. "Brass bibliography: 1957, and addenda, 1956." *Brass Quarterly* 2 (1958): 12–19.

50 Rasmussen, Mary. "Brass bibliography: 1958, and addenda, 1956–1957." *Brass Quarterly* 3 (1959): 21–26.

51 Rasmussen, Mary. "Brass bibliography: 1959, and addenda, 1956–1958." *Brass Quarterly* 4 (1960): 30–34.

52   Rasmussen, Mary. "Brass bibliography: 1960, and addenda, 1959." *Brass Quarterly* 5 (1961): 69–72.

53   Rasmussen, Mary. "Brass bibliography: 1961, and addenda, 1958–1960." *Brass Quarterly* 6, no. 1 (1962): 17–22.

54   Rasmussen, Mary. "Brass bibliography: 1962, and addenda, 1959–1961." *Brass Quarterly* 7, no. 1 (1963): 45–49.

      Reynolds, G. E. "New books and methods on brasses." *The School Musician* 36 (Oct. 1964): 14+.

      Riley, Maurice W. "A tentative bibliography of early wind instrument tutors." *Journal of Research in Music Education* 6 (1958): 3–24.

      Roberts, J. "Current research relating to the trombone." *Journal of the International Trombone Association* 12, no. 1 (1984): 31–32.

55   Roznoy, R. T. "A selected bibliography of English language material relevant to the trombone." *Journal of the International Trombone Association* 4 (1976): 23–29.

56   Rutan, Harold Duane. "An annotated bibliography of written material pertinent to the performance of brass and percussion chamber music." Ed.D. diss., University of Illinois, 1960.

57   Rutan, Harold Duane. "An annotated bibliography of written material pertinent to the performance of brass and percussion chamber music." *Dissertation Abstracts* 21 (1961): 3481–3482.

58   Smith, D. L. "A selected periodical index for trumpet." *International Trumpet Guild Newsletter* 7, no. 3 (1981): 24–25.

59   Sorenson, Scott Paul. "Printed trumpet instruction to 1835." *Journal of the International Trumpet Guild* 12, no. 1 (1987): 4–14.

      Streeter, Thomas W. "The historical and musical aspects of the 19th century bass trombone." *Journal of the International Trombone Association* 4 (Jan. 1976): 33–36; 5 (Jan. 1977): 25–35.

60   Streeter, Thomas W. "Survey and annotated bibliography on the historical development of the trombone." *Journal of the International Trombone Association* 7 (1979): 27–32.

61   Stuart, D., comp. "Brass research projects." *Journal of the International Trombone Association* 10, no. 4 (1982): 5–9.

      Turrentine, Edgar M. "The history of brass instruments in ancient times: a bibliographic essay." *NACWPI Journal* 21, no. 3 (Spring 1973): 29–30.

      Turrentine, Edgar M. "The physiological aspect of brasswind performance technique: a bibliographic essay." *NACWPI Journal* 26, no. 2 (Nov. 1977): 3–5.

      Varner, J. L. "Anthology of tuba writings." *Brass and Percussion* 1, no. 5 (1973): 13–14.

62   Vivona, Peter M. "Theater techniques in recent music for the trombone [includes bibliography of theater]." *Journal of the International Trombone Association* 10, no. 2 (1982): 20–25.

      Wekre, Froydis Ree. "The Leningrad school of horn playing." *The Horn Call* 10, no. 1 (Oct. 1979): 92–95.

63   Winter, James H. "Books about the horn." *Woodwind World* 3, no. 3 (1961): 12.

Catalogs/Collections

Anderson, S. C. "Selected works from the 17th century music collection of Prince-Bishop Karl Liechtenstein-Kastelkorn: a study of the soloistic use of the trombone." *Journal of the International Trombone Association* 11, no. 1 (1983): 17–20.

Anderson, S. C. "Selected works from the 17th century music collection of Prince-Bishop Karl Liechtenstein-Kastelkorn: a study of the soloistic use of the trombone." *Journal of the International Trombone Association* 11, no. 2 (1983): 35–38.

Anderson, S. C. "Selected works from the 17th century music collection of Prince-Bishop Karl Liechtenstein-Kastelkorn: a study of the soloistic use of the trombone." *Journal of the International Trombone Association* 11, no. 3 (1983): 29–32.

Anderson, S. C. "Selected works from the 17th century music collection of Prince-Bishop Karl Liechtenstein-Kastelkorn: a study of the soloistic use of the trombone." *Journal of the International Trombone Association* 11, no. 4 (1983): 20–22.

Anderson, S. C. "Selected works from the 17th century music collection of Prince-Bishop Karl Liechtenstein-Kastelkorn: a study of the soloistic use of the trombone." *Journal of the International Trombone Association* 12, no. 1 (1984): 33–37.

Anderson, S. C. "Selected works from the 17th century music collection of Prince-Bishop Karl Liechtenstein-Kastelkorn: a study of the soloistic use of the trombone." *Journal of the International Trombone Association* 12, no. 2 (1984): 32–38.

64   Archambo, L. O. "Dissertation reviews: The Lumir C. Havlicek Band Music Collection at the University of Kansas." *Journal of the International Trumpet Guild* 10, no. 2 (1985): 33–36.

65   "Artifacts in the Military Museum and the National Museum in Budapest." *Brass Bulletin—International Brass Chronicle*, no. 48 (1984): 48–61. Also in French and German.

66   Baines, Anthony. *The Bate Collection of historical wind instruments: catalogue of the instruments*. Oxford: Oxford University Press, 1976.

67   Banks, M. D. "17th- and 18th-century brass instruments at the Shrine to Music Museum." *Brass Bulletin—International Brass Chronicle*, no. 58 (1987): 50–59. Also in French and German.

68   Bell, R. E. "Natural trumpets of Leningrad; a description of the natural trum-

pets in the Exhibition of Musical Instruments of the Leningrad Institute of Theater, Music and Cinematography, Leningrad, U.S.S.R." *Journal of the International Trumpet Guild* 7, no. 4 (1983): 10–11 + .

Bernouilli, W. "Meine Sammlung historischer Blechblasinstrumente und Trommeln." *Brass Bulletin—International Brass Chronicle*, no. 5–6 (1973): 85–92. Also in English and French.

69   "Blechblasinstrumente auf der Messe '87 (Frankfurt)." *Musik International-Instrumentenbau-Zeitschrift* 41 (Mar. 1987): 232 + .

70   Boeringer, J., ed. "Instruments like those of the Twenty-Sixth Regimental Band: a catalogue of the Mark Allen Elrod Collection." *The Moravian Music Foundation Bulletin* 26, no. 3 (1981): 60 + .

Bowsher, J. M., and P. S. Watkinson. "Manufacturers' opinions about brass instruments [catalog excerpts]." *Brass Bulletin—International Brass Chronicle*, no. 38 (1982): 25–30. Also in French and German.

"Catalogue general des cuivres." *Brass Bulletin—International Brass Chronicle*, no. 16 (1976): whole issue. Also in English and German.

Chesebro, Gayle, and Philip Paul. "The International Horn Society Archive—a resource for regional workshops." *The Horn Call* 16, (June 1986): 58–59.

71   Conner, Rex A. "Massed ensemble library." *T.U.B.A. Journal* 7, no. 2 (Fall 1979): 34.

Corley, R., comp. *Brass players' guide to the literature, 1973–74.* North Easton, MA: Robert King Music Company, 1974.

72   "Deutsche Demokratische Republik: Repräsentativer Metallblasinstrumenten-Katalog." *Brass Bulletin—International Brass Chronicle*, no. 35 (1981): 11–111. Also in French and English.

73   Dolak, Deb, comp. "More tapes [IHS Archives]." *The Horn Call* 16, (June 1986): 38–39.

74   Dolak, Deb. "Music listening center [IHS Archives]." *The Horn Call* 16, (June 1986): 32–37.

75   Dressler, John. "The IHS Archive: source for historical research." *The Horn Call* 15, no. 2 (Apr. 1985): 34–35.

76   Dressler, John. "The IHS Archive: source for historical research." *The Horn Call* 16, (June 1986): 56–57. Reprinted from *The Horn Call* 15, no. 2 (Apr. 1985).

"E flat, D, and E flat/D trumpet directory [products available in England]." *Sounding Brass & the Conductor* 6, no. 2 (1977): 62.

77   "E flat soprano cornet directory." *Sounding Brass & the Conductor* 6, no. 3 (1977): 101.

78   Ehnes, Fred Rickard. "A guide to the archive of the International Horn Society 1969–1977 at Alexander M. Bracken Library, Ball State University, Muncie, Indiana." *Dissertation Abstracts* 43 (Sept. 1982): 579A + .

79   Ehnes, Fred Rickard. "A guide to the archive of the International Horn Society 1969–1977 at Alexander M. Bracken Library, Ball State University, Muncie, Indiana." D.A. diss., Ball State University, 1982.

Eliason, Robert E. "The Meachams, musical instrument makers of Hartford and Albany (includes list of known Meacham instruments)." *Journal of the American Musical Instrument Society* 5 (1980–81): 69–70.

80   Farrar, Lloyd P., and Frank Kaderabek. "Sound the trumpet! News from the Trumpet Museum." *Journal of the International Trumpet Guild* 12, no. 1 (1987): 56.

Farrar, Lloyd P. "Sound the trumpet! News from the Trumpet Museum." *Journal of the International Trumpet Guild* 12, no. 2 (1987): 43–44.

Garofalo, R., and M. Elrod. "Heritage Americana: reflections on the performance practices of mid-nineteenth century brass bands." *Journal of Band Research* 7, no. 1 (1981): 1–26. Includes partial listing of Elrod and Garofalo collections.

81   Geiser, Brigitte, and Markus Römer. *Das Alphorn in der Schweiz. Katalog zur Ausstellung im Heimatmuseum Grindelwald Sommer 1972*. Grindelwald: Buchdruckerei Grindelwald, 1972.

82   Haine, M., and I. de Keyser. "Catalogue des instruments Sax au Musee Instrumental de Bruxelles." *Brussels Museum of Musical Instruments* 9–10, nos. 1–2 (1979–1980): entire issue.

83   Halfpenny, Eric. "The Christ Church trophies [zink]." *The Galpin Society Journal* 28 (Apr. 1975): 81–85.

84   Hancock, John M. "The horns of the Stearns Collection." *The Horn Call* 14, no. 2 (Apr. 1984): 60–71.

85   Heyde, Herbert. *Trompeten, Posaunen, Tuben*. Katalog. Musikinstrumenten-Museum der Karl-Marx-Universität, no. 3. Leipzig: VEB Deutscher Verlag für Musik, 1980.

86   Kappel, L. "Die Trompeteninstrumente des Ungarischen Nationalmuseums in Budapest." *Brass Bulletin—International Brass Chronicle*, no. 48 (1984): 64–70. Also in English and French.

87   Kitzel, Larry. "The trombones of the Shrine to Music Museum." *Dissertation Abstracts* 46 (Oct. 1985): 832A.

88   Kitzel, Larry. "The trombones of the Shrine to Music Museum." D.M.A. diss., University of Oklahoma, 1985.

89   Larson, André Pierre. "Catalog of the nineteenth-century British brass instruments in the Arne B. Larson Collection of Musical Instruments." *Dissertation Abstracts* 35 (June 1975): 7946A.

90   Larson, André Pierre. "Catalogue of the nineteenth-century British brass instruments in the Arne B. Larson Collection of Musical Instruments." Ph.D. diss., West Virginia University, 1974.

91   Laudermilch, Kenneth L. "The Streitweiser Trumpet Museum (Pottstown, PA)." *International Trumpet Guild Newsletter* 8, no. 2 (1982): 18–21.

92   McSweeney, A. "Publishers of brass music directory." *Sounding Brass & the Conductor* 7, no. 3 (1978): 95–98.

93   Marsh, Robert E. "IHS Archive update/report." *The Horn Call* 16, (June 1986): 8–9.

94   Mathez, Jean-Pierre. "Trumpet museum Bad Säckingen." *Brass Bulletin—*

International Brass Chronicle, no. 53 (1986): 17–27. Also in French and German.

95 Moege, Gary Ray. "A catalog of the alto brass instruments in the Arne B. Larson Collection of Musical Instruments." *Dissertation Abstracts* 46 (May 1986): 3187A.

96 Moege, Gary Ray. "A catalog of the alto brass instruments in the Arne B. Larson Collection of Musical Instruments." D.M.A. diss., University of Oklahoma, 1985.

97 Older, J. "The lady bugler." *The School Musician* 52 (Oct. 1980): 10–11 + .

98 "Once upon a time there was." *Brass Bulletin—International Brass Chronicle*, no. 18 (1977): 8 + . Excerpt from catalog Fratelli Rossano, Fabbrica di Strumenti Musicali, Bari, Italie du Sud, 1887.

Otto, C. A. "A checklist of compositions with significant trombone parts in the Liechtenstein Music Collection." *Journal of the International Trombone Association* 9 (1981): 11–13.

99 Peterson, Mary. "The Arne B. Larson Collection." *T.U.B.A. Journal* 8, no. 2 (Fall 1980): 5–7.

100 Peterson, Mary. "The Arne B. Larson Collection, part two." *T.U.B.A. Journal* 8, no. 3 (Winter 1981): 15–18.

Peterson, Mary. "Double-bell euphoniums in the Arne B. Larson Collection." *T.U.B.A. Journal* 8, no. 4 (Spring 1981): 4–9.

101 Poole, H. E., and others. "A catalogue of musical instruments offered for sale in 1839 by D'Almaine & Co., 20 Soho Square." *The Galpin Society Journal* 35 (1982): 2–36.

102 Pressley, E. "Musical wind instruments in the Moravian musical archives, Salem, N.C." D.M.A. diss., University of Kentucky, 1975.

103 Rideout, Jeffrey. "Resource Library report." *T.U.B.A. Journal* 9, no. 3 (Winter 1982): 13.

104 Rideout, Jeffrey. "T.U.B.A. Resource Library August, 1983." *T.U.B.A. Journal* 11, no. 2 (Fall 1983): 44–56.

105 Rideout, Jeffrey J. "Annual report of the T.U.B.A. Resource Library—1980." *T.U.B.A. Journal* 8, no. 4 (Spring 1981): 15–22.

Robert, J. "Works with trombone in the Alfred Einstein collection of 16th and 17th century instrumental music: a descriptive catalog." *Journal of the International Trombone Association* 12, no. 4 (1984): 25–32.

106 Roos, W. "The musical instrument collection at Meran." *Galpin Society Journal* 32 (May 1979): 10–23.

107 Scott, Marshall Lynn. "The American piston valved cornets and trumpets of the Shrine to Music Museum (South Dakota)." D.M.A. diss, University of Wisconsin (Madison), 1988.

108 Scott, S. "The Streitweiser Foundation historic Trumpet Museum." *Brass Bulletin—International Brass Chronicle*, no. 39 (1982): 39–43. Also in French and German.

109 *Staatliches Institut für Musikforschung Preussischer Kulturbesitz; Musikinstrumenten-Museum Berlin: Katalog der Blechblasinstrumente (Polsterzungenin-*

strumente). Berlin: Staatliches Institut für Musikforschung Preussischer Kulturbesitz, 1976.

110   Stewart, Gary M. *Keyed brass instruments in the Arne B. Larson collection.* Shrine to Music Museum, Catalog of the Collections, vol. 1, edited by André P. Larson. Vermillion, SD: Shrine to Music Museum, 1980.

111   Swain, John Joseph. "A catalog of the E-flat tubas in the Arne B. Larson collection at the university of South Dakota." *Dissertation Abstracts* 47 (Oct. 1986): 1111A.

112   Swain, John Joseph. "A catalog of the E-flat tubas in the Arne B. Larson Collection at the University of South Dakota." Ph.D. diss., Michigan State University, 1986.

"Technical drawings of historical instruments in the Metropolitan Museum of Art." *American Recorder* 16, no. 3 (1975): 101.

113   Watson, Catherine. "Archive celebration." *The Horn Call* 16, (June 1986): 42–55.

Weber, R. "Some researches into pitch in the 16th century with particular reference to the instruments in the Accademia Filarmonica of Verona." *The Galpin Society Journal* 28 (Apr. 1975): 7–10.

114   Whitwell, D. "Solo wind works in the British Museum." *The Instrumentalist* 31 (Sept. 1976): 96 + .

Young, P. T. "Inventory of instruments: J. H. Eichentopf, Pörschman, Sattler, A. and H. Grenser, Grundmann." *The Galpin Society Journal* 31 (May 1978): 100–134.

Discographies

115   "Addendum to CRI tribute (Journal, Vol. IV) [forty additional chamber works including at least one trumpet]." *International Trumpet Guild Newsletter* 6, no. 2 (1980): 37–40.

116   Anderson, S. C. "Music for alto trombone." *Journal of the International Trombone Association* 13, no. 2 (1985): 42–43.

117   Bahr, Edward R. "A discography of classical trombone/euphonium solo and ensemble music on long-playing records distributed in the United States." *Dissertation Abstracts* 41 (Aug. 1980): 451A.

118   Bahr, Edward R. "A discography of classical trombone/euphonium solo and ensemble music on long-playing records distributed in the United States." D.M.A. diss., University of Oklahoma, 1980.

119   "Bass trombone recording released." *The School Musician* 49 (May 1978): 61.

120   Berger, J. "The virtuoso trumpet [recordings]." *Musical Quarterly* 48, no. 2 (1962): 275–277.

121   Berry, L. "Recorded trumpet albums [includes list]." *Woodwind World—Brass*

and Percussion 19, no. 1 (1980): 18–19.

122   Bishop, Ronald T. "Arnold Jacobs on record: its influence on me." *T.U.B.A. Journal* 15, no. 4 (May 1988): 27–29.

123   Blake, Curtiss, comp. "Jazz discography by (horn) player." *The Horn Call* 13, no. 1 (Oct. 1982): 83–88.

124   Bland, Vurl, and William Bryant. "A catalog of recordings for the tuba." *T.U.B.A. Journal* 15, no. 1 (Aug. 1987): 13–16. Edited by Kenneth Kiesow and Joan Draxler.

125   Boehler, F. W. "Neue Schallplatten: Für Bläser (Blechblasinstrumenten und Orgel)." *Musik und Kirche* 55, no. 5 (1985): 248–250.

126   Bridges, Glenn D. "Early recordings of brass instruments." *Music Journal* 17 (Jan. 1959): 60+.

127   Bryant, William. "Recordings for the euphoniumist." *T.U.B.A. Journal* 13, no. 4 (May 1986): 19–22.

128   Cummings, Barton. "Addenda for tuba record guide." *T.U.B.A. Journal* 4, no. 1 (Fall 1976): 19.

129   Cummings, Barton. "Tuba record guide." *T.U.B.A. Newsletter* 3, no. 1 (Fall 1975): 18–20.

130   Cummings, Barton. "Tuba record guide." *T.U.B.A. Newsletter* 3, no. 3 (Spring/Summer 1976): 6.

131   Ehnes, Fred Rickard. "Record review [two new releases of solo and chamber works]." *The School Musician* 56 (Aug.-Sept. 1984): 58.

Elliott, David G. "The Brahms horn trio and hand horn idiom." *The Horn Call* 10, no. 1 (Oct. 1979): 61–73.

132   Everett, T. "Recent jazz slides on record '79." *International Trombone Association Newsletter* 7, no. 1 (1979): 14+.

133   Everett, Tom. "J. J. Johnson on record: an overview." *Journal of the International Trombone Association* 16, no. 2 (Spring 1988): 34–35.

134   Faulkner, Maurice. "Brass instrument recordings." *The Instrumentalist* 36 (May 1982): 32+.

135   Faulkner, Maurice. "Brass recordings." *The Instrumentalist* 38 (Aug. 1983): 64+.

136   Faulkner, Maurice. "Superb brass recordings: Trumpet solos and brass ensembles." *The Instrumentalist* 36 (Oct. 1981): 54–57.

137   Faulkner, Maurice. "Superb brass recordings: Tuba solos and ensembles." *The Instrumentalist* 36 (Nov. 1981): 79–82.

Ghitalla, Armando. "Fanfare for the trumpet [including a selected trumpet discography]." *American Record Guide* 24 (1957/58): 243–245.

Giddins, G. "Weatherbird: The excitable Roy Eldridge [jazz recordings by Louis Armstrong-influenced trumpeters]." *Village Voice* 26 (May 27, 1981): 76+.

Glover, S. L. "Allen Vizzutti: an interview." *Journal of the International Trumpet Guild* 6 (1981): 18–30. Includes discography.

138   Goldman, Richard Franco. "Reviews of records [Trumpet Concertos]." *Music Quarterly* 52, no. 2 (1966): 266–267.

139 Hansen, J. E., comp. "Discography of trombone solo literature." *Journal of the International Trombone Association* 13, no. 2 (1985): 32–34.

140 Haynie, John J. "A guide to recorded trumpet literature." *The Instrumentalist* 15 (May 1961): 40–41.

141 Hepola, Ralph. "The complete jazz and solo discography of Bill Watrous." *Journal of the International Trombone Association* 14, no. 4 (Fall 1986): 42–45.

142 Hernon, M. *French horn discography*. Westport, CT: Greenwood, 1986.

Hill, J. "Performance practices of the 16th, 17th, and 18th centuries: a few practical references for the trombonist [includes select discography and bibliography]." *Journal of the International Trombone Association* 9 (1981): 20–23.

143 Kehle, Robert. "Addendum to 'Discography of Trombone Literature.' " *Journal of the International Trombone Association* 13, no. 4 (1985): 34–35. Addendum to "Discography of trombone literature," by J. Hansen and J. D. McEniry.

Kipnis, Igor. "A splendid collection of royal brass music [new Nonesuch release]." *HiFi/Stereo Review* 17 (Nov. 1966): 72–73.

Laplace, Michel. "Le trombone dans le jazz et la musique populaire: le pluralisme d'expression a partir de 1945." *Brass Bulletin—International Brass Chronicle*, no. 52 (1985): 20–28. Also in English and German.

144 Laplace, Michel. "The trumpet in the USSR [includes Soviet players discography]." *International Trumpet Guild Newsletter* 4, no. 2 (1978): 19–21.

145 Lowrey, A. L. "Crystal Records—twenty years of excellence [index of repertoire]." *Journal of the International Trumpet Guild* 10, no. 4 (1986): 29–38.

146 Lowrey, A. L. "A feast of recorded baroque trumpet ensemble repertoire." *Journal of the International Trumpet Guild* 6 (1981): 31–33+.

Lowrey, A. L. "Homage to pioneers of trumpet LP's [includes discography]." *Journal of the International Trumpet Guild* 8, no. 1 (1983): 22–25+.

147 Lowrey, A. L. "O Christmas brass, O Christmas brass [recordings]." *Journal of the International Trumpet Guild* 8, no. 2 (1983): 13–16+.

148 Lowrey, A. L., comp. *Trumpet discography*. New York: Colin, 1970.

149 Moore, D. W. "The sound of brass across four centuries [recordings]." *The American Record Guide* 37 (Oct. 1970): 92–94.

150 "Moravian trombone choir music recorded [Music of the Moravian Trombone Choir]." *The Moravian Music Foundation Bulletin* 21, no. 2 (1976): 9.

151 Morgan, R. P. "New music for solo trombone—and for virtuoso trombonist [recording]." *High Fidelity* 19 (Apr. 1969): 64–65.

152 Mueller, Cynthia. "Catalogue of archive tapes of IHS Workshops I-IV and VI." *The Horn Call* 16, (June 1986): 10–31.

153 Musser, G. J. "Brass recording." *Woodwind World—Brass and Percussion* 19, no. 5 (1980): 30–33.

154 "New recordings: brass quintets." *The Instrumentalist* 33 (Mar. 1979): 125–126.

155   "On a new label, five new works for brass ensemble." *The American Record Guide* 31 (May 1965): 816.

156   "Recent jazz 'slides' on record." *Newsletter of the International Trombone Association* 4, no. 3 (1977): 19–21.

"Records: *In Tune* [2-disc set has 'just tuning' for scales and triads for each major and minor key]." *Brass Bulletin—International Brass Chronicle*, no. 33 (1981): 83 + . Also in French and German.

157   Sloan, Gerry. "Suggested listening for jazz trombonists." *The Instrumentalist* 30 (Mar. 1976): 82 + .

158   Uggen, Stuart. "A French horn discography." *The Instrumentalist* 24 (Mar. 1970): 59–61.

Vesely, Stanley J., Jr. "Bibliography of methods, albums and solos related to the bass tuba." Master's thesis, Northwestern University, 1962.

Weerts, R. "Educational solo recordings [wind and percussion instruments]." *The Instrumentalist* 23 (Feb. 1969): 22.

159   Whitaker, Donald. "Brass recordings." *The Instrumentalist* 20 (June 1966):73–78.

160   Winking, C. "A beginning library of solo brass recordings." *The Instrumentalist* 34 (June 1980): 50 + .

161   Winter, D. W. "The band director's guide to euphonium recordings." *The Instrumentalist* 35 (May 1981): 27–28.

162   Winter, Denis, comp. "Euphonium recordings—a discography of selected recordings of euphonium performances." *T.U.B.A. Journal* 7, no. 3 (Winter 1980): 9–14.

Literature Lists

163   Anderson, S. C. "The alto trombone, then and now [includes list of music]." *The Instrumentalist* 40 (Nov. 1985): 54 + .

Baker, J., and others. "Music for horn." *Sounding Brass & the Conductor* 9, no. 3 (1980): 27–28.

Bashford, R. "New music reviewed." *Music Teacher and Piano Student* 64 (July 1985): 23.

164   Bedford, F. "A survey of twentieth century music for brass and harpsichord [includes list]." *Woodwind World—Brass and Percussion* 17, no. 1 (1978): 10–12.

Benshoof, James D. "Brass ensemble music." *NACWPI Journal* 27, no. 2 (Nov. 1978): 61–62.

Benshoof, James D. "Contemporary music for brass ensemble." *NACWPI Journal* 27, no. 1 (Sept. 1978): 46–49.

Bergstone, F. "A recommended selected list of French horn literature." *The*

Instrumentalist 27 (June 1973): 51–53.

165 "A bibliography of chamber music including parts for horn." *Brass Quarterly* 5, no. 1 (1961): 11–33.

166 "A bibliography of chamber music including parts for horn, as compiled from thirteen selected sources." *Brass Quarterly* 4, no. 4 (1961): 159–167.

Bowman, Brian. "New materials—euphonium." *T.U.B.A. Journal* 4, no. 3 (Spring/Summer 1977): 8.

"Brass music for the church." *Church Music [St. L]*, no. 2 (1972): 25–40.

167 "Brass trios in the ITA collection." *Journal of the International Trombone Association* 14, no. 1 (1986): 42.

168 "Briefly noted—unaccompanied solos for brass." *Brass and Woodwind Quarterly* 2, no. 1–2 (1969): 69–70.

169 Briegleb, Arthur, and Wendell Hoss, comps. "Music for ensembles." *The Horn Call* 2, no. 2 (May 1972): 11–18.

Broadwell, R. B. "A selected list of woodwind, brass, and string ensemble literature: its use in high school music." Master's thesis, University of Southern California, 1959.

170 Brown, M. "Repertoire for brass soloists." *The Instrumentalist* 31 (Dec. 1976): 67–68.

171 Brown, M. "Repertoire for brass soloists." *The Instrumentalist* 31 (Dec. 1976): 66–67.

172 Brown, M. "Repertoire for brass soloists." *The Instrumentalist* 31 (Jan. 1977): 51–53.

173 Brown, M. "Trombone solos performed in college student recitals." *Journal of the International Trombone Association* 5 (1977): 22–23.

174 Brüchle, Bernhard. *Music bibliographies for all instruments (Musik-Bibliographien für alle Instrumente)*. Munich 70, Box 700 308, D 8000: The Author, 1976.

175 Call, G. K. "Music for euphonium." *Sounding Brass & the Conductor* 9, no. 3 (1980): 30–31.

176 Cansler, Philip Trent. "An analytical listing of published music of the twentieth century for solo trumpet and organ." D.M.A. diss., University of Oregon, 1984.

Cansler, Philip Trent. "An analytical listing of published music of the twentieth century for solo trumpet and organ." *Dissertation Abstracts* 45 (June 1985): 3474A–3475A.

177 "Catalogue general des cuivres." *Brass Bulletin—International Brass Chronicle*, no. 16 (1976): whole issue. Also in English and German.

178 "Cor-horn." *Brass Bulletin—International Brass Chronicle*, no. 20 (1977): 8–11.

179 Corley, R., comp. *Brass players' guide to the literature, 1973–74*. North Easton, MA: Robert King Music Company, 1974.

180 Cummings, Barton, Sandy Keathley, Gary Buttery, Gary Bird, and Jack Tilbury, eds. "New materials." *T.U.B.A. Journal* 7, no. 1 (Summer 1979): 5–12.

181 Cummings, Barton. "New materials." *T.U.B.A. Journal* 4, no. 1(Fall 1976): 19.

182 Cummings, Barton, ed. "New materials—tuba." *T.U.B.A. Journal* 5, no. 3 (Spring/Summer 1978): 21–23.

183 Cummings, Barton. "New music for tuba." *T.U.B.A. Newsletter* 3, no. 3 (Spring/Summer 1976): 5.

184 Day, D. K. "A comprehensive bibliography of music for brass quintet." *The Instrumentalist* 28 (Nov. 1973): 64–68; 28 (Dec. 1973): 60–64 + .

Day, D. K. "A comprehensive bibliography of music for brass quintet [Addendum]." *The Instrumentalist* 29 (Oct. 1974): 59.

Decker, C. "Popular and folk music of America for brass [includes list of music]." *Woodwind World—Brass and Percussion* 16, no. 6 (1977): 22 + .

185 Decker, R. G. *Music for three brasses; a bibliography of music for three heterogeneous brass instruments alone and in chamber ensembles.* Oneonta, NY: Swift-Dorr, 1976.

186 Devol, J., comp. *Brass music for the church.* Plainview, NY: Branch, 1974.

187 Devol, J., comp. "Music for Easter with brass." *Journal of Church Music* 16 (Jan. 1974): 10–14.

Douglas, Darrell R. "Brass music in the liturgy of the church." *NACWPI Journal* 22, no. 3 (Spring 1974): 20–21.

Dunnick, D. Kim. "Selected literature for trumpet ensemble." *The Instrumentalist* 34 (Mar. 1980): 44 + .

188 Echelard, Donald Joseph. "A thematic dictionary and planning guide of selected solo literature for trumpet." Ed.D. diss., University of Montana, 1969.

189 Echelard, Donald Joseph. "A thematic dictionary and planning guide of selected solo literature for trumpet." *Dissertation Abstracts* 31 (Nov. 1970): 2419A.

190 "Ensembles de cuivres—Blechbläserensembles—brass ensembles." *Brass Bulletin—International Brass Chronicle,* no. 20 (1977): 15–17.

191 Famera, K. M. *Chamber music catalogue.* New York: Pendragon Press, 1978.

Fasthoff, Henry J. "A catalogue of ensemble music for woodwind, brass, and percussion instruments written by composers in the United States." Master's thesis, Florida State University, 1949.

Faulkner, Maurice. "Annual review of solos and studies: trumpet and French horn." *The Instrumentalist* 39 (Feb. 1985): 71–76.

192 Faulkner, Maurice. "Trumpet and horn solos and studies." *The Instrumentalist* 34 (Dec. 1979): 24–26.

Faust, Randall E. "Selected literature for solo brass instruments and electronic media." *NACWPI Journal* 32, no. 1 (1983): 4–17.

193 Faust, Randall Edward. "A comprehensive performance project in horn literature with an essay consisting of three original concertpieces for horn and electronic media, an explanation of techniques used, and a listing of relevant literature." 2 vols. D.M.A. diss., University of Iowa, 1980.

194 Fetter, D. "Johannes Rochut (1881–1952) [includes list of transcriptions]."

Brass Bulletin—International Brass Chronicle, no. 50 (1985): 41–49. In English, French, and German.

Fink, Reginald H. *The trombonist's handbook: a complete guide to playing and teaching the trombone.* Athens, Ohio: Accura, 1977.

Fitzgerald, Bernard. "Chamber music for trumpet—with strings or woodwinds." *The Instrumentalist* 5 (Nov. 1950): 23–25.

195 "Formations diverses—verschiedene Besetzungen—miscellaneous." *Brass Bulletin—International Brass Chronicle*, no. 20 (1977): 18–19.

Gay, B. "New music for the brass band." *Music in Education* 34, no. 341 (1970): 28–29.

George, S. "The trombone choir [includes list of music]." *The Instrumentalist* 29 (May 1975): 44–46.

Gray, R., and Mary Rasmussen, comps. "Three bibliographies of nineteenth- and twentieth-century concertante works; solo parts for the trumpet; solo parts for the trombone; solo parts for more than one different brass instrument." *Brass Quarterly* 6, no. 1 (1962): 10–16.

Gray, S. "The tuba ensemble today [includes list of music]." *The Instrumentalist* 35 (Sept. 1980): 78+.

Gregory, Robin. *The trombone: the instrument and its music.* New York: Praeger; London: Faber & Faber, 1973.

Haynie, John J. "A graded list of trumpet solos." *The Instrumentalist* 18 (Aug. 1963): 47–49.

Heier, Dorothy Ruth. "Selected twentieth-century compositions for trumpet." *Dissertation Abstracts* (Jan. 1964): 2933–2934.

Heier, M. R. "Helping students cope with 20th century trumpet music." *Woodwind World—Brass and Percussion* 16, no. 3 (1977): 32–33+.

196 Heller, G. N. *Ensemble music for wind and percussion instruments; a catalog.* Washington, DC: National Education Association, 1970.

Helm, Sanford M. "Catalog of chamber music for wind instruments." Master's thesis, University of Michigan, 1946.

197 Helm, Sanford M. *Catalog of chamber music for wind instruments.* Ann Arbor: Lithoprinted by Braun-Brumfield, 1952.

198 Herrick, Dennis. "A summary of listings for the year [pieces listed in the Recent Programs column]." *Journal of the International Trumpet Guild* 11, no. 4 (1987): 11–12.

Hoffren, J. "Selected bibliography of music for brass choir." *The Instrumentalist* 15 (Aug. 1961): 36–38.

199 Horton, Ronald Lee. "Music for worship: a compilation of diverse Protestant hymns cross-referenced for service use and scored for intermediate brass ensemble." Ph.D. diss., Columbia Pacific University, 1983.

200 Hummel, Donald A. "A selected list of original works for trombone trio." *Journal of the International Trombone Association* 6 (1978): 16–17.

201 Hummel, Donald Austin. "Abstract: A selected and annotated bibliography of original works for trombone trio." *Missouri Journal of Research in Music Education* 3, no. 5 (1976): 119–120.

Hylander, Martha A. "A selective list of graded trombone methods and solos." Master's thesis, Eastman School of Music, 1948.

Ingalls, David M. "More tuba literature." *The Instrumentalist* 8 (Mar. 1954): 8+.

202   Janetzky, Kurt. "Unmöglich? [18th century brass music]." *Brass Bulletin—International Brass Chronicle*, no. 10 (1975): 34–41. Also in English and French.

Jensen, J. R. "A bibliography of chamber music for French horn." Master's thesis, University of California at Los Angeles, 1962.

Kagarice, Vern. "An annotated bibliography of trombone solo literature with band or orchestra accompaniment." D.Mus. diss., Indiana University, 1973.

Keig, L. "Idiomatic music for small mixed brass ensembles." *Woodwind World—Brass and Percussion* 19, no. 2 (1980): 26–29.

Keig, L. "Idiomatic music for small mixed brass ensembles." *Woodwind World—Brass and Percussion* 19, no. 3 (1980): 6–9+.

203   King, Robert D., comp. *Brass players' guide, 1976–77*. North Easton, MA: Robert King Music, 1977.

Kinney, G. "The brass quintet is an educator's horn of plenty." *Music Educators Journal* 67 (Dec. 1980): 39–41.

204   Klein, Stephen. "How to obtain the music you heard at the Third International Tuba-Euphonium Symposium-Workshop." *T.U.B.A. Journal* 6, no. 3 (Spring 1979): 6–7.

Kleinhammer, Edward. *The art of trombone playing*. Evanston, Ill.: Summy-Birchard, 1963.

Kronholz, K. "Concertos, sonatas, and concert works for trumpet with woodwinds: an index." *International Trumpet Guild Newsletter* 7, no. 1 (1980): 14–16.

205   Kurtz, S. James. "A study and catalog of ensemble music for woodwinds alone or with brass from ca. 1700 to ca. 1825." Ph.D. diss., University of Iowa, 1971.

206   Kurtz, S. James. *A study and catalog of ensemble music for woodwinds alone or with brass from ca. 1700 to ca. 1825*. Iowa City: The author, 1971.

207   Kurtz, S. James. "A study and catalog of ensemble music for woodwinds alone or with brass from ca. 1700 to ca. 1825." *Dissertation Abstracts* 32 (Mar. 1972): 5269A.

Lake, L. "Music for brass ensemble." *Sounding Brass & the Conductor* 3, no. 4 (1974–1975): 125.

Lake, L. "Music for brass ensemble." *Sounding Brass & the Conductor* 5, no. 2 (1976): 60.

Lindner, R. "The junior high school brass choir [includes list of music]." *The Instrumentalist* 23 (Sept. 1968): 85–87.

Louder, Earle L., and David R. Corbin. "Euphonium music guide." *T.U.B.A. Newsletter* 1, no. 3 (Spring 1974): 5.

Lowrey, A. L., comp. "Index of baroque masterpieces for trumpet & organ."

Journal of the International Trumpet Guild 7, no. 3 (1983): 38–39.

McSweeney, A. "Publishers of brass music directory." *Sounding Brass & the Conductor* 7, no. 3 (1978): 95–98.

208 Maldonado, Luis. "Addendum—solo music literature for junior high and high school euphonium and tuba performers." *T.U.B.A. Journal* 15, no. 2 (Nov. 1987): 24–25.

209 Maldonado, Luis. "Ensemble literature for junior high and high school euphonium and tuba performers." *T.U.B.A. Journal* 15, no. 2 (Nov. 1987): 24.

210 Maldonado, Luis. "Solo music literature for junior high and high school euphonium and tuba performers." *T.U.B.A. Journal* 14, no. 4 (May 1987): 39–41.

211 Miller, Robert Melvin. "Abstract: The concerto and related works for low brass: a catalog of compositions from c. 1700 to the present." *Missouri Journal of Research in Music Education* 3, no. 4 (1975): 91.

212 Miller, Robert Melvin. "The concerto and related works for low brass: a catalogue of compositions from c. 1700 to the present." Ph.D. diss., Washington University, 1974.

213 Miller, Robert Melvin. "The concerto and related works for low brass: a catalogue of compositions from c. 1700 to the present." *Dissertation Abstracts* 35 (Mar. 1975): 6185A.

Moody, N. L. "Better brass through ensembles [includes list of suggested music]." *The School Musician* 52 (Feb. 1981): 19.

Moore, R. "Reviews: trumpet duet." *Woodwind World—Brass and Percussion* 19, no. 4 (1980): 28.

Moore, R. "Reviews: trumpet etudes." *Woodwind World—Brass and Percussion* 19, no. 4 (1980): 28.

Moore, R. "Reviews: trumpet trio." *Woodwind World—Brass and Percussion* 19, no. 4 (1980): 28.

Morris, R. Winston. "A basic repertoire and studies for the serious tubist." *The Instrumentalist* 27 (Feb. 1973): 33–34.

Morris, R. Winston. "Music for multiple tubas." *The Instrumentalist* 24 (Apr. 1970): 57–58.

Morris, R. Winston. "New materials—euphonium-tuba." *T.U.B.A. Newsletter* 1, no. 2 (Winter 1974): 10.

Morris, R. Winston. "New materials—euphonium-tuba." *T.U.B.A. Newsletter* 1, no. 3 (Spring 1974): 6–7.

Morris, R. Winston. "New materials—euphonium-tuba." *T.U.B.A. Newsletter* 2, no. 1 (Fall 1974): 4.

Mueller, Herbert C. "Accompanied two trumpet literature—an annotated bibliography [graded]." *Journal of the International Trumpet Guild* 1 (1976): 29.

"Music for bass trombone." *Sounding Brass & the Conductor* 8, no. 4 (1979): 153.

"Music for bass trombone." *Sounding Brass & the Conductor* 9, no. 2 (1980): 31–32.

"Music for brass band." *Sounding Brass & the Conductor* 8, no. 4 (1979): 147–148.

"Music for brass band." *Sounding Brass & the Conductor* 9, no. 3 (1980): 32.

"Music for brass ensemble." *Sounding Brass & the Conductor* 8, no. 4 (1979): 148–149.

"Music for horns." *Sounding Brass & the Conductor* 8, no. 4 (1979): 151.

"Music for trombone." *Sounding Brass & the Conductor* 8, no. 4 (1979): 151–152.

"Music for trumpet." *Sounding Brass & the Conductor* 8, no. 4 (1979): 150–151.

"Music for tuba." *Sounding Brass & the Conductor* 8, no. 4 (1979): 153–154.

Nagel, Robert. "Trumpet ensemble music." *The Instrumentalist* 31 (Apr. 1977): 60. Includes list.

Ode, James. "A selected list of trumpet duet collections [graded]." *Journal of the International Trumpet Guild* 1 (1976): 28.

214 O'Loughlin, N. "Horn." *The Musical Times* 119 (Feb. 1978): 152.

Otto, C. A. "A checklist of compositions with significant trombone parts in the Liechtenstein Music Collection." *Journal of the International Trombone Association* 9 (1981): 11–13.

215 "Partitions—Noten—music." *Brass Bulletin—International Brass Chronicle,* no. 20 (1977): 2–7.

216 "Partitions—Noten—music [cornet music]." *Brass Bulletin—International Brass Chronicle,* no. 20 (1977): 5–6.

217 Pietrachowicz, J. "Polish chamber music for brass instruments since 1945." *Journal of the International Trombone Association* 6 (1978): 3–5.

Pinkow, James David. "A selected and annotated bibliography of music for horn and piano with analyses of representative works." *Dissertation Abstracts* 45 (Apr. 1985): 3023A.

Popiel, P. "The solo tuba and Walter Hartley." *The Instrumentalist* 24 (1970): 63–68.

218 Pruzin, R. S. "Brass quintet." *Woodwind World—Brass and Percussion* 19, no. 5 (1980): 33–35.

219 Rasmussen, Mary. "A bibliography of 'symphonies concertantes,' 'concerti grossi,' etc., including solo parts for the horn, as compiled from twenty selected sources." *Brass Quarterly* 5, no. 2 (1961): 62–68.

Rasmussen, Mary. "A bibliography of 19th- and 20th-century music for male voices with wind- or brass-ensemble accompaniment." *Brass Quarterly* 7, no. 2 (1963): 66–77; 7, no. 3 (1964): 124–132.

Rasmussen, Mary, comp. "A bibliography of 19th- and 20th-century music for mixed voices with wind- or brass-ensemble accompaniment." *Brass Quarterly* 6, no. 3 (1963): 120–130.

Rasmussen, Mary. "A bibliography of 19th- and 20th-century music for mixed voices with wind- or brass-ensemble accompaniment." *Brass*

Quarterly 7, no. 1 (1963): 34–44.

Rasmussen, Mary. "A bibliography of choral music with trombone ensemble accompaniment, as compiled from eleven selected sources." *Brass Quarterly* 5, no. 4 (1962): 153–159.

220 Rasmussen, Mary. *A teacher's guide to the literature of brass instruments.* Durham, NH: Brass Quarterly, 1964.

221 Reifsnyder, Robert. "The Paris Conservatory solos, 1897–1945." *Journal of the International Trombone Association* 14, no. 2 (Spring 1986): 44–47.

222 Reifsnyder, Robert. "The Romantic trombone: Part two." *Journal of the International Trombone Association* 15, no. 3 (Summer 1987): 32–37.

Revelli, William D. "A study program for the cornet or trumpet." *Etude* 73 (Nov. 1955): 19 + .

Reynolds, G. E. "New brass ensemble publications." *The School Musician* 35 (Oct. 1963): 28 + .

223 Reynolds, G. E. "New brass publications." *The School Musician* 37 (Feb. 1966): 14 + ; (June-July 1966): 12 + .

224 Richardson, W. "Trombone and baritone solo and study materials." *The Instrumentalist* 32 (Feb. 1978): 60–61.

Robert, J. "Works with trombone in the Alfred Einstein collection of 16th and 17th century instrumental music: a descriptive catalog." *Journal of the International Trombone Association* 12, no. 4 (1984): 25–32.

Roberts, J. E. "A preliminary list of seventeenth-century chamber music employing the trombone." *Journal of the International Trombone Association* 8 (1980): 19–22.

225 Sears, L. "Classic trumpet tunes." *Musart* 20, no. 3 (1968): 24.

Senff, Thomas Earl. "An annotated bibliography of the unaccompanied solo repertoire for trombone." *Dissertation Abstracts* 37 (July 1976): 28A.

Shoemaker, J. R. "Music for brass comes into its own." *Music Education Journal* 58 (Sept. 1971): 36–39.

226 Shoemaker, John Rogers. "A selected and annotated listing of 20th century ensembles published for three or more heterogeneous brass instruments." Ed.D. diss., Washington University, 1968.

227 Shoemaker, John Rogers. "A selected and annotated listing of 20th century ensembles published for three or more heterogeneous brass instruments." *Dissertation Abstracts* 29 (June 1969): 4519A.

Smith, G. P. "Original unaccompanied trombone ensemble music." *The Instrumentalist* 28 (Feb. 1974): 52–54.

228 Smith, G. P. "Paris National Conservatory contest pieces for trombone." *Journal of the International Trombone Association* 5 (1977): 23–24.

Spongberg, Ralph D. "Bibliography of the literature for the B-flat cornet or trumpet." Master's thesis, Northwestern University, 1950.

Swett, J. "A selected, annotated list of published trombone literature." *The Instrumentalist* 28 (Feb. 1974): 76 + .

Tarr, Edward H. "Original Italian baroque compositions for trumpet and organ." *Diapason* 61 (Apr. 1970): 27–29.

229 Tesch, John A. "An annotated bibliography of selected trombone duets." D.M.A. diss., University of Arizona, 1987.

Thrall, R. S. "Reviews: tuba review." *Woodwind World—Brass and Percussion* 19, no. 3 (1980): 35.

Thrall, R. S. "Reviews: tuba solo." *Woodwind World—Brass and Percussion* 19, no. 4 (1980): 28.

230 Tilbury, Jack, ed. "New materials—brass quintet." *T.U.B.A. Journal* 6, no. 1 (Fall 1978): 35.

231 Tilbury, Jack, ed. "New materials—brass quintet." *T.U.B.A. Journal* 6, no. 2 (Winter 1979): 17.

232 Tilbury, Jack, ed. "New materials—brass quintet." *T.U.B.A. Journal* 6, no. 3 (Spring 1979): 14–15.

Troiano, William. "The New York State School Music Association contest list for tuba solos and tuba ensembles." *T.U.B.A. Journal* 14, no. 2 (Nov. 1986): 20–24.

233 "Trombone-posaune." *Brass Bulletin—International Brass Chronicle*, no. 20 (1977): 11–14.

234 "Trombone trios in the ITA collection." *Journal of the International Trombone Association* 14, no. 1 (1986): 41–42.

235 "Tuba." *Brass Bulletin—International Brass Chronicle*, no. 20 (1977): 14–15.

Walker, B. H. "Brass sextets." *The School Musician* 21 (Jan. 1950): 36.

Walker, B. H. "Christmas solo and ensemble material for brass instruments." *The School Musician* 25 (Dec. 1953): 37–38.

Walker, B. H. "French horn contest solos, duets and quartets." *The School Musician* 25 (Jan. 1954): 34–36.

Wallace, Paul, comp. "Original manuscript music for wind and percussion instruments." *NACWPI Bulletin* 7 (Mar. 1959): 4–9; (June 1959): 4–12; (Dec. 1959): 6–11.

Whitwell, D. "Early brass manuscripts in Vienna." *The Instrumentalist* 25 (Dec. 1970): 36–37.

Whitwell, D. "Solo wind works in the British Museum." *The Instrumentalist* 31 (Sept. 1976): 96+.

Wiggins, B. "New scores for brass band." *Sounding Brass & the Conductor* 3, no. 4 (1974–1975): 114.

Wiggins, B., and others. "Music for trumpet." *Sounding Brass & the Conductor* 9, no. 3 (1980): 28–30.

Wildman, L. "Wedding music with brass." *Diapason* 55 (Oct. 1964): 20–21.

Winick, Steven. "Contemporary music for unaccompanied trumpet." *The Instrumentalist* 25 (Jan. 1971): 36–38.

Winick, Steven. "Music for brass trio." *The Instrumentalist* 27 (Jan. 1973): 48–53.

236 Winkler, K. "Bibliographie der Kompositionen für Posaune und Orgel." *Brass Bulletin—International Brass Chronicle*, no. 51 (1985): 63–66. Also in English and French.

237 Winkler, K. "Neuausgaben originaler Ensemblemusik des 17. Jahrhunderts

für Blechbläser [includes list of editions examined]." *Brass Bulletin—International Brass Chronicle*, no. 53 (1986): 69–80. Also in English and French.

Wood, Alfred F. "Music for wind ensembles and piano." *The Instrumentalist* 12 (Sept. 1957): 46–47.

Young, Raymond. "Some recommended euphonium music." *T.U.B.A. Newsletter* 1, no. 2 (Winter 1974): 5.

238   Zettler, R. "Ein bunter Literatur-Strauss für Blechbläser." *Neue Musikzeitung* 35 (June-July 1986): 42.

239   Zettler, R. "Neues für einige Blechbläser-Besetzungen." *Neue Musikzeitung* 35 (June-July 1986): 43.

Performer Lists/Directories

240   Amend, J. J. "Trumpet sections of American symphony orchestras: The Detroit Symphony Orchestra." *Journal of the International Trumpet Guild* 1 (1976): 22–23.

241   Amend, J. J. "Trumpet sections of American symphony orchestras: The Philadelphia Orchestra (1900–1977)." *International Trumpet Guild Newsletter* 3, no. 3 (1977): 14–15.

"American composer listing, woodwinds and brass solo and ensemble." *The Triangle of Mu Phi Alpha* 66, no. 2 (1972): 19–25.

242   "B flat trumpet directory." *Sounding Brass & the Conductor* 6, no. 4 (1978): 131–133.

243   Barbour, W. "Orchestral showcase: the Detroit Symphony Orchestra." *Journal of the International Trombone Association* 11, no. 4 (1983): 13–17.

244   Bauer, P., comp. "A complete chronological listing of the trombone and tuba personnel of Stan Kenton's orchestras." *Journal of the International Trombone Association* 11, no. 4 (1983): 24–25.

245   "Boston Symphony Orchestra trombone personnel—1881–1979." *International Trombone Association Newsletter* 6, no. 4 (1979): 39–40.

246   Bowman, Brian, comp. "Euphonium/baritone horn directory." *T.U.B.A. Journal* 6, no. 1 (Fall 1978): 32–33.

247   Chasanov, E. L. "Orchestral showcase: The National Symphony Orchestra." *Journal of the International Trombone Association* 11, no. 1 (1983): 7–12.

248   "Chicago Symphony Orchestra low brass personnel 1891–1979 [list]." *International Trombone Association Newsletter* 7, no. 2 (1980): 14–15.

Clark, K. "From our readers: More trumpeters." *The Instrumentalist* 32 (Nov. 1977): 18+.

249   Clark, K. C. "Trumpet sections of American symphony orchestras: the Bos-

ton Symphony Orchestra." *International Trumpet Guild Newsletter* 5, no. 3 (1979): 6.

250 Clark, K. C. "Trumpet sections of American symphony orchestras: The Chicago Symphony Orchestra." *Journal of the International Trumpet Guild* 8, no. 2 (1983): 17–22.

251 "Cleveland Orchestra trombone personnel." *Newsletter of the International Trombone Association* 6, no. 3 (1979): 16–17.

252 Cooper, I. "Orchestra showcase: the Buffalo Philharmonic Orchestra [interview with low brass players and list of low brass personnel, 1936–1979]." *International Trombone Association Newsletter* 7, no. 1 (1979): 17+.

253 Crowne, David K. "Nicknames of jazz trumpeters." *Journal of the International Trumpet Guild* 12, no. 2 (Dec. 1987): 18–33.

254 Dietrich, K. "Orchestra showcase: The Milwaukee Symphony Orchestra." *Journal of the International Trombone Association* 11, no. 3 (1983): 26–28.

255 *The directory of British brass bands*. Rochdale, England: British Federation of Brass Bands, 1976.

256 "Directory of horn players in American symphony orchestras." *The Instrumentalist* 33 (Apr. 1979): 33.

257 "Directory of music organizations [Tubists Universal Brotherhood Association]." *The Instrumentalist* 38 (Sept. 1983): 110.

258 "Directory of symphony trombonists [U.S. and Canada]." *The Instrumentalist* 40 (Nov. 1985): 40+.

259 "Directory of trumpet players in American symphony orchestras." *The Instrumentalist* 31 (Apr. 1977): 51.

260 Edwards, R. "A postal survey of trombone players in the London area." *Journal of the International Trombone Association* 7 (1979): 15–19.
"An 18th century directory of London musicians." *The Galpin Society Journal* 2 (1949): 27–31.

261 Everett, T., comp. "A survey of orchestral bass trombonists." *Journal of the International Trombone Association* 7 (1979): 23–26.

262 Everett, T., comp. "A survey of studio and big band bass trombonists." *Newsletter of the International Trombone Association* 5, no. 3 (1978): 9–16.

263 Fauntley, B. J. "Orchestral showcase: The CAPAB Orchestra." *Journal of the International Trombone Association* 12, no. 4 (1984): 22–24.

264 Gaska, E. Leslie, comp. "Orchestras in the United States and Canada [horn sections]." *The Horn Call* 12, no. 2 (Apr. 1982): 79–91.

265 Hinterbichler, Karl G. "Orchestral showcase: the Dallas Symphony Orchestra." *Journal of the International Trombone Association* 12, no. 1 (1984): 13–14.

266 Hood, B. "Ten outstanding trumpet players in the Los Angeles area." *Brass Bulletin—International Brass Chronicle*, no. 41 (1983): 43+. Also in French and German.

267 "Horn personnel in orchestras: 1971–72." *The Horn Call* 2, no. 2 (May 1972): 20–21.

268 Horton, D. L., ed. "ITG artist-members." *International Trumpet Guild News-letter* 4, no. 1 (1977): 13–19.

269 Hunt, P. B. "Orchestra showcase: The Denver Symphony Orchestra [includes trombone personnel, 1934–1982]." *Journal of the International Trombone Association* 10, no. 1 (1982): 16–19.

270 "ITG artists-members." *Journal of the International Trumpet Guild* 1 (1976): 42–47.

271 Jameson, P. "Orchestra showcase: The Atlanta Symphony Orchestra." *Journal of the International Trombone Association* 10, no. 4 (1982): 11–13.

272 Johnson, D. "Brass [Cleveland brass section]." *Canadian Musician* 7, no. 1 (1985): 54.

273 Kagarice, Vern, and J. Marcellus, comps. "Trombone personnel of American and Canadian orchestras and service bands." *Journal of the International Trombone Association* 10, no. 1 (1982): 20–21.

274 Kohlenberg, R., and R. Thomas. "Orchestral showcase: The New York Philharmonic Orchestra." *Journal of the International Trombone Association* 11, no. 2 (1983): 16–24.

275 Langwill, Lyndesay G. *An index of musical wind-instrument makers*. Edinburgh: The Author, 1960.

276 Langwill, Lyndesay G. *An index of musical wind-instrument makers*. Second enlarged edition. Edinburgh: The Author, 1962.

277 Langwill, Lyndesay G. *An index of musical wind-instrument makers*. Edinburgh: Author, 1972.

Langwill, Lyndesay G. "Two rare eighteenth-century London directories." *Music and Letters* 30 (1949): 37–43.

278 Langwill, Lyndesay G. *Wood-wind and brass instrument makers*. Edinburgh: the author, 1941.

279 Laplace, Michel, and others. "Trumpet players in Belgium and Switzerland." *International Trumpet Guild Newsletter* 4, no. 5, no. 1 (1978): 7–8.

280 Lucas, D. "Orchestra showcase: The Houston Symphony Orchestra." *Journal of the International Trombone Association* 10, no. 3 (1982): 27–31.

281 Marcellus, John. "Directory of symphony trombonists [U.S. and Canada]." *The Instrumentalist* 28 (Feb. 1974): 55.

Montagu, Jeremy. "Choosing brass instruments [includes list of brass instrument makers and dealers]." *Early Music* 4, no. 1 (1976): 35–38.

282 "Orchestra showcase: The Baltimore Symphony Orchestra." *Journal of the International Trombone Association* 10, no. 2 (1982): 14–19.

283 "Orchestras around the world [horn sections]." *The Horn Call* 3, no. 2 (May 1973): 45–53.

284 "Orchestras around the world [horn sections]." *The Horn Call* 5, no. 2 (Spring 1975): 65+.

285 "Orchestras around the world [horn sections]." *The Horn Call* 6, no. 2 (1976): 76+.

286 "Orchestras around the world [horn sections]." *The Horn Call* 9, no. 1 (Oct.

1978): 90–94.

287 "Orchestras in the U.S. and Canada [horn sections]." *The Horn Call* 7, no. 2 (May 1977): 73–80.

288 "Personnel listing of symphony orchestras (addendum)." *Journal of the International Trombone Association* 12, no. 3 (1984): 44.

"Philadelphia Orchestra trombone personnel 1900–1984." *Journal of the International Trombone Association* 12, no. 3 (1984): 19.

289 "Piccolo trumpet directory." *Sounding Brass & the Conductor* 7, no. 2 (1978): 61.

290 "A pictorial history of low brass players in the Boston Symphony Orchestra, 1887–1986." *Journal of the International Trombone Association* 14, no. 4 (1986): 12–21.

Pietrachowicz, J. "Brass instrumentalists in Poland: education and institution since 1945." *Journal of the International Trombone Association* 5 (1977): 2–3.

291 "Professional euphoniumists in the major U.S. service bands." *T.U.B.A. Journal* 5, no. 2 (Winter 1978): 5.

292 "Professional tubists in the major U.S. service bands." *T.U.B.A. Journal* 6, no. 2 (Winter 1979): 18.

293 Scharnberg, William, comp. "Orchestras around the world: Part II. United States and Canada (a cornographical list)." *The Horn Call* 9, no. 2 (Apr. 1979): 80–88.

Seyfried, Erhard. "Meet the Wiener Waldhornverein!" *The Horn Call* 4, no. 2 (Spr. 1974): 29–32.

294 Tilbury, Jack, David Porter, and Sally Wagner. "The United States Army Band Tuba-Euphonium Conference—February 4–7, 1987: a summary." *T.U.B.A. Journal* 15, no. 2 (Nov. 1987): 14–19.

295 Vach, Milan. "Kaemika Corni." *The Horn Call* 18, no. 2 (Apr. 1988): 31–32.

Vernei, B. W. "American composer listing, for woodwinds and brass." *The Triangle of Mu Phi Epsilon* 64, no. 2 (1970): 17–21.

296 Weber, K. "Die Posaunisten im Festspielorchester Bayreuth." *Das Orchester* 28 (July-Aug. 1980): 581–583.

Wilkie, J. A. "American composer listing, woodwinds and brass solo and ensemble." *The Triangle of Mu Phi Epsilon* 65, no. 2 (1971): 23–28.

297 Yeo, Douglas. "Horn players of the Boston Symphony Orchestra, 1881–1988." *The Horn Call* 18, no. 2 (Apr. 1988): 47–61.

298 Yeo, Douglas, comp. "Personnel listing of symphony, opera and ballet orchestras [international]." *Journal of the International Trombone Association* 12, no. 1 (1984): 15–19.

299 Yeo, Douglas. "A pictorial history of the low brass players in the Boston Symphony Orchestra, 1887–1986." *Journal of the International Trombone Association* 14, no. 4 (Fall 1986): 12–21.

300 Yeo, Douglas. "Tuba players of the Boston Symphony Orchestra, 1913–1987." *T.U.B.A. Journal* 14, no. 4 (May 1987): 14–20.

Research Techniques

Bridges, Glenn D. "Pioneers in Brass [how information was obtained to write the book]." *Journal of Band Research* 3, no. 2 (1967): 40–42.

301   Lindner, Richard John. "A cataloging technique and a computer-aided system for retrieving information about brass music." 2 vols. Ph.D. diss., University of Iowa, 1971.

302   Lindner, Richard John. "A cataloging technique and a computer-aided system for retrieving information about brass music." *Dissertation Abstracts* 35 (Mar. 1972): 5270A.

303   Rasmussen, Mary. "Researchmanship—or, some very random thoughts on theses and thesis writing." *Brass Quarterly* 5, no. 2 (1962): 73–77.

PART II

HISTORY AND MUSIC LITERATURE

General History

304   Ahrens, Christian. *Eine Erfindung und ihre Folgen: Blechblasinstrumente mit Ventilen.* Kassel: Bärenreiter, 1986.

305   Altenburg, Wilhelm. "Adolphe Sax und seine Verdienste um den Instrumentenbau." *Zeitschrift für Instrumentenbau* 32 (1911/12): 1051–1055.

"Artifacts in the Military Museum and the National Museum in Budapest." *Brass Bulletin—International Brass Chronicle*, no. 48 (1984): 48–61. Also in French and German.

306   Asten, O. "Deutsche Blechblasinstrumente." *Das Echo* 44 (1925): 1839.

307   Bachmann, S. "Ueber die Stadtpfeifer bei Alt-St.-Martin." *Fränkische Blätter für Geschichtsforschung und Heimatpflege (Bamberg)* 6, no. 25 (1954): 98–100.

Bahr, Edward R. "Some notes on the early valve." *The Galpin Society Journal* 33 (Mar. 1980): 111–124.

308   Baines, Anthony. *Brass instruments: their history and development.* London: Faber & Faber, 1976.

309   Baines, Anthony. "Brass instruments: their history and development." *International Trumpet Guild Newsletter* 5, no. 3 (1979): 19–21.

310   Baines, Anthony. "James Talbot's manuscript." *The Galpin Society Journal* 1 (1948): 9–26.

311   Bechler, Leo. "Ein schlesischer Berg-Hoboist erfindet die Ventile [Friedrich Blühmel]." *Deutsche Militär-Musiker Zeitung* 58, no. 19 (1936): 8.

312   Bernouilli, W. "Meine Sammlung historischer Blechblasinstrumente und Trommeln." *Brass Bulletin—International Brass Chronicle*, no. 5–6 (1973): 85–92. Also in English and French.

313   Bernsdorff-Engelbrecht, C. "Herforder Bläsertage." *Musik und Kirche* 37, no. 3 (1967): 137–139.

314   Bevan, Clifford. "Background brass." *Sounding Brass & the Conductor* 6, no. 3 (1977): 96–97.

315   Bitthorn, O. *Geschichte der "Schwedischen Reitersignale," welche seit dem Jahr 1632 vom Stadtturm . . . geblasen werden.* 4. Auss. Berlin: n.p., 1910.

316   Bitthorn, O. *Mitteilungen über die "Schwedischen Reiter-Signale," welche seit 276 Jahren vom Stadtthurm zu Delitzsch in der Provinz Sachsen an jeden Sonnabend um 10 Uhr von der Stadt-Kapelle geblasen werden.* 3. Auss. Berlin: n.p., (1909).

317   Blaikley, D. J. "The development of modern wind instruments." *Proceedings of the Musical Association* 12 (1885/86): 125–138.

318   Blankenburg, Walter. "Von der Verwendung von Blechblasinstrumenten in Bachs kirchenmusikalischen Werken und ihrer Bedeutung." *Musik und Kirche* 20 (1950): 65–71.

319   "Das Blech in der Musik." *Allgemeine musikalische Zeitung* 13 (1878): 17–22, 33–38, 49–53.

320   "Die Blechblasinstrumente." *Der Chor* 2 (1950): 126–127.

321   Bonanni, F. *Gabinetto armonico (1723)*. Reprint and summary, with intro-duction and captions by F. L. Harrison and J. Rimmer. New York: Dover, 1964.

322   Bowles, Edmund A. "La hiérarchie des instruments de musique dans l'Europe féodale." *Revue de Musicologie* 42 (1958): 155–169.

323   Bowles, Edmund A. "Unterscheidung der Instrumente Buisine, Cor, Trompe und Trompette." *Archiv für Musikwissenschaft* 18 (1961): 52–72.

       Brand, G. "The brass age." *Music* 4, no. 1 (1970): 36–37.

324   "Brass! Brass!" *Dwight's* 9 (1856): 126.

325   "Brass! Brass! again." *Dwight's* 9 (1856): 141.

326   "Brass! Brass! Brass!" *Dwight's* 13 (1858): 126–127.

327   "Brass instruments—their improvement during the last century." *Musician* 27 (Feb. 1922): 19.

328   Brücker, Fritz. *Die Blasinstrumente in der altfranzösischen Literatur*. Giessener Beiträge zur romanischen Philologie, vol. XIX. Giessen: n.p., 1926.

329   Buhle, Edward. *Musical instruments in the miniatures of the early Middle Ages: with special regard to brass instruments*. Ed. by M. Sändig. Wiesbaden: Breitkopf & Härtel, 1972 (1903).

330   Buhle, Edward. "Musical instruments in the miniatures of the early Middle Ages: with special regard to brass instruments." *Brass Bulletin—International Brass Chronicle*, no. 28 (1979): 77–80.

331   Buhle, Edward. *Die musikalischen Instrumente in den Miniaturen des frühen Mittelalters. Ein Beitrag zur Geschichte der Musikinstrumente, I. Die Blasinstrumente*. Reprint of 1903 edition (Leipzig: Breitkopf & Härtel). Walluf bei Wiesbaden: Sändig, 1972.

332   Buhle, Edward. *Die Musikalischen Instrumente in den Miniaturen des frühen Mittelalters. I. Die Blasinstrumente*. Leipzig: Breitkopf & Härtel, 1903.

333   Bula, Karol. "Blasinstrumente in der polnischen Musikpraxis der ersten Hälfte des 18. Jahrhunderts." In *Die Blasinstrumente und ihre Verwendung . . .* , edited by Eitelfriedrich Thom, 26–32. Magdeburg: Rat des Bezirkes; Leipzig: Zentralhaus für Kulturarbeit, 1977.

334   Carse, Adam. "Brass instruments in the orchestra." *Music & Letters* 3 (1922): 378–382.

335   Carse, Adam. *Musical wind instruments. A history of the wind instruments used in European orchestras and wind-bands from the later Middle Ages up to the present time*. Reprint of the 1939 edition with a new introduction by Himie Voxman. New York: Da Capo, 1973.

336   Carse, Adam. "Wind instruments and inventors." *Musical Opinion* 61 (1937–38): 689–691.

337   Chaussier, Henry. *Notice explicative pour les nouveaux instruments en ut*. Paris: Millereau, 1886.

338   Clappé, Arthur A. *The wind-band and its instruments: their history, construction, acoustics, technique, and combination*. Reprint of the 1911 edition (New York: H. Holt). Portland, Me.: Longwood, 1976.

339   Clappé, Arthur A. *The wind-band and its instruments; their history, construction, acoustics, technique and combination.* New York: H. Holt and Co., 1911.

340   Deisenroth, F. "Die Bläserkultur der Blechblasinstrumente in der Militär-musik unter besonderer Berücksichtigung der Weitmensurierten Bügel-instrumente mit Einschluss der Zug- und Ventilposaunen." *Deutsche Militär-Musiker Zeitung* 60 (1938): 29–30, 41–42.

341   Denis, V. "Musical instruments in fifteenth century Netherlands and Italian art." *The Galpin Society Journal* 2 (1949): 32–46.

       Dieck, A. "Les musiciens ambulants de Salzgitter au XIX siecle [sous l'aspect particulier des cuivres]." *Brass Bulletin—International Brass Chronicle*, no. 13 (1976): 95–115. Also in English and German. Excerpt from his book *Die Wandermusikanten von Salzgitter.*

342   Draper, F. C. "The development of brass wind instruments." In *Brass Today.* Edited by Frank Wright, 90–99. London: Besson, 1957.

343   Drechsel, F. A. "Neue Nachrichten über die Erfinder der Inventionen und Ventile an Blasinstrumenten." *Zeitschrift für Instrumentenbau* 48 (1927–1928): 634–635.

344   Drechsel, F. A. "Zur Geschichte des Instrumentenbaues in Dresden. II. Blasinstrumentenmacher." *Zeitschrift für Instrumentenbau* 49 (1928–1929): 997–1000.

       Eglin, A. "Kirchliche Bläserarbeit." *Musik und Gottesdienst* 18, no. 4 (1964): 113–120.

345   Ehmann, Wilhelm. *Die bläserische Kunst; bläsereigene Satzpraktiken in der ältern Blasmusik.* Kassel: Eichenkreuz-Verlag, 1951.

346   Ehmann, Wilhelm. "Das Blasen auf Metallinstrumenten en Geschichte und Gegenwart." *Junge Musik* (1957): 49–53.

347   Ehmann, Wilhelm. "Blech-Blasen in der kirchenmusikalischen Ausbil-dung." *Musik und Kirche* 34, no. 3 (1964): 120–134; no. 4 (1964): 185–187.

348   Ehmann, Wilhelm. "Formen und Reformen des Blasens." *Neue Zeitschrift für Musik* 118 (1957): 522–524.

349   Ehmann, Wilhelm. "Neue Blechblasinstrumente nach alten Modellen." *Hausmusik* 22 (1958): 79–86. German version of an article which appeared in *Brass Quarterly* 1 (1957/58): 214–225.

350   Ehmann, Wilhelm. "Von alten Blasinstrumenten." *Hausmusik* (1954): 7–10.

351   "An 18th century directory of London musicians." *The Galpin Society Journal* 2 (1949): 27–31.

352   Eliason, Robert E. "Brass instrument key and valve mechanisms made in America before 1875 with special reference to the D. S. Pillsbury collec-tion in Greenfield Village, Dearborn, Michigan." *Dissertation Abstracts* 29 (May 1969): 4036A–4037A.

353   Eliason, Robert E. "Brass instrument key and valve mechanisms made in America before 1875, with special reference to the D. S. Pillsbury Col-lection in Greenfield Village, Dearborn, Michigan." D.M.A. diss., Uni-versity of Missouri (Kansas City), 1969.

       Eliason, Robert E. "Brasses with both keys and valves." *Journal of the Ameri-*

can Musical Instrument Society 2 (1976): 69–85.

Eliason, Robert E. "Dissertation: Brass instrument key and valve mechanisms made in America before 1875, with special reference to the D. S. Pillsbury Collection in Greenfield Village, Dearborn, Michigan [abstract]." *Monthly Journal of Research in Music Education* 2, no. 3 (1969): 81–82.

354 Eliason, Robert E. *Early American brass makers*. Brass Research Series. Nashville: Brass Press, 1979.

355 Eliason, Robert E. "Early American brass makers." *Music Educators Journal* 66 (Sept. 1979): 89.

356 Eliason, Robert E. "Early American valves for brass instruments." *The Galpin Society Journal* 23 (Aug. 1970): 86–96.

Eliason, Robert E. "The Meachams, musical instrument makers of Hartford and Albany (includes list of known Meacham instruments)." *Journal of the American Musical Instrument Society* 5 (1980–81): 69–70.

357 Ernst, Friedrich. "Die Blechblasinstrumentenbauer-Familie Moritz in Berlin [Beitrag zur Geschichte des Berliner Instrumentenbaues]." *Das Musikinstrument* 18, no. 4 (Apr. 1969): 624–626.

358 Evenson, Pattee Edward. "A history of brass instruments, their usage, music, and performance practices in ensembles during the Baroque era." D.M.A. diss., University of Southern California, 1960.

359 Evenson, Pattee Edward. "A history of brass instruments, their usage, music, and performance practices in ensembles during the Baroque era." *Dissertation Abstracts* 22 (1962): 3219.

360 Fallet, Eduard M. "Die Stadtpfeiferei von Neuenburg im 16. und 17. Jahrhundert." *Schweizerische Musikzeitung* 69 (1929): 42–45, 76–80.

Faulkner, Maurice. "Report on European brasses." *The Instrumentalist* 20 (Sept. 1965): 88.

361 Fétis, F. J. "Exposition des produits de l'industrie: Instruments à vent." *Revue musicale* 14 (1834): 171–175.

362 Fétis, F. J. "Facture des instruments à vent sur l'établissement de M. Sax, de Bruxelles." *Revue musicale* 14 (1834): 76–78.

363 Finscher, Ludwig. "Aufführungspraktische Versuche zur geistlichen Musik des 15. und 16. Jhs. im Westdeutschen Rundfunk Köln." *Die Musikforschung* 12 (1959): 480–488.

364 Fitzgibbon, H. Macauley. "Instruments and their music in the Elizabethan Drama." *Musical Quarterly* 17 (1931): 319–329.

Flor, G. J. "Brass workshop: the saxhorn—past and present [Heritage Americana Cornet-Saxhorn Brass Band]." *The School Musician* 54 (May 1983): 26–29.

365 Fox, Lilla M. "Instruments of religion and folklore". Chap. 3 in *History of Musical Instruments*. London: Lutterworth, 1969.

366 Franz, O. "Les nouveaux instruments de musique de Richard Wagner." *L'Echo musical* 16 (1884): 290–293.

367 Fromme, Arnold. "Performance technique on brass instruments during the

seventeenth century." *Journal of Research in Music Education* 20, no. 3 (Fall 1972): 329–343.

368 Frotscher, G. "Turmmusik in alter Zeit." *Musik in Jugen und Volk* 5 (1942): 122.

369 Ganse, A. "Geschichte der Blechbläserfamilie bis zur Entstehung der Blasorchester." *Die Volksmusik—Ausg. A* (1939): 70–74.

  Garlock, F. "Brass instruments in church???" *The School Musician* 36 (Jan. 1965): 70–71.

370 Gauntlett, Helen P. "The sound of the trumpet." *Music Journal* 13 (Sept. 1959): 100.

371 Gifford, Robert Marvin, Jr. "The music and performance practices of the medieval wind band." *Journal of Band Research* 10, no. 2 (Spring 1974): 25–32.

  Gornston, D. "The golden era of brass." *The Instrumentalist* 3 (Nov. 1948): 39.

372 Gurlitt, Wilibald. "Ein Briefwechsel zwischen Paul Hainlein und L. Friedrich Behaim aus den Jahren 1647–1648." *Sammelbände der Internationalen Musikgesellschaft* 14 (1912/13): 491–499.

373 Haensel, R. "Der Stadtpfeifer und die Stadtkapelle in Lobenstein." In *Festschrift zur Ehrung von Heinrich Albert (1604–1651)*, edited by G. Kraft. Weimar: n.p., 1954.

  Haine, M., and I. de Keyser. "Catalogue des instruments Sax au Musee Instrumental de Bruxelles." *Brussels Museum of Musical Instruments* 9–10, nos. 1–2 (1979–1980): entire issue.

374 Haine, M., and I. De Keyser. "Les estampilles des instruments Sax." *Brass Bulletin—International Brass Chronicle*, no. 30 (1980): 43–45 + . Also in English and German.

  Hall, H. H. "Early sounds of Moravian brass music in America: a cultural note from Colonial Georgia." *Brass Quarterly* 7, no. 3 (1964): 115–123.

  Hamilton, D. "The Wagnerian orchestra." *San Francisco Opera Magazine*, no. 10 (Fall 1981): 45–48 + .

375 Hamilton, H. C. "By the help of brass." *Etude* 51 (1933): 341.

376 Harley, John. "Music at the English court in the eighteenth and nineteenth centuries." *Music and Letters* 50, no. 3 (July 1969): 332–351.

377 Hart, G. "Bemerkungen über ältere Blasinstrumentenmacher." *Instrumentenbau-Zeitschrift* 15 (1961): 163–166.

378 Heyler, E. O. "The story of brass wind instruments. A study in the evolution of the orchestra." *Music* (Chicago) 7 (1894/95): 240–248, 349–354.

379 Hickernell, Ross. "The classic brass." *Etude* 49 (1931): 781.

380 Hicks, C. E. "Church music: justification for the use of brass instruments in the church service." *Woodwind World—Brass and Percussion* 20, no. 2 (1981): 12–13 + .

381 Hicks, C. E. "Church music: justification for the use of brass instruments in the Church service." *Woodwind World—Brass and Percussion* 20, no. 3 (1981): 12–14.

382   Hilfiger, J. J. "A history of keyed brass instruments." *NACWPI Journal* 34, no. 4 (1986): 4–7.

383   Hüttl, A. R. "Bessere Ansprache bei Blechblasinstrumenten." *Instrumentenbau-Zeitschrift* 25 (Apr. 1971): 316.

384   "Instruments d'A. Sax." *La Belgique musicale* 5, no. 11 (18 July 1844): 43–44.

385   Jäger, J. "Ansatz und Atmung bei Blechbläsern." *Das Orchester* 28 (Sept. 1980): 693–696.

386   Jähns, F. W. "Parade-Marsch und Horn-Signale der Königl. Sächsischen leichten Infanterie, angeblich von Carl Maria von Weber." *Allgemeine musikalische Zeitung* 13 (1878): 177–183.

387   Jaffee, K. "Divers notes on brass instruments in English periodicals 1678–1719." *Brass Quarterly* 7, no. 4 (1964): 178–193.

388   Kalkbrenner, A. "Die Notation der Ventil-Instrumente (Hörner und Trompeten) in der Orchestermusik." *Neue Zeitschrift für Musik* 83 (1887): 236–237, 321–323.

389   Karstädt, Georg. "Die Bläser in den Instrumentengruppen des Mittelalters." *Die Volksmusik. Ausg. A. Streich- und Blasmusik* 4 (1941): 177–180.

390   Karstädt, Georg. "Blasinstrumente des Barock." *Musica* 4 (1950): 460–462.

391   Karstädt, Georg. "Die Blasmusik und ihre Aufgaben in den alten Reichsstädten." *Die Volksmusik. Ausg. A. Streich- und Blasmusik* 6 (1941): 267–270.

392   Karstädt, Georg. "Die Umbildung des Blasregisters nach Erfindung der Ventile." *Instrumentenbau-Zeitschrift* 15 (1961): 160–163.

393   Karstädt, Georg. "Vom Klappenhorn zum Ventilinstrument." *Die Volksmusik. Ausg. A. Streich- und Blasmusik* 7 (1942): 177–180.

394   Kenton, Egon F. "Nel quarto centenario della nescita di Giovanni Gabrieli." *La Rassegna Musicale* 28 (1958): 26–31.

395   Kimmel, William. *Polychoral music and the Venetian school*. Rochester, NY: University of Rochester Press, 1954.

396   Koch, Hans Oskar. "Die Spezialtypen der Blasinstrumente in der 1. Hälfte des 18. Jahrhunderts im deutschen Sprachraum." Staatsexamensarbeit, Hochschule für Musik und Theater, 1969.

397   Komma, K. M. "Wiederweckung der Turmmusik im Sudentenland." *Musik in Jugend und Volk* 5 (1942): 125.

398   Kramer, William F. "Some highlights in the history of brass instruments." *Southwestern Brass Journal* I (Spring 1957): 31–32; (Fall 1957): 27–29.

399   Krautwurst, Franz. "Musik der 2. Hälfte des 16. und des 17. Jahrhunderts." In *Nürnberg—Geschichte einer europäischen Stadt*, edited by Gerhardt Pfeiffer, 287–291. München: Beck, 1971.

400   Krivin, M. "A century of wind instrument manufacturing in the United States." Ph.D. dissertation, State University of Iowa, 1961. Published. Ann Arbor, Mich.: University Microfilms, 1961.

       Krüger, Walther. "Anforderungen an den heutigen Blasinstrumentenbau unter Berücksichtigung der Aufführungspraxis von Musik des 18. Jahrhunderts." In *Bericht über das 1. Symposium zu Fragen der Anforderungen an den Instrumentenbau: Blankenburg/Harz, 31 Mai 1980*, edited by Eitel-friedrich Thom and Renate Bormann, 10–13.Magdeburg: Rat des Be-zirkes, 1980.

401   Lajarte, E. D. de. *Instruments Sax et fanfares civiles.* Paris: n.p., 1867.

402   Langwill, Lyndesay G. "Instrument-making in Paris in 1839." *Music & Letters* 39 (1958): 135–138.

403   Langwill, Lyndesay G. "London wind-instrument makers of the seventeenth and eighteenth centuries." *Music Review* 7 (1946): 88–102.

404   Langwill, Lyndesay G. "Two rare eighteenth-century London directories." *Music and Letters* 30 (1949): 37–43.

405   Leonards, Petra G. "Artikulation auf Blasinstrumenten im 16. und 17. Jahrhundert. Ein Beitrag zur Spieltechnik der Blasinstrumente vor dem geistesgeschichtlichen Hintergrund dieser Zeit." *Tibia* 5, no. 1 (1980): 1–9.

406   Levy, J. "Die Signalinstrumente in den altfranzösischen Texten." *Sammelbände der Internationalen Musikgesellschaft* 12 (1910/11): 325–330.

407   Levy, J. *Die Signalinstrumente in den altfranzösischen Texten.* Halle: C. A. Kämmerer, 1910.

408   Lewinsky, I. "Ueber den Einfluss der verbesserten Blasinstrumente auf die österreichische Volksmusik." *Allgemeine Wiener Musikzeitung* 2 (1842): 285–286.

409   Limac, O. L. "Falsche Bezeichnungen der Orchester-Instrumente." *Zeitschrift für Instrumentenbau* 34 (1913/14): 295–296.

Limmer, R. "Blechblasinstrumente aus der Musikstadt Graslitz." *Brass Bulletin—International Brass Chronicle*, no. 29 (1980): 41 +. Also in French and English.

410   McCready, Matthew A. "Compensating systems: an historical overview." *T.U.B.A. Journal* 10, no. 4 (Spring 1983): 5–6.

411   MacDonald, Robert J. "François-Joseph Gossec and French instrumental music in the second half of the eighteenth century." Ph.D. diss., University of Michigan, 1968.

412   Mahillon, C. "Réponse à M. Sax, père." *La Belgique musicale* 8, no. 9 (4 Mar. 1847): 1–2.

413   Malson, L. "La génération des 'veloces' n'a pas encore dit son dernier mot." *Jazz Magazine* 5 (July 1959): 26–29.

414   Marquis, A. "Antique instruments: a famous Civil War band lives again." *Hobbies* 75 (Sept. 1970): 48–49 +.

415   Martin, Julius. *Graslitz, seine Anfänge und seine Entwicklung zur Zentrale der Blasinstrumentenindustrie der österreichische-ungarischen Monarchie, 1610–1918.* Wien: n.p., 1957.

416   Mathez, Jean-Pierre. "Les cuivres a Rome [economic aspects]." *Brass Bulletin—International Brass Chronicle*, no. 43 (1983): 18–22 +. Also in English and German.

417   Mathez, Jean-Pierre. "Les petites histoires de la vie des cuivres: 'Le Nouveau.' " *Brass Bulletin—International Brass Chronicle*, no. 55 (1986): 23–24. Also in English and German.

418   Mayerhofer, Götz. "Münchener Turmmusik." *Allgemeine Musikalische Zeitung* 65 (1938): 280–281.

419   Mayerhofer, Götz. "Münchener Turmmusik." *Die Musik-Woche* 6 (1938): 308–309.

420   Mayerhofer, Götz. "Turmmusiken in München." *Deutsche Militär-Musiker Zeitung* 60 (1938): 297.

421   Mende, Emily, and Jean-Pierre Mathez. *Arbre genealogique illustre des cuivres europeens depuis le debut du Moyen Age/Stammbaum der europäischen Blechblasinstrumente in Bildern seit dem frühen Mittelalter/Pictorial family tree of brass instruments in Europe since the early Middle Ages.* Moudon, Switzerland: Editions BIM, 1978.

422   Mende, Emily, and Jean-Pierre Mathez. "Stammbaum der Europäischen Blechblasinstrumente in Bildern seit dem frühen Mittelalter/Pictorial family tree of brass instruments in Europe since the early Middle Ages." *Das Orchester* 27 (Sept. 1979): 680.

423   Mende, Emily. "Pictorial family tree of brass instruments since the early Middle Ages." *International Trumpet Guild Newsletter* 6, no. 1 (1979): 16.

       Menzel, Ursula. "Historische Blechblasinstrumente und Restaurierung." *Brass Bulletin—International Brass Chronicle*, no. 39 (1982): 7–12. Also in French and English.

424   Mertin, Josef. "Das Instrumentarium der alten Musik (Renaissance und Gotik). I: Die Blasinstrumente." *Oesterreichische Musik Zeitschrift* 13 (1958): 409–415.

425   Michaels, Jost. "Die künstlerische Bedeutung der Blasinstrumente und ihrer Literatur." *Das Orchester* 6 (1958): 33–40.

426   Mojsisovics. "Einiges über Turmblasen." *Schlesisches Blatt für evangelische Kirchenmusik* 56 (191?): 8.

427   Mojsisovics. "Turmblasen." *Korrespondenzblatt des evangelischen Kirchengesangvereins für Deutschland* 33 (191-?): 3–4; *Der Kirchenchor* 30 (191-?): 6.

428   Monke, W. "Eine Erfindung setzt sich durch: Über die 150jährige Geschichte des Metallblasinstrumentenventils." *Musikhandel* 16, no. 3 (1965): 98–99.

429   Moritz, Camillo. "Werdegang der Signalinstrumente." *Zeitschrift für Instrumentenbau* 33 (1912/13): 1203–1205, 1244–1245, 1287–1288.

430   "Die 'Münchener Turmmusik.' " *Zeitschrift für Musik* 107 (1940): 625.

431   "Musical instruments of brass." *The Music Trade Review* (June, 1904): 37.

432   "Musiker diskutierten mit Herstellern; Markneukirchener Musiktage 1970." *Instrumentenbau-Zeitschrift* 24 (Aug. 1970): 468 + .

433   Nakayama, F. "Painting from the 18th century [Chinese-derived brass played at the Okinawan court]." *Brass Bulletin—International Brass Chronicle*, no. 35 (1981): 44–45. Also in French and German.

434   Naylor, Tom L. "Battle of the bands [Civil War]." *Woodwind World—Brass and Percussion* 15, no. 4 (1976): 8–9.

435   Nelle. "Vom Blasen von den Türmen bei deutschen Siegen und sonst." *Korrespondenzblatt des evangelischen Kirchengesangvereins für Deutschland* 30 (191?): 12.

436   Nickel, Ekkehart. *Der Holzblas-Instrumentenbau in der Freien Reichsstadt Nürnberg*. Munich: Katzbichler, 1971.

437   Ode, James. *Brass instruments in church services*. Minneapolis: Augsburg, 1970.

Olsen, D. M., and others. "Music in an American frontier communal society (Aurora, Oregon)." *Brass Bulletin—International Brass Chronicle*, no. 34 (1981): 21–22. Adapted from *Oregon Historical Quarterly*.

Olsen, D. M., and others. "Music in an American frontier communal society (Aurora, Oregon)." *Brass Bulletin—International Brass Chronicle*, no. 36 (1981): 64–77. Also in French and German.

438   Olson, R. D. "Correlating scientific writings with music studies." *Newsletter of the International Trumpet Guild* 3, no. 3 (1977): 7–10.

439   "On the cover [history]." *Music Educators Journal* 50, no. 4 (1964): 50.

"Once upon a time there was." *Brass Bulletin—International Brass Chronicle*, no. 18 (1977): 8+. Excerpt from catalog Fratelli Rossano, Fabbrica di Strumenti Musicali, Bari, Italie du Sud, 1887.

440   Orval, Francis. "Aperçu sur la fabrication, le chaudronnage et le montage des cuivres naturels anciens et des trompes de vénerie." *Bulletin de la Société Liégeoise Musicologique* 29 (Apr. 1980): 1–13.

441   "A pictorial history of the brasses." *Bandwagon* (Selmer) 8 (May 1960): 6–7.

442   Pilard, C. *Les Inventions Sax dans les musiques militaires et à l'orchestre*. Paris: E. Vert, 1869.

443   Plass, Ludwig. "Was die Geschichte der Posaunen lehrt. Studie über die ehemalige und gegenwartige Turmmusik." *Allgemeine Musikalische Zeitung* (Berlin) 40 (1913): 445–447, 477–479.

444   Plenckers, L. J. *Brass instruments*. New York: Da Capo, 1970.

445   Polk, Keith. "Municipal wind music in Flanders in the late Middle Ages." *Brass and Woodwind Quarterly* 2, nos. 1–2 (Spring-Summer 1969): 1–15.

446   Poncelet-Lecocq, P. "De la nécessité pour les corps de musique militaire de multiplier les instruments de cuivre intermédiares, afin d'amener une fusion plus parfaite du son entre les cuivres et les bois." *L'Echo musical* 1, no. 2 (15 June 1869).

Pressley, E. "Musical wind instruments in the Moravian musical archives, Salem, N.C." D.M.A. diss., University of Kentucky, 1975.

447   Preuss, D. "Die katholische Griffweise bei einem protestantischen Horn; über Rarität aus dem Bereich des Blechblasinstrumentenbaus." *Das Orchester* 34 (Sept. 1986): 912–914.

Quayle, N. H. "American brass supreme." *Music Journal* 18 (Nov.-Dec. 1960): 50–51+.

448   Rein, Friedrich. "Aus der Geschichte der Turmbläserei." *Die Volksmusik—Ausg. A* (1940): 105–108.

449   Rein, Friedrich. "Aus der Praxis der Turmmusiken." *Die Volksmusik. Ausg. A. Streich- und Blasmusik* 6 (1941): 201.

450   Rein, Friedrich. "Münchener Turmmusik." *Die Musik* 30 (1937): 138–139.

451   Rein, Friedrich. "Münchener Turmmusik." *Allgemeine Musikalische Zeitung*

67 (1940): 305–306.

452   Rein, Friedrich. "Münchener Turmmusik." *Musik in Jugend und Volk* 5 (1942): 127.

453   Reitz, John V. "Brass instruments in the contemporary orchestral situation." Master's thesis, University of Washington, 1950.

454   Richter. "Turmmusik." *Organum* 23 (192-?) 3.

455   Richter. "Turmmusik." *Korrespondenzblatt des ev. Kirchengesangvereins für Deutschland* 36, nos. 1, 3 (192?): n.p.

456   Richter. "Turmmusiken." *Korrespondenzblatt des evangelischen Kirchengesangvereins für Deutschland* 36 (191?): 1/3.

457   Riedl, Alfred. "Graslitzer Blechblasinstrumente und ihre Geschichte." *Instrumentenbau-Zeitschrift* 13 (1959): 274–280.

458   Riehl, Wilhelm Heinrich. "Der Stadpfeifer." In *Deutsche Kurzschrift*. Darmstadt: Winkler, 1950. (Worte und Besinnung, Bd. 655).

459   Riesenfeld, P. "Ausdruckswerte der Blechblasinstrumente in musikgeschichtlicher Beurteilung." *Schweizerische Instrumentalmusik* 28 (1939): 456–459.

460   Riley, Maurice W. "A tentative bibliography of early wind instrument tutors." *Journal of Research in Music Education* 6 (1958): 3–24.

461   Rode, Theodore. "Wiederholter Wunsch zur Gründung einer Militärmusik-Hochschule für die Deutsche Armee in der Metropole Berlin." *Neue Zeitung für Musik* 78 (1882): 267–269. [Includes information on the history of the valve.]

462   Rosenkranz, Marie. "Die Musik als Mitgestalterin am Werden des Menschen. Die Blasinstrumente und das Melos." *Kommenden* 11, no. 13 (1957): 7; no. 14: 10; no. 16: 8.

463   Sachs, Curt. *Die Blechblasinstrument. Revue der Musik-instrumente. Eine Bestandsaufnahme als Umfrage*. Reprinted from the *Frankfurter Zeitung* of Sept. 17, 1930. n.p., 1930.

464   Sachs, Curt. "Die Litui in Bachs Motette 'O Jesu Christ.'" *Bach Jahrbuch* 18 (1921): 96–97.

465   Sachs, Curt. "Die Verwirrung in der Tonlagenbezeichnung der Blasinstrumente." *Zeitschrift für Instrumentenbau* 31 (1910/11): 1226–1227; *Deutsche Militär-Musiker Zeitung* 35 (1913): 83–84.

466   Salmen, W. "Russische Musik und Musiker vor 1700, unter besonderer Berücksichtigung der Blasmusik." *Brass Bulletin—International Brass Chronicle*, no. 7 (1974): 65–74. Also in English and French.

467   Sax, Adolphe. "Un Cartel musical—Les Instruments d'Adolphe Sax." *La Belgique musicale* 7, no. 19 (10 Sept. 1846): 4–8.

468   Sax, Adolphe. "Offenes Sendschreiben an Herrn Wieprecht, General-director der preuss. Militärmusik." *Allgemeine musikalische Zeitung* 48 (1846): 617–620, 643–647, 651–654, 670–672.

469   Sax, [C. -J.]. "Réponse de M. Sax père à M. Wieprecht." *La Belgique musicale* 8, no. 8 (25 Feb. 1847): 2–5.

470   Sch., E. "Vom blasen von den Türmen." *Korrespondenzblatt des evangelischen*

Kirchengesangvereins für Deutschland 31 (191?): 5.

471   Schlenger, Kurt. "Die Blaeser in der Musikausübung des 20. Jahrhunderts." *Die Musik* 30 (1937): 174–179.

472   Schlesinger, Kathleen. "Valves." In *Encyclopaedia Britannica*. 11th ed. New York, 1910–11.

Schmidt, W. C. "Fünf Generationen Mundstück-Spezialisten." *Brass Bulletin—International Brass Chronicle*, no. 29 (1980): 27–29 + . Also in French and English.

473   Schubert, F. L. *Die Blechinstrumente der Musik*. 2. Auss. Leipzig: Merseburger, 1883.

474   Schubert, F. L. *Die Blechinstrumente der Musik, ihre Geschichte, Natur, Handhabung und Verwendung in der Instrumental-, Gesangs-, Militär- und Tanzmusik*. Leipzig: Merseburger, 1866.

475   Schubert, F. L. "Ueber den Gebrauch und Missbrauch der Ventilinstrumente in Verbindung mit anderen Instrumenten." *Neue Zeitschrift für Musik* 61 (1865): 296–297, 304–305, 312–313.

476   Selch, F. R. "The great American marching band [includes history-'backfiring' instruments]." *Ovation* 7 (July 1986): 10.

477   "A short history of brass instruments." *Metronome* 30, nos. 1, 6, 7, 8 (1914).

478   Shoults, C. R. "The brass instruments." *Music Journal* 19 (Sept. 1961): 36.

Simon, George T. *The big bands*. Foreword by Frank Sinatra. New York and London: Macmillan, 1967.

479   "Special DDR: Metallblasinstrumente aus Markneukirchen." *Brass Bulletin—International Brass Chronicle*, no. 60 (1987): 16–20. Also in English and French.

Stewart, Gary M. *Keyed brass instruments in the Arne B. Larson collection*. Shrine to Music Museum, Catalog of the Collections, vol. 1, edited by André P. Larson. Vermillion, SD: Shrine to Music Museum, 1980.

480   Stiegler, Karl. "Turmblasen." *Musikpädagogische-Zeitschrift* 15 (1925): n.p.

481   Suppan, Wolfgang, ed. *Bericht über die erste internationale Fachtagung zur Erforschung der Blasmusik, Graz 1974*. Tutzing: H. Schneider, 1976.

482   Teichmann, Heinz. *Instrumentenkunde. 3. Blechblasinstrumente*. Berlin: Volk und Wissen, 1955.

483   Teuchert, Emil, and Erhard Walter Haupt. *Musik-Instrumente in Wort und Bild. Teil III: Messingblas- und Schlaginstrumente*. 2 Aufl. Leipzig: Breitkopf & Härtel, 1928.

484   Trichet, P. "Des cornets de chasse et autres semblables instruments." *Brass Bulletin—International Brass Chronicle*, no. 47 (1984): 51–54. Also in English and German.

485   Urban, Darrell Eugene. "Stromenti da tirarsi in the cantatas of J. S. Bach [abstract]." *Missouri Journal of Research in Music Education* 4, no. 1 (1977): 125–126.

Urban, Darrell Eugene. " 'Stromenti da tirarsi' in the cantatas of J. S. Bach." Ed.D. diss., Washington University, 1977.

486   Valentin, Erich. "Münchener Turmmusik 1938." *Zeitschrift für Musik* 105 (1938): 642–643.

487   Valentin, Erich. "Zwei Jahre Münchener Turmmusik." *Zeitschrift für Musik* 105 (1938): 769–770.

488   "Vom Werden der Blasinstrumente." *Instrumentenbau-Zeitschrift* 11 (1956–57): 167–168.

489   Wagner, I. L. "Nationalistic practices in brass performance." *The Instrumentalist* 31 (Oct. 1976): 52–53.

490   Walser, Gerold. "Römische und gallische Militärmusik." *Geering Festschrift* (1973): 231–239.

491   Wattenbarger, James A. "The Turmmusik of Johann Pezel." Ph.D. diss., Northwestern University, 1957.

492   Wattenbarger, James A. "The Turmmusik of Johann Pezel." *Dissertation Abstracts* 18 (Feb. 1958): 609.

493   Webb, J. "19th-century keyed brass." *Music Trades* 127 (Feb. 1986): 83–85.

494   Wenke, Wolfgang. "Die Holz- und Metallblasinstrumente der ersten Hälfte des 18. Jahrhunderts im deutschen Sprachgebiet." In *Die Blasinstrumente und ihre Verwendung* . . . , edited by Eitelfriedrich Thom, 17–21. Magdeburg: Rat des Bezirkes; Leipzig: Zentralhaus für Kulturarbeit, 1977.

495   Whitwell, David. *The Renaissance wind band and wind ensemble.* Northridge, CA: Winds, 1983.

496   Wieprecht, [W.]. "Réponse de M. Wieprecht à M. Ad. Sax." *La Belgique musicale* 7, no. 35 (31 Dec. 1846): 2–3.

497   Wilson, J. S. "The development of the odd ball brass [in jazz]." *Down Beat* 27 (Jan. 7, 1960): 24–25.

498   Zahl, Wesley. "Instruments and instrumentation: the brass." *Jacobs' Band Monthly* 17 (Sept. 1932): 6–7+; (Nov. 1932): 6.

499   Zingel, Hans Joachim. "Der Anteil der Blasinstrumente an den Neuausgaben alter Musik." *Die Musik-Woche* 3, no. 33 (1935): 3–5.

500   Zingel, Hans Joachim. "Neues Material zur Geschichte der älteren Blechbläsermusik." *Die Musik-Woche* 4, no. 10 (1936): 3–4.

501   Zwittkovits, Heinrich. "Blasmusik in Oesterreich—ihre historische Basis." *Oesterreichische Blasmusik* 27, no. 7 (Sept. 1979): 1–2, 9–10.

General Literature

502   "American composer listing, woodwinds and brass solo and ensemble." *The Triangle of Mu Phi Alpha* 66, no. 2 (1972): 19–25.

503   Ball, E. "The music of Edward Gregson." *Sounding Brass & the Conductor* 6, no. 3 (1977): 98–100.

504   Barbour, J. Murray. "The use of brass instruments in early scores." *Bulletin*

of the American Musicological Society (Sept. 1940, as of June 1939): 16–17.

505 Bartels, Wolfgang von. "Die Olympiafanfaren." *Zeitschrift für Musik* 103 (1936): 443–445.

506 Bartels, Wolfgang von. "Olympiahymne von Richard Strauss. Paul Winters Olympiafanfaren." *Zeitschrift für Musik* 103 (1936): 1100–1101.

507 Bashford, R. "New music reviewed." *Music Teacher and Piano Student* 64 (July 1985): 23.

Bays, Robert E. "Renaissance and Baroque music as a source for improved brass instruction." Ph.D. diss., George Peabody College for Teachers, 1952.

Bedbrook, Gerald S. "The genius of Giovanni Gabrieli." *Music Review* 8 (1947): 91–101.

Biehle. "Johann Pezel und die Turmsonate." *Schlesisches Blatt für evangelische Kirchenmusik* 56 (191?): 4.

508 Biehle, Herbert. "Johann Pezel und die Turmmusik." *Musik Industrie* 4 (191?): 22.

Blankenburg, Walter. "Von der Verwendung von Blechblasinstrumenten in Bachs kirchenmusikalischen Werken und ihrer Bedeutung." *Musik und Kirche* 20 (1950): 65–71.

509 Borris, Siegfried. "Die Blechbläser im Orchester. Tradition und Defizit." *Das Orchester* 27, no. 9 (1979): 639–645.

Boyd, Edward. "Brass in the concert band." *Southwestern Brass Journal* 1 (Spring, 1957): 37–39.

510 Brand, M. "Trills and other frills in brass literature." *The Instrumentalist* 33 (Sept. 1978): 56+.

511 "Brass music for the church." *Church Music* [St. L], no. 2 (1972): 25–40.

512 Brauer, James Leonard. "Instruments in sacred vocal music at Braunschweig-Wolfenbuttel: a study of changing tastes in the seventeenth century." 2 vols. Ph.D. diss., City University of New York, 1983.

513 Bridge, Joseph. "Town waits and their tunes." *Proceedings of the Musical Association* 54 (1927–1928): 63–92.

"Briefly noted—unaccompanied solos for brass." *Brass and Woodwind Quarterly* 2, no. 1–2 (1969): 69–70.

514 Brodde, Otto. "Kirchenmusik für Sänger und Bläser." *Der Kirchenchor* 21, no. 4 (1961): 60–62.

Buckner, J. F. "A touch of brass." *Journal of Church Music* 18 (Feb. 1976): 11–13.

515 Bumcke, Gustav. "Die Verwendung der Blasinstrumente in Regers Werken." *Der Aufschwung* 1 (May 1925).

516 Castellani, Marcello, and Elio Durante. *Del portar della lingua negli instrumenti di fiato. Per uno corretta interpretazione delle sillabe articolatorie nella trattatistica dei secc. XVI-XVIII.* Firenza: Studio per edizioni scelte, 1979.

"Catalogue general des cuivres." *Brass Bulletin—International Brass Chronicle*, no. 16 (1976): whole issue. Also in English and German.

517 Coe, John W. "A study of five selected contemporary compositions for

brass." D.Mus. diss., Indiana University, 1971.

518 Cummings, Barton. "Contemporary Hungarian brass chamber music." *Woodwind World—Brass and Percussion* 19, no. 2 (1980): 11.

519 Dart, Thurston. "The repertory of the Royal Wind Music." *The Galpin Society Journal* 11 (1958): 70–77.

Devol, J., comp. *Brass music for the church.* Plainview, NY: Branch, 1974.

Devol, J., comp. "Music for Easter with brass." *Journal of Church Music* 16 (Jan. 1974): 10–14.

Douglas, Darrell R. "Brass music in the church." *American Organist* 14 (May 1980): 34–35.

520 Douglas, Darrell R. "Brass music in the liturgy of the church." *NACWPI Journal* 22, no. 3 (Spring 1974): 20–21.

521 E. G. "Turmmusik." *Schweizerische Musikzeitung* 65 (191-?): 16.

522 Eglin, A. "Kirchliche Bläserarbeit." *Musik und Gottesdienst* 18, no. 4 (1964): 113–120.

523 Ehmann, Wilhelm. *Voce et Tuba; gesammelte Reden und Aufsätze.* Edited by D. Berke and others. Kassel: Bärenreiter, 1976.

524 Erdmann, Alfred. "Neue und alte Werke für Blasinstrumente und Bläserkammermusik." *Die Musik-Woche* 4, no. 42 (1936): 2–5.

Evenson, Pattee Edward. "A history of brass instruments, their usage, music, and performance practices in ensembles during the Baroque era." D.M.A. diss., University of Southern California, 1960.

Evenson, Pattee Edward. "A history of brass instruments, their usage, music, and performance practices in ensembles during the Baroque era." *Dissertation Abstracts* 22 (1962): 3219.

525 Fasthoff, Henry J. "A catalogue of ensemble music for woodwind, brass, and percussion instruments written by composers in the United States." Master's thesis, Florida State University, 1949.

526 Faulkner, Maurice. "Wagnerian brass style." *The Instrumentalist* 24 (Sept. 1969): 47–49.

527 Faust, Randall E. "Selected literature for solo brass instruments and electronic media." *NACWPI Journal* 32, no. 1 (1983): 4–17.

528 Favre, G. "La Fanfare de la Peri." *L'Education Musicale* (Apr. 1948).

Fitzgibbon, H. Macauley. "Instruments and their music in the Elizabethan Drama." *Musical Quarterly* 17 (1931): 319–329.

529 Fleury, Louis. "Chamber music for wind instruments." *The Chesterian* 37 (1923/24): 111–116; 144–148.

Gaulden, Robert Luther, Jr. "The historic development of scoring for the wind ensemble." Ph.D. diss., Eastman School of Music, 1958.

530 Geiringer, Karl. "Guillaume Dufays 'Gloria ad modum tubae.' " *Zeitschrift für Musik* 94 (1927): 16–19.

Gifford, Robert Marvin, Jr. "The music and performance practices of the medieval wind band." *Journal of Band Research* 10, no. 2 (Spring 1974): 25–32.

531 Globokar, V. "Ueberlegungen zum Thema Blechbläser." *Das Orchester* 25

(Oct. 1977): 691–695.

532 Grad, Toni. "Die Blasmusik im katholischen Brauchtum." *Musikhandel* 9 (1958): 8–9, 53–54.

Gray, R., and Mary Rasmussen, comps. "Three bibliographies of nineteenth- and twentieth-century concertante works; solo parts for the trumpet; solo parts for the trombone; solo parts for more than one different brass instrument." *Brass Quarterly* 6, no. 1 (1962): 10–16.

Hahn, Robert. *Die saarländische Bergmusik, die Bergkapellen*. Saarbrücken: Minerva-Verlag; Thinnes & Nolte, 1969.

533 Helm, Sanford M. "Catalog of chamber music for wind instruments." Master's thesis, University of Michigan, 1946.

Helm, Sanford M. *Catalog of chamber music for wind instruments*. Ann Arbor: Lithoprinted by Braun-Brumfield, 1952.

534 Henschel. "Von Turm-Musik, Trompeten und Posaunen." *Die Sendung* 7 (191-?): 44.

535 Hess, Howard. "Fanfares by Americans." *Modern Music* 20 (1943): 189–191.

Hicks, C. E. "Church music: justification for the use of brass instruments in the church service." *Woodwind World—Brass and Percussion* 20, no. 2 (1981): 12–13+; no. 3 (1981): 12–14.

536 Hohstadt, Thomas. "Modern concepts in music for brass." D.M.A. diss., University of Rochester, 1962.

537 Hohstadt, Thomas. "Modern concepts in music for brass." *Journal of Band Research* 4, no. 1 (1967): 30–41.

538 Hohstadt, Thomas. "Modern concepts in music for brass." *Journal of Band Research* 4, no. 2 (1968): 6–23.

Jähns, F. W. "Parade-Marsch und Horn-Signale der Königl. Sächsischen leichten Infanterie, angeblich von Carl Maria von Weber." *Allgemeine musikalische Zeitung* 13 (1878): 177–183.

Janetzky, Kurt. "Unmöglich? [18th century brass music]." *Brass Bulletin—International Brass Chronicle*, no. 10 (1975): 34–41. Also in English and French.

539 Kanerva, S. "Special Finland: ein kurzer Blick auf die geschichte der finnische Blechblasmusik." *Brass Bulletin—International Brass Chronicle*, no. 53 (1986): 52–55. Also in English and French.

Kimmel, William. *Polychoral music and the Venetian school*. Rochester, NY: University of Rochester Press, 1954.

540 Kipnis, Igor. "A splendid collection of royal brass music [new Nonesuch release]." *HiFi/Stereo Review* 17 (Nov. 1966): 72–73.

541 Kneller, G. "Music, music, music." *Music* 3, no. 6 (1970): 4–7.

542 LaRue, J., and G. Wolf. "Finding unusual brass music." *Brass Quarterly* 6, no. 3 (1963): 111–119.

Lewy, Rudolf. "The wrong brass? [faithfulness to instrumentation as scored]." *Brass Bulletin—International Brass Chronicle*, no. 41 (1983): 10–15. Also in French and German.

543 Logan, Jackie Dale. "*Mouthpiece* by Kenneth Gaburo: a performer's analysis

of the composition." Ph.D. diss., University of California (San Diego), 1977.

Magnell, Elmer P. "Evaluation of solo brass literature." *The Instrumentalist* 8 (Mar. 1954): 52–53.

544 Manuel, Roland. "Freude an der Musik. 6. Gespräch: Von der Harfe und den Blechinstrumenten." *Lancelot*, no. 22 (1950): 30.

Mayerhofer, Götz. "Münchener Turmmusik." *Allgemeine Musikalische Zeitung* 65 (1938): 280–281.

Mayerhofer, Götz. "Münchener Turmmusik." *Die Musik-Woche* 6 (1938): 308–309.

Mayerhofer, Götz. "Turmmusiken in München." *Deutsche Militär-Musiker Zeitung* 60 (1938): 297.

Michaels, Jost. "Die künstlerische Bedeutung der Blasinstrumente und ihrer Literatur." *Das Orchester* 6 (1958): 33–40.

545 Miller, D. G. "Johann Stoerl and his Six Sonatas for Cornett and Trombones." Master's essay, University of Rochester, 1962.

546 Miller, T. A. "An investigation of Johann Sebastian Bach's Cantata 118 *O Jesu Christ, Meins Lebens Licht*." *Dissertation Abstracts* 32 (Dec. 1971): 3354A.

Mitchell, G. H. "Brass of Peace [integration into worship services]." *Journal of Church Music* 23 (Jan. 1981): 2–3.

"Die 'Münchener Turmmusik.' " *Zeitschrift für Musik* 107 (1940): 625.

547 Music Publishers Association. "The United States Copyright Law—a practical outline." *T.U.B.A. Journal* 13, no. 3 (Feb. 1986): 23–24.

548 "Musiker diskutierten mit Herstellern." *Instrumentenbau-Zeitschrift* 24 (Aug. 1970): 468+.

Musser, W. I. "Increased interest in brass chamber music." *The School Musician* 32 (Apr. 1961): 34–35+.

549 Nelson, Mark Allan. "The brass *Parables* of Vincent Persichetti." D.M.A. diss., Arizona State University, 1985.

550 Nichols, K. "Muted brass." *Storyville*, no. 30 (Aug.-Sept. 1970): 203–206.

551 Nobel, Hans. "Münchener Turmmusiken/ausgeführt von bayerischen Kammermusikern. Heroische Kunst unter freiem Himmel." *Die Musik-Woche* 5, no. 24 (1937): 1–2.

Ode, James. *Brass instruments in church services*. Minneapolis: Augsburg, 1970.

552 Ode, James A. "The use of brass instruments in Lutheran Churches in America." Ph.D. diss., University of Rochester, 1965.

553 Panoff, P. "Mit Pauken und Trompeten. Militärmusik der Völker und Zeiten." *Westermanns illustrierte deutsche Monatshefte* (Nov. 1936): 269.

Rasmussen, Mary. "An introductory index of contemporary chorale settings for brass instruments." *Brass Quarterly* 6, no. 2 (1962): 47–81.

Rasmussen, Mary. *A teacher's guide to the literature of brass instruments*. Durham, NH: Brass Quarterly, 1964.

Rein, Friedrich. "Münchener Turmmusik." *Die Musik* 30 (1937): 138–139.

Rein, Friedrich. "Münchener Turmmusik." *Allgemeine Musikalische Zeitung* 67 (1940): 305–306.

Rein, Friedrich. "Münchener Turmmusik." *Musik in Jugend und Volk* 5 (1942): 127.

Reynolds, G. E. "New brass music reviews." *The School Musician* 34 (Apr. 1963): 26 +.

Reynolds, G. E. "New brass publications." *The School Musician* 37 (Feb. 1966): 14 +; (June-July 1966): 12 +.

Richter. "Turmmusik." *Korrespondenzblatt des ev. Kirchengesangvereins für Deutschland* 36, nos. 1, 3 (192?): n.p.

554   Ridley, E. A. K. *Wind instruments of European art music.* Foreword by David M. Boston. London: Inner London Educational Authority, 1974.

Rosenkranz, Marie. "Die Musik als Mitgestalterin am Werden des Menschen. Die Blasinstrumente und das Melos." *Kommenden* 11, no. 13 (1957): 7; no. 14: 10; no. 16: 8.

Salmen, W. "Russische Musik und Musiker vor 1700, unter besonderer Berücksichtigung der Blasmusik." *Brass Bulletin—International Brass Chronicle,* no. 7 (1974): 65–74. Also in English and French.

555   Schmohl, G. "Blasen—einmal anders." *Gottesdienst und Kirchenmusik,* no. 4 (1966): 138–142.

Schubert, F. L. *Die Blechinstrumente der Musik, ihre Geschichte, Natur, Handhabung und Verwendung in der Instrumental-, Gesangs-, Militär- und Tanzmusik.* Leipzig: Merseburger, 1866.

556   Schütze, Erich. "Blasmusik im Dienst der Gemeinschaft." *Die Musik* 33 (1940–41): 104–105.

557   Schultz, P. M. " 'Praise the Lord with the sound of trumpet' and trombone and horn and tuba." *The School Musician* 44 (Dec. 1972): 48–49.

558   Schumacher, S. E. "An analytical study of published unaccompanied solo literature for brass instruments: 1950–1970." *Dissertation Abstracts* 37 (Feb. 1977): 4689A.

559   Schumacher, Stanley E. "An analytical study of published unaccompanied solo literature for brass instruments." Ph.D. diss., Ohio State University, 1976.

560   Shoemaker, J. R. "Music for brass comes into its own." *Music Education Journal* 58 (Sept. 1971): 36–39.

Smith, Robert D. "Some performance practice problems of 17th-century brass music." *NACWPI Journal* 19, no. 2 (Winter 1970–71): 13–14.

561   Spearman, Fanny Turner. "The sound of trumpets." *The Church Musician* 9 (Oct. 1958): 13–14.

562   Squire, W. Barclay. "Purcell's music for the funeral of Mary II." *Sammelbände der Internationalen Musikgesellschaft* 4 (1902/03): 225–233.

563   Suppan, Wolfgang. "Die Blasmusik—eine eigengeprägte Kunstform?" *Oesterreichische Blasmusik* 28, no. 1 (Jan.-Feb. 1980): 1–3.

564   Suppan, Wolfgang. *Lexicon des Blasmusikwesens.* Freiburg im Breisgau: F. Schulz, 1973.

565   Suppan, Wolfgang. *Lexicon des Blasmusikwesens*. 2nd ed. Freiburg im Breis-
       gau: F. Schulz, 1977.
       Trobian, Helen R. "The brass quartet in the church." *Music Ministry* 2 (July
       1961): 10–11.
566   Vagner, Robert S. "A new look at chamber music for winds." *The Instru-
       mentalist* 13 (June 1959): 70–73.
       Valentin, Erich. "Münchener Turmmusik 1938." *Zeitschrift für Musik* 105
       (1938): 642–643.
       Valentin, Erich. "Zwei Jahre Münchener Turmmusik." *Zeitschrift für Musik*
       105 (1938): 769–770.
       Vernei, B. W. "American composer listing, for woodwinds and brass." *The
       Triangle of Mu Phi Epsilon* 64, no. 2 (1970): 17–21.
567   Vigl, Karl H. "Musizieren im Freien—warum eigentlich nicht? Betrachtun-
       gen und Argumente." *Oesterreichische Blasmusik* 27, no. 4 (May 1979): 1–
       2.
568   Walker, B. H. "Christmas solo and ensemble material for brass instru-
       ments." *The School Musician* 25 (Dec. 1953): 37–38.
569   Wallace, Paul, comp. "Original manuscript music for wind and percussion
       instruments." *NACWPI Bulletin* 7 (Mar. 1959): 4–9; (June 1959): 4–12;
       (Dec. 1959): 6–11.
570   Walls, B. G. "The baryton divertimenti of Haydn; a selected adaptation for
       brass trio." *Dissertation Abstracts* 30 (Aug. 1969): 756A.
       Wattenbarger, James A. "The Turmmusik of Johann Pezel." Ph.D. diss.,
       Northwestern University, 1957.
       Wattenbarger, James A. "The Turmmusik of Johann Pezel." *Dissertation
       Abstracts* 18 (Feb. 1958): 609.
       Waybright, D. "Brass playing in the marching band." *The Instrumentalist* 38
       (June 1984): 12–13.
       "Weber brass sonatas published." *The Moravian Music Foundation Bulletin*
       22, no. 2 (1977): 7.
571   Whitwell, D. "Early brass manuscripts in Vienna." *The Instrumentalist* 25
       (Dec. 1970): 36–37.
572   Whitwell, D. "George Bernard Shaw: the music critic." *The School Musician*
       40 (Dec. 1968): 56–59.
573   Wildman, L. "Wedding music with brass." *Diapason* 55 (Oct. 1964): 20–21.
       Wilkie, J. A. "American composer listing, woodwinds and brass solo and
       ensemble." *The Triangle of Mu Phi Epsilon* 65, no. 2 (1971): 23–28.
574   Wilson, J. R. "A study of brass instrument compositions of the Baroque
       period." Master's thesis, University of Washington, 1958.
575   Yoder, David Winston. "A study and performance of extended sacred choral
       works with brass instruments by contemporary American composers."
       D.M.A. diss., University of Southern California, 1973.
576   Yoder, David Winston. "A study and performance of extended sacred choral
       works with brass instruments by contemporary American composers."
       Dissertation Abstracts 34 (Mar. 1974): 6031A-6032A.

Zingel, Hans Joachim. "Der Anteil der Blasinstrumente an den Neuausgaben alter Musik." *Die Musik-Woche* 3, no. 33 (1935): 3–5.

Zingel, Hans Joachim. "Neues Material zur Geschichte der älteren Blechbläsermusik." *Die Musik-Woche* 4, no. 10 (1936): 3–4.

577   "Zu singen und auf allerley Instrumenten zu gebrauchen; über zusammenwirken von Sängern und Bläsern." *Neue Zeitschrift für Musik* 119 (1958): 475.

Orchestration

578   *8. Tonmeistertagung 19.-22 November 1969 Hamburg.* Durchgeführt vom Verband deutscher Tonmeister und Toningenieure e.V. Köln: Westdeutscher Rundfunk, 1969.

Adams, S. R. "A survey of the use of trombones to depict infernal and horrendous scenes in three representative operas." *Journal of the International Trombone Association* 9 (1981): 16–20.

Adkins, Hector Ernest. *Treatise on the military band.* 2d revised ed. London; New York: Boosey, 1958.

579   Anderson, John Drummond. "Brass scoring techniques in the symphonies of Mozart, Beethoven and Brahms." Ph.D. diss., George Peabody College for Teachers, 1960.

580   Anderson, John Drummond. "Brass scoring techniques in the symphonies of Mozart, Beethoven and Brahms." *Dissertation Abstracts* 21 (1961): 2315.

Barbour, J. Murray. "The use of brass instruments in early scores." *Bulletin of the American Musicological Society* (Sept. 1940, as of June 1939): 16–17.

581   Beauregard, Cherry N. "The tuba: a description of the five orchestral tubas and guidelines for orchestral tuba writing." Ph.D. diss., University of Rochester, Eastman School of Music, 1970.

Bingham, John Joseph. "The innovative uses of the trombone in selected compositions of Vinko Globokar." *Dissertation Abstracts* 45 (May 1985): 3234A-3235A.

Blandford, W. F. H. "Bach's horn parts." *The Horn Call* 9, no. 2 (Apr. 1979): 23–27. Reprinted from *The Musical Times* 77 (Aug. 1936): 748–750.

Blandford, W. F. H. "The fourth horn in the 'Choral Symphony.' " *The Horn Call* 10, no. 2 (Apr. 1980): 52–66. Also in German. Reprinted from *The Musical Times* (Jan. 1925).

Blandford, W. F. H. "Handel's horn and trombone parts." *The Musical Times* 80 (1939): 697–699, 746–747, 794.

Blandford, W. F. H. "Handel's horn and trombone parts." *The Musical Times* 81 (1940): 223.

Blandford, W. F. H. "Studies on the horn. III. The fourth horn in the Choral symphony." *The Musical Times* 66 (1925): 29–32, 124–129, 221–223.

Blandford, W. F. H. "Wagner and the horn parts of Lohengrin." *The Musical Times* 63 (1922): 622–624, 693–397.

582   Bobo, Robert P. "Scoring for the Wagner 'tuben' by Richard Wagner, Anton Bruckner, and Richard Strauss." D.M.A. diss., University of Miami, 1971.

Boer, B. H. "Observations on Bach's use of the horn." *Bach—the quarterly journal of the Riemenschneider Bach Institute* 11, no. 2 (1980): 21–28.

Boer, B. H. "Observations on Bach's use of the horn [includes list of works]." *Bach—the quarterly journal of the Riemenschneider Bach Institute* 11, no. 3 (1980): 9–23.

583   Book, Brian. "Views of Berlioz on the use of the ophicleide and tuba in his orchestral works." *T.U.B.A. Journal* 10, no. 4 (Spring 1983): 10–19.

584   Boone, Dalvin Lee. "The treatment of the trumpet in six published chamber works composed between 1920 and 1929." *Dissertation Abstracts* 33 (Apr. 1973): 5762A.

585   Bostley, Edward John. "Abstract: The horn in the music of Gustav Mahler." *Missouri Journal of Research in Music Education* 4, no. 4 (1980): 74–76.

586   Bostley, Edward John. "The horn in the music of Gustav Mahler." D.M.A. diss., University of Missouri (Kansas City), 1980.

Bostley, Edward John. "The horn in the music of Gustav Mahler." *Dissertation Abstracts* 41 (Apr. 1981): 4205A.

587   Brandon, Stephen Paul. "The tuba: its use in selected orchestral compositions of Stravinsky, Prokofiev, and Shostakovich." *Dissertation Abstracts* 35 (Sept. 1974): 1684A-1685A.

Brandon, Stephen Paul. "The tuba: its use in selected orchestral compositions of Stravinsky, Prokofiev, and Shostakovich." D.M.A. diss., Catholic University of America, 1974.

Braunstein, J. "Scoring for the horn from Haydn to Strauss." *International Musician* 47 (Apr. 1949): 22 + .

588   Brevig, Per. "Let's standardize trombone notation." *Music Journal* 32 (July 1974): 18–20 + . Excerpt from his doctoral dissertation: "Avant-garde techniques in solo trombone music."

589   Broder, Nathan. "The wind-instruments in Mozart's symphonies." *Musical Quarterly* 19 (1933): 235–259.

Brown, Tom. "The hunting horn and the classic style." *The Horn Call* 10, no. 2 (Apr. 1980): 38–51.

Brownlow, A. "The mute in contemporary trumpet performance." *The Instrumentalist* 33 (May 1979): 52 + .

Bryan, Paul. "The horn in the works of Mozart and Haydn: some observations and comparisons." In *Haydn Yearbook* 9 (1975): 189–255. In English with German summary.

590   Butterworth, A. "Brass band scoring." *Sounding Brass & the Conductor* 7, no. 1 (1978): 14 + .

Butterworth, A. "Brass band scoring in the seventies." *Sounding Brass & the*

Conductor 4, no. 3 (1975): 76–77.

Butterworth, A. "Brass band scoring in the seventies." *Sounding Brass & the Conductor* 4, no. 4 (1976): 109 + ; 5, no. 3 (1976): 76–77 + .

591 Butterworth, A. "Brass band scoring in the seventies [role of percussionist]." *Sounding Brass & the Conductor* 6, no. 4 (1978): 136 + .

592 Cailliet, L. "The B-flat bass horn (the miscast instrument)." *The School Musician* 42 (May 1971): 47 + .

Carse, Adam. "Beethoven's trumpet parts." *The Musical Times* 94 (1953): 32.

Carse, Adam. "Brass instruments in the orchestra." *Music & Letters* 3 (1922): 378–382.

593 Christensen, C. J. "Some uses of the trombone in the Mexican symphonic repertoire." *Journal of the International Trombone Association* 4 (1976): 36–37 + .

Coe, John W. "A study of five selected contemporary compositions for brass." D.Mus. diss., Indiana University, 1971.

Coleman, Jack. "The trumpet: its use in selected works of Stravinsky, Hindemith, Shostakovich, and Copland." *Dissertation Abstracts* 26 (Dec. 1965): 3389.

Coleman, Jack. "The trumpet: its use in selected works of Stravinsky, Hindemith, Shostakovich, and Copland." D.M.A. diss., University of Southern California, 1965.

Collins, T. "Observations on the origins and influences leading to Bach's idiomatic writing for the trumpet in 'Grosser Herr, o starker König' from the *Christmas Oratorio*." *Bach—the quarterly journal of the Riemenschneider Bach Institute* 17, no. 2 (1986): 31–45.

594 Collins, William Tracy. "Berlioz and the trombone." D.M.A. diss., University of Texas (Austin), 1985.

595 Collins, William Tracy. "Berlioz and the trombone." *Dissertation Abstracts* 46 (May 1986): 3185A.

Cornfield, C. J. "The notation of brass instruments." *The Musical Times* 74 (1933): 653–654.

Croll, Gerhard. "Blasinstrumente in Mozarts Instrumentalmusik. Diskussion "Horn", "Klarinette" und "Bassetklarinette". Diskussion "Oboe" und "Fagott." *Mozart Jahrbuch* (1968–70): 27–29, 33–34.

596 Cummings, Barton. "New techniques for tuba." *The Composer* 6, no. 15 (1974–1975): 28–32.

597 Cundell, Edric. "Composing for brass band." In *Brass Today*. Edited by Frank Wright, 65–69. London: Besson, 1957.

598 Delp, R. "Studio: contemporary harmony, arranging, harmonizing a melody." *Musician Player & Listener*, no. 2 (Nov. 1979): 82.

Deming, Howard Owen. "The use of the trumpet in selected symphonic works of the late nineteenth and early twentieth centuries." D.Mus. diss., Indiana University, 1969.

599 Dondeyne, D., and F. Robert. *Nouveau traité d'orchestration à l'usage des harmonies, fanfares et musique militaires*. Paris: H. Lemoine, 1969.

600 Douay, J. "Le trombone dans le *Bolero* de Ravel." *Brass Bulletin—International Brass Chronicle*, no. 13 (1976): 59–62.

601 Drew, J. "The emancipation of the trombone in orchestral literature." *Journal of the International Trombone Association* 9 (1981): 2–4.

Droste, Paul. "Arranging string literature for euphonium." *T.U.B.A. Journal* 5, no. 2 (Winter 1978): 6–8.

Eichborn, Hermann Ludwig. *Die Trompete in alter und neuer Zeit. Ein Beitrag zur Musikgeschichte und Instrumentationslehre*. Leipzig: Breitkopf & Härtel, 1881.

602 Estes, David John. "Scoring for wind instruments in the symphonies of Johann Chrisostomus Wolfgang Amadeus Mozart." M.A. diss., California State University at San Diego, 1973.

Faust, Randall E. "Electronic and compositional techniques used in 'Horn Call.' " *The Horn Call* 11, no. 2 (1981): 58–61.

603 Francoeur, Louis-Joseph. *Diapason Général de tous les instruments à vent avec des observations sur chacun d'eux, auquel on a joint un projet nouveau pour simplifier la manière actuelle de copier*. Genève: Minkoff, 1971.

604 Friedman, S. A. "Effective scoring for trumpet ensemble." *International Trumpet Guild Newsletter* 4, no. 2 (1978): 6–10.

Fulkerson, J. "Indeterminate instrumentation: a way of extending instrumental techniques." *Journal of the International Trombone Association* 4 (1977): 3–4.

605 Gaulden, Robert Luther, Jr. "The historic development of scoring for the wind ensemble." Ph.D. diss., Eastman School of Music, 1958.

Golland, J. "Writing for brass band." *Composer*, no. 28 (Summer 1968): 12–15.

606 Greenstone, P. J. "Articulation guide for brass instruments based on common practices of contemporary composers and performers." *Dissertation Abstracts* 47 (Nov. 1986): 1525A.

Gregory, Robin. "The horn in Beethoven's symphonies." *Music and Letters* 33 (1952): 303–310.

Gregory, Robin. "The horn in Beethoven's symphonies." *The Horn Call* 7, no. 2 (May 1977): 25–31.

607 Gregson, E. "The composer speaks; Gordon Jacob [interview]." *Sounding Brass & the Conductor* 1, no. 2 (1972): 41–42 + .

608 Gressang, J. C. "Textural procedures in instrumental ensemble music and chamber music prior to the classic period." *Dissertation Abstracts* 39 (Dec. 1978): 3211A.

609 Hanson, Wesley Luther. "The treatment of brass instruments in the symphonies of Gustav Mahler." *Dissertation Abstracts* 37 (June 1977): 7392A.

610 Hanson, Wesley Luther. "The treatment of brass instruments in the symphonies of Gustav Mahler." D.M.A. diss., University of Rochester, Eastman School of Music, 1977.

Hartman, Mark Shafer. "The use of the alto trombone in symphonic and operatic orchestral literature." *Dissertation Abstracts* 46 (Nov. 1985): 1122A.

611 Henshilwood, Donald. "The instruments of the wind band." *Composer* 79 (Summer 1983): 4–6.

Hildebrandt, Donald Jay. "The bass trombone in the twentieth-century orchestra: its use in twenty-seven representative scores." D.Mus. diss., Indiana University, 1976.

Hiller, A. "Die Trompete in den Werken Jean-Philippe Rameaus." *Brass Bulletin—International Brass Chronicle*, no. 35 (1981): 59–64. Also in French and English.

Hodik, Fritz. "Das Horn bei Richard Wagner." Ph.D. diss., Innsbruck, 1937.

612 Horton, Cynthia. "The identification of idiomatic writing for the horn." *Dissertation Abstracts* 47 (Sept. 1986): 706A.

613 Horton, Cynthia. "The identification of idiomatic writing for the horn." D.M.A. diss., University of Wisconsin (Madison), 1986.

614 Huckeby, Ed. "The fourth horn part of the adagio cantabile movement of Beethoven's Symphony No. 9 (Op. 125) in d minor." *The Horn Call* 13, no. 2 (Apr. 1983): 72–75.

Jahn, A. P. *Anweisung zum Gebrauch des Waldhorns sowohl in der Orchester-, als in der Harmonie-Musik für Componisten welche keine genaue Kenntniss dieses Instruments besitzen.* Leipzig: Breitkopf & Härtel, 1829.

Komorzynski, Egon. "Die Posaunen bei Mozart." *Wiener Figaro* 16 (1947): H. 7/8.

615 Kozma, T. "The horn in Goetterdaemmerung." *Opera News* 16 (Dec. 31, 1951): 24–25.

616 Kozma, T. "The trombone in Aida." *Opera News* 16 (Mar. 3, 1952): 30–31.

Kozma, T. "The trumpet in Carmen." *Opera News* 16 (Feb. 11, 1952): 26–27.

Krenz, Edward B. "The brass sextet: a short history of its component instruments; a discussion of the principles of arranging; and five arrangements by the author." Master's thesis, University of Washington, 1952.

Kuehn, David Laurance. "The use of the tuba in the operas and music dramas of Richard Wagner." D.M.A. diss., University of Rochester, 1974.

Kunitz, H. "Vier Posaunen in Opern Verdis und Puccinis." *Musik und Geschichte* (1957): 29.

617 Kunitz, Hans. *Die Instrumentation, Teil 9: Tuba.* Leipzig: Breitkopf & Härtel, 1968.

Lajarte, T. E. D. F. d. "Introduction du trombone dans l'orchestre de l'opéra." In *Curiosités de l'opéra.* Paris: C. Lévy, 1883.

Laplace, Michel. "Ravel et le 'nouveau' trombone." *Brass Bulletin—International Brass Chronicle*, no. 47 (1984): 34–38. Also in English and German.

Larson, Jacob Francis. "The role of the trumpet in the music of Johann Sebastian Bach: past and present performance considerations through selected works." D.M.A. diss., University of Cincinnati, 1976.

Leuba, Christopher. "Rossini's 'E.' " *The Horn Call* 15, no. 2 (Apr. 1985): 66.

Leuba, Christopher. "Stravinsky's F sharp." *The Horn Call* 12, no. 1 (Oct. 1981): 42–43.

Lewis, H. M. "The natural trumpet in the modern orchestra." *The Instrumentalist* 25 (Oct. 1970): 40–41.

618   Lewy, Rudolf. "The wrong brass? [faithfulness to instrumentation as scored]." *Brass Bulletin—International Brass Chronicle*, no. 41 (1983): 10–15. Also in French and German.

619   McCready, Joan W. "Arranging Christmas carols for the tuba ensemble." *T.U.B.A. Journal* 11, no. 2 (Fall 1983): 2–4.

MacDonald, Robert J. "François-Joseph Gossec and French instrumental music in the second half of the eighteenth century." Ph.D. diss., University of Michigan, 1968.

McNerney Famera, Karen. "Mutes, flutters, and trills: a guide to composers for the horn." M.M. thesis, Yale University, 1967.

Maycock, J. "The Bach trumpet parts." *Musical Opinion* 75 (Mar. 1952): 343+.

Merewether, Richard. "Varying national usages in the music of Rossini." *The Horn Call* 16, no. 2 (Apr. 1986): 18.

Miller, Frederick Staten. "A comprehensive performance project in trombone literature with an essay on the use of trombone in the music of Heinrich Schütz." D.M.A. diss., University of Iowa, 1974.

Miller, Frederick Staten. "A comprehensive performance project in trombone literature with an essay on the use of trombone in the music of Heinrich Schütz." *Dissertation Abstracts* 35 (Jan. 1975): 4595A.

Moore, R. C., ed. *Operatic French horn passages*. Bryn Mawr, PA: Presser, 1971.

620   Morrison, T. L. "The use of timpani and brass by Haydn, Mozart and their predecessors." Dissertation, University of Texas, 1947.

621   Mortenson, Gary Curtiss. "The varied role of the trumpet in the musical textures of Igor Stravinsky." D.M.A. diss., University of Texas (Austin), 1984.

Mortenson, Gary Curtiss. "The varied role of the trumpet in the musical textures of Igor Stravinsky." *Dissertation Abstracts* 45 (Jan. 1985): 1912A.

622   Nellist, R. "Scoring hymn tunes for brass band." *Sounding Brass & the Conductor* 8, no. 2 (1979): 79–80.

Oehlberger, Karl. "Artikulationsprobleme des Bläsers bei der Wiedergabe der Werke Mozarts." *Wiener Figaro* 38 (May 1970): 18–30.

Oneglia, M. F. "Cornets—please!!!" *The Instrumentalist* 25 (June 1971): 58–60.

Paul, Ernst. "Das Horn bei Mozart." *Wiener Figaro* 20 (1952): H. 3.

623   Payne, Dorothy Katherine. "Contrapuntal techniques in the accompanied brass and woodwind sonatas of Hindemith." Ph.D. diss., University of Rochester, 1974.

624 Perl, B. "Les cuivres dans les operas de Berlioz." *Brass Bulletin—International Brass Chronicle*, no. 45 (1984): 18–30. Also in English and German.

625 Phelps, Russell L. "Uses of wind instruments in the classical period—influence on their use today in high school band work." Master's thesis, Northwestern University, 1955.

Pierce, T. "Monteverdi's use of brass instruments." *Journal of the International Trombone Association* 9 (1981): 4–8.

Pirie, J. "Arranging: general observations." *Canadian Musician* 4, no. 5 (1982): 67.

Pizka, Hans, comp. *Das Horn bei Mozart*. Kirchheim bei München: the Compiler, 1980.

626 Prescott, J. "Treatment of the cornet and trumpet in selected twentieth-century band compositions." *Journal of Band Research* 21, no. 1 (1985): 50–60.

Reifsnyder, Robert. "The changing role of the euphonium in contemporary band music." D.Mus. diss., Indiana University, 1980.

627 Reifsnyder, Robert. "Why have composers stopped writing melodically for the euphonium?" *T.U.B.A. Journal* 8, no. 4 (Spring 1981): 13–14.

Richardson, E. "Handel's horn and trombone parts." *The Musical Times* 81 (1940): 180.

Ricks, Robert. "Letters to the editor [Bach's use of 7th, 11th, or 13th partials in writing for natural horn]." *Journal of Music Theory* 5, no. 2 (1961): 334–336.

628 Riddle, P. H. "Scoring for the young French horn section." *The School Musician* 43 (Jan. 1972): 37+.

Rivenberg, L. L. "Scoring for three horns: a study of four examples from Beethoven's works." Master's thesis, University of Rochester, 1961.

629 Roeser, Valentin. *Essai d'instruction à l'usage de ceux qui composent pour la clarinette et le cor (1764)*. Geneva: Minkoff, 1972.

Rohde, F. Virginia. "The use of the French horn in the orchestra as exemplified in the symphonies of Haydn, Mozart and Beethoven." Master's thesis, Eastman School of Music, 1940.

630 Ross, C. "Brass scoring techniques of the 19th century." *Woodwind World—Brass and Percussion* 16, no. 2 (1977): 49–50.

631 Ross, C. "Scoring for the middle school brass & percussion sections." *Woodwind World—Brass and Percussion* 14, no. 5 (1975): 36–37.

Ross, Richard Raymond. "The use of the trombone in the Symphonia Sacre I of Heinrich Schütz." D.M.A. diss., Catholic University of America, 1977.

632 Runyan, William Edward. "Orchestration in five French grand operas." Ph.D. diss., University of Rochester, Eastman School of Music, 1983.

633 Rush, Ralph E. "The brass section—strength of the orchestra." *Etude* 73 (Oct. 1955): 15+.

Russell, Ross. "Brass instrumentation in be-bop." *Record Changer* 8 (Jan. 1949): 9–10, 21.

Sandor, E. P. "Development and use of the chromatic trumpet in the nine-teenth-century orchestra." *NACWPI Journal* 33, no. 4 (1985): 4–12.

634 Sauer, R. C. "Transcription fundamentals." *Brass Bulletin—International Brass Chronicle*, no. 31 (1980): 55–56. Also in French and German.

Sauer, Ralph. "The alto trombone in the symphony orchestra." *Journal of the International Trombone Association* 12, no. 3 (1984): 41.

Schuller, Gunther. "An open letter to composers." *The Instrumentalist* 27 (Feb. 1973): 38.

Scutiero, Amedeo. "Sull'uso del corno dal 1700 a Debussy." *Nuova Rivista Musicali Italiana* 14, no. 3 (July-Sept. 1980): 350–367.

Seiffert, Stephen Lyons. "Johannes Brahms and the French horn." D.M.A. diss., University of Rochester, Eastman School of Music, 1969.

Shawger, J. D. "The uses of the trombone in the modern symphony or-chestra." Master's thesis, University of Washington, 1958.

Sluchin, B. "The trombone in the sacred works of W. A. Mozart." *Brass Bulletin—International Brass Chronicle*, no. 46 (1984): 31–35. Also in French and German.

635 Smith, J. L. "The use of the tuba in the symphonic poems of Richard Strauss." *Dissertation Abstracts* 40 (Aug. 1979): 534A-535A.

636 Smith, J. R. "Changes in the musical treatment of the brass in nineteenth-century symphonic and operatic composition." *Dissertation Abstracts* 35 (Feb. 1975): 5453A-5454A.

637 Smith, J. R. "Dissertation reviews: Changes in the musical treatment of the brass in nineteenth-century symphonic and operatic composition." *Journal of the International Trumpet Guild* 10, no. 1 (1985): 50–51.

638 Smith, John Robert. "Changes in the musical treatment of the brass in nineteenth-century symphonic and operatic composition." D.M.A. diss., University of Texas (Austin), 1974.

Sprung, D. "Wagner and the horn." *San Francisco Opera Magazine* (Apr. 1985): 53–54.

Stacy, William B. "Style and register as correlated factors in the horn parts of selected symphonies by Joseph Haydn." M.A. diss., University of North Carolina at Chapel Hill, 1969.

639 Stafford, James Edward. "Compositional devices employed in scoring for voice and brass combination by selected contemporary American com-posers." Ph.D. diss., Louisiana State University and Agricultural and Mechanical College, 1970.

640 Stafford, James Edward. "Compositional devices employed in scoring for voice and brass combination by selected contemporary American com-posers." *Dissertation Abstracts* 31 (Mar. 1971): 4827A.

641 Stewart, J. "The complete musician: orchestrating for brass." *Guitar Player* 11 (Sept. 1977): 116.

642 Stewart, J. "The complete musician: orchestration—the trumpets." *Guitar Player* 11 (Aug. 1977): 118.

643 Stith, Marice. "New ideas for composers of trumpet music." *The Composer*

6, no. 15 (1974–1975): 12–13.

Sweeney, J. A. "Die Naturtrompete in den Kantaten J. S. Bachs." Dissertation, Freie Univ. Berlin, 1961.

Talma, Louise. "Horns and trumpets as used in the orchestra from 1700–1900." Master's thesis, Columbia University, 1933.

Tanner, James Cornwell, Jr. "Technical and musical uses of the trombone in selected original repertoire for the twentieth-century concert band." *Dissertation Abstracts* 44 (Nov. 1983): 1239A.

Taylor, William A. "The orchestral treatment of the trombone in the 18th and 19th centuries." Master's thesis, Eastman School of Music, 1951.

Thompson, Mark. "Brahms and the light." *The Horn Call* 9, no. 1 (Oct. 1978): 71–72. Also in French and German.

Todd, J. "The trumpet as a solo orchestral color since 1827." Master's thesis, University of Washington, 1961.

644   Tuozzolo, James M. "Trumpet techniques in selected works of four contemporary American composers: Gunther Schuller, Meyer Kupferman, William Sydeman, and William Frabizio." *Dissertation Abstracts* 33 (Dec. 1972): 2972A-2973A.

645   Vandenbroeck, Orthon. *Traité général de tous les instruments à vent à l'usage des compositeurs.* Geneva, Minkoff, 1973.

646   Vernei, B. W. "American composer listing, for woodwinds and brass." *The Triangle of Mu Phi Epsilon* 64, no. 2 (1970): 17–21.

Vincent, Charles, and Sam Cope. *The Brass band and how to write for it.* London[?]: Vincent Music Co., 1908.

647   Wallace, Oliver C. "Problems involved in selecting and transcribing sixteenth century Italian madrigals for brass ensemble use in the high school." Master's thesis, University of Miami (Fla.), 1953.

648   Wallace, S. C. "A study of high school band directors' ability to discriminate between and identify modern cornet and trumpet timbres." *Dissertation Abstracts* 40 (Apr. 1980): 5359A.

649   Walshe, Robert C. "The orchestral horn transpositions of Richard Strauss." *The Horn Call* 17, no. 2 (Apr. 1987): 11–15.

Weingartner. "Horn und Harfe im modernen Orchester." *Signale für die musikalische Welt* 76 (191?): 11, 17.

Weingartner, Felix. "Die Posaunen in Mozarts Requiem." *Die Musik* 5 (1905/06): 41–43.

Wheeler, J. "A curiosity in Schubert's trumpet writing." *The Galpin Society Journal* 21 (Mar. 1968): 185–186.

Whitman, Dale. "The horn in the works of Bach and Handel." D.M.A. diss., Catholic University of America, 1979.

650   Whybrew, William C. "Ravel's use of orchestral brass." Master's thesis, Eastman School of Music, 1947.

651   Wilkie, J. A. "American composer listing, woodwinds and brass solo and ensemble." *The Triangle of Mu Phi Epsilon* 65, no. 2 (1971): 23–28.

652   Williams, Edwin Lynn. "Dissertation reviews: The role of the trumpet and

cornet in the early ballets of Igor Stravinsky." *Journal of the International Trumpet Guild* 10, no. 3 (1986): 25–26.

653   Williams, Edwin Lynn. "The role of the trumpet and cornet in the early ballets of Igor Stravinsky." D.M.A. diss., University of Cincinnati, 1980.

Willis, James D. "A study of Paul Hindemith's use of the trombone as seen in selected chamber compositions." D.M.A. diss., University of Missouri (Kansas City), 1973.

654   Wilson, Cecil Barley. "Berlioz' use of brass instruments." *Dissertation Abstracts* 32 (Sept. 1971): 1558A-1559A.

655   Wilson, Cecil Barley. "Berlioz' use of brass instruments." Ph.D. diss., Case Western Reserve University, 1971.

656   Wise, R. E. "Scoring in the neoclassic woodwind quintets of Hindemith, Fine, Etler, and Wilder." *Dissertation Abstracts* 28 (Oct. 1967): 1462A-1463A.

Wotton, Tom S. "Notation of the horn: some altered meanings." *The Musical Times* 65 (1924): 808–812.

Wotton, Tom S. "Notation of the horn: some altered meanings." *The Musical Times* 66 (1925): 154–155.

Wright, Denis. "Scoring for brass band." *The Musical Times* 73 (1932): 800–803.

657   Wright, Denis. *Scoring for brass band.* 4th ed. London: Baker, 1967.

Wright, Denis. *Scoring for the brass band.* Colne, Lancashire: J. Duckworth, 1935.

Yoder, David Winston. "A study and performance of extended sacred choral works with brass instruments by contemporary American composers." D.M.A. diss., University of Southern California, 1973.

Yoder, David Winston. "A study and performance of extended sacred choral works with brass instruments by contemporary American composers." *Dissertation Abstracts* 34 (Mar. 1974): 6031A-6032A.

Young, Jerry Allen. "The tuba in the symphonic works of Anton Bruckner and Gustav Mahler: a performance analysis." Ed.D. diss., University of Illinois (Urbana-Champaign), 1980.

Young, Jerry Allen. "The tuba in the symphonic works of Anton Bruckner and Gustav Mahler: a performance analysis." *Dissertation Abstracts* 41 (May 1981): 4641A.

Zahl, Wesley. "Instruments and instrumentation: the brass." *Jacobs' Band Monthly* 17 (Sept. 1932): 6–7+; (Nov. 1932): 6.

Zorn, Hans. "Die Trompete in der deutschen Orchestermusik von ca. 1750 bis ins 20. Jahrhundert." Ph.D. diss., Innsbruck, 1973.

658   Agrell, Jeffrey. "Jazz and the horn." *Brass Bulletin—International Brass Chronicle*, no. 40 (1982): 41–45. Also in French and German.

659   Agrell, Jeffrey. "Jazz and the horn: Thomas Bacon." *Brass Bulletin—International Brass Chronicle*, no. 45 (1984): 34. Also in French and German. Reprinted in part from *Brass and Percussion* 1, no. 3 (1973): 6–7.

660   Agrell, Jeffrey. "Jazz and the horn: Tom Varner." *Brass Bulletin—International Brass Chronicle*, no. 47 (1984): 55–57. Also in French and German.

661   Altenburg, Wilhelm. "Die Wagnertuben und ihre Einführung in die Militärmusik." *Zeitschrift für Instrumentenbau* 31 (1910/11): 1105–1107. Subsequent correspondence: 1149–1150 [Max Enders]; 1187–1189 [Gebr. Alexander]; 1230–1231 [Enders]; 1273–1274 [Alexander].

      Altman, Sylvia. "A historical study on the horns and trumpets. Outline of the structural evolution of the instruments. The function and treatment of the horns and trumpets from Bach to Wagner." Master's thesis, Columbia University, 1933.

      Angles, R. "Piano and horn [Barry Tuckwell]." *Music and Musicians* 12 (July 1964): 27.

662   *Anleitung zum Trompetenblasen für die Königlich-preussischen Postillone.* Berlin: A. W. Hayn, 1850. Partially reprinted in: *Schüler, Posthornsignale.*

663   [Bagge, Selmar]. "Important review of Johannes Brahms' Trio for violin, horn and piano, op. 40." *Allgemeine musikalische Zeitung* 2 (1867): 15–17, 24–25.

664   Baines, Anthony. "The William Bull horn." *The Galpin Society Journal* 35 (1982): 157–158.

665   Baker, J., and others. "Music for horn." *Sounding Brass & the Conductor* 9, no. 3 (1980): 27–28.

666   Baltz, K. "Jagdhorn." *Deutsche Jägerzeitung* 68 [1916?]: 534.

667   Barboteu, M. Georges. "Du cor." *The Horn Call* 6, no. 2 (May 1976): 23–32.

668   Barboteu, M. Georges. "Evolution of the horn in France." *The Horn Call* 6, no. 2 (1976): 33–40.

      Barbour, J. Murray. "Trumpet and horn in the church music of Bach and his contemporaries." *Bulletin of the American Musicological Society* (Sept. 1948): 61–62.

669   Barbour, J. Murray. *Trumpets, horns and music.* East Lansing, Mich.: Michigan State University, 1964.

670   Barford, D. C. "The horn concertos of Antonio Rosetti." *Dissertation Abstracts* 41 (Dec. 1980): 2344A.

671   Barford, David. "The horn concertos of Antonio Rosetti." D.M.A. diss., University of Illinois (Urbana-Champaign), 1980.

672   "Barry Tuckwell edits French horn classics." *The School Musician* 48 (June-July 1977): 8 + .

673   Bate, Philip. "An English 'cor omnitonique.' " *The Galpin Society Journal* 2 (1949): 52–54.

674   Bate, Philip. "Horn lore." *The Galpin Society Journal* 31 (May 1978): 150–151.

675   Baumann, Hella. "The horn as a symbol." *The Horn Call* 11, no. 2 (1981): 40–48.

676   Baumann, M. P. "Befragungsmodell und Vergleich; erläutert am Beispiel der Langtrompeten." *Die Musikforschung* 31, no. 2 (1978): 161–176.

677   Bell. "A bibliographic survey of the horn in chamber music, 1950–1830." *The Horn Call* 17, no. 2 (Apr. 1987): 37–44.

678   Bergstone, F. "A recommended selected list of French horn literature." *The Instrumentalist* 27 (June 1973): 51–53.

679   Betts, James Edmond. "A comprehensive performance project in horn literature with an essay consisting of a comparison of concepts of horn technique as expressed in selected instructional materials for horn dating from 1798 to 1960." D.M.A. diss., University of Iowa, 1984.

680   Bevan, Clifford. "Letters: The mellophonium." *Sounding Brass & the Conductor* 9, no. 1 (1980): 6–7.

681   Bienenfeld, Elsa. "Das Waldhorn." *Deutsche Musiker-Zeitung* 64 (1933): 531.

682   Birsak, K. "Musikinstrumente im Tanzmeistersaal." *Mitteilungen der Internationalen Stiftung Mozarteum* 29, no. 3–4 (1981): 16 + .

683   Blaikley, D. J. "The French horn." *Proceedings of the Musical Association* 35 (1908/09): 123–134.

684   Blandford, W. F. H. "Bach's horn parts." *The Musical Times* 77 (1936): 748–750, correction 837.

685   Blandford, W. F. H. "Bach's horn parts." *The Horn Call* 9, no. 2 (Apr. 1979): 23–27. Reprinted from *The Musical Times* 77 (Aug. 1936): 748–750.

686   Blandford, W. F. H. "The fourth horn in the 'Choral Symphony.' " *The Horn Call* 10, no. 2 (Apr. 1980): 52–66. Also in German. Reprinted from *The Musical Times* (Jan. 1925).

687   Blandford, W. F. H. "Handel's horn and trombone parts." *The Musical Times* 80 (1939): 697–699, 746–747, 794.

688   Blandford, W. F. H. "Handel's horn and trombone parts." *The Musical Times* 81 (1940): 223.

689   Blandford, W. F. H. "Studies on the horn." *The Musical Times* 63 (1922): 544–547; 693–697.

690   Blandford, W. F. H. "Studies on the horn. III. The fourth horn in the Choral symphony." *The Musical Times* 66 (1925): 29–32, 124–129, 221–223.

691   Blandford, W. F. H. "Wagner and the horn parts of Lohengrin." *The Musical Times* 63 (1922): 622–624, 693–697.

692   Blechschmidt, M. "Die Russischen Hörner im sächsischen Erzbergbau." *Musikforum* 23, no. 4 (1978): 15–20.

693   Blood, Elsworth F. "The transition from hand horn to valved horn studied through orchestral horn music from 1815–1845." Master's thesis, Eastman School of Music, 1948.

694   "Blow your own whachamacallit." *High Fidelity* 21 (Nov. 1971): 52.

Blyth, A. "Tuckwell's chance choice." *Music and Musicians* 17 (Sept. 1968): 34+.

695 Boer, B. H. "Observations on Bach's use of the horn." *Bach—the quarterly journal of the Riemenschneider Bach Institute* 11, no. 2 (1980): 21–28.

696 Boer, B. H. "Observations on Bach's use of the horn [includes list of works]." *Bach—the quarterly journal of the Riemenschneider Bach Institute* 11, no. 3 (1980): 9–23.

Bostley, Edward John. "Abstract: The horn in the music of Gustav Mahler." *Missouri Journal of Research in Music Education* 4, no. 4 (1980): 74–76.

Bostley, Edward John. "The horn in the music of Gustav Mahler." D.M.A. diss., University of Missouri (Kansas City), 1980.

697 Bostley, Edward John. "The horn in the music of Gustav Mahler." *Dissertation Abstracts* 41 (Apr. 1981): 4205A.

698 Boulton, John. "The horn." *Hallé* (Nov. 1949): 15–17.

699 Bourgue, D. "Le cor en France." *Brass Bulletin—International Brass Chronicle*, no. 1 (1971): 19–27. Includes summaries in English and German.

700 Bourgue, D. "Die Entwicklung des Hornbaues in Frankreich." *Oesterreichische Musikzeitung* 38 (Sept. 1983): 497–498.

701 Bourgue, D. "La trompe de chasse, son histoire, sa technique, sa musique." *Brass Bulletin—International Brass Chronicle*, no. 39 (1982): 26–38. Also in English and French.

Bowles, Edmund A. "Unterscheidung der Instrumente Buisine, Cor, Trompe und Trompette." *Archiv für Musikwissenschaft* 18 (1961): 52–72.

702 Bracegirdle, Lee. "The New York school: its development and relationship to the Viennese style." *The Horn Call* 14, no. 2 (Apr. 1984): 16–24.

703 Bracegirdle, Lee. "Die New Yorker Schule; ihre Entwicklung und ihre Verwandtschaft mit dem Wiener Stil." *Oesterreichische Musikzeitung* 38 (Sept. 1983): 500.

704 Brain, Dennis. "About the French horn." In *Brass Today*. Edited by Frank Wright, 60–63. London: Besson, 1957.

705 Braunstein, J. "Scoring for the horn from Haydn to Strauss." *International Musician* 47 (Apr. 1949): 22+.

Briegleb, Arthur, and Wendell Hoss, comps. "Music for ensembles." *The Horn Call* 2, no. 2 (May 1972): 11–18.

706 "The British French horn." *Music and Musicians* 25 (Sept. 1976): 8+.

Brockpähler, Renate. " 'Signalhorn,' 'Riete,' 'Adventshorn.' Volkstümliche Blasinstrumente in Westfalen." *Rheinisch-Westfälische Zeitschrift für Volkskunde* 24, nos. 1–4 (1978): 30–77.

707 Brockway, Oliver. "Mozart and Haydn: some mis-attributions?" *The Horn Call* 3, no. 2 (May 1973): 16–23.

708 Brockway, Oliver. "Specialist publications for horn: a British contribution." *The Horn Call* 15, no. 2 (Apr. 1985): 62–64.

709 Brown, Thomas Martin, Jr. "Clarino horn, hunting horn, and hand horn: their comparative roles in the classic music of the eighteenth century." D.A. diss., Ball State University, 1978.

710 Brown, Thomas Martin, Jr. "Clarino horn, hunting horn, and hand horn: their comparative roles in the classic music of the 18th-century." *Dissertation Abstracts* 40 (Aug. 1979): 523A-524A.

711 Brown, Tom. "The hunting horn and the classic style." *The Horn Call* 10, no. 2 (Apr. 1980): 38–51.

712 Brüchle, Bernhard. *Horn-Bibliographie, I-II.* Wilhelmshaven: Heinrichshofen, 1970.

713 Brüchle, Bernhard. *Horn-Bibliographie, Band 2: Ergänzungen zur Ausgabe von 1970.* Wilhelmshaven: Heinrichshofen, 1975.

714 Brüchle, Bernhard, and Kurt Janetzky. *Kulturgeschichte des Horns (A pictorial history of the horn).* English translation by C. Baumann. Tutzing: H. Schneider, 1976.

Brüchle, Bernhard, and D. Lienhard. *Horn bibliographie, Band III: Ergänzungen zu den Ausgaben von 1970 und 1975.* Wilhelmshaven: Heinrichshofen, 1983.

715 Brüchle, Bernhard. "An unknown work for horn by Richard Strauss." *The Horn Call* 3, no. 1 (Nov. 1972): 21–23.

716 Bryan, Paul. "The horn in the works of Mozart and Haydn: some observations and comparisons." In *Haydn Yearbook* 9 (1975): 189–255. In English with German summary.

717 Bujanovski, V. "Die Leningrader Hornschule." *Oesterreichische Musikzeitung* 38 (Sept. 1983): 498–499.

718 Butterworth, J. "Music for horn." *Sounding Brass & the Conductor* 5, no. 2 (1976): 61.

719 Cahier. "Cors ou trompes de chasse." *Nouveaux mélanges d'archéologie* 6 (1874): 35.

Cailliet, L. "The B-flat bass horn (the miscast instrument)." *The School Musician* 42 (May 1971): 47 + .

720 Cameron, L. C. R. *The hunting horn.* London: n.p., 1950.

721 Cannan, J. "Around the horn." *Music of the West* 13 (Dec. 1957): 7 + .

722 Capps, William. "Lecture-recital—the uses of the hunting horn and Waldhorn in the orchestra (1639–1865)." Ph.D. diss., Catholic University of America, 1970.

723 Carse, Adam. "The French horn in England." *Hallé* (June 1950): 14–17.

724 Ceccarosi, Domenico. *Le possibilita coloristiche del corno.* Roma: Edizioni musicali *Ortipe*, 1949.

725 Ceccarossi, Domenico. "I concerti per corno di Mozart e la loro interpretazione." *Rivista Italiana Musicologia* 21, no. 1 (1987): 24–34.

726 Chesboro, Gayle. "Horn-Lokk (by Sigurd Berge): an analysis and commentary." *The Horn Call* 6, no. 1 (Nov. 1975): 15–16.

727 Chesebro, Gayle. "An analysis of Bujanovski's Sonata for Horn Solo." *The Horn Call* 7, no. 2 (May 1977): 32–33.

728 Chesebro, Gayle. "An annotated list of original works for horn alone and for horn with one other non-keyboard instrument." D.Mus. diss., Indiana University, 1977.

729   Chesebro, Gayle. "*Laudatio* (Bernhard Krol): an analysis." *The Horn Call* 10, no. 1 (Oct. 1979): 51.

730   Childs, Carroll Arthur. "Literature for the French horn." *Master's thesis, Northwestern University*, 1950.

        Christmann, Arthur. "Horns and trumpets of yesteryear. Instruments without valves." *The Baton* 9, no. 3 (1930): 9+.

731   Civil, Alan. "About the horn." *Composer [London]*, no. 41 (Autumn 1971): 17–20.

732   Civil, Alan. "History of the horn." *Music and Musicians* 19 (May 1971): 24–25.

733   Classens, Gustav. "Robert Schumanns 'Konzertstück für 4 Hörner und grosses Orchester (Werk 86).' " *Die Musik-Woche* 4, no. 14 (1936): 7–8.

734   Clewing, Carl. "Denkmäler deutscher Jagdkultur." In *Auftrag der Deutschen Jägerschaft*. Neudamm, J. Neumann. Kassel: Bärenreiter, c. 1937.

735   Coar, Birchard. *A critical study of the nineteenth century horn virtuosi in France*. DeKalb, Ill.: the author, 1952.

736   Coar, Birchard. *The French horn*. DeKalb, Ill.: the author, 1947.

737   Coerper. "Das Klappenhorn." *Zeitschrift für Instrumentenbau* 39 (191-?): 11–12.

738   Collorafi, Jim. "On reconstructing Mozart's unfinished horn concerti." *The Horn Call* 12, no. 2 (Apr. 1982): 13–17.

739   Collorafi, Jim. "Schubert's alla breve symbol." *The Horn Call* 16, no. 2 (Apr. 1986): 62–63.

740   "Le Cor." *Schweizerische Instrumentalmusik* 27 (1938): 328, 351–352, 400–401.

741   Cox, P. W. L., Jr. "The neglected second horn." *Music Educators Journal* 25 (Sept. 1938): 45+.

742   Croll, Gerhard. "Blasinstrumente in Mozarts Instrumentalmusik. Diskussion 'Horn,' 'Klarinette' und 'Bassetklarinette.' Diskussion 'Oboe' und 'Fagott.' " *Mozart Jahrbuch* (1968–70): 27–29, 33–34.

743   Dahlstrom, J. F. "History and development of the horn." *The School Musician* 41 (Feb. 1970): 52–53.

        Damm, Peter. "300 Jahre Waldhorn." *Brass Bulletin—International Brass Chronicle*, no. 31 (1980): 19–20+. Also in English and French.

        Damm, Peter. "300 Jahre Waldhorn." *Brass Bulletin—International Brass Chronicle*, no. 32 (1980): 19+. Also in English and French.

744   Damm, Peter. "Did Mozart really compose only four horn concertos?" *The Horn Call* 10, no. 2 (Apr. 1980): 23–24. Also in German.

745   Damm, Peter. *Gedanken zu den Hornkonzerten von Richard Strauss*. Richard Strauss-Blätter. Neue Folge, IV, ed. by Günter Brosche, 31–42.

746   Damm, Peter. "Hat J. S. Bach die Partie des Corne da Caccia der *Messe h-Moll* BWV 232 für Gottfried Reiche komponiert?" *Brass Bulletin—International Brass Chronicle*, no. 58 (1987): 63–65+. Also in English and French.

747   Damm, Peter. "Hat J. S. Bach die Partie des Corne da Caccia der *Messe h-Moll* BWV 232 für Gottfried Reiche komponiert?" *Brass Bulletin—Inter-*

national Brass Chronicle, no. 56 (1986): 61 + . Also in English and French.

748 Damm, Peter. "Hat J. S. Bach die Partie des Corne da Caccia der *Messe h-Moll* BWV 232 für Gottfried Reiche komponiert?" *Brass Bulletin—International Brass Chronicle*, no. 57 (1987): 67–76 + . Also in English and French.

749 Damm, Peter. "Das Horn in der ersten Hälfte des 18. Jahrhunderts. Versuche der interpretation hoher Hornpartien." In *Die Blasinstrumente und ihre Verwendung* . . . , edited by Eitelfriedrich Thom, 37–41. Magdeburg: Rat des Bezirkes; Leipzig: Zentralhaus für Kulturarbeit, 1977.

750 Damm, Peter. "On the articulation marks in Mozart's horn concerti." *The Horn Call 9*, no. 1 (Oct. 1978): 37–46.

751 Damm, Peter. "Verzierungen in Hornkonzerten des 18. Jahrhunderts." *Brass Bulletin—International Brass Chronicle*, no. 42 (1983): 12–15. Also in English and French.

752 Damm, Peter. "Verzierungen in Hornkonzerten des 18. Jahrhunderts." *Brass Bulletin—International Brass Chronicle*, no. 44 (1983): 48–52. Also in English and French.

753 Damm, Peter. "Verzierungen in Hornkonzerten des 18. Jahrhunderts; Veränderungen und Modifikationen des Tempos." *Brass Bulletin—International Brass Chronicle*, no. 45 (1984): 46–54. Also in English and French.

754 Daubeny, Ulric. "The horn." *Musical Opinion* 37 (1914): 361–362.

755 Daubeny, Ulric. "A descriptive chapter about the French horn." *Metronome* 40 (Feb. 1924): 78–79.

756 Davis, Shelley G. "The hunt, the keyboard and J. G. Lang's *Concerto da caccia*." *Music Review* 39, nos. 3–4 (Aug.-Nov. 1978): 162–177.

757 Delano, Alice. "Mozart 'Horn Concerto K. 495': a study of editions." *The Horn Call 18*, no. 1 (Oct. 1987): 25–29.

Delp, R. "Studio: contemporary harmony, arranging, harmonizing a melody." *Musician Player & Listener*, no. 2 (Nov. 1979): 82.

758 der Meer, John Henry van. "Wide sockets on 18th-century horns." *The Galpin Society Journal* 36 (1983): 28.

759 Detourbet, A. *Remarques sur la trompe de chasse, le ton de vénerie et l'interpretation des fanfares, avec un historique abrégé de l'instrument et des conseils pour son emploi en forêt*. Autun: Imprimerie Notre-Dame des Anges, 1929.

760 Devemy, Jean. "Du cor d'harmonie." *Musique & Radio* 36 (1945): 137–138.

761 Doelger, F. A. "Das Horn als Trauerinstrument." In *Antike und Christentum*, by F. J. Dölger, II, 4, 316.

Dressler, J. "Materials for horn auditions: band and orchestra." *The Instrumentalist* 36 (Jan. 1982): 65–67.

762 Dressler, John C. "The cadenzas in Mozart's horn concerti." *The Horn Call 15*, no. 1 (Oct. 1984): 47–51.

763 Dullat, G. "Vom Contrahorn über den 16füssigen Orgelbass und den Contra-Bassophon zum Claviatur-Contrafagott." *Tibia—Magazin für Freunde alter und neuer Bläsermusik 9*, no. 2 (1984): 99–105.

764 Dunn, Richard. "Linguistic notes on brass technique." *The Horn Call 2*, no.

2 (May 1972): 52–53.

765   Dunn, Richard. "Mozart's unfinished horn concertos: the 'fifth' and 'sixth' concertos." *The Horn Call* 13, no. 1 (Oct. 1982): 16–26.

766   Durday, James Clark. "Music for the French horn from the late Romantic period and the twentieth-century." M.A. thesis, California State University (Long Beach), 1977.

767   Dutlenhoefer, Marie. "Gebr. Alexander, Mainz 1782–1982." *The Horn Call* 13, no. 1 (Oct. 1982): 28–35.

768   Eger, J. "Around the horn." *Musical Courier* 156 (Nov. 1, 1957): 10–11.

769   Eichborn, Hermann Ludwig. "Die Einführung des Horns in die Kunstmusik." *Monatshefte für Musikgeschichte* 21 (1889): 80–88.

770   Eichborn, Hermann Ludwig. "Einige Worte über russiche Jagdhorn-Musik." *Zeitschrift für Instrumentenbau* 13 (1892/93): 133–134.

771   Eisenschink, Alfred. *Der Jäger und sein Horn.* 4th ed. Munich: BLV, 1975.

772   Elliott, David G. "The Brahms horn trio and hand horn idiom." *The Horn Call* 10, no. 1 (Oct. 1979): 61–73.

773   Erdmann, Alfred. "Die Bedeutung der gestopften und gedämpften Waldhörner. Ein neuer Waldhorndämpfer." *Die Musik-Woche* 3, no. 10 (1935): 3–6.

774   Erdmann, Alfred. "Zweifelhafte Bezeichnungen in den Hornstimmen. Internationale einheitliche Bezeichnung des Notenmaterials wäre erforderliche." *Die Musik-Woche* 5, no. 9 (1937): 3–4 + .

775   Fako, Nancy. "In memoriam: Carl Geyer." *The Horn Call* 4, no. 1 (Autumn 1973): 52–54.

776   Fardell, J. M. "The Ripon hornblower." *English Dance and Song* 35, no. 1 (1973): 11.

777   Farkas, Philip. "Horn excerpt clinic: 'Till.' " *The Horn Call* 15, no. 1 (Oct. 1984): 55–57.

778   Farkas, Philip, and Lawrence Sansone, Jr. "In memoriam, Lorenzo Sansone." *The Horn Call* 6, no. 1 (Nov. 1975): 17–18.

779   Farnsley, Stephen H. "Gunther Schuller's Concerto for Horn and Orchestra: an unpublished, youthful masterpiece." *The Horn Call* 17, no. 1 (Oct. 1986): 17–23.

        Faulkner, Maurice. "Annual review of solos and studies: trumpet and French horn." *The Instrumentalist* 39 (Feb. 1985): 71–76.

780   Faulkner, Maurice. "Solos and studies for trumpet and horn." *The Instrumentalist* 32 (Feb. 1978): 56 + .

        Faulkner, Maurice. "Trumpet and French horn [1982–83 publications]." *The Instrumentalist* 38 (Dec. 1983): 42 + .

        Faulkner, Maurice. "Trumpet and French horn [annual review of solos and studies]." *The Instrumentalist* 35 (Dec. 1980): 33–34.

781   Faulkner, Maurice. "Trumpet and French horn (some of the more interesting selections we found)." *The Instrumentalist* 36 (Dec. 1981): 65–66.

782   Faulkner, Maurice. "Trumpet and French horn solos and studies." *The Instrumentalist* 33 (Jan. 1979): 80 + .

Faulkner, Maurice. "Trumpet and horn solos and studies." *The Instrumentalist* 34 (Dec. 1979): 24–26.

783 Faust, Randall E. "Electronic and compositional techniques used in 'Horn Call.' " *The Horn Call* 11, no. 2 (1981): 58–61.

Faust, Randall Edward. "A comprehensive performance project in horn literature with an essay consisting of three original concertpieces for horn and electronic media, an explanation of techniques used, and a listing of relevant literature." 2 vols. D.M.A. diss., University of Iowa, 1980.

784 Fehr, Max. *Musikalische Jagd*. Zürich: Hug, 1954.

785 Fétis, F. -J. "Cor-solo de Dujariez." *Gazette musicale de Belgique* (5 June 1834).

786 Fétis, F. J. "Concert de cors russes." *Revue musicale* 13 (1833): 284–285.

787 Fétis, F. J. "Cors à pistons." *Revue musicale* 2 (1828): 153–162.

788 Fétis, F. J. "Nouveau cor omnitonique." *Revue musicale* 13 (1833): 172–174.

789 Fitzpatrick, Horace. "Blasinstrumente in Mozarts Instrumentalmusik [instrumentenbau und Spieltechnik]. Das Waldhorn der Mozartzeit und seine geschichtliche Grundlage." *Mozart Jahrbuch* (1968–70): 21–27.

790 Fitzpatrick, Horace. *The horn and horn-playing and the Austro-Bohemian tradition from 1680 to 1830*. New York: Oxford University Press, 1970.

791 Fitzpatrick, Horace. *The horn and horn-playing and the Austro-Bohemian tradition from 1680 to 1830*. London: Oxford University Press, 1971.

792 Fitzpatrick, Horace. "Notes on the Vienna horn." *The Galpin Society Journal* 14 (Mar. 1961): 49–51.

793 Fitzpatrick, Horace. "The Waldhorn and its associations in Bach's time." *Royal Musical Association Research Chronicle*, no. 3 (1963): 51–54.

Fleischhauer, G. "Bucina und Cornu." *Wissenschaftliche Zeitschrift der Martin-Luther-Universität* (1960): 501–506.

794 Francis, George. "Horn notes." *Monthly Musical Record* 62 (1932): 105–106.

795 Fransman, H. "Das Waldhornspiel in Finnland." *Oesterreichische Musikzeitung* 38 (Sept. 1983): 499.

796 Freedman, R. S. "Bits 'n' pieces 'bout horns 'n' trumpets." *Music Journal* 30 (Dec. 1972): 28+.

797 Freedman, R. S. "One-note musicians [horn bands]." *The Instrumentalist* 36 (Nov. 1981): 120–121.

798 Frevert, Walter. *Die deutschen Jagdsignale und Brackenjagdsignale. Mit Merkversen*. Berlin: P. Parey, 1951.

799 Friese, Ernst August. "Klappenhorn und Klappentrompete." *Musica* 4 (1950): 224–225.

800 Gassel, Otto. "Von den Jagdhornbläser-Korps." *Wild und Hund* 61 (1958): 529–530.

801 Gaubert, H. "Trompes de chasse." *Musica* (Chaix) 66 (Sept. 1959): 35–42.

802 Gaubert, Henri. "Trompes de chasse." *The Horn Call* 11, no. 2 (1981): 31–35. Reprinted from *Musica* 66 (Sept. 1959).

803 Götz, Robert, ed. *Jagdsignale, Jagdfanfaren, Jagdfanfarenmärsche, Jagdweisen und Jägerlieder*. Plauen i. V.: G. Wolff, 1936.

804   Gottron, Adam Bernhard. *Das Waldhornbüchlein*. Würtzburg: St. Ritaverlag, 1925.

805   Greenberg, Norman C. "Anthropology and the horn." *The Horn Call* 11, no. 1 (Oct. 1980): 64–74.

806   Greene, G. J. "Louis François Dauprat; his life and works." *Dissertation Abstracts* 31 (June 1971): 6647A.

807   Greene, Gary A. "Response to Johnson's article concerning the Strauss concerti." *The Horn Call* 12, no. 2 (Apr. 1982): 40–41.

808   Greene, Gary Allen. "Richard Strauss: the two concertos for horn and orchestra." M.M. thesis, Butler University, 1978.

       Greenfield, E. "London report [Barry Tuckwell]." *High Fidelity* 18 (Mar. 1968): MA30.

809   Gregory, Robin. "Full score: the horn." *Philharmonic Post* 5 (Sept.-Oct. 1949): 8–10.

810   Gregory, Robin. "The horn in Beethoven's symphonies." *Music and Letters* 33 (1952): 303–310.

811   Gregory, Robin. "The horn in Beethoven's symphonies." *The Horn Call* 7, no. 2 (May 1977): 25–31.

812   Gregory, Robin. *The horn; a comprehensive guide to the modern instrument and its music*. 2d ed. London: Faber and Faber, 1969.

       Gregory, Robin. *The horn; a guide to the modern instrument*. London: Faber and Faber, 1961.

813   Greissle, Felix. "Die formale Grundlagen des Bläserquintetts von Arnold Schönberg." *Musikblätter des Anbruch* (Feb. 1925).

814   Gumbert, Friedrich. *Posthornschule und Posthorn-Taschenliederbuch nebst Abriss der Geschichte des Posthorns und Sammlung historischer Posthornstücke von K. Thierme*. Leipzig: C. Merseburger, 1903.

815   Haeffner, R. "Stopphornet—Waldhornet." *Musikern* 38, no. 13/14 (1945): 9–11.

816   Halfpenny, Eric. "Smith, London." *The Galpin Society Journal* 21 (Mar. 1968): 105–107.

817   Halfpenny, Eric. "Tantivy: an exposition of the 'Ancient hunting notes.' " *Proceedings of the Royal Musical Association* 80 (1953–54): 43–58.

       Hancock, John M. "The horns of the Stearns Collection." *The Horn Call* 14, no. 2 (Apr. 1984): 60–71.

       Hardin, Burton E. "Character of the French horn." *The Instrumentalist* 19 (Feb. 1965): 32+.

818   Hardin, Burton E. "Komm süsser Tod." *The Horn Call* 9, no. 1 (Oct. 1978): 47–49.

819   Hardin, Peter. "The Beethoven solo works for horn." *NACWPI Journal* 19, no. 4 (Summer 1971): 31–32.

820   Hare, Robert Y. "A study of the French horn in orchestral music." Master's thesis, Wayne University, 1950.

821   Haynes, S. W. "A survey of solo literature for French horn and piano." Master's thesis, University of Washington, 1960.

822   Heiss, H. "Musik und Jägerei." *Völkische Musik-Erziehung* 4 (1938): 164–166.
823   Helfritz. "Die Blasinstrumente des Orchesters [Horn]." *Zeitschrift des Reichsbundes Deutscher Orchestervereine* 3 (1930): 6.
       Henschel, A. K. "Hörner und Trompeter." *Die Sendung* 9 (1932): 112.
824   Hervé, A. "La chasse et la musique—Le cor." *La revue musicale* 6 (1906): 461–466.
825   Heuser, W. "Musik und Jagd." *Deutsches Adelsblatt* 55 (193-?): 1458.
826   Heyde, Herbert. "Nochmals: Zwischen Hörnern und Jägertrompeten." *Brass Bulletin—International Brass Chronicle*, no. 58 (1987): 101. Also in English and French.
827   Heyde, Herbert. "Zwischen Hörner und Jägertrompeten." *Brass Bulletin—International Brass Chronicle*, no. 55 (1986): 42–56. Also in English and French.
828   Hiller, A. *Das grosse Buch vom Posthorn.* Wilhelmshaven: Heinrichshofen, 1985.
829   Hiller, A. "Das Inventions-Posthorn des frühen 19.Jahrhunderts." *Brass Bulletin—International Brass Chronicle*, no. 59 (1987): 27–34. Also in English and French.
830   Hiller, A. "Das Posthorn der Königlich Bayerischen Post des 19. Jahrhunderts im Dienste der Volksmusik." *Brass Bulletin—International Brass Chronicle*, no. 50 (1985): 52–65. Also in English and French.
831   Hodik, Fritz. "Das Horn bei Richard Wagner." Ph.D. diss., Innsbruck, 1937.
832   Hoeltzel, Michael. "Gibt es noch einen deutschen Hornton?" *Oesterreichische Musikzeitschrift* 38 (Sept. 1983): 493–494.
833   Hoeltzel, Michael. "Rund um das Horn [Hamburger Jägerschaft]." *Brass Bulletin—International Brass Chronicle*, no. 44 (1983): 16–21. Also in English and French.
834   Hogarth, G. "Musical instruments: the horn." *Musical World* 4 (1837): 81–85.
835   Holmes, John Clellom. *The horn.* New York: Random House, 1958.
       Hoover, W. "The French horn and the alto horn." *The Instrumentalist* 23 (Dec. 1968): 23.
       "Horn personnel in orchestras: 1971–72." *The Horn Call* 2, no. 2 (May 1972): 20–21.
836   "The horn since Gabriel." *The School Musician* 30 (Dec. 1958): 24–25 +.
       Horton, Cynthia. "The identification of idiomatic writing for the horn." *Dissertation Abstracts* 47 (Sept. 1986): 706A.
       Horton, Cynthia. "The identification of idiomatic writing for the horn." D.M.A. diss., University of Wisconsin (Madison), 1986.
837   Horvath, Roland. "Das Horn—Was ist es? Was kann es?" *Oesterreichische Musikzeitung* 38 (Sept. 1983): 466–471.
838   Horvath, Roland. "The Wagnertuba." *Oesterreichische Musikzeitung* 38 (Sept. 1983): 472–473.
839   Hoss, Wendell. "The development of the French horn." *The Instrumentalist* 3 (May-June 1949): 14–16.

840   House, R. Edmund. "The German style of horn playing: myth or method?" *The Horn Call* 9, no. 2 (Apr. 1979): 29–45. Also in French and German.

841   Howe, W. F. *French horns*. Lecture. Brighton, 1886.

842   Hoza, V. "Tower-watchmen and night-watchmen in Bohemia." *Brass Bulletin—International Brass Chronicle*, no. 29 (1980): 57–60. Also in French and German.

Huckeby, Ed. "The fourth horn part of the adagio cantabile movement of Beethoven's Symphony No. 9 (Op. 125) in d minor." *The Horn Call* 13, no. 2 (Apr. 1983): 72–75.

843   "In memoriam: Anton Horner." *The Horn Call* 2, no. 2 (May 1972): 22–23.

844   "Inventionshorn, einwendig, ausgemalt mit Chinoiserie, 19. Jh." *Brass Bulletin—International Brass Chronicle*, no. 4 (1973): 51. Also in English and French.

845   "Inventionshorn ohne festes Mundrohr, einwendig." *Brass Bulletin—International Brass Chronicle*, no. 4 (1973): 19. Also in English and French.

846   Jacob, Heinrich. *Anleitung zum Jagdhornblasen*. 3. neubearbeitet Auflage. Hamburg and Berlin: P. Parey, 1954.

847   Jacob, Heinrich. "Jagdhorn." *Wild und Hund* 41 (1935): 354–356.

848   Jacob, Heinrich. *So blasen die Jäger! Anleitung zum Jagdhornblasen mit den bei der deutschen Jägerschaft gebräuchlichen Signalen*. Berlin: P. Parey, 1936.

849   Jaenicke, Bruno. "The horn." *The Horn Call* 2, no. 1 (Nov. 1971): 58–60. Reprint from 1930's article.

Jaenicke, Bruno. "Double, double, toil and burble." *Woodwind Magazine* 5 (June 1953): 4–5.

850   Jaenicke, Bruno. "The horn." *The Ensemble News* 2, no. 2 (1927): 11–13.

851   "Jagdhorn, sechswindig, mit getriebenem Silberrand: Jagdszenen 1860." *Brass Bulletin—International Brass Chronicle*, no. 4 (1973): 27. Also in English and French.

852   "Jagdmusik." *Der Volksgesang* (1894).

853   Jahn, A. P. *Anweisung zum Gebrauch des Waldhornes sowohl in der genaue Kenntniss dieses Instruments besitzen*. Leipzig: Breitkopf & Härtel, [1829].

854   Jahn, A. P. *Anweisung zum Gebrauch des Waldhorns sowohl in der Orchester-, als in der Harmonie-Musik für Componisten welche keine genaue Kenntniss dieses Instruments besitzen*. Leipzig: Breitkopf & Härtel, [1829].

855   James, Eric. "Who is Carl Oestreich and why is he important to horn players?" *The Horn Call* 14, no. 2 (Apr. 1984): 53–58.

856   Janetzky, Kurt. "300 Jahre Horn in Böhmen: zu unserem Titebild." *Brass Bulletin—International Brass Chronicle*, no. 31 (1980): 3–4. Also in English and French. Excerpt from *Kulturgeschichte des Horns*, by Brüchle and Janetzky.

857   Janetzky, Kurt, and Bernhard Brüchle. *Das Horn. Eine kleine Chronik seines Werdens und Wirkens*. Bern and Stuttgart: Hallwag, 1977.

858   Janetzky, Kurt, and Bernhard Brüchle. *Le cor*. Transl. by L. Jospin. Lausanne: Payot, 1978.

859   Janetzky, Kurt, and Bernhard Brüchle. *The horn*. Portland, OR: Amadeus Press, 1988.

860   Janetzky, Kurt. "A closer look, past and future, at the re-enlivening of the clarin register for horn music from 1720–1780." *The Horn Call* 12, no. 1 (Oct. 1981): 31–35. Also in German.

861   Janetzky, Kurt. "Metamorphoses of possibilities." *The Horn Call* 2, no. 2 (May 1972): 77–88. Translated by Cecilia C. Baumann.

862   Janetzky, Kurt. "Two interesting double concerti [Johann Beer, Michael Haydn]." *The Horn Call* 4, no. 1 (Autumn 1973): 67–70.

863   Janetzky, Kurt. "Vom steten Wandel: Gedankensplitter zur Geschichte des Horns." *Das Orchester* 28 (Mar. 1980): 194–198.

864   Janetzky, Kurt. "Das Waldhorn-Quartett: von der Kuriosität zur künstlerischen Erfüllung." *Musica* 8 (1954): 142–144.

865   Janetzky, Kurt. "Zwei Interessante Doppelkonzerte [Johann Beer/Michael Haydn]." *The Horn Call* 4, no. 1 (Autumn 1973): 62–66.

866   Jensen, J. R. "A bibliography of chamber music for French horn." Master's thesis, University of California at Los Angeles, 1962.

867   Jensen, R. "The pre-orchestral horn." *The Instrumentalist* 23 (Apr. 1969): 44–45.

868   Jeurissen, Herman. "An unknown horn concerto by W. A. Mozart [an attempt at a reconstruction]." *The Horn Call* 10, no. 2 (Apr. 1980): 12–14.

869   Johnson, Bruce Chr. "Richard Strauss's horn concerti: signposts of a career." *The Horn Call* 12, no. 1 (Oct. 1981): 58–67.

870   Johnson, Keith M. "The classical horn concerto cadenza." D.Mus. diss., Indiana University, 1976.

871   Jung, K. F. *Frankreichs Bracken- und Brackenjagdausdrücke*. n.p.: Privatdruck, [192-?].

872   Jung, K. F. "Geläut und Glocken." *Deutsche Jägerzeitung* 80, no. 10 (1922).
      Kalkbrenner, A. "Die Notation der Ventil-Instrumente (Hörner und Trompeten) in der Orchestermusik." *Neue Zeitschrift für Musik* 83 (1887): 236–237, 321–323.

873   Kampen, Paul. "The Ripon horn." *The Horn Call* 17, no. 1 (Oct. 1986): 38–39.

874   Kandler, Georg. "Zur Geschichte der alten Jägermusik." *Deutsche Militär-Musiker Zeitung* 58 (1936, Nr. 21): 2–4.
      Karstädt, Georg. "Aufführungspraktische Fragen bei Verwendung von Naturtrompeten, Naturhörnern und Zinken." In *Kongress—Bericht*, 93–95. Gesellschaft für Musikforschung, 1953.

875   Karstädt, Georg. "Die Besetzung des 'Corno' bei Joh. Seb. Bach." *Die Musikforschung* 4 (1951): 376–377.

876   Karstädt, Georg. "Das Horn und seine Aufgaben im heutigen Orchester." *Allgemeine Musikalische Zeitung* 66 (1939): 525–526.
      Karstädt, Georg. "Horn und Zink bei Johann Sebastian Bach." *Musik und Kirche* 22 (1952): 187–190.

877   [Karstädt, Georg]. "Jagd und Musik." In *Die Jagd*. Bremen: W. Dorn, 1959.

878 Karstädt, Georg. "Mozarts Hornkonzert." *Die Volksmusik—Ausg. A* (1941): 250–253.

879 Karstädt, Georg. "Waldhorn als Solo- und Orchesterinstrument." *Die Volksmusik—Ausg. A* (1940): 173–176.

880 Kearns, Andrew. "The virtuoso horn concertos of Franz Xaver Pokorny." *The Horn Call* 14, no. 1 (Oct. 1983): 33–46.

881 Kimple, Wilbert Kenneth, Jr. "Make it a horn section [four horn parts require different types of players]." *The Instrumentalist* 34 (Jan. 1980): 40+.

882 King, John R. "The technique of writing for the French horn as illustrated in the Trio, opus 40, by Johannes Brahms." Master's thesis, Eastman School of Music, 1946.

883 Kingdon-Ward, Martha. "Mozart and the horn." *Music and Letters* 31 (1950): 318–332.

884 Kleffel, Arno. "Die Notierungsweise des Ventilhorns." *Musik pädagogische Blätter* 36 (1913): 321–322.

885 Kling, H. "Le cor de chasse." *Rivista musicale italiana* 18 (1911): 95–136. Published separately. Turin: Bocca, 1911.

886 Kling, H. "Studie über das Waldhorn." *Neue Zeitschrift für Musik* 94 (1898): 509–511, 535, 545–546.

Kling, Henri. "Giovanni Punto, célèbre corniste." *Bulletin français de la S. I. M.* 4 (1908): 1066–1082.

Knott, Handel. "The horn." *Music and Letters* 32 (1951): 200–201.

Koch, Hans Oskar. "Die Spezialtypen der Blasinstrumente in der 1. Hälfte des 18. Jahrhunderts im deutschen Sprachraum." Staatsexamensarbeit, Hochschule für Musik und Theater, 1969.

887 Köhler, Augustus Charles. *The coach horn. What to blow, and how to blow it. By an Old Guard.* London: Köhler & Son, 1888.

888 Körner, Friedrich. "Ein Horn von Michael Nagel in Graz." *Historisches Jahrbuch der Stadt Graz* 2 (1969): 87–96.

889 Kopsch, J. "Das Waldhorn und Richard Strauss." *Internationale Richard-Strauss-Gesellschaft*, Mitteilungen 24 (Mar. 1960): 3–6.

890 Kouloff. "From the F Sharp of the Russian Imperial Horn Music." *Harmonicon* 2 (1824): 104.

Kozma, T. "The horn in Goetterdaemmerung." *Opera News* 16 (Dec. 31, 1951): 24–25.

891 Kunitz, Hans. *Die Instrumentation. Ein Hand- und Lehrbuch. Teil VI: Horn.* Leipzig: VEB Breitkopf & Härtel, 1957.

892 La Roche, Charles, Boursier de. *Les plus belles fanfares de chasses, transcrites et revues. Précedées d'une étude sur les cornures par Jean des Airelles et d'une introduction historique et bibliographique par le Commandant G. de Marolles.* Paris: E. Nourry, 1930.

893 "Landeswettbewerb im Jagdhornblasen in Bayern." *Der deutsche Jäger* 79, no. 24 (1962).

894 Larkey, Amy. "Gustav Heim and The Waldhorn Quartette." *The Horn Call* 7, no. 1 (Nov. 1976): 34–41.

895   Leavis, Ralph. "Mozart's last horn concerto." *Music and Letters* 34 (1953): 315–318.

896   Leeson, Daniel N. "Whatever happened to the 'sinfonie concertante?' " *The Horn Call* 16, no. 2 (Apr. 1986): 68–74.

       Leipp, Emile, and Lucien Thevet. "Le cor." *Bulletin du Groupe d'acoustique musicale* 41 (May 1969): 1–23.

897   Leuba, C. "The Viennese 'Pumpenhorn.' " *The Instrumentalist* 16 (1961): 34 +.

898   Leuba, Christopher. "Comment on, and an index of the Gumbert excerpt series." *The Horn Call* 10, no. 1 (Oct. 1979): 19–21.

899   Leuba, Christopher. "The descant horn." *The Instrumentalist* 26 (Feb. 1972): 46–49; (Mar. 1972): 70–73.

900   Leuba, Christopher. "The horn concertos of Franz Anton Rossler ("Rosetti")." *The Horn Call* 8, no. 2 (1978): 42–56.

901   Leuba, Christopher. "Performing the brass quintets of Victor Ewald." *The Horn Call* 16, no. 1 (Oct. 1985): 36.

902   Leuba, Christopher. "Rossini's 'E.' " *The Horn Call* 15, no. 2 (Apr. 1985): 66.

903   Leuba, Christopher. "Stravinsky's F sharp." *The Horn Call* 12, no. 1 (Oct. 1981): 42–43.

904   Leuba, Julian Christopher. "Orchestral excerpt clinic: the 'Andante cantabile' from Tschaikowsky's Fifth Symphony." *The Horn Call* 16, no. 2 (Apr. 1986): 64–67.

905   Lewis, Paul. "Early valve horns." *The Galpin Society Journal* 36 (1983): 128–129.

906   Lewis, Peter. *A fox-hunter's anthology.* New York: Macmillan, 1935.

       Limouzin, C. *Eugène Vivier, la vie et les aventures d'un corniste, 1817–1852.* Paris: Marpon, 1888.

907   Lockhart, K. "Pit stop: "The Ring." *San Francisco Opera Magazine* (Apr. 1985): 50–52.

908   McCann, William J. "Lecture recital: A short history of the natural horn and its use by Haydn and Mozart." D.M.A. diss., Catholic University of America, 1974.

909   McConathy, O. W. "Great horn virtuosi of the past." *Symphony* 4 (Apr. 1950): 12–13.

910   McConathy, O. W. "Great horn virtuosi of the past." *Woodwind World* 3 (Sept. 15, 1959): 14; (Dec. 1, 1959): 11.

911   MacDonald, James. "Leutgeb's legacy: the Mozart horn masterpieces." *The Horn Call* 5, no. 2 (Spring 1975): 29–35.

       MacDonald, Robert J. "François-Joseph Gossec and French instrumental music in the second half of the eighteenth century." Ph.D. diss., University of Michigan, 1968.

912   Machala, Kazimierz Wieslaw. "The horn concertos of Francesco Antonio Rosetti." D.M.A. diss., Juilliard School, 1978.

913   McMullan, Andrew J. "Mozart's music for the horn." Master's thesis, East-

man School of Music, 1947.

914 McNerney Famera, Karen. "Mutes, flutters, and trills: a guide to composers for the horn." M.M. thesis, Yale University, 1967.

915 Mahillon, Victor Charles. *Le cor.* Brussels: Mahillon, 1907.

916 Mahillon, Victor Charles. "The horn—its history, its theory, its construction." *Dominant* 16, nos. 10–11 (1908); 17, nos. 1–2, 5 (1909).

917 Mahillon, Victor Charles. "Les musiques de chasses russes." *L'Echo musical* 24 (1894): 1–6.

918 Mann, William. "Hindemith's horn concerto." *London Musical Events* 6 (Apr. 1951).

Maret, H. "Les cors de Potemkin." *Chronique musicale* 10 (1875): 13–16.

919 Marolles, G. de. *Essai de monographie sur la trompe de chasse.* Privately printed, ca. 1910-ca. 1920.

920 Marolles, G. de. *Monographie abrégée de la trompe de chasse.* Privately printed, ca. 1910-ca. 1920.

921 Marolles, G. de. *Trois questions relatives a l'historique de la trompe de chasse.* Privately printed, ca. 1910-ca. 1920.

922 Martell, Paul. "Zur Geschichte des Waldhorns." *Deutsche Militär-Musiker Zeitung* 52 (1930): 29.

923 Martin, D. L. "Placing the horns; thoughts and opinions from seven directors." *The Instrumentalist* 39 (Aug. 1984): 64–65.

924 Marx, Josef. *W. A. Mozart's twelve Duos for two French horns.* New York: McGinnis & Marx, 1947. Introduction.

925 Mathez, Jean-Pierre. "Editorial: Corno da caccia—for trumpeters or horn players? A debate for experts only?" *Brass Bulletin—International Brass Chronicle,* no. 54 (1986): 3–4. Also in French and German.

926 Mathis, W. E. "Peck-horns and other castoffs." *The Instrumentalist* 35 (Feb. 1981): 30–31.

927 Maximilian v. Bayern, Herzog, ed. *Posthornklänge (für das chromatische Horn. Mit Reisebildern von Carl Stieler).* Munich: Braun & Schneider, [c. 1860].

928 Meek, Harold. "The horn!" *The Horn Call* 1, no. 2 (May 1971): 19–21. Reprinted from *Music Educators Journal* (Nov. 1970).

929 Meek, Harold. "The horn!" *Music Education Journal* 57 (Nov. 1970): 9 + .

930 Mende, Emily. "The hunting horn in Europe." *The Horn Call* 8, no. 2 (1978): 58–64.

931 Merewether, Richard. "Varying national usages in the music of Rossini." *The Horn Call* 16, no. 2 (Apr. 1986): 18.

932 Merewether, Richard. "The Vienna-horn—and some thoughts on its past fifty years." *The Horn Call* 15, no. 1 (Oct. 1984): 31–35.

933 Michel, A. "Posthornsignale, eine historische Volksmusikpraxis." *Musikforum* 31, no. 4 (1986): 11–17.

934 Miller, James Earl. "The life and works of Jan Vaclav Stich (Giovanni Punto)—a check-list of eighteenth-century concertos and players—an edition for study and performance of the Concerto No. VI in E-flat by Giovanni Punto." 2 vols. Ph.D. diss., University of Iowa, 1962.

935   Miller, James Earl. "The life and works of Jan Vaclav Stich (Giovanni Punto): a check-list of eighteenth-century horn concertos and players." *Dissertation Abstracts* 24 (Aug. 1963): 768–769.

936   Mitchell, J. Harris. "The use of the French horn from Bach through Schumann." Master's thesis, University of North Carolina, 1956.

937   Montagu, G., and Jeremy Montagu. "Beverley Minster reconsidered." *Early Music* 6, no. 3 (1978): 406–408.

938   Moore, R. C., ed. *Operatic French horn passages*. Bryn Mawr, PA: Presser, 1971.

939   Morley-Pegge, Reginald. "Callcott's radius French horn." *The Galpin Society Journal* (Mar. 1950): 49–51.

940   Morley-Pegge, Reginald. "The degenerate horn." *Music and Letters* 32 (1951): 94–96.

941   Morley-Pegge, Reginald. "The evolution of the modern French horn from 1750 to the present day." *Musical Association Proceedings, Session* 69 (1943): 35–55.

942   Morley-Pegge, Reginald. *The French horn*. London: E. Benn, 1960; New York: Philosophical Library, 1960.

943   Morley-Pegge, Reginald. *The French horn; some notes on the evolution of the instrument and its technique*. London: E. Benn, 1960.

944   Morley-Pegge, Reginald. *The French horn: some notes on the evolution of the instrument and of its technique*. 2d ed. London: Benn, 1973.

945   Morley-Pegge, Reginald. "The orchestral French horn; its origin and evolution." In *Seventh Music Book*, 195–219. London: Hinrichsen, 1952.

946   Morley-Pegge, Reginald. "The French horn." *Brass Bulletin—International Brass Chronicle*, no. 25 (1979): 75.

947   Moser, Hans Joachim. " 'Hörner aufsetzen,' ein Waldhornschern seit Mozart." *Das Orchester* 7, no. 12 (1950): 344–345.

948   Muenster, Georg, Graf zu. *Der Hirschruf*. Leipzig: Weber, 1921.

949   Murray, S. E. "The double horn concerto: a specialty of the Oettingen-Wallerstein Court [appendix lists concerto repertory]." *The Journal of Musicology* 4, no. 4 (1985–1986): 507–534.

950   Murray, Thomas. "The four Mozart Horn Concertos." *The Horn Call* 7, no. 2 (May 1977): 18–20.

951   "Music for horns." *Sounding Brass & the Conductor* 8, no. 4 (1979): 151.

952   Nadaf, G. "Music for horn—some new, some old." *The School Musician* 44 (Mar. 1973): 14 + .

953   Neefe, K. "Sind die alt-sachsischen Hornsignale von Carl Maria von Weber?" *Neue Zeitschrift für Musik* 91 (1895): 13–14, 25–26.

954   Neitzel, O. "Die Horn-Notirung—eine brennende Frage." *Neue Zeitschrift für Musik* 87 (1891): 61–62, 73–74, 85–87.

955   Netto. "Von Hörnern, Posaunen und Trompeten aus alter und neuer Zeit." *Deutsche Mititär-Musiker Zeitung* 28 (1906): 73–74.

956   "A new double French horn." *Metronome* 23, no. 1 (1907): 12.

957   "New horn set in corno da caccia style." *Musik International-Instrumentenbau-*

Zeitschrift 37 (Dec. 1983): 745–746.

958   Newbould, B. "Mozart, the hand horn and K.447." *Music Teacher and Piano Student* 57 (Sept. 1978): 17–18.

"Notice sur l'introduction des cors, des clarinettes et des trombones dans les orchestres français, extraite des manuscrits autographes de Gossec." *Revue musicale* 5 (1829): 217–223.

959   O'Connor, Edward Joseph Patrick. "A recital and a study of Paul Hindemith's style in his compositions for solo French horn." *Dissertation Abstracts* 28 (Oct. 1967): 1460A.

960   O'Connor, Edward Joseph Patrick. "A recital and a study of Paul Hindemith's style in his compositions for solo French horn." Ed.D. diss., Columbia University, 1967.

961   Ohlsson, Eric Paul. "The quintets for piano, oboe, clarinet, horn and bassoon by Wolfgang Amadeus Mozart and Ludwig van Beethoven." D.M.A. diss., Ohio State University, 1980.

Oldeberg, Andreas. "Vorgeschichtliche Blashörner." *Musica* (Apr. 1952): 149–152.

962   O'Loughlin, N. "Horn." *The Musical Times* 125 (Feb. 1984): 99–100.

963   Oosting, Stephen. "Text-music relationships in Benjamin Britten's 'Serenade for Tenor, Horn, and Strings.' " D.M.A. diss., University of Rochester, Eastman School of Music, 1985.

"Orchestras around the world [horn sections]." *The Horn Call* 6, no. 2 (1976): 76+.

964   Paul, E. "Das Horn und seine Entwicklung vom Natur- zum Ventilinstrument." Dissertation, Vienna, 1932.

965   Paul, E. "Jagd und Musik." *Musikerziehung* 15 (1962): 174–177.

966   Paul, E. "Oesterreichische Jagdmusik." *Oesterreichische Musik Zeitschrift* 12 (1957): 230–236.

967   Paul, Ernst. "Austrian hunting music." *The Horn Call* 2, no. 1 (Nov. 1971): 32–39. Translated by Bernhard Bruechle.

968   Paul, Ernst. "Das Horn bei Mozart." *Wiener Figaro* 20 (1952): H. 3.

969   Paul, Ernst. "Das Horn des Wiener Klangstils." *Oesterreichische Musikzeitschrift* 24, no. 12 (Dec. 1969): 698–702.

970   Paul, Ernst. "Das Horn des Wiener Klangstils." *The Horn Call* 3, no. 2 (May 1973): 29–32.

971   Paul, Ernst. "Oesterreichische Jagdmusik." *The Horn Call* 2, no. 1 (Nov. 1971): 23–31.

972   Paul, Ernst. "The Viennese horn style." *The Horn Call* 3, no. 2 (May 1973): 33–36. Translated by Oliver Brockway.

973   Paul, Ernst. "Das Waldhorn." *Musikerziehung* (Sept. 1949): 28–30.

"The Pavahn Trio [piano, violin and French horn]." *Woodwind World* 5, no. 4 (1964): 5.

974   Pease, Edward. "Performing the Brahms Horn Trio." *The Horn Call* 4, no. 1 (Autumn 1973): 44–51.

975   Pénable, Jean Lazare. "Le cor." In *Encyclopédie de la musique et dictionnaire*

du Conservatoire. 2. ptie, vol. 3 (1927). Paris: Delagrave, 1913–1931.

976 Pendergast, D. J. "The horn, a fearsome beast." *Music Journal* 29 (Apr. 1971): 47+.

977 Piersig, Fritz. *Die Einfürung des Hornes in die Kunstmusik und seine Verwendung bis zum Tode J. S. Bachs*. Halle: Niemeyer, 1927.

978 Pilkova, Zkenka. "Das Waldhorn in böhmischen Quellen des 18. Jahrhunderts." *Die Musikforschung* 35, no. 3 (1982): 262–266. Translated by Rudolf Toman.

979 Pinkow, David James. "A selected and annotated bibliography of music for horn and piano with analyses of representative works." D.M.A. diss., University of Maryland, 1983.

980 Pinkow, James David. "A selected and annotated bibliography of music for horn and piano with analyses of representative works." *Dissertation Abstracts* 45 (Apr. 1985): 3023A.

981 Pizka, Hans, comp. *Das Horn bei Mozart*. Kirchheim bei München: the Compiler, 1980.

982 Pompecki, Bernhard. *Jagd- und Waldhornschule . . . nebst Jagd-Signalbuch. Mit einer gesch. Abhandlung über die Hörner im allgem. und die Jagd- und Jägerhörner im besond*. 2. unveränd. Auss. Neudamm: J. Neudamm, [1926].

983 Poncet, J. "De la sensibilité des instruments de cuivre [hunting horns]." *Brass Bulletin—International Brass Chronicle*, no. 28 (1979): 29+. Also in English and German.

984 Poncet, J. "La trompe de chasse." *Brass Bulletin—International Brass Chronicle*, no. 39 (1982): 45–47. Also in English and German.

Pottag, Max. "Reflections on the history of the horn ensemble." *The Instrumentalist* 13 (Aug. 1959): 36.

985 Rahles, F. "Deutsches Horn (Cor allemand) das von Hrn. L. A. Schröder in Köln neu effundene Blech-Instrument." *Neue Zeitschrift für Musik* 28 (1848): 23.

986 Rasmussen, Mary. "The Manuscript Kar. Wenster Litt. I/1–17b (Universitensbiblioteket, Lund)—a contribution to the history of the baroque horn concerto." *Brass Quarterly* 5, no. 4 (1962): 135–152. Includes music.

987 Rdt, C. "Ueber die Verbreitung des chromatischen oder Ventilhorns." *Neue Zeitschrift für Musik* 2 (1835): 177–178.

988 Redslob, Kurt. *Deutsch Jagdsignale mit Merksprüchen*. Neudamm: J. Neudamm, 1930.

989 Reich, Dr. "Noch einmal: die Russischen Hörner im sächsischen Erzbergbau." *Musikforum* 24, no. 3 (1979): 30.

990 Reissiger, C. G. "Ueber Ventil-Hörner und Klappen-Trompeten." *Allgemeine musikalische Zeitung* 39 (1837): 608–610.

991 Rennert, G. "Posthorn—Posthornklänge." *Archiv für Postgeschichte in Bayern* (1931): 74–85.

992 Reumont, René. "Le cor et son évolution." *Musique & Radio* 41 (1951): 325+.

993 Richardson, E. "Handel's horn and trombone parts." *The Musical Times* 81 (1940): 180.

994 Ricks, Robert. "Letters to the editor [Bach's use of 7th, 11th, or 13th partials in writing for natural horn]." *Journal of Music Theory* 5, no. 2 (1961): 334–336.

995 Ricks, Robert. "Russian horn bands." *Musical Quarterly* 55, no. 3 (July 1969): 364–371.

996 Riggio, Suzanne. "Hornists vote to remove French from horn name." *The School Musician* 43 (Aug.-Sept. 1971): 25.

997 Righini, Pietro. *Il corno.* Ancona: Bèrben, 1972.

998 Ringer, Alexander L. "The Chasse as a musical topic of the 18th century." *Journal of the American Musicological Society* 6 (1953): 148–159.

999 Ringer, Alexander L. "The chasse; historical and analytical bibliography of a musical genre." Ph.D. diss., Columbia University, 1955.

1000 Rivenberg, L. L. "Scoring for three horns: a study of four examples from Beethoven's works." Master's thesis, University of Rochester, 1961.

1001 Rode, Theodore. "Die russische Jagdmusik." *Neue Zeitschrift für Musik* 50 (1859): 242–244.

1002 Rode, Theodore. "Zur Geschichte des Horns." *Neue berliner Musikzeitung* 14 (1860): 242.

Roeser, Valentin. *Essai d'instruction à l'usage de ceux qui composent pour la clarinette et le cor (1764).* Geneva: Minkoff, 1972.

1003 Rohde, F. Virginia. "The use of the French horn in the orchestra as exemplified in the symphonies of Haydn, Mozart and Beethoven." Master's thesis, Eastman School of Music, 1940.

1004 Rosenthal, Irving. "Music in 'Down Under' land." *The Horn Call* 4, no. 2 (Spr. 1974): 19–21.

1005 Rosenthal, Irving. "New Zealand, music, and the horn." *The Horn Call* 4, no. 2 (Spr. 1974): 17–19.

1006 Rosner, J. *Jagd-Signale und Fanfaren, zusammengestellt und rhythmisch geordnet.* 19. Auss. Pless: A. Krummer, 1902.

1007 Rudolph. "Doppelhorn oder B-Horn mit Quint-Ventil?" *Deutsche Militär-Musiker Zeitung* 54 (191-?): 19.

1008 Rudolz, Rudolf. "Entgegnung über die Notierungsweisen der Ventilhorns." *Musikpädagogische Blätter* 36 (1913): 279–280.

1009 Rühlmann, J. "Das Waldhorn." *Neue Zeitschrift für Musik* 66 (1870): 293–295, 301–303, 309–311, 317–320, 325–327; 68 (1872): 399–401, 411–414, 422–423, 431–433, 483–485, 496–498; 69 (1873): 255–257, 265–266, 277–279, 285–287.

1010 Ruff, Willie. "Paul Hindemith and the sound of the horn." *The Horn Call* 17, no. 1 (Oct. 1986): 52–54.

1011 "Russian horn music." *Harmonicon* (1831): 11–12.

1012 Sacchi, Leo Joseph. "Studies on the natural horn." M.Mus. thesis, University of Houston, 1968.

Saenger, Gustav. "The growing popularity of French horns." *Metronome* 43 (Jan. 15, 1927): 23+.

1013 Saenger, Gustav. "History and development of the French horn." *Met-*

ronome 22, no. 2 (1906).

1014 Saint-Foix, Georges de. "Les concertos pour cor de Mozart." *Revue de Musicologie* 13 (1929): 239–245.

1015 "St. Paul Chamber Orchestra." *The Horn Call* 4, no. 1 (Autumn 1973): 34–35.

1016 Sansone, Lorenzo. *French horn music literature, with composers' biographical sketches.* New York: Sansone, 1962.

1017 Sargeant, W. "Profiles: something I could do." *The New Yorker* 53 (Mar. 14, 1977): 45–46+.

1018 Sargent, George Quinby. "The evolution of the chromatic scale on the French horn from 1700 to 1850." M.M. thesis, Indiana University, 1959.

1019 Schaberg, A. L. "A study of the treatment of the horn in the Quintet, K. 407, for horn and strings by Wolfgang Amadeus Mozart." Master's essay, University of Rochester, 1961.

1020 Scharnberg, William. "A colonial slave horn player." *The Horn Call* 13, no. 1 (Oct. 1982): 62–63.

1021 Scharnberg, William. "The hornist's nemisis [sic]: marching band." *NACWPI Journal* 34, no. 1 (1985): 10–11.

1022 Scharnberg, William. "The Manuscript Katalog Wenster Litteratur I/1–17b." *The Horn Call* 8, no. 2 (1978): 79–83.

1023 Scharnberg, William Michael. "A comprehensive performance project in horn literature with an essay including performance editions of four works for horn selected from the manuscript *Katalog Wenster Litteratur I/1–17b.*" D.M.A. diss., University of Iowa, 1977.

1024 Scharnberg, William Michael. "A comprehensive performance project in horn literature with an essay including performance editions of four works for horn selected from the manuscript *Katalog Wenster Litteratur I/1–17b.*" *Dissertation Abstracts* 38 (Jan. 1978): 3797A.

1025 Schlesinger, Kathleen. "Horn." In *Encyclopaedia Britannica.* 11th ed. New York, 1910–11.

1026 Schmidt, J. "Von meinen Jagdhörnern." *Wild und Hund* 64, no. 13 (1961): 428–429.

1027 Schüler, Karl. *Posthornsignale.* Plauen i. V.: G. Wolff, 1934.

1028 Schünemann, Georg. "Die ältesten Jagdfanfaren." *Die Musik* 33 (1940–41): 66–67.

1029 Schultz, Donald G. "Style of French horn composition, 1720–1770." Master's thesis, Northwestern University, 1956.

1030 Schultz, K. "The French horn, a right handed instrument." *Monthly Journal of Research in Music Education* 1, no. 4 (1965): 23–35.

Schultz, P. M. " 'Praise the Lord with the sound of trumpet' and trombone and horn and tuba." *The School Musician* 44 (Dec. 1972): 48–49.

1031 Schwarzl, Siegfried. "Das Wiener F-Horn und seine Zukunstaufgabe." *Das Orchester* 18 (May 1970): 227–230.

1032 Schweikert, Norman. "Jonathan Boen premiers Jan Bach's Horn Concerto." *The Horn Call* 14, no. 1 (Oct. 1983): 64–69.

1033   Schweikert, Norman. "Gumpert, not Gumbert!" *The Horn Call* 1, no. 2 (May 1971): 45.

Schweikert, Norman. "A history of the organized horn ensemble in the United States." *The Horn Call* 16, no. 1 (Oct. 1985): 20–32.

1034   Schweikert, Norman. "Horns across the sea." *The Horn Call* 2, no. 2 (May 1972): 54–60.

1035   Schweikert, Norman. "Veteran hornist Joseph Mourek retires." *The Horn Call* 6, no. 1 (Nov. 1975): 21.

1036   Scutiero, Amedeo. "Sull'uso del corno dal 1700 a Debussy." *Nuova Rivista Musicali Italiana* 14, no. 3 (July-Sept. 1980): 350–367.

1037   Seaman, Gerald. "The Russian horn band." *Monthly Musical Record* 89 (1959): 93–99.

1038   Seidel, Hans. "Horn und Trompete im alten Israel unter Berücksichtigung der 'Kriegsrolle' von Qumran." *Wissenschaftliche Zeitschrift der Universität Leipzig* 4 (1956/57): 5.

1039   Seidl, Bartholomäus. *Der Fall Bach-Trompete und Corno da Caccia.* Hittis'au: Vorarlberg, Seidl, 1955.

1040   Seiffert, Stephen Lyons. "Johannes Brahms and the French horn." D.M.A. diss., Eastman School of Music (University of Rochester), 1969.

1041   Seyfried, Erhard. "Concerning the article by Richard Merewether: The Vienna-horn—and some thoughts on its past fifty years." *The Horn Call* 16, no. 1 (Oct. 1985): 34–35.

1042   Shears, L. A. "The Romantic Waldhornlied." *Monatshefte für deutschen Unterricht* 27 (1935): 307–311.

1043   Sheppard, L. "The French horn." *Music Teacher* 48 (Apr. 1969): 23 + .

1044   Shone, A. B. "Coaching calls." *The Musical Times* 92 (1951): 256–259.

1045   Short, Lee W. "The history and development of the French horn." Master's thesis, Illinois Wesleyan University, 1952.

1046   Smith, H. Clifford. "An engraved horn now in the possession of Miss Martineau." *Proceedings of the Society of Antiquaries* 27 (1915): 138–142.

1047   "Les sonneurs de cor." *L'Echo musical* 24 (1894): 33–34.

1048   Souhart, R. *Bibliographie général des ouvrages sur la chasse, la vénerie et la fauconnerie.* Paris: P. Rouquette, 1886.

1049   Sprung, D. "Wagner and the horn." *San Francisco Opera Magazine* (Apr. 1985): 53–54.

1050   Stacy, William B. "Style and register as correlated factors in the horn parts of selected symphonies by Joseph Haydn." M.A. diss., University of North Carolina at Chapel Hill, 1969.

1051   Stegemann, M. "Vivaldi und das Horn: Mutmassungen über die Genese der *Concerti RV 538* und *RV 539.*" *Informazioni e Stui Vivaldiani* 7 (1986): 62–71. Includes summary in Italian.

Steinberg, Lester Simon. "The treatment of the natural horns and trumpets in the symphonies of the Mannheim school, Haydn, Mozart, and Beethoven." Honors thesis, Harvard University, 1937.

1052   Stewart, Milton L. "Chamber music for voices with French horn: performance problems for French horn, Part 1." *The Horn Call* 18, no. 2 (Apr. 1988): 63–71.

1053   Stoddard, Hope. "The French horn in our orchestras." *International Musician* 47 (Apr. 1949): 19.

1054   Stout, L. J. "The history and development of the horn." *Woodwind World* 10, no. 4 (1971): 11–12.

1055   Streitweiser, Franz X. "Original instrument, modern copy, re-creation with modern technique, or modern instrument? [clarinhorn]." *Newsletter of the American Musical Instrument Society* 16, no. 2 (1987): 6–7.

1056   Suppan, Wolfgang, ed. *Bericht über die vierte internationale Fachtagung zur Erforschung der Blasmusik.* Tutzing: H. Schneider, 1984.

       Talma, Louise. "Horns and trumpets as used in the orchestra from 1700–1900." Master's thesis, Columbia University, 1933.

       Tarr, Edward H. "Das gewundene Jagdinstrument von J. W. Haas." *Brass Bulletin—International Brass Chronicle*, no. 54 (1986): 8–22. Also in English and German.

1057   Tarr, Edward H. "Handel horn duo located in South America." *Brass Bulletin—International Brass Chronicle*, no. 49 (1985): 41–44. Also in French and German.

       Tarr, Edward H. "Why do I—a trumpeter—play the horn?" *International Trumpet Guild Newsletter* 3, no. 2 (1977): 6.

1058   Taut, Kurt. *Die Anfänge der Jagdmusik.* Leipzig: the author, [ca. 1927].

1059   Taut, Kurt. *Beiträge zur Geschichte der Jagdmusik.* Leipzig, Radelli & Hille, 1927.

       Thayer, Robert W. "The literature of the French horn: Its use in teaching." Master's thesis, University of Wichita, 1955.

1060   Thelander, Kristin Pederson. "The solo horn writing of Carl Oestreich (1800–1840) and critical editions of three works for horn and orchestra." *Dissertation Abstracts* 48 (Sept. 1987): 511A.

1061   Thelander, Kristin Pederson. "The solo horn writing of Carl Oestreich (1800–1840) and critical editions of three works for horn and orchestra." D.M.A. diss, University of Wisconsin (Madison), 1987.

1062   Thomason, G. "Selected solo and ensemble literature for the French horn." *The Instrumentalist* 16, no. 11 (Aug. 1962): 33–38.

1063   Thompson, Mark. "Brahms and the light." *The Horn Call* 9, no. 1 (Oct. 1978): 71–72. Also in French and German.

1064   Thompson, Virginia M. Weichman. "A comprehensive performance project in horn literature with an essay consisting of a comparison of selected writings on melodic interpretation." D.M. diss., University of Iowa, 1987.

1065   Thompson, Virginia M. Weichman. "A comprehensive performance project in horn literature with an essay consisting of a comparison of selected writings on melodic interpretation." *Dissertation Abstracts* 48 (Jan. 1988): 1581A.

1066   "300 years of the French horn in Bohemia." *The Horn Call* 11, no. 2 (1981): 19.

1067   Tovey, Donald F. "Schumann's concerto for four horns and orchestra, op. 86." *Monthly Musical Record* 1 (1940): 310–312.

1068   Trenner, Franz, and Bernhard Bruechle. "Franz Strauss." *The Horn Call* 2, no. 2 (May 1972): 61–65. Reprinted and translated from *Neue Zeitschrift für Musik* (1955).

       Trichet, P. "Des cornets de chasse et autres semblables instruments." *Brass Bulletin—International Brass Chronicle*, no. 47 (1984): 51–54. Also in English and German.

1069   Truger, W. "Des Jägers Ruf—das Jagdhorn." *Anblick* 17 (1962): 319–320.

1070   Tuckwell, Barry. "The horn." *Music Teacher and Piano Student* 55 (Oct., Nov., Dec. 1976): 9–10, 10, 14.

1071   Tuckwell, Barry. "The horn." *The Australian Journal of Music Education*, no. 19 (Oct. 1976): 11–12.

1072   Tuckwell, Barry. *Horn.* Yehudi Menuhin music guides. London: MacDonald, 1983.

1073   Turbeville, George. *Noble art of Venerie (1576).* Facsimile reprint. Oxford: n.p., 1908.

       Uggen, Stuart. "A French horn discography." *The Instrumentalist* 24 (Mar. 1970): 59–61.

1074   Unger, Hermann. "Das Horn." *Die Musik-Woche*, no. 18 (1951): 141.

1075   Vach, Milan. "About the horn in Bohemia from 'Hudebni Nastroje.' " *The Horn Call* 17, no. 2 (Apr. 1987): 30–33.

1076   van Norman, Clarendon Ess, Jr. "The French horn—its use and development in musical literature." *Dissertation Abstracts* 26 (Nov. 1965): 2798.

1077   van Norman, Clarendon Ess, Jr. "The French horn—its use and development in musical literature." Ed.D. diss., Columbia University, 1965.

       "A virtuoso on the French horn." *The Harbinger* 2, no. 16 (18 Mar. 1846): 256.

1078   "Vom Doppelhorn." *Schweizerische Instrumentalmusik* 26 (1937): 440–441.

1079   Wakefield, David A. "A chronological list of horn tutors." *The Horn Call* 17, no. 2 (Apr. 1987): 69–72.

1080   *Das Waldhorn in der Geschichte und Gegenwart der tschechischen Musik (Materialy z mezinarodniho sympozia olesnim rohu JAMU Brno, 25.-27.9.1981).* Prague: Ceska Hudebni Spolecnost, 1983.

       Waln, G. "The beginnings and development of the woodwind quintet." *The Instrumentalist* 22 (Oct. 1967): 64–6.

1081   Walshe, Robert C. "The autograph of Richard Strauss's 'First Horn Concerto.' " *The Horn Call* 15, no. 2 (Apr. 1985): 57–61.

1082   Walshe, Robert C. "Hand technique and the hand horn." *The Horn Call* 16, no. 2 (Apr. 1986): 57–61.

       Walshe, Robert C. "The orchestral horn transpositions of Richard Strauss." *The Horn Call* 17, no. 2 (Apr. 1987): 11–15.

1083   Walshe, Robert C. "The transition from hand horn to valve horn in Germany." *The Horn Call* 17, no. 1 (Oct. 1986): 25–26.

1084   Weber, G. "Ueber Ventilhorn und Ventiltrompete mit drei Ventilen." *Caecilia* 17 (1835): 73–105.

1085   [Weber, Gottfried]. "Review of F. D. Weber's Trois Quatuors pour quatre Cors chromatiques." *Caecilia* 18 (1836): 265–267.

1086   Weingartner. "Horn und Harfe im modernen Orchester." *Signale für die musikalische Welt* 76 (191-?): 11, 17.

1087   Weiss, Wisso. "Das Posthorn." *Gutenberg Jahrbuch* (1944–1949): 39–46.

1088   Welcker, H. "Hundelaut und Hornsignale." *Wild und Hund* 62, no. 1 (1959): 17.

     "Wettbewerb der Jagdhornbläser in Hessen." *Wild und Hund* 61 (1958): 248.

1089   Whitman, Dale. "The horn in the works of Bach and Handel." D.M.A. diss., Catholic University of America, 1979.

     Whitwell, D. "Solo wind works in the British Museum." *The Instrumentalist* 31 (Sept. 1976): 96 +.

     Widholm, G. "Untersuchungen zum Wiener Klangstil." *Oesterreichische Musikzeitschrift* 38 (Jan. 1983): 18–27.

1090   Wildenhaag, Archibald, Freiherr von. "Das Jagdhorn." *Wild und Hund* 28, nos. 50–51 (1922).

1091   Wilson, J. S. "The horn that nobody wants." *Downbeat* 26 (Sept. 17, 1959): 15 +.

1092   Wörner, Karl H. "Hindemiths neues Oktett." *Melos* 25 (1958): 356–359.

     Wolf, W. "Corni da caccia mit neuer Technik." *Musik International-Instrumentenbau-Zeitschrift* 37 (May 1983): 368 +.

1093   Wotton, Tom S. "Notation of the horn: some altered meanings." *The Musical Times* 65 (1924): 808–812.

1094   Wotton, Tom S. "Notation of the horn: some altered meanings." *The Musical Times* 66 (1925): 154–155.

1095   Wüerst, Richard. "Ueber Ventil-Hörner und -Trompeten." *Neue Berliner Musikzeitung* 28 (1874): 353–354.

     Wulstan, D. "The sounding of the shofar." *The Galpin Society Journal* 26 (May 1973): 29–46.

1096   Zielinski, Jaroslaw de. "Russian hunting music." *Musical Quarterly* 3 (1917): 53–59.

1097   Zilliacus, Laurin. *Mail for the world: from the courier in the University postal union.* New York: J. Day, 1953.

Cornet/Bugle/Flugelhorn

1098   Allen, Don Edward. "A compiled and annotated listing of materials available for the cornet ensemble." Master's thesis, University of South Dakota, 1951.

Anon. *Tutor for the royal keyed bugle*. London: Z. T. Purday, [ca. 1835].

1099 "Au phonographe [print of 1885 recording session]." *Brass Bulletin—International Brass Chronicle*, no. 42 (1983): 31.

1100 Baird, Frank W. "A history and annotated bibliography of tutors for trumpet and cornet." *Dissertation Abstracts* 44 (Dec. 1983): 1719A.

1101 Baird, Frank W. "A history and annotated bibliography of tutors for trumpet and cornet." Ph.D. diss., University of Michigan, 1983.

1102 Beck, Frederick Allan. "The flugelhorn: its history and literature." D.M.A. diss., University of Rochester, Eastman School of Music, 1979.

1103 Bevan, Clifford. "Background brass [flugelhorn]." *Sounding Brass & the Conductor* 7, no. 1 (1978): 15+.

1104 Bieber, R. J. "From our readers: Whose cornet? [140 year old rotary valve cornet]." *The Instrumentalist* 20 (May 1966): 6.

1105 Brancour, René. *Notice historique sur les cornets*. Paris: n.p., 1912.

1106 Bridges, Glenn D. "Pioneer cornetists. Mathew Arbuckle." *The School Musician* 27 (Nov. 1955): 20.

Brockpähler, Renate. " 'Signalhorn,' 'Riete,' 'Adventshorn.' Volkstümliche Blasinstrumente in Westfalen." *Rheinisch-Westfälische Zeitschrift für Volkskunde* 24, nos. 1–4 (1978): 30–77.

Brother, Arthur. "May we present our Canadian bugle and drum band." *The School Musician* 25 (Sept. 1953): 20–21.

Bruggman, Joseph E. "A compendium of selected solo cornet/trumpet literature for students and teachers." Ed.D. diss., Columbia University Teachers College, 1949.

1107 Burum, H. *J. B. Arban; ausführliche Anleitung zum Selbstunterricht der Trompetenschule*. Hofheim: Hofmeister, 1976.

1108 Cailliet, L. "The flugelhorn." *The Instrumentalist* 16 (Dec. 1961): 32.

Clarke, Herbert L. *The cornet and the cornetist; historical series of cornet talks*. Compiled by G. D. Bridges. Detroit: The compiler, 1970.

1109 "The Cornet." *American Musician* 29, no. 19 (1913): 10–11.

1110 "The Cornet and its music." *Metronome* 23, no. 3 (1907).

1111 "Cornet directory." *Sounding Brass & the Conductor* 3, no. 4 (1974–1975): 123.

1112 Daubeny, Ulric. "The bugle and the cavalry trumpet." *Metronome* 40 (Aug. 1924): 65+.

1113 Daubeny, Ulric. "A descriptive chapter about the cornet." *Metronome* 41 (Jan. 1, 1925): 76–77.

Deisenroth, F. "Die Bläserkultur der Blechblasinstrumente in der Militärmusik unter besonderer Berücksichtigung der Weitmensurierten Bügelinstrumente mit Einschluss der Zug- und Ventilposaunen." *Deutsche Militär-Musiker Zeitung* 60 (1938): 29–30, 41–42.

Döring, C., comp. *Signale; die umfassendste Sammlung aller bei der Wehrmacht, Marine, Post, Feuerwehr, und bei der Jagd gebräuchlichen Musik-Signal*. Erweitert von P. Merkelt. Leipzig: W. Gebauer, [194-?].

Dominy, Micky. "An analysis of the cornet solos contained on the class I University Interscholastic League List of the school year 1953–54." Master's thesis, Sam Houston State Teachers College, 1954.

1114 Dudgeon, R. T. "The keyed bugle, its history, literature and technique." *Dissertation Abstracts* 41 (Oct. 1980): 1271A.

1115 "Editor's preface: The development of the cornet [Facsimile of pages II-V of 1907 Hawkes & Son edition of Cornet Method by Arban]." *International Trumpet Guild Newsletter* 4, no. 3 (1978): 8–11.

1116 Eliason, Robert E. "Communication [keyed bugle]." *Journal of the American Musical Instrument Society* 4 (1978): 143.

1117 Eliason, Robert E. "The Dresden keyed bugle." *Journal of the American Musical Instrument Society* 3 (1977): 57–63.

1118 Eliason, Robert E. *Keyed bugles in the United States.* Washington, DC: Smithsonian Institution Press, 1972.

1119 Feltz, J. "Cornet in concert band and its mouthpiece." *The School Musician* 57 (Apr. 1986): 30–31.

1120 Flor, G. J. "Brass workshop: The bugle past and present." *The School Musician* 56 (May 1985): 30–31.

1121 "Flugel directory." *Sounding Brass & the Conductor* 4, no. 1 (1975): 26.

1122 Gauffriau, J. M. "Cover [engraved 1895 Couesnon]." *Brass Bulletin—International Brass Chronicle*, no. 38 (1982): 3. Also in French and German.

1123 Gay, B. "Cornet high and dry." *Sounding Brass & the Conductor* 6, no. 3 (1977): 101.

1124 Gerson-Kiwi, Edith. "With trumpets and sound of cornet." *Tatzlil*, no. 3 (1963): 210 + . In Hebrew, with English abstract.

1125 Gouse, Charles Frederick. "The cornett: its history, literature and performance praxis including a practical tutor for developing performance skills." *Dissertation Abstracts* 34 (June 1974): 7806A.

1126 Green, K. "Taps: the song of the universal soldier—a Memorial Day perspective on an American musical tradition." *International Musician* 78 (May 1980): 6.

Greissinger, F. Henri. *Instructions for the trumpet and drum; together with the full code of signals and calls used by the United States army and navy.* Revised and enlarged by W. F. Smith. New York: Carl Fischer, [1900].

1127 Hall, J. "The saga of the cornet and six of its outstanding artists." *Brass Bulletin—International Brass Chronicle*, no. 12 (1975): 19–35. Also in French and German.

1128 Hemming, Katharine D. "The bugle and its calls." *Etude* 59 (1941): 455 + .

1129 Horwood, W. "The vulgar cornet." *Crescendo International* 15 (Jan. 1977): 4.

Irish Free State. Dept. of Defence. *Trumpet and bugle calls.* Defence Force Regulations. Dublin: Stationery Office, 1926.

1130 Jacobsen, Samuel L. "The cornet." *Music* 13 (1897): 622–629.

1131 Jenkins, H. "The cornet—a damsel in distress." *The Instrumentalist* 22 (Oct. 1967): 77–79.

1132 Johnson, K. "The cornet today." *The Instrumentalist* 33 (May 1979): 76.

1133   Keck, F. A. "The flugelhorn as an orchestral instrument." *Woodwind World—Brass and Percussion* 17, no. 2 (1978): 22–23+.

Köhler, Augustus Charles. *The coach horn. What to blow, and how to blow it. By an Old Guard.* London: Köhler & Son, 1888.

LaBrew, A. *Francis Johnson (1792–1844): a study in 19th century military and terpsichorean music history.* Detroit, 13560 Goddard Street: The Author, 1974.

1134   Lanshe, R. "The cornet: its origin and development." *Woodwind World—Brass and Percussion* 17, no. 4 (1978): 34–35+.

1135   Laplace, Michel. "La trompette et le cornet dans le jazz et la musique populaire." *Brass Bulletin—International Brass Chronicle*, no. 42 (1983): 16–30. Also in English and German.

1136   Laplace, Michel. "La trompette et le cornet dans le jazz et la musique populaire." *Brass Bulletin—International Brass Chronicle*, no. 45 (1984): 38–44. Also in English and German.

1137   Laplace, Michel. "La trompette et le cornet dans le jazz et la musique populaire [1927–1945]." *Brass Bulletin—International Brass Chronicle*, no. 43 (1983): 44–65. Also in English and German.

1138   Laplace, Michel. "La trompette et le cornet dans le jazz et la musique populaire [1945-present]." *Brass Bulletin—International Brass Chronicle*, no. 44 (1983): 54–60. Also in English and German.

1139   Lillya, Clifford P. "About that famous letter [H. L. Clarke to E. Benge]." *Journal of the International Trumpet Guild* 12, no. 2 (Dec. 1987): 12–13+.

1140   Lillya, Clifford P. "The laughing cornet (and all that Jaz)." *Journal of the International Trumpet Guild* 13, no. 2 (Dec. 1988): 21+.

Logier. *A complete introduction to the art of playing on the keyed bugle.* London: Clementi, 1820.

Lombard, N. C. *The trumpeter's manual, for the use of trumpeters in the military and naval forces of the United States.* 2d ed. Boston: Lombard, 1911.

Mahan, Frederick A. "Trumpeters and buglers." *Metronome* 23, no. 11 (1907): 11–12.

Marshall, B. "Rhode Island leap." *Crescendo International* 10 (Nov. 1971): 27.

1141   Mathis, W. E. "Peck-horns and other castoffs." *The Instrumentalist* 35 (Feb. 1981): 30–31.

1142   May, E. C. "America falls in step to the call of drum and bugle." *Popular Science* 125 (Sept. 1934): 49–52.

1143   Morris, E. J. "Is the cornet an endangered species?" *The School Musician* 54 (Dec. 1982): 38–40.

1144   Mullady, F., and W. H. Kofoed. "The story of taps." *Coronet* 50 (May 1961): 81.

1145   Oneglia, M. F. "Cornets—please!!!" *The Instrumentalist* 25 (June 1971): 58–60.

1146   Oster, Raymond. "A survey of selected cornet literature." Master's thesis,

Arthur Jordan Conservatory of Music, 1937.

1147 Ostling, A. "Why not cornets and trumpets? [in bands]." *The Instrumentalist* 21 (June 1967): 37–39.

Otis. "Cornet versus trumpet." *The Musical Times* 58 (1917): 409–410.

"Partitions—Noten—music [cornet music]." *Brass Bulletin—International Brass Chronicle*, no. 20 (1977): 5–6.

1148 Peterson, O. A. "Historical outline of cornet from 'The Cornet.' " *Jacobs' Band Monthly* 22 (Sept. 1937): 4.

1149 Pierce, Edwin H. "On some old bugle-calls of the U.S. Navy." *Musical Quarterly* 18 (1932): 134–139.

1150 Poncelet-Lecocq, P. "Du bugle alto." *L'Echo musical* 1, no. 7 (15 Aug. 1869).

Poole, H. E., and others. "A catalogue of musical instruments offered for sale in 1839 by D'Almaine & Co., 20 Soho Square." *The Galpin Society Journal* 35 (1982): 2–36.

Prescott, J. "Treatment of the cornet and trumpet in selected twentieth-century band compositions." *Journal of Band Research* 21, no. 1 (1985): 50–60.

Quayle, N. H. "The cornet's sole survivor." *Music Journal* 19 (Sept. 1961): 44+.

1151 Rorick, David R. "Nineteenth-century American cornet/brass band music." D.M.A. diss., Catholic University of America, 1979.

1152 Sander, Rudolf. " 'Ein neues Kornett' und andere Verbesserungs-Bestrebungen im Blechblas-Instrumentenbaue." *Zeitschrift für Instrumentenbau* 23 (1903): 469–471+.

Sandor, E. P. "Development and use of the chromatic trumpet in the nineteenth-century orchestra." *NACWPI Journal* 33, no. 4 (1985): 4–12.

1153 Schiedel, A. "The trumpet and the cornet." *Woodwind World—Brass and Percussion* 18, no. 3 (1979): 16+.

1154 Schlesinger, Kathleen. "Cornet." In *Encyclopaedia Britannica*. 11th ed. New York, 1910–11.

Schüler, Karl. *Posthornsignale*. Plauen i. V.: G. Wolff, 1934.

1155 Sheblessy, S. K. "Taps—a military tone poem." *American Music Teacher* 23, no. 3 (1974): 35.

1156 Soracco, Joseph P. "A descriptive analysis of bugles and a survey determining their prevalence and status in the public schools of Massachusetts." Master's thesis, Boston University, 1953.

Sousa, John Philip. *A book of instruction for the field-trumpet and drum, together with the trumpet and drum signals now in use in the Army, Navy and Marine Corps of the United States*. New York: Carl Fischer, 1886.

"Del Staigers—world famous cornetist." In *White Way News*. Cleveland: H. N. White Co., 1930.

1157 Suppan, Wolfgang. "Steirische Flügelhorn-Ländler." *Sänger- und Musikantenzeitung* 11, no. 5 (Sept.-Oct. 1968): 103–110.

Tamplini, G. *The Bandsman*. Book 15: "The Bugle Major." Book 16: "The

Trumpet Major." London: n.p., ca. 1856.

1158   Taranto, V. A. "Cornet comeback." *The Instrumentalist* 33 (Oct. 1978): 128.

1159   Taylor, L. "Heyday of the keyed-bugle." *Music Journal* 11 (July, 1953): 16–17+.

Tetzlaff, Daniel B., and John J. Haynie. "Materials for trumpet and cornet." *The Instrumentalist* 14 (Nov. 1959): 44–45+.

Trumpet and bugle sounds for the army, with instructions for the training of trumpeters and buglers. London: Eyre & Spottiswoode, [1903].

"The trumpeter and trumpet calls (from *The Journal of the Military Service Institution)." Metronome* 27, no. 5 (1911): 18–19.

Tully. *Tutor for the Kent bugle.* London: R. Cocks, [ca. 1838].

1160   U.S. Bureau of Naval. *Manual for buglers, U.S. Navy.* Washington: U.S. Government Printing Office, 1953.

U.S. War Department. *Field manual.* Technical manual 20, no. 250. Washington: GPO, 1940.

Wallace, S. C. "A study of high school band directors' ability to discriminate between and identify modern cornet and trumpet timbres." *Dissertation Abstracts* 40 (Apr. 1980): 5359A.

War office trumpet and bugle sounds for the army. With instructions for training of trumpeters and buglers. London: H. M. Stationery Office, ca. 1929.

Webb, J. "19th-century keyed brass." *Music Trades* 127 (Feb. 1986): 83–85.

1161   Webb, J. "Bradshaw's serpentine valved cornopean." *The Galpin Society Journal* 35 (1982): 154–156.

1162   Webb, J. "Four keyed bugles by Greenhill." *Journal of the International Trumpet Guild* 10, no. 3 (1986): 14–18.

1163   Whear, Paul W. "Bugles in the marching band." *The Instrumentalist* 12 (Sept. 1957): 43.

1164   Wheeler, J. "New light on the 'regent's bugle'; with some notes on the keyed-bugle." *The Galpin Society Journal* 19 (Apr. 1966): 65–70.

1165   Whiting, C. E. "Then and now [comparison between young cornetists of the 1930s and today]." *The School Musician* 41 (Aug.-Sept. 1969): 78–80.

Williams, Edwin Lynn. "Dissertation reviews: The role of the trumpet and cornet in the early ballets of Igor Stravinsky." *Journal of the International Trumpet Guild* 10, no. 3 (1986): 25–26.

Williams, Edwin Lynn. "The role of the trumpet and cornet in the early ballets of Igor Stravinsky." D.M.A. diss., University of Cincinnati, 1980.

1166   Woodard, William H. "Bugle and drum corps." *The School Musician* 23 (Nov. 1951): 11+.

1167   Woodard, William H. "You can play real music on the modern bugles." *The School Musician* 23 (Apr. 1952): 13.

1168   Wright, G. "Judith Plant and the keyed bugle." *The School Musician* 46 (Jan. 1975): 44–45.

Zilliacus, Laurin. *Mail for the world: from the courier in the University postal union.* New York: J. Day, 1953.

1169   "Die achttönige Martin-Trompete—auch sie hat ihre Geschichte und Literatur." *Instrumentenbau Musik International* 30, no. 12 (1976): 751–752.

1170   Acton, Ellen Hall. "A history of the cornett." M.M. thesis, University of Cincinnati College-Conservatory, 1973.
"Addendum to CRI tribute (Journal, Vol. IV) [forty additional chamber works including at least one trumpet]." *International Trumpet Guild Newsletter* 6, no. 2 (1980): 37–40.

1171   Adkins, C., and A. Dickinson. "A trumpet by any other name: toward an etymology of the trumpet marine." *Journal of the American Musical Instrument Society* 8 (1982): 5–15.

1172   Altenburg, Detlef. "Dissertationen: Untersuchungen zur Geschichte der Trompete im Zeitalter der Clarinblaskunst (1500–1800)." *Die Musikforschung* 28, no. 2 (1975): 209–210.

1173   Altenburg, Detlef. "Special presentation: 'useful annotations on the privileged free art of the trumpeters' (shortly after 1650)." *Brass Bulletin—International Brass Chronicle*, no. 14 (1976): 29–31. Also in French and German. Condensed and trans. from *Untersuchungen zur Geschichte der Trompete im Zeitalter der Clarinblaskunst (1500–1800)*.

1174   Altenburg, Detlef. "Untersuchungen zur Geschichte der Trompete im Zeitalter der Clarinblaskunst (1500–1800)." Ph.D. diss., Universität Köln, 1973.

1175   Altenburg, Detlef. *Untersuchungen zur Geschichte der Trompete im Zeitalter der Clarinblaskunst (1500–1800)*. No. 75 in Kölner Beiträge zur Musikforschung. Regensburg: Bosse; Nashville: Brass Press, 1973.

1176   Altenburg, Johann Ernst. *Essay on an introduction to the heroic and musical trumpeters' and kettledrummers' art (1795)*. Translated by Edward H. Tarr. Nashville: Brass Press, 1974.

1177   Altenburg, Johann Ernst. *Versuch einer Anleitung zur heroisch-musikalischen Trompeter- und Pauker-Kunst*. Halle: J. C. Hendel, 1795. Facsimile reprint. Dresden: R. Bertling, 1911.

1178   Altenburg, Johann Ernst. *Versuch einer Anleitung zur heroisch-musikalischen Trompeter- und Pauker-Kunst*. Monuments of Music and Music Literature in Facsimile. New York: Broude Bros., 1966.

1179   Altenburg, Johann Ernst. *Versuch einer Anleitung zur heroisch-musikalischen Trompeter- und Pauker-Kunst*. Reprint of original edition, Halle, 1795. Amsterdam: Antiqua, 1966.

1180   Altenburg, Johann Ernst. *Versuch einer Anleitung zur heroisch-musikalischen Trompeter- und Paukerkunst*. Edited and with an afterword by Frieder Zschoch. Leipzig: VEB Deutscher Verlag für Musik, 1972.

1181   Altenburg, Johann Ernst. *Versuch einer Anleitung zur heroisch-musikalischen Trompeter- und Paukerkunst (1795)*. Edited by Frieder Zschoch. Leipzig:

Deutscher Verlag für Musik, 1973.

1182   Altenburg, Johann Ernst. *Versuch einer Anleitung zur heroisch-musikalischer trompeter- und pauker-kunst, zu mehrerer aufnahme deselben historisch, theoretisch und praktisch beachten und mit exempeln erlautert von Johann Ernst Altenburg.* Halle: J. C. Hendel, 1795.

1183   Altenburg, Wilhelm. "Ein kleiner Nachtrag zu dem Artikel in Nr. 6: Die hohen Bach-Trompeten." *Zeitschrift für Instrumentenbau* 30 (1909/10): 227–228.

1184   Altenburg, Wilhelm. "Richard Wagner und die Holztrompete." *Zeitschrift für Instrumentenbau* 21 (1900/01): 375–376, 461.

1185   Altenburg, Wilhelm. "Zur Aufklärung über die hohen F-Trompeten." *Deutsche Militär-Musiker Zeitung* 31 (1909): 687–688.

1186   Altman, Sylvia. "A historical study on the horns and trumpets. Outline of the structural evolution of the instruments. The function and treatment of the horns and trumpets from Bach to Wagner." Master's thesis, Columbia University, 1933.

        Amend, J. J. "Trumpet sections of American symphony orchestras: The Detroit Symphony Orchestra." *Journal of the International Trumpet Guild* 1 (1976): 22–23.

        Amend, J. J. "Trumpet sections of American symphony orchestras: The Philadelphia Orchestra (1900–1977)." *International Trumpet Guild Newsletter* 3, no. 3 (1977): 14–15.

1187   Anderson, Ronald Kent. "An historical and stylistic study of selected trumpet literature for performance and teaching." Ed.D. diss., Columbia University, 1970.

        Anderson, Ronald Kent. "An historical and stylistic study of selected trumpet literature for performance and teaching." *Dissertation Abstracts* 31 (Jan. 1971): 3578A.

1188   Andrus, Wayne Edmond. "The evolution of the the Italian Baroque solo trumpet sonata." M.A. thesis, West Texas State University, 1977.

1189   Arfinengo, Carlo. *La tromba e il trombone.* Ancona; Milano: Bèrben, 1973.

1190   Awouters, M. "X-raying musical instruments: a method in organological study." *Revue Belge de Musicologie* 36–38 (1982–1984): 203–214 + .

        Bach, Vincent. "Bach's 'Brandenburg concerto no. 2'; who can play the trumpet part." *The Instrumentalist* 15 (Sept. 1960): 94–96.

1191   Bach, Vincent. "The history of the trumpet." *Jacobs' Band Monthly* 10 (Dec. 1925): 8–9.

        "Bachtrompeten—eine Forderung des Tages." *Deutsche Militär-Musiker Zeitung* 52 (1930): 11.

1192   Bagans, K. "On the trumpet, as at present employed in the orchestra." *Harmonicon* (1830): 23.

1193   Bagans, K. "Ueber die Trompete in ihrer heutigen Anwendbarkeit im Orchester, mit einem Rückblick auf die frühere Behandlungsart derselben." *Berliner allgemeine musikalische Zeitung* 6 (1829): 337–341.

1194   Baines, Anthony. "The evolution of trumpet music up to Fantini." *Royal*

Musical Association Proceedings 10 (1974–1975): 1–9.

1195   Baines, Anthony. "The Galpin cornett." *The Galpin Society Journal* 29 (May 1976): 125–126.

Baird, Frank W. "A history and annotated bibliography of tutors for trumpet and cornet." *Dissertation Abstracts* 44 (Dec. 1983): 1719A.

Baird, Frank W. "A history and annotated bibliography of tutors for trumpet and cornet." Ph.D. diss., University of Michigan, 1983.

1196   Baldwin, David. "Bach arias for trumpet [includes list and some thematic excerpts]." *Journal of the International Trumpet Guild* 2 (1977): 26–27.

1197   Ballou, Richard. "The history, technique, and literature of the trumpet." Master's thesis, Brigham Young University, 1953.

1198   Barbour, J. Murray. "Trumpet and horn in the church music of Bach and his contemporaries." *Bulletin of the American Musicological Society* (Sept. 1948): 61–62.

Barbour, J. Murray. *Trumpets, horns and music.* East Lansing, Mich.: Michigan State University, 1964.

"Baroque trumpet mouthpieces." *International Trumpet Guild Newsletter* 4, no. 1 (1977): 5.

1199   Bartolatta, William S. "Lecture recital: Late seventeenth-century trumpet pieces by the composers at San Petronio in Bologna." D.M.A. diss., Catholic University of America, 1974.

1200   Bate, Philip. *The trumpet and trombone; an outline of their history, development and construction.* London: E. Benn; New York: W. W. Norton, 1966.

1201   Bate, Philip. *The trumpet and trombone; an outline of their history, development, and construction.* 2d ed. London: Benn; New York: Norton, 1972.

Baumann, M. P. "Befragungsmodell und Vergleich; erläutert am Beispiel der Langtrompeten." *Die Musikforschung* 31, no. 2 (1978): 161–176.

1202   Beese. "Die neue Jazz-Trompete." *Das Orchester* 8 (1931): 20.

Bell, R. E. "Natural trumpets of Leningrad; a description of the natural trumpets in the Exhibition of Musical Instruments of the Leningrad Institute of Theater, Music and Cinematography, Leningrad, U.S.S.R." *Journal of the International Trumpet Guild* 7, no. 4 (1983): 10–11+.

1203   Bendinelli, Cesare. *Tutta l'arte della trombetta, 1614.* Facsimile edition. Edited by Edward H. Tarr. Kassel: Bärenreiter, 1975.

Bennett, J. G. "A guide for the performance of trumpet mariachi music in schools." *Dissertation Abstracts* 40 (Jan. 1980): 3859A+.

1204   Bentschitsch, Maria. "Die Trompeterkunst bis zum 18. Jahrhundert." M.A. diss., Hochschule für Musik Mozarteum, Salzburg, 1982.

1205   Berger, Jean. "Notes on some 17th-century compositions for trumpets and strings in Bologna." *Musical Quarterly* 37 (1951): 354–367.

Berger, Melvin. *The trumpet book.* New York: Lothrop, Lee & Shepard, 1978.

1206   Bernstein, Harry Marvin. "Alessandro Stradella's serenata, *Il Barcheggio* (Genoa, 1681): a modern edition and commentary with emphasis on the use of the cornetto and the trumpet." D.M.A. diss., Stanford University, 1979.

1207   Bernstein, Harry Marvin. "Alessandro Stradella's serenata, *Il Barcheggio* (Genoa, 1681): a modern edition and commentary with emphasis on the use of the cornetto and the trumpet." *Dissertation Abstracts* 40 (Jan. 1980): 3610A.

1208   *Bestimmungen für Musik- und Trompeterkorps des Heeres.* Berlin: Verlag "Offene Wort," 1936.

1209   "Bilder zur Musik." *Musik und Bildung* 12 (Oct. 1980): 593.

1210   Birkemeier, Richard P. "The history and music of the orchestral trumpet of the nineteenth century." *Journal of the International Trumpet Guild* 9, no. 3 (1985): 22–39.

1211   Birkemeier, Richard P. "The history and music of the orchestral trumpet of the nineteenth century." *Journal of the International Trumpet Guild* 9, no. 4 (1985): 13–27.

1212   Blackinton, David P. "Lecture recital: An analysis of the work *Something Else* for solo trumpet and electronic tape by Edward Diemente." D.M.A. diss., Catholic University of America, 1974.

1213   Blandford, W. F. H. "The 'Bach trumpet.' " *Monthly Musical Record* 65 (1935): 49–51, 73–76, 97–100.

1214   Blandford, W. F. H. "The 'Bach trumpets.' " *The Musical Times* 33 (1892): 682–683.

1215   Blandford, W. F. H. "Bach's trumpets." *Monthly Musical Record* 61 (1931): 44–45.

1216   Blandford, W. F. H. "Bach's trumpets." *Monthly Musical Record* 61 (1931): 201–204.

1217   Blandford, W. F. H. "Clarino and trumpet." *The Musical Times* 81 (1940): 32. Letter to the editor.

1218   Blandford, W. F. H. "The Regent's bugle." *The Musical Times* 66 (1925): 442–443.

1219   Blémant, Louis. *Méthode de clarion, contenant toutes les sonneries réglementaires en usage dans l'armée ainsi que des exercises, marches, récréations, etc.* Paris: G. Gross, 1934.

1220   Bolen, Charles W. "Equestrian ballets of the baroque." *American Music Teacher* 5 (May 1956): 2.

1221   Bolte, Johannes. "Texte zu militärischen Signalen und Märschen." *Zeitschrift für Volkskunde* 2 (1930): 83–92.

1222   Bond, Gareth H. "The history of the clarino as related to the analyzation and performance of the Telemann *Concerto in D Major:* the contemporary trumpet: a synthesis of earlier mechanical innovations, as related to the analyzation and performance of Wildgans, *The Mystical Trumpeter.*" Ph.D. diss., Catholic University of America, 1972.

1223   Boone, Dalvin Lee. "The treatment of the trumpet in six published chamber works composed between 1920 and 1929." Ed.D. diss., University of Illinois (Urbana-Champaign), 1972.

       Boone, Dalvin Lee. "The treatment of the trumpet in six published chamber works composed between 1920 and 1929." *Dissertation Abstracts* 33 (Apr. 1973): 5762A.

1224 Boulton, John. "The trumpet." *Hallé* (Jan. 1950): 10–11.

Bowles, Edmund A. "Eastern influences on the use of trumpets and drums during the Middle Ages." *Annuario musical* 27 (1972): 3–28.

1225 Bowles, Edmund A. "Iconography as a tool for examining the loud consort in the fifteenth century." *Journal of the American Musical Instrument Society* 3 (1977): 100–121.

Bowles, Edmund A. "Unterscheidung der Instrumente Buisine, Cor, Trompe und Trompette." *Archiv für Musikwissenschaft* 18 (1961): 52–72.

1226 Bowman, Brian. "The bass trumpet and tenor tuba in orchestral and operatic literature." D.M.A. diss., Catholic University of America, 1975.

Boyle, P. "The skoonum horn." *Jazz Forum*, no. 29 (June 1974): 15–16.

Brahmstedt, Howard Kenneth. "The application of trumpet studies to performance problems in twentieth-century music." D.Mus. diss., Indiana University, 1973.

1227 Bravington, E. "Full score: the trumpet." *Philharmonic Post* 5 (Sept.-Oct. 1950): 3–5.

1228 Brischle, A. "Zum Gebrauch der Trompete bei J. S. Bach." *Archiv für Musikwissenschaft* 44, no. 4 (1987): 306–312.

1229 Brofsky, H. "Padre Martini's Sonata for Four Trumpets and Strings." *Brass Quarterly* 5, no. 2 (1961): 58–61.

1230 Browne, James A. "Handel's trumpeter." *Monthly Musical Record* 39 (1909): 8–9.

1231 Bruger. "Der Werdegang der Trompete." *Evangelische Musikzeitung* 17, no. 11f (192-?).

1232 Bruggman, Joseph E. "A compendium of selected solo cornet/trumpet literature for students and teachers." Ed.D. diss., Columbia University Teachers College, 1949.

1233 Brungess, Kenneth Lee. "A recital of twentieth-century trumpet and wind literature." M.A. thesis, California State University (Long Beach), 1974.

1234 Brunner, Lowell Henry. "The evolution of the trumpet as a solo instrument and a descriptive account of trumpet solo literature." Master's thesis, Northwestern University, 1957.

1235 Büttner, Manfred. "Studien zur Geschichte der Trompete." Dissertation, Münster, 1953.

1236 Burkart, Richard E. "The trumpet in England in the seventeenth century with emphasis on its treatment in the works of Henry Purcell and a biography of the Shore family of trumpeters." *Dissertation Abstracts* 32 (Apr. 1972): 5822A-5823A.

1237 Burkart, Richard Edgar. "The trumpet in England in the seventeenth century with emphasis on its treatment in the works of Henry Purcell and a biography of the Shore family of trumpeters." Ph.D. diss., University of Wisconsin (Madison), 1972.

1238 Burkett, E., and S. Trinkle. "A review of the Johann Ernst Altenburg treatise, *Essay on an Introduction to the Heroic and Music Trumpeters' and Kettledrummers' Art*, from the timpanists' perspective." *NACWPI Journal* 32, no. 2 (1984–1985): 19–27.

1239 Byrd, Donaldson Toussaint, II. "The performance and analysis of an original Afro-American musical composition for trumpet and orchestra." Ed.D. diss., Columbia University Teachers College, 1983.

Byrne, M. "The Goldsmith-trumpet-makers of the British Isles." *The Galpin Society Journal* 19 (Apr. 1966): 71–83.

1240 Candelaria, Leonard Anthony. "An overview of performance practices relating to seventeenth- and eighteenth-century trumpet music: considerations for modern performance." D.M. diss., Northwestern University, 1985.

1241 Candelaria, Leonard Anthony. "An overview of performance practices relating to seventeenth- and eighteenth-century trumpet music: considerations for modern performance." *Dissertation Abstracts* 47 (June 1987): 4225A-4226A.

Cansler, Philip Trent. "An analytical listing of published music of the twentieth century for solo trumpet and organ." D.M.A. diss., University of Oregon, 1984.

1242 Cansler, Philip Trent. "An analytical listing of published music of the twentieth century for solo trumpet and organ." *Dissertation Abstracts* 45 (June 1985): 3474A-3475A.

1243 Carnovale, A. N. "A comprehensive performance project in trumpet literature with an essay on published music composed since ca. 1900 for solo trumpet accompanied by orchestra." *Dissertation Abstracts* 35 (July 1974): 494A.

1244 Carnovale, August Norbert. "A comprehensive performance project in trumpet literature with an essay on published music composed since ca. 1900 for solo trumpet accompanied by orchestra." D.M.A. diss., University of Iowa, 1973.

1245 Carnovale, N. *Twentieth-century music for trumpet and orchestra: an annotated bibliography*. Nashville: Brass Press, 1975.

1246 Carse, Adam. "Beethoven's trumpet parts." *The Musical Times* 94 (1953): 32.

1247 Carse, Adam. "Clarino and trumpet." *The Musical Times* 81 (1940): 33.

1248 Carse, Adam. "The trumpet makers of Nuremberg." *Monthly Musical Record* 67 (1937): 203–204.

1249 Cecconi-Bates, A. "B-flat trumpets used in *Paragraphs and Fugue*." *Woodwind, Brass and Percussion* 22, no. 8 (1983): 14–16.

1250 Charlesworth, C. "Better things are electric." *Melody Maker* 46 (Sept. 11, 1971): 30.

1251 Chladni, E. F. F. "Nachrichten von einigen . . . neueren Erfindungen und Verbesserungen musikalischer Instrumente." *Allgemeine musikalische Zeitung* 23 (1821): 393–398, 411.

1252 Christmann, Arthur. "Horns and trumpets of yesteryear. Instruments without valves." *The Baton* 9, no. 3 (1930): 9 + .

1253   Ciurczak, Peter L. "The trumpet in baroque opera: its use as a solo, ob-
        bligato, and ensemble instrument." *Dissertation Abstracts* 35 (June 1975):
        7941A.

1254   Ciurczak, Peter L. "The trumpet in baroque opera: its use as a solo, ob-
        bligato, and ensemble instrument." *Journal of the International Trumpet
        Guild* 10, no. 4 (1986): 39–73 + .

1255   Ciurczak, Peter L. "The trumpet in Baroque opera: its use as a solo, ob-
        bligato, and ensemble instrument." 2 vols. Ph.D. diss., North Texas
        State University, 1974.

1256   Ciurczak, Peter L. "The trumpet in baroque opera: its use as a solo, ob-
        bligato, and ensemble instrument." *Journal of the International Trumpet
        Guild* 6 (1981): 2–17. Musical examples, pp. 54–68.

1257   Ciurczak, Peter L. "The trumpet in Baroque opera: its use as a solo, ob-
        bligato, and ensemble instrument. The technical details of trumpet
        style." *Journal of the International Trumpet Guild* 13, no. 1 (Sept. 1988): 4–
        39.

1258   "Clarino-Ensemble setzt Reihe der Klosterkonzerte in Maulbronn fort."
        Das Orchester 33 (Jan. 1985): 43.

        Clark, K. C. "Trumpet sections of American symphony orchestras: The
        Chicago Symphony Orchestra." *Journal of the International Trumpet Guild*
        8, no. 2 (1983): 17–22.

1259   Clendenin, W. Ritchie, and William R. Clendenin. *A modern edition of Gi-
        rolamo Fantini's trumpet method (1638).* Boulder, CO: Empire, 1977.

1260   Coleman, Jack. "The trumpet: its use in selected works of Stravinsky,
        Hindemith, Shostakovich, and Copland." *Dissertation Abstracts* 26 (Dec.
        1965): 3389.

1261   Coleman, Jack. "The trumpet: its use in selected works of Stravinsky,
        Hindemith, Shostakovich, and Copland." D.M.A. diss., University of
        Southern California, 1965.

1262   Collins, T. "Observations on the origins and influences leading to Bach's
        idiomatic writing for the trumpet in 'Grosser Herr, O starker König'
        from the *Christmas Oratorio.*" *Bach—the quarterly journal of the Riemen-
        schneider Bach Institute* 17, no. 2 (1986): 31–45.

1263   "Les cornettistes du nord." *L'Echo musical* 18 (1886): 97.

1264   Cudworth, C. L. "Some new facts about the Trumpet Voluntary." *The
        Musical Times* 94 (1953): 401–403.

1265   Cudworth, C. L., and F. B. Zimmerman. "The trumpet voluntary." *Music
        & Letters* 41 (1960): 342–348.

1266   Dahlqvist, Rene. "Johann-Georg Albrechtsberger Concertino for 'Chro-
        matic Trumpet.' " *Brass Bulletin—International Brass Chronicle*, no. 1
        (1971): 9–18. Also in French and German.

1267   Dahlqvist, Rene. *The keyed trumpet and its greatest virtuoso, Anton Weidinger.*
        Nashville, Brass Press, 1975.

        Dahlqvist, Rene. "Some notes on the early valve." *The Galpin Society Journal*

33 (1980): 111–124.

1268   Dahlstrom, J. E. "History and development of the trumpet." *The School Musician* 41 (Jan. 1970): 58–59.

Dale, Delbert A. *Trumpet technique.* London; New York: Oxford University Press, 1965.

1269   Daniels, E. S. "Military calls." *The Instructor* 70 (Feb. 1961): 16.

Daubeny, Ulric. "The bugle and the cavalry trumpet." *Metronome* 40 (Aug. 1924): 65+.

1270   Davenay, R. "Heures et visages de Paris—les sonneurs de trompe." *L'Illustration* 187 (Apr. 21, 1934): 452–453.

De Jong, William Donai. "The earliest trumpet method book extant." *Dissertation Abstracts* 32 (Oct. 1971): 2116A-2117A.

1271   De Jong, William Donai. "The earliest trumpet method book extant: a lecture recital; together with three other recitals." D.M.A. diss., North Texas State University, 1971.

1272   de Pascual, B. Kenyon. "Jose de Juan Martinez's tutor for the circular hand-stopped trumpet (1830)." *Brass Bulletin—International Brass Chronicle*, no. 57 (1987): 50–54+. Also in French and German.

1273   Decker, C. F. "Trumpet research: a selective bibliography." *The Instrumentalist* 27 (May 1973): 56+.

1274   Del Borgo, E. "The baroque trumpet." *The Instrumentalist* 22 (Oct. 1967): 70–73.

1275   Demaret, G. "Cloches, sonneurs et sonneries." *Revue liturgique et musicale* (1931).

1276   Deming, Howard Owen. "The use of the trumpet in selected symphonic works of the late nineteenth and early twentieth centuries." D.Mus. diss., Indiana University, 1969.

1277   Deppe, Frithjof. "Die Fanfare im Lager- und Fahrtenleben." *Die Spielschar* 9 (1936): 170–174.

1278   Detel, Adolf. "Zinken bei den Hamburger Buxtehude-Feiern." *Hausmusik—Zeitschrift für Hausmusik* 7 (1938): 144–145.

1279   Detourbet, A. *La trompe enchantée, ses traditions, ses ressources, son avenir; avec l'analyse de 57 chefs d'oeuvre suivie de 26 fanfares, la plupart inédites, et d'une galerie illustrée de sonneurs célèbres.* Dijon: E. Rebourseau, 1942.

"Directory of trumpet players in American symphony orchestras." *The Instrumentalist* 31 (Apr. 1977): 51.

1280   Döring, C., comp. *Signale; die umfassendste Sammlung aller bei der Wehrmacht, Marine, Post, Feuerwehr, und bei der Jagd gebräuchlichen Musik-Signal.* Erweitert von P. Merkelt. Leipzig: W. Gebauer, [194?].

1281   Dorsam, Paul James. "Some solutions to the problem of transcribing Corelli's opera quinta church sonatas for trumpet and piano." Mus.A.D. diss., Boston University School for the Arts, 1974.

1282   Douglass, Robert. "The first trumpet method: Girolamo Fantini's modo per imparare a sonare di tromba (1638)." *Journal of Band Research* 7, no. 2 (Spring 1971): 18–22.

1283   Douglass, Robert S. "The history of the trumpet through the Baroque era." Master's thesis, North Texas State College, 1954.

1284   Downey, P. "A Renaissance correspondence concerning trumpet music." *Early Music* 9, no. 3 (1981): 325–329.

1285   Downey, P. "The Renaissance slide trumpet, fact or fiction?" *Early Music* 12, no. 1 (1984): 26–33.

1286   Drake, Julian. "The Christ Church cornetts, and the ivory cornett in the Royal College of Music, London." *The Galpin Society Journal* 34 (1981): 44–50.

1287   DuBose, C. B., and H. M. Lewis. "From our readers: Natural trumpets." *The Instrumentalist* 26 (May 1972): 9.

1288   Dudgeon, R. T. "A handbook for the cornetto." *Journal of the International Trumpet Guild* 1 (1976): 30–34.

1289   Duffy, Thomas Christopher. "*Triptych for Brass Quintet* (1962) by Charles Allen Whittenberg: an analysis." D.M.A. diss., Cornell University, 1986.

        Dunnick, D. Kim. "Selected literature for trumpet ensemble." *The Instrumentalist* 34 (Mar. 1980): 44 + .

        Echelard, Donald Joseph. "A thematic dictionary and planning guide of selected solo literature for trumpet." Ed.D. diss., University of Montana, 1969.

        Echelard, Donald Joseph. "A thematic dictionary and planning guide of selected solo literature for trumpet." *Dissertation Abstracts* 31 (Nov. 1970): 2419A.

        Ehmann, Wilhelm. "Der Bach-Trompeter Gottfried Reiche; seine Quatricinien und seine Trompete." *Der Kirchenmusiker* 12 (1961): 49–55.

1290   Ehmann, Wilhelm. "Neue Trompeten und Posaunen." In *Kirchenmusik, Vermächtnis und Aufgabe*, edited by W. Ehmann, 58–63. Darmstadt: K. Merseburger, 1958.

1291   Eichborn, Hermann Ludwig. *Das alte Clarinblasen auf Trompeten*. Leipzig: Breitkopf & Härtel, 1894.

1292   Eichborn, Hermann Ludwig. *Das alte Clarinblasen auf Trompeten*. Reprint of the 1894 edition. Nashville: Brass Press, 1973.

1293   Eichborn, Hermann Ludwig. "Das beste praktische Werke über die Trompete." *Zeitschrift für Instrumentenbau* (1900/01): 804–806, 831–832.

1294   Eichborn, Hermann Ludwig. "Die Clarintrompeterei." *Musikalisches Wochenblatt* 16 (1885): 622–624, 638–639.

        Eichborn, Hermann Ludwig. "Girolamo Fantini, ein Virtuos des siebzehnten Jahrhunderts und seine Trompeten-Schule." *Monatshefte für Musikgeschichte* 22 (1890): 112–138.

1295   Eichborn, Hermann Ludwig. "Grade Zinken und Jägertrompete im musikhistorischen Museum von Paul de Wit in Leipzig." *Zeitschrift für Instrumentenbau* 15 (1894/95): 813–815, 839–842, 867–869.

1296   Eichborn, Hermann Ludwig. *Die Trompete in alter und neuer Zeit. Ein Beitrag zur Musikgeschichte und Instrumentationslehre*. Leipzig: Breitkopf & Härtel, 1881.

1297   Eichborn, Hermann Ludwig. *Die Trompete in alter und neuer Zeit. Ein Beitrag zur Musikgeschichte und Instrumentationslehre.* Wiesbaden: Sändig, 1968. Reprint of the 1881 Breitkopf & Härtel publication.

1298   Eitner, R. "Wer hat die Ventiltrompete erfunden?" *Monatshefte für Musikgeschichte* 13 (1881): 41–47.

Ellis, J. R. "Pedagogical topics for trumpet: baroque performance styles." *Journal of the International Trumpet Guild* 9, no. 3 (1985): 48–51.

1299   Ellis, John Robert. "Treatment of the trumpet in the Bible and its relationship to the sacred solo arias with obbligato trumpet by Johann Sebastian Bach." *Dissertation Abstracts* 45 (Oct. 1984): 981A.

1300   Ellis, John Robert. "Treatment of the trumpet in the Bible and its relationship to the sacred solo arias with obbligato trumpet by Johann Sebastian Bach." D.M.A. diss., Arizona State University, 1984.

1301   Enders, Max. "Erwiderung auf die Ausführungen von Dr. R. Strauss über hohe Bach-Trompeten und Bläser derselben." *Zeitschrift für Instrumentenbau* 30 (1909/10): 228–229.

England, W. L. "Northampton Cornetto Weekend." *Recorder and Music* 5, no. 11 (1977): 363.

1302   Enrico, E. "Torelli's trumpet music: a structural analysis." *Journal of the International Trumpet Guild* 2 (1977): 2–23. Chapter 5 of his dissertation, 1970.

1303   Enrico, E. "Torelli's trumpet music: the primary sources." *Journal of the International Trumpet Guild* 3 (1978): 4–14.

1304   Enrico, Eugene Joseph. "Giuseppe Torelli's instrumental ensemble music with trumpet." Ph.D. diss., University of Michigan, 1970.

1305   Fantini, Girolamo. *A modern edition of Girolamo Fantini's trumpet method (1638).* Edited by W. R. and W. R. Clendenin. Boulder, CO: Empire, 1977.

1306   Fantini, Girolamo. *Modo per imparare a sonare di tromba.* Frankfurt: D. Vuastch, 1638. Facsimile reprint. Milan: Bollettino Bibliografico Musicale, 1934.

1307   Fantini, Girolamo. *Modo per imparare a sonare di tromba (1638).* Facsimile. Nashville: Brass Press, 1972.

1308   Fantini, Girolamo. *Modo per imparare a sonare di tromba (1638).* Transl. by Edward Tarr. Nashville: Brass Press, 1978.

1309   Farmer, H. G. "Crusading martial music." *Music and Letters* 30 (1949): 243–249.

1310   Faulkner, Maurice. "300 years later: what trumpet to play?" *The Instrumentalist* 40 (Dec. 1985): 68–69.

1311   Faulkner, Maurice. "Annual review of solos and studies: trumpet and French horn." *The Instrumentalist* 39 (Feb. 1985): 71–76.

Faulkner, Maurice. "The rotary valve trumpet and the Vienna style." *The Instrumentalist* 26 (Jan. 1972): 28–29.

Faulkner, Maurice. "Solos and studies for trumpet and horn." *The Instrumentalist* 32 (Feb. 1978): 56+.

Faulkner, Maurice. "Trumpet and French horn [1982–83 publications]." *The Instrumentalist* 38 (Dec. 1983): 42 + .

1312 Faulkner, Maurice. "Trumpet and French horn [annual review of solos and studies]." *The Instrumentalist* 35 (Dec. 1980): 33–34.

Faulkner, Maurice. "Trumpet and French horn [some of the more interesting selections we found]." *The Instrumentalist* 36 (Dec. 1981): 65–66.

Faulkner, Maurice. "Trumpet and French horn solos and studies." *The Instrumentalist* 33 (Jan. 1979): 80 + .

Faulkner, Maurice. "Trumpet and horn solos and studies." *The Instrumentalist* 34 (Dec. 1979): 24–26.

1313 Feather, Leonard. "The trumpet in jazz." *Downbeat* 25 (Jan. 23, 1958): 14–16 + .

1314 Federhofer, Hellmut. "Die landschaftlichen Trompeter und Heerpauker in Steiermark." *Zeitschrift des historischen Vereines für Steiermark* 40 (1949): 63–102.

1315 Fitzgerald, Bernard. "Chamber music for trumpet—with strings or woodwinds." *The Instrumentalist* 5 (Nov. 1950): 23–25.

1316 Fitzgerald, Bernard. "Solo literature for the trumpet." *The Instrumentalist* 2 (Nov. 1947): 28.

1317 "$500 donation from ITG helps Edison Institute acquire rare early American trumpet [made by Samuel Graves & Co.]." *International Trumpet Guild Newsletter* 7, no. 3 (1981): 7.

Fleischhauer, G. "Bucina und Cornu." *Wissenschaftliche Zeitschrift der Martin-Luther-Universität* (1960): 501–506.

1318 Flowers, David M. "Lecture recital: The unaccompanied trumpet." D.M.A. diss., Catholic University of America, 1974.

1319 Foss, George Dueward, Jr. "The stylistic problems to be considered in performing music from the trumpet repertoire of earlier periods on the modern instrument." M.A. thesis, American University, 1962.

1320 France. Ministère de la guerre. *Instruction du 18 juin 1912 sur les batteries et sonneries (Commune à toutes les armes). A jour avec modificatif no 1 du 15 octobre 1933.* Paris: Charles-Lavauzelle, 1949.

1321 Franquin, M. "La trompette à pistons." *Schweizerische Instrumentalmusik* 27 (1938): 64–65, 89–90, 113–114, 138.

1322 Frasch, C. C. "The late medieval trumpet." *Journal of the Graduate Music Students at the Ohio State University,* no. 5 (Spr. 1975): 16–25.

Freedman, R. S. "Bits 'n' pieces 'bout horns 'n' trumpets." *Music Journal* 30 (Dec. 1972): 28 + .

1323 Freeman, Jess B. "Origin and development of the trumpet." Master's thesis, Ohio State University, 1947.

Friese, Ernst August. "Klappenhorn und Klappentrompete." *Musica* 4 (1950): 224–225.

1324 Friese, Ernst August. "Die klassische Trompete." *Der Berufsmusiker* 3 (1950): 158–159.

1325   Friese, Ernst August. "Die klassische Trompete." *Die Musik-Woche*, no. 20 (1951): 158–159.

Gagne, J. "La trompette marine." *Carnet Musical*, no. 9 (July 1973): 14–16.

1326   Gardner, M. "Forgotten trumpet school." *Melody Maker* 45 (Sept. 26, 1970): 32.

1327   Gardner, N. "Trumpet and piano [repertoire]." *Journal of the International Trumpet Guild* 9, no. 2 (1984): 31–36.

1328   Gardner, Ned. "In search of the Renaissance slide trumpet." *Journal of the International Trumpet Guild* 12, no. 2 (Dec. 1987): 4–9.

1329   Garlepp, Bruno. *Die Geschichte der Trompete nebst eine Biographie J. Koslecks.* Hannover: L. Oertel, 1914.

1330   Garlepp, Bruno. "Die Trompete und ihre Bedeutung im Volksleben." *Allgemeine Musikzeitung* (Berlin) 31 (1904): 61–63, 79–81, 99–101, 119–121.

1331   Garlepp, Bruno. "Die Trompete. Ihre Geschichte und Bedeutung für das Volk." *Deutsche Militär-Musiker Zeitung* 28 (1906): 445–446, 463–464, 479–480, 495–496.

1332   Garrett, Stephen Craig. "A comprehensive performance project in trumpet repertoire; a discussion of the twentieth-century concerto for trumpet and orchestra; an investigative study of concertos by Alexander Arutunian, Henry Tomasi, Charles Chaynes, and André Jolivet; and a bibliography of concertos for trumpet and orchestra . . . from 1904 to 1983." D.M.A. diss., University of Southern Mississippi, 1984.

1333   Garrett, Stephen Craig. "A comprehensive performance project in trumpet repertoire; a discussion of the twentieth-century concerto for trumpet and orchestra; an investigative study of concertos by Alexander Arutunian, Henry Tomasi, Charles Chaynes, and André Jolivet; and a bibliography of concertos for trumpet and orchestra . . . from 1904 to 1983." *Dissertation Abstracts* 46 (Dec. 1985): 1434A-1435A.

Gates, C. R. "A selective annotated bibliography of articles published in English concerning history, development, and use of soprano brass instruments in the nineteenth century." *Journal of the International Trumpet Guild* 11, no. 2 (1986): 30–33.

1334   Gaudet, A. "The trumpet through the ages." *Brass and Percussion* 2, no. 5 (1974): 6–7+; Woodwind World—Brass and Percussion 14, no. 1, 2 (1975): 36–3.

1335   Geiringer, Karl. "Haydn's trumpet concerto." *The Musical Times* 81 (1940): 83.

1336   "Geretsried (B. R. Deutschland) [Meinl and Lauber making exact copy of trumpet by Joh. Leonhard Ehe (III), 1746]." *Brass Bulletin—International Brass Chronicle*, no. 5–6 (1973): 114. Also in English and French.

Gerson-Kiwi, Edith. "With trumpets and sound of cornet." *Tatzlil*, no. 3 (1963): 210+. In Hebrew, with English abstract.

1337   Ghitalla, Armando. "Fanfare for the trumpet [including a selected trumpet discography]." *American Record Guide* 24 (1957/58): 243–245.

1338   Ghitalla, Armando. "The repertoire of trumpet solos." *Music Journal* 16

(Sept. 1958): 54–55 + .

Gifford, Robert Marvin, Jr. "The music and performance practices of the medieval wind band." *Journal of Band Research* 10, no. 2 (Spring 1974): 25–32.

1339   Girschner, O. "Die alte Feldtrompete." *Harmonie* 7, no. 86 (1894); *Der Volksgesang* (1894).

1340   Glover, S. L. "Early trumpet music in Schwerin [with list]." *Brass Bulletin— International Brass Chronicle*, no. 23 (1978): 35 + . Also in French and German.

Gourlay, K. A. "Long trumpets of northern Nigeria—in history and today." *African Music* 6, no. 2 (1982): 48–72.

1341   Gouse, Charles Frederick. "The cornett: its history, literature and performance praxis including a practical tutor for developing performance skills." Mus.A.D. diss., Boston University, 1974.

1342   Gray, R., and Mary Rasmussen, comps. "Three bibliographies of nineteenth- and twentieth-century concertante works; solo parts for the trumpet; solo parts for the trombone; solo parts for more than one different brass instrument." *Brass Quarterly* 6, no. 1 (1962): 10–16.

1343   Green, Jane. "Trumpets, literal and figurative." *Notes & Queries* 173 (1937): 2–5, corrigenda 90, additions 119.

1344   Gregory, Robin. "Characteristics of the trumpet." *Philharmonic Post* 5 (Sept.-Oct. 1950): 5.

1345   Greissinger, F. Henri. *Instructions for the trumpet and drum; together with the full code of signals and calls used by the United States army and navy.* Revised and enlarged by W. F. Smith. New York: Carl Fischer, [1900].

1346   Gretton, P. "Cornet and sackbut." *International Trumpet Guild Newsletter* 6, no. 1 (1979): 15–16.

1347   Güttler, Ludwig. "Möglichkeiten und Probleme bei der Wiedergabe hoher Trompetenpartien der ersten Hälfte des 18. Jahrhunderts aus der Sicht des heutigen Spielers. In *Die Blasinstrumente und ihre Verwendung . . . ,* edited by Eitelfriedrich Thom, 22–25. Magdeburg: Rat des Bezirkes; Leipzig: Zentralhaus für Kulturarbeit, 1977.

1348   Guichon, Alfred. "La trompette." *Chronique musicale* 10 (1895): 49–58.

1349   Hänsel, R. "Ein Trompeter-Lehrbrief aus Auma." *Jahrbuch des Kreismuseums Hohenleuben-Reichenfels* 6 (1957): 43–45.

1350   Hahn, W. "Vom alten 'Trompeterrecht.' " *Die Musik-Woche* 3, no. 2 (1935): 2–3.

Halary. *Clavitube ou Trompette à clefs.* [Paris?]: n.p., 1821.

Halfpenny, Eric. "British trumpet mouthpieces: addendum to 'Early British trumpet mouthpieces.' " *The Galpin Society Journal* 21 (Mar. 1968): 185.

1351   Halfpenny, Eric. "William Bull and the English baroque trumpet." *The Galpin Society Journal* 15 (Mar. 1962): 18–24.

1352   Halfpenny, Eric. "The Christ Church trophies [zink]." *The Galpin Society Journal* 28 (Apr. 1975): 81–85.

1353   Halfpenny, Eric. "Cotgrave and the 'sourdine.' " *The Galpin Society Journal*

23 (Aug. 1970): 116–117.

1354 Halfpenny, Eric. "Early British trumpet mouthpieces." *The Galpin Society Journal* 20 (Mar. 1967): 76–88.

1355 Halfpenny, Eric. "Four seventeenth-century British trumpets." *The Galpin Society Journal* 22 (Mar. 1969): 51–57.

1356 Halfpenny, Eric. "Musicians at James II's coronation." *Music and Letters* 32 (1951): 103–114.

1357 Halfpenny, Eric. "Notes on two later British trumpets." *The Galpin Society Journal* 24 (July 1971): 79–83.

1358 Halfpenny, Eric. "William Shaw's 'harmonic trumpet.' " *The Galpin Society Journal* 13 (1960): 7–12.

1359 Halfpenny, Eric. "Two Oxford trumpets." *The Galpin Society Journal* 16 (May 1963): 49–62.

1360 Hall, Ernest. "Bach's trumpets." *Monthly Musical Record* 61 (1931): 78.

1361 Hall, J. "Is the band really ready for the trumpet?" *Woodwind World—Brass and Percussion* 17, no. 1 (1978): 29–30 + .

Hall, J. "The rotary valve trumpet—an American revival." *The Instrumentalist* 26 (Jan. 1972): 29–30.

1362 Harbach, H. C. "Hark the drums and trumpets." *Etude* 55 (1937): 305 + .

1363 Harkins, E. "Aspects of 'Kryl', a trumpet piece." *Journal of the International Trumpet Guild* 5 (1980): 22–28 + .

1364 Haynie, John J. "A graded list of trumpet solos." *The Instrumentalist* 18 (Aug. 1963): 47–49.

Head, Emerson Williams. "An evaluation of the use of vibrato in trumpet performance with historical and pedagogical perspectives." D.M.A. diss., Catholic University of America, 1980.

1365 Hebrok, F. "Die Wiederentdeckung der Clarintrompete und ihre Neukonstruktion." *Instrumentenbau-Zeitschrift* 15 (1961): 212 + .

1366 Heier, Dorothy Ruth. "Selected twentieth-century compositions for trumpet." Ed.D. diss., Columbia University, 1963.

1367 Heier, Dorothy Ruth. "Selected twentieth-century compositions for trumpet." *Dissertation Abstracts* (Jan. 1964): 2933–2934.

Heier, M. R. "Helping students cope with 20th century trumpet music." *Woodwind World—Brass and Percussion* 16, no. 3 (1977): 32–33 + .

1368 Hein, Sister Emmanuella Mary. "The trumpet sonatas of the Bologna School and their relationship to the solo concerto." Master's thesis, College of the Holy Names, 1962.

1369 "Heisse Trompeten." *Vier Viertel* 3, no. 2 (1949): 4.

1370 Henderson, Hubert P. "A study of the trumpet in the 17th century: its history, resources, and use." Master's thesis, University of North Carolina, 1949.

1371 Hendrich, Robert. "Trommeln und Fanfaren im Jungvolk." *Musik und Volk* 3 (1935): 77–80.

Henschel. "Von Turm-Musik, Trompeten und Posaunen." *Die Sendung* 7 (1930): 44.

1372   Henschel, A. K. "Hörner und Trompeter." *Die Sendung* 9 (1932): 112.
        Herrick, Dennis. "A summary of listings for the year [pieces listed in the
        Recent Programs column]." *Journal of the International Trumpet Guild* 11,
        no. 4 (1987): 11–12.

1373   Herrick, Dennis. "Ten years of programs [summary of compositions per-
        formed]." *Journal of the International Trumpet Guild* 10, no. 4 (1986): 12–
        15+.

1374   Heyde, Herbert. "Eine Geschäftskorrespondenz von Johann Wilhelm Haas
        aus dem Jahre 1719." In *Aufsätze und Jahresbericht* 1976, 32–38. 1977.
        Heyde, Herbert. "Medieval trumpets and trumpet playing in Europe (The-
        sis, Leipzig, 1965)." *Brass Bulletin—International Brass Chronicle*, no. 17
        (1977): 74–79.
        Heyde, Herbert. "Nochmals: Zwischen Hörnern und Jägertrompeten."
        Brass Bulletin—International Brass Chronicle, no. 58 (1987): 101. Also in
        English and French.

1375   Heyde, Herbert. "Die Sensation mit den Dresdner Silbertrompeten." *Das
        Orchester* 34 (Mar. 1986): 304–306.

1376   Heyde, Herbert. "Trompete und Trompetenblasen im europäischen Mit-
        telalter." *Die Musikforschung* 19, no. 1 (1966): 57–58. Ph.D. diss., Leipzig,
        1965.

1377   Heyde, Herbert. "Die Unterscheidung von Klarin- und Prinzipaltrompete.
        Zum Problem des Klarinblasens." *Beiträge zur Musikwissenschaft* 9 (1967):
        55–61.
        Heyde, Herbert. "Zwischen Hörner und Jägertrompeten." *Brass Bulletin—
        International Brass Chronicle*, no. 55 (1986): 42–56. Also in English and
        French.

1378   Hickman, David R. "Charles Schlueter on orchestral trumpet playing." *The
        Instrumentalist* 31 (Sept. 1976): 58+.
        Hiller, A. "Jean Baptiste Prin: ein Virtuose der Trompette marine." *Brass
        Bulletin—International Brass Chronicle*, no. 39 (1982): 53–58.

1379   Hiller, A. "Die Trompete im Dienst der norddeutschen Postverwaltungen
        des 19. Jahrhunderts." *Brass Bulletin—International Brass Chronicle*, no.
        47 (1984): 12–18. Also in English and French.

1380   Hiller, A. "Die Trompete in den Werken Jean-Philippe Rameaus." *Brass
        Bulletin—International Brass Chronicle*, no. 35 (1981): 59–64. Also in French
        and English.

1381   "Historische Musikinstrumente." *Musikhandel* 17, no. 8 (1966): 385–386.
        Hitt, George Lynn. "The lead trumpet in jazz (1924–1970)." D.Mus. diss.,
        Indiana University, 1976.

1382   Höfler, Janez. "Der 'Trompette de menestrels' und sein Instrument."
        Tijdschrift van de Vereniging voor Nederlandse Musiekgeschiedenis 29, no. 2
        (1979): 92–132.

1383   Hoffren, J. "Selected bibliography of music for brass choir." *The Instru-
        mentalist* 15 (Aug. 1961): 36–38.

1384   Hofmann, Richard. "Die F-Trompete im 2. Brandenburgischen Konzert von Joh. Seb. Bach." *Bach Jahrbuch* 13 (1916): 1–7.

1385   Hogarth, G. "Musical instruments: the trumpet, trombone, serpent and ophicleide." *Musical World* 4 (1837): 129–133.

1386   "Die hohen Bach-Trompeten." *Zeitschrift für Instrumentenbau* 30 (1909/10): 194–195.

1387   Hohstadt, Thomas. *Solo literature for the trumpet.* F. E. Olds Music Education Library. Fullerton, Calif.: F. E. Olds, 1959.

1388   Holman, P. "The trumpet sonata in England." *Early Music* 4, no. 4 (1976): 424–429.

    Hood, B. "Ten outstanding trumpet players in the Los Angeles area." *Brass Bulletin—International Brass Chronicle*, no. 41 (1983): 43 + . Also in French and German.

1389   Hoover, Cynthia A. "The slide trumpet of the nineteenth century." *Brass Quarterly* 6, no. 4 (1963): 159–178.

1390   Hoover, Cynthia A. "A trumpet battle at Niblo's Pleasure Garden." *Musical Quarterly* 55, no. 3 (July 1969): 384–395.

1391   Howard, Beverly A. "Texture in selected twentieth-century program music for trumpet and organ, a lecture recital, together with three recitals of selected works of J. Alain, J. S. Bach, G. Böhm, N. Degrigny, H. Distler, N. Duruflé, J. Guillou, A. Heller, W. A. Mozart, E. Raxache, M. Reger, L. Vierne." D.M.A. diss., North Texas State University, 1986.

1392   Howard, Beverly A. "Texture in selected twentieth-century program music for trumpet and organ, a lecture recital, together with three recitals of selected works of J. Alain, J. S. Bach, G. Böhm, N. Degrigny, H. Distler, N. Duruflé, J. Guillou, A. Heller, W. A. Mozart, E. Raxache, M. Reger, L. Vierne." *Dissertation Abstracts* 47 (Feb. 1987): 2790A + .

1393   Howell, S. "Paulus Paulirinus of Prague on musical instruments." *Journal of the American Musical Instrument Society* 5–6 (1980–81): 14 + .

1394   Humfeld, Neill H. "The history and construction of the cornett." Dissertation, University of Rochester, 1962.

1395   Hunsberger, Donald R. "The bass trumpet: from Wagner until today." *The Instrumentalist* 19 (Apr. 1965): 99–102.

1396   Hyatt, Jack René. "The soprano and piccolo trumpets: their history, literature, and a tutor." D.M.A. diss., Boston University, 1974.

1397   "Instruments nouveaux . . . Trompette à coulisse de M. Buhl." *Revue musicale* 13 (1833): 123–124.

1398   Irish Free State. Dept. of Defence. *Trumpet and bugle calls.* Defence Force Regulations. Dublin: Stationery Office, 1926.

    "ITG artists-members." *Journal of the International Trumpet Guild* 1 (1976): 42–47.

1399   Jackson, David Lee. "Late seventeenth-century Italian trumpet concertos of the Bologna school." *Dissertation Abstracts* 35 (Mar. 1975): 6182A.

1400   Jackson, David Lee. "Late seventeenth-century Italian trumpet concertos of the Bologna school: a lecture recital; together with three other recitals." D.M.A. diss., North Texas State University, 1974.

1401   Jähns, Friedrich Wilhelm. "Ein Freischütz-Curiosum. Mitt. über das 50jähr. Dienst-Jubiläum des Trompeters A. Metzkopp, der ununterbrochen durch die 50 Jahre der Freischütz-Auff. jedesmal in dem Bauern-Marsch die Solo-Trp. blies." *Vossische Zeitung* 81 (1872): Sonntags-Beil. 14.

1402   Jahn, Fritz. "Beiträge zur Geschichte des Nürnberger Musikinstrumenten-baues. Trompeten- und Posaunenmacher im 16. Jh." Dissertation, Erlangen, ca. 1923.

1403   Jahn, Fritz. "Die Nürnberger Trompeten- und Posaunenmacher im 16. Jahrhundert." *Archiv für Musikwissenschaft* 7 (1925): 23–52.

1404   Janetzky, Kurt. "Die Trompete: eine Ausstellung im Trompeterschloss zu Säckingen." *Brass Bulletin—International Brass Chronicle*, no. 29 (1980): 103–105. Also in French and English.

1405   Jarcho, Saul. "Two kinds of trumpet." *Bulletin of the New York Academy of Medicine* 47, no. 4 (Apr. 1971): 428–430.

1406   Jenny, W. A. v. "Zur Herkunft des Trompetenornaments." *Jahrbuch für prähistorische Kunst* 10 (1935): 31–48.

1407   K., J. *Die Ton- oder Musiksprache und ihre Anwendeng als musikalische Telegraphie.* Prague: J. Posp'isil, 1855.

        K., R. "Ein Altmeister deutscher Trompeterkunst [Julius Kosleck]." *Neue Zeitschrift für Musik* 93 (1897): 525–526.

        Kalkbrenner, A. "Die Notation der Ventil-Instrumente (Hörner und Trompeten) in der Orchestermusik." *Neue Zeitschrift für Musik* 83 (1887): 236–237, 321–323.

1408   Kalkbrenner, A. "Ueber die Signale der Infanterie." *Militär-Wochenblatt* (1881).

1409   Karstädt, Georg. "Anleitung zum Zinkenspiel." *Hausmusik—Zeitschrift für Hausmusik* 8 (1939): 50–53.

1410   Karstädt, Georg. "Aufführungspraktische Fragen bei Verwendung von Naturtrompeten, Naturhörnern und Zinken." In *Kongress—Bericht*, 93–95. Gesellschaft für Musikforschung, 1953.

1411   Karstädt, Georg. "Horn und Zink bei Johann Sebastian Bach." *Musik und Kirche* 22 (1952): 187–190.

1412   Karstädt, Georg. "Trompeter und Zinkenisten. Eine soziologische Betrachtung." *Deutsche Musikkultur* 2 (1937): 205–209.

1413   Karstädt, Georg. "Die Verwendung der Zinken in der Hausmusik." *Hausmusik—Zeitschrift für Hausmusik* 15 (1951): 125–127.

1414   Karstädt, Georg. "Zur Geschichte des Zinken und seiner Verwendung in der Musik des 16. bis 18. Jahrhunderts." Dissertation, Berlin, 1935.

1415   Karstädt, Georg. "Zur Geschichte des Zinken und seiner Verwendung in der Musik des 16. bis 18. Jhs." *Archiv für Musikforschung* 2 (1937): 385–432.

1416   Karstädt, Georg. *Zur Geschichte des Zinken und seiner Verwendung in der Musik des 16. bis 18. Jhs.* Leipzig: Breitkopf & Härtel, 1937.

1417   Kemenater, H. "Nur der Edle sei Trompeter." *Instrumentenbau-Zeitschrift* 14 (1960): 124 + .

1418   Kenton, Egon F. "A lexicographical communication on a non-existent composer [Scipione Bargagli]." *Acta Musicologica* 26 (1954): 129.

1419   Kinsky, Georg. "Zur Frage der Ausführung der Trompetenpartien in Bachschen Werken." *Allgemeine Musikzeitung* (Berlin) 36 (1909): 966–967.

1420   "Kirchenmusik mit Zinken." *Musik und Kirche* 10 (1938): 46–47.

1421   Kirchmeyer, H. "Die Rekonstruktion der Bachtrompete." *Neue Zeitschrift für Musik* 122 (1961): 137–145.

1422   Kirchner, T. "Mit Pauken und Trompeten." *Deutsche Militär-Musiker Zeitung* 62 (1940): 222.

1423   Kobbe, G. "The trumpet in camp and battle." *Century Magazine* 56 (1898): 537–543.

        Koch, Hans Oskar. "Die Spezialtypen der Blasinstrumente in der 1. Hälfte des 18. Jahrhunderts im deutschen Sprachraum." Staatsexamensarbeit, Hochschule für Musik und Theater, 1969.

1424   Körner, F. "Die Trompete im 20. Jahrhundert." *Instrumentenbau-Zeitschrift* 24 (June 1970): 369–370.

1425   Kozma, T. "The trumpet in Carmen." *Opera News* 16 (Feb. 11, 1952): 26–27.

        Krautwurst, Franz. "Musik der 2. Hälfte des 16. und des 17. Jahrhunderts." In *Nürnberg—Geschichte einer europäischen Stadt*, edited by Gerhardt Pfeiffer, 287–291. München: Beck, 1971.

1426   Kronholz, K. "Concertos, sonatas, and concert works for trumpet with woodwinds: an index." *International Trumpet Guild Newsletter* 7, no. 1 (1980): 14–16.

1427   Kunitz, Hans. *Die Instrumentation. Ein Hand- und Lehrbuch. Teil VII: Trompete.* Leipzig: VEB Breitkopf & Härtel, 1958.

1428   "Ein kurfürstlich sächsischer Erlass gegen das unbefugte Trompeten-Blasen und Heerpauken-Schlagen." *Zeitschrift für Instrumentenbau* 14, no. 2 (1893/94).

1429   Labella, Peter. "The transition from natural trumpet to valve trumpet studied in the symphonic and operatic orchestra from 1817–1849." Master's thesis, Eastman School of Music, 1948.

1430   Landy, E. *Méthode de clarion . . . avec vignette et description de l'instrument.* Paris: Gallet, [1903].

        Laplace, Michel. "Les fondateurs de l'ecole française de trompette Merri Franquin, Eugene Foveau et Raymond Sabarich." *Brass Bulletin—International Brass Chronicle*, no. 29 (1980): 67–69+. Also in German and English. Expanded from *International Trumpet Guild Newsletter* 3, no. 3 (1977): 13–14.

1431   Laplace, Michel. "A tribute to the British trumpet tradition." *Journal of the International Trumpet Guild* 3 (1978): 2–4+.

        Laplace, Michel. "La trompette et le cornet dans le jazz et la musique populaire." *Brass Bulletin—International Brass Chronicle*, no. 42 (1983): 16–30. Also in English and German.

        Laplace, Michel. "La trompette et le cornet dans le jazz et la musique populaire." *Brass Bulletin—International Brass Chronicle*, no. 45 (1984): 38–44. Also in English and German.

Laplace, Michel. "La trompette et le cornet dans le jazz et la musique populaire (1927–1945)." *Brass Bulletin—International Brass Chronicle*, no. 43 (1983): 44–65. Also in English and German.

Laplace, Michel. "La trompette et le cornet dans le jazz et la musique populaire (1945-present)." *Brass Bulletin—International Brass Chronicle*, no. 44 (1983): 54–60. Also in English and German.

Laplace, Michel. "The trumpet in the USSR [includes Soviet players discography]." *International Trumpet Guild Newsletter* 4, no. 2 (1978): 19–21.

1432 Larson, Jacob Francis. "The role of the trumpet in the music of Johann Sebastian Bach: past and present performance considerations through selected works." D.M.A. diss., University of Cincinnati, 1976.

1433 Laudermilch, Kenneth Lee. "The keyed trumpet." D.M.A. diss., Catholic University of America, 1976.

1434 Lautenschlager, Kurt March. "The cornett: classification, history, uses and performance practices." M.A. thesis, California State University (Fullerton), 1976.

1435 Lederer, L. "Eros brachte die Trompete aus Kreta zurück." *Instrumentenbau-Zeitung* 29, no. 8 (1975): 569.

1436 Leech-Wilkinson, D. "Il libro di appunti di un suonatore di tromba del quindicesimo secolo." *Rivista Italiana di Musicologia* 16, no. 1 (1981): 16–39.

1437 Lessmann, Otto. "[An account of a demonstration of clarino playing by Julius Kosleck]." *Neue Berliner Musikzeitung* (1871): 431.

1438 Lewis, H. M. "Authentic baroque interpretation for trumpet." *The Instrumentalist* 32 (Feb. 1978): 44–45.

1439 Lewis, H. M. "Extra-harmonic trumpet tones in the baroque era—natural trumpet vs. tromba da tirarsi." *Journal of the International Trumpet Guild* 5 (1980): 39–45.

1440 Lewis, H. M. "French trumpet ensemble music of the late seventeenth century." *Journal of the International Trumpet Guild* 7, no. 4 (1983): 12–17.

1441 Lewis, H. M. "The natural trumpet in the modern orchestra." *The Instrumentalist* 25 (Oct. 1970): 40–41.

1442 Lewis, H. M. "The trumpet in the romantic era—a forgotten instrument." *The Instrumentalist* 26 (Jan. 1972): 26–27.

1443 Lewis, H. M. " 'The Trumpet Shall Sound' [aria by Handel]." *The Instrumentalist* 31 (Apr. 1977): 49–51.

1444 Lewis, Horace Monroe. "The problem of the 'tromba da tirarsi' in the works of J. S. Bach." Ph.D. diss., Louisiana State University, 1975.

1445 Lewis, Horace Monroe. "The problem of the tromba da tirarsi in the works of J. S. Bach." *Dissertation Abstracts* 36 (Oct. 1975): 1893A.

1446 Limac, O. L. "Die Trompete als Kircheninstrumente." *Zeitschrift für Instrumentenbau* 30 (1909/10): 1209.

1447 Littleton, W. S. *Trumpeter's handbook and instructor.* Kansas City, Kansas:

Hudson-Kimberly Pub. Co., [1902].

1448   Logan, J. D. "*Mouth-Piece* by Kenneth Gaburo: a performer's analysis of the composition." *Dissertation Abstracts* 38 (Aug. 1977): 539A.

1449   Lombard, N. C. *The trumpeter's manual, for the use of trumpeters in the military and naval forces of the United States.* 2d ed. Boston: Lombard, 1911.

1450   Lord, Jewel W. "The trumpet: its history, literature and place in the public school." Master's thesis, University of Southern California, 1949.

Lowrey, A. L. "A feast of recorded baroque trumpet ensemble repertoire." *Journal of the International Trumpet Guild* 6 (1981): 31–33 + .

Lowrey, A. L. "Homage to pioneers of trumpet LP's [includes discography]." *Journal of the International Trumpet Guild* 8, no. 1 (1983): 22–25 + .

1451   Lowrey, A. L., comp. "Index of baroque masterpieces for trumpet & organ." *Journal of the International Trumpet Guild* 7, no. 3 (1983): 38–39.

1452   McCready, M. "An idiomatic view of the keyed trumpet through two concerti." *Journal of the International Trumpet Guild* 9, no. 1 (1984): 46–52.

1453   McGrady, R. "The court trumpeters of Charles I and Charles II." *The Music Review* 35, no. 3–4 (1974): 223–230.

1454   McNaught, W. "Clarino and trumpet." *The Musical Times* 81 (1940): 83.

McRae, B. "Arena: trumpet no end [decline as innovative force in jazz]." *Jazz Journal* 29 (Dec. 1976): 12.

1455   Mahan, Frederick A. "Trumpeters and buglers." *Metronome* 23, no. 11 (1907): 11–12.

1456   Mahan, Frederick A. "Trumpeters and trumpet calls." *Journal of the Mil. Ser. Inst. of the U.S.* 43 (1908): 297–302.

1457   Mahillon, Victor Charles. "Une découverte intéressant." *L'Echo musical* 3, no. 11 (15 Nov. 1871); 4, no. 1 (15 Jan. 1872).

1458   Mahillon, Victor Charles. *La trompette.* Brussels: Mahillon, 1907.

1459   Mahillon, Victor Charles. "The trumpet—its history—its theory—its construction." *Dominant* 16, nos. 7–9 (1908).

1460   Mang, Walter. "Zur Neubelebung des alten Zinks." *Zeitschrift für Instrumentenbau* 57 (1936–37): 116–117.

1461   Mariconda, Dominick J. "The trumpet—its history, care, repertoire and method of performance." Master's thesis, Hartt College of Music, 1952.

Markl, Jaroslav. "Kesselmundstückinstrumente und das Hirtenblasen in Böhmen." *Emsheimer Festschrift* (1974): 123–130.

1462   Martell, Paul. "Zur Geschichte der Trompete." *Musik Industrie* 5, no. 7 (n.d.).

1463   Martell, Paul. "Zur Geschichte der Trompete." *Das Orchester* 4 (1927): 125, 141.

1464   Martell, Paul. "Zur Geschichte der Trompete." *Die Musik-Woche* 3, no. 13 (1935): 5–7.

Mathez, Jean-Pierre. "Editorial: Corno da caccia—for trumpeters or horn players? A debate for experts only?" *Brass Bulletin—International Brass Chronicle*, no. 54 (1986): 3–4. Also in French and German.

1465   Mathez, Jean-Pierre. "Les petites histoires de la vie des cuivres: une petite musique de trompette." *Brass Bulletin—International Brass Chronicle*, no. 50 (1985): 81 +. Also in English and German.

Mathez, Jean-Pierre. "Trumpet museum Bad Säckingen." *Brass Bulletin—International Brass Chronicle*, no. 53 (1986): 17–27. Also in French and German.

Mathis, W. E. "Peck-horns and other castoffs." *The Instrumentalist* 35 (Feb. 1981): 30–31.

1466   Maycock, J. "The Bach trumpet parts." *Musical Opinion* 75 (Mar. 1952): 343 +.

1467   McCarthy, Albert J. *The trumpet in jazz*. London: Citizen Press, 1945.

1468   Meister, Hans. "Die Entwicklung der Trompete von der Barockzeit bis zur Romantik und ihre solistische wie orchestrale Verwendung in der Kunstmusik." *Das Orchester* 31, no. 6 (1983): 541–546.

1469   Menke, Werner. *History of the trumpet of Bach and Handel*. Nashville: Brass Press, 1972.

1470   Menke, Werner. *History of the trumpet of Bach and Handel*. Reprint of 1934 English translation by G. Abraham. Nashville: Brass Press, 1985.

1471   Menke, Werner. *History of the trumpet of Bach and Handel; a new point of view and new instruments; forming a history of the trumpet and its music, from its earliest use as an artistic instrument to the middle of the eighteenth century. Special reference given to its employment by Bach and Handel*. Translated by Gerald Abraham. London: W. Reeves, 1934.

1472   Menke, Werner. "Probleme der Bachtrompeten und Vorschläge für die Posaunenmission." *Kirchenchor* 45 (1934): 22.

1473   Menke, Werner. "Rekonstruktion der Bachtrompeten in D und F." *Musik und Kirche* 6 (1934): 89–93.

1474   Meredith, Henry M. "Baroque trumpet ornamentation: another view." *International Trumpet Guild Newsletter* 7, no. 3 (1981): 22–23.

1475   Meredith, Henry M. "Girolamo Fantini's Trumpet Method: a practical edition." 2 vols. D.A. diss., University of Northern Colorado, 1984.

1476   Meredith, Henry M. "Girolamo Fantini's trumpet method: a practical edition." *Dissertation Abstracts* 46 (Oct. 1985): 835A.

1477   *Metronome* 68 (1952). May issue devoted to trumpets and trumpeters.

1478   Meyer, Clemens. "Ein historisches dokument [Trompeter-lehrbrief, Schwerin, 1762]." *Deutsche Musiker-Zeitung* 61 (1930): 168–169.

1479   Meyer, Lawrence James. "The adaptation of selected American folk tunes for solo trumpet with instrumental accompaniment." *Dissertation Abstracts* 25 (July 1964): 522–523.

1480   Meyer, Lawrence James. "The adaptation of selected American folk tunes for solo trumpet with instrumental accompaniment." Ed.D. diss., University of Northern Colorado, 1964.

1481   Michel, Paul. "Hof- und Feldtrompeter in Thüringen. Ein Beitrag zur Sozialgeschichte des Musikers." *Senn Festschrift* (RILM76 4857): 135–141.

1482   Michel, Paul. "Hof- und Feldtrompeter in Thüringen." *Heimat* (Weimar) 3 (1958): 75–84.

Miller, D. G. "Johann Stoerl and his Six Sonatas for Cornett and Trombones." Master's essay, University of Rochester, 1962.

Miller, K. E. "Instruments of the baroque era." *Choral Journal* 7, no. 5 (1967): 16.

1483   Mitchell, G. "The United States Army Herald Trumpets." *The Instrumentalist* 27 (Apr. 1973): 32–33.

1484   Modell, Ron. "The ITL draft." *The Instrumentalist* 30 (Jan. 1976): 24–25.

1485   Mönkemeyer, Helmut. *Spielanleitung für Zinken in d' und a/How to play the cornett in D and A.* Celle: Moeck, 1978.

1486   Mörtzsch, Otto. "Die Dresdener Hoftrompeter." In *Musik im alten Dresden; Drei Abhandlungen.* Dresden: Verlag des Vereins für Geschichte Dresdens, 1921.

Monk, C. "First steps towards playing the cornett." *Early Music* 3, no. 2, 3 (1975): 132–133, 244–248.

Montagu, G., and Jeremy Montagu. "Beverley Minster reconsidered." *Early Music* 6, no. 3 (1978): 406–408.

Montagu, Jeremy. "One of Tutankhamon's trumpets." *The Galpin Society Journal* 29 (May 1976): 115–117.

1487   Montagu, Jeremy. "The Society's first foreign tour." *The Galpin Society Journal* 21 (Mar. 1968): 6–8 + .

1488   Moore, Albert Lee. "Two anonymous eighteenth-century manuscripts for trumpet with oboe ensemble from the Lilien part-books (Sonsfeld Collection): a lecture recital; together with three other recitals." D.M.A. diss., North Texas State University, 1981.

1489   Moore, R. "Reviews: trumpet duet." *Woodwind World—Brass and Percussion* 19, no. 4 (1980): 28.

1490   Moore, R. "Reviews: trumpet etudes." *Woodwind World—Brass and Percussion* 19, no. 4 (1980): 28.

1491   Moore, R. "Reviews: trumpet trio." *Woodwind World—Brass and Percussion* 19, no. 4 (1980): 28.

1492   Morley, M. L. "Authentic ornamentation practice in baroque trumpet arias." *International Trumpet Guild Newsletter* 6, no. 2 (1980): 17–21.

1493   Morley, M. L. "The trumpet arias in the oratorios of George Frederic Handel." *Dissertation Abstracts* 40 (Jan. 1980): 3619A + .

1494   Morley, M. L. "The trumpet arias in the oratorios of George Frederic Handel." *Journal of the International Trumpet Guild* 5 (1980): 14–19.

1495   Morley, Max Lynn. "The trumpet arias in the oratorios of George Frederic Handel: a lecture recital; together with three other recitals." D.M.A. diss., North Texas State University, 1979.

1496   Morley-Pegge, R. "Clarino and trumpet." *The Musical Times* 81 (1940): 32–33.

1497   Morrione, Phillip Richard. "A Baroque trumpet recital." M.A. thesis, California State University (Long Beach), 1973.

1498   Morrow, W. "The trumpet as an orchestral instrument." *Proceedings of the Musical Association* 21 (1894/95): 133–147.

Mortenson, Gary Curtiss. "The varied role of the trumpet in the musical textures of Igor Stravinsky." D.M.A. diss., University of Texas (Austin), 1984.

1499 Mortenson, Gary Curtiss. "The varied role of the trumpet in the musical textures of Igor Stravinsky." *Dissertation Abstracts* 45 (Jan. 1985): 1912A.

1500 Muckelroy, Roby Kenneth. "A brief history of the trumpet and an annotated bibliography of studies for the trumpet." M.Mus. thesis, University of Houston, 1968.

1501 Mueller, Herbert C. "Accompanied two trumpet literature—an annotated bibliography [graded]." *Journal of the International Trumpet Guild* 1 (1976): 29.

1502 Müller, S. "Die A-Trompete." *Die Posaune* 20 (1936): 45–46.

1503 Müller, Ulrich Robert. "Dissertationen: Untersuchungen zu den Strukturen von Klängen der Clarin- und Ventiltrompete." *Die Musikforschung* 25, no. 3 (1972): 352–353.

Mullady, F., and W. H. Kofoed. "The story of taps." *Coronet* 50 (May 1961): 81.

1504 "Music for trumpet." *Sounding Brass & the Conductor* 8, no. 4 (1979): 150–151.

1505 Nagel, Robert. "The I.T.G. Trumpet Composition Contest." *International Trumpet Guild Newsletter* 3, no. 3 (1977): 11–12.

1506 Nagel, Robert. "Trumpet ensemble music." *The Instrumentalist* 31 (Apr. 1977): 60. Includes list.

1507 "Naturtrompete der Bachzeit neugebaut." *Hausmusik* 25, no. 2 (1961): 60.

1508 Naylor, Tom L. *The trumpet and trombone in graphic arts: 1500–1800.* Nashville: Brass Press, 1979.

1509 Neff, Carolyn Hope. "A study of trumpet pedagogy and repertoire in the United States and Scandinavia." D.M.A. diss., University of Oregon, 1974.

Netto. "Von Hörnern, Posaunen und Trompeten aus alter und neuer Zeit." *Deutsche Mititär-Musiker Zeitung* 28 (1906): 73–74.

1510 Neukomm, E. "Sonneries de trompettes." *Le Menéstrel* 59, no. 35 (189-?).

1511 Neuss, Heinrich Georg. *Musica parabolica, oder parabolische music, das ist, erorterung etlicher gleichnisse und figuren, die in der music, absonderlich an der trommete befindlich,. . . .* Leipzig: Bey Heinsius erben, 1754.

1512 Nicholas, M. R. "Establishing and expanding an early music consort [cornetto, sackbut]." *The Instrumentalist* 32 (Mar. 1978): 36–39.

1513 Nickel, Ekkehart. *Der Holzblasinstrumentenbau in der Freie Reichsstadt Nürnberg.* Giebing: Katzbichler, 1970.

1514 Nowak, Leopold. "Beethovens *Fidelio* und die österreicheschen Militärsignale." *Oesterreichische Musik Zeitschrift* 10 (1955): 373–375.

Nussbaum, Jeffrey. "An interview with Don L. Smithers." *Journal of the International Trumpet Guild* 13, no. 2 (Dec. 1988): 11–20+.

1515 Nuys, Robert Copeland Van. "The history and nature of the trumpet as applied to the sonatas of Giuseppi Torelli." D.M.A. diss., University of Illinois, 1969.

1516   Ochs, Traugott. "Wie sind die hohen Trompeten der alten Komponisten zu ersetzen?" *Allgemeine Musikzeitung* (Berlin) 37 (1910): 160.

1517   Ode, James. "A selected list of trumpet duet collections [graded]." *Journal of the International Trumpet Guild* 1 (1976): 28.

1518   O'Loughlin, N. "Modern trumpet." *The Musical Times* 125 (Dec. 1984): 711.

1519   O'Loughlin, N. "Trumpet." *The Musical Times* 125 (Apr. 1984): 217.

1520   Olson, R. D. "The present state of prose writings concerning the trumpet." *Music Educators Journal* 51, no. 2 (1964): 73–75.

1521   Oman, Charles. "The insignia and civic plate of the city of Bristol: the insignia." *Connoisseur* 182, no. 733 (Mar. 1973): 169–176.

1522   Oneglia, Mario Francesco. "The trumpet in chamber music other than brass ensemble." Ed.D. diss., Columbia University, 1966.

1523   Oneglia, Mario Francesco. "The trumpet in chamber music other than brass ensemble." *Dissertation Abstracts* 27 (June 1967): 4287A-4288A.

1524   Ornelas, R. S. "A comprehensive performance project in trumpet repertoire; an essay on Eugene Bozza's published compositions for solo trumpet with piano or orchestra and an analysis of representative compositions." *Dissertation Abstracts* 47 (May 1987): 3905A.

1525   Ornelas, Raul Sosa. "A comprehensive performance project in trumpet repertoire; an essay on Eugene Bozza's published compositions for solo trumpet with piano or orchestra and an analysis of representative compositions." D.M.A. diss., University of Southern Mississippi, 1986.

Oster, Raymond. "A survey of selected cornet literature." Master's thesis, Arthur Jordan Conservatory of Music, 1937.

Ostling, A. "Why not cornets and trumpets? [in bands]." *The Instrumentalist* 21 (June 1967): 37–39.

1526   Otis. "Cornet versus trumpet." *The Musical Times* 58 (1917): 409–410.

1527   Overton, Friend Robert. *Der Zink.* Mainz: Schott, 1982.

1528   Overton, Friend Robert. *Der Zink. Geschichte, Bauweise und Spieltechnik eines historischen Musikinstruments.* Mainz: Schott, 1981.

1529   Overton, Friend Robert. "Der Zink: Neue Entwicklungen und Forschungen." *Das Orchester* 29, no. 2 (Feb. 1981): 97–101.

"Partitions-Noten-music." *Brass Bulletin—International Brass Chronicle*, no. 20 (1977): 2–7.

1530   Payne, James Farwell. "Johann Nepomuk Hummel's *Concerto a tromba principale*: a lecture recital; together with three other recitals." D.M.A. diss., North Texas State University, 1980.

Peterson, O. A. "Historical outline of cornet from *The Cornet*." *Jacobs' Band Monthly* 22 (Sept. 1937): 4.

1531   Pfannenstiel. "Von der Trompete." *Deutsche Militär-Musiker Zeitung* 46 (191-?): 1.

1532   Pichler, F. "Von Trompetern und Paukern." *Carinthia* 47 (1857): 65f.

1533   Pickard, Alexander L., Jr. "A practical edition of the trumpet sonatas of

Giuseppe Jacchini." D.M.A. diss., University of Rochester, Eastman School of Music, 1974.

1534 Pier, Fordyce Chilcen. "Italian Baroque instrumental music with solo trumpet from the Emilian School: Cazzati to Torelli." Mus.A.D. diss., Boston University School for the Arts, 1979.

1535 Pierce, T. "Monteverdi's use of brass instruments." *Journal of the International Trombone Association* 9 (1981): 4–8.

1536 Pietzsch, Hermann. "Nochmals die Bach-Trompetenfrage." *Zeitschrift für Instrumentenbau* 30 (1909/10): 375–378.

1537 Pietzsch, Hermann. *Die Trompete als Orchester-Instrument und ihre Behandlung in den verschiedenen Epochen der Musik.* Heilbronn: C. F. Schmidt, 1901.

1538 Pietzsch, Hermann. "Trompetenblasen in alter und neuer Zeit." *Deutsche Musiker-Zeitung* 40 (1909): 2.

Plass, Ludwig. "Joh. Seb. Bach's Clarintrompeter (Gottfried Reiche) und seine Kunst." *Allgemeine Musikalische Zeitung* 54 (1927): 1121–1123.

"Pop goes the trumpet [trumpeters as singers]." *Melody Maker* 43 (Sept. 7, 1968): 12.

Prescott, J. "Treatment of the cornet and trumpet in selected twentieth-century band compositions." *Journal of Band Research* 21, no. 1 (1985): 50–60.

1539 Preston, N. "Trumpet, the melody instrument of knights." *Etude* 54 (1936): 485+.

1540 "Race track trumpeters." *International Musician* 48 (Mar. 1950): 14+.

1541 Rasmussen, Mary. "Bach-trumpet madness; or, A plain and easy introduction to the attributes, causes and cure of a most mysterious musicological malady." *Brass Quarterly* 5, no. 1 (1961): 37–40.

1542 Rasmussen, Mary. "A concertino for chromatic trumpet by Johann Georg Albrechtsberger." *Brass Quarterly* 5, no. 3 (1962): 104–108.

1543 Rasmussen, Mary. "English trumpet concertos in some eighteenth-century printed collections." *Brass Quarterly* 5, no. 2 (1961): 51–57.

1544 Rasmussen, Mary. "New light on some unusual seventeenth-century French trumpet parts." *Brass Quarterly* 6, no. 1 (1962): 9. Includes music.

Reissiger, C. G. "Ueber Ventil-Hörner und Klappen-Trompeten." *Allgemeine musikalische Zeitung* 39 (1837): 608–610.

1545 Reissmann, A. "Mit Pauken und Trompeten." *Neue Berliner Musikzeitung* 42 (1888): 339–341, 349–351.

1546 Remsen, Lester E. "A study of the natural trumpet and its modern counterpart." D.M.A. diss., University of Southern California, 1960.

1547 Remsen, Lester E. "A study of the natural trumpet and its modern counterpart." *Dissertation Abstracts* 21 (1961): 1587.

1548 Rhodes, Emil. *Les trompettes du Roi.* Paris: A. Picard, 1909.

1549 Richard, Leon. "The literature of the trumpet as a solo and obbligato instrument in combination with soprano voice in works of the Italian, English, and German schools during the Baroque period." D.M.A. diss.,

Memphis State University, 1984.

1550 Richard, Leon Richard. "The literature of the trumpet as a solo and obligato instrument in combination with soprano voice in works of the Italian, English, and German schools during the baroque period." *Dissertation Abstracts* 45 (Apr. 1985): 3024A.

1551 Richter, P. E. "Eine zweiventilige Trompete aus dem Jahre 1806 und die Wiener Instrumentenbacher Kerner." *Zeitschrift für Instrumentenbau* 30 (1909/10): 36–38.

1552 Richter, P. F. "Das alte Clarin-Blasen auf Trompeten." *Monatshefte für Musikgeschichte* 27 (1895): 75–76.

Roos, W. "The musical instrument collection at Meran." *Galpin Society Journal* 32 (May 1979): 10–23.

1553 Rowlette, T. W. "The history of the trumpet." *The School Musician* 26 (Jan. 1955): 20–21.

Roy, and Muller. *Tutor for the keyed trumpet*. London: n.p., (183-?).

1554 Rywosch, Bernhard. "Pfeifer und Trompeter." *Die Musik* 21 (1929): 352–354.

1555 Sachs, Curt. "Bachs 'Tromba da tirarsi.' " *Bach Jahrbuch* 5 (1908): 141–143.

1556 Sachs, Curt. "Die Basstrompete." *Deutsche Militär-Musiker Zeitung* 35 (1913): 597.

1557 Sachs, Curt. "Chromatic trumpets in the Renaissance." *Musical Quarterly* 36 (1950): 62–66.

Sachs, Curt. "Die Litui in Bachs Motette 'O Jesu Christ.' " *Bach Jahrbuch* 18 (1921): 96–97.

1558 Sachs, Curt. "Eine unkritische Kritik des Klarinblasens." *Archiv für Musikwissenschaft* 2 (1920): 335–336.

1559 Sandor, E. P. "Development and use of the chromatic trumpet in the nineteenth-century orchestra." *NACWPI Journal* 33, no. 4 (1985): 4–12.

1560 Savitt, Ronald Keith. "A recital: music in the twentieth century for trumpet." M.A. thesis, California State University (Long Beach), 1977.

Schering, Arnold. "Zu Gottfried Reiches Leben und Kunst." *Bach Jahrbuch* 15 (1918): 133–140.

1561 Schiedel, A. "The trumpet and the cornet." *Woodwind World—Brass and Percussion* 18, no. 3 (1979): 16+.

1562 Schlesinger, Kathleen. "Bach's trumpets." *Monthly Musical Record* 61 (1931): 108–109.

1563 Schlesinger, Kathleen. "Cornet [Zink]." In *Encyclopaedia Britannica*. 11th ed. New York, 1910–11.

1564 Schlesinger, Kathleen. "Trumpet." In *Encyclopaedia Britannica*. 11th ed. New York, 1910–11.

1565 Schneider-Cuvay, M. M., and others, eds. *Denkmäler der Musik in Salzburg, Band I: Aufzüge für Trompeten und Pauken/Musikstücke für mechanische Orgelwerke*. Munich: Katzbichler, 1977.

1566 Schünemann, Georg. *Deutsche Fanfaren und Feldstücke aus alter Zeit*. Kassel: n.p., 193?.

1567 Schünemann, Georg. "Fanfaren und Feldstücke aus alter Zeit." *Deutsche Musikkultur* 1 (1936): 179–181.

1568 Schünemann, Georg. "Sonaten und Feldstücke der Hoftrompeter." *Zeitschrift für Musikwissenschaft* 17 (1935): 147–170.

1569 Schünemann, Georg. *Trompeterfanfaren, Sonaten und Feldstücke.* Part 1. Vol. 7 of *Das Erbe Deutscher Musik.* Kassel: Bärenreiter, 1936.

Schultz, P. M. " 'Praise the Lord with the sound of trumpet' and trombone and horn and tuba." *The School Musician* 44 (Dec. 1972): 48–49.

1570 Scott, B. "Twentieth-century compositions for trumpet & strings: critiques, comments & criticisms." *American String Teacher* 30, no. 4 (1980): 19–23.

1571 Scott, B. "Twentieth-century compositions for trumpet and strings." *International Trumpet Guild Newsletter* 7, no. 2 (1981): 7–11.

Scott, S. "The Streitweiser Foundation historic Trumpet Museum." *Brass Bulletin—International Brass Chronicle*, no. 39 (1982): 39–43. Also in French and German.

Sears, L. "Classic trumpet tunes." *Musart* 20, no. 3 (1968): 24.

1572 "Seele im Blech." *Vier Viertel* 3, no. 2 (1949): 6.

Seidel, Hans. "Horn und Trompete im alten Israel unter Berücksichtigung der 'Kriegsrolle' von Qumran." *Wissenschaftliche Zeitschrift der Universität Leipzig* 4 (1956/57): 5.

1573 Seidl, Bartholomäus. *Der Fall Bach-Trompete und Corno da Caccia.* Hittis'au: Vorarlberg, Seidl, 1955.

1574 Seidler, R. D. "Vivaldi's 'thirteen' concertos for trumpet(s)." *NACWPI Journal* 24, no. 1 (1975): 13–17.

1575 Seidler, R. D. "Vivaldi's 'thirteen' concertos for trumpet(s)." *International Trumpet Guild Newsletter* 6, no. 2 (1980): 15–17.

1576 Shainman, Irwin. "The changeover from the natural to the valved trumpet as seen in the 19th century orchestration." Master's thesis, Columbia University, 1948.

Sim, A. C. "The Wanstead Trumpet Quartet." *Music in Education* 30, no. 322 (1966): 298–299.

1577 Simmonds, R. "How high the C?" *Crescendo International* 11 (Mar. 1973): 10–11.

1578 Sittard, J. "Hochfürstlich Württembergische neue Zinckenisten-Ordnung von 1721 sowie einige Urkunden bezüglich der Anstellung der alten Instrumentalisten in Stuttgart." *Monatshefte für Musikgeschichte* 18 (1886): 27–38.

1579 Sittard, J. "Den Trompetern, Pfeiffern und Lautenschlägern wird vom Grafen Ulrich v. Württemberg 'ihre gemachte Gesellschaft bestetigt' 1458." *Monatshefte für Musikgeschichte* 19 (1887): 4–7.

"Slide trumpets inspired by old prototypes from Egger & Co." *Musik International-Instrumentenbau-Zeitschrift* 39 (Oct. 1985): 687.

Slone, K., and Jamie Aebersold, eds. "28 modern jazz trumpet solos." *Jazz Journal International* 33 (Feb. 1980): 19.

1580 Smimov, B. "The Russian folk cornett, or rozhok." *The Galpin Society Journal*

14 (Mar. 1961): 76–78.

1581   Smith, D. "A short history of the trumpet." *The Instrumentalist* 26 (Jan. 1972): 20–25.

1582   Smith, D. L. "A selected periodical index for trumpet." *International Trumpet Guild Newsletter* 7, no. 3 (1981): 24–25.

1583   Smith, Norman E. "Opinions of contemporary European trumpet players." *NACWPI Journal* 24, no. 4 (1976): 3–11; 25, no. 1 (1976): 34–38; 25, no. 2 (1976–1977): 8–24.

1584   Smith, Norman E. "Opinions of contemporary European trumpet players." *Journal of the International Trumpet Guild* 1 (1976): 5–19+. Reprinted in part from *NACWPI Journal* (1976).

1585   Smithers, Donald L. "The Baroque trumpet after 1721—some preliminary observations. I: Science and practice." *Early Music* 5, no. 2 (Apr. 1977): 177–183.

1586   Smithers, Donald L. "The Baroque trumpet after 1721—some preliminary observations. II: Function and use." *Early Music* 6, no. 3 (July 1978): 356–361.

1587   Smithers, Donald L. "The Hapsburg Imperial 'Trompeter' and 'Heerpaucker' privileges of 1653." *The Galpin Society Journal* 24 (July 1971): 84–95.

1588   Smithers, Donald L. *The music and history of the Baroque trumpet before 1721.* Foreword by Percy Young. Syracuse, NY: Syracuse University; London: Dent & Sons, 1973.

1589   Smithers, Donald L. "Scholarship and performance [theory and practice in relation to the baroque trumpet]." *Music and Musicians* 18 (Nov. 1969): 28–29.

1590   Smithers, Donald L. "Seventeenth-century English trumpet music." *Music and Letters* 48, no. 4 (1967): 358–365.

1591   Smithers, Donald L. "The trumpets of J. W. Haas: a survey of four generations of Nuremberg brass instrument makers." *The Galpin Society Journal* 18 (Mar. 1965): 23–41.

        Smoker, Paul Alva. "A comprehensive performance project in trumpet literature with a survey of some recently developed trumpet techniques and effects appearing in contemporary music." *Dissertation Abstracts* 35 (Oct. 1974): 2328A.

        Smoker, Paul Alva. "A comprehensive performance project in trumpet literature with a survey of some recently developed trumpet techniques and effects appearing in contemporary music." D.M.A. diss., University of Iowa, 1974.

1592   Solomon, John. "Bach's trumpets." *Monthly Musical Record* 61 (1931): 43–44.

1593   "Sonneries de trompettes." *L'Echo musical* 23 (1893): 253–255.

1594   Sorenson, Scott Paul. "Thomas Harper, Sr. (1786–1835): trumpet virtuoso and pedagogue." *Dissertation Abstracts* 48 (Sept. 1987): 510A.

        Sorenson, Scott Paul. "Printed trumpet instruction to 1835." *Journal of the*

International Trumpet Guild 12, no. 1 (1987): 4–14.

Sousa, John Philip. *A book of instruction for the field-trumpet and drum, together with the trumpet and drum signals now in use in the Army, Navy and Marine corps of the United States.* New York: Carl Fischer, 1886.

1595   Spongberg, Ralph D. "Bibliography of the literature for the B-flat cornet or trumpet." Master's thesis, Northwestern University, 1950.

1596   Staples, J. "Reaching our coda." *Crescendo International* 20 (June 1982): 37.

1597   Staples, J. "The trumpet quartet." *Crescendo International* 20 (Nov. 1981): 37.

1598   Staples, J. "The trumpet quartet." *Crescendo International* 20 (Dec. 1981): 37.

1599   Staples, J. "The trumpet quartet." *Crescendo International* 20 (Jan. 1982): 37.

1600   Staples, J. "The trumpet quartet." *Crescendo International* 20 (Feb. 1982): 37.

1601   Staples, J. "The trumpet quartet." *Crescendo International* 20 (Mar. 1982): 37.

1602   Stedron, Bohumìr. "Die Landschaftstrompeter und Tympanisten im alten Brünn. Zur Entwicklungsgeschichte einer unbekannten Musikgesellschaft im 17. und 18. Jahrhundert." *Die Musikforschung* 21, no. 4 (Oct.–Dec. 1968): 438–458.

1603   Steinberg, Lester Simon. "The treatment of the natural horns and trumpets in the symphonies of the Mannheim school, Haydn, Mozart, and Beethoven." Honors thesis, Harvard University, 1937.

1604   Sternfield, Frederick W. "The dramatic and allegorical function of music in Shakespeare's tragedies: The symbolism of trumpets—Pipes versus strings—Music of the spheres—Sweet and harsh tuning." *Annales Musicologiques* 3 (1955): 265–282.

1605   Stevens, Thomas. "I chose to address myself to new music rather than new trumpet." *Brass Bulletin—International Brass Chronicle*, no. 5–6 (1973): 47–70.

1606   Stevens, Thomas. "New trumpet music: basic performance elements." *Journal of the International Trumpet Guild* 1 (1976): 24–27.

Stewart, J. "The complete musician: orchestration—the trumpets." *Guitar Player* 11 (Aug. 1977): 118.

1607   Stibler, Robert J. "The trumpet/cornetto sonatas of Johann Heinrich Schmelzer at Kromeriz." D.M.A. diss., Catholic University of America, 1979.

1608   Stiehl, C. "Die Lübeckischen Stadt- und Feldtrompeter." *Mitteilungen des Vereins für Lübeckische Geschichte und Altertumsdkunde* 6, no. 9 (May-June 1894).

Stith, Marice. "New ideas for composers of trumpet music." *The Composer* 6, no. 15 (1974–1975): 12–13.

1609   Stoddard, Hope. "The trumpet in our orchestras and bands." *International Musician* 48 (Mar. 1950): 20–22.

1610   Stöver, Walter. "Die Problematischen hohen Trompeten." *Neue Musikzeitschrift München* (May 1950): 130.

1611   "The story of the trumpet." *Metronome* 40 (Feb. 1924): 38+.

1612   "Die Story von der Jazztrompete [jazz trumpeters' styles in cartoon form]."
        Jazz Podium 24 (Nov. 1975): 21.

1613   Struth, S. "Alte Meister: Bachs Trompeter, Gottfried Reiche." *Das Musik-
        leben* 6 (1953): 171–172.

1614   Sweeney, J. A. "Die Naturtrompete in den Kantaten J. S. Bachs." Disser-
        tation, Freie Univ. Berlin, 1961.

1615   Talma, Louise. "Horns and trumpets as used in the orchestra from 1700–
        1900." Master's thesis, Columbia University, 1933.

1616   Tamplini, G. *The Bandsman*. Book 15: "The Bugle Major." Book 16: "The
        Trumpet Major." London: n.p., ca. 1856.

1617   Tarr, Edward H. "The baroque trumpet, the high trumpet, and the so-
        called Bach trumpet." *Brass Bulletin—International Brass Chronicle*, no. 2,
        3 (1972): 25–42, 39–57.

1618   Tarr, Edward H. "Die Musik und die Instrumente der *Charamela real* in
        Lissabon." *Forum Musicologie* 2 (1980): 181–229.

1619   Tarr, Edward H. "The *New Grove* and the trumpet." *International Trumpet
        Guild Newsletter* 8, no. 2 (1982): 12–13.

1620   Tarr, Edward H. "Original Italian baroque compositions for trumpet and
        organ." *Diapason* 61 (Apr. 1970): 27–29.

1621   Tarr, Edward H. *Die Trompete; ihre Geschichte und Spieltechnik von der Antike
        bis zur Gegenwart*. Bern: Hallwag, 1977.

1622   Tarr, Edward H. *La trompette*. Transl. by L. Jospin. Lausanne: Payot, 1977.

1623   Tarr, Edward H. *The trumpet*. Portland, OR: Amadeus Press, 1988.

1624   Tarr, Edward H. "The trumpets and music of the Charamela real." *Journal
        of the International Trumpet Guild* 1 (1976): 38–39.

1625   Tarr, Edward M. *Die Trompete*. Bern; Stuttgart: Hallwag, 1977.

1626   Taylor, P. "Would someone like to take up the cornetto?" *Recorder and
        Music* 4, no. 12 (1974): 433–435. Reprinted in *American Recorder* 16, no.
        2 (1975): 46–48.

1627   Taylor, T. F. "Jeremiah Clarke's trumpet tunes: another view of origins."
        Musical Quarterly 56, no. 3 (1970): 455–462.

1628   "Technical drawings of historical instruments in the Metropolitan Museum
        of Art." *American Recorder* 16, no. 3 (1975): 101.

1629   Terry, C. Sanford. "The tromba da tirarsi." *Monthly Musical Record* 61 (1931):
        141.

1630   Tetzlaff, Daniel B., and John J. Haynie. "Materials for trumpet and cornet."
        The Instrumentalist 14 (Nov. 1959): 44–45+.

1631   Theurer, Britton. "An interpretive discussion of the solo passages most
        frequently requested at orchestral trumpet auditions." *International
        Trumpet Guild Newsletter* 7, no. 3 (1981): 9–21.

1632   "Thomas Harper." *Musical World* 2 (1836): xi. With a frontispiece depicting
        Harper with Clara Novello.

1633   Tiedt. "Die Bach-Trompete." *Deutsche Musiker-Zeitung* 51 (191?): 6.

1634   Tilmouth, M. "Corelli's trumpet sonata." *Monthly Musical Record* 90 (1960): 217–221.

1635   Titcomb, Caldwell. "Baroque court and military trumpets and kettledrums: Technique and music." *The Galpin Society Journal* 9 (1956): 56–81.

1636   Titcomb, Caldwell. "Carrousel music at the court of Louis XIV." In *Essays on music in honor of Archibald Thompson Davidson by his associates*. Pp. 205–213. Cambridge, Mass.: Harvard University Department of Music, 1957.

1637   Titcomb, Caldwell. "The kettledrums in Western Europe: Their history outside the orchestra." Ph.D. diss., Harvard University, 1952.

1638   Todd, J. "The trumpet as a solo orchestral color since 1827." Master's thesis, University of Washington, 1961.

1639   Trichet, P. "Du cornet à bouquin et du serpent." *Brass Bulletin—International Brass Chronicle*, no. 46 (1984): 12–13+. Also in English and German.

1640   Trobian, Helen R. "With sound of trumpet." *Music Ministry* 2 (June 1961): 4–5+.

1641   "Trompeten für Bachpartituren." *Instrumentenbau-Zeitschrift* 26 (Apr. 1972): 304.

1642   "Trompeten und Posaunen." *Musik International-Instrumentenbau-Zeitschrift* 38 (Aug. 1984): 561–565+.

1643   "La trompette." *Journal Musical Français*, nos. 159–160 (July-Aug. 1967): 45–46.

1644   "Des trompettes." *Brass Bulletin—International Brass Chronicle*, no. 49 (1985): 31–33. Also in English and German.

1645   *Trumpet and bugle sounds for the army, with instructions for the training of trumpeters and buglers*. London: Eyre & Spottiswoode, [1903].

1646   *The trumpet—a fragment dedicated to the Wesleyan Society*. London: Hatchard, 1830.

1647   "The trumpet in Australia." *International Trumpet Guild Newsletter* 3, no. 1 (1976): 2–3.

1648   "The trumpet in Austria." *International Trumpet Guild Newsletter* 3, no. 1 (1976): 2.

1649   "The trumpet in Norway." *International Trumpet Guild Newsletter* 3, no. 1 (1976): 3.

1650   "The trumpeter and trumpet calls [from *The Journal of the Military Service Institution*]." *Metronome* 27, no. 5 (1911): 18–19.

1651   "Trumpets of the 17th century." *Boston Symphony Orchestra Programs, 47th season* (1927–1928): 748–756.

        Tuozzolo, James M. "Trumpet techniques in selected works of four contemporary American composers: Gunther Schuller, Meyer Kupferman, William Sydeman, and William Frabizio." *Dissertation Abstracts* 33 (Dec. 1972): 2972A-2973A.

        Tuozzolo, James M. "Trumpet techniques in selected works of four contemporary American composers: Gunther Schuller, Meyer Kupferman, William Sydeman, and William Fabizio." D.M.A. diss., University of Miami, 1972.

1652   Turrentine, Edgar M. "Notes on the ancient Olympic trumpet blowing contests." *The Instrumentalist* 23 (Apr. 1969): 42–43.

1653   Turrentine, Edgar M. "The trumpet's day." *The Instrumentalist* 19 (Mar. 1965): 72–73.

1654   Unger, Hermann. "Die Trompete." *Die Musik-Woche*, no. 16 (1951): 121–122.

1655   Urban, D. E. "Gottfried Reiche; notes on his art, life, instruments, and music." *Monthly Journal of Research in Music Education* 1, no. 5 (1966): 14–55.

1656   Urban, Darrell Eugene. "Stromenti da tirarsi in the cantatas of J. S. Bach." *Dissertation Abstracts* 38 (Oct. 1977): 1733A.

        Urban, Darrell Eugene. "Stromenti da tirarsi in the cantatas of J. S. Bach [abstract]." *Missouri Journal of Research in Music Education* 4, no. 1 (1977): 125–126.

1657   Urban, Darrell Eugene. " 'Stromenti da tirarsi' in the cantatas of J. S. Bach." Ed.D. diss., Washington University, 1977.

        U.S. Bureau of Naval. *Manual for buglers, U.S. Navy.* Washington: U.S. Government Printing Office, 1953.

1658   U.S. Marine Corps. *Manual for drummers, trumpeters and fifers.* Washington, DC: Government Printing Office, 1935.

        U.S. War Department. *Field manual.* Technical manual 20, no. 250. Washington: GPO, 1940.

1659   Valenti, Tommaso. "Cantratto di un maestro di tromba di Trevi dell' Umbria (1537)." *Note d'Archivio* 3 (Mar. 1926): 62–65.

1660   Van Nuys, Robert Copeland. "The history and nature of the trumpet as applied to the sonatas of Giuseppe Torelli." *Dissertation Abstracts* 30 (Feb. 1970): 3498A.

1661   Van Nuys, Robert Copeland. "The history and nature of the trumpet as applied to the sonatas of Giuseppi Torelli." D.M.A. diss., University of Illinois (Urbana-Champaign), 1969.

1662   Vetter, W. *Die Trompeten in Bachs dritter Orchester-Ouverture.* Bach-Jahrbuch, 1953.

1663   Vogel, M. "Eine schwierige Trompetenstelle; zum Problem der Intonation im Orchester." *Das Orchester* 11 (Jan. 1963): 7–11.

1664   Voigt, Alban. "Der Zinken oder Cornett." *Deutsche Instrumentenbau Zeitschrift* 37 (1936): 163–164.

1665   Voigt, Alban. "Zur Geschichte der Trompete." *Deutsche Instrumentenbau Zeitschrift* 37 (1936): 261.

1666   von Witzleben, D. "Die Bestimmungen für die Trompeterkorps im neuen Exerzier-Reglement für die Kavallerie." *Deutsche Militär-Musiker Zeitung* 31 (1909): 249–250.

1667   Vuilleumier, H. "Les trompettes d'église." *Revue historique vaudoise* 1 (1893): 129.

1668   Wagner, Ernst. "Die alte Trompete in neuerer Zeit." *Musikalisches Wochenblatt* 15 (1884): 481–483, 497–499, 509–511.

1669   Wakser, David. "A study of the implications of history and tradition as a contributing factor to the style of orchestral trumpet performance." Master's thesis, Ohio State University, 1947.

1670   Walcha, Helmut. "Das Trompetenportativ im 2. Brandenburgischen Konzert." *Musik und Kirche* 22 (1952): 66–67.

1671   Walker, B. H. "Trumpet quartets." *The School Musician* 21 (Jan. 1950): 36–37.

1672   Walser, Robert. "Musical imagery and performance practice in J. S. Bach's arias with trumpet." *Journal of the International Trumpet Guild* 13, no. 1 (Sept. 1988): 62–77.

1673   Walter, E. "Dialogue—Andre Bernard: le renouveau de la trompette [interview]." *Harmonie*, no. 126 (Sept. 1977): 42–49.

1674   *War office trumpet and bugle sounds for the army. With instructions for training of trumpeters and buglers.* London: H. M. Stationery Office, ca. 1929.

        Weber, G. "Ueber Ventilhorn und Ventiltrompete mit drei Ventilen." *Caecilia* 17 (1835): 73–105.

1675   Weber, R. "Some researches into pitch in the 16th century with particular reference to the instruments in the Accademia Filarmonica of Verona." *The Galpin Society Journal* 28 (Apr. 1975): 7–10.

1676   Weber-Robiné, Friedrich. "Die Trompete als Kircheninstrument." *Zeitschrift für Instrumentenbau* 30 (1909/10): 1171–1172.

1677   Weber-Robiné, Friedrich. "Die Trompete im Lichte des Fortschritts." *Deutsche Militär-Musiker Zeitung* 31 (1909): 625, 638.

1678   "Chris Welch [use of trumpet in rock music]." *Melody Maker* 50 (Aug. 2, 1975): 22.

        Werner, Arno. "Johann Ernst Altenburg, der letzte Vertreter der heroischen Trompeter- und Paukerkunst." *Zeitschrift für Musikwissenschaft* 15 (1932–1933): 258–274.

1679   Werner, E. "Die Bedeutung der Totenmeerrollen für die Musikgeschichte." *Studia Musica* 4, no. 1–2 (1963): 21–35.

1680   Werner, Eric. "Musical aspects of the Dead Sea scrolls." *Musical Quarterly* 43 (1957): 21–37.

1681   Werner, M. "Trompeter, Trommler und Pfeifer." *Deutsche Militär-Musiker Zeitung* 60 (1938): 393.

        Wheeler, J. "Further notes on the classic trumpet." *The Galpin Society Journal* 18 (Mar. 1965): 14–22.

1682   White, Edna. "Why the trumpet is king of instruments." *Musical Observer* 30 (May 1931): 28–30.

        Whitwell, D. "Solo wind works in the British Museum." *The Instrumentalist* 31 (Sept. 1976): 96+.

1683   Wiggins, B., and others. "Music for trumpet." *Sounding Brass & the Conductor* 9, no. 3 (1980): 28–30.

1684   Wildvogel, Christian. *Dissertatio inauguralis iuridica de buccinatoribus eorumque iure, Vom Recht der Trompeter, quam . . . sub praesidio Christiani Wildvogelii . . . placidae eruditorum disquisitioni submittit Christianus Bantz-*

land. . . . Jena: Typis Mullerianis, 1711.

Williams, Edwin Lynn. "Dissertation reviews: The role of the trumpet and cornet in the early ballets of Igor Stravinsky." *Journal of the International Trumpet Guild* 10, no. 3 (1986): 25–26.

Williams, Edwin Lynn. "The role of the trumpet and cornet in the early ballets of Igor Stravinsky." D.M.A. diss., University of Cincinnati, 1980.

1685   Williams, R. "Names that blew the trumpet sky high." *Melody Maker* 46 (Sept. 11, 1971): 30+.

1686   Winick, Steven. "Contemporary music for unaccompanied trumpet." *The Instrumentalist* 25 (Jan. 1971): 36–38.

1687   Winick, Steven. "Trumpet music by Carl Maria von Weber: a tusch, a canon, and a march." *Journal of the International Trumpet Guild* 12, no. 4 (May 1988): 4–29.

1688   Witzenhausen, A. "Die Trompete." *Allgemeine Volksmusik Zeitung* 10 (1960): 146–148.

1689   Worthmüller, Willi. "Die Instrumente der Nürnberger Trompeten- und Posaunenmacher." In *Mitteilungen des Vereins für Geschichte der Stadt Nürnberg*, 372–480. 1955.

1690   Worthmüller, Willi. "Die Nürnberger Trompeten- und Posaunenmacher des 17. und 18. Jahrhunderts." In *Mitteilungen des Vereins für Geschichte der Stadt Nürnberg*, 208–325. 1954.

Wüerst, Richard. "Ueber Ventil-Hörner und -Trompeten." *Neue Berliner Musikzeitung* 28 (1874): 353–354.

X., P. Y. "Orchestral Sketches, no. 1: Mr. Harper." *The Dramatic and Musical Review* 3 (1844): 200–201.

Zak, Sabine. *Studien zur Musik als "Ehr und Zier" im mittelalterlichen Reich. Music im höfischen Leben, Recht und Zeremoniell.* Neuss: Peter Päffigen, 1978.

1691   Zimmerman, G. E. "Off-stage trumpet." *The Instrumentalist* 27 (Nov. 1972): 43–46.

1692   Zimmermann, Josef. *Von Zinken, Flöten und Schalmeien.* Düren: Bezani, 1967.

1693   Zolnay, L. "Feldtrompeter und Kriegsmusiker im ungarischen Mittelalter." *Studia Musicologica* 16, no. 1–4 (1974): 151–178.

1694   Zorn, Hans. "Die Trompete in der deutschen Orchestermusik von ca. 1750 bis ins 20. Jahrhundert." Ph.D. diss., Innsbruck, 1973.

1695   Zschoch, Frieder. "Zur Aufführungspraxis der Trompetenpartien in Werken Bachs, Händels und Telemanns." *Zu Fragen der Aufführungspraxis und Interpretation von Instrumentalmusik in der ersten Hälfte des 18. Jahrhunderts* (RILM76 2263): 29–34.

1696   Adams, S. R. "Some thoughts on solo trombone literature." *The School Musician* 48 (Nov. 1976): 8+.

1697   Adams, S. R. "A survey of the use of trombones to depict infernal and horrendous scenes in three representative operas." *Journal of the International Trombone Association* 9 (1981): 16–20.

Adams, S. R. "Trombones in the orchestra [learning the orchestral music repertoire]." *The School Musician* 47 (Mar. 1976): 8+.

1698   Allsen, J. M. "Frescobaldi's 'Canzonas for Basso Solo' (1628–1634)." *Journal of the International Trombone Association* 12, no. 3 (1984): 36–40.

Anderson, S. C. "The alto trombone, then and now [includes list of music]." *The Instrumentalist* 40 (Nov. 1985): 54+.

Anderson, S. C. "Music for alto trombone." *Journal of the International Trombone Association* 13, no. 2 (1985): 42–43.

1699   Anderson, S. C. "Selected works from the 17th century music collection of Prince-Bishop Karl Liechtenstein-Kastelkorn: a study of the soloistic use of the trombone." *Journal of the International Trombone Association* 11, no. 1 (1983): 17–20.

1700   Anderson, S. C. "Selected works from the 17th century music collection of Prince-Bishop Karl Liechtenstein-Kastelkorn: a study of the soloistic use of the trombone." *Journal of the International Trombone Association* 11, no. 2 (1983): 35–38.

1701   Anderson, S. C. "Selected works from the 17th century music collection of Prince-Bishop Karl Liechtenstein-Kastelkorn: a study of the soloistic use of the trombone." *Journal of the International Trombone Association* 11, no. 3 (1983): 29–32.

1702   Anderson, S. C. "Selected works from the 17th century music collection of Prince-Bishop Karl Liechtenstein-Kastelkorn: a study of the soloistic use of the trombone." *Journal of the International Trombone Association* 11, no. 4 (1983): 20–22.

1703   Anderson, S. C. "Selected works from the 17th century music collection of Prince-Bishop Karl Liechtenstein-Kastelkorn: a study of the soloistic use of the trombone." *Journal of the International Trombone Association* 12, no. 1 (1984): 33–37.

1704   Anderson, S. C. "Selected works from the 17th century music collection of Prince-Bishop Karl Liechtenstein-Kastelkorn: a study of the soloistic use of the trombone." *Journal of the International Trombone Association* 12, no. 2 (1984): 32–38.

1705   Anderson, S. C. "Selected works from the seventeenth century music collection of Prince-Bishop Karl Liechtenstein-Kastelkorn: a study of the soloistic use of the trombone and modern editions." *Dissertation Abstracts* 38 (Oct. 1977): 1722A-1723A.

1706   Anderson, S. C. "The soloistic use of the alto and tenor trombones in the choral music of Franz Ignaz Tuma." *Journal of the International Trombone Association* 14, no. 3 (1986): 48–53.

1707   Anderson, Stephen Charles. "Selected works from the seventeenth-century music collection of Prince-Bishop Karl Liechtenstein-Kastelkorn: a study of the soloistic use of the trombone and modern editions." D.M.A. diss., University of Oklahoma, 1977.

Appert, D. L. "The alto-trombone—its uses, problems, and solutions." *Journal of the International Trombone Association* 8 (1980): 13–14.

Arfinengo, Carlo. *La tromba e il trombone*. Ancona; Milano: Bèrben, 1973.

Arling, H. J. *Trombone chamber music: an annotated bibliography*. Nashville: Brass Press, 1978.

Arling, H. J. "Trombone chamber music: an annotated bibliography." *Music Educators Journal* 66 (Sept. 1979): 88.

Arling, H. J. *Trombone chamber music: an annotated bibliography*. Enlarged 2nd edition. Nashville: Brass Press, 1983.

1708   "B flat trombone directory." *Sounding Brass & the Conductor* 4, no. 4 (1976): 124–125.

Bachmann, Friedrich. "Pastor D. Johannes Kuhlo und das deutsche Posaunenwerk." *Musik und Kirche* 13 (1941): 87–90.

Back, J. "From our readers: The 'now' trombone." *The Instrumentalist* 25 (Dec. 1970): 8.

1709   Bahr, Edward R. "Idiomatic similarities and differences of the trombone and euphonium in history and performance." *Journal of the International Trombone Association* 6 (1978): 31–36.

Baker, David. *Jazz styles and analysis: trombone*. Chicago: Downbeat Music Workshop, 1973.

Barbour, W. "Orchestral showcase: the Detroit Symphony Orchestra." *Journal of the International Trombone Association* 11, no. 4 (1983): 13–17.

Bate, Philip. *The trumpet and trombone; an outline of their history, development and construction*. London: E. Benn; New York: W. W. Norton, 1966.

Bate, Philip. *The trumpet and trombone; an outline of their history, development, and construction*. 2d ed. London: E. Benn; New York: Norton, 1972.

Bauer, P., comp. "A complete chronological listing of the trombone and tuba personnel of Stan Kenton's orchestras." *Journal of the International Trombone Association* 11, no. 4 (1983): 24–25.

1710   Bellay, F. "Le pupitre des trombones." *Musique & radio* 50 (1960): 211–212.

1711   Besseler, Heinrich. "Die Entstehung der Posaune." *Acta Musicologica* 22 (1950): 8–35.

1712   Bevan, Clifford. "On the cimbasso trail." *Sounding Brass & the Conductor* 8, no. 2 (1979): 57–58+.

1713   Beyer, W. "Reminiszenz an Posaunisten der Vergangenheit." *Brass Bulletin—International Brass Chronicle*, no. 22 (1978): 37+. Also in English and French.

1714   Bingham, John Joseph. "The innovative uses of the trombone in selected compositions of Vinko Globokar." Ed.D. diss., University of Illinois (Urbana-Champaign), 1984.

1715 Bingham, John Joseph. "The innovative uses of the trombone in selected compositions of Vinko Globokar." *Dissertation Abstracts* 45 (May 1985): 3234A-3235A.

1716 Blanchard, Henri. "Le trombone." *Revue et gazette musicale de Paris* 20 (1853): 374.

Blandford, W. F. H. "Handel's horn and trombone parts." *The Musical Times* 80 (1939): 697–699, 746–747, 794.

Blandford, W. F. H. "Handel's horn and trombone parts." *The Musical Times* 81 (1940): 223.

Bock, E. "Posaunen und Harfen." *Christengemeinschaft* 16 (1939–40): 229–232.

"Boston Symphony Orchestra trombone personnel—1881–1979." *International Trombone Association Newsletter* 6, no. 4 (1979): 39–40.

1717 Boulton, John. "The trombone." *Hallé* (May 1950): 12–14.

Bovermann, P. "Nochmal 'Posaunenmusik.' " *Zeitschrift für Kirchenmusiker* 11 (1929): 59.

Bowles, Edmund A. "Iconography as a tool for examining the loud consort in the fifteenth century." *Journal of the American Musical Instrument Society* 3 (1977): 100–121.

1718 Brant, H. "A new spatial symphony for eighty trombones." *Newsletter of the International Trombone Association* 5, no. 2 (1977): 9–11.

1719 Brehm, K. "Die Zugposaune." *Schweizerische Instrumentalmusik* 27 (1938): 7–8.

Brevig, Per. "Let's standardize trombone notation." *Music Journal* 32 (July 1974): 18–20+. Excerpt from his doctoral dissertation: "Avant-garde techniques in solo trombone music."

1720 Brevig, Per Andreas. "Avant-garde techniques in solo trombone music; problems of notation and execution." Ph.D. diss., Juilliard School, 1971.

1721 Brown, Leon F. "Favorite studies and solos for trombone." *Journal of the International Trombone Association* 12, no. 1 (1984): 28–31.

1722 Brown, Leon F. "Trombone forum." *Southwestern Brass Journal* 1 (Spring 1957): 15–19.

Brown, M. "Trombone solos performed in college student recitals." *Journal of the International Trombone Association* 5 (1977): 22–23.

1723 Bryan, P. "A look at some 18th century source material for the trombone." *Journal of the International Trombone Association* 4 (1976): 6–7.

1724 Buss, H. J. "Trombone theatre pieces [includes list]." *Journal of the International Trombone Association* 6 (1978): 6–10.

1725 Callison, Hugh Anthony. "Nineteenth-century orchestral trombone playing in the United States." D.A. diss., Ball State University, 1986.

1726 Cardew, C. "Music in London." *The Musical Times* 110 (Jan. 1969): 50–51.

1727 Carter, J. "Up the pole." *Crescendo International* 13 (June 1975): 19.

1728 Casamorata, L. F. "Del trombone e dei suoi perfezionamenti e trasformazioni in propositio della recente invenzione del bimbonifono." *Atti dell' Accademia del R. Istituto musicale di Firenze* 13 (1875): 32–53.

1729 "Caught [third annual Sackbut week]." *Down Beat* 42 (Aug. 14, 1975): 34–35.

Cecil, Herbert M. "A treatise on the trombone." Master's thesis, Eastman School of Music, 1947.

1730 Chambers, Robert Lee. "Selected trombone virtuosi of the nineteenth century and their solo repertoire." *Dissertation Abstracts* 47 (Sept. 1986): 704A.

1731 Chambers, Robert Lee. "Selected trombone virtuosi of the nineteenth century and their solo repertoire." D.M.A. diss., University of Oklahoma, 1986.

Chasanov, E. L. "Orchestral showcase: The National Symphony Orchestra." *Journal of the International Trombone Association* 11, no. 1 (1983): 7–12.

"Chicago Symphony Orchestra low brass personnel 1891–1979 [list]." *International Trombone Association Newsletter* 7, no. 2 (1980): 14–15.

Christensen, C. J. "Some uses of the trombone in the Mexican symphonic repertoire." *Journal of the International Trombone Association* 4 (1976): 36–37+.

1732 Christie, J. M. "Music for bass trombone." *The Instrumentalist* 15 (Mar. 1961): 44–45.

Collins, William Tracy. "Berlioz and the trombone." D.M.A. diss., University of Texas (Austin), 1985.

Collins, William Tracy. "Berlioz and the trombone." *Dissertation Abstracts* 46 (May 1986): 3185A.

1733 Conger, Robert Brian. "J. S. Bach's *Six Suites for Solo Violoncello*, BWV 1007–1021; their history and problems of transcription and performance for the trombone, a lecture recital, together with three recitals of selected works by Paul Hindemith, Georg Christoph Wagenseil, Richard Monaco, Darius Milhaud, Nino Rota, and others." D.M.A. diss., North Texas State University, 1983.

Cooper, I. "Orchestra showcase: the Buffalo Philharmonic Orchestra [interview with low brass players and list of low brass personnel, 1936–1979]." *International Trombone Association Newsletter* 7, no. 1 (1979): 17+.

1734 Cox, Joseph Lee. "The solo trombone works of Kazimierz Serocki, a lecture recital, together with three recitals of selected works by W. Hartley, P. Dubois, H. Duttileux, H. Tomasi, G. Jacob, L. Grondahl, J. Aubain and others." D.M.A. diss., North Texas State University, 1981.

1735 Crees, E. "Trombone evolution." *Sounding Brass & the Conductor* 4, no. 3 (1975): 83–84.

1736 Crees, E. "Trombone evolution." *Sounding Brass & the Conductor* 4, no. 4 (1976): 106–108; 5, no. 2 (1976): 45.

1737 Crees, E. "Trombone evolution." *Sounding Brass & the Conductor* 5, no. 4 (1977): 116; 6, no. 2 (1977): 49–50.

1738   Dahlstrom, J. F. "History and development of the trombone." *The School Musician* 41 (Mar. 1970): 64+.

1739   Dehn. "Bei Gelegenheit eines Konzertino für die Tenorbassposaune." *Berliner allgemeine musikalische Zeitung* 3 (1826): 391–392. (See also pp. 351, 383.)

Deisenroth, F. "Die Bläserkultur der Blechblasinstrumente in der Militärmusik unter besonderer Berücksichtigung der Weitmensurierten Bügelinstrumente mit Einschluss der Zug- und Ventilposaunen." *Deutsche Militär-Musiker Zeitung* 60 (1938): 29–30, 41–42.

1740   Dempster, Stuart. *The modern trombone: a definition of its idioms.* The New Instrumentation, no. 3. Berkeley: University of California Press, 1979.

1741   Dennis, W. "The history of the trombone." *Metronome* 74 (Mar. 1957): 34–35.

Dietrich, K. "Orchestra showcase: The Milwaukee Symphony Orchestra." *Journal of the International Trombone Association* 11, no. 3 (1983): 26–28.

"Directory of symphony trombonists [U.S. and Canada]." *The Instrumentalist* 40 (Nov. 1985): 40+.

1742   "Un document extraordinaire: Le Tromboniste [first reproduction of 1637 charcoal drawing by C. Saftleven]." *Brass Bulletin—International Brass Chronicle*, no. 11 (1975): 80–81.

Douay, J. "Le trombone dans le *Bolero* de Ravel." *Brass Bulletin—International Brass Chronicle*, no. 13 (1976): 59–62.

Drew, J. "The emancipation of the trombone in orchestral literature." *Journal of the International Trombone Association* 9 (1981): 2–4.

1743   Drew, John Robert. "Classic elements in selected sonatas for trombone and piano by 20th-century American composers." *Dissertation Abstracts* 39 (Dec. 1978): 3208A.

1744   Drew, John Robert. "Classic elements in selected sonatas for trombone and piano by twentieth-century American composers." D.M.A. diss., University of Kentucky, 1978.

1745   Duerksen, George L. "The history and acoustics of the trombone." Master's thesis, University of Kansas, 1956.

1746   Duerksen, George L. "The voice of the trombone." *The Instrumentalist* 19 (Oct. 1964): 98–101.

1747   Eccott, D. J. "The missing trombone." *Delius Society Journal*, no. 48 (July 1975): 5–13.

Ehmann, Wilhelm. "Ein Brief von Johannes Zahn an Eduard Kuhlo." *Jahrbuch für Liturgik und Hymnologie* 4 (1958/59): 135.

Ehmann, Wilhelm. "Neue Trompeten und Posaunen." In *Kirchenmusik, Vermächtnis und Aufgabe*, edited by W. Ehmann, 58–63. Darmstadt: K. Merseburger, 1958.

Ehmann, Wilhelm. *Tibilustrium. Das geistliche Blasen, Formen und Reformen.* Kassel and Basel: Bärenreiter, 1950.

1748   Ehmann, Wilhelm. "Was guett auff Posaunen ist." *Zeitschrift für Musikwissenschaft* 17 (1935): 171–175.

Ehrmann, Alfred von. "Von Posaunisten und Tubabläsern." *Die Musik* 28 (1935–1936): 201–203.

1749 Eliason, Robert E. "The trombone in nineteenth century America." *Journal of the International Trombone Association* 10, no. 1 (1982): 6–10.

English, J. "Some solo works for the trombonist [contemporary]." *International Trombone Association Newsletter* 7, no. 1 (1979): 12–13.

1750 Everett, T. "Solo literature for the bass trombone." *The Instrumentalist* 26 (Dec. 1971): 43–47.

1751 Everett, T. G. *Annotated guide to bass trombone literature*. 2nd ed. Nashville: Brass Press, 1979.

1752 Farnham, Dean A. "The twentieth century trombone sonata." Ph.D. diss., Boston University Graduate School, 1969.

1753 Faulds, John. "The trombone ensemble." In *Brass Today*. Edited by Frank Wright, 111–112. London: Besson, 1957.

Fauntley, B. J. "Orchestral showcase: The CAPAB Orchestra." *Journal of the International Trombone Association* 12, no. 4 (1984): 22–24.

Fink, Reginald H. *The trombonist's handbook: a complete guide to playing and teaching the trombone*. Athens, Ohio: Accura, 1977.

1754 Fischer, H. G. *The Renaissance sackbut and its use today*. New York: Metropolitan Museum of Art, 1984.

1755 Flandrin, G. P. A. L. "Le trombone." In *Encyclopédie de la musique et dictionnaire du Conservatoire*. 2. ptie, vol. 3 (1927). Paris: Delagrave, 1913–1931.

Flor, G. J. "Brass workshop: The trombone mute [includes history]." *The School Musician* 51 (Jan. 1980): 34–36.

1756 Flor, G. J. "Reviews: trombone solo." *Woodwind World—Brass and Percussion* 19, no. 4 (1980): 28.

Fulkerson, J. "Indeterminate instrumentation: a way of extending instrumental techniques." *Journal of the International Trombone Association* 4 (1977): 3–4.

1757 Gagne, J. "Le sacqueboute." *Carnet Musical*, no. 6 (Dec. 1972): 19–20.

1758 Galpin, F. W. "The sackbut." *The Musical Times* 47, no. 766; 768 (1906): 828–829; 110.

1759 Galpin, F. W. "The sackbut, its evolution and history. Illustrated by an instrument of the sixteenth century." *Musical Association of London Proceedings* (1907): Session 33, 1–25.

1760 George, Stanley Paul. "A descriptive list of Baroque solo editions which may be practically integrated into the solo literature for trombone." M. A. thesis, The American University, 1969.

1761 Giddins, G. "Weatherbird: The trombone's connected to the. . . . " *Village Voice* 25 (Sept. 3, 1980): 56–57.

1762 Gifford, Robert Marvin, Jr. "A comprehensive performance project in trombone literature with an essay consisting of a survey of the use of the trombone in chamber music with mixed instrumentation composed since 1956." D.M.A. diss., University of Iowa, 1978.

1763   Gifford, Robert Marvin, Jr. "A comprehensive performance project in trombone literature with an essay consisting of a survey of the use of the trombone in chamber music with mixed instrumentation composed since 1956." *Dissertation Abstracts* 39 (Mar. 1979): 5198A.

Gifford, Robert Marvin, Jr. "The music and performance practices of the medieval wind band." *Journal of Band Research* 10, no. 2 (Spring 1974): 25–32.

1764   "Glory of jazz—Trombonists, old and new." *Music U.S.A.* 76 (May 1959): 15–16.

1765   Goodwin, Peter. "Venice preserved." *Journal of the International Trombone Association* 15, no. 2 (Spring 1987): 24–26.

1766   Gotthold, J. "Reflexions sur le trombone basse." *Brass Bulletin—International Brass Chronicle*, no. 39 (1982): 49–51. Also in English and German.

Gray, R., and Mary Rasmussen, comps. "Three bibliographies of nineteenth- and twentieth-century concertante works; solo parts for the trumpet; solo parts for the trombone; solo parts for more than one different brass instrument." *Brass Quarterly* 6, no. 1 (1962): 10–16.

1767   Gray, Robert. "The trombone in contemporary chamber music." *Brass Quarterly* 1, no. 1 (Sept. 1957): 10–19.

1768   Gregory, Robin. *The trombone: the instrument and its music.* New York: Praeger; London: Faber & Faber, 1973.

Gretton, P. "Cornet and sackbut." *International Trumpet Guild Newsletter* 6, no. 1 (1979): 15–16.

1769   Grubb, Marion. "Trombone town, (Bethlehem) Pennsylvania." *Etude* 60 (1942): 378+.

1770   Gugler, B. "Sind im zweiten Finale des Don Juan die Posaunen von Mozart?" *Allgemeine musikalische Zeitung* 2 (1867): 2–4, 13–15, 21–24, 35, 59.

1771   Guion, David M. "French military music and the rebirth of the trombone." *Journal of Band Research* 21, no. 2 (1986): 31–36.

1772   Guion, David M. "The pitch of Baroque trombones." *Journal of the International Trombone Association* 8 (Mar. 1980): 24–28.

1773   Guion, David M. "The seven positions: Joseph Froehlich's New Trombone Method." *Journal of the International Trombone Association* 14, no. 2 (1986): 50–53.

1774   Guion, David Michael. "The trombone and its music, 1697–1811." *Dissertation Abstracts* 46 (Dec. 1985): 1435A.

1775   Guion, David Michael. "The trombone and its music, 1697–1811." Ph.D. diss., University of Iowa, 1985.

Hammerbacher, J. "Wert oder Unwert der Posaunenmusik." *Zeitschrift für evangelische Kirchenmusik* 6 (1928): 91–95, 120–124.

Harlow, L. "We called them trombets [E-flat valve trombone]." *The Instrumentalist* 23 (Aug. 1968): 73–76.

1776   Hartman, Mark Shafer. "The use of the alto trombone in symphonic and operatic orchestral literature." *Dissertation Abstracts* 46 (Nov. 1985): 1122A.

1777 Hartman, Mark Shafer. "The use of the alto trombone in symphonic and operatic orchestral literature." D.M.A. diss., Arizona State University, 1985.

Hartzell, L. W. "Trombones in Ohio [initial Moravian settlements]." *The Moravian Music Foundation Bulletin* 28, no. 4 (1983): 72–74.

Haupt, P. "Die Posaunen von Jericho." *Wiener Zeitschrift für die Kunde des Morgenlandes* 23 (1909): 355.

Heckman, D. "Jazz trombone—five views." *Down Beat* 32 (Jan. 28, 1965): 17–19.

Henschel. "Von Turm-Musik, Trompeten und Posaunen." *Die Sendung* 7 (1930): 44.

1778 Herbert, T. "Solo trombone." *The Musical Times* 127 (Sept. 1986): 502.

"Herr M. Schmidt, Tonkünstler auf der Posaune." *Monatsbericht der Gesellschaft der Musikfreunde* (1830): 8–9.

Hey, Dean Edgar, Jr. "Etudes for trombone using avant-garde techniques." *Dissertation Abstracts* 34 (Feb. 1974): 5229A.

1779 Highfill, Joe R. "The history of the trombone from the Renaissance to the early romantic period." Master's thesis, North Texas State University, 1952.

1780 Hildebrandt, Donald Jay. "The bass trombone in the twentieth-century orchestra: its use in twenty-seven representative scores." D.Mus. diss., Indiana University, 1976.

1781 Hill, J. "Performance practices of the 16th, 17th, and 18th centuries: a few practical references for the trombonist [includes select discography and bibliography]." *Journal of the International Trombone Association* 9 (1981): 20–23.

1782 Hills, Ernie M., III. "The use of trombone in the Florentine intermedii, 1516–1589." D.M.A. diss., University of Oklahoma, 1984.

1783 Hills, Ernie M., III. "The use of trombone in the Florentine intermedii, 1518–1589." *Dissertation Abstracts* 45 (Feb. 1985): 2296A.

1784 Hinterbichler, Karl G. "Evolution of the role of the solo trombone in the nineteenth and twentieth centuries." *Dissertation Abstracts* 35 (Jan. 1975): 4587A-4588A.

1785 Hinterbichler, Karl G. "Evolution of the role of the solo trombone in the nineteenth-century and twentieth-century." D.M.A. diss., North Texas State University, 1974.

Hinterbichler, Karl G. "Orchestral showcase: the Dallas Symphony Orchestra." *Journal of the International Trombone Association* 12, no. 1 (1984): 13–14.

1786 "Historique du trombone." *Musique & Radio* 48 (1958): 443.

1787 "Historische Musikinstrumente." *Musikhandel* 17, no. 8 (1966): 386.

Höfler, Janez. "Der 'Trompette de menestrels' und sein Instrument."

Tijdschrift van de Vereniging voor Nederlandse Musiekgeschiedenis 29, no. 2 (1979): 92–132.

1788   Hofacre, Marta Jean. "The use of tenor trombone in twentieth-century brass quintet music; a brief historical overview with comprehensive listing of original, published twentieth-century quintets and a discussion of tenor trombone excerpts from selected compositions." D.M.A. diss., University of Oklahoma, 1986.

1789   Hofacre, Marta Jean. "The use of tenor trombone in twentieth-century brass quintet music; a brief historical overview with comprehensive listing of original, published twentieth-century quintets and a discussion of tenor trombone excerpts from selected compositions." *Dissertation Abstracts* 47 (Jan. 1987): 2362A-2363A.

Hogarth, G. "Musical instruments: the trumpet, trombone, serpent and ophicleide." *Musical World* 4 (1837): 129–133.

1790   Howey, Henry Eugene. "A comprehensive performance project in trombone literature with an essay consisting of a translation of Daniel Speer's *Vierfaches musikalisches Kleeblatt* (Ulm, 1697)." D.M.A. diss., University of Iowa, 1971.

1791   Huber, H. "Die Posaunenzüge im Wandel der Zeit." *Brass Bulletin—International Brass Chronicle*, no. 11 (1975): 83–94. Also in English and French.

1792   Hübler, K. K. "Die polyphone Posaune: ein Vorschlag zur Notation." *Brass Bulletin—International Brass Chronicle*, no. 45 (1984): 31–33. Also in English and French.

1793   Humfeld, Neill H. "Bordogni 'Vocalise': exercise, etude or solo?" *Journal of the International Trombone Association* 12, no. 1 (1984): 25–26.

1794   "Humfeld's rare species." *Ovation* 4 (Mar. 1984): 7.

Hummel, Donald A. "A selected list of original works for trombone trio." *Journal of the International Trombone Association* 6 (1978): 16–17.

Hummel, Donald Austin. "Abstract: A selected and annotated bibliography of original works for trombone trio." *Missouri Journal of Research in Music Education* 3, no. 5 (1976): 119–120.

Hunt, P. B. "Orchestra showcase: The Denver Symphony Orchestra [includes trombone personnel, 1934–1982]." *Journal of the International Trombone Association* 10, no. 1 (1982): 16–19.

Hylander, Martha A. "A selective list of graded trombone methods and solos." Master's thesis, Eastman School of Music, 1948.

Ioakimidis, D. "Trombonisti di ieri e di oggi." *Musica Jazz* 20 (June 1964): 26–31; 20 (July 1964): 29–33.

1795   Isaacson, Charles Frank. "A study of selected music for trombone and voice." D.M.A. diss., University of Illinois (Urbana-Champaign), 1981.

1796   Isaacson, Charles Frank. "A study of selected music for trombone and voice." *Dissertation Abstracts* 42 (1982): 3802A.

Jahn, Fritz. "Die Nürnberger Trompeten- und Posaunenmacher im 16. Jahrhundert." *Archiv für Musikwissenschaft* 7 (1925): 23–52.

1797   Jameson, P., comp. "Guide to orchestral excerpts." *Journal of the International Trombone Association* 13, no. 4 (1985): 29–30.

Jameson, P. "Orchestra showcase: The Atlanta Symphony Orchestra." *Journal of the International Trombone Association* 10, no. 4 (1982): 11–13.

Jenkins, R. M. "An annotated bibliography of periodical articles related to the bass trombone." *Journal of the International Trombone Association* 11, no. 4 (1983): 7–12.

1798   Jungheinrich, H. K. "Der entfesselte Posaunenbass; 'Cimbasso'—eine Erfindung, über die man spricht." *Das Orchester* 13 (Mar. 1965): 92.

1799   Kagarice, Vern. "An annotated bibliography of trombone solo literature with band or orchestra accompaniment." D.Mus. diss., Indiana University, 1973.

1800   Kagarice, Vern. *Annotated guide to trombone solos with band and orchestra.* Lebanon, IN: Studio/PR, 1974.

Kagarice, Vern, and J. Marcellus, comps. "Trombone personnel of American and Canadian orchestras and service bands." *Journal of the International Trombone Association* 10, no. 1 (1982): 20–21.

1801   Kagarice, Vern, and others. *Solos for the student trombonist: an annotated bibliography.* Nashville: Brass Press, 1979.

1802   Kaplan, Allan Richard. "A performance analysis of five major recital works: concerti for solo trombone and orchestra." Ph.D. diss., New York University, 1978.

1803   Kaplan, Allan Richard. "A performance analysis of five major recital works: concerti for solo trombone and orchestra." *Dissertation Abstracts* 39 (Feb. 1979): 4582A.

1804   Kehrberg, Robert Wayne. "Nine original trombone solos incorporating twentieth century compositional techniques graded for the first ten years of playing." *Dissertation Abstracts* 44 (Nov. 1983): 1236A.

1805   Kerschagl, and Weidemann. "Das Posaunen-Problem (Eine Wagner-Reminiszenz)." *Neue Musikzeitung* (Stuttgart) 42 (191?): 11, 14.

1806   Kidwell, James Kent. "An annotated performance-recording project of selected solo music for trombone with band accompaniment." D.M.A. diss., University of Oklahoma, 1976.

1807   Kidwell, James Kent. "An annotated performance-recording project of selected solo music for trombone with band accompaniment." *Dissertation Abstracts* 37 (June 1977): 7394A.

1808   Kingdon-Ward, Martha. "In defense of the trombone." *Monthly Musical Record* 80 (1950): 228–233.

1809   Kingdon-Ward, Martha. "In defense of the trombone." *Symphony* 5 (July-Aug. 1951): 14–15.

Kitzel, Larry. "The trombones of the Shrine to Music Museum." *Dissertation Abstracts* 46 (Oct. 1985): 832A.

Kohlenberg, R. "Preliminary results of a survey of trombone related research." *Journal of the International Trombone Association* 15, no. 2 (1987): 18–19.

Kohlenberg, R., and R. Thomas. "Orchestral showcase: The New York Philharmonic Orchestra." *Journal of the International Trombone Association* 11, no. 2 (1983): 16–24.

1810 Komorzynski, Egon. "Die Posaunen bei Mozart." *Wiener Figaro* 16 (1947): H. 7/8.

Kozma, T. "The trombone in Aida." *Opera News* 16 (Mar. 3, 1952): 30–31.

1811 Kröger, E. *Die Posaune im Jazz.* Vienna: Universal, 1972.

Kuhlo, Johannes. *Posaunen-Fragen beantwortet.* Gütersloh: C. Bertelsmann, 1933.

Kuhlo, Johannes. *Posaunen-Fragen, beantwortet.* 3. Auss. Bethel bei Bielefeld: Buchh. de Anstalt Bethel, 1909.

1812 Kunitz, H. "Vier Posaunen in Opern Verdis und Puccinis." *Musik und Geschichte* (1957): 29.

1813 Lajarte, T. E. D. F. d. "Introduction du trombone dans l'orchestre de l'opéra." In *Curiosités de l'opéra.* Paris: C. Lévy, 1883.

Lane, George B. "Instrument manufacturers and specifications." *Journal of the International Trombone Association* 4 (1976): 8–16.

1814 Lane, George B. "Orchestral repertoire for civic symphony trombonists." *NACWPI Journal* 25, no. 1 (1976): 38–40.

1815 Lane, George B. *The trombone in the Middle Ages and the Renaissance.* Bloomington: Indiana University Press, 1982.

1816 Lane, George Bertram. "The trombone: its musical environment from the late Middle Ages through the late renaissance." *Dissertation Abstracts* 37 (Dec. 1976): 3259A.

1817 Lane, George Bertram. "The trombone: its musical environment from the late Middle Ages through the late Renaissance." D.M.A. diss., University of Texas (Austin), 1976.

1818 Laplace, Michel. "Ravel et le 'nouveau' trombone." *Brass Bulletin—International Brass Chronicle,* no. 47 (1984): 34–38. Also in English and German.

1819 Laplace, Michel. "Le trombone dans le jazz et la musique populaire." *Brass Bulletin—International Brass Chronicle,* no. 50 (1985): 36–40. Also in English and German.

1820 Laplace, Michel. "Le trombone dans le jazz et la musique populaire: la periode classique Armstrongienne (1927–1945)." *Brass Bulletin—International Brass Chronicle,* no. 51 (1985): 40–46. Also in English and German.

1821 Laplace, Michel. "Le trombone dans le jazz et la musique populaire: le pluralisme d'expression a partir de 1945." *Brass Bulletin—International Brass Chronicle,* no. 52 (1985): 20–28. Also in English and German.

"Leading trombonists meet Buddy Morrow." *Crescendo International* 10 (Sept. 1971): 8.

1822 Leisenring, John Robert. "Twentieth-century trombone concerti." D.M.A. diss., University of Illinois (Urbana-Champaign), 1974.

1823 Leisenring, John Robert. "Twentieth-century trombone concerti." *Dissertation Abstracts* 35 (Jan. 1975): 4591A.

1824 Lemke, Jeffrey J. "French tenor trombone solo literature and pedagogy since 1836." *Dissertation Abstracts* 44 (Sept. 1983): 698A.

1825   Lemke, Jeffrey J. "French tenor trombone solo literature and pedagogy since 1836." A.Mus.D. diss., University of Arizona, 1983.

1826   Lester, Raymond David. "The emergence of the bass trombone in recent music literature." M.A. thesis, California State University (Long Beach), 1981.

1827   Lewis, Michael. "The sacbut, instrument of kings (once you get used to it)." *Journal of the International Trombone Association* 10, no. 2 (1982): 12–13. Reprinted from *The Christian Science Monitor*.

1828   Lewy, Rudolf. "Trombone basso." *Journal of the International Trombone Association* 5 (1977): 10–22.

Lister, R. "The contrabass sackbut—a modern copy." *Brass Bulletin—International Brass Chronicle*, no. 31 (1980): 71 +. Also in French and German.

Lister, R. "The contrabass sackbut—a modern copy." *Journal of the International Trombone Association* 9 (1981): 23.

Lucas, D. "Orchestra showcase: The Houston Symphony Orchestra." *Journal of the International Trombone Association* 10, no. 3 (1982): 27–31.

1829   Lück, R. "Von der Tuba mirum zur verfremdeten Posaune—ein Werkstattgespräch mit Vinko Globokar." *Neue Zeitschrift für Musik* 131 Sept. 1970): 439–444.

1830   Lupica, Benedict. *The magnificent bone: a comprehensive study of the slide trombone.* New York: Vantage, 1974.

1831   Lyttelton, Humphrey. *I play as I please; the memoirs of an old Etonian trumpeter.* London: MacGibbon & Kee, 1954.

MacDonald, Robert J. "François-Joseph Gossec and French instrumental music in the second half of the eighteenth century." Ph.D. diss., University of Michigan, 1968.

1832   McGee, T. J., and S. E. Mittler. "Information on instruments in Florentine Carnival songs." *Early Music* 10, no. 4 (1982): 452–461.

1833   McGrannahan, A. Graydon, III. "The trombone in German and Austrian ensemble sonatas of the late seventeenth century: a lecture recital, together with three recitals of selected works of Presser, Bozza, George, Beethoven, Stevens, Wilder, White, Spillman, Tuthill and others." D.M.A. diss., North Texas State University, 1981.

1834   Magliocco, H. "Literature reviews." *Newsletter of the International Trombone Association* 6, no. 1 (1978): 23–29.

1835   Magliocco, H. "The Renaissance trombone." *Brass and Percussion* 1, no. 3 (1973): 6–7.

1836   Mahillon, Victor Charles. *Le trombone.* Brussels: Mahillon, 1907.

Mahrenholz, C. "Ueber Posaunenmusik." *Musik und Kirche* 1 (1929): 132–137, 163–173, 261–267.

1837   Malterer, Edward Lee. "The employment of ornamentation in present day trombone performance of transcriptions of Baroque literature." *Dissertation Abstracts* 41 (Jan. 1981): 2823A.

Marcellus, John. "Directory of symphony trombonists [U.S. and Canada]." *The Instrumentalist* 28 (Feb. 1974): 55.

1838 Martell, Paul. "Zur Geschichte der Posaune." *Die Musik-Woche* 3, no. 4 (1935): 5–6.

"Martin Schlee zum 65. Geburtstag." *Gottesdienst und Kirchenmusik* (1954): 143–145.

1839 Masson, Gabriel. "Historique du trombone." *Musique & Radio* 52, no. 619 (Nov. 1962): 41.

1840 Mater, F. "Die Behandlung der Posaune im Symphonie- und Opernorchester." *Deutsche Militär-Musiker-Zeitung* 63 (1941): 51.

1841 Maxted, George. *Talking about the trombone*. London: John Baker, 1970.

1842 Mehl, J. G. "Der Gottesdienst an Bezirksposaunentagen." *Gottesdienst und Kirchenmusik* 2 (1964): 65–69.

1843 Mehl, J. G. "Der Gottesdienst an Bezirksposaunentagen." *Gottesdienst und Kirchenmusik* 5 (1964): 195–199.

1844 Meinerzhagen, Fritz. "Das Posaunenregister im Orchester." *Deutsche Militär-Musiker Zeitung* 27 (1905): 105–106, 120–121.

1845 Mertens, A. "Le trombone en Belgique." *Brass Bulletin—International Brass Chronicle*, no. 5–6 (1973): 93–96. Also in German and English.

Miller, D. G. "Johann Stoerl and his Six Sonatas for Cornett and Trombones." Master's essay, University of Rochester, 1962.

1846 Miller, Frederick Staten. "A comprehensive performance project in trombone literature with an essay on the use of trombone in the music of Heinrich Schütz." D.M.A. diss., University of Iowa, 1974.

1847 Miller, Frederick Staten. "A comprehensive performance project in trombone literature with an essay on the use of trombone in the music of Heinrich Schütz." *Dissertation Abstracts* 35 (Jan. 1975): 4595A.

1848 Miller, K. E. "Instruments of the baroque era." *Choral Journal* 7, no. 5 (1967): 16.

Miller, Robert Melvin. "Abstract: The concerto and related works for low brass: a catalog of compositions from c. 1700 to the present." *Missouri Journal of Research in Music Education* 3, no. 4 (1975): 91.

Miller, Robert Melvin. "The concerto and related works for low brass: a catalogue of compositions from c. 1700 to the present." Ph.D. diss., Washington University, 1974.

Miller, Robert Melvin. "The concerto and related works for low brass: a catalogue of compositions from c. 1700 to the present." *Dissertation Abstracts* 35 (Mar. 1975): 6185A.

1849 Mitchell, Arthur B. "The trombone: A short historical background with suggested methods and materials for its instruction in public schools." Master's thesis, University of Wichita, 1954.

"Moravian trombone choir music recorded [Music of the Moravian Trombone Choir]." *The Moravian Music Foundation Bulletin* 21, no. 2 (1976): 9.

1850 Müller, S. "Die Ventilposaune." *Evangelische Musik-Zeitung* 30 (1936): 33–34.

1851 "Music for bass trombone." *Sounding Brass & the Conductor* 8, no. 4 (1979): 153.

1852 "Music for bass trombone." *Sounding Brass & the Conductor* 9, no. 2 (1980): 31–32.

1853 "Music for trombone." *Sounding Brass & the Conductor* 8, no. 4 (1979): 151–152.

"Musician extraordinary [Jaroslav Cimera]." *The Instrumentalist* 8 (Dec. 1953): 35.

1854 Myers, Richmond E. "Two centuries of trombones." *Etude* 73 (Apr. 1955): 12+.

1855 Nash, H. "The better half." *Sounding Brass & the Conductor* 2, no. 2 (1973): 62–63.

1856 Nash, H. "Trombones on trial." *Sounding Brass & the Conductor* 1 (Apr. 1972): 21–22.

Naylor, Tom L. *The trumpet and trombone in graphic arts: 1500–1800.* Nashville: Brass Press, 1979.

Netto. "Von Hörnern, Posaunen und Trompeten aus alter und neuer Zeit." *Deutsche Mititär-Musiker Zeitung* 28 (1906): 73–74.

1857 "News from Carsten Svanberg [Danish music for trombone]." *Newsletter of the International Trombone Association* 5, no. 3 (1978): 4–5.

Nicholas, M. R. "Establishing and expanding an early music consort [cornetto, sackbut]." *The Instrumentalist* 32 (Mar. 1978): 36–39.

1858 Nicholson, Joseph M. "The development and use of the Renaissance trombone." *Monthly Journal of Research in Music Education* 2, no. 1 (1967): 58–68.

1859 Nicholson, Joseph M. "The history of the trombone as a solo instrument." *Journal of the International Trombone Association* 16, no. 3 (Summer 1988): 34–36.

1860 Nicholson, Joseph M. "Performance considerations of early music for the trombone with other instruments." *Journal of the International Trombone Association* 4 (1976): 20–21.

1861 Nicholson, Joseph M. "The trombone and its solo literature." *Woodwind World—Brass and Percussion* 14, no. 3 (1975): 38+.

1862 Nicholson, Joseph M. "The trombone—its evolution and history." *Music Journal* 25 (Oct. 1967): 70–73+.

1863 Nicholson, Joseph Milford. "A historical background of the trombone and its music." D.M.A. diss., University of Missouri (Kansas City), 1967.

1864 Nicholson, Joseph Milford. "A historical background of the trombone and its music." *Dissertation Abstracts* 28 (Mar. 1968): 3706A.

"1977 Boston Sackbut Week." *Newsletter of the International Trombone Association* 5, no. 1 (1977): 5.

1865 "Notations." *Composer [U.S.]* 2, no. 3 (1970): 68–71.

1866 "Notice sur l'introduction des cors, des clarinettes et des trombones dans les orchestres français, extraite des manuscrits autographes de Gossec." *Revue musicale* 5 (1829): 217–223.

1867   O'Loughlin, N. "Trombone." *The Musical Times* 125 (Apr. 1984): 217.

"Orchestra showcase: The Baltimore Symphony Orchestra." *Journal of the International Trombone Association* 10, no. 2 (1982): 14–19.

1868   Otto, C. A. "A checklist of compositions with significant trombone parts in the Liechtenstein Music Collection." *Journal of the International Trombone Association* 9 (1981): 11–13.

P., I. "On the serpent, bass-horn and trombone." *Harmonicon* (1834): 234.

"Personnel listing of symphony orchestras [addendum]." *Journal of the International Trombone Association* 12, no. 3 (1984): 44.

1869   Pethel, Stanley Robert. "Contemporary composition for the trombone." D.M.A. diss., University of Kentucky, 1981.

1870   Pethel, Stanley Robert. "Contemporary composition for the trombone: a survey of selected works." *Dissertation Abstracts* 42 (Jan. 1982): 2928A.

1871   "Philadelphia Orchestra trombone personnel 1900–1984." *Journal of the International Trombone Association* 12, no. 3 (1984): 19.

Pierce, T. "Monteverdi's use of brass instruments." *Journal of the International Trombone Association* 9 (1981): 4–8.

1872   Pierce, T. "The trombone in the eighteenth century." *Journal of the International Trombone Association* 8 (1980): 6–10.

Plass, Ludwig. "Was die Geschichte der Posaunen lehrt. Studie über die ehemalige und gegenwartige Turmmusik." *Allgemeine Musikalische Zeitung* (Berlin) 40 (1913): 445–447, 477–479.

Polk, Keith. "Municipal wind music in Flanders in the late Middle Ages." *Brass and Woodwind Quarterly* 2, nos. 1–2 (Spring-Summer 1969): 1–15.

1873   Polk, Keith. "The trombone in archival documents—1350–1500." *Journal of the International Trombone Association* 15, no. 3 (Summer 1987): 24–31.

1874   Polk, Keith. "Wind bands of medieval Flemish cities." *Brass & Woodwind Quarterly* 1, nos. 3–4 (1968): 93–113.

"Die Posaune und einer ihrer Pioniere [Prof. Friedrich Mater]." *Die Musik-Woche* 9 (1941): 21–23.

"Posaunenmusik." *Zeitschrift für Kirchenmusiker* 10 (1928): 184.

1875   Pulver, G. "The Sackbut." *The Sackbut* 3, no. 8 (192-?).

1876   Rasmussen, Mary. "A bibliography of choral music with trombone ensemble accompaniment, as compiled from eleven selected sources." *Brass Quarterly* 5, no. 4 (1962): 153–159.

1877   Raum, J. Richard. "Extending the solo and chamber repertoire for the alto trombone from the late Baroque and early Classical periods (1720–1780)." *Journal of the International Trombone Association* 16, no. 2 (Spring 1988): 11–23.

"Recent jazz 'slides' on record." *Newsletter of the International Trombone Association* 4, no. 3 (1977): 19–21.

1878   Reichel, W. C. *Something about trombones and The Old Mill at Bethlehem.* Edited by J. W. Jordan. Bethlehem, Pa.: Moravian Publications Office, 1884.

1879   Reifsnyder, Robert. "A closer look at recent recital programs." *Journal of the International Trombone Association* 11, no. 1 (1983): 25–27.

1880   Reifsnyder, Robert. "The Romantic trombone: Part one." *Journal of the International Trombone Association* 15, no. 2 (Spring 1987): 20–23.

1881   Reifsnyder, Robert. "The Romantic trombone: Part two." *Journal of the International Trombone Association* 15, no. 3 (Summer 1987): 32–37.

1882   Reynolds, J. C. "The trombone in Moravian life." *Moravian Music Journal* 32, no. 1 (1987): 7–11.

Richardson, E. "Handel's horn and trombone parts." *The Musical Times* 81 (1940): 180.

1883   Richardson, W. "Annual review of solos and studies: Trombone and euphonium." *The Instrumentalist* 39 (Feb. 1985): 77–79.

1884   Richardson, W. "Annual review of solos and studies: Trombone/Euphonium." *The Instrumentalist* 37 (Jan. 1983): 52–55.

1885   Richardson, W. "Trombone [annual review of solos and studies]." *The Instrumentalist* 35 (Dec. 1980): 34–36.

Richardson, W. "Trombone and baritone solo and study materials." *The Instrumentalist* 32 (Feb. 1978): 60–61.

1886   Richardson, W. "Trombone/baritone [recent publications]." *The Instrumentalist* 36 (Dec. 1981): 66–68.

1887   Richardson, William Wells. "Lecture-recital—new directions in trombone literature and the techniques needed for its performance." Ph.D. diss., Catholic University of America, 1970.

1888   Robert, J. "Works with trombone in the Alfred Einstein collection of 16th and 17th century instrumental music: a descriptive catalog." *Journal of the International Trombone Association* 12, no. 4 (1984): 25–32.

1889   Roberts, J. "Current research relating to the trombone." *Journal of the International Trombone Association* 12, no. 1 (1984): 31–32.

1890   Roberts, J. E. "A preliminary list of seventeenth-century chamber music employing the trombone." *Journal of the International Trombone Association* 8 (1980): 19–22.

1891   Rode, Theodore. "Die Zug- oder Natur-Posaune unter den Chromatikern bei der Militärmusik." *Neue Zeitschrift für Musik* 62 (1866): 78–79.

1892   Rodin, J. "Bass trombone-perspective." *The School Musician* 47 (May 1976): 20+.

Rohner, Traugott. "Introducing the F-alto trombone." *The Instrumentalist* 4 (Nov. 1949): 18–19.

1893   Ross, Richard Raymond. "The use of the trombone in the Symphonia Sacre I of Heinrich Schütz." D.M.A. diss., Catholic University of America, 1977.

Roznoy, R. T. "A selected bibliography of English language material relevant to the trombone." *Journal of the International Trombone Association* 4 (1976): 23–29.

1894   Roznoy, R. T. "Thoughts on contest performances: music for trombone/euphonium." *The Instrumentalist* 37 (Feb. 1983): 73–77.

1895   Roznoy, Richard Thomas. "A stylistic adaptation of the piano accompaniment of Paul Hindemith's *Sonata for Trombone and Piano*, for wind ensemble." Ph.D. diss., University of Wisconsin (Madison), 1976.

Ruh. "Ueber die Verwendung der Posaunen." *Evangelische Musikzeitung* 21 (191?): 3.

1896   Runyan, W. E. "The alto trombone and contemporary concepts of trombone timbre." *Brass Bulletin—International Brass Chronicle*, no. 28 (1979): 43–45 + . Also in French and German.

1897   Ryon, James P. "The use of the trombone as a solo and ensemble instrument in selected works of the seventeenth-century Moravian court composer, Pavel Josef Vejvanousky." D.M.A. diss., Catholic University of America, 1978.

1898   Sager, D. "Of ear, heart and arm—a tale of the slide trombone in early jazz." *The Second Line* 37 (Winter 1985): 36–43.

1899   Samball, Michael Loran. "The influence of jazz on French solo trombone repertory." *Dissertation Abstracts* 48 (Sept. 1987): 509A.

1900   Samball, Michael Loran. "The influence of jazz on French solo trombone repertory." D.M.A. diss., North Texas State University, 1987.

1901   Sanger, Robert. "The evolution and growth of the trombone and its influence on musical composition and performance." Master's thesis, Northwestern University, 1953.

1902   Sauer, Ralph. "The alto trombone in the symphony orchestra." *Journal of the International Trombone Association* 12, no. 3 (1984): 41.

1903   Schaefer, J. D. "The use of the trombone in the 18th century." *The Instrumentalist* 22 (Apr. 1968): 51–53; (May 1968): 100–102; (June 1968): 61–63.

1904   Schlesinger, Kathleen. "Sackbut." In *Encyclopaedia Britannica*. 11th ed. New York, 1910–11.

1905   Schlesinger, Kathleen. "Trombone." In *Encyclopedia Britannica*. 11th ed. New York, 1910–11.

1906   Schreiber, E. A. "Trombone after-life." *Journal of the International Trombone Association* 12, no. 4 (1984): 43.

Schultz, P. M. " 'Praise the Lord with the sound of trumpet' and trombone and horn and tuba." *The School Musician* 44 (Dec. 1972): 48–49.

1907   Schwartz, H. W. "Slip horn developed from tpt. tuning slide." *Metronome* 54 (Mar. 1938): 17 + .

1908   Senff, Thomas Earl. "An annotated bibliography of the unaccompanied solo repertoire for trombone." *Dissertation Abstracts* 37 (July 1976): 28A.

1909   Senff, Thomas Earl. "An annotated bibliography of the unaccompanied solo repertoire for trombone." D.M.A. diss., University of Illinois (Urbana-Champaign), 1976.

1910   Shawger, J. D. "The uses of the trombone in the modern symphony orchestra." Master's thesis, University of Washington, 1958.

1911   Shoemaker, J. R. "The sackbut in the school." *The Instrumentalist* 26 (Sept. 1971): 40–42.

1912   Sluchin, B. "Eberlin and his contribution to the soloistic use of the trombone." *Journal of the International Trombone Association* 13, no. 4 (1985): 36.

1913 Sluchin, B. "Un martyr de trombone [includes A. Leonard's 1846 address to L'Academie des Beaux-Arts]." *Brass Bulletin—International Brass Chronicle*, no. 31 (1980): 57–59 + . Also in English and German.

1914 Sluchin, B. "The trombone in the sacred works of W. A. Mozart." *Brass Bulletin—International Brass Chronicle*, no. 46 (1984): 31–35. Also in French and German.

1915 Smith, David Bruce. "Trombone technique in the early seventeenth century." *Dissertation Abstracts* 42 (May 1982): 4642A.

1916 Smith, David Bruce. "Trombone technique in the early seventeenth century." D.M.A. diss., Stanford University, 1982.

Smith, G. P. "Paris National Conservatory contest pieces for trombone." *Journal of the International Trombone Association* 5 (1977): 23–24.

1917 Snyder, F. "How to acquire a better trombone section." *Woodwind World— Brass and Percussion* 14, no. 2 (1975): 45 + .

Sommerhalder, M. "Posaunen-Arbeit." *Brass Bulletin—International Brass Chronicle*, no. 34 (1981): 55–59. Also in French and English.

1918 Stevens, Milton. "150 difficult excerpts for the orchestral trombonist." *Newsletter of the International Trombone Association* 8, no. 1 (1980): 30–31.

1919 Stewart, Gary M. "The restoration of a 1608 trombone by Jacob Bauer, Nuremberg." *Journal of the American Musical Instrument Society* 8 (1982): 79–92.

1920 Stoddard, Hope. "The trombone in our orchestras." *International Musician* 48 (Nov. 1949): 20–22 + .

1921 "The story of the trombone." *Metronome* 40 (Sept. 1924): 87 + .

1922 Streeter, Thomas W. "The historical and musical aspects of the 19th century bass trombone." *Journal of the International Trombone Association* 4 (Jan. 1976): 33–36; 5 (Jan. 1977): 25–35.

1923 Streeter, Thomas W. "Lecture-recital—the historical and musical aspects of the 19th century bass trombone." Ph.D. diss., Catholic University of America, 1971.

Streeter, Thomas W. "Survey and annotated bibliography on the historical development of the trombone." *Journal of the International Trombone Association* 7 (1979): 27–32.

1924 Struck-Schlön, M. "Zwischen Möbelmusik und Zwölftonkonzert: die Posaune im Kammerensemble am Beginn der Neuen Musik (1913–1934)." *Brass Bulletin—International Brass Chronicle*, no. 56 (1986): 24–32. Also in English and French.

1925 Struck-Schlön, M. "Zwischen Möbelmusik und Zwölftonkonzert: die Posaune im Kammerensemble am Beginn der Neuen Musik (1913–1934)." *Brass Bulletin—International Brass Chronicle*, no. 55 (1986): 6–14. Also in English and French.

1926 Stuart, David Henry. "A comprehensive performance project in trombone literature with an essay consisting of the use of the trombone in selected chamber compositions of Biagio Marini." D.M.A. diss., University of Iowa, 1981.

1927 Swett, J. "A selected, annotated list of published trombone literature." *The Instrumentalist* 28 (Feb. 1974): 76+.

1928 Tanner, James Cornwell, Jr. "Technical and musical uses of the trombone in selected original repertoire for the twentieth-century concert band." *Dissertation Abstracts* 44 (Nov. 1983): 1239A.

1929 Tanner, James Cornwell, Jr. "Technical and musical uses of the trombone in selected original repertoire for the twentieth-century concert band." Ed.D. diss., Columbia University Teachers College, 1983.

1930 Taylor, William A. "The orchestral treatment of the trombone in the 18th and 19th centuries." Master's thesis, Eastman School of Music, 1951.

1931 Tennyson, Robert Scott. "Five anonymous seventeenth-century chamber works with trombone parts, from the castle archives of Kromeriz." *Dissertation Abstracts* 34 (Dec. 1973): 3459A.

1932 Tennyson, Robert Scott. "Five anonymous seventeenth-century chamber works with trombone parts, from the Castle Archives of Kromeriz." D.M.A. diss., University of Maryland, 1973.

1933 Tepperman, B. "Rudd, Moncur and some other stuff." *Coda—Canada's Jazz Magazine* 10, no. 2 (1971): 8–11.

Tesch, John A. "An annotated bibliography of selected trombone duets." D.M.A. diss., University of Arizona, 1987.

1934 Thein, H. "Die Kontrabassposaune; Bild—Abriss unter besonderer Berücksichtigung der bautechnischen Aspekte (1973)." *Brass Bulletin—International Brass Chronicle*, no. 23 (1978): 55–61+. Also in English and French.

Thein, M., and H. Thein. "Neues über Alt-Posaune." *Brass Bulletin—International Brass Chronicle*, no. 40 (1982): 33. Also in English and French.

1935 Thomas, T. D. "Michael Haydn's "Trombone" Symphony." *Brass Quarterly* 6, no. 1 (1962): 3–8. Includes music.

1936 Trichet, P. "De la saqueboute ou trompette harmonique (vers 1640)." *Brass Bulletin—International Brass Chronicle*, no. 45 (1984): 10–12. Also in English and German.

1937 "The trombone." *American Musician* 29, no. 20 (1913): 10.

1938 "The trombone." *Metronome* 30, no. 6 (1914): 26; no. 11 (1914): 30–31.

1939 "Le trombone." *Schweizerische Instrumentalmusik* 32 (1943): 363.

1940 "The trombone, a brief history." *The Instrumentalist* 28 (Feb. 1974): 41.

1941 "Trombonists talk with Buddy Morrow." *Crescendo International* 10 (Oct. 1971): 22.

"Trompeten und Posaunen." *Musik International-Instrumentenbau-Zeitschrift* 38 (Aug. 1984): 561–565+.

1942 Tucker, Wallace Edward. "The solo tenor trombone works of Gordon Jacob, a lecture recital, together with three recitals of selected works by L. Bassett, W. Hartley, B. Blacher, E. Bloch, D. White, F. David, G.

Wagenseil, and others." D.M.A. diss., North Texas State University, 1987.

1943 Tuersot, A. "Le trombone basse." *Musique & Radio* 51 (1961): 291 + . [French and English text.]

1944 Turrentine, Edgar M. "A translation of the trumpet articles in the "Dictionnaire des Antiquites." *Journal of the International Trumpet Guild* 9, no. 2 (1984): 14–28.

1945 Unger, Hermann. "Die Posaune—ein Instrument des Ueberpersönlichen." *Das neue Blasorchester*, no. 10 (1951): 75.

Venglovsky, V. "Trombone school of the Petersburg-Petrograd-Leningrad Conservatory." *Journal of the International Trombone Association* 12, no. 2 (1984): 26–28.

Vivona, Peter M. "Theater techniques in recent music for the trombone [includes bibliography of theater]." *Journal of the International Trombone Association* 10, no. 2 (1982): 20–25.

Voce, S. "It don't mean a thing." *Jazz Journal* 28 (Apr. 1975): 20–21.

Wagner, I. L. "International news: trombone activities in China [formation of Chinese Trombone Association]." *Journal of the International Trombone Association* 13, no. 4 (1985): 41–42.

1946 Wagner, I. L. "A new, original, 17th century solo: a sonata for trombone and basso continuo." *Journal of the International Trombone Association* 5 (1977): 41–43.

1947 Wagner, I. L. "Trombone ensemble music." *The Instrumentalist* 26 (Aug. 1971): 80–81.

Weber, K. "Die Posaunisten im Festspielorchester Bayreuth." *Das Orchester* 28 (July-Aug. 1980): 581–583.

1948 Weber, K. "Die zweitälteste Posaune (von 1557)." *Das Orchester* 35 (May 1987): 511–512.

1949 Weed, L. "Ferdinand David's *Concertino for Trombone and Orchestra, Op. 4.*" *Journal of the International Trombone Association* 9 (1981): 26–27.

1950 Weeks, D. G. "A review and evaluation of selected contemporary literature for unaccompanied trombone." *Journal of the International Trombone Association* 7 (1979): 21–23.

1951 Weiner, H. "The trombone: changing times, changing slide positions." *Brass Bulletin—International Brass Chronicle*, no. 36 (1981): 52–63.

1952 Weingartner, Felix. "Die Posaunen in Mozarts Requiem." *Die Musik* 5 (1905/06): 41–43.

1953 Wessely, Othmar. "Zur Geschichte des Equals." *Beethoven Festschrift* (1971): 341–360.

1954 Westrup, J. A. "The misuse of the trombone." *The Musical Times* 66 (1925): 524–525.

1955 "The Wetherill trombone or slide flute." *Musical Standard* 31 (1928): 43–44, 59.

1956 Wigness, C. Robert. "The soloistic use of the trombone in 18th-century

Vienna." *Journal of the International Trombone Association* 6, no. 2 (1978): 20–21.

1957   Wigness, C. Robert. "The soloistic use of the trombone in 18th-century Vienna." *Notes* 36, no. 1 (1979): 103.

1958   Wigness, C. Robert. *The soloistic use of the trombone in eighteenth century Vienna*. Brass Research Series, no. 2. Nashville: Brass Press, 1978.

1959   Wigness, Clyde Robert. "A comprehensive performance project in trombone literature with an essay on the soloistic use of the trombone in selected works of eighteenth-century Viennese Imperial Court composers." D.M.A. diss., University of Iowa, 1970.

1960   Wigness, Clyde Robert. "A comprehensive performance project in trombone literature with an essay on the soloistic use of the trombone in selected works of eighteenth-century Viennese Imperial Court composers." *Dissertation Abstracts* 31 (Mar. 1971): 4828A-4829A.

1961   Williams, Jeffrey Price. "The trombone in German and Austrian concerted church music of the Baroque period." *Dissertation Abstracts* 36 (Mar. 1975): 6188A.

1962   Williams, Jeffrey Price. "The trombone in German and Austrian concerted church music of the Baroque period, a lecture recital, together with three recitals of selected works of L. Bassett, L. Grondahl, W. Hartley, V. Persichetti, K. Serocki, H. Tomasi, D. White and others." D.M.A. diss., North Texas State University, 1974.

1963   Willis, James D. "A study of Paul Hindemith's use of the trombone as seen in selected chamber compositions." D.M.A. diss., University of Missouri (Kansas City), 1973.

Winkler, K. "Bibliographie der Kompositionen für Posaune und Orgel." *Brass Bulletin—International Brass Chronicle*, no. 51 (1985): 63–66. Also in English and French.

1964   Winkler, K. "Posaune und orgel: Dialog zweier instrumente." *Brass Bulletin—International Brass Chronicle*, no. 56 (1986): 75 +. Also in English and French.

1965   Wolfinbarger, S. "The solo trombone music of Arthur Pryor: early trombone soloists with band." *Journal of the International Trombone Association* 11, no. 2 (1983): 27–29.

"Works for solo trombone and mixed ensembles performed during the 1975 National Trombone Festival." *Newsletter of the International Trombone Association* 3, no. 2 (1976): 25 +.

Worthmüller, Willi. "Die Instrumente der Nürnberger Trompeten- und Posaunenmacher." In *Mitteilungen des Vereins für Geschichte der Stadt Nürnberg*, 372–480. 1955.

Worthmüller, Willi. "Die Nürnberger Trompeten- und Posaunenmacher des 17. und 18. Jahrhunderts." In *Mitteilungen des Vereins für Geschichte der Stadt Nürnberg*, 208–325. 1954.

Wulstan, D. "The sounding of the shofar." *The Galpin Society Journal* 26 (May 1973): 29–46.

1966   Yeo, Douglas. "The bass trombone: innovations on a misunderstood instrument." *The Instrumentalist* 40 (Nov. 1985): 22–26 + .

Yeo, Douglas, comp. "Personnel listing of symphony, opera and ballet orchestras [international]." *Journal of the International Trombone Association* 12, no. 1 (1984): 15–19.

1967   Zola, L. "The trombone: the phenomenon of a musical sound." *Journal of the International Trombone Association* 11, no. 2 (1983): 29–31.

Zwerin, M. "Ca bouge dans la coulisse." *Jazz Magazine*, no. 277 (July-Aug. 1979): 46–47.

Baritone/Euphonium

1968   "B-flat baritone directory." *Sounding Brass & the Conductor* 4, no. 3 (1975): 95.

1969   "B-flat euphonium directory." *Sounding Brass & the Conductor* 5, no. 1 (1976): 23.

Bahr, Edward R. "Idiomatic similarities and differences of the trombone and euphonium in history and performance." *Journal of the International Trombone Association* 6 (1978): 31–36.

1970   Bahr, Edward R. "Orchestral literature including euphonium or tenor tuba." *T.U.B.A. Journal* 7, no. 2 (Fall 1979): 13–14.

1971   Bevan, Clifford. "Background brass." *Sounding Brass & the Conductor* 7, no. 3 (1978): 100 + .

Bowman, Brian. "The bass trumpet and tenor tuba in orchestral and operatic literature." D.M.A. diss., Catholic University of America, 1975.

1972   Bowman, Brian. "The euphonium—extinct or extant?" *The Instrumentalist* 30 (Dec. 1975): 32.

1973   Bowman, Brian. "New materials—euphonium." *T.U.B.A. Journal* 4, no. 3 (Spring/Summer 1977): 8.

1974   Bowman, Brian. "Reflections on: Euphonium Concert Tour, Japan 1984." *T.U.B.A. Journal* 12, no. 4 (May 1985): 17–19.

1975   Bowman, Brian. "You play a what?" *Brass and Percussion* 1, no. 2 (1973): 12–13 + .

1976   Bryant, William. "Research for tuba and euphonium." *T.U.B.A. Journal* 13, no. 2 (Nov. 1985): 25.

1977   Call, G. K. "Music for euphonium." *Sounding Brass & the Conductor* 9, no. 3 (1980): 30–31.

1978   Campbell, Larry, ed. "New materials—euphonium." *T.U.B.A. Journal* 5, no. 3 (Spring/Summer 1978): 26–27.

1979   Campbell, Larry, ed. "New materials—euphonium." *T.U.B.A. Journal* 6, no. 2 (Winter 1979): 13–16.

1980   Campbell, Larry, ed. "New materials—euphonium." *T.U.B.A. Journal* 6, no. 3 (Spring 1979): 16.

Corwell, Neal. "Using lieder as euphonium literature." *T.U.B.A. Journal* 9, no. 2 (Fall 1981): 20–22.

1981   Cummings, Barton, Brian Bowman, and Larry Campbell. "New materials—tuba and euphonium." *T.U.B.A. Journal* 5, no. 2 (Winter 1978): 34–37.

1982   Cummings, Barton. "New material for tuba and euphonium." *T.U.B.A. Newsletter* 3, no. 2 (Winter 1976): 6.

1983   Droste, Paul. "Begged, borrowed, and stolen solo euphonium literature." *The Instrumentalist* 35 (May 1981): 30–32.

1984   Falcone, Leonard. "Is the baritone horn dying? Let's hope not—but it looks that way." *The School Musician* 46 (May 1975): 40–41.

Floyd, J. R. "The baritone horn versus the euphonium." *Woodwind World— Brass and Percussion* 20, no. 3 (1981): 8–9.

1985   Heinkel, Peggy. "Analysis for interpretation: Samuel Adler's *Dialogues for Euphonium and Marimba*." *T.U.B.A. Journal* 13, no. 3 (Feb. 1986): 10–16.

1986   Hinterbichler, Karl G. "A future for the euphonium?" *The Instrumentalist* 33 (Jan. 1979): 11.

1987   Hvizdos, J. "The euphonium—dead or alive?" *Woodwind World—Brass and Percussion* 15, no. 2 (1976): 54.

1988   "Invention of the baritone." *The Instrumentalist* 17 (April 1963): 30 + .

1989   Louder, Earle L., and David R. Corbin. "Euphonium music guide." *T.U.B.A. Newsletter* 1, no. 3 (Spring 1974): 5.

1990   Louder, Earle L. "Euphonium future bright." *The Instrumentalist* 33 (Jan. 1979): 11.

1991   Louder, Earle L. "Euphonium literature; original solo literature and study books for euphonium." *The Instrumentalist* 35 (May 1981): 29–30.

1992   Louder, Earle Leroy. "An historical lineage of the modern baritone horn and euphonium." D.Mus. diss., Florida State University, 1976.

Maldonado, Luis. "Solo music literature for junior high and high school euphonium and tuba performers." *T.U.B.A. Journal* 14, no. 4 (May 1987): 39–41.

1993   Morris, R. Winston. "New materials—euphonium-tuba." *T.U.B.A. Newsletter* 1, no. 2 (Winter 1974): 10.

1994   Morris, R. Winston. "New materials—euphonium-tuba." *T.U.B.A. Newsletter* 1, no. 3 (Spring 1974): 6–7.

1995   Morris, R. Winston. "New materials—euphonium-tuba." *T.U.B.A. Newsletter* 2, no. 1 (Fall 1974): 4.

1996   Mortimer, Alex. "The bigger brasses—euphoniums and basses." In *Brass Today*. Edited by Frank Wright, 49–52. London: Besson, 1957.

Nash, E. W. "The euphonium: its history, literature and use in American Schools." Master's thesis, University of Southern California, 1962.

1997   Naylor, J. J. "The English euphonium: its development and use." *T.U.B.A. Journal* 9, no. 4 (Spring 1982): 17.

1998   Peterson, M. "A brief history of the euphonium." *The Instrumentalist* 35 (May 1981): 16–17.

Peterson, Mary. "Baritones and euphoniums of European origins." *T.U.B.A. Journal* 9, no. 1 (Summer 1981): 3–7.

Popiel, Peter. "Thirty years of periodical articles concerning the baritone horn and euphonium: a compilation indexed by author." *T.U.B.A. Journal* 10, no. 3 (Winter 1983): 6–7.

1999   Reifsnyder, Robert. "The changing role of the euphonium in contemporary band music." D.Mus. diss., Indiana University, 1980.

2000   Reifsnyder, Robert. "The romantic trombone and its place in the German solo tradition." *Journal of the International Trombone Association* 15, no. 3 (1987): 32–37.

2001   Reifsnyder, Robert. "A short history of the euphonium in America." *Brass Bulletin—International Brass Chronicle*, no. 35 (1981): 13 +. Also in French and German. Excerpt from "The changing role of the euphonium in contemporary band music," D.Mus. diss., Indiana University.

Reifsnyder, Robert. "Why have composers stopped writing melodically for the euphonium?" *T.U.B.A. Journal* 8, no. 4 (Spring 1981): 13–14.

Richardson, W. "Annual review of solos and studies: Trombone and euphonium." *The Instrumentalist* 39 (Feb. 1985): 77–79.

Richardson, W. "Annual review of solos and studies: Trombone/Euphonium." *The Instrumentalist* 37 (Jan. 1983): 52–55.

Richardson, W. "Trombone and baritone solo and study materials." *The Instrumentalist* 32 (Feb. 1978): 60–61.

Richardson, W. "Trombone/baritone [recent publications]." *The Instrumentalist* 36 (Dec. 1981): 66–68.

Roznoy, R. T. "Thoughts on contest performances: music for trombone/euphonium." *The Instrumentalist* 37 (Feb. 1983): 73–77.

"Some baritone solos." *The School Musician* 21 (June 1950): 26–28.

2002   Steinberger, Karl Thomas. "A performance analysis of five recital works for euphonium." *Dissertation Abstracts* 42 (Aug. 1981): 448A.

2003   Steinberger, Karl Thomas. "A performance analysis of five recital works for euphonium." Ph.D. diss., New York University, 1981.

Torchinsky, Abe, and Roger Oyster. "Utilizing the euphonium." *T.U.B.A. Journal* 10, no. 1 (Summer 1982): 4.

2004   "Tuba und Euphonium heute—Von Willson-Band Instruments, Flums, Schweiz." *Instrumentenbau Musik International* 31, no. 4 (1977): 375.

2005   Weerts, R. "Educational solo recordings [wind and percussion instruments]." *The Instrumentalist* 23 (Feb. 1969): 22.

2006   Werden, David R. "Does the euphonium have a future?" *T.U.B.A. Journal* 10, no. 3 (Winter 1983): 11–12.

2007   Winslow, Stephen P. "Historical comparisons of the euphonium and baritone horn." *T.U.B.A. Journal* 5, no. 3 (Spring/Summer 1978): 5–9.

2008   Young, R. G. "Euphonium—well sounding." *The Instrumentalist* 18 (Mar. 1964): 72–2.

2009 Young, Raymond. "Euphoniums—what's happening!" *T.U.B.A. Newsletter* 1, no. 3 (Spring 1974): 10.

2010 Young, Raymond. "Some recommended euphonium music." *T.U.B.A. Newsletter* 1, no. 2 (Winter 1974): 5.

"Zur Geschichte des Tenorhorns und des Barytons." *Schweizerische Instrumentalmusik* 25 (1936): 460–462.

Tuba/Serpent/Ophicleide

2011 Altenburg, Wilhelm. "Der Serpent und seine Umbildung in das chromatische Basshorn und die Ophikleide." *Zeitschrift für Instrumentenbau* 31 (1910–11): 668–671.

Altenburg, Wilhelm. "Die Wagnertuben und ihre Einführung in die Militärmusik." *Zeitschrift für Instrumentenbau* 31 (1910/11): 1105–1107. Subsequent correspondence: 1149–1150 [Max Enders]; 1187–1189 [Gebr. Alexander]; 1230–1231 [Enders]; 1273–1274 [Alexander].

2012 Altenburg, Wilhelm. "Zur Kenntnis des Serpents." *Deutsche Militär-Musiker Zeitung* 31 (1909): 577–578, 590.

2013 Badarak, Mary Lynn. " 'Valse-to-BaB.' " *T.U.B.A. Newsletter* 3, no. 3 (Spring/Summer 1976): 7.

Bahr, Edward R. "Orchestral literature including euphonium or tenor tuba." *T.U.B.A. Journal* 7, no. 2 (Fall 1979): 13–14.

2014 "Dave Baker's *Sonata for Tuba and String Quartet* for Harvey Phillips (second movement)." *Down Beat* 43 (Oct. 7, 1976): 43.

2015 Bate, Philip. "A 'serpent d'eglise': notes on some structural details." *The Galpin Society Journal* 29 (May 1976): 47–50.

2016 Bate, Philip. "Some further notes on serpent technology." *Galpin Society Journal* 32 (May 1979): 124–129.

Beauregard, Cherry N. "The tuba: a description of the five orchestral tubas and guidelines for orchestral tuba writing." Ph.D. diss., University of Rochester, Eastman School of Music, 1970.

2017 Benson, Warren. "Serpentine shadows." *T.U.B.A. Newsletter* 1, no. 2 (Winter 1974): 3.

2018 Bevan, Clifford. "The bass tuba." *Sounding Brass & the Conductor* 8, no. 1 (1979): 23–24.

2019 Bevan, Clifford. "Letters to the editor: Brass [ophicleide]." *The Musical Times* 127 (May 1986): 254–255.

2020 Bevan, Clifford. "On the cimbasso trail." *Sounding Brass & the Conductor* 8, no. 2 (1979): 57–58+.

2021 Bevan, Clifford. *The tuba family*. London: Faber; New York: Scribner's, 1978.

Bobo, Robert P. "Scoring for the Wagner 'tuben' by Richard Wagner, Anton

Bruckner, and Richard Strauss." D.M.A. diss., University of Miami, 1971.

2022 Bobo, Roger. "Tuba: word with a dozen meanings." *Musical Opinion* 99 (May 1976): 366–367.

2023 Bobo, Roger. "Tuba: a word of many meanings." *The Instrumentalist* 15 (Apr. 1961): 65–67.

2024 Bobo, Roger. "Yes or no? Beware! [transcriptions]." *Brass Bulletin—International Brass Chronicle*, no. 21 (1978): 33–35. Also in French and German.

Book, Brian. "Views of Berlioz on the use of the ophicleide and tuba in his orchestral works." *T.U.B.A. Journal* 10, no. 4 (Spring 1983): 10–19.

2025 Boulton, John. "Know your orchestra: The tuba." *Hallé* (Sept. 1950): 14–17.

2026 Bowers, R. E. "Summer heat and the tuba—reply to G. Fry." *Saturday Review of Literature* 24 (Aug. 9, 1941): 9.

2027 Brandon, S. P. "The French tuba." *Woodwind World—Brass and Percussion* 15, no. 5 (1976): 38.

Brandon, Stephen Paul. "The tuba: its use in selected orchestral compositions of Stravinsky, Prokofiev, and Shostakovich." *Dissertation Abstracts* 35 (Sept. 1974): 1684A-1685A.

2028 Brandon, Stephen Paul. "The tuba: its use in selected orchestral compositions of Stravinsky, Prokofiev, and Shostakovich." D.M.A. diss., Catholic University of America, 1974.

2029 "Brass tuba directory." *Sounding Brass & the Conductor* 5, no. 3 (1976): 88–89.

2030 Brousse, Joseph. "Le tuba." In *Encyclopédie de la musique et dictionnaire du Conservatoire*. 2. ptie, vol. 3 (1927). Paris: Delagrave, 1913–1931.

2031 Brown, Leon F. "Materials for Tuba." *The Instrumentalist* 10 (Nov. 1955): 37–40.

Brüchle, Bernhard. "Eine Tuba der Superlative, von historischer Bedeutung. . . . " *Brass Bulletin—International Brass Chronicle*, no. 9 (1974): 41–43. Also in English and French.

Brüchle, Bernhard. "Zumindest noch höhere." *Brass Bulletin—International Brass Chronicle*, no. 7 (1974): 112–113. Also in English and French.

2032 Bryant, Raymond. "The Wagner tubas." *Monthly Musical Record* 67 (1937): 151–153.

Bryant, William. "Research for tuba and euphonium." *T.U.B.A. Journal* 13, no. 2 (Nov. 1985): 25.

2033 Catelinet, Philip. "The truth about the Vaughan Williams *Tuba Concerto*." *T.U.B.A. Journal* 14, no. 2 (Nov. 1986): 30–33.

"Chicago Symphony Orchestra low brass personnel 1891–1979 [list]." *International Trombone Association Newsletter* 7, no. 2 (1980): 14–15.

2034 Chieffi, Brady. "The true (?) roots of the tuba family tree." *T.U.B.A. Journal* 9, no. 3 (Winter 1982): 41.

Cummings, Barton, Brian Bowman, and Larry Campbell. "New materials—tuba and euphonium." *T.U.B.A. Journal* 5, no. 2 (Winter 1978): 34–37.

Cummings, Barton. "A brief summary of new techniques for tuba." *Numus-West*, no. 5 (1974): 62–63.

Cummings, Barton, Sandy Keathley, Gary Buttery, Gary Bird, and Jack Tilbury, eds. "New materials." *T.U.B.A. Journal* 7, no. 1 (Summer 1979): 5–12.

Cummings, Barton. "New material for tuba and euphonium." *T.U.B.A. Newsletter* 3, no. 2 (Winter 1976): 6.

Cummings, Barton. "New materials." *T.U.B.A. Journal* 4, no. 1 (Fall 1976): 19.

Cummings, Barton, ed. "New materials—tuba." *T.U.B.A. Journal* 5, no. 3 (Spring/Summer 1978): 21–23.

2035 Cummings, Barton, ed. "New materials—tuba." *T.U.B.A. Journal* 6, no. 3 (Winter 1979): 9–12.

Cummings, Barton. "New music for tuba." *T.U.B.A. Newsletter* 3, no. 3 (Spring/Summer 1976): 5.

Cummings, Barton. "New techniques for tuba." *The Composer* 6, no. 15 (1974–1975): 28–32.

2036 Cummings, Barton. "Tuba and percussion: are they compatible?" *Woodwind World—Brass and Percussion* 15, no. 6 (1976): 40–41 + .

2037 Cummings, Barton. "Tuba innovations [role in early jazz]." *Woodwind World—Brass and Percussion* 17, no. 5 (1978): 8–11.

2038 Dahlstrom, J. F. "History and development of the tuba." *The School Musician* 41 (Apr. 1970): 60–61.

2039 Davis, Ron. " 'F-E' Suite for tuba (by A. Wildest)." *T.U.B.A. Newsletter* 2, no. 3 (Spring 1975): 8.

2040 de Broekert, Gary. "The tuba; a historical and functional consideration." Master's research project, University of Oregon, 1957.

2041 Dibley, Tom. "The serpents of Beauchamp House." *Journal of the International Trumpet Guild* 12, no. 4 (May 1988): 46–47.

"Directory of music organizations [Tubists Universal Brotherhood Association]." *The Instrumentalist* 38 (Sept. 1983): 110.

2042 Droste, Paul. "Arranging string literature for euphonium." *T.U.B.A. Journal* 5, no. 2 (Winter 1978): 6–8.

2043 Eastep, Michael. "Authentic performance of Verdi." *T.U.B.A. Journal* 4, no. 2 (Winter 1977): 18.

Ehrmann, Alfred von. "Von Posaunisten und Tubabläsern." *Die Musik* 28 (1935–1936): 201–203.

2044 Eliason, Robert E. "Keyed serpent." *T.U.B.A. Journal* 4, no. 1 (Fall 1976): 17–18.

2045 Eliason, Robert E. "A pictorial history of the tuba and its predecessors." *T.U.B.A. Newsletter* 2, no. 1 (Fall 1974): 6. Appears in subsequent issues through Summer, 1976.

2046 Eliason, Robert E. "A pictorial history of the tuba and its predecessors."

T.U.B.A. Journal 4, no. 1 (Fall 1976): 14–15. Appears in subsequent issues through 13, no. 3 (Feb. 1986).

Ernst, Friedrich. "Die Blechblasinstrumentenbauer-Familie Moritz in Berlin [Beitrag zur Geschichte des Berliner Instrumentenbaues]." *Das Musikinstrument* 18, no. 4 (Apr. 1969): 624–626.

2047 Fletcher, John. "Even more tuba talk." *Sounding Brass & the Conductor* 2, no. 4 (1973–1974): 110–112+.

2048 Fletcher, John. "Is the tuba really a solo instrument?" *Sounding Brass & the Conductor* 5, no. 1, 2 (1976): 13+, 54+.

2049 Fletcher, John. "More tuba talk." *Sounding Brass & the Conductor* 2, no. 3 (1973): 78–79+.

2050 Fletcher, John. "Thoughts on the tuba." *Composer [London]*, no. 44 (Summer 1972): 5–12.

2051 Fletcher, John. "The tuba in Britain." *T.U.B.A. Journal* 5, no. 2 (Winter 1978): 22–23.

2052 Fletcher, John. "Tuba talk." *Sounding Brass & the Conductor* 2, no. 2 (1973): 59–61.

2053 Fletcher, John. "Yet further tuba talk." *Sounding Brass & the Conductor* 3, no. 4 (1974–1975): 116–117.

2054 Fry, G. "Review of History of the Tuba, by K. H. Durtmann." *Saturday Review of Literature* 24 (July 26, 1941): 6+.

2055 George, Thom Ritter. "A visit with friends." *T.U.B.A. Journal* 12, no. 1 (Aug. 1984): 26.

2056 Girschner, C. "Bemerkungen über Musik-Instrumenten-Bau." *Berliner allgemeine musikalische Zeitung* 6 (1829): 13–15.

2057 Gottfried, K. H. "Die Ophikleide." *Das Orchester* 26 (Oct. 1978): 759–764.

2058 Grace, Harvey. "A note on the serpent." *The Musical Times* 57 (1916): 500–501.

2059 Gray, S. "The tuba ensemble today [includes list of music]." *The Instrumentalist* 35 (Sept. 1980): 78+.

2060 Greenstone, Paul. "Expanding the tuba repertoire." *T.U.B.A. Journal* 12, no. 3 (Feb. 1985): 9–10.

2061 Griffith, Bobby. "Development of the tuba in the Romantic period." *T.U.B.A. Journal* 11, no. 4 (Spring 1984): 2–5.

2062 Hadfield, J. M. "The serpent." *The Musical Times* 58 (1917): 22, 264.

Halfpenny, Eric. "Lament for *Fusedule Tecil* [serpent]." *The Galpin Society Journal* 17 (Feb. 1964): 113–114.

2063 Halfpenny, Eric. "Playing the serpent." *Symphony* (Apr. 1952): 9.

2064 Heinroth. "Beschreibung und Empfehlung eines von G. Streitwolf in Göttingen verfertigten chromatischen Basshorns." *Allgemeine musikalische Zeitung* 22 (1820): 688–689.

2065 Hellwig, F. "To the editor [serpent]." *The Galpin Society Journal* 23 (Aug. 1970): 173–174.

2066 "Herkunft der Ophikleide." *Musik International-Instrumentenbau-Zeitschrift* 34 (Jan. 1980): 24.

Hilfiger, J. J. "A history of keyed brass instruments." *NACWPI Journal* 34, no. 4 (1986): 4–7.

2067 Hiller, Lejaren. *"Malta for tuba and tape* 1975." *T.U.B.A. Newsletter* 3, no. 3 (Spring/Summer 1976): 7.

2068 Hillsman, W. "Accompagnement instrumental du plain-chant en France depuis la fin du XVIIIe siecle [ophicleide]." *Jeunesse et Orgue*, no. 51 (1982): 11–14.

Hogarth, G. "Musical instruments: the trumpet, trombone, serpent and ophicleide." *Musical World* 4 (1837): 129–133.

2069 Holmes, Brian. "The tuba and Madame Mao: a tale of the Cultural Revolution." *T.U.B.A. Journal* 13, no. 4 (May 1986): 23–26. Illustrated by Justin Novak.

2070 Holmes, William Dewey. "Style and technique in selected works for tuba and electronic prepared tape: a lecture recital, together with three recitals of selected works of V. Persichetti, A. Capuzzi, E. Gregson, W. Ross, N. K. Brown, and others." D.M.A. diss., North Texas State University, 1985.

2071 Homo. "The ophicleide." *Musical World* 16 (1841): 215, 494.

Horvath, Roland. "The Wagnertuba." *Oesterreichische Musikzeitung* 38 (Sept. 1983): 472–473.

2072 Horwood, W. "Musical musings: Grappling with the past [ophicleide]." *Crescendo International* 22 (June-July 1984): 4.

2073 Hunt, E. "Serpent in the midst." *Recorder and Music* 9, no. 2 (1987): 35–36.

Ingalls, David M. "More tuba literature." *The Instrumentalist* 8 (Mar. 1954): 8+.

Jungheinrich, H. K. "Der entfesselte Posaunenbass; 'Cimbasso'—eine Erfindung, über die man spricht." *Das Orchester* 13 (Mar. 1965): 92.

2074 Keathley, Gilbert Harrell. "The tuba ensemble." D.M.A. diss., University of Rochester, Eastman School of Music, 1982.

2075 Keathley, Gilbert Harrell. "The tuba ensemble." *Dissertation Abstracts* 43 (Feb. 1983): 2488A.

2076 Keays, James Harvey. "An investigation into the origins of the Wagner tuba." D.M.A. diss., University of Illinois (Urbana-Champaign), 1977.

2077 Keays, James Harvey. "An investigation into the origins of the Wagner tuba." *Dissertation Abstracts* 38 (Apr. 1978): 5789A.

2078 Kingdon-Ward, Martha. "In defense of the ophicleide." *Monthly Musical Record* 82 (1952): 199–205.

Kirk, Paul Judson, Jr. "The orchestral tuba player: the demands of his literature compared and contrasted with tuba training materials." *Dissertation Abstracts* 37 (Oct. 1976): 1865A.

Klein, Stephen. "How to obtain the music you heard at the Third International Tuba-Euphonium Symposium-Workshop." *T.U.B.A. Journal* 6, no. 3 (Spring 1979): 6–7.

Krush, Jay. "Wingbolt Double-Bell Eight-Valve CC-BB Natural Deluxe Supertuba." *T.U.B.A. Newsletter* 2, no. 1 (Fall 1974): 8.

2079 Kuehn, David Laurance. "The use of the tuba in the operas and music dramas of Richard Wagner." D.M.A. diss., University of Rochester, 1974.

Kunitz, Hans. *Die Instrumentation, Teil 9: Tuba.* Leipzig: Breitkopf & Härtel, 1968.

2080 Laplace, Michel. "Les tubas dans le jazz et dans les musiques populaires." *Brass Bulletin—International Brass Chronicle,* no. 56 (1986): 18–22. Also in English and German.

2081 Laplace, Michel. "Les tubas dans le jazz et dans les musiques populaires." *Brass Bulletin—International Brass Chronicle,* no. 57 (1987): 84–88. Also in English and German.

2082 Leavis, Ralph. "More light on the cimbasso." *The Galpin Society Journal* 34 (Mar. 1981): 151–152.

2083 Lelong, F., and R. Coutet. "Le tuba en France." *Brass Bulletin—International Brass Chronicle,* no. 13 (1976): 26–35. Also in English and German.

2084 Levine, J. A. "Tuba boom: oom-pah-pah fades." *The Christian Science Monitor* 68 (Jan. 29, 1976): 2.

2085 Lewy, Rudolf. "Cimbasso—Verdi's bass." *T.U.B.A. Journal* 15, no. 2 (Nov. 1987): 32–33.

2086 Liagra, D. "Le tuba." *Musique & Radio* 47 (1957): 213–214.

2087 "The London Serpent Trio." *Music and Musicians* 24 (Mar. 1976): 8+.

Lonnman, G. G. "The tuba ensemble: its organization and literature." *Dissertation Abstracts* 35 (June 1975): 7947A.

2088 Lonnman, Gregory George. "The tuba ensemble: its organization and literature." D.M.A. diss., University of Miami, 1974.

2089 Lorenz, J. "Aus dem Leben der Tuba." *Das Orchester* 8 (1960): 1–5.

Maldonado, Luis. "Solo music literature for junior high and high school euphonium and tuba performers." *T.U.B.A. Journal* 14, no. 4 (May 1987): 39–41.

2090 "Manuscripts for tuba." *T.U.B.A. Newsletter* 2, no. 1 (Fall 1974): 5.

2091 Megules, K. I. "Tuba performance—background & history." *Woodwind World—Brass and Percussion* 14, no. 4 (1975): 40+.

2092 Mende, Emily. "Die Tuba, Benjamin der Blechblasinstrumente." *Brass Bulletin—International Brass Chronicle,* no. 17 (1977): 11–14. Also in French and English.

Miller, Robert Melvin. "Abstract: The concerto and related works for low brass: a catalog of compositions from c. 1700 to the present." *Missouri Journal of Research in Music Education* 3, no. 4 (1975): 91.

Miller, Robert Melvin. "The concerto and related works for low brass: a catalogue of compositions from c. 1700 to the present." Ph.D. diss., Washington University, 1974.

Miller, Robert Melvin. "The concerto and related works for low brass: a catalogue of compositions from c. 1700 to the present." *Dissertation Abstracts* 35 (Mar. 1975): 6185A.

2093   Mills, D. L. "The winds of change [obsolete wind instruments]." *The Instrumentalist* 41 (Sept. 1986): 38+.

2094   Monk, C. "The London Serpent Trio." *Woodwind, Brass and Percussion* 20, no. 5 (1981): 16–17.

2095   Monk, C. "The serpent." *Woodwind World—Brass and Percussion* 20, no. 2 (1981): 6–8+.

2096   Morley-Pegge, R. "The 'Anaconda.' " *The Galpin Society Journal* 12 (1959): 53–56.

2097   Morley-Pegge, R. "The evolution of the large-bore bass mouthpiece instrument." *Musical Progress & Mail* (Mar.–July 1940): n.p.

        Morris, R. Winston. "A basic repertoire and studies for the serious tubist." *The Instrumentalist* 27 (Feb. 1973): 33–34.

2098   Morris, R. Winston. "Music for multiple tubas." *The Instrumentalist* 24 (Apr. 1970): 57–58.

2099   Morris, R. Winston. "New literature for tuba." *The Instrumentalist* 38 (Apr. 1984): 48+.

        Morris, R. Winston. "New materials—euphonium-tuba." *T.U.B.A. Newsletter* 1, no. 2 (Winter 1974): 10.

        Morris, R. Winston. "New materials—euphonium-tuba." *T.U.B.A. Newsletter* 1, no. 3 (Spring 1974): 6–7.

        Morris, R. Winston. "New materials—euphonium-tuba." *T.U.B.A. Newsletter* 2, no. 1 (Fall 1974): 4.

2100   Morris, R. Winston. "New solos and studies for tuba." *The Instrumentalist* 32 (Feb. 1978): 61.

2101   Morris, R. Winston. "Tuba [recent publications]." *The Instrumentalist* 36 (Dec. 1981): 68–70.

2102   Morris, R. Winston. "The tuba family." *The Instrumentalist* 27 (Feb. 1973): 33.

2103   Morris, R. Winston. *Tuba music guide.* Evanston, IL: Instrumentalist, 1973.

2104   Morris, R. Winston. "Tuba solos and studies." *The Instrumentalist* 33 (Jan. 1979): 80.

        Mortimer, Alex. "The bigger brasses—euphoniums and basses." In *Brass Today.* Edited by Frank Wright, 49–52. London: Besson, 1957.

2105   "Music for tuba." *Sounding Brass & the Conductor* 8, no. 4 (1979): 153–154.

2106   Nelson, Mark. "The real date of the Hindemith Tuba Sonata." *T.U.B.A. Journal* 9, no. 4 (Spring 1982): 18.

2107   Nelson, Mark E. "The history and development of the serpent." *T.U.B.A. Journal* 10, no. 1 (Summer 1982): 10–14.

2108   "1920 tuba ensemble." *T.U.B.A. Newsletter* 1, no. 2 (Winter 1974): 6.

2109   Nowicke, C. Elizabeth. "A pictorial history of the tuba and its sordid past." *T.U.B.A. Newsletter* 3, no. 2 (Winter 1976): 12–13.

2110   "One step for intonation; one giant step for the serpent." *Journal of the International Trumpet Guild* 11, no. 2 (1986): 9.

2111   "Die Ophicleide." *Caecilia* 9 (1828): 130.

2112   "Ophicleide in Australien." *Instrumentenbau Musik International* 30, no. 6

(1976): 456. Also in English.

2113   "Overshoulder tuba." *T.U.B.A. Newsletter* 2, no. 1 (Fall 1974): 7.

2114   P., I. "On the serpent, bass-horn and trombone." *Harmonicon* (1834): 234.

Pacey, Robert. "An unusual serpent." *The Galpin Society Journal* 33 (Mar. 1980): 132–133.

2115   Page, C. "Early 15th-century instruments in Jean de Gerson's *Tractatus de Canticis* [includes text in Latin with translation]." *Early Music* 6, no. 3 (1978): 339–349.

Perantoni, Daniel. "Contemporary systems and trends for the tuba." *The Instrumentalist* 27 (Feb. 1973): 24–27.

"Performance tasks encountered in selected twentieth-century band excerpts for tuba: their identification, categorization, and analysis." *Dissertation Abstracts* 42 (1981): 441A.

2116   Phillips, Harvey. "Tuba Recital Series." *T.U.B.A. Newsletter* 3, no. 2 (Winter 1976): 1.

2117   Pirie, J. "Arranging: general observations." *Canadian Musician* 4, no. 5 (1982): 67.

2118   Poncelet-Lecocq, P. "Du basso profondo." *L'Echo musical* 1, no. 7 (15 Nov. 1869).

Poole, H. E., and others. "A catalogue of musical instruments offered for sale in 1839 by D'Almaine & Co., 20 Soho Square." *The Galpin Society Journal* 35 (1982): 2–36.

2119   Popiel, P. "The solo tuba and Walter Hartley." *The Instrumentalist* 24 (1970): 63–68.

Popiel, P. J. "The tuba and transposition." *The School Musician* 38 (Aug.-Sept. 1966): 88–89.

Randolph, David M. "Avant-garde effects for tuba—music or noise?" *T.U.B.A. Journal* 8, no. 3 (Winter 1981): 19–23.

2120   Randolph, David M. "A tubist's introduction to the avant-garde." *NACWPI Journal* 28, no. 2 (1980–81): 4–11.

Rasmussen, Mary. "Building a repertoire for the tuba student." *The Instrumentalist* 8 (Jan. 1954): 36–37.

2121   Reed, David F. "Vaughan Williams' *Tuba Concerto*—a retrospective look upon its 25th anniversary." *T.U.B.A. Journal* 8, no. 1 (Summer 1980): 13–14.

Reimer, Mark U. "Brass choir: a new challenge for the tubist." *T.U.B.A. Journal* 11, no. 4 (Spring 1984): 9–10.

2122   "Ein Riesen-Blasinstrument." *Brass Bulletin—International Brass Chronicle*, no. 38 (1982): 4 News Suppl. Also in French and English.

2123   Ross, Walter. "Multiple tuba parts for the orchestra." *T.U.B.A. Newsletter* 2, no. 1 (Fall 1974): 9.

2124   Rowe, Clement E. "The tuba." *Etude* 52 (1934): 405 + .

2125   Rozen, Jay. "The Virgil Thomson commission." *T.U.B.A. Journal* 13, no. 2 (Nov. 1985): 17.

2126   Rudoff, H. "Informal history of the tuba." *Music Journal* 28 (May 1970): 56.

2127 Saltzman, Joe. "How Tubby was born." *T.U.B.A. Journal* 9, no. 4 (Spring 1982): 2–3.

Sander, Rudolf. " 'Ein neues Kornett' und andere Verbesserungs-Bestrebungen im Blechblas-Instrumentenbaue." *Zeitschrift für Instrumentenbau* 23 (1903): 489–471.

2128 Schlesinger, Kathleen. "Bombardon." In *Encyclopaedia Britannica*. 11th ed. New York, 1910–11.

2129 Schlesinger, Kathleen. "Ophicleide." In *Encyclopaedia Britannica*. 11th ed. New York, 1910–11.

2130 Schmidt, J. B. "Ueber die chromatische Bass-Tuba und das neu erfundene Holz-Bass-Blas-Instrument, genannt Bathyphon." *Allgemeine musikalische Zeitung* 42 (1840): 1041–1042.

2131 Schuller, Gunther. "An open letter to composers." *The Instrumentalist* 27 (Feb. 1973): 38.

Schultz, P. M. " 'Praise the Lord with the sound of trumpet' and trombone and horn and tuba." *The School Musician* 44 (Dec. 1972): 48–49.

2132 Schultz, Russ Allan. "The serpent: its characteristics, performance problems, and literature: a lecture recital, together with three recitals of selected works of Stevens, Frescobaldi, Spillman, Wilder, Riter-George, Russell, and others." D.M.A. diss., North Texas State University, 1978.

2133 Schulz, Charles A. "Ancestors of the tuba." *T.U.B.A. Journal* 9, no. 2 (Fall 1981): 3–7.

2134 Schulz, Charles A. "Ancestors of the tuba, Part II." *T.U.B.A. Journal* 9, no. 3 (Winter 1982): 10–12.

2135 Schulz, Charles August. "Two European traditions of tuba playing as evidenced in the solo tuba compositions of Ralph Vaughan Williams and Paul Hindemith, a lecture recital, together with three recitals of selected works of W. Ross, R. Beasley, A. Russell, V. Persichetti, W. S. Hartley, N. K. Brown, J. S. Bach, and others." D.M.A. diss., North Texas State University, 1980.

2136 Schweizer, G. "Ein neues Instrument [Basstuba]." *Musica* 19, no. 3 (1965): 182.

2137 Self, James M. "Reclaiming our heritage." *T.U.B.A. Journal* 5, no. 3 (Spring/Summer 1978): 12–14.

Siener, M. "Thoughts about the tuba." *The School Musician* 38 (Feb. 1967): 44–46 + .

2138 Skowronnek, K. "100 Jahre Basstuba." *Die Musik* 27 (1935): 515–516.

Smith, Claude B. "1936 Bill Bell interview." *T.U.B.A. Newsletter* 1, no. 3 (Spring 1974): 9.

Smith, J. L. "The use of the tuba in the symphonic poems of Richard Strauss." *Dissertation Abstracts* 40 (Aug. 1979): 534A-535A.

2139 Smith, John Lee, Jr. "The use of the tuba in the symphonic poems of Richard Strauss." D.M.A. diss., University of Missouri (Kansas City), 1979.

Sprung, D. "Wagner and the horn." *San Francisco Opera Magazine* (Apr. 1985): 53–54.

2140 Starmer, W. W. "The serpent." *The Musical Times* 57 (1916): 549–550.

2141 Stauffer, Donald W. "A treatise on the tuba." Master's thesis, Eastman School of Music, 1942.

2142 Stauffer, Donald W. *A treatise on the tuba.* Rochester, N.Y.: University of Rochester Press, 1961. Microcard.

2143 Stewart, Gary M. "Clean that old York on a Sunday afternoon." *T.U.B.A. Journal* 14, no. 4 (May 1987): 28–30.

2144 Stewart, Gary M., ed. "Tuba history." *T.U.B.A. Journal* 14, no. 1 (Aug. 1986): 40; no. 2 (Nov. 1986): 34; 15, no. 1 (Aug. 1987): 26–27.

2145 Stewart, Gary M., ed. "Tuba history." *T.U.B.A. Journal* 15, no. 1 (Aug. 1987): 26–27.

2146 Stewart, Gary M., ed. "Tuba history." *T.U.B.A. Journal* 15, no. 3 (Feb. 1988): 26–27.

2147 Stoddard, Hope. "The tuba and its players in our bands and orchestras." *International Musician* 48 (Jan. 1950): 20–22.

2148 Swift, R. F. "Extinct instruments [serpent]." *Woodwind World* 12, no. 2 (1973): 11+.

2149 Thrall, R. S. "Reviews: tuba review." *Woodwind World—Brass and Percussion* 19, no. 3 (1980): 35.

2150 Thrall, R. S. "Reviews: tuba solo." *Woodwind World—Brass and Percussion* 19, no. 4 (1980): 28.

2151 Tilbury, Jack. "Annual review of solos and studies: Tuba." *The Instrumentalist* 39 (Feb. 1985): 79–80+.

2152 Torchinsky, Abe. "Tuba trends." *The Instrumentalist* 18 (Apr. 1964): 86–87.

Trichet, P. "Du cornet à bouquin et du serpent." *Brass Bulletin—International Brass Chronicle*, no. 46 (1984): 12–13+. Also in English and German.

2153 Troiano, William. "The New York State School Music Association contest list for tuba solos and tuba ensembles." *T.U.B.A. Journal* 14, no. 2 (Nov. 1986): 20–24.

2154 "Tuba renaissance." *The Instrumentalist* 40 (Dec. 1985): 16–18.

"Tuba und Euphonium heute—Von Willson-Band Instruments, Flums, Schweiz." *Instrumentenbau Musik International* 31, no. 4 (1977): 375.

2155 "Tubas once struck a low note in China." *Variety* 288 (Oct. 19, 1977): 2.

2156 Tucci, Robert. "The tuba in Europe." *Brass Bulletin—International Brass Chronicle*, no. 11 (1975): 67–79. Also in French and German.

2157 Tucci, Robert. "The tuba in Europe." *T.U.B.A. Journal* 4, no. 3 (Spring/ Summer 1977): 2–3.

2158 Vaillant, Joseph. "The evolution of the tuba in France." *T.U.B.A. Journal* 5, no. 3 (Spring/Summer 1978): 17–18.

2159 Varner, J. L. "Anthology of tuba writings." *Brass and Percussion* 1, no. 5 (1973): 13–14.

2160 Vaughan, Rodger. "Fiftieth birthday tuba recital (2–2–82)." *T.U.B.A. Journal* 10, no. 2 (Fall 1982): 13.

2161 Voigt, Alban. "Das Serpent." *Deutsche Instrumentenbau Zeitschrift* 38 (1937): 282.

2162 W. St. "Was wissen Sie von der Tuba? Des Basses Grundgewalt." *Neues Musikblatt* 15, no. 18 (1936): 5.

2163 Wagener, H. "Zur Choralbegleitung im 19./20. Jahrhundert [serpent]." *Kirchenmusikalische Jahrbuch* 55 (1971): 61–62.

2164 "Wagnerian tubens are growing in popularity." *The School Musician* 42 (Nov. 1970): 66.

Webb, J. "19th-century keyed brass." *Music Trades* 127 (Feb. 1986): 83–85.

2165 Weckerlin, J. -B. "Le serpent." In *Dernier musiciana.* Paris: Garnier Frères, 1899.

2166 Weldon, Constance J., and Greg Lonnman. "The evolution of the tuba ensemble." *T.U.B.A. Journal* 7, no. 1 (Summer 1979): 2–3.

Weldon, Constance J. "The tuba ensemble." *The Instrumentalist* 27 (Feb. 1973): 35–36.

2167 Weston, Stephen J. "Improvements to the nine-keyed ophicleide." *The Galpin Society Journal* 36 (Mar. 1983): 109–114.

2168 Weston, Stephen J. "The untimely demise of the ophicleide." *Brass Bulletin—International Brass Chronicle*, no. 43 (1983): 10–17. Also in French and German.

2169 Westrup, J. A. "Sidelights on the serpent." *The Musical Times* 68 (1927): 635–637.

2170 Yarham, E. R. "Serpents in church." *Music Journal* 21 (Jan. 1963): 76+.

Yeo, Douglas. "Tuba players of the Boston Symphony Orchestra, 1913–1987." *T.U.B.A. Journal* 14, no. 4 (May 1987): 14–20.

Yingst, G. L. "A history of the bass and contrabass tuba with an analytical survey of six selected beginning bass and contrabass instruction books." Master's thesis, Northwestern University, 1960.

2171 Young, Jerry A. "Coordinator of Composer Friends report." *T.U.B.A. Journal* 11, no. 1 (Summer 1983): 19.

2172 Young, Jerry Allen. "The tuba in the symphonic works of Anton Bruckner and Gustav Mahler: a performance analysis." Ed.D. diss., University of Illinois (Urbana-Champaign), 1980.

2173 Young, Jerry Allen. "The tuba in the symphonic works of Anton Bruckner and Gustav Mahler: a performance analysis." *Dissertation Abstracts* 41 (May 1981): 4641A.

2174 "Zur Geschichte des Tenorhorns und des Barytons." *Schweizerische Instrumentalmusik* 25 (1936): 460–462.

Ancient, Non-Western, or Unusual Instruments

2175   Adler, C. "The Shofar, its use and origin." *Journal of the American Oriental Society* 14 (1890): 171–175.

2176   Adler, C. "The Shofar, its use and origin." In *Report of the U.S. National Museum*, 1892. Washington: n.p., 1892. Offprint: Washington, 1894.

2177   Ahrens, Christian. "Instrumentale Musikstile an der osttürkischen Schwarzmeerküste; eine vergleichende Untersuchung der Spielpraxis von 'davul-zurna,' 'kemençe,' und 'tulum.' " Ph.D. diss., Freie Universität Berlin, 1970.

2178   Ahrens, Christian. "Volksmusik der Gegenwart als erkenntnisquelle für Musik der Antike." *Die Musikforschung* 29, no. 1 (Jan.-Mar. 1976): 37–45.

2179   "Das Alphornblasen in den Alpen." *Der Volksgesang* (1894).

2180   "Das Antilopenhorn." *Zeitschrift für Instrumentenbau* 16 (1895/96): 974.

2181   Arom, Simkha. "Instruments de musique particuliers à certaines ethnies de la République Centrafricaine." *Journal of the International Folk Music Council* 19 (1967): 104–108.

        Arom, Simkha. "The music of the Banda-Linda horn ensembles: form and structure." *Selected Reports in Ethnomusicology* 5 (1984): 173–193.

2182   "Art du faiseur d'instruments de musique: *Encyclopedie methodique*, Paris, 1795." *Brass Bulletin—International Brass Chronicle*, no. 56 (1986): 15–16. Also in English and German.

2183   "Australian ghost drums, trumpets and poles." *Anthropos* (Fribourg) 48 (1953): fasc. 1–2.

2184   Baily, J. "A description of the naqqarakhana of Herat, Afghanistan." *Asian Music* 11, no. 2 (1980): 1–10.

2185   Balfour, Henry. "Three Bambu trumpets from Northern Territory, South Australia." *Man* 1 (1901).

2186   Barwise, M. M. "The bronze lur." *Bulletin (The Dolmetsch Foundation)*, no. 19 (1972): back cover.

2187   Baumann, Max Peter. "Funktion und Symbol: Zum Paradigma 'Alphorn.' " *Studia instrumentorum musicae popularis* 5 (1977): 27–32.

2188   Becker, Erich. "Von der Herstellung der alten Luren." *Zeitschrift für Instrumentenbau* 56 (1935–36): 268–270.

2189   Behn, Fr. "Die musikwissenschaftliche Bedeutung der Luren von Daberkow." *Praehistorische Zeitschrift* 7 (1915).

2190   Bierl, Albert, and B. v. Pressentin-Rauter. *Die Jagd mit Lockinstrumenten.* Clöthen: Paul Schettlers Erben, 1924.

2191   Bock, F. "Ueber den Gebrauch der Hörner in Altertum." In *Mittelalterliche Kunstdenkmäler Oesterreichs*, by G. Heider, 127. Vol. II (1860).

2192   Bowles, Edmund A. "Eastern influences on the use of trumpets and drums during the Middle Ages." *Annuario musical* 27 (1972): 3–28.

2193   Briard, Jacques. "Instruments musicaux de l'Age du Bronze." *Bulletin de la societe préhistorique français* 66 (1969): 126–127.

2194   Bridge, Joseph C. "Horns." *Journal of the Chester and North Wales Architectural, Archaeological and Historical Society* 11 [new series] (1905): 85–166.

2195   Brockpähler, Renate. " 'Signalhorn,' 'Riete,' 'Adventshorn.' Volkstümliche Blasinstrumente in Westfalen." *Rheinisch-Westfälische Zeitschrift für Volkskunde* 24, nos. 1–4 (1978): 30–77.

2196   Cherbuliez, A. E. "Systematisches und Geschichtliches zur Alphornmelodik." *Schweizerische Musik-Zeitung*, no. 5 (1949).

2197   Choisy, F. "Les instruments prehistoriques scandinaves, les 'Lurs.' " *Le guide musical* (1895): 321.

2198   Christy, Miller. "The harvest horn in Essex." *Essex Review* 32 (Jan. 1923): 1–3.

2199   Closs, A. "Gotisches Rufhorn." *Zeitschrift für Historischen Waffen- und Kostümkunde*, N.F. 3 (1931): 66–94.

2200   Closson, Ernest. "L'Olifant." *La revue musicale belge* 2 (1926): 446–456.

2201   Coles, John M. "Some Irish horns of the late Bronze age." *Journal of the Royal Society of Antiquaries in Ireland* 97, no. 2 (1967): 113–117.

2202   Cuming, H. S. "On phonic horns." In *Journal of the British Archaeological Association* 5 (1850): 119–132.

2203   "Curiosite instrumental; le cor des Alpes." *Instrumentenbau-Zeitschrift* 25 (Nov. 1971): 543.

2204   Dalton, O. M. "The Clephane horn." *Archaeologia* 65 (1914): 213–222.

2205   Devic, Dragoslav. "Hirtentrompeten in Nordostserbien." *Studia Instrumentorum Musicai Popularis* 5 (1977): 76–80.

2206   du Mège. "Mémoire sur quelques châsses ou reliquaires, oliphants. . . ." *Mémoires de la Société archéologique du midi de la France* 3 (1836/37): 305.

2207   Eichenauer, Richard. "Die Luren." *Musik und Volk* 4 (1936–37): 182–187.

2208   Elkan, S. "Alphorn." *Garbe* 13 (1931): 66–94.

2209   Ellis, A. E. "Shells as musical instruments." *Conchologists' Newsletter* 55 (Dec. 1975): 460–461.

2210   Emsheimer, Ernst. "Zur Typologie der schwedischen Holztrompeten." *Studia instrumentorum musicae popularis* 1 (1971): 87–97.

2211   Eppelsheim, Jürgen. "Berlioz' 'Petit Saxhorn Suraigu.' " In *Bericht über den Internationalen Musikwissenschaftlichen Kongress-Bericht Berlin 1974*, 586–591.

       Ewers, Karl. "Zur Frage des Alts im Blasorchester. Die 'Lurette' als Beitrag zur Lösung des Problems." *Die Musik-Woche* 6 (1938): 742.

2212   Fagan, B. M., and J. Kirkman. "An ivory trumpet from Sofala, Mozambique." *Ethnomusicology* 11, no. 3 (1967): 368–374.

2213   Falke, O. V. "Elfenbeinhörner. I. Aegypten und Italien." *Pantheon* 2 (1929): 511–517.

2214   Farmer, Henry G. "The horn of Alexander the Great." *Journal—Royal Asiatic Society* (1926): 500–503.

2215   Fétis, F. J. "Note sur une trompette romaine trouvée récemment aux environs de Bavay." *Bulletin de l'Académie royale de Belgique* 13 (1846).

2216   Finesinger, Sol Baruch. "The shofar." *Hebrew Union College Annual* 8/9 (1931–1932): 193–228.

2217   Fleischhauer, G. "Bucina und Cornu." *Wissenschaftliche Zeitschrift der Martin-Luther-Universität* (1960): 501–506.

Fox, Lilla M. "Instruments of religion and folklore." Chap. 3 in *History of Musical Instruments*. London: Lutterworth, 1969.

2218   Foy, W. "Zur Frage nach der Herkunft einiger alter Jagdhörner aus Elfenbein: Portugal oder Benin?" *Abhandlungen und Berichte der Museen für Tierkunde und Völkerkunde* (Dresden) 9 (1900/01).

2219   Gagne, J. "La trompette marine." *Carnet Musical*, no. 9 (July 1973): 14–16.

2220   Gassmann, Alfred Leonz. *Das Alphorn in den Bergen*. Zurich: Musica Aeterna, 1948.

2221   Gassmann, Alfred Leonz. *Blast mir das Alphorn noch einmal! Was der Alphorner von seinem Naturinstrument wissen muss*. Zurich: Gebr. Hug, 1938.

2222   Geiser, Brigitte. *Das Alphorn in der Schweiz*. Bern: Haupt, 1976.

2223   Geiser, Brigitte. "Das Alphorn in der Schweiz." In *Schweizer Heimatbücher* 177/178. Bern: Haupt, 1978.

2224   Geiser, Brigitte, and Markus Römer. *Das Alphorn in der Schweiz. Katalog zur Ausstellung im Heimatmuseum Grindelwald Sommer 1972*. Grindelwald: Buchdruckerei Grindelwald, 1972.

2225   Geiser, Brigitte. "Volksmusikinstrumente der Schweiz." In *Bericht über den Internationalen Musikwissenschaftlichen Kongress-Bericht Berlin 1974*, 596–599.

2226   Geiser, K. "Ein Alphornbläser aus dem 16. Jahrhundert." *Berner Taschenbuch* (1894): 113.

2227   Gerson-Kiwi, Edith. "Horn und Trompete im Alten Testament—Mythos und Wirklichkeit." *Emsheimer Festschrift* (1974): 57–60.

2228   Gessler, E. A. *Die Harschhörner von Uri*. Historisches Neujahrsblatt (herausgegeben vom Verein für Geschichte von Uri) 33 (1929): 1–24.

2229   Gottschick, Anna Martina. "Das Alphorn." *Hausmusik* 16 (1952): 78–79.

2230   Gourlay, K. A. "Long trumpets of northern Nigeria—in history and today." *African Music* 6, no. 2 (1982): 48–72.

2231   Günther. "Herstellung eines Signalhorn." *Zeitschrift für Instrumentenbau* 55 (1935): 323–324.

2232   Gysi, Fritz. "Herkunft und Verbreitung des Alphorns." *Heimatleben* 28, no. 2 (1955).

2233   Habenicht, G. "Caracteristici stilistice zonale ale semnalelor de bucium." *Revista de Etnografie si Folclor* 12, no. 4 (1967): 261–276.

2234   Habenicht, G. "Musik der rumänischen Hirtentrompeten." *Demos* 9 (1968): 135–136.

2235   Hall, B. "Musical roundabout [alphorn]." *Music Teacher and Piano Student* 41 (Apr. 1962): 179.

2236   Hammerich, A., and C. Elling. "Studien über die altnordischen Lüren im Nationalmuseum zu Kopenhagen." *Zeitschrift für Instrumentenbau* 14

(1893/94): 622–626, 647–649.

2237 Hammerich, A., and C. Elling. "Studien über die altnordischen Lüren im Nationalmuseum zu Kopenhagen." *Vierteljahrsschrift für Musikwissenschaft* 10 (1894): 1–32.

2238 Hammerich, A. *Les lurs de l'âge de bronze, au Musée national de Copenhague.* Copenhagen: Tr. E. Beauvois, 1894.

2239 Haupt, P. "Die Posaunen von Jericho." *Wiener Zeitschrift für die Kunde des Morgenlandes* 23 (1909): 355.

2240 Heim, E. "Das Alphorn." *Neue Alpenpost* (1880).

2241 Heim, E. "Bericht über die Wiedereinfuehrung des Alphorns." *Schweizerische Alpenzeitung* 1 (1883): 229.

2242 Henggeler, Joe. "Ivory trumpets of the Mende." *African Arts* 14, no. 2 (Feb. 1982): 59–63.

2243 Hickman, Hans. "Die kultische Verwendung der altägyptischen Trompete." *Die Welt des Orients* (1950): 351–355.

2244 Hickmann, Hans. *La trompette dans l'Egypte ancienne.* Cairo: Impr. de l'Institute d'archéologie orientale, 1946.

Höfler, Janez. "Der 'Trompette de menestrels' und sein Instrument." *Tijdschrift van de Vereniging voor Nederlandse Musiekgeschiedenis* 29, no. 2 (1979): 92–132.

2245 Holmes, Peter, and J. M. Coles. "Prehistoric brass instruments." *World Archaelolgy* 12, no. 3 (Feb. 1981): 280–286.

2246 Huggler, Rudolf. "Das Alphorn im Berner Oberland." *Heimatleben* 28, no. 2 (1955).

2247 "Instrumentale Kuriosität im Konzertsaal; das Alphorn." *Instrumentenbau-Zeitschrift* 25 (July 1971): 316–317.

2248 Jones, Trevor A. "The 'yiraki' ('didjeridu') in north-east Arnhem Land: techniques and styles." In *The Australian Aboriginal heritage: an introduction through the arts,* edited by R. M. Berndt and E. S. Phillips, 269–274. Sydney: Ure Smith, 1973.

2249 "Jüdische Tempelinstrumente—Schofar und Hazozerah." *Zeitschrift für Instrumentenbau* 53 (1932–1933): 194–195.

Kampen, Paul. "The Ripon horn." *The Horn Call* 17, no. 1 (Oct. 1986): 38–39.

2250 Kandler, Georg. " 'Lurette'—ein neuer Alt-/Blechblasinstrument." *Die Musik-Woche* 6 (1938): 742–743.

2251 Kaupert, W. "Das Alphorn, ein Hirteninstrument." *Musica* 23, no. 2 (1969): 157–158.

2252 Kendrick, T. D. "The horn of Ulph." *Antiquity* 11 (1937): 278–282.

2253 Kirby, Percival R. "Ancient Egyptian trumpets." In *Seventh Music Book,* 250–255. London: Hinrichsen, 1952.

2254 Klier, Karl M. "Etwas vom Alphorn." *Der Bergsteiger* 8 (1937): 526–533. Reprint. Wien: A. Holzhausens Nachf., 1937.

2255 Kohlbach, Berthold. "Das Widderhorn [Schofar]." *Beiträge zur jüdischen Volkskunde* 26 (1916): 113–128.

2256   Komorzynski, E. R. v. "Trompete als Signalinstrumente im altägyptischen Heer." *Archiv für ägypt. Archaeologie* 1 (1938): 155–197.

2257   Kühnel, E. "Die sarazenischen Olifanthörner." *Jahrbuch der Berliner Museen* 1 (1959): 33–50.

2258   Langeron, O. "La trompette d'argent." *Mémoires de la Commission des antiquitiés du départment de la Côte d'or* 14 (1901–05).

Leipp, Emile, and Lucien Thevet. "Le cor." *Bulletin du Groupe d'acoustique musicale* 41 (May 1969): 1–23.

2259   Lipp, Franz. "Die 'Drilutn,' das Alphorn des Böhmerwaldes." In *Jahrbuch des Oesterreichischen Volksliedwerkes*, 20 (1971). Edited by Leopold Nowak and Leopold Schmidt. Vienna: Bundesministerium für Unterricht, 1971.

2260   Loomis, R. S., and J. St. Lindsay. "The magic horn and cup in Celtic and grail tradition." *Romanische Forschungen* 45 (1931): 66–94.

2261   "Die Luren—altgermanische Musikinstrumente." *Deutsche Musiker-Zeitung* 64 (1933): 417.

2262   Macak, Ivan. "Ueber die Möglichkeiten zur Erforschung der Geschichte der Hirtenmusikinstrumente in der Slowakei." *Studia Instrumentorum Musicae Popularis* 5 (1977): 71–75.

2263   Maier, J. E. *Bizarre brass of four millenniums; or, Arcane artifacts and indigenous instruments.* Humorous. Old Greenwich, CT: Spratt Music, 1976.

2264   Mang, Walter. "Die 'alteste' Trompete der Welt." *Schweizerische Instrumentalmusik* 27 (1938): 397.

2265   Markl, Jaroslav. "Kesselmundstückinstrumente und das Hirtenblasen in Böhmen." *Emsheimer Festschrift* (1974): 123–130.

Mathez, Jean-Pierre. "Les cuivres a Rome [economic aspects]." *Brass Bulletin—International Brass Chronicle*, no. 43 (1983): 18–22 + . Also in English and German.

Mattison, D. "Sweet old tunes [Indian brass bands of British Columbia]." *Brass International* 10, no. 3 (1982): 14–15 + .

Matzke, H. "Von den alten Luren—Betrachtungen anlässlich des Neubaus von 'Ventilluren.' " *Zeitschrift für Instrumentenbau* 56 (1935–36): 150–151.

2266   Mbati-Katana, S. "Similarities of musical phenomena over a large part of the African continent as evidenced by the 'irambo' and 'empango' side-blown trumpet styles and drum rhythms." *African Urban Notes* 5, no. 4 (Winter 1970): 25–41.

2267   Meucci, R. "Riflessioni di archeologia musicale: gli strumenti militari romani e il lituus." *Rivista Italiana di Musicologia* 19, no. 3 (1985): 383–394.

2268   Meucelin-Roeser, M. "Der Einsiedler 'Cantus Paschalis' und die Alphornweise: eine Richtigstellung." *Archiv für Musikwissenschaft* 29, no. 3 (1972): 209–212.

2269   Meyling, A. C. "Bazuinen over Alpen en Lage Landen." *Töristen Kampiön*, no. 10 (1954).

2270   Montagu, Jeremy. "The conch in prehistory: pottery, stone and natural." *World Archaeology* 12, no. 3 (Feb. 1981): 273–279.

2271   Montagu, Jeremy. "One of Tutankhamon's trumpets." *The Galpin Society*

Journal 29 (May 1976): 115–117.

2272 Moser, H. J. *Die Luren von Daberkow*. Berlin: n.p., 1939. (Kleine Kostbarkeiten.)

2273 Moyle, Alice. "The Australian 'didjeridu': a late musical intrusion." *World Archaeology* 12, no. 3 (Feb. 1981): 321–331.

2274 "Music of antiquity [bronze horns or Lurar]." *Canon* 12 (Sept. 1958): 55.

2275 Nef, Karl. "Die Verbreitung des Alphorns." *Schweizerische Musikzeitung* 47 (1907): 248, 272.

2276 "Ein neues Blasinstrument." *Zeitschrift für Blasinstrument* 16 (1895/96): 554, 565.

2277 Newman, A. K. "On the musical notes and other features of the long Maori trumpet." *Transactions and Proceedings of the New Zealand Institute* 38 (new series vol. 21) (1905).

2278 O'Callaghan, Donal. "A Brudevaelte lur re-examined: the evidence for ritual music in the Scandinavian late Bronze Age." *The Galpin Society Journal* 36 (Mar. 1983): 104–108.

2279 Oldeberg, Andreas. "Vorgeschichtliche Blashörner." *Musica* (Apr. 1952): 149–152.

2280 Olhausen. "Im Norden gefundene vergeschichtliche Trompeten." *Zeitschrift für Ethnologie* 23 (1891): 847–861.

2281 Olshausen, O. "Im Norden gefundene vorgeschichtliche Trompeten." *Zeitschrift für Ethnologie* 23 (1891): 847–861; *Verhandlungen der Berliner anthropolog. Gesellschaft* (1891): 847.

2282 "On the Ranz des vaches." *Harmonicon* 2 (1824): 37–39, 58–59.

2283 Pagenkopf, W. "Instrumente der Kriegsmusik in Altertum. Lituus, Cornu, Bucina und Tuba." *Deutsche Militär-Musiker Zeitung* 63 (1941) or 62 (1940): 28.

2284 Panke, W. "Von Berg-Jazz und Grubenklang-Orchester: Jazzer im deutschsprachigen Raum besinnen sich auf Originäres." *Neue Musikzeitung* 34 (June-July 1985): 14.

2285 Pfleger, A. "Das Schweizer Alphorn in den Hochvogesen." *Schweizer Archiv für Volkskunde* 49 (1953): 34–50.

2286 Phene, J. S. "On the . . . Keltic horn." *Journal of the British Archaeological Association* 33 (1877): 395–400.

2287 Piggott, S. "The carnyx in early iron age Britain." *The Antiquaries Journal* 39, nos. 1–2 (1959).

2288 Pilipczuk, A. *Elfenbeinhörner im sakralen Königtum Schwarzafrikas*. Bonn: Verlag für systematische Musikwissenschaften, 1985.

2289 Prague, H. "Le Schophar; esquisse critique et historique." *Archives Israelites* (1883). Offprint. Paris: n.p., 1883.

2290 Regner, Hermann. "Ein altes instrument wird neu entdeckt." *Pro musica*, no. 4 (1958): 101 +.

2291 Righini, Pietro. "Dalle trombe egizie per l'Aida alle trombe di Tut-Ankh-Amon." *Nuova Revista Musicale Italiana* 11, no. 4 (Oct.-Dec. 1977): 591–605.

2292   Rindlisbacher, O. "Alphorn—unique Swiss instrument." *Etude* 47 (1929): 108.

2293   Ringbom, Lars Ivar. "Gallenhushornens Bilder." In *Acta academise aboensis humaniora Abo*, vol.18, 258–304. Abo: Abo akademi, 1949.

2294   Rusch, R. "Haller Heerhorn." *Tiroler Heimatblätter* 12 (1934): 186.

2295   "Die Russische Hornmusik." *Zeitschrift für Instrumentenbau* 52 (1931–1932): 367.

2296   Sachs, Curt. "Lituus und Carnyx." In *Festschrift zum 90. Geburtstag . . . Rochus Freiherrn von Liliencron*, 241–246. Leipzig: Breitkopf & Härtel, 1910.

2297   Schlesinger, Kathleen. "Buccina." In *Encyclopaedia Britannica*. 11th ed. New York, 1910–11.

2298   Schmidt, C. E. "Interlocking techniques in Kpelle music." *Selected Reports in Ethnomusicology* 5 (1984): 194–216.

2299   Schmidt, H. "Die Luren von Daberkow." *Praehistorische Zeitschrift* 7 (1915).

2300   Schweeger-Exeli, Anne Marie. "Ein Elfenbeinblashorn aus Benin." *Archiv für Völkerkunde* 13 (1958): 227–235.

2301   "Seances de la Societe [alphorn]." *Revue de Musicologie* 59, no. 2 (1973): 320.

        Seidel, Hans. "Horn und Trompete im alten Israel unter Berücksichtigung der 'Kriegsrolle' von Qumran." *Wissenschaftliche Zeitschrift der Universität Leipzig* 4 (1956/57): 5.

2302   Sinor, Denis. "La Mort de Batu et les trompettes mues par le vent chez Herberstein." *Journal Asiatique* 233 (1941–42): 201–208. [Concerns a central Asiatic legend of huge wind-blown trumpets.]

        Smimov, B. "The Russian folk cornett, or rozhok." *The Galpin Society Journal* 14 (Mar. 1961): 76–78.

2303   Teichmann, Eduard. "Zur Deutung der Worte 'dein eyn' auf dem Tragbande des sogenannten Karlshornes." *Aachener Geschichtsverein Zeitschrift* 25 (1903): 1–27.

2304   Tomescu, Vasile. "Musica Daco-Romana. Buccina." *Muzica* 30 (Mar. 1980): 37–44.

2305   Tomescu, Vasile. "Musica Daco-Romana. Cornul." *Muzica* 30 (Apr. 1980): 39–46.

2306   Turrentine, Edgar M. "The history of brass instruments in ancient times: a bibliographic essay." *NACWPI Journal* 21, no. 3 (Spring 1973): 29–30.

        Turrentine, Edgar M. "Notes on the ancient Olympic trumpet blowing contests." *The Instrumentalist* 23 (Apr. 1969): 42–43.

2307   V., E. "Le cor des alpes." *La Belgique musicale* 6, no. 3 (22 May 1845): 10–11.

2308   Völckers, J. "Alphorn Trio für Touristikwerbung." *Instrumentenbau-Zeitung* 28, no. 8 (1974): 601.

2309   Voigt, Alban. "Das Alphorn." *Deutsche Instrumentenbau Zeitschrift* 35 (1934): 99–100.

2310   Voigt, Alban. "Das Alphorn." *Zeitschrift für Instrumentenbau* 60 (1940): 186–187.

2311 Voigt, Alban. "Die alt-agyptische Trompete." *Deutsche Instrumentenbau Zeitschrift* 34 (1933): 70.

2312 Voigt, Alban. "Altrömische Blasinstrumente. Der Lituus." *Zeitschrift für Instrumentenbau* 52 (1931–1932): 152–153.

2313 Voigt, Alban. "Altrömische Blasinstrumente. Die Tuba." *Zeitschrift für Instrumentenbau* 52 (1931–1932): 278.

2314 Voigt, Alban. "Der Carnyx." *Deutsche Instrumentenbau Zeitschrift* 34 (1933): 254.

2315 Voigt, Alban. "Der Carnyx." *Deutsche Instrumentenbau Zeitschrift* 38 (1937): 90.

2316 Voigt, Alban. "Der Carnyx—ein altrömisches Instrument." *Deutsche Instrumentenbau Zeitschrift* 39 (1938): 20.

2317 Voigt, Alban. "Ein letztes Wort über den Lituus." *Deutsche Instrumentenbau Zeitschrift* 38 (1937): 260.

2318 Voigt, Alban. "Der Lituus." *Deutsche Instrumentenbau Zeitschrift* 38 (1937): 60.

2319 Voigt, Alban. "Der Lur." *Deutsche Instrumentenbau Zeitschrift* 33 (1932): 385.

2320 Voigt, Alban. "Die Signalinstrumente des römischen Heeres und der Lituus." *Deutsche Instrumentenbau Zeitschrift* 34 (1933): 347.

2321 Voigt, Alban. "What was the Roman lituus?" *Discovery* 16 (Dec. 1935): 367.

2322 Vorreiter, Leopold. "Die Musikinstrumente Europas im Altertum—welche Erkenntnisse vermitteln sie der Gegenwart." *Archiv für Musikorganologie* 1, no. 1 (Dec. 1976): 34–48.

Walser, Gerold. "Römische und gallische Militärmusik." *Geering Festschrift* (1973): 231–239.

2323 Weckerlin, J. -B. "Les lurs." In *Dernier musiciana*. Paris: Garnier Frères, 1899.

2324 Widmer, M. "Swiss alphorn in legend and in fact." *School Arts* 43 (1944): 218, 227–228.

2325 Wind, Tage. "Die ältesten brauchbaren Musikinstrumente der Welt [lur]." *Volkslied und Hausmusik* 3 (1936): 122–125.

2326 Winternitz, Emanuel. "Strange musical instruments in the Madrid notebooks of Leonardo da Vinci." *Metropolitan Museum Journal* 2 (1969): 115–126.

2327 Wulstan, D. "The sounding of the shofar." *The Galpin Society Journal* 26 (May 1973): 29–46.

2328 Zagiba, Franz. "Von der Keltischen Carnyx I zum Alphorn." *Wiora Festschrift* (1970): 609–612.

2329 Zak, Sabine. *Studien zur Musik als "Ehr und Zier" im mittelalterlichen Reich. Music im höfischen Leben, Recht und Zeremoniell.* Neuss: Peter Päffigen, 1978.

2330 Zemp, Hugo. "Trompes sénoufo." *Annales de l'Universite d'Abidjan* (1969): 25–50.

2331 Zerries, Otto. "Drei alte, figürlich verzierte Holztrompeten aus Brasilien in den Museen zu Kopenhagen, Leiden und Oxford." *Ethnologische Zeitung* 1 (1977): 77–89.

Ensembles

2332 "A propos de l'orchestre de cuivre." *Schweizerische Instrumentalmusik* 30 (1941): 94.

2333 Adkins, Hector Ernest. *Treatise on the military band.* 2d revised ed. London; New York: Boosey, 1958.
"American composer listing, woodwinds and brass solo and ensemble." *The Triangle of Mu Phi Alpha* 66, no. 2 (1972): 19–25.

2334 Arnold, M. "Annual review of solos and studies: brass ensemble music." *The Instrumentalist* 39 (May 1985): 59–62.

2335 Arom, Simkha. "The music of the Banda-Linda horn ensembles: form and structure." *Selected Reports in Ethnomusicology* 5 (1984): 173–193.

2336 Arwood, Jeff, ed. "United States Military Bands." *T.U.B.A. Journal* 14, no. 3 (Feb. 1987): 20–71.

2337 Ayres, T. A. "The woodwind quintet." *The Instrumentalist* 20 (Feb. 1966): 61–62.

2338 Back, Jean. "Vergleichende Uebersicht über die instrumentale Zusammensetzung grosser europäischer Harmonie- und Blechmusikkorps." *Schweizerische Instrumentalmusik* 26 (1937): 340–341, 366–367.

2339 Baer, Douglas Milton. "The brass trio: a comparative analysis of works published from 1924 to 1970." Ph.D. diss., Florida State University, 1970.

2340 Baer, Douglas Milton. "The brass trio: a comparative analysis of works published from 1924 to 1970." *Dissertation Abstracts* 31 (Mar. 1971): 4812A.

2341 Bahr, Edward R. "The brass trio repertoire." *Woodwind, Brass and Percussion* 24, no. 2 (1985): 15–16.
Bauer. "Neue Turmmusik." *Schlesisches Blatt für evangelische Kirchenmusik* 61, no. 7/8 (n.d.).

2342 Becker, William R. "Transcription of early instrumental music for brass ensemble, a style analysis and suggestions for modern use." Master's thesis, Iowa State Teachers College, 1954.

2343 Bedford, F. "A survey of twentieth century music for brass and harpsichord [includes list]." *Woodwind World—Brass and Percussion* 17, no. 1 (1978): 10–12.

2344 Benshoof, James D. "Brass ensemble music." *NACWPI Journal* 27, no. 2 (Nov. 1978): 61–62.

2345 Benshoof, James D. "Contemporary music for brass ensemble." *NACWPI Journal* 27, no. 1 (Sept. 1978): 46–49.

2346 Bird, G. J. "Brass ensemble; guidelines to achievement." *Brass and Percus-*

sion 1, no. 4 (1973): 22+.

2347 Block, Nancy Cochran. "Ensemble etiquette." *The Horn Call* 16, no. 2 (Apr. 1986): 51–53.

2348 Bloomquist, K. "The brass choir, what and why?" *The Instrumentalist* 18 (Feb. 1964): 73–75.

2349 Blümel, C. "Leserbriefe [Response to 'Neuausgaben originaler Ensemble-musik des 17. Jahrhunderts für Blechbläser,' by K. Winkler]." *Brass Bulletin—International Brass Chronicle*, no. 55 (1986): 109+. Also in English and French.

Boeringer, J., ed. "Instruments like those of the Twenty-Sixth Regimental Band: a catalogue of the Mark Allen Elrod Collection." *The Moravian Music Foundation Bulletin* 26, no. 3 (1981): 55–57.

2350 Boyd, Edward. "Brass in the concert band." *Southwestern Brass Journal* 1 (Spring, 1957): 37–39.

2351 Braathen, Sverre O. *Here comes the circus! The rise and fall of the circus band.* Evanston, Ill.: Instrumentalist, 1958.

"Brass trios in the ITA collection." *Journal of the International Trombone Association* 14, no. 1 (1986): 42.

Briegleb, Arthur, and Wendell Hoss, comps. "Music for ensembles." *The Horn Call* 2, no. 2 (May 1972): 11–18.

2352 Brother, Arthur. "May we present our Canadian bugle and drum band." *The School Musician* 25 (Sept. 1953): 20–21.

2353 Brown, Leon F. "The brass choir." *The Instrumentalist* 11 (Feb. 1957): 22–23.

Carlson, C. A., and E. R. Currier. "Music for choir and brass ensemble." *Music Journal* 18 (Nov.-Dec. 1960): 10–11+.

Clappé, Arthur A. *The wind-band and its instruments: their history, construction, acoustics, technique, and combination.* Reprint of the 1911 edition (New York: H. Holt). Portland, Me.: Longwood, 1976.

Clappé, Arthur A. *The wind-band and its instruments; their history, construction, acoustics, technique and combination.* New York: H. Holt and Co., 1911.

2354 Crouch, Rebekah Ellen. "The contributions of Adolphe Sax to the wind band." Ph.D. diss., Florida State University, 1968.

Cummings, Barton. "Contemporary Hungarian brass chamber music." *Woodwind World—Brass and Percussion* 19, no. 2 (1980): 11.

2355 Currier, E. R. "The history of brass ensemble literature." Ed.D. diss., Columbia University, 1959.

Day, D. K. "A comprehensive bibliography of music for brass quintet." *The Instrumentalist* 28 (Nov. 1973): 64–68; 28 (Dec. 1973): 60–64+.

2356 Day, D. K. "A comprehensive bibliography of music for brass quintet [Addendum]." *The Instrumentalist* 29 (Oct. 1974): 59.

2357 Decker, C. "Popular and folk music of America for brass [includes list of music]." *Woodwind World—Brass and Percussion* 16, no. 6 (1977): 22+.

Decker, R. G. *Music for three brasses; a bibliography of music for three hetero-*

geneous brass instruments alone and in chamber ensembles. Oneonta, NY: Swift-Dorr, 1976.

2358 Douglas, Darrell R. "Brass music in the church." *American Organist* 14 (May 1980): 34–35.

2359 Dunnick, D. Kim. "Selected literature for trumpet ensemble." *The Instrumentalist* 34 (Mar. 1980): 44+.

2360 Eglin, A. "Kirchenchor und Bläsergruppe." *Der Evangelische Kirchenchor* 72, no. 3 (1967): 45–51.

2361 Ehmann, Wilhelm, ed. *Der Bläserchor-Besinnung und Aufgabe.* Kassel: Bärenreiter, 1969.

2362 Ehmann, Wilhelm. "Dienst und Klang—Der Kirchenmusiker und der Blechbläserchor." *Der Kirchenmusiker* 27, no. 4 (1976): 123–124.

Elliot, J. H. "The all-brass ensemble." *Music & Letters* 12 (1931): 30–34.

Elliot, J. H. "Brass music in development." *Monthly Musical Record* 67 (1937): 34–35.

2363 Elliot, J. H. "The evolution of music for brass." *The Musical Times* 77 (1936): 885–887.

Elliot, J. H. "Music for brass." *Monthly Musical Record* 62 (1932): 105–106.

Erdmann, Alfred. "Neue und alte Werke für Blasinstrumente und Bläserkammermusik." *Die Musik-Woche* 4, no. 42 (1936): 2–5.

2364 Evans, Eliot D. "All you ever wanted to know about the Washington D. C. military bands." *T.U.B.A. Journal* 8, no. 1 (Summer 1980): 2–12.

2365 Faulkner, Maurice. "The brass choir." *Music Educators Journal* 25 (Dec. 1938): 70–71.

2366 Fitzgerald, Bernard. "The small brass ensemble." *The Instrumentalist* 6 (Oct. 1951): 22–25.

Fleck, Hattie C. "The oldest American brass band [East Barrington, N. H.]." *Etude* 5 (1937): 304.

2367 Fosse, John B. "The transcription of Baroque music for the use of school brass ensembles." Master's thesis, University of Southern California, 1955.

Frayling-Kelly, F. "Brass band and concert band review." *Musical Opinion* 105 (Dec. 1981): 95.

Freedman, R. S. "One-note musicians [horn bands]." *The Instrumentalist* 36 (Nov. 1981): 120–121.

Friedman, S. A. "Effective scoring for trumpet ensemble." *International Trumpet Guild Newsletter* 4, no. 2 (1978): 6–10.

2368 Fromme, Arnold. "The compositions for three choirs in the *Canzoni et Sonate* (Venice, 1615) of Giovanni Gabrieli: a critical and performing edition." Ph.D. diss., New York University, 1980.

2369 Fromme, Arnold. "New interest in the brass quintet." *Music Journal* 23 (Jan. 1965): 50+.

2370 Garlock, F. "Brass instruments in church???" *The School Musician* 36 (Jan. 1965): 70–71.

2371 Getchell, Robert W. "The modern brass choir." Master's thesis, Eastman

School of Music, 1941.

Gifford, Robert Marvin, Jr. "The music and performance practices of the medieval wind band." *Journal of Band Research* 10, no. 2 (Spring 1974): 25–32.

2372   Glover, Ernest N. "The brass ensemble." *Symphony* 6 (Jan. 1953): 11–12.

2373   Glover, Ernest N. "The Thor Johnson brass composition awards." *Symphony* 8 (Nov. 1954): 9.

Gray, S. "The tuba ensemble today [includes list of music]." *The Instrumentalist* 35 (Sept. 1980): 78+.

Gressang, J. C. "Textural procedures in instrumental ensemble music and chamber music prior to the classic period." *Dissertation Abstracts* 39 (Dec. 1978): 3211A.

2374   Hahn, Robert. *Die saarländische Bergmusik, die Bergkapellen.* Saarbrücken: Minerva-Verlag; Thinnes & Nolte, 1969.

2375   Hall, H. H. "Early sounds of Moravian brass music in America: a cultural note from Colonial Georgia." *Brass Quarterly* 7, no. 3 (1964): 115–123.

Hall, H. H. "Early sounds of Moravian brass music in America; a cultural note from colonial Georgia." *The Moravian Music Foundation Bulletin* 15, no. 1–2 (1970): 1–4. Reprinted from *Brass Quarterly.*

2376   Hall, J. "Trends of the brass ensemble." *The Instrumentalist* 31 (May 1977): 42–43.

Harley, John. "Music at the English court in the eighteenth and nineteenth centuries." *Music and Letters* 50, no. 3 (July 1969): 332–351.

2377   Hauk, Carl. "Die Bläsergemeinschaft." *Die Volksmusik—Ausg. A* (1943): 37–42.

2378   Heinkel, Peggy. "A look at the Tokyo Bari-Tuba Ensemble." *T.U.B.A. Journal* 14, no. 2 (Nov. 1986): 18–19.

Heller, G. N. *Ensemble music for wind and percussion instruments; a catalog.* Washington, DC: National Education Association, 1970.

Helm, Sanford M. "Catalog of chamber music for wind instruments." Master's thesis, University of Michigan, 1946.

Helm, Sanford M. *Catalog of chamber music for wind instruments.* Ann Arbor: Lithoprinted by Braun-Brumfield, 1952.

2379   Hind, Harold C. "Brass and woodwind." *Music in Education* 27, no. 302 (1963): 111.

Hofacre, Marta Jean. "The use of tenor trombone in twentieth-century brass quintet music; a brief historical overview with comprehensive listing of original, published twentieth-century quintets and a discussion of tenor trombone excerpts from selected compositions." D.M.A. diss., University of Oklahoma, 1986.

Hofacre, Marta Jean. "The use of tenor trombone in twentieth-century brass quintet music; a brief historical overview with comprehensive listing of original, published twentieth-century quintets and a discussion of tenor trombone excerpts from selected compositions." *Dissertation Abstracts* 47 (Jan. 1987): 2362A-2363A.

Hoffren, J. "Selected bibliography of music for brass choir." *The Instrumentalist* 15 (Aug. 1961): 36–38.

2380 Hohstadt, Thomas. "A history of the modern brass ensemble." *Music Journal* 26 (Jan. 1968): 34 + .

2381 Holz, Ronald Walker. "A history of the Hymn Tune Meditation and related forms in Salvation Army instrumental music in Great Britain and North America, 1880–1980." Ph.D. diss., University of Connecticut, 1981.

Horton, Ronald Lee. "Music for worship: a compilation of diverse Protestant hymns cross-referenced for service use and scored for intermediate brass ensemble." Ph.D. diss., Columbia Pacific University, 1983.

2382 Howarth, Elgar. "By arrangement." *Sounding Brass & the Conductor* 7, no. 3 (1978): 105 + .

Hummel, Donald Austin. "Abstract: A selected and annotated bibliography of original works for trombone trio." *Missouri Journal of Research in Music Education* 3, no. 5 (1976): 119–120.

2383 Husted, B. F. *The brass ensemble: its history and music.* 2 vols. Rochester, N.Y.: University of Rochester Press, 1961 (microcard). Ph.D. diss., 1961.

2384 Husted, Benjamin. "The brass ensemble—its history and music." Ph.D. diss., Eastman School of Music, 1955.

2385 Ithaca Brass Quintet. "Faculty brass performance, results of a survey." *Journal of the International Trumpet Guild* 1 (1976): 35.

2386 James, Eric D. "The horn in ensemble—some alternatives." *The Horn Call* 13, no. 1 (Oct. 1982): 44–47.

Janetzky, Kurt. "Das Waldhorn-Quartett: von der Kuriosität zur künstlerischen Erfüllung." *Musica* 8 (1954): 142–144.

2387 Jepson, Barbara. "Brass quintet: too good to play second fiddle." *The Wall Street Journal* 64 (Feb. 28, 1984): 30.

Joseph, J. "The Fine Arts Brass Ensemble." *Music Teacher and Piano Student* 62 (Sept. 1983): 25.

Kanerva, S. "Special Finland: ein kurzer Blick auf die geschichte der finnische Blechblasmusik." *Brass Bulletin—International Brass Chronicle*, no. 53 (1986): 52–55. Also in English and French.

2388 Karasick, S. "The brass ensemble and brass choir." *Music Journal* 24 (Jan. 1966): 38–39.

2389 Karjalainen, K. "The brass septet tradition in Finland." *Brass Bulletin—International Brass Chronicle*, no. 21 (1978). Also in French and German.

2390 Karjalainen, K. "Special Finland: Brass achieves respectability." *Brass Bulletin—International Brass Chronicle*, no. 53 (1986): 36–38. Also in French and German.

2391 Keig, L. "Idiomatic music for small mixed brass ensembles." *Woodwind World—Brass and Percussion* 19, no. 2 (1980): 26–29.

2392 Keig, L. "Idiomatic music for small mixed brass ensembles." *Woodwind World—Brass and Percussion* 19, no. 3 (1980): 6–9 + .

2393 King, Robert D. "Brass ensemble or brass choir?" *Southwestern Brass Journal* 1 (Fall 1957): 30–32.

2394   Kiser, Daniel Wayne. "A musical and pedagogical classification of selected brass quintet literature." D.M.A. diss., University of Illinois, 1987.

2395   Koch, W. "Begründete Vorbehalte? Fragen um Sänger und Bläser." *Der Kirchenchor* 28, no. 2 (1968): 23–24.

2396   Krenz, Edward B. "The brass sextet: a short history of its component instruments; a discussion of the principles of arranging; and five arrangements by the author." Master's thesis, University of Washington, 1952.

2397   Kuehn, David L. "The brass choir: suggestions for its continued success." *The Instrumentalist* 31 (May 1977): 43–45.

Kurtz, S. James. "A study and catalog of ensemble music for woodwinds alone or with brass from ca. 1700 to ca. 1825." Ph.D. diss., University of Iowa, 1971.

Kurtz, S. James. *A study and catalog of ensemble music for woodwinds alone or with brass from ca. 1700 to ca. 1825.* Iowa City: The author, 1971.

Kurtz, S. James. "A study and catalog of ensemble music for woodwinds alone or with brass from ca. 1700 to ca. 1825." *Dissertation Abstracts* 32 (Mar. 1972): 5269A.

2398   Lake, L. "Music for brass ensemble." *Sounding Brass & the Conductor* 3, no. 4 (1974–1975): 125.

2399   Lake, L. "Music for brass ensemble." *Sounding Brass & the Conductor* 5, no. 2 (1976): 60.

2400   Lake, L. "Vive l'ensemble." *Sounding Brass & the Conductor* 4, no. 3 (1975): 86–87.

2401   Lange, Stephen Reynolds. "An analysis of *Concerto for Brass, Organ, and Percussion* by Robert Elmore, *Concerto for Brass and Organ* by Seth Bingham, and *Concerto for Organ and Brasses* by Normand Lockwood." Ph.D. diss., Michigan State University, 1978.

2402   Langhans, F., and D. Schuberth. "Dienst und Klang—der Kirchenmusiker und der Blechblaserchor." *Der Kirchenmusiker* 27, no. 1 (1976): 1–10.

Larkey, Amy. "Gustav Heim and The Waldhorn Quartette." *The Horn Call* 7, no. 1 (Nov. 1976): 34–41.

Lewis, H. M. "French trumpet ensemble music of the late seventeenth century." *Journal of the International Trumpet Guild* 7, no. 4 (1983): 12–17.

2403   Lonnman, G. G. "The tuba ensemble: its organization and literature." *Dissertation Abstracts* 35 (June 1975): 7947A.

2404   Lüttmann, Reinhard. "Bläserdidaktik im Spannungsfeld des heitigen Musiklebens." *Musikpädagogik und gesellschaftliche Wirklichkeit* (1977): 62–66.

McCready, Joan W. "Arranging Christmas carols for the tuba ensemble." *T.U.B.A. Journal* 11, no. 2 (Fall 1983): 2–4.

2405   Marciniak, F. "The community brass ensemble." *The Instrumentalist* 22 (Apr. 1968): 26.

2406   Maret, H. "Les cors de Potemkin." *Chronique musicale* 10 (1875): 13–16.

2407   Mari, P. "La musique de chambre." *La Revue Musicale*, no. 316–317 (1978): 145–151.

2408   Marquis, A. "A great Civil War band lives again [First Brigade Band, Milwaukee]." *The Instrumentalist* 25 (June 1971): 26–27.

May, E. C. "America falls in step to the call of drum and bugle." *Popular Science* 125 (Sept. 1934): 49–52.

Metcalf, Owen Wells. "The New York Brass Quintet; its history and influence on brass literature and pedagogy." D.Mus. diss., Indiana University, 1978.

2409   Milligan, Terry Gilbert. "Charles Ives: a study of the works for chamber ensemble written between 1898 and 1908 which utilize wind instruments." D.M.A. diss., University of Texas (Austin), 1978.

2410   Milligan, Terry Gilbert. "Charles Ives: a study of the works for chamber ensemble written between 1898 and 1908 which utilize wind instruments." *Dissertation Abstracts* 39 (Oct. 1978): 1919A.

2411   Mincarelli, D. "Blazing brasses." *Woodwind, Brass and Percussion* 24, no. 2 (1985): 14.

2412   Mitchell, G. H. "Brass of Peace [integration into worship services]." *Journal of Church Music* 23 (Jan. 1981): 2–3.

2413   Moody, N. L. "Better brass through ensembles [includes list of suggested music]." *The School Musician* 52 (Feb. 1981): 19.

2414   Morris, R. Winston. "The Tennessee Technological University Tuba Ensemble." *Woodwind World—Brass and Percussion* 14, no. 1 (1975): 32 + .

2415   "Music for brass ensemble." *Sounding Brass & the Conductor* 8, no. 4 (1979): 148–149.

2416   "Music for brass ensembles." *The Music Review* 40, no. 3 (1979): 235–236.

"Music in the open air—Brass bands and bands non-military." *Dwight's* 9 (1856): 93–94.

2417   Musser, W. I. "Increased interest in brass chamber music." *The School Musician* 32 (Apr. 1961): 34–35 + .

2418   Nelson, Mark A. "Developing the beginning tuba/euphonium ensemble." *T.U.B.A. Journal* 9, no. 3 (Winter 1982): 14–16.

2419   Nelson, S. "The brass trio." *Woodwind World—Brass and Percussion* 18, no. 1 (1979): 6.

Nicholas, M. R. "Establishing and expanding an early music consort [cornetto, sackbut]." *The Instrumentalist* 32 (Mar. 1978): 36–39.

"1920 tuba ensemble." *T.U.B.A. Newsletter* 1, no. 2 (Winter 1974): 6.

2420   O'Loughlin, N. "Brass ensemble." *The Musical Times* 125 (Apr. 1984): 217.

2421   Olson, Kenneth Elmer. "Yankee bands of the Civil War." Ph.D. diss., University of Minnesota, 1971.

Polk, Keith. "Municipal wind music in Flanders in the late Middle Ages." *Brass and Woodwind Quarterly* 2, nos. 1–2 (Spring-Summer 1969): 1–15.

Polk, Keith. "Wind bands of medieval Flemish cities." *Brass & Woodwind Quarterly* 1, nos. 3–4 (1968): 93–113.

Poncelet-Lecocq, P. "De la nécessité pour les corps de musique militaire de multiplier les instruments de cuivre intermédiares, afin d'amener une fusion plus parfaite du son entre les cuivres et les bois." *L'Echo musical* 1, no. 2 (15 June 1869).

2422   Porter, Andrew. "Musical events: Java sparrows." *The New Yorker* 51 (Feb. 2, 1976): 75–78.

2423   "Posaunenwerk der EKD als Konkurrent." *Musikhandel* 30, no. 7 (1979): 408.

2424   Posten, R. "A view from below [two trombone brass quintets]." *Journal of the International Trombone Association* 5 (1977): 43–44.

Pottag, Max. "The French horn ensemble." *Symphony* 6 (Dec. 1952): 9.

Pottag, Max. "The French horn ensemble." *Woodwind World* 3 (Jan.-Feb. 1959): 6.

Pottag, Max. "Reflections on the history of the horn ensemble." *The Instrumentalist* 13 (Aug. 1959): 36.

2425   Poulin, Pamela Lee. "Three stylistic traits in Poulenc's chamber works for wind instruments." Ph.D. diss., University of Rochester, Eastman School of Music, 1983.

2426   Price, Jeffrey Keith. "Abstract: A study of selected twentieth-century compositions for heterogeneous brass ensemble and organ by United States composers." *Missouri Journal of Research in Music Education* 3, no. 5 (1976): 117–119.

2427   Price, Jeffrey Keith. "A study of selected twentieth-century compositions for heterogeneous brass ensemble and organ by United States composers." *Dissertation Abstracts* 37 (Nov. 1976): 2484A.

2428   Price, Jeffrey Keith. "A study of selected twentieth-century compositions for heterogeneous brass ensemble and organ by United States composers." D.M.A. diss., University of Missouri (Kansas City), 1976.

Pruzin, R. S. "Brass quintet." *Woodwind World—Brass and Percussion* 19, no. 5 (1980): 33–35.

2429   Raph, A. "Brass ensemble programming." *The Instrumentalist* 19 (Feb. 1965): 66–67.

2430   Rasmussen, Mary. "A bibliography of 19th- and 20th-century music for male voices with wind- or brass-ensemble accompaniment." *Brass Quarterly* 7, no. 2 (1963): 66–77; 7, no. 3 (1964): 124–132.

2431   Rasmussen, Mary, comp. "A bibliography of 19th- and 20th-century music for mixed voices with wind- or brass-ensemble accompaniment." *Brass Quarterly* 6, no. 3 (1963): 120–130.

2432   Rasmussen, Mary. "A bibliography of 19th- and 20th-century music for mixed voices with wind- or brass-ensemble accompaniment." *Brass Quarterly* 7, no. 1 (1963): 34–44.

2433   Rasmussen, Mary. "An introductory index of contemporary chorale settings for brass instruments." *Brass Quarterly* 6, no. 2 (1962): 47–81.

2434   Reed, David F. "Victor Ewald and the Russian chamber brass school." D.M.A. diss., University of Rochester, 1979.

2435   Reed, David F. "Victor Ewald and the Russian chamber brass school." *Dissertation Abstracts* 40 (May 1980): 5644A.

2436   Reimer, Mark U. "Brass choir: a new challenge for the tubist." *T.U.B.A. Journal* 11, no. 4 (Spring 1984): 9–10.

2437   Reynolds, G. E. "New brass ensemble publications." *The School Musician* 35 (Oct. 1963): 28 + .

2438   Reynolds, G. E. "New brass music reviews." *The School Musician* 34 (Apr. 1963): 26 + .

2439   Reynolds, George. "Brass ensembles." *The School Musician* 29 (Nov. 1957): 14 + .

2440   Richards, John K. "Brass ensembles foster permanent interest in music." *The Instrumentalist* 8 (Jan. 1954): 24–25 + .

Ricks, Robert. "Russian horn bands." *Musical Quarterly* 55, no. 3 (July 1969): 364–371.

2441   Romersa, Henry J. "A study of Giovanni Gabrieli (1557–1612) with particular emphasis on six compositions by Giovanni Gabrieli." 2 vols. Master's thesis, Oberlin College, 1955.

2442   Ross, Walter Beghtol. "Part I: *Concerto for Brass Quintet and Orchestra* [original composition]. Part II: Principles of melodic construction in Paul Hindemith's Chamber Concerti, Opus 36." D.M.A. diss., Cornell University, 1966.

2443   Schaefer, J. D. "The brass ensemble—why bother?" *The Instrumentalist* 21 (Mar. 1967): 14 + .

2444   Schaffer, W. A. "The brass choir in the band." *The Instrumentalist* 20 (Sept. 1965): 52–53.

2445   Schmidt, C. E. "Interlocking techniques in Kpelle music." *Selected Reports in Ethnomusicology* 5 (1984): 194–216.

2446   Schweikert, Norman. "A history of the organized horn ensemble in the United States." *The Horn Call* 16, no. 1 (Oct. 1985): 20–32.

Seaman, Gerald. "The Russian horn band." *Monthly Musical Record* 89 (1959): 93–99.

2447   Sebby, R. W. "Balancing the brass section of the American concert band." *Woodwind World—Brass and Percussion* 14, no. 2 (1975): 42–43.

Shoemaker, John Rogers. "A selected and annotated listing of 20th century ensembles published for three or more heterogeneous brass instruments." Ed.D. diss., Washington University, 1968.

Shoemaker, John Rogers. "A selected and annotated listing of 20th century ensembles published for three or more heterogeneous brass instruments." *Dissertation Abstracts* 29 (June 1969): 4519A.

2448   Smith, D. "The birth of four-plus brass." *The Instrumentalist* 35 (Feb. 1981): 27–28.

"Special hongrie: Barcs 1984; brass ensemble seminar." *Brass Bulletin—International Brass Chronicle*, no. 48 (1984): 28–29. Also in French and German.

Staples, J. "Reaching our coda." *Crescendo International* 20 (June 1982): 37.

Staples, J. "The trumpet quartet." *Crescendo International* 20 (Nov. 1981): 37.

Staples, J. "The trumpet quartet." *Crescendo International* 20 (Dec. 1981): 37.

Staples, J. "The trumpet quartet." *Crescendo International* 20 (Jan. 1982): 37.

Staples, J. "The trumpet quartet." *Crescendo International* 20 (Feb. 1982): 37.

Staples, J. "The trumpet quartet." *Crescendo International* 20 (Mar. 1982): 37.

2449 Starkey, Williard A. "The history and practice of ensemble music for lip-reed instruments." Ph.D. diss., State University of Iowa, 1955.

2450 Stivers, Davison L., and brass choir: history. "The brass choir: its instruments, history, literature and value to school instrumental music." Master's thesis, University of Southern California, 1954.

2451 Stoddard, Hope. "Brass ensembles—twentieth century specialty." *The International Musician* 56 (Feb. 1958): 22–23 + .

Struck-Schlön, M. "Zwischen Möbelmusik und Zwölftonkonzert: die Posaune im Kammerensemble am Beginn der Neuen Musik (1913-1934)." *Brass Bulletin—International Brass Chronicle*, no. 55 (1986): 6–14. Also in English and French.

2452 "Summit Brass: national brass ensemble formed." *The School Musician* 57 (Oct. 1985): 9.

2453 Swift, Arthur G., Jr. "Twentieth-century brass ensemble music: a survey with analyses of representative compositions." Ph.D. diss., University of Iowa, 1969.

2454 Swift, Arthur G., Jr. "Twentieth-century brass ensemble music; a survey with analyses of representative compositions." *Dissertation Abstracts* 30 (Mar. 1970): 3978A-3979A.

Tilbury, Jack, ed. "New materials—brass quintet." *T.U.B.A. Journal* 6, no. 1 (Fall 1978): 35.

Tilbury, Jack, ed. "New materials—brass quintet." *T.U.B.A. Journal* 6, no. 2 (Winter 1979): 17.

Tilbury, Jack, ed. "New materials—brass quintet." *T.U.B.A. Journal* 6, no. 3 (Spring 1979): 14–15.

2455 Trobian, Helen R. "Brass ensembles in church services." *The Instrumentalist* 6 (Oct. 1951): 12 + .

2456 Trobian, Helen R. "The brass quartet in the church." *Music Ministry* 2 (July 1961): 10–11.

Troiano, William. "The New York State School Music Association contest list for tuba solos and tuba ensembles." *T.U.B.A. Journal* 14, no. 2 (Nov. 1986): 20–24.

2457 Tunnell, Michael Hilton. "A comprehensive performance project in trumpet literature; an essay on selected trumpet excerpts from brass quintets by Ingolf Dahl, Gunther Schuller, Alvin Etler, and Jan Bach; and a bibliography of brass quintets written by American composers from 1938 to 1980." D.M.A. diss., University of Southern Mississippi, 1982.

2458 Tunnell, Michael Hilton. "An essay on selected trumpet excerpts from brass quintets by Ingolf Dahl, Gunther Schuller, Alvin Etler, and Jan Bach." *Journal of the International Trumpet Guild* 8, no. 3 (1984): 14–38.

2459 Turrentine, Edgar M. "A study of 12 tower sonatas by Johann Pezel for public school brass ensemble." 2 vols. Master's thesis, Oberlin College, 1952.

2460 "25 years of the Philip Jones Brass Ensemble." *The Gramophone* 54 (Dec. 1976): 972 + .

2461 Uber, David. "Antiphonal music for brass choirs." *The Instrumentalist* 17 (Apr. 1963): 69–71.

2462 Uber, David. "Notes on brass ensemble music." *The Instrumentalist* 37 (Sept. 1982): 38 + .

2463 Uber, David Albert. "The brass choir in antiphonal music." *Dissertation Abstracts* 26 (Nov. 1965): 2797–2798.

2464 Uber, David Albert. "The brass choir in antiphonal music." Ed.D. diss., Columbia University, 1965.

2465 Upchurch, John David. "A manual for college brass quintet performance and its application to selected works of Nicola Vincentino." D.Mus. diss., Indiana University, 1970.

Vagner, Robert S. "A new look at chamber music for winds." *The Instrumentalist* 13 (June 1959): 70–73.

2466 van Ess, Donald Harrison. "The stylistic evolution of the English brass ensemble." Ph.D. diss., Boston University Graduate School, 1963.

2467 van Ess, Donald Harrison. "The stylistic evolution of the English brass ensemble." *Dissertation Abstracts* 24 (Nov. 1963): 2074–2075.

2468 Varasdy, F. "The history of brass ensemble music in Hungary." *Journal of the International Trombone Association* 13, no. 1 (1985): 46–47.

2469 Varasdy, F. "Special hongrie: brass chamber music in Hungary." *Brass Bulletin—International Brass Chronicle*, no. 48 (1984): 42–47. Also in French and German.

2470 Walker, B. H. "Brass sextets." *The School Musician* 21 (Jan. 1950): 36.

Wallace, Paul, comp. "Original manuscript music for wind and percussion instruments." *NACWPI Bulletin* 7 (Mar. 1959): 4–9; (June 1959): 4–12; (Dec. 1959): 6–11.

Walls, B. G. "The baryton divertimenti of Haydn; a selected adaptation for brass trio." *Dissertation Abstracts* 30 (Aug. 1969): 756A.

2471 Walls, Billy G. "The baryton divertimenti of Haydn: a selected adaptation for brass trio." Ph.D. diss., Florida State University, 1968.

2472 Waln, G. "The beginnings and development of the woodwind quintet." *The Instrumentalist* 22 (Oct. 1967): 64–6.

2473 Waln, G. "The woodwind quintet: its development and music." *The Instrumentalist* 19 (Apr. 1965): 90 + .

2474 "Weber brass sonatas published." *The Moravian Music Foundation Bulletin* 22, no. 2 (1977): 7.

2475 Weisensee, W. "Landesposaunentag 1971 in Nürnberg—Festtag der Siebentausend." *Gottesdienst und Kirchenmusik*, no. 3 (May-June 1971): 83–87.

2476 Weiss, Bernard. "The brass ensemble." *Music Educators Journal* 34 (Nov.-Dec. 1947): 44–45.

2477 Weldon, Constance J. "The tuba ensemble." *The Instrumentalist* 27 (Feb. 1973): 35–36.

Weldon, Constance J., and Greg Lonnman. "The evolution of the tuba ensemble." *T.U.B.A. Journal* 7, no. 1 (Summer 1979): 2–3.

2478 Whitaker, Donald. "Brass ensembles." *The Instrumentalist* 21 (June 1967): 20+.

2479 White, Edna. "Reviving the brass quartet—its early history and possibilities." *Musical Observer* 30 (July 1931): 30–31.

Whitwell, David. *The Renaissance wind band and wind ensemble.* Northridge, CA: Winds, 1983.

Williams, Arthur L. "For musical reasons—should the drum and bugle corps be replaced by the brass band?" *The Instrumentalist* 14 (Nov. 1959): 89–90.

2480 Williams, J. Clifton. "New horizons for the brass choir." *Southwestern Brass Journal* 1 (Spring 1957): 6–8.

2481 Winick, Steven. "Music for brass trio." *The Instrumentalist* 27 (Jan. 1973): 48–53.

Winkler, K. "Neuausgaben originaler Ensemblemusik des 17. Jahrhunderts für Blechbläser [includes list of editions examined]." *Brass Bulletin—International Brass Chronicle*, no. 53 (1986): 69–80. Also in English and French.

Wise, R. E. "Scoring in the neoclassic woodwind quintets of Hindemith, Fine, Etler, and Wilder." *Dissertation Abstracts* 28 (Oct. 1967): 1462A–1463A.

2482 Wolf, Edward C. "An introductory study of brass ensemble music in the baroque era." Master's thesis, Northwestern University, 1955.

2483 Wolf, U. "Leserbriefe [Response to 'Neuausgaben originaler Ensemblemusik des 17. Jahrhunderts für Blechbläser,' by K. Winkler]." *Brass Bulletin—International Brass Chronicle*, no. 55 (1986): 109. Also in English and French.

2484 Wood, Alfred F. "Music for wind ensembles and piano." *The Instrumentalist* 12 (Sept. 1957): 46–47.

Woodard, William H. "Bugle and drum corps." *The School Musician* 23 (Nov. 1951): 11+.

2485 Zoppoth, Marguerite. "Materials for elementary brass ensembles." Master's thesis, Eastman School of Music, 1950.

"Zum Repertoire des reinen Blechmusikkorps." *Schweizerische Instrumentalmusik* 27 (1938): 147–149.

Brass Band

"A propos de l'orchestre de cuivre." *Schweizerische Instrumentalmusik* 30 (1941): 94.

2486   "Annual brass band contest at the Zoological Gardens, Bellevue, Manchester." *Musical World* 50 (1872): 607–608.

2487   "Ausbau der Besetzung des Blechmusikkorps." *Schweizerische Instrumentalmusik* 32 (1943): 214.

2488   Avis, R. "The British brass band." *The Instrumentalist* 24 (Nov. 1969): 57–61.

2489   B., Ch. "La Question des fanfares." *L'Echo musical* 11, no. 16 (2 Aug. 1879); 11, no. 17 (16 Aug. 1879).

2490   Back, Jean. "Vergleichende Uebersicht über die instrumentale Zusammensetzung grosser europäischer Harmonie- und Blechmusikkorps." *Schweizerische Instrumentalmusik* 26 (1937): 340–341, 366–367.

2491   Ball, E. "The nature of the brass band." *Sounding Brass & the Conductor* 1 (Apr. 1972): 13 + .

2492   Bashford, R. "Repertory: brass band." *Music in Education* 42, no. 349 (1978): 249–250.

2493   Berger, K. "The American brass band? Yes!" *The Instrumentalist* 15 (Nov. 1960): 44.

2494   Boult, A. "Required reading." *Sounding Brass & the Conductor* 8, no. 3 (1979): 118–119.

2495   Brand, G. "The brass age." *Music* 4, no. 1 (1970): 36–37.

2496   Brand, V. "British brass bands—amateur music with a professional touch." *The Instrumentalist* 26 (Apr. 1972): 18–21.

2497   "Brass aus England—in Deutschland und Oesterreich immer beliebter." *Musik International-Instrumentenbau-Zeitschrift* 40 (July 1986): 468–469.

2498   "Brass aus England—auch in Deutschland immer beliebter." *Musik International-Instrumentenbau-Zeitschrift* 39 (Apr. 1985): 340 + .

2499   "The brass band as a social factor." *Music* (Chicago) 20 (1901): 242–244.

2500   *Brass band tuning.* Reprinted from the *Brass Band News.* Liverpool: Wright & Round, 1933.

2501   Brayley, Arthur W. "The first brass band instruments. Giving a history of the first brass band, its members, etc." *The American Music Journal* 5, nos. 7–12 (1905/06); 6, no. 1 (1906/07).

2502   Bright, C. "The school brass band in high pitch [lowering pitch to 440]." *Music in Education* 30, no. 317 (1966): 30–31.

2503   "British brass band to invade Raleigh [WRAL British Brass Band]." *The School Musician* 58 (Oct. 1986): 21.

"Broadcasting brass [viewpoints from producers and musicians]." *Brass International* 10, no. 2 (1982): 4–7 + .

Butterworth, A. "Brass band scoring." *Sounding Brass & the Conductor* 7, no. 1 (1978): 14 + .

2504 Butterworth, A. "Brass band scoring in the seventies." *Sounding Brass & the Conductor* 4, no. 3 (1975): 76–77.

2505 Butterworth, A. "Brass band scoring in the seventies." *Sounding Brass & the Conductor* 4, no. 4 (1976): 109 + ; 5, no. 3 (1976): 76–77 + .

Butterworth, A. "Brass band scoring in the seventies [role of percussionist]." *Sounding Brass & the Conductor* 6, no. 4 (1978): 136 + .

2506 Butterworth, A. "The brass band—a cloth cap joke?" *Music in Education* 34, no. 342 (1970): 78–79 + ; no. 343 (1970): 152–153.

2507 Butterworth, A. "Programme notes." *Sounding Brass & the Conductor* 6, no. 3 (1977): 91–92.

2508 Caisley, L. "Brass bands in school." *Sounding Brass & the Conductor* 1 (Apr. 1972): 23.

2509 Caisley, L. "Coming of age." *Sounding Brass & the Conductor* 2, no. 3 (1973): 91–92 + .

2510 Carse, Adam. "Brass bands." *Monthly Musical Record* 58 (1928): 327.

2511 Catelinet, Philip. "The British concept of brass." *The School Musician* 29 (Feb. 1958): 10 + .

2512 Catelinet, Philip. "The editor's opus." *Sounding Brass & the Conductor* 9, no. 2 (1980): 35.

2513 Colin, S. *And the bands played on*. London: Elm Tree; North Pomfret, VT: David & Charles, 1979.

2514 Cook, Kenneth. *The Bandsman's everything within*. London: Hinrichsen, 1950.

2515 Cook, Kenneth. "The brass band repertory." *The Musical Times* 90 (1949): 243–244.

2516 Cook, Kenneth, and Lance Caisley. *Music through the brass band*. National School Brass Band Association. Handbook No. 1. London: Hinrichsen, 1953.

2517 Cook, Kenneth. *Oh, listen to the band! A brass band miscellany*. London: Hinrichsen, 1950.

2518 Copley, I. A. "Warlock and the brass band." *The Musical Times* 109 (Dec. 1968): 1115–1116.

Cotterrell, R. "Mike Westbrook: taking music to the people [interview]." *Jazz Forum*, no. 39 (1976): 38–41.

2519 Cruft, J. "Art and Cruft; brass bands and the Arts Council." *Sounding Brass & the Conductor* 3, no. 2 (1974): 55–56.

Cundell, Edric. "Composing for brass band." In *Brass Today*. Edited by Frank Wright, 65–69. London: Besson, 1957.

2520 "Czech brass band music." *Music News from Prague*, no. 2–3 (1981): 6.

2521 Dallas, K. "Brass bound." *Melody Maker* 49 (Sept. 7, 1974): 41.

2522 "Desire Dondeyne prodigue ses conseils aux fanfares du Quebec." *Vie Musicale*, no. 4 (1966): 8–10.

2523 Dieck, A. "Les musiciens ambulants de Salzgitter au XIX siecle [sous l'aspect particulier des cuivres]." *Brass Bulletin—International Brass Chronicle*, no. 13 (1976): 95–115. Also in English and German. Excerpt from his book, *Die Wandermusikanten von Salzgitter*.

The directory of British brass bands. Rochdale, England: British Federation of Brass Bands, 1976.

2524 Dutton, Brent. "British brass band championships." *T.U.B.A. Journal* 7, no. 4 (Spring 1980): 11–14.

2525 Egli, E. "Die Instrumental-Besetzung der Blasmusik verschiedener Länder." *Deutsche Militär-Musiker Zeitung* 28 (1906): 210–211.

2526 Elliot, J. H. "The all-brass ensemble." *Music & Letters* 12 (1931): 30–34.

2527 Elliot, J. H. "Brass music in development." *Monthly Musical Record* 67 (1937): 34–35.

Elliot, J. H. "The evolution of music for brass." *The Musical Times* 77 (1936): 885–887.

2528 Elliot, J. H. "Music for brass." *Monthly Musical Record* 62 (1932): 105–106.

Eskdale, George. "Brass band to symphony orchestra." In *Brass Today*. Edited by Frank Wright, 81–83. London: Besson, 1957.

2529 Farringdon, H. "Export brass." *Sounding Brass & the Conductor* 2, no. 3 (1973): 80–81 + .

2530 Fleck, Hattie C. "The oldest American brass band [East Barrington, N. H.]." *Etude* 5 (1937): 304.

2531 Flor, G. J., ed. "Brass workshop: The British brass band in the United States [selected list]." *The School Musician* 58 (Dec. 1986): 18–20.

2532 Flor, G. J. "Brass workshop: the saxhorn—past and present [Heritage Americana Cornet-Saxhorn Brass Band]." *The School Musician* 54 (May 1983): 26–29.

2533 Frak, C. A. "The American brass band—it makes great sense." *The Instrumentalist* 15 (Apr. 1961): 32.

2534 Fransman, H. "Special Finland: Die Tradition der Blasmusiken [the septet]." *Brass Bulletin—International Brass Chronicle*, no. 53 (1986): 49–51. Also in English and French.

2535 Frayling-Kelly, F. "Brass band and concert band review." *Musical Opinion* 105 (Dec. 1981): 95.

2536 Gähwiler, A. *Zum 100jahr. Bestehen der Blechharmonie Kirchberg*. Kirchberg: n.p., 1943, 1944.

2537 Garofalo, R., and M. Elrod. "Heritage Americana: reflections on the performance practices of mid-nineteenth century brass bands." *Journal of Band Research* 7, no. 1 (1981): 1–26. Includes partial listing of Elrod and Garofalo collections.

2538 Garofalo, R., and M. Elrod. "Mostly for brasses." *Woodwind World—Brass and Percussion* 20, no. 1 (1981): 8–10.

2539 Gay, B. "The brass band: what now?" *Music in Education* 34, no. 344 (1970): 205.

2540 Gay, B. "Eurobands." *Sounding Brass & the Conductor* 7, no. 4 (1978): 132–133.

2541   Gay, B. "New music for the brass band." *Music in Education* 34, no. 341 (1970): 28–29.

2542   Gay, B. "The view from Soho Square." *Sounding Brass & the Conductor* 1, no. 2 (1972): 39–40.

2543   Gerschefski, Edwin. "To the brass band." *Modern Music* 14 (1937): 189–192.

2544   Glover, Ernest N. "The Salvation Army International Staff Band." *The Instrumentalist* 11 (June 1957): 25.

2545   Golland, J. "Writing for brass band." *Composer*, no. 28 (Summer 1968): 12–15.

2546   "Great Britain: Wesite's Jazz Cabaret." *Jazz Forum—the magazine of the European Jazz Federation*, no. 60 (1979): 12.

Gregson, E. "The composer speaks; Gordon Jacob [interview]." *Sounding Brass & the Conductor* 1, no. 2 (1972): 41–42+.

2547   Gregson, E. "Music for today." *Sounding Brass & the Conductor* 9, no. 1 (1980): 8–9+. Reprinted from *Brass Bands in the 20th Century*.

2548   Hailstone, Alf. "The British bandsman." *T.U.B.A. Journal* 14, no. 2 (Nov. 1986): 16.

2549   Hanci, T. "Brass bands in Czechoslovakia." *Journal of Band Research* 6, no. 1 (1969): 42–45.

2550   Hanci, T. "A green light for Czechoslovak brass bands." *Music News from Prague*, no. 4 (1971): 1–2.

2551   Harratt, P. "The 'soul-saving' brassmen." *Sounding Brass & the Conductor* 9, no. 2 (1980): 20–22.

2552   Hazell, C. "Not so much a brass band, more a way of life." *Sounding Brass & the Conductor* 1, no. 3 (1972): 84–87.

2553   Hazelman, H. "The British brass band." *The Instrumentalist* 16 (Sept. 1961): 59–60.

2554   Henshaw, L., and C. Hayes. "So you wanna be a rock 'n' roll star?" *Melody Maker* 47 (Nov. 18, 1972): 36–37.

2555   Hind, Harold C. *The brass band*. Foreword by Walter Reynolds. London: Hawkes & Son, 1934.

2556   Hind, Harold C. "The British wind band." In *Seventh Music Book*, 183–194. London: Hinrichsen, 1952.

2557   Hind, Harold C. "The British wind band." In *Waits—Wind Band—Horn*. London: Hinrichsen, 1952.

2558   Holz, Richard E. "The brass band tradition." *Music Journal* 19 (Apr. 1961): 63+.

2559   Holz, Richard E. "The Salvation Army's premier band—The International Staff Band of London, England." *The School Musician* 28 (Apr. 1957): 24–25+.

2560   Horwood, W. "A blitz on the diehards." *Crescendo International* 20 (Feb. 1982): 4.

2561   Horwood, W. "Musical musings [National Brass Band Championships of Great Britain]." *Crescendo International* 21 (Dec. 1982): 8+.

2562 Horwood, W. "Transposition—the logical approach [working with a brass band]." *Crescendo International* 10 (Jan. 1972): 39.

2563 Jacobs, A. "Music in London [National Brass Band Festival Concert]." *The Musical Times* 113 (Dec. 1972): 1214.

2564 James, I. "What's it all about?" *Sounding Brass & the Conductor* 3, no. 2 (1974): 44–45 +.

2565 Jameson, I. "Bandkraft [brass band music series]." *Music Teacher and Piano Student* 58 (July 1979): 25.

2566 Johnson, W. V. "The British brass band." *The Instrumentalist* 34 (Nov. 1979): 25–29.

2567 Johnstone, W. "The brass band movement." *Making Music*, no. 77 (Autumn 1971): 10–12.

2568 Johnstone, W. "The brass band movement." *Sounding Brass & the Conductor* 2, no. 4 (1973–1974): 116–118.

2569 Kalkbrenner, A. *Die Organisation der Militärmusikchöre aller Länder*. Hannover: L. Oertel, [188?].

2570 Kemp, C. "A 'brash' American meets British brass." *Brass and Percussion* 1, no. 1 (1973): 16 +.

2571 "Klare konzeption—Grundlage für effektive Arbeitsergebnisse; zum Arbeitsplan der BAG Blasmusik Karl-Marx-Stadt." *Musikforum* 16 (Sept. 1971): 1–2.

2572 Koenig, K. "Four country brass bands [Louisiana]." *The Second Line* 36 (Fall 1984): 18–20.

2573 Koenig, K. "Louisiana brass bands and history in relation to jazz history." *The Second Line* 35 (Summer 1983): 7–15.

2574 Koenig, K. "The plantation belt brass bands and musicians: professor James B. Humphrey." *The Second Line* 33 (Fall 1981): 24–40.

2575 Koenig, K. "Professor Robert Hingle and the Sweet Sixteen Brass Band of Point a la Hache (Louisiana)." *The Second Line* 35 (Fall 1983): 4–13.

2576 Lacome, P. "Reorganisation des musique militaires. Les instruments à six pistons." *Le Ménestrel* (c.1873).

2577 Leidzen, E. "Some brass tacks about brass bands." *The Instrumentalist* 15 (Nov. 1960): 45–46 +.

2578 Lewis, W. J. "The origin of village bands." *Sounding Brass & the Conductor* 1, no. 2 (1972): 49.

2579 Lodge, E. A. *The brass band at a glance*. Huddersfield: The Author, [1896].

2580 Mamminga, Michael Arthur. "British brass bands." *Music Education Journal* 58 (Nov. 1971): 82–83.

2581 Mamminga, Michael Arthur. "British brass bands." *Dissertation Abstracts* 34 (Oct. 1973): 1953A.

2582 Mamminga, Michael Arthur. "British brass bands." Ph.D. diss., Florida State University, 1973.

2583 Mattison, D. "Sweet old tunes [Indian brass bands of British Columbia]." *Brass International* 10, no. 3 (1982): 14–15 +.

2584 Mattison, D. "Sweet old tunes [nineteenth-century missionaries spread brass bands as well as the gospel]." *Brass International* 10, no. 2 (1982): 16–18.

2585 Middendorf, J. W. "The rebirth of the big brass band [keynote address at ACBA Convention, 1979]." *Woodwind World—Brass and Percussion* 18, no. 4 (1979): 4–6.

2586 Morris, E. Vaughan. "The National Brass Band Festival." In *Brass Today*. Edited by Frank Wright, 31–36. London: Besson, 1957.

2587 Mortimer, Harry. "Bands at the microphone." In *Brass Today*. Edited by Frank Wright, 21–23. London: Besson, 1957.

2588 "Music for brass band." *Sounding Brass & the Conductor* 8, no. 4 (1979): 147–148.

2589 "Music for brass band." *Sounding Brass & the Conductor* 9, no. 3 (1980): 32.

2590 "Music in the open air—Brass bands and bands non-military." *Dwight's* 9 (1856): 93–94.

2591 Nash, H. "Swedish rhapsody." *Sounding Brass & the Conductor* 1, no. 2 (1972): 51–54.

2592 "The National Youth Brass Band of Switzerland." *Brass Bulletin—International Brass Chronicle*, no. 32 (1980): 16–17. Also in French and German.

2593 Neefe, K. "Die historische Entwickelung der Königl. Sächs. Infanterie- und Jägermusik im 19. Jh." *Neue Zeitschrift für Musik* 92 (1896): 357–358, 365–366, 373–374, 381–382, 389–390, 397–398, 405–406.

2594 Neefe, K. "Die Sächsische Cavalleriemusik in ihrer geschichtlichen Entwickelung." *Neue Zeitschrift für Musik* 91 (1895): 521–522, 533–535.

2595 Neilson, James. "The salvation army band." *Etude* 67 (Jan. 1949): 19–20; (Feb. 1949): 81+.

Nellist, R. "Scoring hymn tunes for brass band." *Sounding Brass & the Conductor* 8, no. 2 (1979): 79–80.

2596 New, L. J. "Problems of an African band." *Music Teacher and Piano Student* 52 (Dec. 1973): 10–11.

2597 Newsome, R. "The suite." *Sounding Brass & the Conductor* 7, no. 4 (1978): 134–137.

2598 Newsome, Ralph. "The development of brass band music." *Sounding Brass & the Conductor* 8, no. 3 (1979): 102–104.

2599 Newson, Jon. "The American brass band movement." *Quarterly Journal of the Library of Congress* 36, no. 2 (Spring 1979): 114–139.

2600 Olsen, D. M., and others. "Music in an American frontier communal society (Aurora, Oregon)." *Brass Bulletin—International Brass Chronicle*, no. 34 (1981): 21–22. Adapted from *Oregon Historical Quarterly*.

2601 Olsen, D. M., and others. "Music in an American frontier communal society (Aurora, Oregon)." *Brass Bulletin—International Brass Chronicle*, no. 36 (1981): 64–77. Also in French and German.

Olson, Kenneth Elmer. "Yankee bands of the Civil War." Ph.D. diss., University of Minnesota, 1971.

2602 O'Steen, K. "Brass Band scores abroad, but still awaits breakthrough in U.S." *Variety* 325 (Jan. 7, 1987): 136.

2603   Pacchiana, J. "Battle of the brass bands [England]." *The Instrumentalist* 41 (May 1987): 80+.

2604   Parker, P. "Kontakt mit der Zeit: zum 3. zentralen Leistungsvergleich der Blasorchester der DDR." *Musikforum* 25, no. 3 (1980): 27–28.

2605   Perrins, B. "Programme building for the brass band." *Sounding Brass & the Conductor* 2, no. 3 (1973): 85–86.

2606   Perrins, B. "What is a brass band?" *Brass Bulletin—International Brass Chronicle*, no. 25 (1979): 63–65+.

2607   Rankl, Karl. "Conducting brass." In *Brass Today*. Edited by Frank Wright, 11–13. London: Besson, 1957.

2608   "The Redbridge phenomenon." *Sounding Brass & the Conductor* 1 (Apr. 1972): 11–12.

2609   Renton, F. "Sad sounds of the eighties." *Sounding Brass & the Conductor* 9, no. 2 (1980): 16–17.

2610   Reynolds, G. "The American brass band." *The School Musician* 32 (Feb. 1961): 16+.

2611   Ridgeon, John. "Inaugural concert of the City of London Band." *Sounding Brass & the Conductor* 1, no. 2 (1972): 58–59.

2612   Rimmer, Drake. "Percussion: its place in the brass band." In *Brass Today*. Edited by Frank Wright, 100–102. London: Besson, 1957.

2613   Rode, Theodore. "Eine einheitliche deutsche Militär-Instrumentirung und -Stimmung als nothwendige Consequenz eines einheitlichen Deutschlands." *Neue Zeitschrift für Musik* 79 (1883): 46.

2614   Rode, Theodore. "Entwurf und Vorschläge zu einer Normalinstrumentirung der deutschen Militärmusik." *Neue Zeitschrift für Musik* 78 (1882): 121–124.

2615   Rode, Theodore. *Eine neue Regiments-Hornisten-Infanterie-Musik*. Leipzig: Kahnt, 1850.

2616   Rode, Theodore. "Zur Geschichte der königl. preussischen Infanterie-, Jäger- und Cavalleriemusik." *Neue Zeitschrift für Musik* 51 (1859): 71–72, 85–86, 92–93.

2617   Rohner, Traugott. "Let's examine the possibilities of the American brass band." *The Instrumentalist* 15 (Sept. 1960): 50–51+.

        Rorick, David R. "Nineteenth-century American cornet/brass band music." D.M.A. diss., Catholic University of America, 1979.

2618   Rose, A. S. *Talks with bandsmen; A Popular handbook for brass instrumentalists*. London: W. Rider, [1895].

2619   Rosenbaum, D. "Die Entwicklung der Preussischen Militär-Musik." *Deutschen Militär-Musiker Zeitung* 28 (1906): 101–103.

2620   Russell, John Frederick, and J. H. Elliot. *The brass band movement*. London: J. M. Dent, 1936.

2621   Rutland, Harold. "Resounding brass." *The Musical Times* 99 (1958): 315–316.

2622   Satoh, T. "Salvation Army in Japan." *Brass Bulletin—International Brass Chronicle*, no. 52 (1985): 30–34. Also in French and German.

2623   Sawhill, Clarence. "A famous brass band festival." *Music Journal* 13 (1959): 16+.

2624   Schafer, W. J., and R. B. Allen. *Brass bands and New Orleans jazz*. Baton Rouge: Louisiana State University Press, 1977.

2625   Schafer, W. J., and R. B. Allen. "Brass bands and New Orleans jazz." *Footnote* 9, no. 2 (1978): 18.

2626   Schafer, W. J. *Brass bands and New Orleans jazz*. Baton Rouge: Louisiana State University Press, 1979.

2627   Scott, J. "The history of the brass band and its literature in South Yorkshire." Ph.D. diss., Sheffield, 1970.

2628   Smith, Bernard J. "The Salvation Army brass band." *The Instrumentalist* 5 (Nov. 1950): 12–14; (Jan.-Feb. 1951): 30+.

2629   Stewart, John H. "The British brass band." *Music Educators Journal* 37 (Apr.-May 1951): 30+.

2630   "Talking point: Spit and polish [the brass band tradition]." *Music in Education* 42, no. 390 (1978): 74.

2631   Taylor, A. "Brass on the box; a personal view of brass bands in general, and the Granada Band of the Year Contest in particular." *Sounding Brass & the Conductor* 2, no. 2 (1973): 56–58.

2632   Taylor, A. R. "Brass bands." *Sounding Brass & the Conductor* 8, no. 2 (1979): 69–70.

2633   "The [thirty-first] National Brass Band Festival." *The Musical Times* 77 (1936): 936–937.

2634   Thomson, Maud. "The national youth brass band." *The Musical Times* 93 (1952): 493–495.

2635   Turner, J. "Should brass bands play to entertain or educate?" *Sounding Brass & the Conductor* 7, no. 2 (1978): 76.

van Ess, Danald Harrison. "The stylistic evolution of the English brass ensemble." Ph.D. diss., Boston University Graduate School, 1963.

2636   Vincent, Charles, and Sam Cope. *The Brass band and how to write for it*. London[?]: Vincent Music Co., 1908.

2637   Walmsley, P. "An Australian's impressions of a day at the National." *Sounding Brass & the Conductor* 6, no. 4 (1978): 128–129.

2638   Walters, H. "The American brass band is ready for the downbeat." *The Instrumentalist* 15 (Dec. 1960): 29–30.

2639   Weber, A., and A. Renggli. *50 Jahre Metallharmonie Bern*. Bern: n.p., 1941.

2640   West, M. "March of the brass band." *Munsey* 25 (1901): 640–645.

2641   Whittaker, L. "Fairview Baptist Church Christian Band." *Footnote* 3, no. 6 (1972): 15–17.

2642   Wiggins, A. R. *Salvation army music and song*. n.p.: Hinrichsen's Musical Yearbook, 1945–46.

2643   Wiggins, B. "New scores for brass band." *Sounding Brass & the Conductor* 3, no. 4 (1974–1975): 114.

2644   Williams, Arthur L. "For musical reasons—should the drum and bugle corps be replaced by the brass band?" *The Instrumentalist* 14 (Nov. 1959): 89–90.

2645   Wright, Denis. *The brass band conductor.* London: J. Duckworth, 1948.

2646   Wright, Denis. "Brass colour contrasts." In *Brass Today.* Edited by Frank Wright, 53–55. London: Besson, 1957.

2647   Wright, Denis. *The complete bandmaster.* London: Pergamon, 1963.

2648   Wright, Denis. "Scoring for brass band." *The Musical Times* 73 (1932): 800–803.

Wright, Denis. *Scoring for brass band.* 4th ed. London: Baker, 1967.

2649   Wright, Denis. *Scoring for the brass band.* Colne, Lancashire: J. Duckworth, 1935.

2650   Wright, Frank. "Brass band." *Musik der Zeit* 4 (1953): 40–41.

2651   Wright, Frank. "Who wants to be an adjudicator?." In *Brass Today.* Edited by Frank Wright, 15–19. London: Besson, 1957.

2652   Zealley, Alfred. "The great British brass band movement." *Etude* 66 (1948): 534–35 + .

2653   "Zum Repertoire des reinen Blechmusikkorps." *Schweizerische Instrumentalmusik* 27 (1938): 147–149.

Trombone Choir

2654   Aring, J. "Aus der Arbeit evangelischer Posaunenchöre." *Rheinland* 8 (1928): 120.

Arling, H. J. *Trombone chamber music: an annotated bibliography.* Nashville: Brass Press, 1978.

Arling, H. J. *Trombone chamber music: an annotated bibliography.* Enlarged 2nd edition. Nashville: Brass Press, 1983.

Arling, H. J. "Trombone chamber music: an annotated bibliography." *Music Educators Journal* 66 (Sept. 1979): 88.

2655   "Aus der Arbeit des Posaunenwerkes in der Kirchenprovinz Sachsen und Anhalt." *Musik und Kirche* 21 (1951): 35.

2656   Bachmann, F. "Aus der Arbeit der Posaunenchöre." *Musik und Kirche* 30 (1960): 33–36.

2657   Bachmann, F., and W. Koch, eds. *Dortmund, 5.-8. Oktober 1956. Aus Anlass des 100 Geburtstages von D. Johannes Kuhlo.* Deutscher Evangelischer Posaunentag, vol. 2. Dortmund: Deutscher Evangelischer Posaunentag, 1956.

2658   Bachmann, Fritz. "13. Bayerischer Landesposaunentag in Rothenburg o.d.T." *Gottesdienst und Kirchenmusik* 4 (1953): 187–188.

2659   Bachmann, Fritz. "Aus Geschichte und Wollen der Posaunenchöre." *Der Evangelische Kirchenmusiker* 21 (1937): 45–46.

2660 Bachmann, Fritz. "Ein Blick in die Arbeit der Posaunenchöre." *Spielet dem Herrn* 18 (1937): 7–9.

2661 Bachmann, Fritz. *Neue Bestrebungen auf dem Gebiete der Blasmusik, Ein Blick in die Arbiet der evangelischen Posaunenchöre*. Vortrag auf dem Fest der deutschen Kirchenmusik 1937 in Berlin. Hamburg, 1937.

2662 Bachmann, Fritz. "Der Posaunenchor, ein treuer Helfer im pfarramtlichen Dienst." *Deutsches Pfarrerblatt* 43 (1939): 396.

2663 Bauer, and Jaehnig. "Posaunenmusik und Kirchenmusik." *Neues sächsisches Kirchenblatt* (1929): 785.

2664 Bauer. "Neue Turmmusik." *Schlesisches Blatt für evangelische Kirchenmusik* 61, no. 7/8 (192?).

2665 Bauer. "Posaunenchor-Leiterkursus." *Zeitschrift für Kirchenmusiker* 11 (191?): 3.

2666 Beckerath, Alfred von. "Festliche Tage neuer Blasmusik in Marktoberdorf." *Musik im Unterricht* 48, no. 5 (1957): 157.

2667 "Bläser-Musik in der Jugend auf neuen Wegen." *Hausmusik—Zeitschrift für Hausmusik* 18 (1954): 16.

2668 "Bläsertagung in Lindau." *Hausmusik* 21 (1957): 129.

2669 Bock, E. "Posaunen und Harfen." *Christengemeinschaft* 16 (1939–40): 229–232.

2670 Bodelschwingh, F. v. "Lobet den Herrn mit Posaunen." *Bote von Bethel*, no. 168 (1936): 2–14.

2671 Bovermann, P. "Nochmal 'Posaunenmusik.' " *Zeitschrift für Kirchenmusiker* 11 (1929): 59.

2672 Branstine, Wesley R. "The Moravian Church and its trombone choir in America, a lecture recital, together with three recitals of selected works by W. Presser, R. Monaco, L. Bassett, P. Bonneau, E. Bozza, R. Dillon and others." D.M.A. diss., North Texas State University, 1984.

2673 Brodde, Otto. "Bedenken und Fragen zu Erich Grubers Bericht 'Der gegenwärtige Stand der Posaunenarbeit.' " *Musik und Kirche* 23 (1953): 106–109.

Brodde, Otto. "Kirchenmusik für Sänger und Bläser." *Der Kirchenchor* 21, no. 4 (1961): 60–62.

2674 Brodde, Otto. "Lass dir unser Lob gefallen! Gedanken zu einem neuen Posaunenbuch von Fritz Bachmann." *Deutsches Pfarrerblatt* (Essen) 51 (1951): 230.

2675 Bubmann, O. "100 Jahre Posaunenchor in Neuendettelsau." *Gottesdienst und Kirchenmusik* 4 (1965): 147–152.

2676 "Burgsteinfurter Bläserwoche." *Hausmusik—Zeitschrift für Hausmusik* 18 (1954): 149.

2677 de Fries, F. "Unsere Posaunenchöre." *Monatsschrift für Gottesdienst und kirchliche Kunst* 34 (1929): 47–50.

2678 Denks. "Einst und jetzt. Ein Beitrag zur Geschichte der Posaunenchöre." *Spielet dem Herrn* 17 (1936): 84–87.

2679 Dierks, Werner, and Martin Goldstein. "Göttinger Posaunenmission."

Neubau. Blätter für neues Leben aus Wort und Geist (München) 7 (1952): 208–214, 247–255.

2680   Dress, Heinrich. *Loben den Herrn! 25jährige Jubel-Festschrift der evang. luth. Freikirchlichen Posaunenchöre der Provinz Hannover.* Hörpel über Soltau: Dress, 1946.

2681   Duwe, W. "Ein Vorschlag zur planmässigen Arbeit unserer (Posaunen-) Chöre." *Spielet dem Herrn* 18 (1937): 70–72.

2682   Ehmann, Wilhelm. *Die bläsereigene Satzpraktiken in der älteren Blasmusik.* n.p.: Tagungsbericht der Betheler Bläsertage, 1949.

Ehmann, Wilhelm. "Ein Brief von Johannes Zahn an Eduard Kuhlo." *Jahrbuch für Liturgik und Hymnologie* 4 (1958/59): 135.

2683   Ehmann, Wilhelm. "Hundert Jahre Kuhlo-Posaunenbuch; zum 125. Geburtstag und 40. Todestag Johannes Kuhlos." *Der Kirchenmusiker* 32, no. 5 (1981): 152–156.

2684   Ehmann, Wilhelm. *Johannes Kuhlo, ein Spielmann Gottes.* Stuttgart: Kreuz-Verlag, 1951.

2685   Ehmann, Wilhelm. *Johannes Kuhlo, ein Spielmann Gottes.* 2 vols. Wittenburg: Luther Verlag, 1956.

2686   Ehmann, Wilhelm. *Johannes Kuhlo, ein Spielmann Gottes.* 5th ed. Wittenburg: Luther, 1974.

2687   Ehmann, Wilhelm. "Die Kantoreipraxis in unseren Posaunenchören." *Der Chorleiter* 3 (1957): 1.

2688   Ehmann, Wilhelm. "Neue Wege der Blasmusik." *Das Musikleben* 4 (1951): 208–210.

2689   Ehmann, Wilhelm. *Tibilustrium. Das geistliche Blasen, Formen und Reformen.* Kassel and Basel: Bärenreiter, 1950.

2690   Ehmann, Wilhelm. "Zum 10-jährigen Todestag von Johannes Kuhlo." *Musik und Kirche* 21 (1951): 189–190.

2691   Ehmann, Wilhelm. "Zur Geschichte des Posaunenblasens." *Pastoralblätter. Monatsschrift für den Gesamtbereich des evangelischen Pfarrantes* (Stuttgart) (1951): 766–771.

2692   "Entschliessung des Posaunenwerkes der Evangelischen Kirche in Deutschland." *Musik und Kirche* 21 (1951): 278–279.

2693   Everett, Tom. "The literature of the Ars Antigua Trio: a ten year commissioning project." *Journal of the International Trombone Association* 15, no. 3 (1987): 44–47.

Faulds, John. "The trombone ensemble." In *Brass Today.* Edited by Frank Wright, 111–112. London: Besson, 1957.

2694   Felgenhauer, Siegfried. "Gedanken zur Literatur unserer Posaunenchöre." *Spielet dem Herrn* 19 (1938): 72–74.

2695   Fliedner, K. T. "Der Posaunenchor als volksmissionarisches und kirchenmusikalisches Instrument." *Spielet dem Herrn* 19 (1938): 72–74.

2696   Folgner, Karl-Joachim. "1. Sing- Bläserwoche in Schmie (Württ.) vom 25.8.1951 bis 1.9.1951." *Musik und Kirche* 21 (1951): 297–298.

2697   Franke, Christoph. "Die Kantoreipraxis in den Posaunenchören." *Der Kir-*

chenmusiker VII (1956): 80–83.

2698 "Der 15. bayerische Landesposaunentag." *Gottesdienst und Kirchenmusik* (1957): 135–138.

2699 Gadsch, H. "Verwendungsmöglichkeiten eines Posaunenchores." *Zeitschrift für Kirchenmusiker* 22 (1940): 31.

2700 George, S. "The trombone choir [includes list of music]." *The Instrumentalist* 29 (May 1975): 44–46.

2701 Görisch. "Der volksmissionarische Dienst der Posaunenchöre." *Spielet dem Herrn* 17 (1936): 187–191.

2702 Greifenstein, Hermann. "14. Landesposaunentag in Regensburg." *Gottesdienst und Kirchenmusik* (1955): 122–124.

2703 Grosch, Georg. "Der Dienst der Posaunenchöre auf dem Münchner Kirchentag (12. bis 16. August 1959)." *Gottesdienst und Kirchenmusik* (1959): 88–91.

2704 Grosch, Georg. "Die instrumentale Besetzung eines evangelischen Posaunerchors." *Gottesdienst und Kirchenmusik* 6 (1964): 253–255.

2705 Gruber, Erich. "Der gegenwärtige Stand der Posaunenarbeit." *Musik und Kirche* 23 (1953): 11–19.

2706 Haffner, W. "Der neue Schrei; Posaunenchor und Barockinstrumente." *Gottesdienst und Kirchenmusik*, no. 1 (1966): 17–19.

      Hall, H. H. "Early sounds of Moravian brass music in America: a cultural note from Colonial Georgia." *Brass Quarterly* 7, no. 3 (1964): 115–123.

2707 Hall, H. H. "Early sounds of Moravian brass music in America: a cultural note from colonial Georgia." *The Moravian Music Foundation Bulletin* 15, no. 1–2 (1970): 1–4. Reprinted from *Brass Quarterly*.

2708 Hall, H. H. "The Moravian trombone choir: a conspectus of its early history and the traditional death announcement." *The Moravian Music Foundation Bulletin* 26, no. 1 (1981): 5–8.

2709 Hammerbacher, J. "Wert oder Unwert der Posaunenmusik." *Zeitschrift für evangelische Kirchenmusik* 6 (1928): 91–95, 120–124.

2710 Hart, G. "Hausmusik und Posaunenchor." *Hausmusik* 16 (1952): 48–50.

2711 Hartzell, L. W. "Trombones in Ohio [initial Moravian settlements]." *The Moravian Music Foundation Bulletin* 28, no. 4 (1983): 72–74.

2712 Henschel. "Von Turm-Musik, Trompeten und Posaunen." *Die Sendung* 7 (1930): 44.

2713 Honemeyer, Karl. *Die Posaunenchöre im Gottesdienst.* Schriften reihe der Westfälischen Landeskirchenmusikschule in Herford, H. 3. Gütersloh: Rufer-Verlag, 1951.

2714 Hummel, Donald Austin. "A selected and annotated bibliography of original works for trombone trio." D.M.A. diss., University of Missouri (Kansas City), 1976.

2715 Iskraut, Paul. *Mit Posaunen durch Siebenbürgen, Ungarn und Tschechei.* Hamburg: Buchhandlung des Nordbundes, [ca. 1935].

2716 Jenssen. "Allerlei Gedanken eines Posaunenchorleiters." *Spielet dem Herrn* 17 (1936): 22–25.

2717   *Johannes Kuhlo, ein Spielmann Gottes.* Gütersloh: Rufer, 1947.

2718   Kämper, Karl. "Die Entstehung des ersten Posaunenchors im Ravensberger Lande. Ein Beitrag zur Geschichte der deutschen Posaunenchöre." *Spielet dem Herrn* 17 (1936): 141–142, 156–157; *Singet dem Herrn* 39 (1937): 26–27.

2719   Kessler, F. "Vom Posaunenwerk der evangelische Kirche." *Weg und Wahrheit* 2 (1948): 308.

2720   "Kleine Betrachtung zum Landesposaunentag in Ulm." *Württembergische Blätter für Kirchenmusik* (Stuttgart) (1954): 75–77.

2721   Klenner, Gottfried. "Wie ein Knabenposaunenchor entsteht." *Mitteilungsblatt der Sächsischen Posaunenmission*, no. 37 (1936): 1–2.

2722   Klingemann. "Aufgabe der Posaunchöre." *Kirchenmusik* 7 (1926): 1195.

2723   Klupsch, Theodor. *Posaunenchöre und Kirchenchöre; das Amt des Kantors und Organisten.* Hrsg. Oberkirchenrat d. Ev.-Luth. Landeskirche Mecklenburgs. Schwerin: Mecklenburgische Kirchenzeitung, 1952.

2724   Koch, J. H. "Ergebnisse der Tagung 'Sänger und Bläser.'" *Musik und Kirche* 31 (1961): 120–124.

2725   Koch, Wilhelm. "Posaunenchöre—klingende Botschafter?" *Der Kirchenmusiker* 9 (1958): 187–190.

2726   Koch, Wilhelm. "Posaunenmission Heute." *Der Kirchenchor* 19 (1959): 66–67.

2727   Küster, M. "Aus der Arbeit Ländlicher Posaunenchöre." *Psalter und Harfe* 10 (1937): 35–36.

2728   Kuhlo, Johannes. *Posaunen-Fragen beantwortet.* Gütersloh: C. Bertelsmann, 1933.

2729   Kuhlo, Johannes. *Posaunen-Fragen beantwortet.* 3. Auss. Bethel bei Bielefeld: Buchh. de Anstalt Bethel, 1909.

2730   Kuhlo, Johannes. *Das Wichtigste zur Schulung der Bläser.* Gütersloh: Rufer, 1947.

2731   "Landesposaunentag am 2./3. Juni 1951 in Rostock." *Musik und Kirche* 21 (1951): 287–288.

2732   Lange, Hans Jürgen. "Fortbildungslehrgang für Mitarbeiter und Reichsposaunenratssitzung in Neuhaus (Schliersee) vom 17.-23. September 1951." *Musik und Kirche* 22 (1952): 69–71.

2733   Lange, Hans Jürgen. "Gegenwärtige Probleme der Posaunenarbeit." *Musik und Kirche* 24 (1954): 37–40.

2734   Lange, Hans Jürgen. "Kantoreipraxis und Posaunenchor." *Gottesdienst und Kirchenmusik* (1958): 187–192.

2735   Lange, Hans Jürgen. "Kirchenmusiker und Posaunenchor." *Gottesdienst und Kirchenmusik* 3 (1960): 68–79.

2736   Lange, Hans Jürgen. "Obmänner- und Berufsarbeitertagung und Ratssitzung des Posaunenwerkes im evangelischen Jugendhof Sachsenhain bei Verden/Aller vom 6. dis 11. Oktober 1952." *Musik und Kirche* 22 (1952): 267–269.

2737   Lange, Hans Jürgen. "Zweiter Deutscher Evangelischer Posaunentag in

Dortmund vom 5.-7. Oktober 1956." *Musik und Kirche* 27 (1957): 147–150.

2738 Leaman, J. "The trombone choir of the Moravian Church." *The Moravian Music Foundation Bulletin* 20, no. 1 (1975): 2–7.

2739 Leaman, J. "The trombone choir of the Moravian Church." *Journal of the International Trombone Association* 5 (1977): 44–49. Reprinted from *Moravian Music Foundation Bulletin* 20, no. 1.

2740 Leib, Walter. "Turmblasen." *Süddeutsche Sänger-Zeitung* 30 (1936): 71–72.

2741 Ley, W. *50 Jahre Posaunenchor Thierseifen*. Waldbröl: Haupt, 1932.

2742 Lobitz, Carl McComb. "Problems in transcribing and composing music for trombone choir." *Dissertation Abstracts* 30 (Nov. 1969): 2062A.

2743 Lobitz, Carl McComb. "Problems in transcribing and composing music for trombone choir." D.Mus.A. diss., University of Oklahoma, 1969.

2744 Lutschewitz, Martin. "Der Chorleiter und seine Aufgaben im Posaunenchor." *Der Kirchenmusiker* 7 (1956): 76–79.

2745 Lutschewitz, Martin. "Geistliches Blasen." *Gottesdienst und Kirchenmusik* (1955): 79–82.

2746 Lutschewitz, Martin. "Das Posaunenchoralbuch." *Gottesdienst und Kirchenmusik* (1955): 151–153.

Lutschewitz, Martin. "Probe des Posaunenchores—Wesen und Aufgabe." *Gottesdienst und Kirchenmusik* (1956): 81–84.

2747 Lutschewitz, Martin. "Ueber die Arbeit an Choralsätzen mit Bläsern." *Gottesdienst und Kirchenmusik* (1956): 48–52.

2748 Luz. *Posaunenchöre*. Stuttgart: Holland & Josenhaus, 1910.

2749 Mahrenholz, C. "Ueber Posaunenmusik." *Musik und Kirche* 1 (1929): 132–137, 163–173, 261–267.

2750 Matthes, Wilhelm. "Der 12. bayerische Landesposaunentag in Bayreuth." *Gottesdienst und Kirchenmusik* 2 (1951): 158–159.

2751 Matthes, Wilhelm. "Das grosse Bläsertreffen in Bayreuth." *Musik und Kirche* 21 (1951): 289–290.

2752 Maurer, Joseph A. "The Moravian trombone choir." *The Historical Review of Berks County* 20 (Oct.-Dec. 1954): 2–8.

Mehl, J. G. "Der Gottesdienst an Bezirksposaunentagen." *Gottesdienst und Kirchenmusik* 2 (1964): 65–69.

Mehl, J. G. "Der Gottesdienst an Bezirksposaunentagen." *Gottesdienst und Kirchenmusik* 5 (1964): 195–199.

2753 Mehl, J. G. "Zur Lage und Geschichte Passaus." *Gottesdienst und Kirchenmusik*, nos. 4–5 (1966): 153–154.

Menke, Werner. "Probleme der Bachtrompeten und Vorschläge für die Posaunenmission." *Kirchenchor* 45 (1934): 22.

2754 Meyer, J. H. "Kirchlicher Stosstrupp der Posaunenchöre." *Die Dorfkirche* 23 (1930): 206.

2755 Mrozek, Hans. "Landesposaunentag in Ulm 1950." *Musik und Kirche* 20 (1950): 138–139.

2756 Mrozek, Hans. "Studientagung für Bläsermusik in Schmie vom 19. bis 28.

März 1953." *Musik und Kirche* 23 (1953): 119.

2757 Mühleisen, Hermann. "Posaunen-Vorspiel zum Choral bezw. zum Gemeindegesang." *Musik und Kirche* 6 (1934): 319–320.

2758 Müller, A. "Kirchenmusikalische Bedeutung der Posaunenchöre." *Bausteine* 61 (1931): 189–193.

2759 Müller, A. "Posaunenchöre in der Kirchenmusik." *Sächsisches Kirchenblatt* 79 (1931): 670, 685.

Müller, A. "Schule für Posaunenchöre." *Bausteine* 54 (1922): 29.

2760 Müller, A. *Unsere Posaunenchöre.* Dresden: Verbandsbuchhandlung, (1905).

2761 Müller, Adolf. "Die Posaunenchöre Deutschlands." *Allgemeine Musikalische Zeitung* 67 (1940): 42–43.

2762 Müller, Adolf. "Die Posaunenchöre und die Kirchenmusik." *Zeitschrift für Kirchenmusiker* 10 (1928–29): 133, 141. Reprint. Dresden: Zu beziehen durch die Posaunenmission, (193-?).

2763 Müller, Adolf. *Die Posaunenchöre und die Kirchenmusik.* Dresden-A: Zu beziehen durch die Posaunenmission, [193?].

2764 Müller, Adolf. "Posaunenmission." *Baustein* 56 (1924): 5.

2765 Müller, Adolf. "Posaunenmission." *Der Kirchenchor* 36 (1926): 27–30.

2766 Müller, Adolf. *Die Posaunenmission als Liedbewegung in der Kirche.* Dresden and Sächs: Posaunenmission, 1930.

2767 Müller, Adolf. "Wirkungsmöglichkeit der Posaunenchöre." *Bausteine* 62 (1930): 17–20.

2768 Müller, O. "Posaunenmission." *Zeitschrift für Kirchenmusiker* 10 (1928): 184.

2769 Müller, S. *Der Verband schweizer Posaunenchöre.* Adliswil bei Zürich: Verlag des Verb., 1941.

2770 Müller, S. "Der VI. Schweizerische Posaunentag am 9./10. Mai 1936 in Zürich." *Evangelische Musikzeitung* 30 (1936): 37–42.

2771 Müller, S. "Wie man einen figurierten Choral einüben sollte." *Die Posaune* 20 (1936): 34–35.

2772 Nelle, K. "Vorschläge für die Turm-musik." *Spielet dem Herrn* 17 (1936): 12–13, 63, 80, 95.

2773 Nethercutt, R. "Trombone trios." *Journal of the International Trombone Association* 7 (1979): 19–21.

2774 "Neue Literatur für Posaunenchöre." *Monatsschrift für Gottesdienst und kirchliche Kunst* 36 (1931): 97.

2775 "Posaunenchöre und ihre Verwendung." *Zeitschrift für Kirchenmusiker* 10 (1928): 60.

2776 "Der Posaunenchor als pädagogisch-psychologische Aufgabe." *Gottesdienst und Kirchenmusik,* no. 4–5 (July-Oct. 1975): 120–124.

2777 "Posaunenchor und Volkslied." *Die Dorfkirche* 26 (1933): 26.

2778 "Posaunenchorfrage." *Zeitschrift für Kirchenmusiker* 10 (1928): 152.

2779 "Posaunenmission und Kirche." *Der Kirchenmusiker* 2 (1951): 153–154.

2780 "Posaunenmusik." *Zeitschrift für Kirchenmusiker* 10 (1928): 184.

Rasmussen, Mary. "A bibliography of choral music with trombone ensemble accompaniment, as compiled from eleven selected sources." *Brass*

Quarterly 5, no. 4 (1962): 153–159.

Reichel, W. C. *Something about trombones and The Old Mill at Bethlehem.* Edited by J. W. Jordan. Bethlehem, Pa.: Moravian Publications Office, 1884.

2781   Reynolds, J. C. "The Moravian trombone choir." *Newsletter of the International Trombone Association* 8, no. 1 (1980): 24–25.

Reynolds, J. C. "News on the trombone front ["Moravian sized" trombones available]." *The Moravian Music Foundation Bulletin* 28, no. 4 (1983): 74–75.

Reynolds, J. C. "The trombone in Moravian life." *Moravian Music Journal* 32, no. 1 (1987): 7–11.

2782   Richter, L. "Zur Posaunenchorfrage." *Zeitschrift für Kirchenmusiker* 11 (1929): 19.

2783   "Richtlinien für die Gewährleistung einheitlicher Arbeit der Bezirke des Verbandes evang. Posaunenchöre in Bayern." *Gottesdienst und Kirchenmusik* 5 (1950): 33–34.

2784   [Rieckmann, Adolf]. *Geschichte des Posaunenchores Fliegenberg, 1876–1926.* Winsen a. L.: Gebr. Ravens, (1926).

2785   Riesenfeld, Paul. "Der Werdegang des Wortes 'Posaune.' " *Evangelische Musikzeitung* 30 (1936): 20.

2786   Roland, K. "Zur Geschichte der Posaunenchor." *Zeitschrift für Instrumentenbau* 53 (1932–1933): 300–301.

2787   Roth, Erich. "Für die Freunde der Posaunenmusik. Bericht über die Obmänner- und Berufsarbeitertagung des Posaunenwerkes der EKD im Hause der Begegnung zu Mülheim, Ruhr vom 14.-20. Sept. 1953." *Der Kirchenmusiker* 4 (1953): 156–158.

2788   Roth, Erich. "Mit Jubelklang, mit Instrumenten schön, in Chören ohne Zahl . . . Dankbare und kritische Erinnerung. Der zweite Deutsche Evangelische Posaunentag." *Der Kirchenmusiker* 8 (1957): 46–48.

2789   Ruh. "Ueber die Verwendung der Posaunen." *Evangelische Musikzeitung* 21 (191-?): 3.

2790   Rustler, H. "Landesposaunentag in Passau eine ökumenische Begegnung." *Gottesdienst und Kirchenmusik,* nos. 4–5 (1966): 149–153.

2791   Saam, J. "Der bayerische Landesposaunentag in Passau 14. bis 15. Mai 1966." *Gottesdienst und Kirchenmusik,* nos. 4–5 (1966): 144–149.

2792   Schieber, Ernst. "Blasmusik im Gottesdienst." *Musik und Kirche* 11 (1939): 174–178.

2793   Schlee, Martin. "[Posaunenchor]. Eine Anfrage und eine Anregung." *Gottesdienst und Kirchenmusik* (1954): 124–125.

2794   Schlee, Martin. "2. Deutscher Evangelischer Posaunentag." *Gottesdienst und Kirchenmusik* 7 (1956): 184–186.

2795   Schlee, Martin. "30 Jahre Verband evangelischer Posaunenchöre in Bayern." *Gottesdienst und Kirchenmusik* 3 (1952): 31–37, 75–78.

2796   Schlee, Martin. "Das Blasinstrument in der Jugendarbeit." *Gottesdienst und Kirchenmusik* (1957): 201.

2797   Schlee, Martin. "Einige Gedanken über das Instrumentarium unserer Posaunenchöre." *Gottesdienst und Kirchenmusik* 3 (1952): 186–188.

2798   Schlee, Martin. "Tagung der Obmänner und Berufsarbeiter im Posaunenwerk der EKD 14.-21.9.1953 in Mülheim, Ruhr." *Gottesdienst und Kirchenmusik* 4 (1953): 213–215.

2799   Schlee, Martin. "Die Verwendung der Posaunenchöre im Gottesdienst." *Gottesdienst und Kirchenmusik* (1950): 7–9.

2800   Schlee, Martin. "Was ist bei der Grundung eines Posaunenchores zu denken." *Gottesdienst und Kirchenmusik* 2 (1951): 76–78.

2801   Schlee, Martin. "Was ist von der Gründung eines Posaunenchores zu bedenken?" *Gottesdienst und Kirchenmusik* (1957): 170–171.

2802   Smith, G. P. "Original unaccompanied trombone ensemble music." *The Instrumentalist* 28 (Feb. 1974): 52–54.

2803   Sommerhalder, M. "Posaunen-Arbeit." *Brass Bulletin—International Brass Chronicle*, no. 34 (1981): 55–59. Also in French and English.

2804   Stahl. "Turmmusik in Lübeck." *Korrespondenzblatt des evangelischen Kirchengesangvereins für Deutschland* 31 (191?): 9–10.

2805   Stober, Berthold. "Vorwärts in der Posaunenmission!" *Spielet dem Herrn* 18 (1937): 23–26.

2806   Stober, Emil. "Instrumentalmusik im Kirchenraum III. Die Aufgabe der Posaunenchöre." *Evangelische Kirchenmusiker* 30 (1953): 10–13.

2807   Strecker, O. *Geschichte der Posaunenvereine in der hannoverschen lutherischen Landeskirche in ihren ersten 50 Jahren.* Hannover: The Author, 1899.

2808   Stroschein, G. "Lehrgang für Posaunenchorleiter in Rozyscze." *Luthererbe in Polen* 2 (1939): 4 +.

2809   Stroschein, G. "Ueber die Posaunenarbeit in Wolhynien." *Spielet dem Herrn* 18 (1937): 169–171.

       Tanner, P. "A versatile trombone ensemble." *Music Journal* 13 (Apr.-May 1959): 36 +.

2810   Teichert. "Die Aufgaben der Posaunenmission." *Mitteilungsblatt der Sächsischen Posaunenmission*, no. 30 (1935): 1–3; and *Die Posaune* 20 (1936): 18–21.

       "Trombone trios in the ITA collection." *Journal of the International Trombone Association* 14, no. 1 (1986): 41–42.

2811   Tucker, W. E. "The trombone quartet, its appearance and development throughout history: the trombone quartet in chamber music, early twentieth century [includes list]." *Journal of the International Trombone Association* 8 (1980): 2–5.

2812   Tucker, W. E. "The trombone quartet: its appearance and development throughout history." *Journal of the International Trombone Association* 7 (1979): 2–7.

       Ueberwasser, A. B. . . . *Orientierungsbuch und Schule für Posaunen- oder Bläser-Chöre.* Markneukirchen: B. Ueberwasser, 1913.

2813   Unger, Ludwig, and Martin Schlee. "Eine Aufrage und eine Anregung: Posaunenchöre." *Gottesdienst und Kirchenmusik* 5 (1954): 124–125.

2814 Unger, Robert. "Heinrich Schütz und die Posaunenchöre." *Spielet dem Herrn* 17 (1936): 130–132.

2815 "Unsere Pfarrbläserchöre." *Musik und Altar* (Freibg. i. Br.) 6 (1953–54): 230–232.

2816 Utz, Kurt. "Grundsätzliches zur Literaturfrage der evangelischen Posaunenchöre." *Musik und Kirche* 9 (1937): 122–130.

2817 Utz, Kurt. "Ueber das sakrale Amt des Posaunenchores." *Spielet dem Herrn* 17 (1936): 157–160.

2818 Utz, Kurt. "Ueber das Verhältnis vom Ton zum Wort." *Spielet dem Herrn* 18 (1937): 130–132, 147–149.

2819 "Der Verband evangelischer Posaunenchöre in Bayern e. V." *Gottesdienst und Kirchenmusik*, nos. 4–5 (1966): 155.

2820 "Vom dreyfachen Auftrag der Posaunenmusik." *Evangelische Welt* (Bethel) 5 (1951): 653.

2821 "Vorschläge zur Turmmusik." *Mitteilungsblatt der Sächsischen Posaunenmission*, nos. 34–37 (1936).

Wagner, I. L. "Trombone ensemble music." *The Instrumentalist* 26 (Aug. 1971): 80–81.

Weisensee, W. "Landesposaunentag 1971 in Nürnberg—Festtag der Siebentausend." *Gottesdienst und Kirchenmusik*, no. 3 (May-June 1971): 83–87.

2822 Weiss. "Posaunenchöre im Dienste der Volksmission!" *Spielet dem Herrn* 18 (1936): 88–90.

2823 Winking, C. "The trombone choir in Moravian liturgies." *The School Musician* 49 (Jan. 1978): 54–55.

2824 Würz, A. "Schwingt euch auf, Posaunenchöre." *Münchner Mosaik* 1 (1938): 278.

2825 Zacharias, E. *Die Posaunenchöre, ihre Entstehung und Ausbreitung.* Dresden: Verbandsbuchhandlung, 1902.

Jazz/Popular Styles

Agrell, Jeffrey. "Jazz and the horn." *Brass Bulletin—International Brass Chronicle*, no. 40 (1982): 41–45. Also in French and German.

Agrell, Jeffrey. "Jazz and the horn: Thomas Bacon." *Brass Bulletin—International Brass Chronicle*, no. 45 (1984): 34. Also in French and German. Reprinted in part from *Brass and Percussion* 1, no. 3 (1973): 6–7.

Agrell, Jeffrey. "Jazz and the horn: Tom Varner." *Brass Bulletin—International Brass Chronicle*, no. 47 (1984): 55–57. Also in French and German.

2826 Baker, David. *Jazz styles and analysis: trombone.* Chicago: Downbeat Music Workshop, 1973.

"Dave Baker's *Sonata for Tuba and String Quartet* for Harvey Phillips (second movement)." *Down Beat* 43 (Oct. 7, 1976): 43.

Beese. "Die neue Jazz-Trompete." *Das Orchester* 8 (1931): 20.

Berendt, J. "Jazz in Germany." *Jazz Journal International* 32 (Aug. 1979): 7.

2827 Boyle, P. "The skoonum horn." *Jazz Forum*, no. 29 (June 1974): 15–16.

2828 "Brass in pop groups." *Jazz & Pop* 9 (Nov. 1970): 32–33.

2829 Brunn, H. O. *The story of the original Dixieland jazz band.* Reprint. Baton Rouge: Louisiana State University, 1969.

2830 Burns, J. "Dem bones, dem bones, dem bopping bones!" *Jazz and Blues* 2 (Oct. 1972): 16–19.

2831 Collier, James Lincoln. *Louis Armstrong, an American genius.* New York: Oxford University Press, 1983.

Cummings, Barton. "Tuba innovations [role in early jazz]." *Woodwind World—Brass and Percussion* 17, no. 5 (1978): 8–11.

2832 Davison, Michael Allyn. "A motivic study of twenty improvised solos of Randy Brecker between the years of 1970–1980." D.M. diss., University of Wisconsin (Madison), 1987.

2833 De Lagueronniere, C. "Some instruments to be included in jazz exhibit [photo essay]." *The Second Line* 35 (Winter 1983): 22–23.

Fairweather, D. "Troublesome trumpet." *Jazz Journal International* 32 (May 1979): 15.

Farrow, Bill. "Brass instruments in the dance band." *Southwestern Brass Journal* 1 (Fall 1957): 15–16.

Feather, Leonard. "La coulisse, le swing, et l'embouchure." *Jazz Magazine* 8 (Oct. 1962): 20–25.

2834 Feather, Leonard. "Giants of jazz: the trombonists." *International Musician* 61 (July 1962): 12–13+.

2835 Feather, Leonard. "Giants of jazz: The trumpeters." *International Musician* 61 (Sept. 1962): 12–13+.

Feather, Leonard. "Le piston, le swing et l'embouchure." *Jazz Magazine* 9 (Apr. 1963): 20–25.

Feather, Leonard. "The trumpet in jazz." *Downbeat* 25 (Jan. 23, 1958): 14–16+.

2836 Giddins, G. "Weatherbird: Celebration in the mainstream [Tubajazz Consort]." *Village Voice* 23 (Sept. 18, 1978): 106.

"Glory of jazz—Trombonists, old and new." *Music U.S.A.* 76 (May 1959): 15–16.

"Goodbye to those dance band days says Jimmy Knepper." *Crescendo International* 19 (June 1981): 16–17.

2837 Hall, M. E. "Brass instruments in the dance band." *Southwestern Brass Journal* 1 (Spring 1957): 27–31.

2838 Heckman, D. "Jazz trombone—five views." *Down Beat* 32 (Jan. 28, 1965): 17–19.

2839 Heckman, D. "Miscellaneous brass [jazz brass]." *Down Beat* 30 (Jan 31, 1963): 16–17.

Henshaw, L., and C. Hayes. "So you wanna be a rock 'n' roll star?" *Melody Maker* 47 (Nov. 18, 1972): 36–37.

2840 Hitt, George Lynn. "The lead trumpet in jazz (1924–1970)." D.Mus. diss., Indiana University, 1976.

2841 Horwood, W. "Musical musings: Brief moments of glory [unusual instruments in jazz]." *Crescendo International* 22 (Mar.-Apr. 1985): 8.

2842 Kernfeld, Barry Dean. "Adderley, Coltrane, and Davis at the twilight of bebop: the search for melodic coherence (1958–59)." 2 vols. Ph.D. diss., Cornell University, 1981.

Koenig, K. "Louisiana brass bands and history in relation to jazz history." *The Second Line* 35 (Summer 1983): 7–15.

Kröger, E. *Die Posaune im Jazz*. Vienna: Universal, 1972.

Lambert, G. E. "Trumpets no end [Ellington's trumpeters]." *Jazz Journal* 14 (Jan. 1961): 8–10.

Laplace, Michel. "Le trombone dans le jazz et la musique populaire." *Brass Bulletin—International Brass Chronicle*, no. 50 (1985): 36–40. Also in English and German.

Laplace, Michel. "Le trombone dans le jazz et la musique populaire: la periode classique Armstrongienne (1927–1945)." *Brass Bulletin—International Brass Chronicle*, no. 51 (1985): 40–46. Also in English and German.

Laplace, Michel. "Le trombone dans le jazz et la musique populaire: le pluralisme d'expression a partir de 1945." *Brass Bulletin—International Brass Chronicle*, no. 52 (1985): 20–28. Also in English and German.

Laplace, Michel. "La trompette et le cornet dans le jazz et la musique populaire." *Brass Bulletin—International Brass Chronicle*, no. 42 (1983): 16–30. Also in English and German.

Laplace, Michel. "La trompette et le cornet dans le jazz et la musique populaire." *Brass Bulletin—International Brass Chronicle*, no. 45 (1984): 38–44. Also in English and German.

Laplace, Michel. "La trompette et le cornet dans le jazz et la musique populaire (1927–1945)." *Brass Bulletin—International Brass Chronicle*, no. 43 (1983): 44–65. Also in English and German.

Laplace, Michel. "La trompette et le cornet dans le jazz et la musique populaire (1945-present)." *Brass Bulletin—International Brass Chronicle*, no. 44 (1983): 54–60. Also in English and German.

Laplace, Michel. "Les tubas dans le jazz et dans les musiques populaires." *Brass Bulletin—International Brass Chronicle*, no. 56 (1986): 18–22. Also in English and German.

Laplace, Michel. "Les tubas dans le jazz et dans les musiques populaires." *Brass Bulletin—International Brass Chronicle*, no. 57 (1987): 84–88. Also in English and German.

"Lead trumpet, Lenton '71, M. Vax." *Crescendo International* 10 (Nov. 1971): 20–22.

Lillya, Clifford P. "About that famous letter [H. L. Clarke to E. Benge]." *Journal of the International Trumpet Guild* 12, no. 2 (Dec. 1987): 12–13 + .

2843   McCarthy, Albert. *Big band jazz*. London: Barrie & Jenkins; New York: Putnam, 1974.

2844   McRae, B. "Arena: trumpet no end [decline as innovative force in jazz]." *Jazz Journal* 29 (Dec. 1976): 12.

        Malson, L. "La génération des 'veloces' n'a pas encore dit son dernier mot." *Jazz Magazine* 5 (July 1959): 26–29.

        McCarthy, Albert J. *The trumpet in jazz*. London: Citizen Press, 1945.

        Panke, W. "Von Berg-Jazz und Grubenklang-Orchester: Jazzer im deutschsprachigen Raum besinnen sich auf Originäres." *Neue Musikzeitung* 34 (June-July 1985): 14.

2845   Russell, Ross. "Brass instrumentation in be-bop." *Record Changer* 8 (Jan. 1949): 9–10, 21.

        Sager, D. "Of ear, heart and arm—a tale of the slide trombone in early jazz." *The Second Line* 37 (Winter 1985): 36–43.

        Samball, Michael Loran. "The influence of jazz on French solo trombone repertory." *Dissertation Abstracts* 48 (Sept. 1987): 509A.

        Samball, Michael Loran. "The influence of jazz on French solo trombone repertory." D.M.A. diss., North Texas State University, 1987.

        Schafer, W. J., and R. B. Allen. *Brass bands and New Orleans jazz*. Baton Rouge: Louisiana State University Press, 1977.

        Schafer, W. J., and R. B. Allen. "Brass bands and New Orleans jazz." *Footnote* 9, no. 2 (1978): 18.

        Schafer, W. J. *Brass bands and New Orleans jazz*. Baton Rouge: Louisiana State University Press, 1979.

        Siders, H. "Splendor in the brass [interview]." *Down Beat* 40 (Feb. 1, 1973): 13–16+.

2846   Simon, George T. *The big bands*. Foreword by Frank Sinatra. New York and London: Macmillan, 1967.

2847   Sloan, Gerry. "Brass roots [jazz innovators]." *Educator* 7, no. 2 (1974–1975): 33.

2848   Slone, K., and Jamie Aebersold, eds. "28 modern jazz trumpet solos." *Jazz Journal International* 33 (Feb. 1980): 19.

2849   Stewart, Milton L. "Review of jazz French horn." *The Horn Call* 18, no. 1 (Oct. 1987): 47–53.

        "Die Story von der Jazztrompete [jazz trumpeters' styles in cartoon form]." *Jazz Podium* 24 (Nov. 1975): 21.

        Voce, S. "It don't mean a thing." *Jazz Journal* 28 (Apr. 1975): 20–21.

        "Chris Welch [use of trumpet in rock music]." *Melody Maker* 50 (Aug. 2, 1975): 22.

2850   Wilmer, V. "Trois jeunes tambours." *Jazz Magazine*, no. 202 (July 1972): 10–13+.

        Wilson, J. S. "The development of the odd ball brass [in jazz]." *Down Beat* 27 (Jan. 7, 1960): 24–25.

        Wilson, J. S. "The horn that nobody wants." *Downbeat* 26 (Sept. 17, 1959): 15+.

2851   Zwerin, M. "Ca bouge dans la coulisse." *Jazz Magazine*, no. 277 (July–Aug. 1979): 46–47.

Biography/Performers

2852   Aebi, Franz. "In memoriam: [Willi] Aebi." *The Horn Call* 18, no. 1 (Oct. 1987): 54–55.

Agrell, Jeffrey. "Jazz and the horn: Tom Varner." *Brass Bulletin—International Brass Chronicle*, no. 47 (1984): 55–57. Also in French and German.

Aitken, T. "Tuba Britannica: John Fletcher [interview]." *Brass Bulletin—International Brass Chronicle*, no. 47 (1984): 19–24.

Altenburg, Wilhelm. "Adolphe Sax und seine Verdienste um den Instrumentenbau." *Zeitschrift für Instrumentenbau* 32 (1911/12): 1051–1055.

Amend, J. J. "Trumpet sections of American symphony orchestras: The Detroit Symphony Orchestra." *Journal of the International Trumpet Guild* 1 (1976): 22–23.

Amend, J. J. "Trumpet sections of American symphony orchestras: The Philadelphia Orchestra (1900–1977)." *International Trumpet Guild Newsletter* 3, no. 3 (1977): 14–15.

2853   Angles, R. "Piano and horn [Barry Tuckwell]." *Music and Musicians* 12 (July 1964): 27.

2854   "Anton Horner—An interview with the great master of the horn." *Symphony* 5 (Nov. 1951): 7–8.

Arfinengo, Carlo. *La tromba e il trombone*. Ancona; Milano: Bèrben, 1973.

2855   Bach, M. "Women and brass: three portraits." *Brass Bulletin—International Brass Chronicle*, no. 31 (1980): 97. Also in French and German.

2856   Bachmann, Friedrich. "Pastor D. Johannes Kuhlo und das deutsche Posaunenwerk." *Musik und Kirche* 13 (1941): 87–90.

2857   Baker, William F. "T.U.B.A. profile—George Black." *T.U.B.A. Journal* 7, no. 2 (Fall 1979): 2–5.

Ball, E. "The music of Edward Gregson." *Sounding Brass & the Conductor* 6, no. 3 (1977): 98–100.

Balmuth, Jerry. "An interview with Domenico Ceccarossi." *The Horn Call* 3, no. 1 (Nov. 1972): 53–58.

2858   Baltzer, B. " 'Ich hasse die imperialen Gesten': ein Gespräch mit dem Trompeter Ludwig Güttler." *Neue Zeitschrift für Musik* 149 (Jan. 1988): 30–32.

2859   Barrow, Gary. "Col. Earl D. Irons and the evolution of cornet pedagogy." *Journal of the International Trumpet Guild* 10, no. 2 (1985): 24–32.

2860   Barrow, Gary Wayne. "Colonel Earl D. Irons: his role in the history of music education in the southwest to 1958." Ph.D. diss., North Texas State University, 1982.

2861 Bate, Philip. "In memoriam: Reginald F. Morley-Pegge." *The Horn Call* 3, no. 1 (Nov. 1972): 18–19.

Bate, Philip. *The trumpet and trombone; an outline of their history, development, and construction.* 2d ed. London: Benn; New York: Norton, 1972.

Bechler, Leo. "Ein schlesischer Berg-Hoboist erfindet die Ventile [Friedrich Blühmel]." *Deutsche Militär-Musiker Zeitung* 58, no. 19 (1936): 8.

2862 Becknell, Nancy. "Louis François Dauprat (1781–1886)." *The Horn Call* 11, no. 2 (1981): 55–57.

2863 Bedbrook, Gerald S. "The genius of Giovanni Gabrieli." *Music Review* 8 (1947): 91–101.

2864 Behrend, Roger, ed. "T.U.B.A. tribute to Dr. Leonard Falcone and Harold Brasch." *T.U.B.A. Journal* 13, no. 4 (May 1986): 14–18.

Beyer, W. "Reminiszenz an Posaunisten der Vergangenheit." *Brass Bulletin—International Brass Chronicle*, no. 22 (1978): 37 + . Also in English and French.

2865 Biehle. "Johann Pezel und die Turmsonate." *Schlesisches Blatt für evangelische Kirchenmusik* 56 (191-?): 4.

2866 Biehle, Herbert. "Johann Pezel." *Leipziger Neueste Nachrichten* (June 23, 1927): n.p.

2867 Biehle, Herbert. "Johann Pezel und die Turmmusik." *Musik-Industrie* 4 (191?): 22.

2868 Blain, B. "There's more to music than rock." *Melody Maker* 45 (Oct. 31, 1970): 35.

Blair, Stacy. "Studying with Maurice Andre." *International Trumpet Guild Newsletter* 6, no. 3 (1980): 11.

2869 Blyth, A. "Tuckwell's chance choice." *Music and Musicians* 17 (Sept. 1968): 34 + .

2870 Bowman, Brian. "T.U.B.A. euphonium profile—Leonard Falcone." *T.U.B.A. Journal* 5, no. 2 (Winter 1978): 2–4.

Bradle, S. "Carole Reinhart, solo trumpeter supreme [interview]." *The Instrumentalist* 37 (Nov. 1982): 34–39.

2871 Braun, Elaine. "Profile: Ifor James." *The Horn Call* 12, no. 1 (Oct. 1981): 22–29.

2872 Bridges, Glenn D. "Simone Mantia (1873–1951)—a short biography." *T.U.B.A. Journal* 4, no. 3 (Spring/Summer 1977): 4.

2873 Bridges, Glenn D. "Ole June May—a short biography." *T.U.B.A. Journal* 7, no. 2 (Fall 1979): 15.

2874 Bridges, Glenn D. "Pioneer cornetist . . . Benjamin C. Bent." *The School Musician* 25 (Feb. 1954): 15.

2875 Bridges, Glenn D. "Pioneer cornetist . . . Jules Levy." *The School Musician* 25 (May 1954): 11 + .

2876 Bridges, Glenn D. "Pioneer cornetist . . . W. Paris Chambers." *The School Musician* 25 (Mar. 1954): 16.

2877 Bridges, Glenn D. "Pioneer cornetist . . . Walter Emerson." *The School Musician* 25 (Nov. 1953): 17.

2878 Bridges, Glenn D. "Pioneer cornetist . . . William Northcott." *The School Musician* 25 (Dec. 1953): 13+.

2879 Bridges, Glenn D. "Pioneer cornetists. Allesandro Liberati." *The School Musician* 27 (Sept. 1955): 27.

2880 Bridges, Glenn D. "Pioneer cornetists. David Wallace Reeves." *The School Musician* 27 (Dec. 1955): 18.

2881 Bridges, Glenn D. "Pioneer cornetists. Louis Schreiber." *The School Musician* 27 (Oct. 1955): 14.

2882 Bridges, Glenn D. *Pioneers in brass*. Detroit, The author, 1965.

2883 Bridges, Glenn D. "Pioneers in Brass." *Music Journal* 25 (April 1967): 40–41+.

2884 Bridges, Glenn D. *Pioneers in brass*. Revised. Detroit: Glenn D. Bridges, 1968.

2885 Bridges, Glenn D. "Pioneers in brass." *Journal of Band Research* 6, no. 2 (1970): 13–18. Excerpts from his book.

2886 Bridges, Glenn D. "Pioneers in Brass [how information was obtained to write the book]." *Journal of Band Research* 3, no. 2 (1967): 40–42.

2887 "Briefe von Jorg Neuschel in Nürnberg, nebst einigen anderen." *Monatshefte für Musikgeschichte* 9 (1877): 149–159.

2888 Britten, Benjamin. "Dennis Brain (1921–1957)." *Tempo* 46 (Winter 1958): 5–6.

2889 Browne, James A. "Handel's trumpeter." *Monthly Musical Record* 39 (1909): 8–9.

2890 Burkart, Richard E., comp. "Other tributes to Leon Rapier." *Journal of the International Trumpet Guild* 12, no. 4 (May 1988): 37–39.

Burkart, Richard E. "The trumpet in England in the seventeenth century with emphasis on its treatment in the works of Henry Purcell and a biography of the Shore family of trumpeters." *Dissertation Abstracts* 32 (Apr. 1972): 5822A-5823A.

Burkart, Richard Edgar. "The trumpet in England in the seventeenth century with emphasis on its treatment in the works of Henry Purcell and a biography of the Shore family of trumpeters." Ph.D. diss., University of Wisconsin (Madison), 1972.

Burns, J. "Dem bones, dem bones, dem bopping bones!" *Jazz and Blues* 2 (Oct. 1972): 16–19.

Burum, H. J. B. Arban; ausführliche Anleitung zum Selbstunterricht der Trompetenschule. Hofheim: Hofmeister, 1976.

2891 Carse, Adam. "Adolphe Sax and the Distin family." *Music Review* 6 (1945): 193–201.

2892 Castil-Blaze, F. "Actéon, Paer, E. Vivier." *La France musicale* (14 May 1843).

2893 "V. F. Cerveny [obituary]." *Zeitschrift für Instrumentenbau* 16 (1895/96): 333–335.

2894 Cerveny, J. *Ehrenkranz für V. F. Cerveny*. Prague: n.p., 1883.

2895 Chambers, Jack. *Milestones*. 2 vols. Toronto: University of Toronto Press, 1983.

Chambers, Robert Lee. "Selected trombone virtuosi of the nineteenth century and their solo repertoire." *Dissertation Abstracts* 47 (Sept. 1986): 704A.

Chambers, Robert Lee. "Selected trombone virtuosi of the nineteenth century and their solo repertoire." D.M.A. diss., University of Oklahoma, 1986.

Civil, Alan, and others. "Solo voices [interview with players]." *Sounding Brass & the Conductor* 9, no. 3 (1980): 15–17.

2896　Clark, K. "From our readers: More trumpeters." *The Instrumentalist* 32 (Nov. 1977): 18+.

2897　Clarke, Herbert L. "A cornet playing pilgrim's progress." *Jacobs' Band Monthly* 12 (Aug. 1927)–15 (Sept. 1930). Published in 24 irregular installments.

2898　Clarke, Herbert L. "Famous cornetists of the past—Matthew Arbuckle." *Jacobs' Band Monthly* 16 (Mar. 1931): 8–9.

2899　Clarke, Herbert L. "Famous cornetists of the past—Ezra M. Bagley." *Jacobs' Band Monthly* 16 (Aug. 1931): 6–7.

2900　Clarke, Herbert L. "Famous cornetists of the past—Herman Bellstedt." *Jacobs' Band Monthly* 17 (Jan. 1932): 10–11.

2901　Clarke, Herbert L. "Famous cornetists of the past—Benjamin C. Bent." *Jacobs' Band Monthly* 16 (June 1931): 9.

2902　Clarke, Herbert L. "Famous cornetists of the past—W. Paris Chambers." *Jacobs' Band Monthly* 16 (Dec. 1931): 4–5.

2903　Clarke, Herbert L. "Famous cornetists of the past—Walter Emerson." *Jacobs' Band Monthly* 16 (Oct. 1931): 4–5.

2904　Clarke, Herbert L. "Famous cornetists of the past—Jules Levy." *Jacobs' Band Monthly* 16 (Apr. 1931): 6–7+.

2905　Clarke, Herbert L. "Famous cornetists of the past—Allesandro Liberati." *Jacobs' Band Monthly* 16 (Nov. 1931): 6–7+.

2906　Clarke, Herbert L. "Famous cornetists of the past—William Northcott." *Jacobs' Band Monthly* 17 (May 1932): 4+.

2907　Clarke, Herbert L. "Famous cornetists of the past—St. Jacome." *Jacobs' Band Monthly* 16 (Jan. 1931): 8–9.

2908　Clarke, Herbert L. "Famous cornetists of the past—Louis Schreiber." *Jacobs' Band Monthly* 17 (Oct. 1932): 4–5.

2909　Clarke, Herbert L. "Famous cornetists of the past—David Wallace Reeves." *Jacobs' Band Monthly* 17 (Mar. 1932): 8+.

2910　Clarke, Herbert L. "Famous cornetists of the past. Foreword." *Jacobs' Band Monthly* 15 (Nov. 1930): 8–9.

2911　Clarke, Herbert L. "Famous cornetists of the past. Jean Baptiste Arban." *Jacobs' Band Monthly* 15 (Dec. 1930): 8–9+.

2912　Clarke, Herbert L. *How I became a cornetist; the autobiography of a cornet-playing pilgrim's progress.* St. Louis: J. L. Huber, 1934.

2913　Clarke, Herbert L. "The road to success—an autobiographical series." *Jacobs' Band Monthly* 21 (Sept. 1936) to 25 (June 1940). Appears rather regularly throughout these issues.

Coar, Birchard. *A critical study of the nineteenth century horn virtuosi in France.* DeKalb, Ill.: the author, 1952.

2914 Cobb, David. "In memoriam—Robert A. Lewis." *T.U.B.A. Journal* 10, no. 1 (Summer 1982): 19.

2915 Coghill, Gene. "My first teacher: Arcady Yegudkin—'The General.' " *The Horn Call* 15, no. 1 (Oct. 1984): 15–19.

Collier, James Lincoln. *Louis Armstrong, an American genius.* New York: Oxford University Press, 1983.

2916 Colnot, C., and B. Dobroski. "Bill Watrous [interview]." *Accent* 1, no. 1 (1976): 11–13.

2917 Comettant, J. P. O. *Histoire d'un inventeur au XIXe siècle. Adolphe Sax: ses ouvrages et ses luttes.* Paris: Pagnerre, 1860.

Conner, Rex A. "Ben Gossick—musician/engineer." *The Instrumentalist* 27 (May 1973): 42–43.

Copley, I. A. "Warlock and the brass band." *The Musical Times* 109 (Dec. 1968): 1115–1116.

2918 Cotterrell, R. "Mike Westbrook: taking music to the people [interview]." *Jazz Forum*, no. 39 (1976): 38–41.

Cowan, Thomas. "Profile: interview with Charles Kavaloski." *The Horn Call* 7, no. 1 (Nov. 1976): 62–67.

2919 Cowan, Thomas. "Profile: Interview with Norman Schweikert." *The Horn Call* 6, no. 2 (1976): 56–61.

Cowan, Thomas. "Profile: interview with Philip Farkas." *The Horn Call* 8, no. 1 (Nov. 1977): 60–68.

Crouch, Rebekah Ellen. "The contributions of Adolphe Sax to the wind band." Ph.D. diss., Florida State University, 1968.

Crowne, David K. "Nicknames of jazz trumpeters." *Journal of the International Trumpet Guild* 12, no. 2 (Dec. 1987): 18–33.

2920 Daellenbach, Charles. "Renold Schilke 1910–1982—the Schilke legacy." *T.U.B.A. Journal* 10, no. 4 (Spring 1983): 2–4.

Dahlqvist, Rene. *The keyed trumpet and its greatest virtuoso, Anton Weidinger.* Nashville: Brass Press, 1975.

2921 Davidson, Louis. *Trumpet profiles.* Bloomington, IN: The Author, 1975.

2922 Davis, Ron. "T.U.B.A. profile: Tommy Johnson." *T.U.B.A. Journal* 9, no. 3 (Winter 1982): 2–6.

2923 Decker, Richard. "Profile: a tribute to Richard Moore." *The Horn Call* 16, no. 2 (Apr. 1986): 29–41.

"Desire Dondeyne prodigue ses conseils aux fanfares du Quebec." *Vie Musicale*, no. 4 (1966): 8–10.

Dobroski, B. "*Accent* interviews Doc." *The Instrumentalist* 31 (Jan. 1977): 74–78. Reprinted from *Accent* (Sept.-Oct. 1976).

2924 Dokshitser, Timofey. "Mail: In the Soviet Union we also have similar activities." *Brass Bulletin—International Brass Chronicle*, no. 15 (1976): 71–72. Also in French and German.

2925   Dudgeon, R. T. "Joseph Haliday, inventor of the keyed bugle." *Journal of the American Musical Instrument Society* 9 (1983): 53–67.

2926   Edwards, H. S. "Eugene Vivier." *The Musical Times* 36 (1895): 87–89.

2927   Egeland, O. "Meet Philip Jones." *The Instrumentalist* 37 (Apr. 1983): 28 +.

2928   Ehmann, Wilhelm. "Der Bach-Trompeter Gottfried Reiche; seine Quatricinien und seine Trompete." *Der Kirchenmusiker* 12 (1961): 49–55.

2929   Ehmann, Wilhelm. "Ein Brief von Johannes Zahn an Eduard Kuhlo." *Jahrbuch für Liturgik und Hymnologie* 4 (1958/59): 135.

Ehmann, Wilhelm. "Hundert Jahre Kuhlo-Posaunenbuch; zum 125. Geburtstag und 40. Todestag Johannes Kuhlos." *Der Kirchenmusiker* 32, no. 5 (1981): 152–156.

Ehmann, Wilhelm. *Johannes Kuhlo, ein Spielmann Gottes*. Stuttgart: Kreuz-Verlag, 1951.

Ehmann, Wilhelm. *Johannes Kuhlo, ein Spielmann Gottes*. 2 vols. Wittenburg: Luther Verlag, 1956.

Ehmann, Wilhelm. *Johannes Kuhlo, ein Spielmann Gottes*. 5th ed. Wittenburg: Luther, 1974.

Ehmann, Wilhelm. "Zum 10-jährigen Todestag von Johannes Kuhlo." *Musik und Kirche* 21 (1951): 189–190.

2930   Ehrmann, Alfred von. "Von Posaunisten und Tubabläsern." *Die Musik* 28 (1935–1936): 201–203.

2931   Eichborn, Hermann Ludwig. "Girolamo Fantini, ein Virtuos des siebzehnten Jahrhunderts und seine Trompeten-Schule." *Monatshefte für Musikgeschichte* 22 (1890): 112–138.

Erb, R. H. "The Arnold Jacobs legacy." *The Instrumentalist* 41 (Apr. 1987): 22–24 +.

2932   "Ernest Clarke—ace trombonist and trombone instructor." *Jacobs' Band Monthly* 25 (June 1940): 7.

Everett, T. "A survey of orchestral bass trombonists." *Journal of the International Trombone Association* 8 (1980): 23–24.

2933   Everett, Tom. "A conversation with Frank Rehak." *Journal of the International Trombone Association* 15, no. 2 (Spring 1987): 36–45.

Everett, Tom. "J. J. Johnson—on the road again [interview]." *Journal of the International Trombone Association* 16, no. 3 (Summer 1988): 22–29.

2934   Everett, Tom. "J. J. Johnson: architect of the modern jazz trombone." *Journal of the International Trombone Association* 16, no. 2 (Spring 1988): 30–33.

Fako, Nancy. "In memoriam: Carl Geyer." *The Horn Call* 4, no. 1 (Autumn 1973): 52–54.

Farkas, Philip, and Lawrence Sansone, Jr. "In memoriam, Lorenzo Sansone." *The Horn Call* 6, no. 1 (Nov. 1975): 17–18.

2935   Farnsley, Stephen H. "Gunther Schuller: his influence on the French horn." D.A. diss., Ball State University, 1985.

2936   Farnsley, Stephen H. "Gunther Schuller: his influence on the French horn." *Dissertation Abstracts* 47 (Sept. 1986): 705A.

2937 Farrar, Lloyd P. "Ferdinand Coeuille: maker of The Telescope Cornets and Trumpets." *Journal of the International Trumpet Guild* 13, no. 2 (Dec. 1988): 41+.

2938 Farrar, Lloyd P. "Ellis Pugh and his convertible trumpet." *Journal of the International Trumpet Guild* 13, no. 2 (Dec. 1988): 45+.

2939 Faulkner, Maurice. "Report on European brasses." *The Instrumentalist* 20 (Sept. 1965): 88.

Feather, Leonard. "Giants of jazz: the trombonists." *International Musician* 61 (July 1962): 12–13+.

Feather, Leonard. "Giants of jazz: the trumpeters." *International Musician* 61 (Sept. 1962): 12–13+.

2940 Fétis, F. J. "Martin Joseph Mengal." In *Annuaire de l'Académie royale de Belgique* (1859).

Fetter, D. "Johannes Rochut (1881–1952) [includes list of transcriptions]." *Brass Bulletin—International Brass Chronicle,* no. 50 (1985): 41–49. In English, French, and German.

Fladmoe, G. G. "The contributions to brass instrument manufacturing of Vincent Bach, Carl Geyer, and Renold Schilke." *Dissertation Abstracts* 36 (Mar. 1976): 5904A-5905A.

2941 Frizane, Daniel Evans. "Arthur Pryor (1870–1942) American trombonist, bandmaster, composer." D.M.A. diss., University of Kansas, 1984.

Garlepp, Bruno. *Die Geschichte der Trompete nebst eine Biographie J. Koslecks.* Hannover: L. Oertel, 1914.

2942 Giddins, G. "Weatherbird: The excitable Roy Eldridge [jazz recordings by Louis Armstrong-influenced trumpeters]." *Village Voice* 26 (May 27, 1981): 76+.

2943 Gilson, P., and A. Remy. *Adolphe Sax.* Brussels: Institut National Belge de Radiodiffusion, 1938–39.

2944 Globokar, Vinko. "Reflexions sur le joueur de cuivre." *Brass Bulletin—International Brass Chronicle,* no. 17 (1977): 47–59. Also in English and German.

2945 Goldman, Edwin Franko. "Arban and his method." *Metronome* 31, no. 5 (1915): 16.

Greene, G. J. "Louis François Dauprat; his life and works." *Dissertation Abstracts* 31 (June 1971): 6647A.

2946 Greenfield, E. "London report [Barry Tuckwell]." *High Fidelity* 18 (Mar. 1968): MA30.

Hall, J. "The saga of the cornet and six of its outstanding artists." *Brass Bulletin—International Brass Chronicle,* no. 12 (1975): 19–35. Also in French and German.

2947 Haugan, Paul W. "T.U.B.A. profile—Arnold M. Jacobs, tubist of the Chicago Symphony Orchestra." *T.U.B.A. Journal* 4, no. 2 (Winter 1977): 2–10.

2948 Hauprich, Donna J. "T.U.B.A. profile—Abe Torchinsky." *T.U.B.A. Journal* 6, no. 1 (Fall 1978): 2–5.

Heckman, D. "Jazz trombone—five views." *Down Beat* 32 (Jan. 28, 1965): 17–19.

Heinkel, Peggy. "Sensei [Toru Miura, euphonium teacher]." *T.U.B.A. Journal* 14, no. 4 (May 1987): 23.

2949 Hepola, Ralph. "Looking at Dennis Brain." *T.U.B.A. Journal* 12, no. 4 (May 1985): 10–11.

2950 "Herr M. Schmidt, Tonkünstler auf der Posaune." *Monatsbericht der Gesellschaft der Musikfreunde* (1830): 8–9.

2951 Hester, Steven. "Joe Tarto: titan of the tuba." *T.U.B.A. Journal* 15, no. 1 (Aug. 1987): 11–12.

2952 Heuberger, Richard. "Anton Weidinger." *Die Musik* 7 (1907/08): 162–166.

2953 Heuchamps, Edgar. "Quelques aspects de la vie toumentée et féconde d'Ad. Sax." In *Revue catholique des idées et des faits.* n.p., 1938.

2954 Heyde, Herbert. "Medieval trumpets and trumpet playing in Europe (Thesis, Leipzig, 1965)." *Brass Bulletin—International Brass Chronicle*, no. 17 (1977): 74–79.

Hill, Douglas. "Impossible Dreams or Great Expectations?" *The Instrumentalist* 33 (May 1979): 36–37.

2955 Hill, Elicia. "A tribute to Betty Glover." *Journal of the International Trombone Association* 14, no. 2 (Spring 1986): 12–15.

2956 Hiller, A. "Jean Baptiste Prin: ein Virtuose der Trompette marine." *Brass Bulletin—International Brass Chronicle*, no. 39 (1982): 53–58.

Hood, B. "Ten outstanding trumpet players in the Los Angeles area." *Brass Bulletin—International Brass Chronicle*, no. 41 (1983): 43 + . Also in French and German.

2957 Horton, D. L., ed. "ITG artist-members [The Brass Consort]." *Journal of the International Trumpet Guild* 5, no. 1 (1978): 10.

2958 Horvath, Roland. "In memory of Friedrich Reithofer." *The Horn Call* 18, no. 2 (Apr. 1988): 23.

2959 Horwood, W. "The distinguished Distins?" *Crescendo International* 13 (May 1975): 4.

2960 "In memoriam—Alec Wilder and Eddie Sauter." *T.U.B.A. Journal* 9, no. 1 (Summer 1981): 19.

"In memoriam: Anton Horner." *The Horn Call* 2, no. 2 (May 1972): 22–23.

2961 "In memoriam—Donald R. Baird." *T.U.B.A. Journal* 7, no. 1 (Summer 1979): 18.

2962 "In memoriam: Forrest W. Standley." *The Horn Call* 17, no. 1 (Oct. 1986): 28.

2963 "In memoriam—Ira D. Lee." *T.U.B.A. Journal* 8, no. 3 (Winter 1981): 50.

2964 "In memoriam: James Buffington (1922–1981)." *The Horn Call* 12, no. 1 (Oct. 1981): 21.

2965 "In memoriam—John Bambridge." *T.U.B.A. Journal* 5, no. 2 (Winter 1978): 21.

2966 "In memoriam: Merrill Ellis." *T.U.B.A. Journal* 9, no. 4 (Spring 1982): 23.

2967 "In memoriam—Ray McLaughlin." *T.U.B.A. Journal* 12, no. 4 (May 1984): 8.

2968 Ioakimidis, D. "Trombonisti di ieri e di oggi." *Musica Jazz* 20 (June 1964): 26–31; 20 (July 1964): 29–33.

2969 Jacobson, B. "New god for Fridays [Barry Tuckwell]." *Music and Musicians* 13 (Nov. 1964): 35.

2970 Jacobson, S. L. "Eminent cornet virtuosi, past and present [A. Liberati, Herman Bellstedt, Jr.]." *Music* (Chicago) 15 (1898): 60–64.

James, Eric. "Who is Carl Oestreich and why is he important to horn players?" *The Horn Call* 14, no. 2 (Apr. 1984): 53–58.

2971 Jameson, Philip, and David Mathie. "The National Music Camp at age 60: a retrospective look at its trombone teachers and students from 1928–1988." *Journal of the International Trombone Association* 16, no. 3 (Summer 1988): 32–33.

2972 Jensen, Svend Kragelund. "Portrait of Ingbert Michelsen." *The Horn Call* 12, no. 2 (Apr. 1982): 42–43. Translated by Anna Brakstad.

Johannes Kuhlo, ein Spielmann Gottes. Gütersloh: Rufer, 1947.

Johnson, D. "Brass [Cleveland brass section]." *Canadian Musician* 7, no. 1 (1985): 54.

2973 K., R. "Ein Altmeister deutscher Trompeterkunst [Julius Kosleck]." *Neue Zeitschrift für Musik* 93 (1897): 525–526.

2974 Kalkbrenner, A. *Wilhelm Wieprecht, sein Leben und Wirken.* Berlin: n.p., 1882.

2975 Kampen, Paul A. "Profile: Farquharsen Cousins." *The Horn Call* 16, no. 2 (Apr. 1986): 19–23.

2976 Kemp, Stephen. "How Vincent Bach started in the business." *Metronome* 44 (Nov. 1928): 25+.

2977 Kemp, Stephen. "There were many obstacles in Vincent Bach's path to success." *Metronome* 44 (Mar. 1928): 29+.

Kenton, Egon F. "Nel quarto centenario della nescita di Giovanni Gabrieli." *La Rassegna Musicale* 28 (1958): 26–31.

2978 Kenyon, Dave. "A cornetist confesses—Del Staigers tells a few on himself." *Metronome* 49 (Dec. 1933): 25+.

Kernfeld, Barry Dean. "Adderley, Coltrane, and Davis at the twilight of bebop: the search for melodic coherence (1958–59)." 2 vols. Ph.D. diss., Cornell University, 1981.

2979 Klee, J. H. "Tuba talk with Howard Johnson." *Down Beat* 39 (Feb. 3, 1972): 16+.

2980 Kling, Henri. "Giovanni Punto, célèbre corniste." *Bulletin français de la S. I. M.* 4 (1908): 1066–1082.

Koenig, K. "The plantation belt brass bands and musicians: Professor James B. Humphrey." *The Second Line* 33 (Fall 1981): 24–40.

Koenig, K. "Professor Robert Hingle and the Sweet Sixteen Brass Band of Point a la Hache (Louisiana)." *The Second Line* 35 (Fall 1983): 4–13.

2981 LaBrew, A. *Francis Johnson (1792–1844): a study in 19th century military and terpsichorean music history*. Detroit, 13560 Goddard Street: The Author, 1974.

2982 Lambert, G. E. "Trumpets no end [Ellington's trumpeters]." *Jazz Journal* 14 (Jan. 1961): 8–10.

2983 Langenus, Gustave. "Bruno Jaenicke." *The Ensemble News* 2, no. 2 (1927): 11.

2984 Lantz, Evans. "Responses to Coghill's article on Arcady Yegudkin: another view of the General." *The Horn Call* 15, no. 2 (Apr. 1985): 11–12.

2985 Laplace, Michel. "Les fondateurs de l'ecole française de trompette Merri Franquin, Eugene Foveau et Raymond Sabarich." *Brass Bulletin—International Brass Chronicle*, no. 29 (1980): 67–69+. Also in German and English. Expanded from *International Trumpet Guild Newsletter* 3, no. 3 (1977): 13–14.

2986 Laplace, Michel. "Introduction to the French trumpet stars." *International Trumpet Guild Newsletter* 3, no. 2 (1977): 4–6.

2987 Laplace, Michel. "Introduction to the French trumpet stars: Eugene and Raymond." *International Trumpet Guild Newsletter* 3, no. 3 (1977): 13–14.

2988 "The late Thomas Harper [obituary]." *Dwight's* 2 (1852): 194.

"Lead trumpet, Lenton '71, M. Vax." *Crescendo International* 10 (Nov. 1971): 20–22.

2989 "Leading trombonists meet Buddy Morrow." *Crescendo International* 10 (Sept. 1971): 8.

2990 Leuba, Julian Christopher. "Responses to Coghill's article on Arcady Yegudkin: survival of the fittest." *The Horn Call* 15, no. 2 (Apr. 1985): 10.

2991 Limouzin, C. *Eugène Vivier, la vie et les aventures d'un corniste, 1817–1852*. Paris: Marpon, 1888.

2992 Loucas, Paul. "T.U.B.A. profile—Joe Tarto." *T.U.B.A. Journal* 5, no. 3 (Spring/Summer 1978): 2–3.

2993 Lowrey, A. "Maurice Andre—a French performing model." *The Instrumentalist* 23 (Apr. 1969): 68–69+.

2994 Lowrey, A. "Homage to pioneers of trumpet LP's [includes discography]." *Journal of the International Trumpet Guild* 8, no. 1 (1983): 22–25+.

McConathy, O. W. "Great horn virtuosi of the past." *Symphony* 4 (Apr. 1950): 12–13.

McConathy, O. W. "Great horn virtuosi of the past." *Woodwind World* 3 (Sept. 15, 1959): 14; (Dec. 1, 1959): 11.

MacDonald, James. "Leutgeb's legacy: the Mozart horn masterpieces." *The Horn Call* 5, no. 2 (Spring 1975): 29–35.

McGrady, R. "The court trumpeters of Charles I and Charles II." *The Music Review* 35, no. 3–4 (1974): 223–230.

2995 Marcellus, John. "Blow freely: a salute to William F. Cramer." *Journal of the International Trombone Association* 15, no. 3 (Summer 1987): 14–16.

2996 Marshall, B. "Rhode Island leap." *Crescendo International* 10 (Nov. 1971): 27.

2997   "Martin Schlee zum 65. Geburtstag." *Gottesdienst und Kirchenmusik* (1954): 143–145.

2998   Mathez, Jean-Pierre. *Joseph Jean-Baptiste Laurent Arban (1825–1889).* Moudon, Switzerland: Editions BIM, 1977.

2999   Mathez, Jean-Pierre. "Arban (1825–1889)." *Brass Bulletin—International Brass Chronicle,* no. 15 (1976): 15+. Also in French and German.

3000   Meek, Harold. "In memoriam: Max Gustav Hess." *The Horn Call* 5, no. 1 (Autumn 1974): 40–42.

3001   Mende, Emily. "In memoriam: The Rev. Dr. h.c. Wilhelm Bernoulli (30 June 1904–25 Nov. 1980)." *The Horn Call* 11, no. 2 (1981): 36.

3002   Metcalf, Owen Wells. "The New York Brass Quintet; its history and influence on brass literature and pedagogy." D.Mus. diss., Indiana University, 1978.

3003   *Metronome* 54 (Nov. 1938) issue devoted to Bix Biederbecke.

3004   Miles, R. P. "Clay Smith, composer, trombonist and man." *Metronome* 43 (Aug. 15, 1927): 7+.

       Miller, D. G. "Johann Stoerl and his Six Sonatas for Cornett and Trombones." Master's essay, University of Rochester, 1962.

       Miller, James Earl. "The life and works of Jan Vaclav Stich (Giovanni Punto)—a check-list of eighteenth-century concertos and players—an edition for study and performance of the Concerto No. VI in E-flat by Giovanni Punto." 2 vols. Ph.D. diss., University of Iowa, 1962.

3005   Miller, James Earl. "The life and works of Jan Vaclav Stich (Giovanni Punto): a check-list of eighteenth-century horn concertos and players." *Dissertation Abstracts* 24 (Aug. 1963): 768–769.

       Mitchell, G. "The United States Army Herald Trumpets." *The Instrumentalist* 27 (Apr. 1973): 32–33.

3006   Morgenstern, D. "Armstrong at 85: The big band years." *Village Voice* 30 (Aug. 27, 1985): 70+.

3007   "R. Morley-Pegge." *The Horn Call* 1, no. 2 (May 1971): 44. [Photograph only].

3008   Morris, R. Winston. "T.U.B.A. tuba profile: Allan Jaffe and Anthony 'Tuba Fats' Lacen." *T.U.B.A. Journal* 9, no. 2 (Fall 1981): 11–16.

3009   Mudge, Susan. "Conversations in Los Angeles with Charlie Loper, Dick Nash, Bill Booth, Roy Main, and Morris Repass." *Journal of the International Trombone Association* 11, no. 1 (1983): 21–24; no. 3 (1983): 32–35.

3010   Mudge, Susan. "Arthur Pryor: this is your life!" *Journal of the International Trombone Association* 15, no. 2 (Spring 1987): 28–29.

3011   Mueller, John. "T.U.B.A. euphonium profile: Harold Brasch." *T.U.B.A. Journal* 9, no. 4 (Spring 1982): 4–5.

3012   Murrow, Richard. "August Helleberg, Sr. Part I." *T.U.B.A. Journal* 10, no. 1 (Summer 1982): 2–3.

       "Musician extraordinary [Jaroslav Cimera]." *The Instrumentalist* 8 (Dec. 1953): 35.

       Nash, H. "Colin Davis talks to Sounding Brass [interview]." *Sounding Brass*

& the Conductor 1, no. 4 (1973): 116–117+.

Neidig, K. L. "Philip Farkas: master horn teacher [interview]." *The Instrumentalist* 33 (Apr. 1979): 16–23.

Neidig, K. L. " 'Man alive, what a kick this is!'—an interview with Adolph 'Bud' Herseth." *The Instrumentalist* 31 (Apr. 1977): 38–44.

3013   Nussbaum, Jeffrey. "An interview with Don L. Smithers." *Journal of the International Trumpet Guild* 13, no. 2 (Dec. 1988): 11–20+.

Olsen, Paul. "Trumpet player's answer man [Elden Benge]." *Etude* 68 (Dec. 1950): 24.

3014   Otto, A. S. "Reminiscing in tempo [notes on the Ellington band and its personnel]." *Educator* 11, no. 2 (1978–1979): 10–12.

3015   *The outstanding brass and wind players and teachers at the Moscow Conservatory.* Moscow: Muzyka, 1979.

3016   Parramon, H. "Pierre Vilhardin de Belleau, trompetiste de Louis XV." *Brass Bulletin—International Brass Chronicle*, no. 59 (1987): 70–81. Also in English and German.

3017   "The Pavahn Trio [piano, violin and French horn]." *Woodwind World* 5, no. 4 (1964): 5.

3018   Paxman, Bob, James H. Winter, Barry Tuckwell, B. Lee Roberts, Dale Clevenger, Burton E. Hardin, John Wates, and Helen Ghiradella. "In memoriam: Richard Merewether." *The Horn Call* 16, no. 2 (Apr. 1986): 13–16.

3019   Pease, Edward. "Some first-hand impressions of brass playing in Moscow and Leningrad, Winter, 1976." *NACWPI Journal* 25, no. 1 (1976): 3–7.

3020   Pennell, Harriet B. "Making a career as a cornetist. An interview with Herbert L. Clarke." *Etude* 50 (1932): 332+.

3021   Phillips, Harvey. "Tribute to friends." *T.U.B.A. Journal* 9, no. 4 (Spring 1982): 19–22.

"A pictorial history of low brass players in the Boston Symphony Orchestra, 1887–1986." *Journal of the International Trombone Association* 14, no. 4 (1986): 12–21.

3022   Pierce, Robert O. "In memoriam: Willem Adriaan Valkenier." *The Horn Call* 17, no. 1 (Oct. 1986): 29–33.

3023   Pietrachowicz, J. "Brass instrumentalists in Poland: education and institution since 1945." *Journal of the International Trombone Association* 5 (1977): 2–3.

"Pilafian tames titanic tuba." *The Instrumentalist* 34 (Jan. 1980): 90.

3024   Pizka, Hans. "In memoriam: Fritz Huth." *The Horn Call* 11, no. 1 (Oct. 1980): 35.

3025   Pizka, Hans. "Jubilee with the Siegfried call [Gerd Seifert]." *The Horn Call* 15, no. 2 (Apr. 1985): 79–80.

3026   Pizka, Hans. "Karl Stiegler (1876–1932)." *The Horn Call* 10, no. 1 (Oct. 1979): 24–28. Also in German.

3027   Plass, Ludwig. "Joh. Seb. Bach's Clarintrompeter (Gottfried Reiche) und seine Kunst." *Allgemeine Musikalische Zeitung* 54 (1927): 1121–1123.

3028   "Pop goes the trumpet [trumpeters as singers]." *Melody Maker* 43 (Sept. 7, 1968): 12.

3029   "Die Posaune und einer ihrer Pioniere [Prof. Friedrich Mater]." *Die Musik-Woche* 9 (1941): 21–23.

      Pratt, Bill. "Dr. Hermann Moeck talks about his firm." *American Recorder* 14, no. 1 (Feb. 1973): 3–8.

3030   Q. "M. Vivier." *Musical World* 18 (1843): 331–332.

3031   Quayle, N. H. "American brass supreme." *Music Journal* 18 (Nov.-Dec. 1960): 50–51 +.

3032   Quayle, N. H. "The cornet's sole survivor." *Music Journal* 19 (Sept. 1961): 44 +.

3033   Quayle, N. H. "A master of the cornet [H. L. Clarke]." *Music Journal* 19 (Mar. 1961): 46 +.

3034   Rackett, Arthur H. "Bert Brown—cornet virtuoso." *Jacobs' Band Monthly* 12 (Oct. 1927): 6–7.

3035   Rackett, Arthur H. "Edward B. Llewellyn, master of the cornet and trumpet." *Jacobs' Band Monthly* 10 (Sept. 1925): 8.

3036   Rasmussen, Mary. "Two early nineteenth-century trombone virtuosi: Carl Traugott Queisser and Friedrich August Belcke." *Brass Quarterly* 5, no. 1 (1961): 3–17.

      Reed, David F. "Victor Ewald and the Russian chamber brass school." D.M.A. diss., University of Rochester, 1979.

      Reed, David F. "Victor Ewald and the Russian Chamber Brass School." *Dissertation Abstracts* 40 (May 1980): 5644A.

3037   "Rex Connor and friend." *T.U.B.A. Newsletter* 2, no. 1 (Fall 1974): 10.

3038   Richardson, Lee. "T.U.B.A. tuba profile: Fred Pfaff." *T.U.B.A. Journal* 11, no. 1 (Summer 1983): 2–5.

      Romersa, Henry J. "A study of Giovanni Gabrieli (1557–1612) with particular emphasis on six compositions by Giovanni Gabrieli." 2 vols. Master's thesis, Oberlin College, 1955.

3039   Rosenthal, Irving. "An Englishman with a French horn [Dennis Brain]." *Woodwind Magazine* 5 (Dec. 1952): 8–9 +.

3040   Rosenthal, Irving. "The extraordinary Mr. Punto [Wenzel Stich]." *Woodwind Magazine* 7 (Oct. 1954): 12–14.

3041   Rosenthal, Irving. "Man of the horn [Carl Geyer]." *Woodwind Magazine* 6 (Nov. 1953): 7.

3042   Rosenthal, Irving. "Of brass and Brain [Alfred Brain]." *Woodwind Magazine* 6 (Oct. 1953): 9–10 +.

      "St. Paul Chamber Orchestra." *The Horn Call* 4, no. 1 (Autumn 1973): 34–35.

      Sansone, Lorenzo. *French horn music literature, with composers' biographical sketches.* New York: Sansone, 1962.

3043   Sansone, Lorenzo. "The inimitable Xavier Reiter." *Symphony* 3 (Nov. 1949): n.p.

3044   Saxton, S. Earl. "In memoriam, Malcolm Colby Henderson." *The Horn Call*

6, no. 1 (Nov. 1975): 19–20.

3045　Scharnberg, William. "William C. Robinson, founder of the IHS, retires." *The Horn Call* 17, no. 1 (Oct. 1986): 12–15.

3046　Scharnberg, William. "Upon the retirement of Clyde Miller." *The Horn Call* 14, no. 2 (Apr. 1984): 98–100.

3047　Scharnberg, William. "Upon the retirement of James Winter." *The Horn Call* 18, no. 1 (Oct. 1987): 21–24.

3048　Schering, Arnold. "Zu Gottfried Reiches Leben und Kunst." *Bach Jahrbuch* 15 (1918): 133–140.

3049　Schulman, Michael. "T.U.B.A. profile—Charles Daellenbach." *T.U.B.A. Journal* 6, no. 3 (Spring 1979): 2–4.

3050　Schweikert, Norman. "America's first important professional hornist [Victor Pelissier]." *The Horn Call* 1, no. 1 (Feb. 1971): 15–17.

3051　Schweikert, Norman. "Frank Brouk retires from the Chicago Symphony." *The Horn Call* 9, no. 2 (Apr. 1979): 75–78.

　　　Schweikert, Norman. "Gumpert, not Gumbert!" *The Horn Call* 1, no. 2 (May 1971): 45.

3052　Schweikert, Norman. "Wendell Hoss [in memoriam]." *The Horn Call* 11, no. 1 (Oct. 1980): 36–51.

　　　Schweikert, Norman. "Veteran hornist Joseph Mourek retires." *The Horn Call* 6, no. 1 (Nov. 1975): 21.

　　　Selyanin, A. "Emile Joseph Trognee (1868–1942): discovery of unpublished trumpet studies." *Brass Bulletin—International Brass Chronicle*, no. 51 (1985): 68–69. Also in French and German.

3053　Shapiro, Harry. "In memoriam: James Stagliano." *The Horn Call* 18, no. 1 (Oct. 1987): 57.

3054　Sherman, Roger. "The legacy of Bernard Adelstein." *Journal of the International Trumpet Guild* 13, no. 2 (Dec. 1988): 5–10.

　　　Siders, H. "Splendor in the brass [interview]." *Down Beat* 40 (Feb. 1, 1973): 13–16+.

　　　Simon, George T. *The big bands*. Foreword by Frank Sinatra. New York and London: Macmillan, 1967.

　　　Sloan, Gerry. "Brass roots [jazz innovators]." *Educator* 7, no. 2 (1974–1975): 33.

3055　Sloan, Gerry. "You're in Teagarden country." *Journal of the International Trombone Association* 14, no. 2 (Spring 1986): 27–32.

　　　Sluchin, B. "Eberlin and his contribution to the soloistic use of the trombone." *Journal of the International Trombone Association* 13, no. 4 (1985): 36.

　　　Sluchin, B. "Un martyr de trombone [includes A. Leonard's 1846 address to L'Academie des Beaux-Arts]." *Brass Bulletin—International Brass Chronicle*, no. 31 (1980): 57–59+. Also in English and German.

3056　Smith, Clay. "Jaroslav Cimera—great trombone soloist and artist." *Metronome* 43 (July 15, 1927): 11+.

3057   Smith, Clay. "Herbert L. Clark [sic]—self-made man." *Metronome* 44 (May 1928): 28+.

Smith, M. "A matter of application." *Sounding Brass & the Conductor* 2, no. 1 (1973): 28–29+.

3058   Solti, Georg, and others. "Who is Arnold Jacobs?" *T.U.B.A. Journal* 15, no. 4 (May 1988): 30–34.

Sorenson, Scott Paul. "Thomas Harper, Sr. (1786–1835): trumpet virtuoso and pedagogue." *Dissertation Abstracts* 48 (Sept. 1987): 510A.

3059   Sorenson, Scott Paul. "Thomas Harper, Sr. (1788–1853): trumpet virtuoso and pedagogue." Ph.D. diss., University of Minnesota, 1987.

3060   Spearman, Andrew. "In memoriam: Herbert E. Holtz (May 24, 1894-July 2, 1980)." *The Horn Call* 11, no. 2 (1981): 37.

3061   Spilka, Bill. "Small makes it big in the Big Apple." *Journal of the International Trombone Association* 16, no. 3 (Summer 1988): 17–21.

Staigers, Del. "A world famous cornetist tells how he got that way." *Metronome* 47 (July 1931): 15+.

3062   "Del Staigers—world famous cornetist." In *White Way News*. Cleveland: H. N. White Co., 1930.

Stamm, Marv. "Getting to the top." *NAJE Educator* 9, no. 4 (1977): 16+.

3063   Stewart, Bob. "The legitimate jazz artist: an interview with Earl McIntyre." *T.U.B.A. Journal* 12, no. 1 (Aug. 1984): 5–8.

3064   Stewart, M. Dee. "An Arnold Jacobs biography." *T.U.B.A. Journal* 15, no. 4 (May 1988): 14–17.

3065   Stork, Karl. "Friedrich August Belcke. Der erste Virtuose auf der Zugposaune (1795–1874)." *Deutsche Musiker-Zeitung* 62 (1931): 672–673.

3066   Stork, Karl. "Robert Müller (Dem Andenken des Posaunen-Virtuosen und -Lehrers, 1849–1909)." *Deutsche Musiker-Zeitung* 63 (1932): 232–233.

3067   Stork, Karl. "Carl Traugott Queisser; zum Gedächtnis des berühmten Posaunen-Virtuosen (1800–1846)." *Deutsche Musiker-Zeitung* 61 (1930): 856–858.

Stork, Karl. "Zu einer Blechinstrumentenmacher-Werkstätte. Bei Meister Max Enders in Mainz." *Die Musik-Woche* 6 (1938): 137.

Struth, S. "Alte Meister: Bachs Trompeter, Gottfried Reiche." *Das Musikleben* 6 (1953): 171–172.

3068   Sudhalter, Richard M., Philip R. Evans, and William Dean-Myatt. *Bix; man and legend*. London: Quartet, 1974.

3069   Tarr, Edward H. "Cesare Bendinelli." *Brass Bulletin—International Brass Chronicle*, no. 17 (1977): 31–39+.

3070   Taylor, John M. "Reminiscences of the man and his horn." *T.U.B.A. Journal* 9, no. 2 (Fall 1981): 2.

3071   Temming, Fritz. *Edward Kuhlo*. Gütersloh: n.p., 1924.

Tepperman, B. "Rudd, Moncur and some other stuff." *Coda—Canada's Jazz Magazine* 10, no. 2 (1971): 8–11.

3072   Theurer, Britton. "Donald Bullock: in memoriam." *Journal of the International Trumpet Guild* 13, no. 2 (Dec. 1988): 24–27.

3073   "Thomas Harper." *Musical World* 2 (1836): xi. With a frontispiece depicting
        Harper with Clara Novello.

3074   Toeplitz, Uri. "The two brothers Lewy." *The Horn Call* 11, no. 1 (Oct. 1980):
        75–76.

        Trenner, Franz, and Bernhard Bruechle. "Franz Strauss." *The Horn Call* 2,
        no. 2 (May 1972): 61–65. Reprinted and translated from *Neue Zeitschrift
        für Musik* (1955).

        "Trombonists talk with Buddy Morrow." *Crescendo International* 10 (Oct.
        1971): 22.

3075   Tunnell, Michael. "Leon Rapier: a tribute." *Journal of the International Trum-
        pet Guild* 12, no. 4 (May 1988): 30–37.

        Urban, D. E. "Gottfried Reiche; notes on his art, life, instruments, and
        music." *Monthly Journal of Research in Music Education* 1, no. 5 (1966): 14–
        55.

3076   Uustalu, U. "Recalling Prof. Jaan Tamm (1875–1933)." *The Horn Call* 15,
        no. 1 (Oct. 1984): 82–86.

3077   "A virtuoso on the French horn." *The Harbinger* 2, no. 16 (18 Mar. 1846):
        256.

3078   "Vivier." *Musical World* 23 (1848): 737–739.

3079   Wald, A. H. "Sumner Erickson, tuba prodigy." *The Instrumentalist* 37 (May
        1983): 36+.

        Walter, E. "Dialogue—Andre Bernard: le renouveau de la trompette [in-
        terview]." *Harmonie*, no. 126 (Sept. 1977): 42–49.

3080   Watson, Catherine. "An interview with Richard Merewether." *The Horn
        Call* 15, no. 1 (Oct. 1984): 87–89.

3081   Watson, Catherine. "An interview with William Karl Ver Meulen." *The
        Horn Call* 14, no. 2 (Apr. 1984): 41–44.

3082   Watson, Catherine. "A profile of Harold Meek." *The Horn Call* 17, no. 1
        (Oct. 1986): 41–46.

3083   Watson, Catherine. "Profile of Morris Secon." *The Horn Call* 15, no. 2 (Apr.
        1985): 67–72.

3084   Welch, C. "Making music: brass, woodwinds, reeds." *Melody Maker* 48
        (Nov. 17, 1973): 42–43.

3085   Werner, Arno. "Johann Ernst Altenburg, der letzte Vertreter der he-
        roischen Trompeter- und Paukerkunst." *Zeitschrift für Musikwissenschaft*
        15 (1932–1933): 258–274.

3086   Wheeler, J. "Denis Stevens and the trumpet." *Musical Opinion* 83 (1959):
        95+.

        White, Jack Okey. "Renold Otto Schilke: his contributions to the devel-
        opment of the trumpet." *Dissertation Abstracts* 41 (Aug. 1980): 458A.

3087   White, Jack Okey. "Renold Otto Schilke: his contributions to the devel-
        opment of the trumpet." D.A. diss., New York University, 1980.

3088   Whitfield, Edward J. "Remembrances and recollections of Arnold M. Ja-
        cobs." *T.U.B.A. Journal* 12, no. 4 (May 1985): 7.

        Whiting, C. E. "Then and now [comparison between young cornetists of the 1930s and today]." *The School Musician* 41 (Aug.-Sept. 1969): 78–80.

3089 Whitman, Dale. "In memoriam: Joseph Singer." *The Horn Call* 9, no. 2 (Apr. 1979): 21–22.

Whitwell, D. "George Bernard Shaw: the music critic." *The School Musician* 40 (Dec. 1968): 56–59.

3090 Whitworth, W. "Lead player [Bernie Glow]." *International Trumpet Guild Newsletter* 5, no. 2 (1979): 9–12.

3091 Wilder, Alec. "In memoriam—John R. Barrows." *The Horn Call* 4, no. 2 (Spring 1974): 22–25.

Williams, R. "Names that blew the trumpet sky high." *Melody Maker* 46 (Sept. 11, 1971): 30+.

Wilmer, V. "Trois jeunes tambours." *Jazz Magazine*, no. 202 (July 1972): 10–13+.

3092 Wilson, George C. "Harvey Phillips and Rex Conner—a perspective from their teacher." *T.U.B.A. Journal* 15, no. 3 (Feb. 1988): 25.

3093 Winter, James H. "In memoriam: [Willi] Aebi." *The Horn Call* 18, no. 1 (Oct. 1987): 55–56.

3094 Woelber, Henry. "Walter Milton Smith." *Jacobs' Band Monthly* 22 (Nov. 1937): 6+.

Wolfinbarger, S. "The solo trombone music of Arthur Pryor: early trombone soloists with band." *Journal of the International Trombone Association* 11, no. 2 (1983): 27–29.

Wright, G. "Judith Plant and the keyed bugle." *The School Musician* 46 (Jan. 1975): 44–45.

3095 X., P. Y. "Orchestral Sketches, no. 1: Mr. Harper." *The Dramatic and Musical Review* 3 (1844): 200–201.

3096 Yancich, Milan. "The Carl Geyer story." *Woodwind World* 3, no. 11 (1961): 14–15.

Yancich, Milan. "Carl Geyer—the mouthpiece man." *NACWPI Bulletin* 10, no. 3 (Mar. 1962): 16–19.

3097 Yancich, Milan. "Willem A. Valkenier—a profile." *The Horn Call* 14, no. 1 (Oct. 1983): 51–55.

Yeo, Douglas. "Horn players of the Boston Symphony Orchestra, 1881–1988." *The Horn Call* 18, no. 2 (Apr. 1988): 47–61.

Yeo, Douglas. "Tuba players of the Boston Symphony Orchestra, 1913–1987." *T.U.B.A. Journal* 14, no. 4 (May 1987): 14–20.

PART III

PEDAGOGY, STUDY AND TECHNIQUE

General

3098   Aitken, T. "British training." *Brass Bulletin—International Brass Chronicle*, no. 54 (1986): 48–59. Also in French and German.

3099   Aitken, T. " 'What's your proper job?' A social portrait of the British brass player [interview with Maurice Murphy, John Pigneguy, Bill Geldard and James Gourlay]." *Brass Bulletin—International Brass Chronicle*, no. 51 (1985): 14–24. Also in French and German.

3100   Alexik, Frank S. "Rhythmic studies for the beginning brass player." Master's thesis, Boston University, 1953.

3101   Altman, R. J., Jr. "A study to ascertain the commonly preferred elements in a brass warm-up routine." *Missouri Journal of Research in Music Education* 5, no. 3 (1986): 50–76.

3102   Altosino, Leroy F. "A comparative study of breathing in brass instrument playing and singing." Master's thesis, DePaul University, 1951.

3103   Amstutz, A. Keith. "The 'jaw thrust'—some considerations." *NACWPI Journal* 24, no. 2 (1976–1977): 38 + .

3104   Amstutz, A. Keith. "Sibelius #2 blues; or, Is specialization a dead art?" *NACWPI Journal* 25, no. 3 (1977): 57–59.

3105   Arndt, J. "Blechbläser: Theorie und Praxis—Bericht vom dritten Seminar der Musikschule Schaumburg." *Neue Musikzeitung* 35 (Aug.-Sept. 1986): 17.

        Arnold, M. "Annual review of solos and studies: brass ensemble music." *The Instrumentalist* 39 (May 1985): 59–62.

3106   Aurand, Wayne O. *Physical factors in brass instrument playing*. Master's thesis, University of Michigan, 1949.

3107   Bach, Vincent. "The proper care of a brass instrument." *Metronome* 45 (July 1929): 20; (Aug. 1929): 23 + .

3108   Baird, F. J. "Transposition of brasswinds." *The School Musician* 36 (Dec. 1964): 8 + .

3109   Baker, K. "My way [warm up exercises]." *Sounding Brass & the Conductor* 5, no. 3 (1976): 74–75.

3110   Barlow, Harry. "Concerning the brass." *Monthly Musical Record* 61 (1931): 131–132.

        Barrow, Gary Wayne. "Colonel Earl D. Irons: his role in the history of music education in the southwest to 1958." Ph.D. diss., North Texas State University, 1982.

3111   Bays, Robert E. "Renaissance and Baroque music as a source for improved brass instruction." Ph.D. diss., George Peabody College for Teachers, 1952.

3112   Beauregard, Cherry. "Psychology in pedagogy." *T.U.B.A. Journal* 9, no. 3 (Winter 1982): 18.

3113   Belfrage, B. "Blechbläser—Sportler." *Das Orchester* 25 (May 1977): 337–339.

3114 Belfrage, B. "Blechbläser—Sportler." *Brass Bulletin—International Brass Chronicle*, no. 21 (1978): 45–52. Also in English and French.

3115 Belfrage, B. *Uebungsmethodik für Blechbläser auf der Basis von physiologischen Faktoren*. Frankfurt am Main: Hansen, 1984.

3116 Bell, Clarence W. "Fundamental problems of teaching brass instruments." Master's thesis, Eastman School of Music, 1945.

3117 Bellamah, J. L. *Brass facts. A survey of the playing and teaching methods of the leading brass authorities*. San Antonio, Tex.: The Author, 1960.

3118 Berry, Lemuel, Jr. "Improving the applied brass curriculum." *NACWPI Journal* 27, no. 1 (Sept. 1978): 19–21.

3119 Biggie, L. H. "Sing ye brass!" *Woodwind, Brass and Percussion* 24, no. 1 (1985): 3.

3120 Biggs, Millard Robert. "An evaluation of a technique employing the use of the magnetic tape recorder in teaching of students of brass instruments." *Dissertation Abstracts* 21 (1961): 1961.

3121 Biggs, Millard Robert. "An evaluation of a technique employing the use of the magnetic tape recorder in teaching of students of brass instruments." Ph.D. diss., State University of Iowa, 1960.

3122 Birch, M. "Strictly instrumental: brass tacks." *Jazz Journal International* 36 (Nov. 1983): 16–17.

3123 Birch, M. "Strictly instrumental: Brass tacks." *Jazz Journal International* 37 (Sept. 1984): 11.

Bird, G. J. "Brass ensemble; guidelines to achievement." *Brass and Percussion* 1, no. 4 (1973): 22+.

3124 Bjurstrom, N. "Orthodontic treatment as a factor in the selection and performance of brass musical instruments." *Missouri Journal of Research in Music Education* 3, no. 2 (1973): 31–57.

3125 Bjurstrom, Neil Albert. "An exploratory investigation of orthodontic treatment as a factor in the selection and performance of brass musical instruments." *Dissertation Abstracts* 32 (June 1972): 7026A.

3126 Bjurstrom, Neil Albert. "An exploratory investigation of orthodontic treatment as a factor in the selection and performance of brass musical instruments." Ph.D. diss., University of Iowa, 1972.

3127 Blaine, Robert J., Jr. "Adaptation of the Suzuki-Kendall method to the teaching of a heterogeneous brass-wind instrument class of trumpets and trombones." Ph.D. diss., Catholic University of America, 1976.

Block, Nancy Cochran. "Ensemble etiquette." *The Horn Call* 16, no. 2 (Apr. 1986): 51–53.

3128 Blume, Hermann. "Blechbläser-Nachwuchs." *Deutsche Militär-Musiker Zeitung* 58, no. 24 (1936): 1–2.

3129 Bouche, R. "Systeme respiratoire pour les cuivres: la 'colonne d'air.' " *Brass Bulletin—International Brass Chronicle*, no. 5–6 (1973): 77–83. Also in English and German.

3130 Bouhuys, A. "Breathing and blowing—Atmung und Spielen auf Blasinstrumenten." *Sonorum Speculum* 13 (Dec. 1962): I-XIII.

3131   Bowie, L. "Intonational problems of young brass players." *The Instrumentalist* 34 (Sept. 1979): 62+.

3132   Bowles, Benjamin Franklin. "Technics of the brass musical instrument." *Metronome* 30, nos. 10, 11, 12 (1914).

3133   Bowles, Benjamin Franklin. *Technics of the brass musical instrument; a condensed instructive treatise on the general construction of brass musical instruments and how to choose them; care of the instruments; and general suggestions on playing, phrasing and practicing.* New York: C. Fischer, 1915.
"Boys and brass." *Music in Education* 31, no. 327 (1967): 579.

3134   Bradley, J. D. "Tips for brass teachers." *Music Journal* 27 (Apr. 1969): 82.

3135   Brandes, Heinz. "Die Stimmung der Blasinstrumente und das Einstimmen." *Die Volksmusik—Ausg. A* (1937): 16–19.

3136   Brandon, S. "Practice hints for performers and students." *Woodwind, Brass and Percussion* 22, no. 6 (1983): 21–23.

3137   Brandon, S. "Practice hints for performers and students." *Woodwind, Brass and Percussion* 22, no. 7 (1983): 14–16+.

3138   Brasch, Harold T. "Discriminating use of the tongue." *The Instrumentalist* 12 (Sept. 1957): 86.
Brasch, Harold T. "How to play the hose." *T.U.B.A. Journal* 9, no. 4 (Spring 1982): 6–7.

3139   Brasch, Harold T. "Producing vibrato." *The Instrumentalist* 12 (Feb. 1958): 48–50.

3140   *Brass anthology: a compendium of articles on the playing of brass instruments (from The Instrumentalist).* Evanston, IL: The Instrumentalist, 1974.

3141   *Brass anthology; 214 articles on brass playing and teaching.* Evanston, IL: Instrumentalist, 1970.

3142   "Brass instrument fingerings." *The Instrumentalist* 8 (Oct. 1953): 28–29.

3143   "Briefly noted—methods and studies for brass." *Brass and Woodwind Quarterly* 2, no. 1–2 (1969): 71–76.

3144   Bright, Lynn Taggart. "A study of methods of teaching the techniques of brass instruments in groups in high schools." Master's thesis, University of Utah, 1955.

3145   "Broadcasting brass [viewpoints from producers and musicians]." *Brass International* 10, no. 2 (1982): 4–7+.

3146   Broucek, Jack W. "The relationship of orthodontics to selection of wind instruments for children." Master's thesis, University of Michigan, 1942.

3147   Burbank, Albert C. "Getting in shape for the contest." *The School Musician* 29 (Mar. 1958): 20+.
Caisley, L. "Brass bands in school." *Sounding Brass & the Conductor* 1 (Apr. 1972): 23.

3148   Carlson, C. A., and E. R. Currier. "Music for choir and brass ensemble." *Music Journal* 18 (Nov.-Dec. 1960): 10–11+.

3149   Carlucci, T. "Brass: developing and improving your sound." *Canadian Musician* 8, no. 5 (1986): 62–63.

3150   Carter, W. "The role of the glottis in brass playing." *The Instrumentalist* 21

(Dec. 1966): 75–79.

Castellani, Marcello, and Elio Durante. *Del portar della lingua negli instrumenti di fiato. Per uno corretta interpretazione delle sillabe articolatorie nella trattatistica dei secc. XVI-XVIII.* Firenza: Studio per edizioni scelte, 1979.

3151   Chase, Deforest R. "Improving brass performance." *The Instrumentalist* 11 (Mar. 1957): 56 + .

3152   Chase, DeForest R. "A test on the fundamentals of brasswind instrument teaching for instrumental music education students." Master's thesis, Ohio State University, 1949.

3153   Cheney, Edward A. "Adaptation to embouchure as a function of dento-facial complex." *American Journal of Orthodontics* 35 (June 1949): 440–443.

3154   Cheney, Edward A., and Byron O. Hughes. "Dento-facial irregularity— How it influences wind instrument embouchure." *Etude* 64 (1946): 379 + , 439–440, 499–500.

3155   Cheyette, Irving. "Why not one system of brass fingering?" *Educational Music Magazine* 31 (Jan. 1952): 18–19.

3156   Ciurczak, P. "How to increase diaphragmatic control." *The Instrumentalist* 14 (June 1960): 51 + .

3157   Civil, Alan. "My way." *Sounding Brass & the Conductor* 4, no. 3 (1975): 84– 85.

3158   Civil, Alan, and others. "Solo voices [interview with players]." *Sounding Brass & the Conductor* 9, no. 3 (1980): 15–17.

Clappé, Arthur A. *The wind-band and its instruments: their history, construction, acoustics, technique, and combination.* Reprint of the 1911 edition (New York: H. Holt). Portland, Me.: Longwood, 1976.

Clappé, Arthur A. *The wind-band and its instruments; their history, construction, acoustics, technique, and combination.* New York: H. Holt and Co., 1911.

3159   Cohen, R. "Playing the softer dynamics." *Brass and Percussion* 1, no. 3 (1973): 20 + .

3160   Cole, H. E. "Advent of brass." *Music in Education* 32, no. 329 (1968): 27– 28.

3161   Colin, Charles. *The brass player.* New York: Colin, 1972.

3162   Colin, Charles. "Range going up?" *The International Musician* 58 (May 1960): 31 + .

3163   Colin, Charles. *Vital brass notes.* Leblanc Education Series. Kenosha, Wisc.: G. Leblanc Corp., 1955.

3164   Comelek, Barbara Kay Zumwalt. "Allusions to the vocal art in selected wind instrument pedagogical sources." D.A. diss., Ball State University, 1985.

Cook, Kenneth, and Lance Caisley. *Music through the brass band.* National School Brass Band Association. Handbook No. 1. London: Hinrichsen, 1953.

3165   Corcoran, G. "Problems with third-valve technique." *The Instrumentalist* 34 (May 1980): 91–92.

3166   Cornfield, C. J. "The notation of brass instruments." *The Musical Times* 74 (1933): 653–654.

3167   Costello, Wm. N. "The big three in playing a brass instrument [power, strength and endurance]." *Metronome* 51 (Apr. 1935): 44+.

3168   Costello, Wm. N. "Developing correct embouchure." *Metronome* 51 (June 1935): 43.

3169   Costello, Wm. N. "An embouchure for any style of playing." *Metronome* 52 (Apr. 1936): 55.

3170   Costello, Wm. N. "Faulty breathing causes 90% of all horn troubles." *Metronome* 51 (Mar. 1935): 20+.

3171   Costello, Wm. N. "Only one correct way to play any brass instrument." *Metronome* 51 (Feb. 1935): 19+.

3172   Costello, Wm. N. "Vibrato for brass players." *Metronome* 52 (Sept. 1936): 48.

3173   Costello, Wm. N. "You can have good breath control and embouchure." *Metronome* 51 (Jan. 1935): 26+.

3174   Cramer, William F. "Blowing with ease and freedom." *The Instrumentalist* 10 (Sept. 1955): 22+.

3175   Cramer, William F. "Determinants of tone quality." *The Instrumentalist* 13 (Nov. 1958): 66–67.

3176   Cramer, William F. "Embouchure control and development." *The Instrumentalist* 12 (Apr. 1958): 46–47.

3177   Cramer, William F. "The initial attack. A good start sets the pattern." *The Instrumentalist* 10 (Oct. 1955): 53–54.

3178   Cramer, William F. "Teaching the brass." *The Instrumentalist* 21 (Oct. 1966): 45–47.

3179   Cuthbert, Frank. "Take care of your instrument." In *Brass Today*. Edited by Frank Wright, 117–119. London: Besson, 1957.

3180   Danner, G. "Extended techniques for brass instruments: some performance considerations." *NACWPI Journal* 35, no. 4 (1987): 4–8.

3181   D'Ath, N. W. "The art of practising." *Making Music* (Autumn 1972): 7–8. Reprinted from *Brass Band News* 2, no. 1 (Jan. 1971).

3182   Davidson, Louis. "Tonguing." *Brass Bulletin—International Brass Chronicle*, no. 44 (1983): 38–42. Also in French and German.

3183   Dehnert, Jerome. "The soft touch in playing brass." *Music Journal* 13 (Oct. 1959): 46.

3184   Deichman, John C. "A handbook for teaching brass instruments in the elementary school, kindergarten through sixth grade." Master's project, University of Southern California, 1956.

        Dekan, Karel. "Auswertung von musikalischen Dynamikbereichen bei verschiedenen Blechblas-Instrumentenspielern und die Klangfarbeänderungen bei Piano, Mezzo-forte und Forte." *IMS Report* 1972 (RILM76 179): 351–355.

3185   DeLamater, E. *Lip science for brass players*. Chicago: Rubank, 1923.

3186   "The denture venture." *International Musician* 56 (July 1957): 28–29.

3187   Deye, H. W. "Developing the brass section." *The Instrumentalist* 1 (Nov. 1947): 8.

3188   Deye, H. W. "The experts disagreed." *The Instrumentalist* 1 (Jan. 1947): 16.

3189   Deye, H. W. "The use of the tongue in brass instruments." *The Instrumentalist* 1 (Mar. 1947): 16.

3190   DeYoung, Derald. "Air velocity." *The Instrumentalist* 32 (Dec. 1977): 71–73.

3191   DeYoung, Derald. "Singing as an aid to brass performance." *The Instrumentalist* 31 (June 1977): 49–50.

3192   DeYoung, Derald. "The videofluorographic technique applied to brass players." *NACWPI Journal* 26, no. 1 (1977): 40–42.

3193   Dietz, Norman C. "Warm-up important for brass players." *The Instrumentalist* 7 (Nov. 1953): 28–29.

3194   Dillon, Robert Morris. "Five original teaching pieces in contemporary styles for brass instruments." Vol. I: text. Vol. II: original composition. D.M.E. diss., University of Oklahoma, 1971.

3195   Dillon, Robert Morris. "Five original teaching pieces in contemporary styles for brass instruments." *Dissertation Abstracts* 32 (Jan. 1972): 4043A.

3196   Dimond, H. L. "Teaching aid for brass instrumentalists." *Brass and Percussion* 2, no. 1 (1974): 16+.

3197   Dise, L. D. "A relaxed approach to brass technique." *The Instrumentalist* 32 (Sept. 1977): 71–73.

3198   Doane, C. "The basic brass embouchure and its adaptation to specific brass instruments." *Dialogue in Instrumental Music Education* 8, no. 2 (1984): 44–54.

3199   Doane, C. "Intonation on brass instruments." *The Instrumentalist* 41 (May 1987): 62+.

3200   "Does playing while marching injure the lips of wind instrument players?" *Jacobs' Band Monthly* 19 (Dec. 1934): 7+; 20 (Jan. 1935): 8+.

        Dokshitser, Timofey. "Mail: In the Soviet Union we also have similar activities." *Brass Bulletin—International Brass Chronicle*, no. 15 (1976): 71–72. Also in French and German.

3201   Douay, J. "Une experience de la chirurgie sur les levres." *Brass Bulletin—International Brass Chronicle*, no. 21 (1978): 53–57. Also in English and German.

3202   Douglass, J. "The embouchure; a written discussion of brass embouchure concepts." *Woodwind World—Brass and Percussion* 15, no. 6 (1976): 36–37+.

3203   Douglass, J. "Warm-up procedures and breath control concepts." *Woodwind World—Brass and Percussion* 17, no. 1 (1978): 34–37.

3204   Drechsler, H. J. "Individualität und Uniformiertheit der Blechbläser." *Brass Bulletin—International Brass Chronicle*, no. 52 (1985): 74–78. Also in English and French.

3205   Dunn, F. Earl. "The brass instrument class—a workbook-text for the teacher or student of the cornet, French horn and trombone." Master's thesis, Iowa State Teachers College, 1954.

3206 Duskin, J. "Tongue placement for brass players." *The Instrumentalist* 31 (Aug. 1976): 12 + .

3207 Eby, Walter M. *Eby's complete scientific method for cornet & trumpet.* Buffalo, N.Y.: Virtuoso Music School, 1926.

3208 Edney, J. "Beginners' page [how to be a brass player]." *Sounding Brass & the Conductor* 4, no. 1 (1975): 32.

3209 Edney, J. "Beginners' page." *Sounding Brass & the Conductor* 4, no. 4 (1976): 128.

3210 Edney, J. "Beginners' page [study material usable for all instruments]." *Sounding Brass & the Conductor* 5, no. 1 (1976): 32.

Egeland, O. "Meet Philip Jones." *The Instrumentalist* 37 (Apr. 1983): 28 + .

3211 Ehmann, Wilhelm. *Bläser-Fibel II.* Kassel: Bärenreiter, 1962.

3212 Ehmann, Wilhelm. *Bläser-Fibel II; Schule bläserischer Gestaltung.* Kassel: Bärenreiter, 1974.

3213 Ehmann, Wilhelm. *Bläser-Fibel; Anleitung für Blechbläser.* Kassel & Basel: Bärenreiter, 1951.

3214 Ehmann, Wilhelm. *Das Bläserspiel.* Kassel: J. Stauda-Verlag, 1960.

3215 Ehmann, Wilhelm. *Schule bläserischer Gestaltung. Bläser-Fibel II.* Kassel: Bärenreiter, 1974.

Eickmann, Paul E., and Nancy L. Hamilton. *Basic acoustics for beginning brass.* Syracuse: Center for Instructional Development, Syracuse University, 1976.

3216 Eiser, M. N. "A refreshing look at brass warm-up." *Woodwind World— Brass and Percussion* 14, no. 3 (1975): 39–40.

3217 Elias, J. "Basics in breathing: an outline to a better sound." *Brass Bulletin— International Brass Chronicle*, no. 32 (1980): 53 + . Also in French and German.

3218 Elsass, J. Frank. "Problems of brass teaching in college." *Southwestern Brass Journal* 1 (Spring 1957): 25–27.

3219 Erb, R. H. "The Arnold Jacobs legacy." *The Instrumentalist* 41 (Apr. 1987): 22–24 + .

3220 Erlenbach, Julius. "A good beginning in four easy steps." *The Instrumentalist* 22 (Mar. 1968): 64–65.

3221 Erlenbach, Julius. "Tonguing." *The Instrumentalist* 26 (Oct. 1971): 19.

3222 Eskdale, George. "Brass band to symphony orchestra." In *Brass Today.* Edited by Frank Wright, 81–83. London: Besson, 1957.

3223 Everett, T. "Get ready, get set, warm-up." *The Instrumentalist* 38 (May 1984): 40–41.

3224 Falcone, R. "The miracle on 46th Street; a profile of Carmine Caruso and his calisthenics for brass." *The Instrumentalist* 38 (June 1984): 54 + .

3225 Farkas, Philip. *The art of brass playing.* Bloomington, Ind.: The Author, 1962.

Farkas, Philip. *L'art de jouer les cuivres. Traité sur la formation et l'utilisation de l'embouchure du musicien jouant un cuivre.* Translated by Alain Maillard. Paris: Leduc, 1981.

Farr, J. W. "Tone production on the cornet or other brass wind instruments." *Metronome* 29, no. 11 (1913): 12.

3226 Farrow, Bill. "Brass instruments in the dance band." *Southwestern Brass Journal* 1 (Fall 1957): 15–16.

3227 Faulkner, Maurice. "The 'breathed attack.' " *The Instrumentalist* 21 (Apr. 1967): 53–54+.

3228 Faulkner, Maurice. "Diagnosing embouchure problems." *The Instrumentalist* 16 (Sept. 1961): 100–102.

3229 Faulkner, Maurice. "Experimentation in breathing as it relates to brass performance." *The Instrumentalist* 21 (Feb. 1967): 9+.

3230 Faulkner, Maurice. "Experimentation in breathing for wind instrumentalists." *The Instrumentalist* 13 (June 1959): 38–39.

3231 Faulkner, Maurice. "The high register—every player's dream." *The Instrumentalist* 39 (Sept. 1984): 96–98.

3232 Faulkner, Maurice. "How to produce a breath attack." *The Instrumentalist* 35 (July 1981): 20+.

3233 Faulkner, Maurice. "Judging the brass soloist in music festivals." *The Instrumentalist* 23 (Apr. 1969): 63–64.

3234 Faulkner, Maurice. "Performing original brass music [17th century]." *The Instrumentalist* 20 (Feb. 1966): 73.

3235 Faulkner, Maurice. "Physical fitness for brass players." *The Instrumentalist* 22 (Sept. 1967): 46+.

Faulkner, Maurice. "Problems of brass intonation." *The Instrumentalist* 20 (Nov. 1965): 69–73.

3236 Faulkner, Maurice. "Style in brass playing." *The Instrumentalist* 18 (Oct. 1963): 95–96; (Nov. 1963): 90–92.

3237 Faulkner, Maurice. "Tips on teaching beginning brass." *The Instrumentalist* 30 (Sept. 1975): 60–62.

3238 Faulkner, Maurice. "Twenty-five years of brass instrument playing." *The Instrumentalist* 25 (Aug. 1970): 39–43.

3239 Fennell, Frederick. "Frederick Fennell on Japan—part one of a series." *T.U.B.A. Journal* 15, no. 2 (Nov. 1987): 26–28.

3240 Fitzgerald, Bernard. "Articulation." *The Instrumentalist* 1 (Nov. 1946): 34.

3241 Fitzgerald, Bernard. "Brass clinic." *The Instrumentalist* 1, no. 1 (1946): 14–15. Bound with vol. 25, no. 1 (Aug. 1970).

3242 Fitzgerald, Bernard. "The brass: cornet, trumpet, French horn, trombone, baritone." *The Instrumentalist* 1 (May 1947): 20.

3243 Fitzgerald, Bernard. "Breathing and embouchure for the brasses." *The Instrumentalist* 1 (Sept. 1946): 14.

3244 Fitzgerald, Bernard. "Criteria for selecting brass solo repertory." *The Instrumentalist* 6 (Mar.-April 1952): 26–27+.

3245 Fitzgerald, Bernard. "Criteria for selecting students adapted to brass instruments." *The Instrumentalist* 1 (Jan. 1947): 34.

3246 Fitzgerald, Bernard. "How to select new instruments." *The Instrumentalist* 6 (Sept. 1951): 18+.

3247 Fitzgerald, Bernard. "Research studies in Brass." *The Instrumentalist* 3 (Nov.-Dec. 1948): 15.

Fitzgerald, Bernard. "The small brass ensemble." *The Instrumentalist* 6 (Oct. 1951): 22–25.

3248 Fitzgerald, Bernard. "Summer study plan." *The Instrumentalist* 1 (May 1947): 20.

3249 Fitzgerald, Bernard. "Teaching problems and techniques." *The Instrumentalist* 5 (Mar.-Apr. 1951): 19+; (May-June 1951): 21+.

3250 Fitzgerald, Bernard. "Tips on teaching young beginners." *The Instrumentalist* 7 (Sept. 1952): 24+.

3251 Fitzgerald, Bernard. "Tone control." *The Instrumentalist* 1 (Sept. 1946): 14.

3252 Fitzgerald, Bernard. "Tone production." *The Instrumentalist* 3 (Jan. 1949): 15–16; (Mar. 1949): 20–21.

3253 Fitzgerald, Bernard. "Tuning problems of brass soloists." *The Instrumentalist* 7 (Nov.-Dec. 1952): 22+.

Flor, G. J. "Compensating devices in brass instruments." *The School Musician* 46 (Nov. 1974): 16+.

Fosse, John B. "The transcription of Baroque music for the use of school brass ensembles." Master's thesis, University of Southern California, 1955.

3254 Fox, Fred. *Essentials of brass playing.* Pittsburg: Volkwein, 1974.

3255 Freedman, Walter J. "The natural scientific system for the playing of brass instruments." Master's thesis, DePaul University, 1943.

3256 Freiberg, Gottfried Ritter von, and Fritz Ramin. "Der Weg zu den Blechblasinstrumenten." In *Hohe Schule der Musik; Handbuch der gesamten Musikpraxis.* Edited by J. Müller-Blattau. Potsdam: Athenaion, 1937.

3257 Frigerio, G. "The Second Summer Academy in Gothenburgh, Sweden, August 11–16, 1986." *Journal of the International Trumpet Guild* 11, no. 3 (1987): 8–9.

3258 Fröhlich, J. *Systematischer Unterricht in den vorzüglichen Orchester-Instrumenten.* Würzburg: F. Bauer, 1829.

Fromme, Arnold. "Performance technique on brass instruments during the seventeenth century." *Journal of Research in Music Education* 20, no. 3 (Fall 1972): 329–343.

3259 Frucht, A. -H. "Blasinstrumentenspiel als Leistungsforderung an Jugendliche." *Musik in der Schule* 9 (1958): 305–307, 352–366.

3260 Garofalo, R. "Using visual aids to teach the acoustical principles of brass instruments." *The Instrumentalist* 24 (Nov. 1969): 77–79.

3261 Gartrell, M. "Getting the best sound from your young band—fast!" *Jazz Educators Journal* 18, no. 2 (1986): 82–85.

3262 Geist, C. "Ueber das richtige Atmen und die Atemeinteilung der Bläser." *Schweizerische Instrumentalmusik* 27 (1938): 29–30.

3263 Germain, Herbert L. "A new approach to beginning brass teaching." Master's thesis, Ohio State University, 1946.

3264 Giangiulio, R. C. "The role of orthodontics in correcting selected embouchure problems." *Journal of the International Trumpet Guild* 4 (1979): 20–21.

3265 Gibson, R. "Tension in brass performance: creative or destructive?" *The Instrumentalist* 31 (Feb. 1977): 65–66.

Globokar, V. "Reflexions sur le joueur de cuivre." *Brass Bulletin—International Brass Chronicle*, no. 17 (1977): 47–59. Also in German and English.

3266 Goldman, Edwin Franko. "Embouchure and its meaning to wind instrument players." *Metronome* 39 (Nov. 1923): 78.

3267 Gornston, D. "The golden era of brass." *The Instrumentalist* 3 (Nov. 1948): 39.

3268 Gorovoy, S. G. "Some ways of improving the development of the lips in brass players." *Brass Bulletin—International Brass Chronicle*, no. 48 (1984): 17–19. Also in French and German.

3269 Graham, J. "Developing a style." *The Instrumentalist* 20 (Mar. 1966): 40 +.

3270 Granger, Robert L. "Studies related to the playing and teaching of brass instruments." Master's thesis, New England Conservatory of Music, 1949.

Greenstone, P. J. "Articulation guide for brass instruments based on common practices of contemporary composers and performers." *Dissertation Abstracts* 47 (Nov. 1986): 1525A.

3271 Greenstone, Paul J. "Articulation guide for brass instruments based on common practices of contemporary composers and performers." Ph.D. diss., University of Florida, 1986.

3272 Grocock, Robert G. "Breath support and tone placement considerations." *The Instrumentalist* 12 (Sept. 1957): 87–88.

3273 Grocock, Robert G. "Teaching of double and triple tonguing." *The Instrumentalist* 8 (Apr. 1954): 28–29.

3274 Groves, S. "A summer school for brass." *Sounding Brass & the Conductor* 3, no. 4 (1974–1975): 119–120 +.

3275 Hall, Jody C. "To 'Ah-ee' or not to 'Ah-ee.' " *The Instrumentalist* 9 (Apr. 1955): 36–39.

3276 Hammer, James W. "The use of method books and photographs to determine good embouchure formation." Master's thesis, University of Kansas, 1951.

3277 Hanson, Fay. "Control of staccato sound production by laryngeal muscles." *Journal of Band Research* 4, no. 1 (1967): 61–64. Documented by R. L. Nichols.

3278 Hanson, G. I. "Marching band and brass embouchure: friend or foe?" *The Instrumentalist* 34 (Oct. 1979): 63–64.

3279 Hardin, Burton E. "Brass embouchure." *The Instrumentalist* 29 (Feb. 1975): 56–57.

3280 Hargreaves, Robert. "A brief treatment of brass instrument fingerings." *Educational Music Magazine* 22 (Jan. 1943): 14 +.

Hargreaves, Robert. "The teaching of brass instruments in school music supervisor's courses." Ph.D. diss., Eastman School of Music, 1941.

3281 Hargreaves, W. "My way [tone production]." *Sounding Brass & the Conductor* 5, no. 4 (1977): 109.

3282 Hargreaves, Walter. "Teaching bandsmen of tomorrow—the first steps." In *Brass Today*. Edited by Frank Wright, 103–105. London: Besson, 1957.

3283 Harmon, Harold D. "Techniques and problems of brass instrument playing." Master's thesis, University of Michigan, 1943.

3284 "Harry James on breathing." *Metronome* 69 (Mar. 1953): 18.

3285 Hatfield, M., and others. "Getting down to brass facts: a roundtable." *Music Educators Journal* 66 (Sept. 1979): 40–47.

3286 Hattwick, Melvin. "The vibrato in wind instruments." In *The Vibrato*, edited by C. E. Seashore, 276–280. University of Iowa Studies in the Psychology of Music, vol. 1, 1932.

3287 Hazelgrove, B. "Brass course at the Guildhall." *Sounding Brass & the Conductor* 2, no. 1 (1973): 19+.

3288 Heath, R. C. "For a better brass sound." *The Instrumentalist* 27 (Mar. 1973): 22+.

3289 Hebson, E. O. "Must tone production be a problem in your brass section?" *The School Musician* 35 (Jan. 1964): 30–31.

3290 Heinkel-Wolfe, Peggy. "Frederick Fennell on the growth of Tokyo Kosei Wind Orchestra—part two of a series." *T.U.B.A. Journal* 15, no. 3 (Feb. 1988): 28–30.

3291 Henshaw, L. "Lets make music." *Melody Maker* 44 (Nov. 22, 1969): 18–21.

3292 Hiigel, Lewis Edward. "The relationship of syllables to pitch and tonguing in brass instrument playing." Ed.D. diss., University of California (Los Angeles), 1967.

3293 Hiigel, Lewis Edward. "The relationship of syllables to pitch and tonguing in brass instrument playing." *Dissertation Abstracts* 28 (Mar. 1968): 3700A.

3294 Hill, Douglas. "Emphasizing the positive." *The Instrumentalist* 42 (Jan. 1988): 16–19.

Hill, Douglas. "Self development and the performance of music." *The Horn Call* 18, no. 2 (Apr. 1988): 45.

3295 Hindsley, M. "Common points in the playing of wind instruments." *Etude* 55 (1937): 645+.

3296 Hoffren, James. "Brass players need a daily practice routine." *The Instrumentalist* 13 (Mar. 1959): 72–74.

3297 Hofmann, H. *Ueber den Ansatz der Blechbläser*. Kassel: Bärenreiter, 1956.

3298 Hofmeister, D. "One step at a time." *The Instrumentalist* 33 (June 1979): 44–45.

3299 Homan, Robert L. "A vocal approach to brass instrument playing." Master's thesis, University of Illinois, 1946.

3300 Hoon, Delbert. "Give the beginning brass player a break." *The School Musician* 27 (Dec. 1955): 12.

3301 Hoover, W. "Preventing lip damage in brass teaching." *The Instrumentalist* 24 (Sept. 1969): 65–68.

3302 Horner, Lenore Kathleen Garman. "A criterion-referenced test in performance-related musical behaviors for instrumentalists in the upper elementary school program." Ed.D. diss., Pennsylvania State University, 1973.

3303 "Horst-Dieter Bolz." *Brass Bulletin—International Brass Chronicle*, no. 45 (1984): 3 News Suppl. Also in French and German.

Horwood, W. "Transposition—the logical approach [working with a brass band]." *Crescendo International* 10 (Jan. 1972): 39.

3304 Hruby, A., and H. E. Kessler. "Dentistry and the musical wind instrument problem." *Dental Radiography & Photography* 32, no. 1 (1959).

3305 Huttlin, Edward John. "A study of lung capacities in wind instrumentalists and vocalists." Ph.D. diss., Michigan State University, 1982.

3306 "International Brass Chamber Music Camp, Competition, and Symposium." *Journal of the International Trombone Association* 13, no. 1 (1985): 48–49.

3307 Irving, David. "Instrumental wind playing and speech production." *The Horn Call* 8, no. 2 (1978): 19–27.

3308 Ischer, R. " 'J'ai forme cet instrument personnellement.' " *Brass Bulletin—International Brass Chronicle*, no. 17 (1977): 29–30. Also in German and English.

3309 Ischer, R. "Sophrologie et musique." *Brass Bulletin—International Brass Chronicle*, no. 54 (1986): 29–36. Also in English and German.

3310 Isley, C. L. "A theory of brasswind embouchure based upon facial anatomy, electromyographic kinesiology, and brasswind embouchure pedagogy." *Dissertation Abstracts* 33 (Feb. 1973): 3956A-3957A.

Ithaca Brass Quintet. "Faculty brass performance, results of a survey." *Journal of the International Trumpet Guild* 1 (1976): 35.

3311 Iveson, John. "Students' page." *Sounding Brass & the Conductor* 5, no. 3 (1976): 96.

3312 Jacobs, Marion L. "Sick embouchures and their cure—a talk to brass players." *Jacobs' Band Monthly* 26 (Apr. 1941): 5+.

Jaeger, Jürgen. "Zur Grundfragen des Blechbläseransatzes am Beispiel der Posaune." *Beiträge zur Musikwissenschaft* 13, no. 1 (1971): 56–73.

3313 Jenkins, H. "Practicing with the mouthpiece." *The Instrumentalist* 18 (Dec. 1963): 71.

3314 Jenkins, H. "Three important concepts." *The Instrumentalist* 24 (May 1970): 69–73.

3315 Jenkins, H. "Two important considerations." *The Instrumentalist* 22 (Jan. 1968): 66+.

3316 Jenkins, M. "Development of the physical aspects of brass playing." *The Instrumentalist* 24 (Jan. 1970): 60–64.

Jenkins, Merlin, Jr. "The pedagogy of brass instruments at the college level." Master's thesis, North Texas State College, 1950.

3317 Johnson, D. "The art of positive teaching." *Canadian Musician* 1, no. 1 (1979): 40+.

3318 Johnson, D. "Brass (the tongue tip spot for correct articulation)." *Canadian*

Musician 6, no. 4 (1984): 78.

Johnson, D. "Brass: Dental habits & labial herpes." *Canadian Musician* 1, no. 5 (1979): 52.

3319 Johnson, D. "Brass: Endurance." *Canadian Musician* 3, no. 3 (1981): 58.

3320 Johnson, D. "Brass: Endurance." *Canadian Musician* 3, no. 4 (1981): 76.

3321 Johnson, D. "Brass: Endurance." *Canadian Musician* 3, no. 5 (1981): 73.

3322 Johnson, D. "Brass: Mouthpiece buzzing." *Canadian Musician* 5, no. 1 (1983): 67.

3323 Johnson, D. "Brass: Multi-tail panic." *Canadian Musician* 4, no. 5 (1982): 63.

3324 Johnson, D. "Brass: No cause for concern?" *Canadian Musician* 3, no. 1 (1981): 58.

3325 Johnson, D. "Brass: Paganini's maxim." *Canadian Musician* 4, no. 4 (1982): 86.

3326 Johnson, D. "Brass: Pedal tones." *Canadian Musician* 4, no. 1 (1982): 62.

3327 Johnson, D. "Brass: Pedal tones." *Canadian Musician* 4, no. 2 (1982): 62.

3328 Johnson, D. "Brass: Schlossberg was right." *Canadian Musician* 6, no. 3 (1984): 69.

3329 Johnson, D. "Brass: Sight reading and phrasing." *Canadian Musician* 3, no. 2 (1981): 58.

3330 Johnson, D. "Brass: Slur concept." *Canadian Musician* 2, no. 6 (1980): 63.

3331 Johnson, D. "Brass: Sound concept." *Canadian Musician* 5, no. 5 (1983): 64.

3332 Johnson, D. "Brass: Sound concept." *Canadian Musician* 5, no. 6 (1984): 64.

3333 Johnson, D. "Brass: Tongue position." *Canadian Musician* 2, no. 3 (1980): 63.

3334 Johnson, D. "Brass: Vibrato." *Canadian Musician* 3, no. 6 (1981): 60.

3335 Johnson, D. "Power below the navel." *Canadian Musician* 2, no. 5 (1980): 63.

3336 Johnson, D. "Realistic thoughts on the art of practicing." *Canadian Musician* 1, no. 2 (1979): 39 + .

3337 Johnson, D. "Tongue conception." *Canadian Musician* 1, no. 3 (1979): 55 + .

3338 Johnson, D. "The total player." *Canadian Musician* 1, no. 4 (1979): 59.

3339 Johnson, K. M. "Basic intonation for brass instruments." *NACWPI Journal* 34, no. 4 (1986): 8–10.

3340 Jones, Charles F. "Comments on brass problems in the high school." *Southwestern Brass Journal* 1 (Spring 1957): 20–25.

3341 Jones, Philip. "My way." *Sounding Brass & the Conductor* 6, no. 1 (1977): 14.

3342 Jones, R. C. "Better brass articulation." *The Instrumentalist* 28 (Sept. 1973): 56–57.

3343 Joseph, J. "The Fine Arts Brass Ensemble." *Music Teacher and Piano Student* 62 (Sept. 1983): 25.

3344 Kacanek, H. S. "Research update: brass performance." *The Instrumentalist* 32 (June 1978): 50–55.

3345 Kanerva, S. "Orivesi-Sommerkurs für Blechbläser." *Brass Bulletin—Inter-*

national Brass Chronicle, no. 4 (1973): 76–78. Also in English and French.

Kenny, P., and J. B. Davies. "The measurement of mouthpiece pressure." *Brass Bulletin—International Brass Chronicle*, no. 37 (1982): 50–54. Also in French and German.

3346 Kessler, Howard E. "Dental factors concerned with instrument playing." *The Instrumentalist* 11 (June 1957): 33–34.

3347 Kinnaman, T. "Changing concepts in brass tone quality." *The Instrumentalist* 22 (Apr. 1968): 24.

3348 Kinney, G. "Articulation and rhythmic precision for the brass player." *The Instrumentalist* 33 (July 1979): 44–48.

3349 Kinyon, John. "Beginning brass class." *The Instrumentalist* 13 (Feb. 1959): 72–73.

3350 Kloss, E. "Pro session—playercise: practice through discovery." *Down Beat* 54 (Jan. 1987): 54–56.

3351 "Eine Knabenblaskapelle und ihre Instrumente." *Instrumentenbau-Zeitschrift* 9 (1954–55): 122–123.

3352 Knaub, D. "Why bother to warm-up?" *The Instrumentalist* 24 (June 1970): 37–38.

3353 Knodt, H. "Gesangsunterricht für Blechbläser?" *Brass Bulletin—International Brass Chronicle*, no. 5–6 (1973): 71–75. Also in English and French.

3354 Koch, Ewald. "Konzeptionelle Fragen der Bläserausbildung." *Forum: Musik in der DDR. Musikschule und Persönlichkeitsbildung* (1975): 127–134.

3355 "Körperliche Eignung zum Bläser." *Schweizerische Instrumentalmusik* 30 (1941): 115.

3356 Koerselman, Herbert Leroy. "A comprehensive performance project in trumpet literature with an annotated bibliography of brass study materials which deal with performance problems encountered in contemporary music." D.M.A. diss., University of Iowa, 1976.

3357 Koerselman, Herbert Leroy. "A comprehensive performance project in trumpet literature with an annotated bibliography of brass study materials which deal with performance problems encountered in contemporary music." *Dissertation Abstracts* 37 (June 1977): 7395A–7396A.

3358 Kohut, Daniel L. "Learning how to perform music." *T.U.B.A. Journal* 15, no. 4 (May 1988): 18–20.

3359 Kramer, S. "Eine praktische Neuerung zur Reinigung und Disinfektion von Metallblasmusikinstrumenten." *Archiv für Hygiene* 125 (1939–40): 347–353.

3360 Kress, V. C. "The voice in brass playing." *The Instrumentalist* 14 (Mar. 1960): 100–103.

Krueger, H. E. "An American trumpet player's impressions of European brass performances." *Brass Bulletin—International Brass Chronicle*, no. 5–6 (1973): 35–46. Also in French and German.

3361 Krumpfer, Hans-Joachim. "III. Internationales Kammermusikseminar in Ungarn." *Brass Bulletin—International Brass Chronicle*, no. 37 (1982): 6–7 News Suppl.

3362 Krumpfer, Hans-Joachim. "Probleme der Unterrichtsmethodik in der Blechbläserausbildung." *Brass Bulletin—International Brass Chronicle*, no. 19 (1977): 51–58. Also in French and English.

3363 Krumpfer, Hans-Joachim. "Zur didaktischen Konzeption des neuen Lehrplans für Blechblasinstrumente unter Berücksichtigung der Unterrichtstätigkeit." *Forum: Musik in der DDR. Musikschule und Persönlichkeitsbildung* (1975): 134–139.

3364 Kubiak, P. V. "Mouthpiece pressure and the brasswind player." *The School Musician* 58 (Nov. 1986): 12–14.

3365 Kuhlo, Johannes. *Das Wichtigste zur Schulung der Bläser.* Gutersloh: Bertelsmann, 1933.

3366 Kwalwasser, Jacob. "Lips of professional wind-instrument players—a photographic study." *Music Publishers Journal* 1 (May-June 1943): 14–15 + .

Lamp, Charles J., and Frances W. Epley. "Relation of tooth evenness to performance on the brass and woodwind instruments." *Journal of the American Dental Association* 22 (1935): 1232–1236.

3367 Lane, George B. "Changing an embouchure." *NACWPI Journal* 24, no. 3 (1976): 38–39.

3368 Law, G. C. "Expression thru articulation techniques." *The Instrumentalist* 15 (May 1961): 65–66; (June 1961): 58–59.

3369 Law, G. C. "Orchestral literature requires development of brass tone." *The Instrumentalist* 15 (Nov. 1960): 72–76.

3370 Lawrence, I. *Brass in your school.* London: Oxford University Press, 1975.

3371 Lee, Ira D. "Vibrato for brasses." *The Instrumentalist* 8 (Mar. 1954): 16–17 + .

3372 Leidig, Vernon F. "A compendium of the technical and tone production factors in wind instruments." Master's thesis, University of Southern California, 1957.

3373 Leidig, Vernon F. *Contemporary brass technique.* Hollywood: Highland Music, 1960.

3374 Leitsinger, Carl. "Is the no-pressure system a fad?" *Metronome* 41 (June 15, 1925): 43.

3375 Leitsinger, Carl. "Triple tongueing." *Metronome* 42 (Aug. 1, 1926): 66.

Leonards, Petra G. "Artikulation auf Blasinstrumenten im 16. und 17. Jahrhundert. Ein Beitrag zur Spieltechnik der Blasinstrumente vor dem geistesgeschichtlichen Hintergrund dieser Zeit." *Tibia* 5, no. 1 (1980): 1–9.

3376 Leuba, Christopher. "Legato." *The Instrumentalist* 35 (Feb. 1981): 58–61.

3377 Leuba, Christopher. "A new look at breath support." *The Instrumentalist* 34 (Apr. 1980): 68 + .

3378 Leuba, Julian Christopher. "The inherent drive of rhythm: a continuation of the discussion." *The Horn Call* 17, no. 1 (Oct. 1986): 64–65.

3379 Lieberman, W. B., and R. C. Jones. "Dental appliances as an aid to brass playing." *The Instrumentalist* 26 (Oct. 1971): 52 + .

3380 Lindlien, Doran Royce. "The design and use of video tape in teaching students the basic care and maintenance of the primary wind instruments." D.M.A. diss., University of Oregon, 1979.

3381 Listiak, Michael. "Vibrato on wind instruments: its use and methods of production." Master's thesis, Eastman School of Music, 1940.

3382 Little, Lowell P. "Some pit-falls facing the young brass student." *The School Musician* 23 (Oct. 1951): 18–19+.

3383 Liva, H. R. "How to develop upper brass range." *The Instrumentalist* 17 (May 1963): 60–62.

3384 Long, Newell. "Development of the embouchure." *Music Educators Journal* 27 (Dec. 1940): 23–24.

3385 Lowrey, A. "Routine for routine's sake [warmup routines]." *The Instrumentalist* 23 (Oct. 1968): 59–62.

Lüttmann, Reinhard. "Bläserdidaktik im Spannungsfeld des heitigen Musiklebens." *Musikpädagogik und gesellschaftliche Wirklichkeit* (1977): 62–66.

3386 Lutschewitz, Martin. "Bläserarbeit in der Schule; Erfahrungen aus Württemberg-Baden." *Neue Zeitschrift für Musik* 118 (1957): 322–323.

3387 Lutschewitz, Martin. "Probe des Posaunenchores—Wesen und Aufgabe." *Gottesdienst und Kirchenmusik* (1956): 81–84.

3388 McBain, D. "Royal Military School of Music [Kneller Hall]." In *Brass Today*. Edited by Frank Wright, 37–42. London: Besson, 1957.

3389 McClintic, Wm. B. "The brass section of the school band; problems in instrumentation, intonation and technique." Master's thesis, University of Southern California, 1958.

3390 McGuffey, P. "Brass pitch in depth." *The Instrumentalist* 27 (June 1968): 34+.

3391 McQueen, William M. "The brass embouchure." Master's thesis, Illinois Wesleyan University, 1945.

3392 Mages, Samuel A. "Avoid lip injuries while marching." *The Instrumentalist* 14 (Sept. 1959): 100–101.

3393 Magnell, Elmer P. "Evaluation of solo brass literature." *The Instrumentalist* 8 (Mar. 1954): 52–53.

3394 Magnell, Elmer P. "Sound that 'tah.' " *The Instrumentalist* 16, no. 6 (Feb. 1962): 58–61.

3395 Maldonado, Luis. "A few guidelines on 'How to practice.' " *T.U.B.A. Journal* 14, no. 1 (Aug. 1986): 41.

Maldonado, Luis. "Long tones, lip slurs, and scales—do we really need them?" *T.U.B.A. Journal* 14, no. 2 (Nov. 1986): 35.

3396 Malek, Vincent F. "The closed throat shuts the door on musical performance." *The Instrumentalist* 11 (May 1957): 34–36.

3397 Malek, Vincent F. "Mastery of the breath, the basis of artistic performance upon brass instruments." Master's thesis, Northwestern University, 1950.

3398 Malek, Vincent F. "Producing tone on brass instruments." *The Instrumentalist* 9 (Dec. 1954): 36–38; (Jan. 1955): 29–32.

Malek, Vincent F. "A study of embouchure and trumpet-cornet mouthpiece measurements." Ph.D. diss., Northwestern University, 1953.

3399   Maljutin, E. N. "Der Einfluss des Blas- und Streichinstrumentspiels auf das Stimmorgan des Spielenden." *Monatsschrift für Ohrenheilkunde* 69 (1935): 658–665.

3400   Manous, C. "Clear thinking on articulation." *The Instrumentalist* 34 (May 1980): 92–94.

3401   Masser, J. "The brass connection [embouchure position and air pressure]." *The Instrumentalist* 32 (Apr. 1978): 89–90.

3402   Masters, Edward L. "Problems of the college brass teacher." *Southwestern Brass Journal* 1 (Fall 1957): 4–6.

3403   Mathez, Jean-Pierre. "Brass techniques: les positions du corps." *Brass Bulletin—International Brass Chronicle*, no. 59 (1987): 36–37. Also in English and German.

3404   Mathez, Jean-Pierre. "Brass techniques: les yeux." *Brass Bulletin—International Brass Chronicle*, no. 60 (1987): 116–117 + .

3405   Mathez, Jean-Pierre. "Brass techniques: the body." *Brass Bulletin—International Brass Chronicle*, no. 55 (1986): 30–31. Also in French and German.

3406   Mathez, Jean-Pierre. "Brass techniques: the brain." *Brass Bulletin—International Brass Chronicle*, no. 54 (1986): 26–27. Also in French and German.

3407   Mathez, Jean-Pierre. "Brass techniques: the ear." *Brass Bulletin—International Brass Chronicle*, no. 56 (1986): 12–14. Also in French and German.

3408   Mathez, Jean-Pierre. "Editorial (practicing to improve, not just maintain, ability)." *Brass Bulletin—International Brass Chronicle*, no. 41 (1983): 7–9. Also in French and German.

3409   Mathez, Jean-Pierre. "La respiration." *Brass Bulletin—International Brass Chronicle*, no. 57 (1987): 80–81. Also in English and German.

3410   Mathez, Jean-Pierre. "La science au service de la musique [interview with Rene Perinelli]." *Brass Bulletin—International Brass Chronicle*, no. 47 (1984): 26–29. Also in English and German.

3411   Mathie, Gordon W. "Teaching musicality to young players." *Journal of the International Trumpet Guild* 5 (1980): 19–21.

3412   Meek, Harold. "Micro-photographic studies of brass." *Symphony* 2 (Sept. 1949): 4.

3413   Meek, Harold. "Tone." *Symphony* 3 (Nov. 1949): 4.

3414   Meidt, Joseph Alexis. "A cinefluorographic investigation of oral adjustments for various aspects of brass instrument performance." *Dissertation Abstracts* 28 (Aug. 1967): 710A-711A.

3415   Meidt, Joseph Alexis. "A cinefluorographic investigation of oral adjustments for various aspects of brass instrument performance." Ph.D. diss., University of Iowa, 1967.

3416   Mellon, Edward K. "The diaphragm and its auxiliaries as related to the embouchure." *The Instrumentalist* 5 (Sept. 1950): 22 + .

3417   Mendez, Rafael. *Prelude to brass playing.* New York: C. Fischer, 1961.

3418   Mendez, Rafael. "Prelude to brass playing." *Brass Quarterly* 5, no. 4 (1962): 165–166.

3419   Mendez, Rafael. "Shop-talk on brass." *Music Journal* 13 (Sept. 1959): 20 + .

3420   Mercer, F. "Blowing brass." *Crescendo International* 12 (July 1974): 37; 13 (Aug., Sept., Oct., Nov. 1974): 35, 35, 34, 36.

3421   Mercer, F. "Blowing brass." *Crescendo International* 13 (Jan., Feb., Mar. 1975): 37, 37, 35.

3422   Mercer, F. "Blowing brass: exercises to strengthen the embouchure." *Crescendo International* 15 (Jan. 1977): 32.

3423   Mercer, F. "Blowing brass: how good is your vibrato?" *Crescendo International* 15 (Mar. 1977): 32.

3424   Mercer, F. "Blowing brass; intervals." *Crescendo International* 14 (Apr., May 1976): 36, 36.

3425   Milak, J. J. "Abstract: A comparison of two approaches of teaching brass instruments to elementary school children." *Missouri Journal of Research in Music Education* 4, no. 4 (1980): 81–83.

3426   Milak, J. J. "A comparison of two approaches of teaching brass instruments to elementary school children." *Dissertation Abstracts* 41 (Sept. 1980): 978A.

3427   Miles, Edgar M. "Beat elimination as a means of teaching intonation to beginning wind instrumentalists." *Journal of Research in Music Education* 20, no. 4 (Winter 1972): 496–500.

3428   Miller, C. *The blues book.* New York, 362 West 52nd St.: The Author, 1979.

3429   Mills, R. "Let's get off the '30-minute' bandwagon [practice time]." *The Instrumentalist* 27 (Oct. 1972): 18 + .

       Mincarelli, D. "Blazing brasses." *Woodwind, Brass and Percussion* 24, no. 2 (1985): 14.

3430   Moeck, W. F. "Brass warm-up." *The Instrumentalist* 16 (Dec. 1961): 60–61.

3431   "Montreux (Switzerland) International Brass Symposium." *Brass Bulletin— International Brass Chronicle*, no. 9 (1974): 35–37. Also in French and German.

       Moody, N. L. "Better brass through ensembles [includes list of suggested music]." *The School Musician* 52 (Feb. 1981): 19.

3432   Moody, William Joseph. "An experimental evaluation of two methods of triple tonguing on brass instruments." Ph.D. diss., University of Minnesota, 1965.

3433   Moody, William Joseph. "An experimental evaluation of two methods of triple tonguing on brass instruments." *Dissertation Abstracts* 26 (Feb. 1966): 4718.

3434   Moog, Helmut. "Der Einsatz von Blasinstrumenten in der Sonderpädagogik." *Musikbildung* 9, no. 9 (1977): 464–469.

3435   Moore, E. C. *The brass book.* Kenosha, Wisc.: G. Leblanc Corp., 1955.

3436   Moore, R. J. "Are college brass players prepared?" *Brass and Percussion* 2, no. 3 (1974): 5–6.

3437   Moore, Ward. "Tone color in brasses." *The Instrumentalist* 6 (Sept. 1951): 40.

       Morehead, T. "Dentures, braces, overlays, and brass." *The Instrumentalist* 36 (Mar. 1982): 38.

3438   Mortenson, Gary Curtiss. "Accuracy and consistency in brass performance." *The School Musician* 57 (Oct. 1985): 4–5.

3439   Moulton, Kenneth E. "The yogi complete breath: a practical application for the brass player." *The Horn Call* 12, no. 2 (Apr. 1982): 35–38.

3440   Müller, Georg. "Die Atemtechnik der Blasinstrumentalisten." *Die Musik-Woche* 6 (1938): 403–404, 419–420; *Deutsche Militär-Musiker Zeitung 6 (1938): 89–92; Die Volksmusik—Ausg. A.* (1938): 261–265 [slightly condensed version].

3441   Müller, Georg. "Grundregeln für das Studium von Blasinstrumenten." *Die Volksmusik—Ausg. A* (1938): 358–361.

3442   Müller, Georg. "Legato und Staccato in der Blasmusik." *Die Volksmusik—Ausg. A* (1938): 209–212.

3443   Müller, Georg. "Studienwerke für Blasinstrumente." *Die Volksmusik—Ausg. A* (1938): 449–452.

3444   Müller, Georg. "Zur Atemtechnik des Bläsers." *Allgemeine Musikalische Zeitung* 64 (1937): 279–281; *Schweizerische Instrumentalmusik* 26 (1937): 293–296.

3445   Musella, Donald F. "The teaching of brass instruments in the public schools using the plan of transferring students of trumpet or cornet to the other brass instruments." Master's thesis, Eastman School of Music, 1957.

        Myers, M. C. "The large brass class." *The Instrumentalist* 17 (Feb. 1963): 57–58.

3446   Myers, Philip F. "The inherent drive of rhythm." *The Horn Call* 15, no. 2 (Apr. 1985): 49 + .

3447   Nadaf, G. "The brass player's warm-up—why, when, and how." *The School Musician* 42 (Oct. 1970): 40 + .

3448   Nadaf, G. "The brass player's warm-up: why, when and how." *The School Musician* 49 (Mar. 1978): 13 + . Reprinted from *The School Musician* 42 (Oct. 1970): 40 + .

3449   Nagel, Robert. "Vibrato and style." *The Instrumentalist* 15 (Mar. 1961): 80–82.

3450   Nash, H. "Colin Davis talks to *Sounding Brass* [interview]." *Sounding Brass & the Conductor* 1, no. 4 (1973): 116–117 + .

3451   Neff, Carolyn Hope. "Embouchure development and the brass mouthpiece." *NACWPI Journal* 36, no. 2 (1987–88): 27–31.

3452   Neilson, James. "How to make the most of practice time." *The Instrumentalist* 5 (Oct. 1950): 20–23.

3453   Neilson, James. "Techniques for the brass section." *The Instrumentalist* 4 (Nov. 1949): 14 + .

3454   Nettaw, J. "Wind instruments and the physical development of children." *The Instrumentalist* 16, no. 1 (Aug. 1962): 25–26.

        Nutaitis, Raymond. "The daily routine—do I need it?" *T.U.B.A. Journal* 8, no. 4 (Spring 1981): 2–3.

3455   Nutt, H. E. "Brasses are the foundation of the band." *The Instrumentalist* 5 (Oct. 1950): 34 + .

3456   O'Donnell, J. F. "Beginning brass instruction: teaching strategies for se-
        lected skills and concepts." *Dissertation Abstracts* 48 (Dec. 1987): 1411A.
3457   Oehlberger, Karl. "Artikulationsprobleme des Bläsers bei der Wiedergabe
        der Werke Mozarts." *Wiener Figaro* 38 (May 1970): 18–30.
3458   Olsen, Walter R. "A new approach to double- and triple-tonguing." *Jacobs'
        Band Monthly* 26 (Jan. 1941): 7.
3459   O'Meara, D. "Brass studies in Australia." *Brass Bulletin—International Brass
        Chronicle*, no. 32 (1980): 75+. Also in French and German.
3460   Orzan, J. J. *L'embouchure de jade, Vol. 1: Principles fondamentaux*. The Author,
        1984.
3461   Otte, Carl, (Wisc.) State Sen. "What difference does it make?" *T.U.B.A.
        Journal* 14, no. 2 (Nov. 1986): 25.
3462   Parker, P. B. "The first consideration." *Sounding Brass & the Conductor* 1
        (Apr. 1972): 19–20.
        Pease, Edward. "Some first-hand impressions of brass playing in Moscow
        and Leningrad, Winter, 1976." *NACWPI Journal* 25, no. 1 (1976): 3–7.
3463   Perrins, B. "Brass players and dynamics." *Sounding Brass & the Conductor*
        1, no. 4 (1973): 114.
3464   Peters, D. "Double tonguing." *The Instrumentalist* 23 (Mar. 1969): 62–63.
3465   Peters, G. D. "What about that pressure?" *The Instrumentalist* 25 (Dec.
        1970): 46–48.
        Peters, George David. "Feasibility of computer-assisted instruction for in-
        strumental music education." Ed.D. diss., University of Illinois at Ur-
        bana-Champaign, 1974.
3466   Peterson, D. "Intonation and brass instruments." *The Instrumentalist* 21
        (Feb. 1967): 44–45.
3467   Petre, L. "Opwarmingsoefeningen bij koperblazers." *Adem* 22, no. 4 (1986):
        196–197. Includes summary in English and French.
3468   Peyron, Victor Lee. "Effects of tension on a lip tone." Master's thesis,
        Illinois State Normal University, 1956.
        Phelps, Russell L. "Uses of wind instruments in the classical period—
        influence on their use today in high school band work." Master's thesis,
        Northwestern University, 1955.
3469   Phillips, Harvey, and W. L. Fowler. "How to aim toward artistry in brass."
        Down Beat 43 (Oct. 7, 1976): 42–43.
3470   Phillips, Harvey. "The International Brass Society." *The Instrumentalist* 29
        (Nov. 1974): 32–34.
3471   Phillips, Harvey. "International brass society." *T.U.B.A. Journal* 13, no. 2
        (Nov. 1985): 16.
3472   Phillips, Harvey. "Toward an international brass society, Part I." *T.U.B.A.
        Journal* 12, no. 4 (May 1985): 16.
3473   Phillips, Harvey. "Toward an international brass society, Part II." *T.U.B.A.
        Journal* 13, no. 1 (Aug. 1985): 11–12.
3474   Piper, E. *The well-tempered player*. London: Crescendo, 1977.

3475 "Pitch chart for treble clef brass instruments." *The Instrumentalist* 8 (Oct. 1953): 30.

Pokorny, Gene. "The tuba and brass pedagogy in Israel." *T.U.B.A. Journal* 8, no. 2 (Fall 1980): 11–14.

3476 Pond, M. J. "Breath focus." *The Instrumentalist* 31 (May 1977): 70 + .

3477 Pond, M. J. "Calisthenics for the brass player." *The Instrumentalist* 33 (Feb. 1979): 46 + .

3478 Pontious, Melvin. "Breath control and the brass." *Music Journal* 13 (Apr.-May 1959): 64 + .

Porter, M. M. "Dental aspects of orchestral wind instrument playing with special reference to the 'embouchure.' " *British Dental Journal* 93 (1952): 66–73.

Porter, Maurice M. "Dental problems in wind instrument playing." *British Dental Journal* 123 (Oct. 1967; Apr. 1968): series of 12 articles.

Porter, Maurice M. *Dental problems in wind instrument playing.* London: British Dental Association, 1968.

3479 Porter, Maurice M. *The embouchure.* London: Boosey & Hawkes, 1967.

3480 Porter, Maurice M. "Problems of the embouchure." In *Brass Today.* Edited by Frank Wright, 106–110. London: Besson, 1957.

3481 Powell, R. E. "Nine myths of brass teaching." *The Instrumentalist* 34 (Nov. 1979): 52–53.

3482 Pruzin, R. S. "Review of a teaching aid." *Woodwind World—Brass and Percussion* 14, no. 4 (1975): 45 + .

3483 Pulling, J. "Les femmes et les cuivres: temoignages." *Brass Bulletin—International Brass Chronicle*, no. 28 (1979): 51–55. Also in English and German.

3484 Puopolo, V. "The development and experimental application of self-instructional practice materials for beginning instrumentalists." *Dissertation Abstracts* 31 (Feb. 1971): 4207A.

3485 "The pupil's the thing. Brass embouchure." *The Instrumentalist* 3 (May 1949): 21.

3486 Purdom, Benjamin A., Jr. "Teaching wind instruments in the elementary school." Master's thesis, DePaul University, 1950.

3487 Quinque, R. "ASA-Methode, ASA-Technik." *Brass Bulletin—International Brass Chronicle*, no. 37 (1982): 45–46. Also in English and French.

3488 Raby, B. "My way [warm-ups for brass instruments in opera]." *Sounding Brass & the Conductor* 8, no. 4 (1979): 134–135.

3489 Rainbow, Edward L. "Instrumental music: recent research and considerations for future investigations." *Council for Research in Music Education Bulletin* 33 (Summer 1973): 8–17.

3490 Ramin, Fritz. "Studien zur Atemtechnik des Bläsers." *Musik und Volk* 4 (1936–37): 187–192.

Rasmussen, Mary. *A teacher's guide to the literature of brass instruments.* Durham, NH: Brass Quarterly, 1964.

3491 "Records: *In Tune* [2-disc set has 'just tuning' for scales and triads for each major and minor key]." *Brass Bulletin—International Brass Chronicle*, no. 33 (1981): 83+. Also in French and German.

3492 Revelli, William D. "Basic qualities viewed in adaptation classes." *The Instrumentalist* 6 (May-June 1952): 16–17+.

3493 Revelli, William D. "Teaching of brass instruments." *Etude* 58 (1940): 383–384+.

3494 Revelli, William D. "Vibratitis." *Etude* 59 (1941): 311–312+.

3495 Reynolds, G. "Brass maintenance." *The School Musician* 31 (Apr. 1960): 14+.

3496 Reynolds, G. "Factors affecting brass tone quality." *The School Musician* 31 (Feb. 1960): 14+.

3497 Reynolds, G. "Setting the cup brass embouchure." *The School Musician* 32 (Apr. 1961): 16+.

3498 Reynolds, G. "Tips on refining your brass." *The School Musician* 31 (Mar. 1960): 18+.

3499 Reynolds, G. E. "In brass, awareness is the answer." *The School Musician* 37 (Apr. 1966): 20+.

3500 Reynolds, G. E. "New books and methods on brasses." *The School Musician* 36 (Oct. 1964): 14+.

3501 Reynolds, George. "Brass tone and embouchure." *The Instrumentalist* 3 (Mar. 1949): 58.

3502 Reynolds, George. "The brass workshop." *The School Musician* 29 (Sept. 1957): 18+.

3503 Reynolds, George. "The brass workshop." *The School Musician* 29 (Oct. 1957): 22+.

3504 Reynolds, George. "Phrasing pointers." *The School Musician* 31 (Nov. 1959): 22+.

Richards, John K. "Brass ensembles foster permanent interest in music." *The Instrumentalist* 8 (Jan. 1954): 24–25+.

3505 Richardson, Claiborne T. "Historical approach to a course of study on the college level for brass wind players." Master's thesis, University of Michigan, 1957.

3506 Richtmeyer, L. "Teaching lip vibrato." *The Instrumentalist* 15 (Jan. 1961): 62+. Correspondence. (Mar. 1961): 6 [D. R. Whitaker]; (Apr. 1961): 4 [P. Labella].

3507 Richtmeyer, Lorin Carol. "A definitive analysis of brass embouchure abnormalcies including recommended remedial techniques." Ph.D. diss., Michigan State University, 1966.

3508 Richtmeyer, Lorin Carol. "A definitive analysis of brass embouchure abnormalcies including recommended remedial techniques." *Dissertation Abstracts* 28 (July 1967): 253A-254A.

3509 Ricquier, M. *L'utilisation de vos ressources interieures.* Paris: Billaudot, 1984.

3510 Ridgeon, John. *Brass for beginners.* London: Boosey & Hawkes, 1977.

3511 Ridgeon, John. "Brass teaching in schools." *Challenges in Music Education* (RILM76 2252): 243–249.

3512   Ridgeon, John. "A change of embouchure?" *Sounding Brass & the Conductor* 6, no. 1 (1977): 22–23.

3513   Ridgeon, John. "The embouchure." *Sounding Brass & the Conductor* 3, no. 3 (1974): 75–77.

3514   Ridgeon, John. *How brass players do it*. Melville, NY: Belwin Mills, 1977.

3515   Ridgeon, John. "Resistance." *Sounding Brass & the Conductor* 3, no. 2 (1974): 52–54.

3516   Riggin, G. W. "Developing instructional materials for beginning students of wind instruments." *Dissertation Abstracts* 19 (1959): 2974.

3517   Righter, Charles B. "The stick-waver talks about the horn-blower. University director lists weaknesses observed in freshman brass players." *The Instrumentalist* 8 (Sept. 1953): 44 + .

Riley, Maurice W. "A tentative bibliography of early wind instrument tutors." *Journal of Research in Music Education* 6 (1958): 3–24.

3518   Robertson, J. "Low brass embouchure control." *The Instrumentalist* 23 (Dec. 1968): 65–67.

Robinson, William C. "The brass and percussion class." *The School Musician* 38 (Jan. 1967): 48–49.

3519   Robinson, William C. "Control your nerves by improving your playing." *The Instrumentalist* 30 (Jan. 1976): 53–56.

3520   Rohner, Traugott. "The fingering relationships of brass instruments." *The Instrumentalist* 10 (Dec. 1955): 30–33.

3521   Rohner, Traugott. "Fingering the brasses." *The Instrumentalist* 7 (Jan.-Feb. 1953): 29–31; (Mar.-Apr. 1953): 35–37.

3522   Rohner, Traugott. "Fingering the brasses." *The Instrumentalist* 33 (Feb. 1979): 30–33.

3523   Rohner, Traugott. "Transposing brass instruments." *The Instrumentalist* 1 (Mar. 1947): 10; (May 1947): 30.

Ross, C. "Scoring for the middle school brass & percussion sections." *Woodwind World—Brass and Percussion* 14, no. 5 (1975): 36–37.

3524   Sandor, E. "A comparison of pitch accuracy in sightreading between singing and brass mouthpiece buzzing." *Dialogue in Instrumental Music Education* 8, no. 1 (1984): 29–35.

3525   Sandor, E. P. "Advanced multiple tonguing for the brasses." *NACWPI Journal* 32, no. 3 (1984): 19–22 + .

3526   Sandor, E. P. "The closed-throat syndrome." *The Instrumentalist* 31 (Nov. 1976): 58 + .

3527   Sandor, E. P. "Dissertation reviews: The effects of two brass pedagogy strategies on the development of auditory discrimination skill." *Journal of the International Trumpet Guild* 10, no. 2 (1985): 36–37.

3528   Sandor, E. P. "The effects of two brass pedagogy strategies on the development of auditory discrimination skills." *Dissertation Abstracts* 44 (1984): 2705A.

3529   Savits, M. F. "Muscle training techniques applicable to methods incorporating myological principles in elementary brass embouchure training curricula." *Dissertation Abstracts* 43 (June 1983): 3838A.

3530 Sawyer, J. R. "Developing the contest winning brass section." *The School Musician* 55 (Jan. 1984): 28–29.

3531 Sax, Adolphe. *Méthode complète pour saxhorn et saxtromba soprano, alto, ténor, baryton, basse et contrebasse à 3, 4 et 5 cylindres; suivie d'exercises pour l'emploi du compensatuer.* Paris: Brandus & Dufour, n.d.

3532 Schaefer, August H. "Varied uses of mute in tone and volume." *The Instrumentalist* 8 (Dec. 1953): 26–27 +.

Schaefer, J. D. "The brass ensemble—why bother?" *The Instrumentalist* 21 (Mar. 1967): 14 +.

3533 Schiedel, A. "Throat tension: causes-effects-remedies." *Woodwind World— Brass and Percussion* 19, no. 4 (1980): 4–5 +.

Schlaefer, Sr. Cecelia Mathilda. "A comparative study of an experimental method for increasing range and endurance on brass instruments [cornet-trumpet]." *Dissertation Abstracts* 36 (Mar. 1976): 5907A.

3534 Schlenger, Kurt. "Berufsstörungen der Bläser." *Die Musik-Woche* 3, no. 22 (1935): 5–7.

3535 Schlenger, Kurt. *Eignung zum Blasinstrumentenspiel.* Schriften zur praktischen Psychologie, vol. 2. Dresden: F. Burgartz, 1935.

3536 Schlenger, Kurt. "Körperliche Eignung zum Bläser." *Die Volksmusik— Ausg. A* (1937): 89–94.

3537 Schlenger, Kurt. "Versuchsmethode zur Untersuchung der Bläseratmung." *Die Musik-Woche* 3, no. 31 (1935): 6–7.

3538 Schlenger, Kurt. "Was ist Bläseransatz?" *Die Musik-Woche* 3, no. 18 (1935): 3–4.

3539 Schmid, W. "Brass articulation." *The Instrumentalist* 22 (Aug. 1967): 83–86.

3540 Schneider, G. A. "Kieferorthopädische Hilfe bei Blasinstrumentalisten." *Fortschritte der Kieferorthopädie* 22 (1962): 483–488.

3541 Scholz, H. G. "Der genaue Bläsereinsatz." *Die Volksmusik—Ausg. A* (1938): 65–67.

3542 Schooley, J. "Studio brass teacher." *Woodwind, Brass and Percussion* 23, no. 3 (1984): 10–11.

3543 Schuhmacher, Franz. "Was der Blechbläser beim Ansatz beachten soll." *Die Volksmusik—Ausg. A* (1938): 67–68.

3544 Schulenburg, Robert. "The care of band instruments." *Music Educators Journal* 27 (Sept. 1940): 29–30 +.

3545 Schultz, H. "Individualizing the brass warm-up." *Woodwind World—Brass and Percussion* 15, no. 1 (1976): 34–35 +.

3546 Schwandt, U. "Letters: the situation of young non-professional brass players." *Brass Bulletin—International Brass Chronicle*, no. 31 (1980): 95. Also in French and German.

3547 Seifers, Heinrich. *Systematik der Blasinstrumente. Eine Instrumentenlehre in Tabellenform.* Frankfurt am Main: Das Musikinstrument, 1967.

3548 Severson, Paul, and Mark McDunn. *Brass wind artistry: master your mind, master your instrument.* Athens, OH: Accura, 1983.

3549   Shew, Bobby. "Freedom from the warm-up syndrome." *Journal of the International Trumpet Guild* 10, no. 4 (1986): 27–28.

3550   Shew, Bobby. "A positive approach to practice." *Crescendo International* 19 (Mar. 1981): 33.

3551   Shoults, C. R. "Analyzing the embouchure." *Music Journal* 19 (May 1961): 42+.

3552   Shoults, C. R. "Brass articulation." *Music Journal* 19 (Oct. 1961): 56–57.

3553   Shoults, C. R. "Wind instrument playing: The art of breathing." *Music Journal* 20, no. 8 (Nov.-Dec. 1962): 60.

3554   Shuck, Lenel. "Press the first valve." *Music Educators Journal* 26 (Oct. 1939): 30–31.

3555   Siders, H. "Splendor in the brass [interview]." *Down Beat* 40 (Feb. 1, 1973): 13–16+.

3556   Sluchin, B. "Playing and singing simultaneously on brass instruments." *Brass Bulletin—International Brass Chronicle*, no. 35 (1981): 5–7+. Also in French and German.

3557   Sluchin, B. "Playing and singing simultaneously on brass instruments." *Brass Bulletin—International Brass Chronicle*, no. 36 (1982): 18–23. Also in French and German.

        Sluchin, B. "Playing and singing simultaneously on brass instruments: acoustical explanation." *Brass Bulletin—International Brass Chronicle*, no. 37 (1982): 20–28. Also in French and German.

3558   Smith, Claude. "Tone control in brass instruments." *Educational Music Magazine* 17 (Jan.-Feb. 1938): 11–13.

3559   Smith, D. "The brass player's pivot." *The Instrumentalist* 22 (Sept. 1967): 95–100.

3560   Smith, John P. "Methods and techniques of teaching brass instruments in the public schools." Master's thesis, University of Southern California, 1951.

3561   Smith, L. "Developing high register." *The International Musician* 58 (Dec. 1960): 20–21.

3562   Smith, Leonard B. "Are you making progress?" *The School Musician* 29 (Dec. 1957): 14+.

3563   Smith, Leonard B. "Understanding 'breath technique.' " *Southwestern Brass Journal* (Spring 1957): 11–14.

3564   Smith, M. "A matter of application." *Sounding Brass & the Conductor* 2, no. 1 (1973): 28–29+.

3565   Smith, Robert D. "Some performance practice problems of 17th-century brass music." *NACWPI Journal* 19, no. 2 (Winter 1970–71): 13–14.

3566   Snapp, Kenneth O. "The 'sotto voce' band." *The Instrumentalist* 8 (Mar. 1954): 28–29+.

3567   Snell, H. "My way [warm up and practicing routine]." *Sounding Brass & the Conductor* 6, no. 3 (1977): 87.

3568   *Something about brass instruments.* New York: C. Fischer, 1928.

3569   Sordillo, Fortunato. "Doubling on brass instruments." *Metronome* 42 (Feb. 15, 1926): 71–72.

3570   Sordillo, Fortunato. "Importance of the proper position of the mouthpiece." *Metronome* 41 (Oct. 15, 1925): 51–52.

Sordillo, Fortunato. "More possibilities on the trombone and other brass instruments." *Metronome* 41 (Jan. 15, 1925).

3571   Sordillo, Fortunato. "The no-pressure system." *Metronome* 41 (Apr. 1925): 27–28.

3572   Sordillo, Fortunato. "Peculiarities and inaccuracies of brass instruments." *Metronome* 42 (July 15, 1926): 42.

3573   Sordillo, Fortunato. "The production of high notes on brass instruments." *Metronome* 41 (Nov. 15, 1925): 58–59.

3574   Sordillo, Fortunato. "What you need as much as playing technic [physical condition]." *Metronome* 41 (June 15, 1925): 46–47.

3575   Sordillo, Fortunato. "Will natural ability supplant teaching?" *Metronome* 41 (Dec. 15, 1925): 62–63.

3576   "Special hongrie: Les etudes musicales des cuivres." *Brass Bulletin—International Brass Chronicle*, no. 48 (1984): 38–39. Also in English and German.

3577   "James Stamp: practical hints." *Brass Bulletin—International Brass Chronicle*, no. 30 (1980): 21. Also in French and German.

3578   "James Stamp: practical hints." *Brass Bulletin—International Brass Chronicle*, no. 31 (1980): 77. Also in French and German.

Starr, N. "Switching brass mouthpieces." *The Instrumentalist* 39 (Nov. 1984): 9.

Stauffer, Donald W. "Intonation deficiencies of wind instruments in ensemble." Ph.D. thesis, Catholic University of America, 1954.

Stauffer, Donald W. *Intonation deficiencies of wind instruments in ensemble.* Washington: Catholic University of America Press, 1954.

3579   Stauffer, Donald W. "The master tuner." *The Instrumentalist* 17 (May 1963): 36–37.

3580   Stevens, John. "Practice for performance." *T.U.B.A. Journal* 10, no. 1 (Summer 1982): 8–9.

3581   Stiman, G. "Checklist for tonal problems [for brass players]." *The School Musician* 44 (Mar. 1973): 22+.

3582   Stiman, H. E. "Some uses of the mouthpiece rim." *The School Musician* 42 (Feb. 1971): 10+.

3583   Stoutamire, A. "Deviled tongue." *The Instrumentalist* 26 (Apr. 1972): 48–51.

3584   Strevens, P. "Beginners please." *Music Teacher and Piano Student* 61 (Nov. 1982): 19.

3585   Stroeher, Michael. "Quality in brass performance." *T.U.B.A. Journal* 11, no. 1 (Summer 1983): 12–13.

3586   Stroessler, J. H. "The class teaching of brass instruments." Master's thesis, University of Washington, 1946.

Stuart, D., comp. "Brass research projects." *Journal of the International Trom-*

bone Association 10, no. 4 (1982): 5–9.

3587 Swallow, John. "Concepts of brass embouchure development." *The Instrumentalist* 42 (Aug. 1987): 12–15.

3588 Sweby, C. "Music through the band." *Music Teacher and Piano Student* 51 (June 1972): 9–10; (July 1972): 15–16; (Aug. 1972): 21; (Sept. 1972): 29; (Oct. 1972): 27 + .

3589 Sweeney, Leslie. *Teaching techniques for the brasses.* Rockville Centre, NY: Belwin, 1953.

3590 Swett, J. P. "Brass tone quality." *The Instrumentalist* 23 (Sept. 1968): 14.

3591 Tapscott, T. "The joy of discovery [teaching tone production to beginners]." *The Instrumentalist* 30 (Apr. 1976): 18.

3592 Taylor, L. "Training the young woodwind quintet." *The Instrumentalist* 18 (Nov. 1963): 76–77; (Dec. 1963): 54–55.

3593 Taylor, Robert Boynton. "A study of the concepts of breathing as presented in literature dealing with tone production for orchestral brass-wind instruments." Ed.D. diss., Columbia University, 1968.

3594 Taylor, Robert Boynton. "A study of the concepts of breathing as presented in literature dealing with tone production for orchestral brass-wind instruments." *Dissertation Abstracts* 29 (Jan. 1969): 2296A.

3595 Teichmann, Heinz. "Dürfen wir die Blasmusik in unseren Schulen vernachlassigen?" *Musik in der Schule* 8 (1957): 122–123.

3596 Tetzlaff, Daniel B. "Bowing and blowing. Analogous approach in teaching strings and brasses." *The Instrumentalist* 12 (Oct. 1957): 64–66.

3597 Tetzlaff, Daniel B. "Brass instrument beginners." *The Instrumentalist* 16, no. 7 (Mar. 1962): 61–62.

3598 Tetzlaff, Daniel B. "Brass playing on the march." *The Instrumentalist* 27 (Oct. 1972): 46–47.

3599 Tetzlaff, Daniel B. "Controlling the low register." *The International Musician* 56 (Sept. 1958): 26–27.

3600 Tetzlaff, Daniel B. "Correcting unmusical starts." *The International Musician* 56 (Mar. 1958): 20–22.

3601 Tetzlaff, Daniel B. "Four steps toward the professional sound." *The Instrumentalist* 9 (Nov. 1954): 36–39.

3602 Tetzlaff, Daniel B. "Go hang—brass mobiles." *The Instrumentalist* 22 (Aug. 1967): 75–78.

3603 Tetzlaff, Daniel B. "How to acquire evenness in tonguing." *The Instrumentalist* 9 (Feb. 1955): 39–40.

3604 Tetzlaff, Daniel B. "Matching tonguing and slurring." *The Instrumentalist* 9 (Mar. 1955): 49 + .

3605 Tetzlaff, Daniel B. "Mostly about lips." *The International Musician* (Apr. 1961): 34–35 + .

3606 Tetzlaff, Daniel B. "Pre-instrument training for brass students." *The International Musician* 58 (Dec. 1959): 28–29 + .

3607 Tetzlaff, Daniel B. "Should I change embouchure?" *The International Musician* 56 (June 1958): 28–30.

3608   Tetzlaff, Daniel B. "Starting the tone." *The International Musician* 56 (Feb. 1958): 18–19 + .

3609   Tetzlaff, Daniel B. "Three more helps for the low register." *The International Musician* 56 (Nov. 1958): 22–23.

3610   Tetzlaff, Daniel B. "Tips on developing the rapid single tongue stroke." *The International Musician* (Jan. 1961): 30–31 + .

3611   Tetzlaff, Daniel B. "Tone and breathing." *The International Musician* (July 1961): 36–37.

3612   Tetzlaff, Daniel B. "Toward a professional sound." *The Instrumentalist* 9 (Oct. 1954): 24 + .

3613   Trickey, Samuel. "An intermediate technical outline for wind instruments." Master's thesis, Eastman School of Music, 1942.

3614   Trobian, Helen R. "Supplemental techniques for beginning brasses." *The Instrumentalist* 13 (Sept. 1958): 55–57.

3615   Trosper, O. W. "The principles and practice of producing vibrato in brass instrument performance." Ed.D. diss., Columbia University, 1962.

3616   Trusheim, William H. "Mental imagery and musical performance: an inquiry into imagery use by eminent orchestral brass players in the United States." Ed.D. diss., Rutgers University, 1987.

        Tucker, A., and others. "Electrocardiography and lung function in brass instrument players." *Journal of the International Trumpet Guild* 5 (1980): 46–52.

3617   "Tune as you play." *The Instrumentalist* 6 (Jan.-Feb. 1952): 10.

3618   Tunison, Earl H. "The embouchure and its effects upon the tone and technique of the brass family." Professional Paper, University of Idaho, 1942.

3619   Turrentine, Edgar M. "The physiological aspect of brasswind performance technique: a bibliographic essay." *NACWPI Journal* 26, no. 2 (Nov. 1977): 3–5.

3620   Umber, W. S. "The use of the brass ensemble at the junior high school level." Master's project report, University of Southern California, 1961.

3621   Usov, Y. "The scientific-theoretical principles of performance for playing brass wind instruments." *Journal of the International Trumpet Guild* 10, no. 2 (1985): 19–21. Translated by J. Cass.

3622   Utgaard, Merton. "Intonation problems of valve instruments." *The Instrumentalist* 11 (June 1957): 32 + .

3623   Van Develde, J. "Cool-down exercises for brass players." *The Instrumentalist* 34 (Dec. 1979): 36–37.

3624   Vesley, T. "Going with the wind." *Music Journal* 13 (June-July 1959): 56.

3625   Waldmann, Guido. "Musikhochschule und Blasmusik." *Junge Musik* (1957): 66–68.

3626   Walker, B. H. "The brass workshop." *The School Musician* 28 (Jan. 1957): 41–43 + .

3627   Walker, B. H. "The brass workshop." *The School Musician* 28 (Feb. 1957): 16 + . [Legato playing on valved instruments.]

3628   Walker, B. H. "The brass workshop." *The School Musician* 28 (Mar. 1957): 16+. [polishing for contest].

3629   Walker, B. H. "The brass workshop." *The School Musician* 28 (Apr. 1957): 46–47. [pressure].

3630   Walker, B. H. "The brass workshop." *The School Musician* 28 (May 1957): 60–61 [tone quality].

3631   Wardle, A. "Behavior modification by reciprocal inhibition of instrumental music performance anxiety." *Journal of Band Research* 11, no. 1 (1974): 18–26.

3632   Waybright, D. "Brass playing in the marching band." *The Instrumentalist* 38 (June 1984): 12–13.

3633   Weast, Robert D. *Brass performance; an analytical text*. New York: McGinnis & Marx, 1961.

3634   Weast, Robert D. *Brass performance; an analytical text of the physical processes, problems and technique of brass*. Second ed. New York: McGinnis & Marx, 1962.

3635   Weast, Robert D. "Development and meaning of breath support." *The Instrumentalist* 14 (Jan. 1960): 56–57.

3636   Weast, Robert D. "The development of range." *The Instrumentalist* 16 (Nov. 1961): 67–68.

3637   Weast, Robert D. *Keys to natural performance for brass players*. Des Moines: Brass World, 1979.

3638   Weast, Robert D. "Relationship between breath support and lip tension." *The Instrumentalist* 13 (Dec. 1958): 52–53.

3639   Weber, Karlheinz. "Der 'druckschwache Ansatz' bei Blechbläsern." *Das Orchester* 27, no. 4 (1979): 267–271.

3640   Weisberg, Arthur. *The art of wind playing*. New York: Schirmer, 1975.

3641   Wekre, Froydis Ree. "After a music review [performing from memory]." *The Horn Call* 13, no. 2 (Apr. 1983): 54.

3642   Wekre, Froydis Ree. "Being a woman brass player—so what?" *Brass Bulletin—International Brass Chronicle*, no. 26 (1979): 51–54. Also in French and German.

        Welch, C. "Making music: brass, woodwinds, reeds." *Melody Maker* 48 (Nov. 17, 1973): 42–43.

3643   Whitcomb, M. R. "Musical performance on wind instruments: a study of interpretive factors." Ed.D. diss., Columbia University, 1959.

3644   Whitehill, C. D. "Some solutions for brass playing problems." *The Instrumentalist* 20 (May 1966): 72+.

3645   Whittacker, Maurice E. "Staccato-Spiel, Doppel- und Flatterzunge auf Blasinstrumente." *Das Schwalbennest* 13, nos. 2 and 4? (1930): n.p.

3646   Whittacker, Maurice E. " 'Tongueing' on wind instruments." *The Musical Times* 67 (1926): 998–999; 68 (1927): 229–230.

3647   Whybrew, William C. "Concerning attack and release." *The Instrumentalist* 12 (Sept. 1957): 89+.

3648   Wiesner, Glenn R., Daniel R. Balbach, and Merrill A. Wilson. *Orthodontics and wind instrument performance.* Washington, D.C.: Music Educators National Conference, 1973.

3649   Wiggins, B. "My way." *Sounding Brass & the Conductor* 8, no. 2 (1979): 54–55.

3650   Wiggins, B. "Practice." *Brass International* 10, no. 1 (1982): 6–8.

3651   Wilbraham, John. "My way [warm-up routines]." *Sounding Brass & the Conductor* 4, no. 2 (1975): 44–45.

     Williams, A. L. "Improving intonation on brass instruments." *Music Journal* (1965): 72+.

3652   Williams, A. L. "Teaching the brass wind instruments." *MTNA Proceedings for 1934* (1934): 243–252.

3653   Willis, L. "Toward better breath control." *The Instrumentalist* 22 (Dec. 1967): 70–71.

3654   Willmann, Paul. "Stadtpfeifereien und Musik-Unterricht." *Zeitschrift für Musik* 92 (1925): 422–425.

3655   Wilson, Harvey LeRoy. "Level method for brasses." *The Instrumentalist* 7 (Sept. 1952): 6+.

3656   Winick, Steven. "Tongue arch: the missing link in brass instrument pedagogy and performance." *Journal of the International Trumpet Guild* 8, no. 2 (1983): 23–26+.

3657   Winslow, R. W., and J. E. Green. *Playing and teaching brass instruments.* Englewood Cliffs, N.J.: Prentice Hall, 1961.

3658   Winter, James H. *The brass instruments; performance and instructional techniques.* Boston: Allyn and Bacon, 1964.

3659   Worrel, J. W. "Quality first." *The School Musician* 30 (Oct. 1958): 18+.

3660   Worrel, J. W. "Quality first." *The School Musician* 32 (Oct. 1960): 12+.

3661   *Wright and Round's amateur band teacher's guide and bandsman's adviser.* Liverpool: Wright and Round, [1889].

3662   Zahl, Wesley. "Addressing the brass." *Jacobs' Band Monthly* 22 (May 1937): 4+.

3663   Zawistowski, J. "Pre-instrument training for beginning brass classes." *The Instrumentalist* 21 (Aug. 1966): 10.

3664   Zazra, H. D. "Purchasing brass instruments." *The Instrumentalist* 27 (Aug. 1972): 18.

     Zoppoth, Marguerite. "Materials for elementary brass ensembles." Master's thesis, Eastman School of Music, 1950.

3665   Zorn, Jay D. "Neglecting the brass ensemble?" *The Instrumentalist* 14 (Nov. 1959): 61–63.

3666   Zorn, Jay D. "The prerehearsal warm up." *The Instrumentalist* 19 (Feb. 1965): 60–63.

3667   Zottola, Frank. "How to improve your 'brass' technique." *The International Musician* 56 (Jan. 1958): 34–35.

3668   Zurcher, Z. W. "The effect of model-supportive practice on beginning brass instrumentalists." *Dissertation Abstracts* 33 (Nov. 1972): 2001A-2002A.

Brass Class (Techniques)

3669   Averyt, Alton R. "An ensemble brass method for college brass classes." Master's thesis, North Texas State College, 1949.

3670   Collins, Thomas C. "A survey and evaluation of the class wind instrument programs in some representative music teacher training institutions, with some suggestions for an ideal course of study." Ph.D. diss., State University of Iowa, 1950.

Dunn, F. Earl. "The brass instrument class—a workbook-text for the teacher or student of the cornet, French horn and trombone." Master's thesis, Iowa State Teachers College, 1954.

Eickmann, Paul E., and Nancy L. Hamilton. *Basic acoustics for beginning brass*. Syracuse: Center for Instructional Development, Syracuse University, 1976.

Elsass, J. Frank. "Problems of brass teaching in college." *Southwestern Brass Journal* 1 (Spring 1957): 25–27.

3671   Hargreaves, Robert. "The teaching of brass instruments in school music supervisor's courses." Ph.D. diss., Eastman School of Music, 1941.

3672   Hargreaves, Robert. *The teaching of brass instruments in school music supervisors' courses*. 4 vols. Rochester, NY: University of Rochester Press, 1953.

Hazelgrove, B. "Brass course at the Guildhall." *Sounding Brass & the Conductor* 2, no. 1 (1973): 19 +.

3673   Hunt, Norman J. *Brass ensemble method for teacher education*. Dubuque, Ia.: W. C. Brown, 1960.

3674   Hunt, Norman J. *Brass ensemble method; beginning class instruction in trumpet, French horn, trombone, baritone, and tuba*. 3rd ed. Dubuque, Ia.: W. C. Brown, 1974.

3675   Hunt, Norman J. *Guide to teaching brass*. 2nd ed. Dubuque Ia.: W. C. Brown, 1978.

3676   Hunt, Norman J. *Guide to teaching brass*. 3rd ed. Dubuque, Ia.: W. C. Brown, 1984.

3677   Huntley, Lawrence D. "A survey of brass techniques classes in the music education curriculum in selected colleges and universities in the United States." *NACWPI Journal* 24, no. 2 (Winter 1975–76): 31–33.

3678   Huntley, Lawrence D. "A survey of brass techniques classes in the music education curriculum of selected colleges and universities in the United States." D.Mus. diss., Indiana University, 1975.

3679   Jenkins, Merlin, Jr. "The pedagogy of brass instruments at the college level." Master's thesis, North Texas State College, 1950.

Kinyon, John. "Beginning brass class." *The Instrumentalist* 13 (Feb. 1959): 72–73.

3680   Lemke, W. R. "A comparison of the effectiveness of a programed instructional technique and a technique using advance organizers and study questions as ancillary learning activities for brass techniques classes at the college level." *Dissertation Abstracts* 40 (June 1980): 6182A.

Masters, Edward L. "Problems of the college brass teacher." *Southwestern Brass Journal* 1 (Fall 1957): 4–6.

3681 Mueller, Herbert C. *Learning to teach through playing.* 2nd edition. Ithaca, NY: The Author, 1986.

3682 Mueller, Herbert C. *Learning to teach through playing: a brass method.* Reading, Mass.: Addison-Wesley, 1968.

3683 Myers, M. C. "The large brass class." *The Instrumentalist* 17 (Feb. 1963): 57–58.

Naylor, Tom L. "A program of study for teaching class trumpet at the college level." Ph.D. diss., Indiana University, 1973.

Power, William B. "A class method for teaching B flat cornet to meet individual differences among students." Master's thesis, University of Arizona, 1952.

3684 Robertson, James David. "The low brass instrumental techniques course: a method book for college level class instruction." D.M.A. diss., University of Northern Colorado, 1983.

3685 Robertson, James David. "The low brass instrumental techniques course: a method book for college level class instruction." *Dissertation Abstracts* 45 (July 1984): 13A-14A.

3686 Robinson, William C. "The brass and percussion class." *The School Musician* 38 (Jan. 1967): 48–49.

Vegna, J. "Elementary class method for the French horn." Master's thesis, Washington University, 1960.

Horn

3687 Aebi, Willi. "Stopped horn." *The Horn Call* 4, no. 2 (Spring 1974): 40–57.

3688 Agrell, Jeffrey. "Dreams and wishes: things I would like to see happen concerning the horn and horn playing." *Brass Bulletin—International Brass Chronicle*, no. 25 (1979): 29 + .

3689 Agrell, Jeffrey. "Jazz and the horn: workshop getting started." *Brass Bulletin—International Brass Chronicle*, no. 42 (1983): 36–40 + . Also in French and German.

3690 Agrell, Jeffrey. "Jazz clinic." *The Horn Call* 16, no. 2 (Apr. 1986): 25–27.

3691 Agrell, Jeffrey. "Practicing without the horn." *Woodwind, Brass and Percussion* 23, no. 3 (1984): 8–9.

3692 Agrell, Jeffrey, and S. Pugh. "Horn auditions: United States orchestras." *Woodwind, Brass and Percussion* 24, no. 4 (1985): 14–15.

3693 Agrell, Jeffrey. "Zen and the art of horn playing." *Brass Bulletin—Inter-*

national Brass Chronicle, no. 22; 23 (1978): 33–36; 69–72. Also in French and German.

3694   Agrell, Jeffrey. "Zen and the art of horn playing." *Brass Bulletin—International Brass Chronicle*, no. 27 (1979): 63 + .

3695   Agrell, Jeffrey. "Zen and the art of horn playing." *Brass Bulletin—International Brass Chronicle*, no. 29 (1980): 35 + . Also in French and German.

3696   *Anweisung zum Gebrauche des Posthorns für die Königlich Hannoverschen Postillons.* Hannover: n.p., 1832.

3697   Baker, J. "My way." *Sounding Brass & the Conductor* 7, no. 3 (1978): 91.

3698   Baker, James. "Horn player's guide to work in Mexico City and Toluca." *The Horn Call* 15, no. 1 (Oct. 1984): 90–91.

3699   Balmuth, Jerry. "An interview with Domenico Ceccarossi." *The Horn Call* 3, no. 1 (Nov. 1972): 53–58.

3700   "Barry Tuckwell at Ithaca College." *Woodwind World—Brass and Percussion* 18, no. 1 (1980): 24–25.

3701   Baumann, Hermann. "Welches Horn für welche Musik?" *Brass Bulletin—International Brass Chronicle*, no. 3 (1972): 13–21. Also in English and French.

3702   Baumann, Hermann. "Wie suche ich ein instrument aus?" *Das Orchester* 34 (Feb. 1986): 127–129.

3703   Beach, Robert F. "A search for better intonation." *The Horn Call* 8, no. 2 (1978): 28–37.

3704   Bertin, J. B. *Nouvelle méthode de trompe ou manuel raisonné à l'usage des veneurs et amateurs de chasse.* . . . Paris: Chez l'auteur, [1844].

3705   Berv, H. *A creative approach to the French horn.* London: Chappell/Presser; Paddock Wood, Tonbridge, Kent, England: A. Kalmus, 1977.

3706   Berv, H. "The temperamental French horn." *Music Journal* 23 (Jan. 1965): 44–45.

      Betts, James Edmond. "A comprehensive performance project in horn literature with an essay consisting of a comparison of concepts of horn technique as expressed in selected instructional materials for horn dating from 1798 to 1960." D.M.A. diss., University of Iowa, 1984.

3707   Bigelow. "On learning the horn." *The Horn Call* 17, no. 2 (Apr. 1987): 48–53.

3708   Bingham, R. D. "A horn symposium: old problems re-visited." *The Instrumentalist* 33 (Apr. 1979): 24–27.

3709   Borden, T. R. "French horn warm-up." *The Instrumentalist* 21 (Nov. 1966): 24.

3710   Bourdess, Jack. "Playing the French horn." *The Instrumentalist* 12 (June 1958): 41–43.

      Bracegirdle, Lee. "The New York school: its development and relationship to the Viennese style." *The Horn Call* 14, no. 2 (Apr. 1984): 16–24.

      Bracegirdle, Lee. "Die New Yorker Schule; ihre Entwicklung und ihre Verwandtschaft mit dem Wiener Stil." *Oesterreichische Musikzeitung* 38 (Sept. 1983): 500.

3711   Bradley, Mary E. "The establishment of performance practice for the horn." *The Horn Call* 7, no. 1 (Nov. 1976): 29–31.

3712   Brain, Aubrey. "The German horn: a comparison." *Monthly Musical Record* 61 (1931): 195.

3713   Brand. *Méthode de trompe.* Paris: J. Meissonnier, 1850.

Braun, Elaine. "Profile: Ifor James." *The Horn Call* 12, no. 1 (Oct. 1981): 22–29.

3714   Braun, Elaine. "Too much too soon?" *Woodwind, Brass and Percussion* 23, no. 5 (1984): 9.

3715   Brooks, Arthur. "Horn playing in the brass quintet context." *The Horn Call* 16, no. 2 (Apr. 1986): 99–100.

3716   Brophy, William R. "Horn players—can you stand to practice?" *Woodwind World—Brass and Percussion* 15, no. 1 (1976): 32–33.

3717   Brophy, William R. "Playing the horn in a woodwind quintet: advice for young performers." *The Instrumentalist* 33 (Aug. 1978): 74+.

3718   Brophy, William R. "The use of third valve fingerings on the horn." *The Horn Call* 7, no. 1 (Nov. 1976): 41–44.

3719   Bürger, E. "Ueber den Anpressdruck des Mundstückes auf die Lippen des Hornbläsers." *Brass Bulletin—International Brass Chronicle*, no. 40 (1982): 27–31.

Bujanovski, V. "Die Leningrader Hornschule." *Oesterreichische Musikzeitung* 38 (Sept. 1983): 498–499.

3720   Bullock, Wilbur W., Jr. "A survey, critical analysis and evaluation of elementary French horn methods now in publication." Master's thesis, Mississippi State College, 1949.

3721   Byrne, Joan S. "Moldau journey." *The Horn Call* 7, no. 2 (May 1977): 65–68.

3722   Carey, Mell C. "The low-register advantage of the setting-on method of mouthpiece placement in French-horn playing." D.Mus. diss., Indiana University, 1975.

3723   Ceccarossi, Domenico. *Il corno; attraverso il suo sviluppo tecnico e coloristico.* Milan: Ricordi, 1957.

3724   Ceccarossi, Domenico. "Il fraseggio." *The Horn Call* 7, no. 1 (Nov. 1976): 51–52.

3725   Ceccarossi, Domenico. "Phrasing." *The Horn Call* 7, no. 1 (Nov. 1976): 53.

3726   Chambers, J. "Horn tone and technique." *Woodwind World* 4, no. 6 (1962): 11–12.

3727   Chambers, J. "Playing the double horn." *Woodwind World* 3 (June 1, 1959): 11–12.

3728   Chambers, John. "Horn tone and technique." *Symphony* 2 (May 1949): 6.

3729   Chambers, John. "Tone and technique." *Woodwind World* 1 (Jan. 1958): 4.

3730   Chenoweth, Richard. "Report from Santa Fe: The twenty-eighth season of the Santa Fe Opera." *The Horn Call* 15, no. 2 (Apr. 1985): 19–27.

Chenoweth, Richard. "The Barry Tuckwell symposium for brass." *The Horn Call* 12, no. 1 (Oct. 1981): 16–19.

Coghill, Gene. "My first teacher: Arcady Yegudkin—'The General.' " *The Horn Call* 15, no. 1 (Oct. 1984): 15–19.

3731 Conti-Entin, Carol. "Two teaching aids for horn [fingerings, index to Pottag-Andraud]." *The Horn Call* 8, no. 1 (Nov. 1977): 70–73.

"Cor-horn." *Brass Bulletin—International Brass Chronicle*, no. 20 (1977): 8–11.

3732 Cornette, Victor. *Méthode de cor.* Paris: Colombier, 1854.

3733 Cousins, Farquharson. "The degenerate horn." *Music and Letters* 31 (1950): 378–380.

3734 Cowan, Thomas. "Profile: Interview with Charles Kavaloski." *The Horn Call* 7, no. 1 (Nov. 1976): 62–67.

Cowan, Thomas. "Profile: Interview with Norman Schweikert." *The Horn Call* 6, no. 2 (1976): 56–61.

3735 Cowan, Thomas. "Profile: Interview with Philip Farkas." *The Horn Call* 8, no. 1 (Nov. 1977): 60–68.

3736 Cox, P. W. L. "Intricacies of the French horn simplified." *The School Musician* 20 (Jan. 1949): 32–33.

3737 Cryder, John Michael. "Some technical considerations of French horn performance in selected twentieth-century compositions." D.M.A. diss., Catholic University of America, 1975.

3738 Dalrymple, Glenn V. "The stuffy horn syndrome: one cause and its cure." *The Horn Call* 2, no. 2 (May 1972): 66–70.

3739 Damm, Peter. "Corni da caccia mit neuer Technik." *Das Orchester* 32 (July–Aug. 1984): 623–624.

Damm, Peter. "Das Horn in der ersten Hälfte des 18. Jahrhunderts. Versuche der interpretation hoher Hornpartien." In *Die Blasinstrumente und ihre Verwendung.* . . , edited by Eitelfriedrich Thom, 37–41. Magdeburg: Rat des Bezirkes; Leipzig: Zentralhaus für Kulturarbeit, 1977.

3740 Dauprat, L. F. *Du cor à pistons, extrait d'un traité théorique et pratique de cet instrument.* Paris: Zetter, 1829.

3741 Dauprat, L. F. *Méthode de cor-alto et cor basse.* Paris: Zetter, [ca. 1824].

3742 De Mersan. *Manuel du chasseur et des gardes-chasses.* Paris: Roret, 1826.

3743 Decker, James C. "Double or nothing: how tight money in Hollywood is popularizing Deskants and Tuben." *The Horn Call* 2, no. 2 (May 1972): 37–40.

3744 Decker, Richard. "Thoughts on auditioning." *The Horn Call* 15, no. 2 (Apr. 1985): 31–32.

3745 Dejonckere, P. H., and others. "Mecanisme oscillatoire de la glotte dans le jeux de cor." *Brass Bulletin—International Brass Chronicle*, no. 41 (1983): 28. Also in English and German.

3746 Dinino, Vincent R. "French horn forum." *Southwestern Brass Journal* 1 (Spring 1957): 39–41.

3747 Dressler, J. "Materials for horn auditions: band and orchestra." *The Instrumentalist* 36 (Jan. 1982): 65–67.

3748 Dressler, John C., comp. "Alphabetical listing of the Chambers/International Music Company orchestral excerpt books for horn, vol. I-VII." *The Horn Call* 18, no. 2 (Apr. 1988): 90.

3749 du Fouilloux, J. *La Vénerie*. Nouv. éd. Angers: n.p., 1844.

3750 Dubernoy, Frederic. *Méthode pour le cor suivie de duo et de trio pour cet instrument*. Genève: Minkoff, 1971.

Dunn, F. Earl. "The brass instrument class—a workbook-text for the teacher or student of the cornet, French horn and trombone." Master's thesis, Iowa State Teachers College, 1954.

3751 Dunn, Richard. "Horror story [stolen horn]." *The Horn Call* 3, no. 2 (May 1973): 24–25.

3752 Dunn, Richard. "Physical stress in horn playing." *The Horn Call* 4, no. 2 (Spring 1974): 26–28.

3753 Duskin, Joel W. "The genius and the hornist." *The Horn Call* 7, no. 2 (May 1977): 20–22.

3754 Earnest, Christopher. "The horn: stopped, muted, and open." *The Horn Call* 7, no. 2 (May 1977): 34–48.

3755 Eger, J. "Breaking the endurance barrier." *Woodwind World* 2 (May 1958): 5–6.

Elliott, David G. "The Brahms horn trio and hand horn idiom." *The Horn Call* 10, no. 1 (Oct. 1979): 61–73.

3756 Erlenbach, Julius. "A checklist for the college-bound horn player." *The School Musician* 44 (Aug.-Sept. 1972): 20+.

3757 Erlenbach, Julius. "Daily warm-ups for the young horn student." *The Instrumentalist* 25 (May 1971): 48–49.

3758 Erlenbach, Julius. "The lower register and the young horn player." *The Horn Call* 2, no. 2 (May 1972): 44–46.

3759 Farkas, Philip. *The art of French horn playing; a treatise on the problems and techniques of French horn playing*. Chicago: C. F. Summy, 1956.

Farkas, Philip. "Horn excerpt clinic: 'Till.' " *The Horn Call* 15, no. 1 (Oct. 1984): 55–57.

3760 Farkas, Philip. "The keystone of good French horn playing." *The School Musician* 24 (Dec. 1952): 13–14+.

3761 Farkas, Philip. *L'art de jouer les cuivres. Traité sur la formation et l'utilisation de l'embouchure du musicien jouant un cuivre*. Translated by Alain Maillard. Paris: Leduc, 1981.

Farkas, Philip. "Medical problems of wind players: a musician's perspective." *The Horn Call* 17, no. 2 (Apr. 1987): 64–68.

3762 Farkas, Philip, Harold Meek, Wendell Hoss, William Muelbe, E. C. Moore, Lloyd Schmidt, and Max Pottag. "Which horn do you prefer—F or Bb? A symposium." *The Instrumentalist* 5 (Jan.-Feb. 1951): 12–16, 38–39.

3763 Farkas, Philip. "The use of the lower lip in horn playing." *The International Musician* 58 (Nov. 1959): 22–23.

3764 Farkas, Philip. "Wet lips versus dry lips." *The International Musician* 59 (Mar. 1961): 42–43.

Farnsley, Stephen H. "Gunther Schuller: his influence on the French horn." D.A. diss., Ball State University, 1985.

Farnsley, Stephen H. "Gunther Schuller: his influence on the French horn." *Dissertation Abstracts* 47 (Sept. 1986): 705A.

3765 Farr, Linda A. "A horn player's guide to orchestral excerpts." *The Instrumentalist* 33 (June 1979): 10.

3766 Farr, Linda A. *A horn player's guide to orchestral excerpts.* Columbia, SC: Broad River Press, 1979.

Faulkner, Maurice. "Annual review of solos and studies: trumpet and French horn." *The Instrumentalist* 39 (Feb. 1985): 71–76.

3767 Faulkner, Maurice. "Horn artistry and vibrato." *The Instrumentalist* 36 (Mar. 1982): 74+.

Faulkner, Maurice. "Solos and studies for trumpet and horn." *The Instrumentalist* 32 (Feb. 1978): 56+.

Faulkner, Maurice. "Trumpet and French horn [annual review of solos and studies]." *The Instrumentalist* 35 (Dec. 1980): 33–34.

Faulkner, Maurice. "Trumpet and French horn solos and studies." *The Instrumentalist* 33 (Jan. 1979): 80+.

Faulkner, Maurice. "Trumpet and horn solos and studies." *The Instrumentalist* 34 (Dec. 1979): 24–26.

Faust, Randall Edward. "A comprehensive performance project in horn literature with an essay consisting of three original concertpieces for horn and electronic media, an explanation of techniques used, and a listing of relevant literature." 2 vols. D.M.A. diss., University of Iowa, 1980.

Fitzpatrick, Horace. *The horn and horn-playing and the Austro-Bohemian tradition from 1680 to 1830.* New York: Oxford University Press, 1970.

3768 Fox, Fred. " 'Bull's eye!' " *The Horn Call* 11, no. 2 (1981): 65–66.

3769 Fox, Fred. "Developing the horn embouchure." *Woodwind World* 7 (Jan. 1955): 5+.

3770 Fox, Fred. "Playing a simple crescendo-diminuendo on middle 'G.' " *The Horn Call* 1, no. 2 (May 1971): 50–51.

3771 Fox, Fred. "A 'sound' formula for the hand position in the bell." *The Horn Call* 9, no. 2 (Apr. 1979): 55–56.

Fransman, H. "Das Waldhornspiel in Finnland." *Oesterreichische Musikzeitung* 38 (Sept. 1983): 499.

3772 Freiberg, Gottfried. "Das Horn." *Oesterreichische Musik Zeitschrift* 13 (1958): 159–161.

3773 Gallay, J. -F. *Méthode pour le cor.* Paris: Schonenberger, [ca. 1845].

3774 Gehner, Robert. "Acquiring air stream control in French horn performance." *NACWPI Journal* 29, no. 3 (May 1981): 14–21.

3775 Göroldt, J. H. *Ausführliche theoretisch-praktische Hornschule vom ersten Elementar-Unterricht, bis zur vollkommensten Ausbildung.* Quedlinburg: Basse, 1830.

3776 Goodwin, Carol G. "An audio-visual method for teaching embouchure and hand position for the French horn using sound tape and slide set." Master's thesis, University of Kansas, 1955.

3777   Gregory, C. "The young player." *Music Teacher and Piano Student* 41 (1962): 233+, 277+.

3778   Gregory, Robin. *The horn; a guide to the modern instrument*. London: Faber and Faber, 1961.
        Gregory, Robin. *The horn; a comprehensive guide to the modern instrument and its music*. 2d ed. London: Faber and Faber, 1969.

3779   Grieve, Alexander. "Craftsmanship: the function of art today (can painting help us?)" *The Horn Call* 5, no. 2 (Spring 1975): 26–28.

3780   Gross, Steve. "Taped orchestra auditions—a report." *The Horn Call* 15, no. 1 (Oct. 1984): 41–43.

3781   Grubert. *Méthode de trompe ou cor de chasse, contenant les études nécessaires pour parvenir à bien jouer*. . . . Paris: Meissonnier, [ca. 1830].

3782   Gugel, H. *Hornschule*. n.p.: n.p., [ca. 1840].

3783   Gustin, Charles E. "The French horn: its effective use in American schools." Master's thesis, University of Southern California, 1954.

3784   Haddad, D. "To sound like a horn player." *The Instrumentalist* 22 (Feb. 1968): 57+.

3785   Hamilton, Elizabeth C. "The pedagogy of the French horn." Master's thesis, Eastman School of Music, 1945.

3786   Hardin, Burton E. "Tracking the wild horn." *The Horn Call* 7, no. 1 (Nov. 1976): 20–24.

3787   Harper, I. "My way [warm-up exercises]." *Sounding Brass & the Conductor* 5, no. 2 (1976): 52–53.

3788   Havens, Kathy Boggs. "A report from Brazil." *The Horn Call* 9, no. 1 (Oct. 1978): 89.

3789   Hdt. "Ueber Klangerzeugung bei Blasinstrumenten, sowie über das sogenannte mehrstimmige Hornblasen." *Allgemeine musikalische Zeitung* 49 (1847): 209–217, 225–228.

3790   Henderson, Malcolm C. "Musical 'Middletown' revisited." *The Horn Call* 5, no. 2 (Spring 1975): 12–16.

3791   Henderson, Malcolm C. "Thinking about stopping: new thoughts on a horny subject." *The Horn Call* 4, no. 1 (Autumn 1973): 25–29.
        Hepola, Ralph. "Looking at Dennis Brain." *T.U.B.A. Journal* 12, no. 4 (May 1985): 10–11.

3792   Hill, Douglas. "Horn playing: a balancing act." *The Horn Call* 14, no. 1 (Oct. 1983): 47–49.

3793   Hill, Douglas. "The IHS and its progress." *The Horn Call* 9, no. 1 (Oct. 1978): 58–60. Also in French and German.

3794   Hill, Douglas. "Impossible Dreams or Great Expectations?" *The Instrumentalist* 33 (May 1979): 36–37.

3795   Hill, Douglas. "The People's Republic of China and Western music [mostly horn]." *The Horn Call* 12, no. 2 (Apr. 1982): 45–49.

3796   Hill, Douglas. "Starting fresh on French horn." *The Instrumentalist* 40 (Oct. 1985): 68+.

3797   Hill, Douglas. "The warm-up as a complete session." *The Horn Call* 5, no.

1 (Autumn 1974): 54–55.

3798   Hipsher, E. "French horn." *Etude* 45 (1927): 506.

3799   Hodges, D. A. "A new way to start the day [warm-up exercises]." *The Instrumentalist* 31 (Mar. 1977): 98–99.

Hoeltzel, Michael. "Gibt es noch einen deutschen Hornton?" *Oesterreichische Musikzeitschrift* 38 (Sept. 1983): 493–494.

3800   Höltzel, Michael. "Meine Kontakte mit den Vereinigten Staaten." *Brass Bulletin—International Brass Chronicle*, no. 17 (1977): 15+. Also in French and English.

Holmes, John Clellom. *The horn*. New York: Random House, 1958.

3801   Hood, Walton Donnie, III. "The beginner and the single F and B-flat French horn." Master's thesis, University of Texas, 1957.

3802   Hopkins, John. "Visit to Melbourne by Hermann Baumann." *The Horn Call* 9, no. 1 (Oct. 1978): 18–19.

3803   Hoss, Wendell. "Drills and devices in playing the horn." *The Horn Call* 7, no. 1 (Nov. 1976): 9–10.

Hoss, Wendell. "Gadgets and gimmicks [as aids to playing the horn]." *The Horn Call* 1, no. 1 (Feb. 1971): 20–22.

3804   Hoss, Wendell. "The horn trill." *The Horn Call* 9, no. 2 (Apr. 1979): 52–53.

3805   Hoss, Wendell. "Making the French horn articulate." *The Instrumentalist* 20 (Jan. 1966): 76.

3806   Hoss, Wendell. "Musical building blocks [in exerpts for the horn]." *The Horn Call* 3, no. 2 (May 1973): 26–27.

3807   Hoss, Wendell. "Stresses in playing the French horn." *The Instrumentalist* 19 (June 1965): 70+.

House, R. Edmund. "The German style of horn playing: myth or method?" *The Horn Call* 9, no. 2 (Apr. 1979): 29–45. Also in French and German.

3808   Hovey, G. " 'The horn, the horn, the lusty horn' [World Horn Workshop]." *The Instrumentalist* 27 (Dec. 1972): 34–35.

3809   Howe, Marvin C. "A critical survey of literature, materials, opinions, and practices related to teaching the French horn." *Dissertation Abstracts* 27 (Apr. 1967): 3481A.

3810   Howe, Marvin C. "A critical survey of literature, materials, opinions, and practices related to teaching the French horn." Ph.D. diss., University of Iowa, 1967.

3811   Howe, Marvin C. "Stopped horn." *The Horn Call* 4, no. 1 (Autumn 1973): 19–24.

3812   Hynninen, Mikko. "Hornplaying in Finland." *The Horn Call* 7, no. 2 (May 1977): 12–15.

3813   Iervolino, Antonio. "Breathing technique (from *The Theoretical and Practical Method for Horn*)." *The Horn Call* 12, no. 2 (Apr. 1982): 19–33. Also in Spanish.

3814   "Is the French horn often played outside the orchestra?" *Canon* 8 (Feb. 1955): 309–310.

3815 Jacobs, Marion L. "Technic of the hand horn." *Jacobs' Band Monthly* 26 (June 1941): 6.

3816 Jacqmin, F. *Méthode complète de premier et de second cor.* Paris: A. Petit, [1832].

3817 Jaenicke, Bruno. "Double, double, toil and burble." *Woodwind Magazine* 5 (June 1953): 4–5.

3818 Jaenicke, Bruno. "Problems of the French horn." *Etude* 59 (1941): 313, 346.

James, Eric D. "The horn in ensemble—some alternatives." *The Horn Call* 13, no. 1 (Oct. 1982): 44–47.

Janetzky, Kurt, and Bernhard Brüchle. *Das Horn. Eine kleine Chronik seines Werdens und Wirkens.* Bern and Stuttgart: Hallwag, 1977.

3819 Janos, O. *Hornschule, Bände I und II.* Budapest: Musica, 1969.

3820 Jensen, R. "Horn technique—muting and stopping." *The Instrumentalist* 22 (Aug. 1967): 30+.

3821 Jepson, Barbara. "Clambake: the dilemma of the horn." *The Horn Call* 17, no. 1 (Oct. 1986): 78–79. Reprinted from *The Wall Street Journal* (July 1, 1986).

3822 Johnson, Eric A. "How to survive as an amateur horn player in the wilderness." *The Horn Call* 13, no. 1 (Oct. 1982): 52–53.

3823 Johnson, K. M. "The horn—mutes and muting." *The School Musician* 52 (Aug.-Sept. 1980): 32–33+.

3824 Johnson, Miles B. "Muting the French horn." *The Instrumentalist* 19 (Jan. 1965): 51–54.

3825 Johnson, Miles B. "Warm-ups for horn." *The Instrumentalist* 24 (Oct. 1969): 56–60.

3826 Jones, Carlberg. "The horn player's right hand." *The Horn Call* 2, no. 1 (Nov. 1971): 61–68.

3827 Jones, M. "Travel notes of a horn player." *Woodwind World* 2 (Sept. 1958): 5–6.

3828 [Jourdain]. *Traité général des chasses à courre et à pied. . . .* Paris: Augdot, 1822.

3829 Kappy, David. "The woodwind quintet: challenges and rewards for the horn player." *The Horn Call* 14, no. 1 (Oct. 1983): 83–84.

3830 Kastner, J. -G. *Méthode élémentaire pour le cor.* Paris: n.p., [ca. 1845].

3831 Kavalovski, Charles. "Orchestral excerpt clinic: Franck 'Symphony in D Minor.' " *The Horn Call* 17, no. 1 (Oct. 1986): 66–67.

3832 Kaza, Roger. "Taking your horn into the wilderness." *The Horn Call* 14, no. 1 (Oct. 1983): 60–62.

3833 Kearns, William K. "Studies in orchestral French horn playing." Master's thesis, Ohio State University, 1954.

Kimple, Wilbert Kenneth, Jr. "Make it a horn section [four horn parts require different types of players]." *The Instrumentalist* 34 (Jan. 1980): 40+.

3834 Kinney, G. "French horn players, arise! [value of standing while performing]." *The Instrumentalist* 32 (May 1978): 68–69.

3835   Kirschen, Jeffry. "Five minutes. . . . " *The Horn Call* 15, no. 2 (Apr. 1985): 53–55.

3836   Klausmeier, C. A. "Beginning horn methods." *The School Musician* 48 (Jan., May 1977): 8+, 16+.

3837   Kling, H. *Praktische Anwendung zum Transponieren.* Hannover: L. Oertel, 1885.

3838   Kling, H. "Ueber gleichzeitige Hervorbringung doppelter und dreifacher Töne auf dem Horn." *Allgemeine musikalische Zeitung* 14 (1879): 504–506.

3839   Klinko, Albert. "Using the 'A' horn." *The Horn Call* 2, no. 1 (Nov. 1971): 42–45.

3840   Knott, Handel. "The horn." *Music and Letters* 32 (1951): 200–201.

3841   [Kresz, Aine]. *Théorie générale de toutes le chasses au fusil, à courre et à tir.* Paris: Corbet, 1823.

3842   Kurth, R. H. "Portrait of a unique instrumentalist [handicapped horn player]." *Medical Problems of Performing Artists* 2, no. 1 (1987): 29–30.

3843   Lanzky-Otto, Ib. "Is a beautiful horn sound really of any importance?" *The Horn Call* 10, no. 2 (Apr. 1980): 35–37.

3844   Lauriston, Michael. "New leadership in the I.H.S." *The Horn Call* 8, no. 1 (Nov. 1977): 52–53.

3845   Lee, Melvin Lewis. "The development of a beginning method of transposition for the orchestral horn." *Dissertation Abstracts* 30 (Nov. 1969): 2061A.

3846   Lee, Melvin Lewis. "The development of a beginning method of transposition for the orchestral horn." D.Mus.Ed. diss., University of Oklahoma, 1969.

3847   Lekvold, A. D. "French horn unique in blending and tone." *The Instrumentalist* 8 (Nov. 1953): 44–45.

3848   Leroux, J. -V. *Nouveau traité de trompe.* Ie recueil. [Paris?]: E. Duverger, 1835.

        "A letter from Dennis Brain." *The Horn Call* 1, no. 2 (May 1971): 48–49.

        Leuba, Christopher. "A centered tone." *Woodwind World—Brass and Percussion* 19, no. 5 (1980): 12–14.

        Leuba, Christopher. "Comment on, and an index of the Gumbert excerpt series." *The Horn Call* 10, no. 1 (Oct. 1979): 19–21.

3849   Leuba, Christopher. "Horn vibrato response." *The Instrumentalist* 36 (July 1982): 68–69.

3850   Leuba, Christopher. "Learning the B flat/F double horn." *The Instrumentalist* 37 (Oct. 1982): 70–72.

3851   Leuba, Christopher. " 'Stopped' playing on the horn." *The Horn Call* 5, no. 2 (Spring 1975): 60–64.

3852   Leuba, Julian Christopher. "Dispute over longer slides." *The Instrumentalist* 34 (May 1980): 110–111.

        Leuba, Julian Christopher. "Orchestral excerpt clinic: the 'Andante cantabile' from Tschaikowsky's Fifth Symphony." *The Horn Call* 16, no. 2 (Apr. 1986): 64–67.

3853 Liese, Ralph. "French horn forum." *Southwestern Brass Journal* 1 (Fall 1957): 41–44.

3854 Lockwood, Ralph. "Taking a new stance." *The Horn Call* 15, no. 1 (Oct. 1984): 58–62.

3855 McCann, William J. "Trumpet and horn: correcting problems early." *The School Musician* 45 (Aug.-Sept. 1973): 20 +.

3856 McConathy, O. W. "Kopprasch etudes develop good technical foundation." *Symphony* 4 (Nov. 1950): 12.

3857 McConathy, Osbourne. "Virtuosity." *The Horn Call* 2, no. 1 (Nov. 1971): 46–48.

3858 McCoy, M. "How to oil rotary valves." *Woodwind World* 3, no. 12 (1961): 5.

3859 McCoy, W. M. "How to preserve lacquer." *Woodwind World* 4, no. 3 (1961): 14.

3860 McKee, W. E. "The use of syllables in playing the French horn." *The Instrumentalist* 16, no. 8 (Apr. 1962): 65–67.

3861 McMullan, A. "Make mine B-flat." *The School Musician* 22 (Sept. 1950): 9.

3862 Magnell, E. P. "Horn in F or B-flat?" *The Instrumentalist* 17, no. 2 (Oct. 1962): 66–67.

3863 Manous, C. "Accuracy for the horn player." *The Instrumentalist* 33 (Nov. 1978): 55–56.

Manous, C. "Clear thinking on articulation." *The Instrumentalist* 34 (May 1980): 92–94.

Mansur, Paul. "Hullabaloo in a horn bell OR the dilemmas of a horn [mutes/stopping]." *The Horn Call* 5, no. 2 (Spring 1975): 39–44.

3864 Mansur, Paul. "Thoughts and observations on Vienna and Vienna horns." *The Horn Call* 14, no. 2 (Apr. 1984): 45–47.

3865 Mansur, Paul. "What is the properest horn to play?" *The Horn Call* 8, no. 2 (1978): 74–78.

3866 Martin, A. "Comment M. Vivier joue du cor." *La Belgique musicale* 4, no. 8 (29 June 1843): 30.

3867 Martin, A. "Le cor de M. Vivier mis à la portée de tout le monde." *La France musicale* (18 June 1843).

3868 Martin, D. L. "Placing the horns; thoughts and opinions from seven directors." *The Instrumentalist* 39 (Aug. 1984): 64–65.

3869 Mathez, Jean-Pierre. "Les petites histoires de la vie des cuivres: une nouvelle place [fiction]." *Brass Bulletin—International Brass Chronicle*, no. 51 (1985): 59–61. Also in English and German.

3870 Matsubara, Chiyo. "Horn situation in Japan." *The Horn Call* 6, no. 1 (Nov. 1975): 51–56.

3871 Matthes, W. "Der Hornist—Musikberuf mit Zukunft; die Kreismusikschule Cloppenburg veranstaltete zum erstenmal die 'Stapeifelder Horntage.' " *Das Orchester* 28 (June 1980): 526–527.

3872 Mattoon, Hubert. "The development and pedagogy of the double French horn." Master's thesis, Illinois Wesleyan University, 1951.

3873   May, Andrew. "Teaching the French horn." Master's thesis, Ohio State University, 1953.

3874   Mayer, Abby, and Lloyd, M.D. Mayer. "Better breathing." *The Horn Call* 2, no. 1 (Nov. 1971): 69–72.

3875   Mayer, Abby. "Summer horn teaching." *The Horn Call* 1, no. 1 (Feb. 1971): 23–27.

3876   Meek, Harold. "Some observations prompted by Hermann Baumann's: 'Welches Horn für welche Musik.' " *Brass Bulletin—International Brass Chronicle*, no. 4 (1973): 21–27. Also in French and German.

3877   Meifred, P. -J. *De l'étendue, de l'emploi et des ressources du cor, en général, et de ses corps de rechange en particulier, avec quelques considerations sur le cor à pistons.* Paris: Launer, [1829].

3878   Meifred, P. -J. *Méthode pour le cor chromatique ou à pistons.* Paris: Richault, [1840].

3879   Mengal, J. *Méthode de cor et cor à pistons.* Paris: Meissonnier, [ca. 1839–40].

3880   Mengal, J. *Méthode de cor, suivie du doigté du Cornet-'a-pistons.* Paris: n.p., [1835?].

3881   Merck, L. H. "A propos de cor." *L'Echo musical* 13 (1881): 159–160.

        Merewether, Richard. " 'Bad notes' in horns." *The Horn Call* 7, no. 1 (Nov. 1976): 26–27.

        Merewether, Richard. *The horn, the horn.* Hornplayer's Companion Series. London: Paxman Musical Instruments Ltd., 1978.

3882   Merewether, Richard. "The question of hand-stopping." *The Horn Call* 5, no. 2 (Spring 1975): 45–59.

        Merewether, Richard. "The Vienna-horn—and some thoughts on its past fifty years." *The Horn Call* 15, no. 1 (Oct. 1984): 31–35.

3883   Merker, Ethyl. "The case for women in brass." *Musart* 28, no. 2 (1975): 30–32. Reprinted from *Leblanc World of Music* (Fall 1975).

3884   Mishori, Yaacov. "Horn playing in Israel." *The Horn Call* 13, no. 2 (Apr. 1983): 40–44.

        Morley-Pegge, Reginald. *The French horn.* London: Benn; New York: Norton, 1960.

        Morley-Pegge, Reginald. *The French horn.* Revised edition. New York: Norton, 1973.

        Morley-Pegge, Reginald. *The French horn: some notes on the evolution of the instrument and of its technique.* 2d ed. London: Benn, 1973.

        Morley-Pegge, Reginald. *The French horn; some notes on the evolution of the instrument and its technique.* London: E. Benn, 1960.

3885   Morrison, P. E. "The French horn in the high school band." *Etude* 47 (1929): 275 + , 355 +.

3886   Murray, T. W. "Pursuing the ideal horn tone." *The Instrumentalist* 31 (Oct. 1976): 58–59.

3887   Nadaf, G. "The horn player's lip trill." *The School Musician* 45 (May 1974): 28–30.

3888   Nadaf, G. "Making music with the horn." *The School Musician* 43 (Aug.–

Sept. 1971): 30+.

3889   Nadaf, G. "Playing the French horn in tune." *The School Musician* 38 (Dec. 1966): 22+.

3890   Nadaf, G. "The right hand and the French horn bell." *The School Musician* 39 (Dec. 1967): 8+.

3891   Nadaf, G. "Teaching the whole horn: some dos and don'ts." *The School Musician* 41 (Dec. 1969): 12+.

3892   Nadaf, G. "Why not the B-flat horn?" *The School Musician* 40 (Oct. 1968): 12.

3893   Neidig, K. L. "Philip Farkas: master horn teacher [interview]." *The Instrumentalist* 33 (Apr. 1979): 16–23.

3894   Nemetz, A. *Hornschule für das Einfache, das Machinen- und das Signal-horn.* Vienna: Diabelli, 1828.

3895   Novikow, C. "A horn apprenticeship [embouchure]." *Brass Bulletin—International Brass Chronicle*, no. 51 (1985): 97. Also in French and German.

3896   "Oberschlesische Förster als Lehrmeister neuer Waldhornbläser." *Der Schlesier Breslauer Nachrichten. Der Heimatbote für alle Nieder- und Oberschlesien* (1955): 3.

3897   O'Connor, Edward Joseph Patrick. "A survey of the warm-up techniques used by five professional French horn players with original warm-up exercises." Master's thesis, Northwestern University, 1962.

3898   Orval, Francis. "Le cor fa/si b 3e piston ascendant d'un ton [includes table of fingerings]." *Brass Bulletin—International Brass Chronicle*, no. 11 (1975): 27–36. Also in English and German.

3899   Orval, Francis. "Lecture at I. H. Workshop IX." *The Horn Call* 8, no. 1 (Nov. 1977): 36–39.

3900   Parshall, Harry E. "The horn and horn playing." *Music Educators Journal* 23 (Oct. 1936): 58+.

Payne, Ian W. "Observations on the stopped notes of the French horn." *Music and Letters* 49, no. 2 (1968): 145–154.

3901   Pease, Edward. "Bodily resonance in horn playing." *The School Musician* 44 (Nov. 1972): 22+.

3902   Pease, Edward. "Bodily resonance in horn playing." *The School Musician* 44 (Jan. 1973): 12+.

3903   Pease, Edward. "Improving French horn accuracy." *The School Musician* 34 (Feb. 1963): 42–43.

Pease, Edward. "Performing the Brahms Horn Trio." *The Horn Call* 4, no. 1 (Autumn 1973): 44–51.

3904   Pease, Edward. "Teaching Mozart Horn Concertos to pre-college performers." *The School Musician* 38 (June-July 1967): 56–57+.

Pendergast, D. J. "The horn, a fearsome beast." *Music Journal* 29 (Apr. 1971): 47+.

3905   Perrini, N. "Basics for beginning French horn students." *The Instrumentalist* 24 (Feb. 1970): 64–70.

3906   Pherigo, J. "A practical guide to hand-stopping the horn." *Dialogue in*

Instrumental Music Education 6, no. 2 (1982): 46–55.

3907　Pherigo, Johnny Lee. "A critical survey of materials and practices related to teaching the horn, 1965–1985." D.M.A. diss., University of Illinois (Urbana-Champaign), 1986.

3908　Pherigo, Johnny Lee. "A critical survey of materials and practices related to teaching the horn, 1965–1985." *Dissertation Abstracts* 47 (Mar. 1987): 3235A.

3909　Pignéguy, John. "News and notes from London." *The Horn Call* 17, no. 1 (Oct. 1986): 85–86.

3910　Pignéguy, John. "Notes from London." *The Horn Call* 16, no. 2 (Apr. 1986): 55–56.

3911　Ploosen, H. -C. de. *Le guide de chasseur ou méthode de trompe de chasse*. Paris: Gauvin, 1848.

3912　Ploosen, H. -C. de. *Nouvelle méthode de trompe ou cor de chasse*. Paris: Veuve Paté, [1848?].

3913　Pottag, Max. "The beginning French horn player." *The Instrumentalist* 1 (Jan. 1947): 10.

3914　Pottag, Max. "Development of good French horn players." *The Instrumentalist* 7 (Mar.-Apr. 1953): 26–27 + .

3915　Pottag, Max. "The fourth horn player." *The School Musician* 44 (Feb. 1973): 42–43.

3916　Pottag, Max. "The French horn ensemble." *Symphony* 6 (Dec. 1952): 9.

3917　Pottag, Max. "The French horn ensemble." *Woodwind World* 3 (Jan.-Feb. 1959): 6.

3918　Pottag, Max. "Reflections on the history of the horn ensemble." *The Instrumentalist* 13 (Aug. 1959): 36.

3919　Pottag, Max, and R. H. Schulze. "Playing the French horn." *The Instrumentalist* 1 (May 1947): 36.

3920　Pottag, Max. "Selecting the right French horn." *The Instrumentalist* 1 (Nov. 1946): 30.

　　　Pruzin, R. S. "Gestopft! Gesundheit!: a discussion of hand-muting for the french horn." *Woodwind, Brass and Percussion* 23, no. 3 (1984): 14–16.

3921　Pruzin, R. S. "Legato style for the French horn." *Brass and Percussion* 2, no. 5 (1974): 10–11 + .

3922　Pruzin, R. S. "A tonguing style for horn." *Woodwind, Brass and Percussion* 24, no. 3 (1985): 10–12.

3923　Pyle, Robert W., Jr. "A theory of hand-stopping." *The Horn Call* 1, no. 2 (May 1971): 53.

3924　Rattner, David. "New trends in horn playing." *Woodwind* (Jan. 1951): 6–7.

3925　Rattner, David. "New trends in horn playing." In *Woodwind Anthology*, 19–20. New York: Woodwind Magazine, 1952.

3926　Rhynard, Maurice L. "The use of special fingerings in selected solo horn literature." *Dissertation Abstracts* 48 (Oct. 1987): 776A.

3927　Rhynard, Maurice L. "The use of special fingerings in selected solo horn literature." D.M.A. diss., Memphis State University, 1987.

3928 Richter, J. "The perils of a free lance horn player." *Woodwind World—Brass and Percussion* 15, no. 3 (1976): 40.

Riddle, P. H. "Scoring for the young French horn section." *The School Musician* 43 (Jan. 1972): 37 + .

3929 Riggio, Suzanne. "An American in Switzerland." *The Horn Call* 7, no. 1 (Nov. 1976): 18–19.

3930 Riggio, Suzanne. "How to finger the double horn." *Woodwind Brass and Percussion* 20, no. 4 (1981): 21–22.

3931 Riggio, Suzanne. "How to put on a horn clinic and concert." *Woodwind World* 11, no. 1 (1972): 10–12 + .

3932 Riggio, Suzanne. "Insights in F." *The Horn Call* 8, no. 1 (Nov. 1977): 22–31.

3933 Riggio, Suzanne. "Notes from a solo hose." *The Horn Call* 11, no. 2 (1981): 89–91.

3934 Riggio, Suzanne. "On which horn, F or B-flat, should a student begin?" *Woodwind World—Brass and Percussion* 20, no. 1 (1981): 12–13.

3935 Riggio, Suzanne. "You say you married a horn player?" *Woodwind World* 13, no. 2 (1974): 10–11.

3936 Riggio, Suzanne. "You say you married a horn player?" *The Horn Call* 5, no. 2 (Spring 1975): 36–38.

Roberts, B. Lee. "Some comments on the physics of the horn and right-hand technique." *The Horn Call* 6, no. 2 (1976): 41–46.

3937 Robinson, William C. "The beginning horn embouchure—pitfalls, problems, and progress." *The Instrumentalist* 22 (Nov. 1967): 68–69.

3938 Robinson, William C. "Daily confrontation with the horn: what do we do next?" *Brass and Percussion* 2, no. 1,2 (1974): 12–13, 14–16 + .

3939 Robinson, William C., and Joseph A. White. "Formation of International Horn Society." *The Horn Call* 1, no. 2 (May 1971): 40.

3940 Roper, H. C. "The note, the right note, and nothing but the right note." *The Instrumentalist* 34 (Dec. 1979): 104.

3941 Rosenthal, Irving. "The horn player who went to heaven." *Woodwind Magazine* 6 (Sept. 1953): 6 + .

3942 Rosevear, Robert A. "Playing the single B-flat horn." *The Instrumentalist* 5 (May-June 1951): 17 + .

3943 Roy, C. *Méthode de cor de signal à clefs.* Mainz: Schott, [ca. 1825].

3944 Rumery, K. R. "Improved use of the double horn." *The Instrumentalist* 29 (Nov. 1974): 61–66.

3945 Rumery, K. R. "Improving the French horn section." *The Instrumentalist* 27 (Apr. 1973): 65–66.

3946 Saenger, Gustav. "The growing popularity of French horns." *Metronome* 43 (Jan. 15, 1927): 23 + .

3947 Saxton, S. Earl. "Horn singing." *Brass Bulletin—International Brass Chronicle*, no. 10 (1975): 17–33. Also in French and German.

3948 Saxton, S. Earl. "The infinite power of self-determination." *The Horn Call*

8, no. 2 (1978): 38–41.

3949 Saxton, S. Earl, and William Morrow. "Do you blow or do you sing on your horn." *The Horn Call* 3, no. 2 (May 1973): 37–44.

3950 Saxton, S. Earl. "The rap session of disabled/handicapped hornists and how they cope." *The Horn Call* 18, no. 1 (Oct. 1987): 31–38.

3951 Saxton, S. Earl. "Singing on the horn." *The Horn Call* 1, no. 2 (May 1971): 22–38.

Scharnberg, William. "The hornist's nemisis [sic]: marching band." *NACWPI Journal* 34, no. 1 (1985): 10–11.

3952 Scharnberg, William. "Underhanded tricks for the hornist [placement and function of right hand in bell]." *The Instrumentalist* 36 (Sept. 1981): 96–99.

3953 Scharnberg, William. "What type of horn should I buy?" *The Horn Call* 18, no. 1 (Oct. 1987): 39–40.

3954 Scheler-Probst, B. "Ueber das B-Horn." *Wild und Hund* 65 (1962): 716–717.

3955 Schmidt, L. "The E-flat horn crook is a crook." *The Instrumentalist* 11 (Jan. 1957): 31–32.

3956 Schmidt, L. "Know the French horns." *The Instrumentalist* 14 (Dec. 1959): 49–53.

3957 Schmoll, Joseph. "Middle and low registers on French horn—using the B-flat side of a double horn." *The Instrumentalist* 12 (Dec. 1957): 38–42.

3958 Schmoll, Joseph. "Playing the French horn." *The Instrumentalist* 13 (Jan. 1959): 54–56.

3959 Schmoll, Joseph. "Problems of French horn playing." *The Instrumentalist* 19 (Feb. 1965): 33.

3960 Schmoll, Joseph. "Start right by teaching the fundamentals of French horn playing." *The Instrumentalist* 15 (Oct. 1960): 95–99.

3961 Schuller, Gunther. *Horn technique*. London: Oxford University Press, 1962.

3962 Schuller, Gunther. "Should horns vibrate?" *Woodwind* (Mar. 1951): 4, 12.

3963 Schuller, Gunther. "Should horns vibrate?." In *Woodwind Anthology*, 17–18. New York: Woodwind Magazine, 1952.

Schultz, K. "The French horn, a right handed instrument." *Monthly Journal of Research in Music Education* 1, no. 4 (1965): 23–35.

3964 Schulze, R. H. "Playing the French horn." *The Instrumentalist* 4 (Mar. 1950): 30–33.

3965 Schweikert, Norman. "Playing assistant first horn." *The Horn Call* 5, no. 1 (Autumn 1974): 43–50.

3966 Secon, Morris. "A response to David Irving on the use of 'DAON' as first suggested by Punto." *The Horn Call* 11, no. 2 (1981): 21–24.

3967 Seifert, Gerd. "Horn excerpts clinic: the Siegfried long call." *The Horn Call* 15, no. 2 (Apr. 1985): 43–45. Also in German.

3968 Seiffert, Elaine. "Forum: the first note." *The Horn Call* 10, no. 2 (Apr. 1980): 68–69.

3969 Seiffert, Stephen L. "The technique of hand stopping." *The Horn Call* 2, no. 2 (May 1972): 47–51.

3970   Seiffert, Stephen L. "Tuning the double horn." *The Horn Call* 4, no. 2 (Spring 1974): 35–39.

3971   Seiffert, Stephen L. "Tuning the double horn." *The Instrumentalist* 29 (Apr. 1975): 54–55.

3972   Seyfried, Erhard. "Meet the Wiener Waldhornverein!" *The Horn Call* 4, no. 2 (Spring 1974): 29–32.

        Shew, Bobby. "A positive approach to practice." *Crescendo International* 19 (Mar. 1981): 33.

3973   Silliman, A. Cutler. "The double horn." *The Instrumentalist* 17 (Mar. 1963): 81–82+.

3974   Silliman, A. Cutler. "The low register of the French horn." *The Instrumentalist* 17, no. 3 (Nov. 1962): 62–64.

3975   Silliman, A. Cutler. "Tuning and intonation on the double French horn." *The Instrumentalist* 13 (Oct. 1958): 69–71.

3976   Singer, J. "The basic rules of horn playing." *Woodwind World* 5 (Sept. 1952): 9+.

3977   "Special RDA: du cor en R.D.A. [interview with Peter Damm]." *Brass Bulletin—International Brass Chronicle*, no. 60 (1987): 33–37. Also in English and German.

3978   Stacy, William B. "Catch those clams." *The Instrumentalist* 30 (Mar. 1976): 71–72.

3979   Stacy, William B. "Elementary horn students need a good start." *The School Musician* 53 (Mar. 1982): 6–7.

3980   Stavens, D. A. "The French horn." *The School Musician* 25 (Dec. 1953): 14+.

3981   Steele-Perkins, C. "Those brain scramble bars." *Sounding Brass & the Conductor* 9, no. 3 (1980): 18–19.

        Stewart, Milton L. "Chamber music for voices with French horn: performance problems for French horn, Part 1." *The Horn Call* 18, no. 2 (Apr. 1988): 63–71.

        Stewart, Milton L. "Review of jazz French horn." *The Horn Call* 18, no. 1 (Oct. 1987): 47–53.

3982   Strevens, Patrick. "A dream come true [London Horn Reunion]." *The Horn Call* 5, no. 2 (Spring 1975): 17–25.

3983   Strevens, Patrick. "A firm foundation." *The Horn Call* 1, no. 1 (Feb. 1971): 8–12.

        Tarr, Edward H. "Handel horn duo located in South America." *Brass Bulletin—International Brass Chronicle*, no. 49 (1985): 41–44. Also in French and German.

3984   Tarr, Edward H. "Why do I—a trumpeter—play the horn?" *International Trumpet Guild Newsletter* 3, no. 2 (1977): 6.

3985   Taylor, L. "Training the young woodwind quintet." *The Instrumentalist* 18 (Nov. 1963): 76–77; (Dec. 1963): 54–55.

3986   Tellier. *Nouveau manuel de veneur contenant les tons et les fanfares de la chasse, précédés des principes de musique et une méthode général pour sonner de la trompe*. Paris: Heugel, [1848].

3987   Thayer, Robert W. "The literature of the French horn: Its use in teaching."
       Master's thesis, University of Wichita, 1955.

3988   Thelander, Kristin P. "A musical tour of the People's Republic of China."
       The Horn Call 11, no. 1 (Oct. 1980): 14–15.

3989   Thévet, Lucien. "Le cor." *Musique & Radio* 47 (1957): 87 + , 91. English and
       French text.

3990   Thomas, Brian, and Seth Orgel. "Auditioning for a horn position in the
       United States." *The Horn Call* 13, no. 2 (Apr. 1983): 56–60.

       Thompson, Virginia M. Weichman. "A comprehensive performance proj-
       ect in horn literature with an essay consisting of a comparison of selected
       writings on melodic interpretation." D.M. diss., University of Iowa,
       1987.

       Thompson, Virginia M. Weichman. "A comprehensive performance proj-
       ect in horn literature with an essay consisting of a comparison of selected
       writings on melodic interpretation." *Dissertation Abstracts* 48 (Jan. 1988):
       1581A.

3991   "Three hundred French hornists perform in concert." *The School Musician*
       46 (Nov. 1974): 38.

3992   Thurmond, J. M. "Teaching the French horn." *Woodwind World* 9, no. 2
       (1970): 12–14; 9, no. 3 (1970): 14–17.

3993   Tritle, Thomas. "On playing horn in Brazil." *The Horn Call* 11, no. 2 (1981):
       50–53.

3994   Trongone, Joseph A. "Breath control for horn players." *Music Educators
       Journal* 34 (Feb. 1948): 40 + .

       Tuckwell, Barry. "The horn." *Music Teacher and Piano Student* 55 (Oct.,
       Nov., Dec. 1976): 9–10, 10, 14.

       Tuckwell, Barry. "The horn." *The Australian Journal of Music Education*, no.
       19 (Oct. 1976): 11–12.

3995   Tuckwell, Barry. "Teaching horn players by the gross." *Music in Education*
       38, no. 369 (1974): 218–220.

3996   Tuttle, William. "How I saved $20.00." *The Horn Call* 7, no. 2 (May 1977):
       16–17.

3997   Uggen, Stuart. "Simple study to help in transition from F horn to double
       horn." *The Horn Call* 1, no. 2 (May 1971): 39.

3998   Urbin, Donatien. *Méthode de cor à trois pistons ou cylindres.* Paris: Richault,
       1852.

3999   V., C. F. *Manuel de veneur, contenant 211 tons et fanfares avec paroles indiquant
       l'action de la chasse. Précédes . . . d'une méthode pour sonner de la trompe.*
       Paris: Jouve, [1835].

4000   Vegna, J. "Elementary class method for the French horn." Master's thesis,
       Washington University, 1960.

4001   Verrier de la Conterie, J. -B. -J. Le. *L'Ecole de la chasse aux chiens courants;
       ou, Vénerie normande.* Nouvelle ed. Paris: Bouchard-Huzard, 1845.

4002   Wadenpfuhl, Karl H. "A fundamental method for the single B-flat French
       horn." Master's thesis, Sam Houston State Teachers College, 1953.

4003   Wadenpfuhl, Raymond John. "A study relating to some common teaching problems of the French horn." Master's thesis, Mississippi Southern College, 1957.

Wakefield, David A. "A chronological list of horn tutors." *The Horn Call* 17, no. 2 (Apr. 1987): 69–72.

4004   Wakefield, David A. "A guide to orchestral excerpt books for horn." D.M.A. diss., Juilliard School, 1981.

4005   Walker, B. H. "French horn contest solos, duets and quartets." *The School Musician* 25 (Jan. 1954): 34–36.

4006   Walker, D. E. "The band director's guide to the stopped horn." *The Instrumentalist* 41 (Nov. 1986): 53.

4007   Walshe, Robert C. "Hand horn technique as a teaching tool." *The Horn Call* 9, no. 2 (Apr. 1979): 73.

Walshe, Robert C. "Hand technique and the hand horn." *The Horn Call* 16, no. 2 (Apr. 1986): 57–61.

Watson, Catherine. "An interview with William Karl Ver Meulen." *The Horn Call* 14, no. 2 (Apr. 1984): 41–44.

4008   Weger, R. J. "Beginning steps on the French horn." *The School Musician* 33 (Nov. 1961): 32 + .

4009   Wekre, Froydis Ree. "The Leningrad school of horn playing." *The Horn Call* 10, no. 1 (Oct. 1979): 92–95.

4010   Wekre, Froydis Ree. "The Leningrad School of horn playing." *Brass Bulletin—International Brass Chronicle*, no. 27 (1979): 45–47 + . Also in French and German.

4011   Werner, Robert J. "Teaching techniques of the French horn." Master's thesis, Northwestern University, 1954.

4012   "Wettbewerb der Jagdhornbläser in Hessen." *Wild und Hund* 61 (1958): 248.

4013   Whaley, David Robert. "The microtonal capability of the horn." D.M.A. diss., University of Illinois (Urbana-Champaign), 1975.

4014   Whaley, David Robert. "The microtonal capability of the horn." *Dissertation Abstracts* 36 (Mar. 1976): 5633A.

4015   "What are the advantages of modern double horns?" *Canon* 8 (May, 1955): 406–407.

4016   Winter, James H. "About lip trills." *Woodwind World* 6, no. 1 (1964): 8.

4017   Winter, James H. "Additional thoughts on notation and transposition." *The Horn Call* 16, no. 1 (Oct. 1985): 38–39.

4018   Winter, James H. "Concerning the 'ring' in horn tone." *Woodwind World* 5, no. 5 (1964): 5.

4019   Winter, James H. "Double-horn intonation." *Woodwind World* 3, no. 8 (1960): 11; no. 9 (1960): 18; no. 10 (1960): 16.

4020   Winter, James H. "Double-horn intonation." *Woodwind World* 3, no. 11 (1961): 18.

4021   Winter, James H. "Philip Farkas on horn playing—an interview." *Woodwind World* 3 (Apr. 1959): 7–8.

4022   Winter, James H. "The hand in the horn bell." *Woodwind World* 3 (Jan.–

Feb. 1959): 17; (June 1, 1959): 17.

4023 Winter, James H. "The horn embouchure in the high register." *Woodwind World* 4, no. 6 (1962): 14.

4024 Winter, James H. "More about the hand in the bell." *Woodwind World* 3 (Apr. 10, 1959): 9.

4025 Winter, James H. "More on horn muting." *Woodwind World* 3 (Dec. 1, 1959): 12–13.

4026 Winter, James H. "More on horn tone." *Woodwind World* 2 (Nov. 1958): 14.

4027 Winter, James H. "Muting the horn." *Woodwind World* 3 (Sept. 15, 1959): 11.

4028 Winter, James H. "Practicing on the horn." *Woodwind World* 4, no. 5 (1962): 20.

4029 Winter, James H. "The problem of accuracy on the French horn." *Woodwind World* 4, no. 2 (1961): 15; no. 1 (1961): 13.

4030 Winter, James H. "Right hand in horn playing." *The Instrumentalist* 9 (May 1955): 38–40.

4031 Winter, James H. "Special problems of hand muting." *Woodwind World* 3 (Feb. 1, 1960): 12.

4032 Winter, James H. "The tone of the horn." *Woodwind World* 2 (Oct. 1958): 14–15.

4033 Winter, James H. "Transposition." *Woodwind World* 4, no. 8 (1962): 8; no. 9 (1963): 16.

4034 Winter, James H. "Variations in horn tone." *Woodwind World* 5, no. 4 (1964): 10+.

4035 Winter, James H. "Where to place the bell." *Woodwind World* 4, no. 4 (1962): 13.

4036 Wise, Ronald. "Horn warm-up: a head trip." *The Horn Call* 4, no. 2 (Spring 1974): 33–34.

4037 Wolf, W. "Corni da caccia mit neuer Technik." *Musik International-Instrumentenbau-Zeitschrift* 37 (May 1983): 368+.

4038 Yancich, Milan. "Carl Geyer—the mouthpiece man." *NACWPI Bulletin* 10, no. 3 (Mar. 1962): 16–19.

4039 Yancich, Milan. *A practical guide to French horn playing.* Bloomington, IN: Wind Music, 1971.

4040 Yancich, Milan. "Starting beginners on French horn." *The Instrumentalist* 13 (Apr. 1959): 57–59.

4041 Yaw, P. H. "Double horn fingering." *Brass and Percussion* 2, no. 3 (1974): 14–16+.

4042 Yaw, P. H. "The horn: right hand position." *Woodwind World—Brass and Percussion* 15, no. 4 (1976): 28–29.

4043 Yaw, P. H. "The single B-flat horn." *Woodwind World—Brass and Percussion* 18, no. 2 (Apr. 1979): 22–23.

4044 Yaw, P. H. "Tuning the double French horn." *The Instrumentalist* 21 (June 1967): 22.

4045   Yeager, G. "Hornist and engineer disagree on hand stopping." *The School Musician* 46 (Aug.-Sept. 1974): 77.

Trumpet

4046   Aitken, Allan Eugene. "A self-instructional audio-imitation method designed to teach trumpet students jazz improvisation in the major mode." Ph.D. diss., University of Oregon, 1975.

4047   Aitken, Allan Eugene. "A self-instructional audio-imitation method designed to teach trumpet students jazz improvisation in the major mode." *Dissertation Abstracts* 37 (July 1976): 18A.

4048   Alexander, John Lee. "Modern D trumpet technique." D.M.A. diss., University of Missouri (Kansas City), 1976.

4049   Alexander, John Lee. "Modern D trumpet technique." *Dissertation Abstracts* 38 (Aug. 1977): 535A.

        Amstutz, A. Keith, and B. H. Kinnie. "Orthodontics and the trumpeter's embouchure—a practical solution." *Journal of the International Trumpet Guild* 7, no. 4 (1983): 18–20.

4050   Amstutz, A. Keith. "A videofluorographic study of the teeth aperture, instrument pivot and tongue arch and their influence on trumpet performance." *Dissertation Abstracts* 31 (Dec. 1970): 2953A.

4051   Amstutz, A. Keith. "A videofluorographic study of the teeth aperture, instrument pivot and tongue arch and their influence on trumpet performance." D.Mus.Ed. diss., University of Oklahoma, 1970.

4052   Amstutz, A. Keith. "A videofluorographic study of the teeth aperture, instrument pivot and tongue arch and their influence on trumpet performance." *Journal of the International Trumpet Guild* 2 (1977): 25–26.

4053   Amstutz, A. Keith. "A videofluorographic study of the teeth aperture, instrument, pivot, and tongue arch and their influence on trumpet performance." *Journal of Band Research* 11, no. 2 (1975): 28–39.

4054   Anderson, P. "Basic concepts in trumpet teaching." *The Instrumentalist* 23 (Feb. 1969): 60–64.

        Anderson, Ronald Kent. "An historical and stylistic study of selected trumpet literature for performance and teaching." Ed.D. diss., Columbia University, 1970.

4055   Anderson, Ronald Kent. "An historical and stylistic study of selected trumpet literature for performance and teaching." *Dissertation Abstracts* 31 (Jan. 1971): 3578A.

4056   Anon. *Tutor for the royal keyed bugle.* London: Z. T. Purday, [ca. 1835].

4057   "The attack." *Brass Bulletin—International Brass Chronicle*, no. 41 (1983): 16–19. Also in French and German.

4058   Austin, J. L., and J. D. Swenson. *Compete conservatory lesson course for the serious trumpet student, Vol. 1.* Houston, TX: Conservatory Publications, 1965.

4059   Autry, B. *Basic guide to trumpet playing.* Chicago: Cole, 1963.

4060   Babcock, L. "Problems of teaching trumpet." *The School Musician* 21 (Sept. 1949): 22.

4061   Bach, Vincent. *The art of trumpet playing.* New York: V. Bach, 1925.

4062   Bach, Vincent. "The art of trumpet playing." *Jacobs' Band Monthly* 13 (Feb. 1928): 64–65.

4063   Bach, Vincent. "Bach's *Brandenburg concerto no. 2;* who can play the trumpet part." *The Instrumentalist* 15 (Sept. 1960): 94–96.

4064   Bach, Vincent. "The cornetist's road to success." *Jacobs' Band Monthly* 13 (Mar. 1928): 56–57.

4065   Bach, Vincent. "The trumpet player." *Jacobs' Band Monthly* 12 (Aug. 1927): 46–47; (Dec. 1927): 72–73.

        Baird, Frank W. "A history and annotated bibliography of tutors for trumpet and cornet." *Dissertation Abstracts* 44 (Dec. 1983): 1719A.

        Baird, Frank W. "A history and annotated bibliography of tutors for trumpet and cornet." Ph.D. diss., University of Michigan, 1983.

4066   Baissières, F. *Méthode simplifiée pour le cornet à pistons, contenant les principes élémentaires de cet instrument.* Paris: Petit, 1839.

4067   Baker, K. "Choosing a trumpet." *Melody Maker* 25 (Sept. 17, 1949): 9.

4068   Baker, K. "There is no easy way to trumpet mastery." *Melody Maker* 26 (Feb. 4, 1950): 8.

4069   Ball, K. "Play-an-instrument month." *Melody Maker* 40 (Nov. 27, 1965): 15.

        Ballou, Richard. "The history, technique, and literature of the trumpet." Master's thesis, Brigham Young University, 1953.

4070   Barber, J. "Trumpet playing: an athletic event." *Woodwind, Brass and Percussion* 24, no. 4 (1985): 12–13.

        Barrow, Gary. "Col. Earl D. Irons and the evolution of cornet pedagogy." *Journal of the International Trumpet Guild* 10, no. 2 (1985): 24–32.

4071   Barrow, Gary. "Con sordino: some thoughts on trumpet muting." *Woodwind, Brass and Percussion* 24, no. 4 (1985): 20–21.

4072   Beauchamp, Malcolm E. "The application of bel canto concepts and principles to trumpet pedagogy and performance." *Dissertation Abstracts* 41 (Oct. 1980): 1269A.

4073   Beauchamp, Malcolm E. "The application of bel canto to trumpet pedagogy." *The Instrumentalist* 38 (Oct. 1983): 64 + .

4074   Beauchamp, Malcolm Eugene. "The application of bel canto concepts and principles to trumpet pedagogy and performance." Ph.D. diss., Louisiana State University and Agricultural and Mechanical College, 1980.

4075   Becker, William R. "The effects of overlearning, initial learning ability and review upon the music memory of junior high school cornet and trumpet players." Ph.D. diss., State University of Iowa, 1962.

4076   Bench, Stephen K. "An analytical study of trumpet teaching with an evaluation of selected elementary methods." Master's thesis, Duquesne University, 1956.

Bendinelli, Cesare. *Tutta l'arte della trombetta, 1614*. Facsimile edition. Edited by Edward H. Tarr. Kassel: Bärenreiter, 1975.

4077   Bennett, J. G. "A guide for the performance of trumpet mariachi music in schools." *Dissertation Abstracts* 40 (Jan. 1980): 3859A+.

4078   Berger, K., and M. S. Hoshiko. "Respiratory muscle action of trumpet players." *The Instrumentalist* 19 (Oct. 1964): 91–94.

4079   Berger, Melvin. *The trumpet book*. New York: Lothrop, Lee & Shepard, 1978.

4080   Berinbaum, M. "Trumpet pedal tones: the key to an expanded range." *The Instrumentalist* 33 (Mar. 1979): 44–46.

4081   Bing, W. W. "Etude scientifique de la fonction pulmonaire; telle qu'elle s'applique aux instruments à vent, avec, en particulier, l'examen de cette fonction chez les trompettistes." *Brass Bulletin—International Brass Chronicle*, no. 13 (1976): 15–26. Also in English and German.

4082   Blair, Stacy. "Studying with Maurice Andre." *International Trumpet Guild Newsletter* 6, no. 3 (1980): 11.

4083   Boley, Donald Henry. "The development and evaluation of the effectiveness of a pilot instructional sound-film for teaching beginning trumpet students with a brief survey of the history of trumpet instruction and the history of educational film research."*Dissertation Abstracts* 31 (Sept. 1970): 1305A.

4084   Boley, Donald Henry. "The development and evaluation of the effectiveness of a pilot instructional sound-film for teaching beginning trumpet students with a brief survey of the history of trumpet instruction and the history of educational film research." Ph.D. diss., University of Iowa, 1970.

4085   Bowles, D. "Circular breathing." *The Instrumentalist* 32 (Jan. 1978): 62–64.

4086   Bradle, S. "Carole Reinhart, solo trumpeter supreme [interview]." *The Instrumentalist* 37 (Nov. 1982): 34–39.

4087   Braff, R. "The rubber embouchure." *Melody Maker* 37 (Oct. 13, 1962): i.

4088   Brahmstedt, Howard Kenneth. "The application of trumpet studies to performance problems in twentieth-century music." D.Mus. diss., Indiana University, 1973.

4089   Briggs, G. V. "Electrophysiological examination of labial function in college-age trumpet performers." *Dissertation Abstracts* 29 (Feb. 1969): 2735A.

4090   Briggs, Guy Vinton. "Electrophysiological examination of labial function in college-age trumpet performers." D.Mus.Ed. diss., University of Oklahoma, 1968.

4091   Brown, B. "In practice." *Sounding Brass & the Conductor* 1, no. 2 (1972): 43–44; 1, no. 3 (1972): 72+.

4092   Browning, Z. D. "Trumpet techniques in the performance of microtones." *International Trumpet Guild Newsletter* 5, no. 2 (1979): 6–9.

4093   Brownlow, A. "The mute in contemporary trumpet performance." *The*

Instrumentalist 33 (May 1979): 52 + .

4094   Brunnenmeyer, C. L. "An important problem in trumpet playing: the embouchure." *The School Musician* 46 (Aug.–Sept. 1974): 18 + .

4095   Bryant, B. "Some parts a studio first trumpet player might be required to play and the reasons why they are difficult." *Down Beat* 41 (Aug. 15, 1974): 40.

4096   Buhl, D. *Méthode de trompette*. Paris: Janet et Cotelle, 1825.

4097   Bullock, Donald. "Alternate fingerings for results." *The Instrumentalist* 19 (Nov. 1964): 72–77.

4098   Burditt, B. A. *The Complete preceptor for the posthorn or cornett, containing all necessary instruction with a large collection of music adapted to the instrument, including some of the most popular pieces of the day*. Boston: E. Howe, [ca. 1850].

Burum, H. *J. B. Arban; ausführliche Anleitung zum Selbstunterricht der Trompetenschule*. Hofheim: Hofmeister, 1976.

4099   Burum, H. "Erlebnisse und Erfahrungen mit Kollegen und Schülern—50 Jahre als Trompeter und Trompetenlehrer." *Das Orchester* 32 (Apr. 1984): 18–22.

4100   Burum, H. "Meine Erlebnisse und Erfahrungen mit Kollegen und Schülern in 50 Jahren als Trompeter und Trompetenlehrer." *Brass Bulletin—International Brass Chronicle*, no. 37 (1982): 58–67. Also in French and English.

4101   Bush, I. "Tell it the way it is: a viewpoint of professional trumpet playing in the United States." *Brass Bulletin—International Brass Chronicle*, no. 22 (1978): 45 + . Also in French and German.

4102   Bush, I. R. *Artistic trumpet technique and study*. Hollywood, Cal.: Highland Music Co., 1962.

4103   Byrd, D. "Talks to young trumpeters." *Down Beat* 28 (Jan. 19, 1961): 18 + .

4104   Cameron, W. C. "Two tips for trumpeters: Tonguing problem?—Maybe not!" *The Instrumentalist* 38 (Mar. 1984): 87–89.

Candelaria, Leonard Anthony. "An overview of performance practices relating to seventeenth- and eighteenth-century trumpet music: considerations for modern performance." D.M. diss., Northwestern University, 1985.

Candelaria, Leonard Anthony. "An overview of performance practices relating to seventeenth- and eighteenth-century trumpet music: considerations for modern performance." *Dissertation Abstracts* 47 (June 1987): 4225A-4226A.

4105   Caputo, C. R. "The development of criteria for measuring the competency of solo trumpet adjudicators." *Dissertation Abstracts* 46 (Sept. 1985): 640A–641A.

4106   Cardoso, W. "Ascending trumpets, vol. 3–4." *Brass Bulletin—International Brass Chronicle*, no. 25 (1979): 75.

4107   Carlucci, T. "Brass: flexibility is the key for freelance trumpet player." *Canadian Musician* 7, no. 6 (1985): 60 + .

4108 Carnovale, N. "Trumpet transpositions." *The Instrumentalist* 14 (May 1960): 60–62.

4109 Carter, J. "The big blow." *Crescendo International* 17 (July 1979): 18–19.

4110 Casto, David D. "A cornet-trumpet manual." Master's thesis, Florida State University, 1956.

4111 Caussinus, V. *Solfège-Méthode . . . de cornet à pistons.* Paris: n.p., 1846.

4112 Chenette, E. "Use that third valve slide!" *The Instrumentalist* 22 (Oct. 1967): 30.

4113 Clappé, A. *Self help to the cornet.* Philadelphia: H. Coleman, 1895.

4114 Clark, K., ed. "Armando Ghitalla on trumpet." *The Instrumentalist* 29 (Nov., Dec. 1974): 72–75, 73–75.

4115 Clarke, Herbert L. *The cornet and the cornetist; historical series of cornet talks.* Compiled by G. D. Bridges. Detroit: The Compiler, 1970.

4116 Clarke, Herbert L. "The proper use of cornet and trumpet." *Musical Observer* 29 (July 1930): 27.

4117 Clarke, Herbert L. "Random talks on the cornet." *Jacobs' Band Monthly* 17 (Dec. 1932): 4–5; (Apr. 1933): 6; (Sept. 1933): 5.

4118 Clarke, Herbert L. "Responsibilities of the cornet soloist." *Etude* 57 (1939): 375–376 + .

Clendenin, W. Ritchie, and William R. Clendenin. *A modern edition of Girolamo Fantini's trumpet method (1608).* Boulder, CO: Empire, 1977.

4119 Cleveland, Dana L. "A convergent approach to teaching the very young student to play the trumpet or cornet." Master's thesis, State College of Washington, 1952.

4120 "Clinic comments from Maynard Ferguson." *The Instrumentalist* 29 (Nov. 1974): 40–41.

4121 Colbert, J. K. "Bob's first cornet lesson." *The School Musician* 26 (Sept. 1954): 24–25.

4122 Cooper, M. A. "Eliminating pressure in trumpet performance." *The School Musician* 58 (Nov. 1986): 29–31.

Corcoran, G. "Problems with third-valve technique." *The Instrumentalist* 34 (May 1980): 91–92.

4123 "Cornets and clarinets—in A or B-flat?—Our readers speak their minds." *Jacobs' Band Monthly* 19 (Mar. 1934): 8 + ; (Apr. 1934): 8; (June 1934): 31; (Oct. 1934): 30.

4124 Courtade, Alexandre. *Méthode de trompette de cavalerie.* Paris: Evette & Schaeffer, ca. 1924.

4125 Crown, T. "Chicago: Brass Seminar—The Trumpet." *Brass Bulletin—International Brass Chronicle*, no. 4 (1973): 67–76. Also in French and German.

4126 Curson, T. "Trumpet." *Musician Player & Listener*, no. 12 (May-June 1979): 48–49.

4127 Curson, T. "Trumpet lip flexibilities." *Musician Player & Listener*, no. 17 (Mar.-Apr. 1979): 17–78.

4128   Curson, T. "Trumpet: chords." *Musician Player & Listener*, no. 16 (Jan.-Feb. 1979): 68.

4129   Dale, Delbert A. *Trumpet technique*. London; New York: Oxford University Press, 1965.

4130   D'Ath, N. W. *Cornet playing*. London: Hawkes, 1960.

4131   Daubenny, Ulric. "Practical trumpet and cornet playing." *Musical News* 42 (1912): 16, 18.

4132   Dauverné, F. G. A. *Méthode pour la trompette*. Paris: Brandus, Dufour et Cie, 1857.

4133   Davidson, Louis. "The 'art' in articulation; a discussion of some fine points of trumpet playing." *Symphony* 7 (Dec. 1953): 7.

4134   Davidson, Louis. "The trumpet attack." *Woodwind World—Brass and Percussion* 16, no. 1 (1977): 30–31.

        Davidson, Louis. *Trumpet profiles*. Bloomington, IN: The Author, 1975.

4135   Davidson, Louis. *Trumpet techniques*. Bloomington, IN: Wind Music, 1971.

4136   Davies, J. B., and others. "A psychological investigation of the role of mouthpiece force in trumpet performance." *Council for Research in Music Education Bulletin*, no. 91 (Spring 1987): 23–30.

4137   Dayley, K. Newell. "Trumpet vibrato: pedagogical significance of correlations between acoustical and physical variants." D.A. diss., University of Northern Colorado, 1986.

4138   Dayley, K. Newell. "Trumpet vibrato: pedagogical significance of correlations between acoustical and physical variants." *Dissertation Abstracts* 47 (Mar. 1987): 3229A.

4139   De Jong, William Donai. "The earliest trumpet method book extant." *Dissertation Abstracts* 32 (Oct. 1971): 2116A-2117A.

        de Pascual, B. Kenyon. "Jose de Juan Martinez's tutor for the circular hand-stopped trumpet (1830)." *Brass Bulletin—International Brass Chronicle*, no. 57 (1987): 50–54+. Also in French and German.

4140   Deming, H. O. "Trumpet/cornet intonation problems." *The Instrumentalist* 13 (June 1959): 52–53.

4141   Deming, H. O. "Why so many cornet-trumpet misfits?" *The Instrumentalist* 11 (Feb. 1957): 48–49.

4142   Deutsch, Maury. "Basic foundations of trumpet playing." *The Instrumentalist* 8 (Oct. 1953): 24–25+.

4143   Deutsch, Maury. "New directions in trumpet/cornet playing." *Down Beat* 48 (Aug. 1981): 58–59.

4144   Deutsch, Maury. "Theory of trumpet intonation." *Down Beat* 47 (June 1980): 72–73.

4145   Develde, J. A. Van. "Doing double duty on the lip waistline." *The Instrumentalist* 36 (Nov. 1981): 54.

4146   Dibbell, D. G. "Can surgery improve trumpet playing?" *NACWPI Journal* 27, no. 1 (1978): 24–25.

4147   Dibbell, D. G. "The incompetent palate: a trumpeting disaster." *Journal of the International Trumpet Guild* 2 (1977): 37–38.

4148   "A discussion of trumpet tone qualities." *The School Musician* 33 (May 1962): 28–28+. Reprinted from October 1959 issue.

4149   Dobroski, B. *"Accent* interviews Doc." *The Instrumentalist* 31 (Jan. 1977): 74–78. Reprinted from *Accent* (Sept.-Oct. 1976).

4150   Doksider, T. "Artikulationsarten: die 'Bogenstriche des Trompeters.' " *Brass Bulletin—International Brass Chronicle,* no. 30 (1980): 23–27+. Also in French and English.

4151   Dominy, Micky. "An analysis of the cornet solos contained on the class I University Interscholastic League List of the school year 1953–54." Master's thesis, Sam Houston State Teachers College, 1954.

Douglass, Robert. "The first trumpet method: Girolamo Fantini's *Modo per imparare a sonare di tromba (1638)." Journal of Band Research* 7, no. 2 (Spring 1971): 18–22.

4152   Drewes, Barry H. "Transposition and its application to the trumpet." Master's thesis, Juilliard School of Music, 1941.

4153   Drucker, V. "Nobility of tone on the trumpet." *Symphony* 5 (Apr. 1951): 10.

4154   Drushler, Paul F. "Programmed instruction: teaching fingerings and pitch notation." *Journal of Band Research* 11, no. 1 (Fall 1974): 8–11.

4155   Drushler, Paul F. "A study comparing programmed instruction with conventional teaching of instrument fingerings and music pitch notation for beginning students of clarinet, flute, and trumpet in a flexible scheduled curriculum." Ed.D. diss., State University of New York (Buffalo), 1972.

4156   Dunlap, N. "Doc Severinsen: 'ideal model.' " *Down Beat* 36 (Jan. 9, 1969): 16–17.

Dunn, F. Earl. "The brass instrument class—a workbook-text for the teacher or student of the cornet, French horn and trombone." Master's thesis, Iowa State Teachers College, 1954.

Eby, Walter M. *Eby's complete scientific method for cornet & trumpet.* Buffalo, N.Y.: Virtuoso Music School, 1926.

Echelard, Donald Joseph. "A thematic dictionary and planning guide of selected solo literature for trumpet." Ed.D. diss., University of Montana, 1969.

Echelard, Donald Joseph. "A thematic dictionary and planning guide of selected solo literature for trumpet." *Dissertation Abstracts* 31 (Nov. 1970): 2419A.

4157   Edris, David Michael. "Ranked orchestral excerpts from selected symphonic repertoire for trumpet." D.M.A. diss., University of Missouri (Kansas City), 1972.

4158   Edris, David Michael. "Ranked orchestral excerpts from selected symphonic repertoire for trumpet." *Dissertation Abstracts* 34 (Sept. 1973): 1311A-1312A.

Eichborn, Hermann Ludwig. *Die Trompete in alter und neuer Zeit. Ein Beitrag zur Musikgeschichte und Instrumentationslehre.* Wiesbaden: Sändig, 1968. Reprint of the 1881 Breitkopf & Härtel publication.

4159   "Elevating the cornet." *The Instrumentalist* 4 (Sept. 1949): 36.

4160   Elgas, Richard Gerald. "A method for the development of flexibility and endurance in the upper partials of the B flat trumpet." M.A. thesis, California State University (Fullerton), 1969.

4161   Ellis, J. R. "Pedagogical topics for trumpet: baroque performance styles." *Journal of the International Trumpet Guild* 9, no. 3 (1985): 48–51.

4162   Ellis, J. R., ed. "Pedagogical topics for trumpet: the embouchure change: difficult decisions for teachers." *Journal of the International Trumpet Guild* 11, no. 3 (1987): 25–27 +.

4163   "Un entretien avec Rolf Quinque." *Brass Bulletin—International Brass Chronicle*, no. 14 (1976): 19–21. Also in English and German.

4164   "Fainting trumpeter." *Scientific American* 200 (June 1959): 86.

4165   Fairweather, D. "Troublesome trumpet." *Jazz Journal International* 32 (May 1979): 15.

Fantini, Girolamo. *A modern edition of Girolamo Fantini's trumpet method (1638).* Edited by W.R. and W.R. Clendenin. Boulder, CO: Empire, 1977.

Fantini, Girolamo. *Modo per imparare a sonare di tromba (1638).* Facsimile. Nashville: Brass Press, 1972.

Fantini, Girolamo. *Modo per imparare a sonare di tromba (1638).* Transl. by Edward Tarr. Nashville: Brass Press, 1978.

4166   Farr, J. W. "One who has changed the position of his cornet mouthpiece." *Metronome* 30, no. 10 (1914): 30.

4167   Farr, J. W. "Tone production on the cornet or other brass wind instruments." *Metronome* 29, no. 11 (1913): 12.

Faulkner, Maurice. "300 years later: what trumpet to play?" *The Instrumentalist* 40 (Dec. 1985): 68–69.

Faulkner, Maurice. "Annual review of solos and studies: trumpet and French horn." *The Instrumentalist* 39 (Feb. 1985): 71–76.

4168   Faulkner, Maurice. "Let that trumpet sing." *The Instrumentalist* 36 (June 1982): 50–51.

4169   Faulkner, Maurice, and E. P. Sharpey-Schafer. "Circulatory effects of trumpet playing." *International Trumpet Guild Newsletter* 8, no. 2 (1982): 22–23 +.

Faulkner, Maurice. "Solos and studies for trumpet and horn." *The Instrumentalist* 32 (Feb. 1978): 56 +.

Faulkner, Maurice. "Trumpet and French horn [annual review of solos and studies]." *The Instrumentalist* 35 (Dec. 1980): 33–34.

Faulkner, Maurice. "Trumpet and French horn solos and studies." *The Instrumentalist* 33 (Jan. 1979): 80 +.

Faulkner, Maurice. "Trumpet and horn solos and studies." *The Instrumentalist* 34 (Dec. 1979): 24–26.

4170   Faulkner, Maurice. "Why American orchestras need rotary-valve trumpets." *The Instrumentalist* 39 (Feb. 1985): 98.

4171   Feather, Leonard. "Le piston, le swing et l'embouchure." *Jazz Magazine* 9 (Apr. 1963): 20–25.

4172   Fernandes, G. M. "The oscilloscope as an aid in changing tone quality in the performance of junior high school cornet and trumpet students." *Dissertation Abstracts* 41 (Dec. 1980): 2491A-2492A.

        Figgs, Linda Drake. "Critique: Qualitative differences in trumpet tones as perceived by listeners and by acoustical analysis (Ed.D. diss., Univ. of Kansas, 1978)." *Council for Research in Music Education Bulletin*, no. 64 (Fall 1980): 67–72. Reviewed by L. B. Hilton.

4173   Finley, S. "Methodology: turning off the XEROX." *International Trumpet Guild Newsletter* 5, no. 3 (1979): 10–11.

4174   Fiske, Harold Eugene, Jr. "Judge-group differences in the rating of secondary school trumpet performances." Ph.D. diss., University of Connecticut, 1972.

4175   Fiske, Harold Eugene, Jr. "Judge-group differences in the rating of secondary school trumpet performances." *Journal of Research in Music Education* 28, no. 3 (1975): 186–196.

4176   Fiske, Harold Eugene, Jr. "Judge-group differences in the rating of secondary school trumpet performances." *Dissertation Abstracts* 33 (June 1973): 6950A–6951A.

4177   Fitzgerald, Bernard. "Pedal tones on the trumpet and cornet." *The Instrumentalist* 2 (May 1948): 38.

4178   Fitzgerald, Bernard. "Teaching materials for beginning trumpet students." *The Instrumentalist* 4 (Sept. 1949): 20+.

4179   Folts, Melvin Lyle. "The relative effect of two procedures, as followed by flute, clarinet, and trumpet students while practicing, on the development of tone quality and on selected performance skills: an experiment in student use of sound-recorded practice material." Ed.D. diss., New York University, 1973.

4180   Forestier, J. *Méthode complète . . . pour le cornet chromatique à pistons (ou cylindres)*. Paris: Meissonnier, [1844].

        Foss, George Dueward, Jr. "The stylistic problems to be considered in performing music from the trumpet repertoire of earlier periods on the modern instrument." M.A. thesis, American University, 1962.

4181   Fowler, W., and Dominic Spera. "How to polish your brass [playing techniques]." *Down Beat* 41 (Feb. 14, 1974): 32.

4182   Franklin, L. "Breathing." *The School Musician* 49 (Aug.-Sept. 1977): 8+. Reprinted from *The School Musician* (Mar. 1972).

4183   Franklin, L. L. "Basic physical aspects of trumpet playing." *The School Musician* 38 (June-July 1967): 20+.

4184   Frei, H. "Die Stellung der Trompete in der heutigen Instrumentalpädagogik." *Schweizerische Musikzeitung* 120, no. 4 (1980): 228+. Includes summary in French.

4185   Friestadt, H. "Notes on the Schlossberg method." *Symphony* 8 (May 1954): 11.

4186   *Fundamentals of brass instruments. Part I. Trumpet and cornet*. Lincoln, Neb.: University of Nebraska Bureau of Visual Education, 1948. Mimeo. booklet with filmstrip.

4187   Gengler, John C. "A study of advanced trumpet technique through the use of thematic literature." Master's thesis, Illinois Wesleyan University, 1948.

4188   Gibson, Daryl J. *A textbook for trumpet.* Minneapolis: Schmitt, Hall & McCreary, 1962.

4189   Gibson, Daryl Robert. "A photographic study of twelve professional trumpet embouchures while playing from the low to the extreme upper register." Ph.D. diss., University of Minnesota, 1973.

4190   Gibson, R. "How the professional trumpeters play double high C." *The Instrumentalist* 29 (Dec. 1974): 58–61.

4191   Glantz, Harry. "Trends in trumpet playing." *Symphony* 5 (Oct. 1951): 9.

4192   Glantz, Harry. "Trumpet player—or artist?" *Symphony* 7 (Feb. 1953): 9.

4193   Gleason, Kenneth. "An elementary trumpet method." Master's thesis, Northeast Missouri State Teachers College, 1953.

4194   Glover, S. L. "Allen Vizzutti: an interview." *Journal of the International Trumpet Guild* 6 (1981): 18–30. Includes discography.

4195   Goldfarb, S. "Gimmicks for the cornet." *Brass International* 10, no. 1 (1982): 4–5. Edited by P. Catelinet.

       Goldman, Edwin Franko. "Arban and his method." *Metronome* 31, no. 5 (1915): 16.

4196   Goldman, Edwin Franko. "Common mistakes of cornetists." *Metronome* 29, nos. 2, 4–8 (1913).

4197   Goldman, Edwin Franko. "The cornet and trumpet—Differences between the two instruments—Uses and abuses of each." *Metronome* 44 (July 1928): 14. Reprinted from *The White Way.*

4198   Goldman, Edwin Franko. "Famous songs and how to play them on the cornet." *Metronome* 27, nos. 5–9, 12 (1911); 28, no. 1 (1912).

       Goldman, Edwin Franko. "How to test a cornet." *Metronome* 33, no. 5 (1917): 20–21.

4199   Goldman, Edwin Franko. "The tongue as a factor in cornet playing." *Metronome* 27, no. 1 (1911): 16.

4200   "Goodbye to those dance band days says Jimmy Knepper." *Crescendo International* 19 (June 1981): 16–17.

       Gouse, Charles Frederick. "The cornett: its history, literature and performance praxis including a practical tutor for developing performance skills." *Dissertation Abstracts* 34 (June 1974): 7806A.

4201   Graban, R. D. "The development of a beginning trumpet method book using Christian materials of Protestant fundamentalists groups as the primary didactic source." *Dissertation Abstracts* 46 (June 1986): 3643A.

4202   Grabel, V. "The cornet and trumpet in band and orchestra." *Etude* 47 (1929): 27.

4203   Grafmyer, James Boyd. *Trumpet: a collection of different ideas of trumpet practice.* 2151 Newton St., Denver, CO: The author, 1975.

       Greissinger, F. Henri. *Instructions for the trumpet and drum; together with the full code of signals and calls used by the United States army and navy.* Revised and enlarged by W. F. Smith. New York: Carl Fischer, [1900].

4204   Grey, Al, and M. Grey. "Plunger techniques; the Al Grey plunger method for trombone and trumpet." Introduction by I. Gitler. New York: Second Floor Music, 1987.

4205   Grin, Fred. "Interpretation and the chances for an American musician in Europe." *Journal of the International Trumpet Guild* 12, no. 3 (Feb. 1988): 12–15+. Edited by Frederick Beck.

4206   Guerin, R. "Quelle trompette?" *Jazz Magazine*, no. 281 (Dec. 1979): 60–62.

        Güttler, Ludwig. "Möglichkeiten und Probleme bei der Wiedergabe hoher Trompetenpartien der ersten Hälfte des 18. Jahrhunderts aus der Sicht des heutigen Spielers. In *Die Blasinstrumente und ihre Verwendung. . . ,* edited by Eitelfriedrich Thom, 22–25. Magdeburg: Rat des Bezirkes; Leipzig: Zentralhaus für Kulturarbeit, 1977.

        Haack, P. A. "Mouthpieces and tone quality: a research review." *Journal of Band Research* 15, no. 2 (1980): 50–52.

4207   Halary. *Clavitube ou Trompette à clefs.* [Paris?]: n.p., 1821.

        Hall, Jody C. "Effect of the oral and pharyngeal cavities on trumpet tone quality." *Journal of the Acoustical Society of America* 27 (1955): 996.

4208   Hall, Jody C. "A radiographic, spectrographic, and photographic study of the non-labial physical changes which occur in the transition from middle to low and middle to high registers during trumpet performance." Ph.D. diss., Indiana University, 1954.

        Hall, Jody C. "A radiographic, spectrographic, and photographic study of the non-labial physical changes which occur in the transition from the middle to low and middle to high registers during trumpet performance." *Dissertation Abstracts* 14 (Nov. 1954): 2086–2087.

        Hanson, Fay. "Control of staccato sound production by laryngeal muscles." *Journal of Band Research* 4, no. 1 (1967): 61–64. Documented by R. L. Nichols.

4209   Harding, J. "The lead trumpet player: a survey of training, practice, and equipment." *Brass Bulletin—International Brass Chronicle*, no. 4 (1973): 29–51. Also in French and German.

4210   Harper, Thomas. *Instructions for the trumpet.* London: T. Harper, [ca. 1836].

4211   Harris, Samuel G. "The progress and value of modern methods and concepts in trumpet techniques." Master's thesis, University of South Dakota, 1954.

4212   Haynie, John J., and L. A. Candelaria, comps. "Course of study, North Texas State University School of Music." *Journal of the International Trumpet Guild* 7, no. 3 (1983): 20–24.

4213   Haynie, John J. "A course of study for the trumpet." *The Instrumentalist* 13 (Nov. 1958): 40–41.

4214   Haynie, John J. "How to play the *Carnival of Venice* in four easy lessons." *The Instrumentalist* 21 (May 1967): 63–67.

4215   Head, Emerson Williams. "An evaluation of the use of vibrato in trumpet performance with historical and pedagogical perspectives." D.M.A. diss., Catholic University of America, 1980.

4216   Heier, M. R. "Helping students cope with 20th century trumpet music." *Woodwind World—Brass and Percussion* 16, no. 3 (1977): 32–33 + .

4217   Helinski, Joseph. "Intonation problems of trumpet performance in relation to the player and the instrument." Master's thesis, Duquesne University, 1956.

4218   Henderson, Hayward W. "An experimental study of trumpet embouchure." *Journal of the Acoustical Society of America* 14 (1942): 58–64.

Henderson, Hayward W. "An experimental study of trumpet embouchure." *Bulletin of the American Musicological Society* (Oct. 1945): 11–12.

4219   Henderson, W. A. "EMG potentials of the sternocleid-mastoid muscle during trumpet performance." *Journal of the International Trumpet Guild* 4 (1979): 30–35 + .

Heyde, Herbert. "Die Unterscheidung von Klarin- und Prinzipaltrompete. Zum Problem des Klarinblasens." *Beiträge zur Musikwissenschaft* 9 (1967): 55–61.

4220   Hickernell, Ross. "Cornet and trumpet—What's the difference?" *Musical Observer* 30 (Mar. 1931): 42 + .

4221   Hickman, David R. "The classical trumpet soloist." *Woodwind World—Brass and Percussion* 16, no. 2 (1977): 32 + .

4222   Hickman, David R. "A natural approach to trumpet playing." *The Instrumentalist* 34 (Aug. 1979): 79–85.

Hickman, David R. "Charles Schlueter on orchestral trumpet playing." *The Instrumentalist* 31 (Sept. 1976): 58 + .

4223   Hightshoe, Robert B. "The development of a standard for accrediting a four year program of trumpet study on a college level." Master's thesis, Ohio State University, 1948.

4224   Holdsworth, E. I. "Neuromuscular activity and covert musical psychomotor behavior: an electromyographic study." *Dissertation Abstracts* 36 (July 1975): 167A.

4225   Hollander, A. "Higher and louder [effect of difficult jazz charts on young players]." *The School Musician* 46 (Nov. 1974): 47.

4226   Horacek, Leo. "A study of vocal and cornet performance intervals." Master's thesis, University of Kansas, 1949.

4227   Horn, Claire H. "The correlation between observable classroom conduct and satisfying experience on violin, clarinet, or trumpet at the fifth and sixth-grade level." M.A. thesis, California State University (Fullerton), 1982.

4228   Horvath, S. M., and Maurice Faulkner. "Physiological observations on French horn players." *The Instrumentalist* 35 (Oct. 1980): 72 + .

4229   House, H. L., comp. "A survey of 43 orchestra audition lists for trumpet." *International Trumpet Guild Newsletter* 7, no. 2 (1981): 28.

4230   Howarth, Elgar. "Performers' platform: some aspects of trumpet playing." *Composer* (Summer 1969): 13–17.

Hyatt, Jack René. "The soprano and piccolo trumpets: their history, literature, and a tutor." D.M.A. diss., Boston University, 1974.

4231 Immer, F. "Basistechniken der naturtrompete." *Brass Bulletin—International Brass Chronicle*, no. 51 (1985): 70–73. Also in English and French.

4232 "Inflated trumpeter." *Time* 73 (Apr. 6, 1959): 62.

4233 Jacobson, S. "The cornet." *Music* (Chicago) 13 (1897/98): 622–629.

Jacobson, Samuel L. "The cornet." *Music* 13 (1897): 622–629.

4234 Jacoby, D. "The importance of sound." *The International Musician* 58 (July 1959): 18–19.

4235 Jenkins, H. "How high is high?" *The Instrumentalist* 18 (Sept. 1963): 96–98.

4236 Jenkins, H. "Playing the small trumpets." *The Instrumentalist* 31 (Jan. 1977): 26–27.

4237 Jenkins, H. "Studies with Schlossberg." *The Instrumentalist* 35 (Apr. 1981): 36+.

Johnson, D. "Brass: Vibrato." *Canadian Musician* 3, no. 6 (1981): 60.

4238 Johnson, K. "Basic skills for young trumpet players." *The School Musician* 54 (June 1983): 12–13.

4239 Johnson, Keith. *The art of trumpet playing*. Ames: Iowa State University Press, 1981.

4240 Johnson, Keith. "Playing the piccolo trumpet." *NACWPI Journal* 27, no. 1 (Sept. 1978): 25–27.

4241 Jones, E. W. "Charming cornets or thrilling trumpets?" *The School Musician* 27 (Sept. 1955): 29+.

4242 Kase, R. "The trumpet section of a jazz ensemble." *The School Musician* 48 (Apr. 1977): 38–39+.

4243 Kastner, J. -G. *Méthode élémentaire de cornet à pistons*. Paris: n.p., [ca. 1837–38].

4244 Knoll, Allan. "Studies in cornet and trumpet pedagogy." Master's thesis, Michigan State College, 1939.

4245 Krauss, S. "On trumpet embouchure." *Symphony* 2 (Mar. 1949): 6.

4246 Krauss, S. "Trumpet valve technique." *Symphony* 4 (Feb. 1950): 12.

4247 Krauss, S. "Tuning the trumpets." *Symphony* 6 (Mar. 1952): 12.

4248 Krueger, H. E. "An American trumpet player's impressions of European brass performances." *Brass Bulletin—International Brass Chronicle*, no. 5–6 (1973): 35–46. Also in French and German.

4249 Krumpfer, Hans-Joachim. *Trompetenschule für Anfänger*. Leipzig: Deutscher Verlag für Musik, 1967.

4250 Kugler, Roger Thomas. "A beginning method for trumpet." D.M.A. diss., University of Oregon, 1975.

4251 Kyme, G. H. "Cornets and trumpets." *The Instrumentalist* 11 (Apr. 1957): 60–62.

4252 Kynaston, T. "Pro session: Randy Brecker's solo on *I Can't Get Started*, a trumpet transcription." *Down Beat* 51 (May 1984): 64–65.

4253 Lacey, Robert M. "The teaching of trumpet using special material." Ed.D.

diss., Boston University School of Education, 1969.

4254 Lacey, Robert M. "The teaching of trumpet using special material." *Dissertation Abstracts* 31 (Aug. 1970): 787A.

Landy, E. *Méthode de clarion . . . avec vignette et description de l'instrument.* Paris: Gallet, [1903].

4255 Lang, W. "My way." *Sounding Brass & the Conductor* 4, no. 4 (1976): 118–119.

4256 Lanshe, R. "Trumpet teaching and the band method approach." *Woodwind World—Brass and Percussion* 15, no. 3 (1976): 36–38 + .

Laplace, Michel. "Les fondateurs de l'ecole française de trompette Merri Franquin, Eugene Foveau et Raymond Sabarich." *Brass Bulletin—International Brass Chronicle,* no. 29 (1980): 67–69 + . Also in German and English. Expanded from *International Trumpet Guild Newsletter* 3, no. 3 (1977): 13–14.

4257 Laplace, Michel. "La trompette et le cornet dans le jazz et la musique populaire: la respiration." *Brass Bulletin—International Brass Chronicle,* no. 46 (1984): 23–30. Also in English and German.

4258 Laplace, Michel. "La trompette et le cornet dans le jazz et la musique populaire: techniques particulieres de jazz." *Brass Bulletin—International Brass Chronicle,* no. 47 (1984): 39–45. Also in English and German.

4259 Laudermilch, Kenneth L. "Long tones for the trumpeter." *The Instrumentalist* 25 (Nov. 1970): 48.

4260 "Lead trumpet, Lenton '71, M. Vax." *Crescendo International* 10 (Nov. 1971): 20–22.

4261 Leitsinger, Carl. "Double tonguing on the trumpet." *Metronome* 41 (July 15, 1925): 42–43.

4262 Leitsinger, Carl. "Interpretation of studies and melodies for trumpet." *Metronome* 41 (Aug. 15, 1925): 61 + .

4263 Leitsinger, Carl. "Interval study for the trumpet player." *Metronome* 41 (Nov. 15, 1925): 50–51.

4264 Leitsinger, Carl. "Overcoming stumbling blocks on the trumpet." *Metronome* 42 (Jan. 15, 1926): 44–45.

4265 Leitsinger, Carl. "Regarding certain points in trumpet playing." *Metronome* 42 (July 15, 1926): 51–52.

4266 Leitsinger, Carl. "Some trumpet queries answered." *Metronome* 41 (Oct. 15, 1925): 58–59.

4267 Leitsinger, Carl. "Transposition for trumpet players." *Metronome* 42 (Dec. 1, 1926): 37–38.

4268 Leitsinger, Carl. "Trumpet talks." *Metronome* 41 (Jan. 15, 1925): 66–67 [melody practice]; (Feb. 15, 1925); 52 [rhythm]; (Apr. 15, 1925); (May 15, 1925): 52 [double tonguing].

4269 Leitsinger, Carl. "The value of interval practice for the trumpet player." *Metronome* 41 (Dec. 15, 1925): 64–65.

4270 Lemasters, D. "Embouchure." *The School Musician* 24 (June-July 1968): 24 + .

4271 Lemasters, D. "For the trumpet player—tongue position." *The School Mu-*

sician 40 (June-July 1969): 44–46.

4272   Lemasters, D. "Tongue position for the trumpet player." *The School Musician* 49 (Nov. 1977): 22. Reprinted from *The School Musician* (June 1969).

4273   Lemasters, D. "Trumpet breathing." *The School Musician* 41 (June-July 1970): 4+.

4274   Lemasters, Donald G. "The art of the trumpet." Master's thesis, Northwestern University, 1949.

4275   Leroy. *Méthode de trompette simple et à 5 clefs.* Mainz: [Schott?], 1823.

4276   Lewis, E. L. "A photographic study of the body positions of sixteen trumpet virtuosi while playing selected exercises." *Dissertation Abstracts* 46 (June 1986): 3644A.

        Lewis, H. M. "Authentic baroque interpretation for trumpet." *The Instrumentalist* 32 (Feb. 1978): 44–45.

4277   Lienerth, R. "Musiker schreiben für Schüler: die Trompete." *Musik und Bildung* 20 (Jan. 1988): 44–45.

4278   Ligotti, A. F., and E. D. Voth. "An orthodontic aid for young trumpeters." *The Instrumentalist* 29 (Sept. 1974): 51–52.

4279   Lillya, Clifford P. "Improving intonation with the third valve slide and first valve trigger." *The Instrumentalist* 11 (June 1957): 44–47.

4280   Lillya, Clifford P. "Trumpet talk for teachers." *The Instrumentalist* 30 (Dec. 1975): 75–76.

4281   Lillya, Clifford P. "Trumpet talk for teachers." *Journal of the International Trumpet Guild* 4 (1979): 17–19.

4282   Lindskoog, W. "Polishing the trumpet player." *The Instrumentalist* 14 (Feb. 1960): 76–79.

        Littleton, W. S. *Trumpeter's handbook and instructor.* Kansas City, Kansas: Hudson-Kimberly Pub. Co., [1902].

4283   Logier. *A complete introduction to the art of playing on the keyed bugle.* London: Clementi, 1820.

        Lord, Jewel W. "The trumpet: its history, literature and place in the public school." Master's thesis, University of Southern California, 1949.

        Lowrey, A. "Maurice Andre—a French performing model." *The Instrumentalist* 23 (Apr. 1969): 68–69+.

4284   Luty, B. "Concert jazz embellishments." *The Instrumentalist* 36 (Nov. 1981): 98+.

        McCann, William J. "Trumpet and horn: correcting problems early." *The School Musician* 45 (Aug.-Sept. 1973): 20+.

4285   McCann, William J. "Trumpet and horn: correcting problems early." *The School Musician* 49 (May 1978): 6+. Reprinted from *The School Musician* 45 (Aug.–Sept. 1973): 20+.

4286   McCauley, John Willys. "Jazz improvisation for the B-flat soprano trumpet: an introductory text for teaching basic theoretical and performance principles." Ph.D. diss., Louisiana State University and Agricultural and Mechanical College, 1973.

4287   McCauley, John Willys. "Jazz improvisation for the B-flat soprano trumpet:

an introductory text for teaching basic theoretical and performance principles." *Dissertation Abstracts* 35 (Aug. 1974): 1145A.

4288 McGuffey, P. "A trumpeter's approach to the orchestra." *International Trumpet Guild Newsletter* 6, no. 1 (1979): 16.

4289 Madsen, C. K., and J. M. Geringer. "Preferences for trumpet tone quality versus intonation." *Council for Research in Music Education Bulletin*, no. 46 (Spring 1976): 13–22.

4290 Malek, Vincent F. "Embouchures of professional trumpet-cornet players." *The Instrumentalist* 9 (Sept. 1954): 48 + .

4291 Malek, Vincent F. "An interview with Harry James on trumpet technique." *The Instrumentalist* 13 (Sept. 1958): 60 + .

Mariconda, Dominick J. "The trumpet—its history, care, repertoire and method of performance." Master's thesis, Hartt College of Music, 1952.

4292 Markley, R. "The difference between trumpet and cornet tone." *The School Musician* 20 (May 1949): 12 + .

4293 Mathez, Jean-Pierre. *Méthode de trompette. Méthodes Instrumentales Viennoises*. Vienna: Universal, 1977.

4294 Mathez, Jean-Pierre. *Trompetenschule für Trompete beliebiger Stimmung, auch geeignet für Kornett und Fluegelhorn, Bände 1–3: Schülerheft, Beiheft, Lehrerheft*. Vienna: Universal, 1976.

Mathie, Gordon W. "Teaching musicality to young players." *Journal of the International Trumpet Guild* 5 (1980): 19–21.

4295 Mathie, Gordon W. "Trumpet transposition: One teacher's approach." *Brass and Percussion* 2, no. 4 (1974): 18–19 + . Includes bibliography.

4296 Mathie, Gordon William. "A theoretical basis for college trumpet study." Ed.D. diss., University of Illinois (Urbana-Champaign), 1969.

4297 Mathie, Gordon William. "A theoretical basis for college trumpet study." *Dissertation Abstracts* 30 (Jan. 1970): 3043A.

4298 Mendez, Rafael. "Successful trumpet playing." *The International Musician* 58 (Oct. 1959): 18.

Meredith, Henry M. "Baroque trumpet ornamentation: another view." *International Trumpet Guild Newsletter* 7, no. 3 (1981): 22–23.

Meredith, Henry M. "Girolamo Fantini's Trumpet Method: a practical edition." 2 vols. D.A. diss., University of Northern Colorado, 1984.

Meredith, Henry M. "Girolamo Fantini's Trumpet Method: a practical edition." *Dissertation Abstracts* 46 (Oct. 1985): 835A.

4299 Merriman, L. C., and J. A. Meidt. "A cinefluorographic investigation of brass instrument performance." *Journal of Research in Music Education* 16, no. 1 (1968): 31–38.

Meyer, L. "Trumpet and cornet tone quality." *The Instrumentalist* 23 (Jan. 1969): 62–67.

4300 Miller, Fred. "Cornets vs. trumpets." *The Instrumentalist* 12 (Dec. 1957): 12. Letter to the editor.

4301 Miller, T. W. "Developing the trumpet embouchure." *The Instrumentalist* 18 (May 1964): 72–73; 18 (June 1964): 62–63.

4302   Mitchell, G. "The teacher, the magic ingredient in teaching." *The School Musician* 7 (Feb. 1975): 38–39.

4303   Mönkemeyer, Helmut. "How to play the cornet in D and A." *American Recorder* 19, no. 4 (1979): 176–177.

Mönkemeyer, Helmut. *Spielanleitung für Zinken in d' und a/How to play the cornett in D and A*. Celle: Moeck, 1978.

4304   Monk, C. "First steps towards playing the cornett." *Early Music* 3, no. 2, 3 (1975): 132–133, 244–248.

4305   Moorehead, J. K. "Embouchures: their assets and liabilities—an interview with Armando Ghitalla." *Journal of the International Trumpet Guild* 11, no. 3 (1987): 17–19 + .

4306   Moulton, Kenneth E. "Training the school orchestra trumpeter." *National School Orchestra Association* 20, no. 1 (1978): 6; no. 2 (1978): 5.

Muckelroy, Roby Kenneth. "A brief history of the trumpet and an annotated bibliography of studies for the trumpet." M.Mus. thesis, University of Houston, 1968.

Musella, Donald F. "The teaching of brass instruments in the public schools using the plan of transferring students of trumpet or cornet to the other brass instruments." Master's thesis, Eastman School of Music, 1957.

4307   Musser, W. I. "The larger trumpet sound." *The Instrumentalist* 15 (Feb. 1961): 42 + .

4308   Myers, W. J. "A photographic, air flow direction, and sound spectra analysis of two trumpet embouchure techniques." *Dissertation Abstracts* 40 (Apr. 1980): 5357A.

4309   Nagel, Robert. "Better sound for trumpet ensembles." *The Instrumentalist* 30 (Apr. 1976): 20.

4310   Naylor, Tom L. "A program of study for teaching class trumpet at the college level." Ph.D. diss., Indiana University, 1973.

4311   Neff, Carolyn Hope. "A study of trumpet pedagogy and repertoire in the United States and Scandinavia." *Dissertation Abstracts* 35 (Dec. 1974): 3796A–3797A.

Neff, Carolyn Hope. "A study of trumpet pedagogy and repertoire in the United States and Scandinavia." D.M.A. diss., University of Oregon, 1974.

4312   Neidig, K. L. " 'Man alive, what a kick this is!'—an interview with Adolph 'Bud' Herseth." *The Instrumentalist* 31 (Apr. 1977): 38–44.

4313   Neilson, James. "Teaching the cornet in beginning classes." *The Instrumentalist* 6 (Jan.–Feb. 1952): 21–22 + .

4314   Nelson, T. "A trumpet warm-up." *The Instrumentalist* 31 (Nov. 1976): 28 + .

4315   Nemetz, A. *Neueste Trompetenschule*. Vienna: Diabelli, 1828.

4316   Noble, C. E. *The psychology of cornet and trumpet playing*. Missoula, MT: Mountain, 1964.

4317   Noblet. *Nouvelle méthode de bugle (ou trompette à clefs) (Klapphorn-Schule) contenant: la tablature, les gammes et les exercises pour se familiariser dans toutes les difficultés de cet instrument, suivis de plusiers morceaux pour un ou deux bugles*. Bonn: Simrock, [1831]; Paris: Aulagnier [1831].

4318   Olson, R. D. "Extended trumpet range." *The Instrumentalist* 17, no. 1 (Sept. 1962): 72–74.

4319   Olson, R. D. "Trumpet pedal register unveiled." *The Instrumentalist* 19 (Sept. 1964): 57+.

4320   Oneglia, M. F. "Mouthpiece change—trauma or triumph." *The Instrumentalist* 30 (Apr. 1976): 46+.

4321   Oneglia, M. F. "The perfect trumpet lesson." *The Instrumentalist* 28 (Apr. 1974): 74–77.

4322   Oneglia, M. F. "Some thoughts on trumpet pedal tones." *The Instrumentalist* 27 (Sept. 1972): 56–57.

4323   Osterhoudt, P. *Trumpet topics*. Logan, Utah: The Author, 1962.

    Overton, Friend Robert. *Der Zink. Geschichte, Bauweise und Spieltechnik eines historischen Musikinstruments*. Mainz: Schott, 1981.

4324   Overton, W. J. "On learning to play the trumpet." *Music Teacher and Piano Student* 41 (1962): 317+.

4325   Patnoe, Herb. "Range problems (how to play high without getting a hernia!)" *The School Musician* 51 (Feb. 1980): 33+.

4326   Peretz, M. H. "An analysis of the writings of Arthur W. Foshay, Bruce R. Joyce, and James B. MacDonald with applications to beginning trumpet method books." *Dissertation Abstracts* 39 (May 1979): 6620A.

4327   Perinelli, R. "Mes dents." *Brass Bulletin—International Brass Chronicle*, no. 11 (1975): 37–40+. Also in English and German.

4328   Peters, George David. "Feasibility of computer-assisted instruction for instrumental music education." *Dissertation Abstracts* 35 (Sept. 1974): 1478A–1479A.

4329   Peters, George David. "Feasibility of computer-assisted instruction for instrumental music education." Ed.D. diss., University of Illinois at Urbana-Champaign, 1974.

4330   Peterson, O. A. *The cornet*. Boston: W. Jacobs, 1934.

4331   Peterson, O. A. *The cornet; practical advice on tone production, valve limitations, mouthpieces, mutes and other invaluable information to the cornetist*. New York: W. Jacobs, 1957.

4332   Pizer, R. A. "Fourth graders vs. band instruments." *The Instrumentalist* 33 (Sept. 1978): 30–31.

4333   Placek, R. W. "Floppy discography ['Micro-trumpet' program reviewed]." *Music Educators Journal* 72 (Oct. 1985): 20+.

4334   Poe, Gerald D. "Basic intonation tendencies of the trumpet-cornet." *The School Musician* 49 (May 1978): 70–71.

4335   Poe, Gerald D. "Trumpet pedagogy." D.M.A. diss., University of Colorado at Boulder, 1973.

4336   Power, William B. "A class method for teaching B flat cornet to meet individual differences among students." Master's thesis, University of Arizona, 1952.

4337   Quinque, R. "ASA methode." *Brass Bulletin—International Brass Chronicle*, no. 29 (1980): 19+. Also in German and English.

4338   Radau, W. "Trompetenkurse mit Jerome Callet." *Jazz Podium* 24 (Mar. 1975): 20.

4339   Ramin, Fritz. "Weg zu den Blechblasinstrumenten [Trompete]." In *Hohe Schule der Musik*, vol. 4, 134–156. Potsdam: n.p., 1936–37.

4340   Rea, Ralph C. "An experimental program for improving the sight-reading ability of cornet and clarinet players." Ph.D. diss., State University of Iowa, 1954.

4341   Remsen, Lester E. "A suggested syllabus for the teaching of the trumpet." Master's thesis, University of Southern California, 1951.

4342   Revelli, William D. "A study program for the cornet or trumpet." *Etude* 73 (Nov. 1955): 19+.

4343   Reyman, Randall. "Chromatic embellishment in jazz trumpet improvisation." *Journal of the International Trumpet Guild* 12, no. 2 (Dec. 1987): 14–16.

4344   Reynolds, G. "A discussion of trumpet tone qualities." *The School Musician* 31 (Oct. 1959): 8+.

4345   Reynolds, G. "A discussion of trumpet tone qualities." *The School Musician* 33, no. 9 (May 1962): 28–29+.

4346   Reynolds, G. "Use of alternate fingerings." *The School Musician* 31 (Dec. 1959): 10+.

4347   Reynolds, George. "The trumpet or the cornet?" *The School Musician* 29 (Jan. 1958): 10+.

4348   Richter, A. "Jerome Callets Zauberformel: Trompeten-Kurs in Solingen." *Das Orchester* 34 (July-Aug. 1986): 815.

4349   Riehl, James O. "A transitional method for school cornetists." Master's thesis, University of Idaho, 1950.

4350   Roche, W. "The trumpet tone." *The School Musician* 45 (Nov. 1973): 12–14.

4351   Roche, W. W. "Fingering technique and the learning process." *The School Musician* 45 (Mar. 1974): 6+.

4352   Roche, W. W. "The mechanism of tone production." *The School Musician* 45 (Jan. 1974): 4+.

4353   Rockey, Robert D. "The importance of the tone center in playing the trumpet." Master's thesis, Ohio State University, 1948.

4354   Rohner, Traugott. "Cornet parts in C." *The Instrumentalist* 2 (Jan. 1948): 37.

4355   Roy, and Muller. *Tutor for the keyed trumpet*. London: n.p., (183-?).

4356   Ruettiger, J. *Technique of tone production for trumpet*. New York: Vantage, 1976.

4357   Ruhnke, Darwin R. "The extent of the use of the melody method of instruction of beginners on the cornet and trumpet." Master's thesis, University of Kansas, 1955.

4358   Sabarich, Raymond. "La trompette." *Musique & Radio* 46 (1956): 413+, 419+. English and French text.

4359   Sabarich, Raymond. "La trompette et les trompettistes aujourd'-hui." *Mu-*

sique & Radio 41 (1951): 357+.

4360 Sanders, J. "Pedal tones for trumpeters." *Brass and Percussion* 2, no. 1 (1974): 6–7.

4361 Sanders, J. C. "Long tones for trumpeters." *Woodwind World—Brass and Percussion* 18, no. 5 (1979): 30–31.

4362 Schlaefer, Sr. Cecelia Mathilda. "A comparative study of an experimental method for increasing range and endurance on brass instruments [cornet-trumpet]." *Dissertation Abstracts* 36 (Mar. 1976): 5907A.

4363 Schorge, J. "High C or bust?" *The Instrumentalist* 30 (May 1976): 16+.

4364 Scimonelli, Frank J. "Problems of teaching cornet and trumpet in the school instrumental program." Master's thesis, Catholic University of America, 1954.

4365 Selyanin, A. "The peculiarities of trumpet method development for trumpet playing in Russia." *Journal of the International Trumpet Guild* 8, no. 1 (1983): 40–45+.

4366 Selyanin, A. "Emile Joseph Trognee (1868–1942): discovery of unpublished trumpet studies." *Brass Bulletin—International Brass Chronicle*, no. 51 (1985): 68–69. Also in French and German.

4367 Severinson, C. "Why warm up?" *The School Musician* 39 (Aug.-Sept. 1967): 68–69.

4368 Shelswell-White, E. R. "An open letter to the beginning trumpet student." *The Instrumentalist* 31 (May 1977): 34+.

4369 Shepard, Hayden. "Forming a good trumpet embouchure." *Metronome* 50 (Oct. 1934): 19+.

4370 Shepard, Hayden. "The keys to trumpet playing, no. 1—endurance." *Metronome* 45 (May 1929): 38. Reprint. "Building up endurance in trumpet playing." *Metronome* 46 (July 1930): 24–25.

4371 Shepard, Hayden. "The keys to trumpet playing—fingering." *Metronome* 46 (May 1930): 34–35.

4372 Shepard, Hayden. "The keys to trumpet playing—tonguing." *Metronome* 46 (Apr. 1930): 29.

4373 Shepard, Hayden. "What makes a good trumpet embouchure, anyway?" *Metronome* 50 (Sept. 1934): 36–37.

4374 Sherman, R. *The trumpeter's handbook.* Athens, OH: Accura Music, 1979.

Sherman, Roger. "The legacy of Bernard Adelstein." *Journal of the International Trumpet Guild* 13, no. 2 (Dec. 1988): 5–10.

4375 Shew, Bobby. "Big band lead trumpet playing." *Crescendo International* 18 (Feb. 1980): 31.

4376 Shew, Bobby. "Big band lead trumpet playing." *Crescendo International* 18 (Mar. 1980): 31.

4377 Shew, Bobby. "Developing the trumpet section." *Crescendo International* 18 (Apr. 1980): 31.

4378 Shew, Bobby. "Developing the trumpet section." *Crescendo International* 18 (May 1980): 31.

4379   Shew, Bobby. "Practising for the jazz player." *Crescendo International* 19 (Sept. 1980): 31.

4380   Shuebruk, Richard. *The Cornet player's guide; or, when, what, how to practise upon the cornet or trumpet.* New York: The Author, 1910.

4381   Siegrist, Frank. *Trumpet playing up to date; technic and special features of modern trumpet and cornet playing.* New York: C. Fischer, 1925.

4382   Sim, A. C. "The Wanstead Trumpet Quartet." *Music in Education* 30, no. 322 (1966): 298–299.

        Simmonds, R. "How high the C?" *Crescendo International* 11 (Mar. 1973): 10–11.

4383   Smith, D. "Trumpet embouchure change." *The Instrumentalist* 26 (June 1972): 46–49.

4384   Smith, Ken. "Enharmonic fingering—its uses and advantages." In *Brass Today.* Edited by Frank Wright, 71–73. London: Besson, 1957.

4385   Smith, M. "My way." *Brass International* 10, no. 3 (1982): 32–33.

4386   Smith, M. "Putting your head on the block." *Brass International* 10, no. 2 (1982): 20–22.

4387   Smith, Norman E. "Opinions of contemporary European trumpet players." *NACWPI Journal* 24, no. 4 (1976): 3–11; 25, no. 1 (1976): 34–38; 25, no. 2 (1976–1977): 8–24.

        Smith, Norman E. "Opinions of contemporary European trumpet players." *Journal of the International Trumpet Guild* 1 (1976): 5–19 + . Reprinted in part from *NACWPI Journal* (1976).

4388   Smith, Norman Edward. "A study of certain expressive-acoustic equivalents in the performance styles of five trumpet players." Ph.D. diss., Florida State University, 1968.

4389   Smith, Norman Edward. "A study of certain expressive-acoustic equivalents in the performance styles of five trumpet players." *Dissertation Abstracts* 30 (May 1970): 5021A-5022A.

        Smithers, Donald L. "The baroque trumpet after 1721—some preliminary observations: science and practice." *Early Music* 5, no. 2 (1977): 177–179 + .

4390   Smoker, Paul Alva. "A comprehensive performance project in trumpet literature with a survey of some recently developed trumpet techniques and effects appearing in contemporary music." *Dissertation Abstracts* 35 (Oct. 1974): 2328A.

4391   Smoker, Paul Alva. "A comprehensive performance project in trumpet literature with a survey of some recently developed trumpet techniques and effects appearing in contemporary music." D.M.A. diss., University of Iowa, 1974.

        Snyder, F. "How to acquire a better trombone section." *Woodwind World— Brass and Percussion* 14, no. 2 (1975): 45 + .

4392   Snyder, William P. "Trumpet forum." *Southwestern Brass Journal* 1 (Spring 1957): 3–6.

        Soracco, Joseph P. "A descriptive analysis of bugles and a survey determining their prevalence and status in the public schools of Massachusetts." Master's thesis, Boston University, 1953.

4393   Sordillo, Fortunato. "Avoiding pressure playing on the trumpet." *Metronome* 42 (Feb. 1, 1926): 68–69.

Sorenson, Scott Paul. "Thomas Harper, Sr. (1786–1835): trumpet virtuoso and pedagogue." *Dissertation Abstracts* 48 (Sept. 1987): 510A.

Sorenson, Scott Paul. "Printed trumpet instruction to 1835." *Journal of the International Trumpet Guild* 12, no. 1 (1987): 4–14.

4394   Sousa, John Philip. *A book of instruction for the field-trumpet and drum, together with the trumpet and drum signals now in use in the Army, Navy and Marine corps of the United States.* New York: Carl Fischer, 1886.

4395   Sousa, John Philip. *The trumpet and the drum.* Reprint. Chicago: WFL Drum Co., 1954.

4396   Staigers, Del. "A world famous cornetist tells how he got that way." *Metronome* 47 (July 1931): 15+.

4397   Stamm, Marv. "Getting to the top." *NAJE Educator* 9, no. 4 (1977): 16+.

4398   "Start off with the right tuition." *Melody Maker* 42 (Nov. 11, 1967): 14.

Stevens, A. "Who'd be a lead trumpet! [health problems incurred from playing]." *Crescendo International* 14 (July 1976): 16.

Stevens, Thomas. "New trumpet music: basic performance elements." *Journal of the International Trumpet Guild* 1 (1976): 24–27.

4399   Stevens, Thomas. "The trumpet in the USA: the piston C trumpet in American orchestras." *Brass Bulletin—International Brass Chronicle*, no. 28 (1979): 35+. Also in French and German.

4400   Stith, Marice. "Trumpet embouchure and related areas." *Woodwind World—Brass and Percussion* 16, no. 4 (1977): 30–31+.

4401   Stoll, Forrest D. "Pedagogy of the trumpet." Master's thesis, Eastman School of Music, 1947.

4402   Stuart, G. "How to make it as a lead trumpet player." *The Instrumentalist* 31 (Apr. 1977): 58–59.

4403   Stuart, G. "To be 'lead trumpet' in a jazz orchestra." *Brass Bulletin—International Brass Chronicle*, no. 10 (1975): 43–47. Also in French and German.

4404   Stubbins, W. H., Clifford P. Lillya, and J. R. Fredrick. "Effects of blowing pressure and embouchure factors on trumpet tone production." *Journal of the Acoustical Society of America* 28 (1956): 769.

4405   "Survey of audition material for trumpet from 33 USA orchestra auditions 1973–1977 [with list]." *Brass Bulletin—International Brass Chronicle*, no. 26 (1979): 16.

4406   Sutherland, Harvey. "The knack of corneting." *Comfort* (April 1904): 10.

4407   Tarr, Edward H. "Cesare Bendinelli—the trumpet method." *Brass Bulletin—International Brass Chronicle*, no. 21 (1978): 13–25. Also in French and German.

Tarr, Edward H. *Die Trompete; ihre Geschichte und Spieltechnik von der Antike bis zur Gegenwart.* Bern: Hallwag, 1977.

Tarr, Edward H. *La trompette*. Transl. by L. Jospin. Lausanne: Payot, 1977.

Tarr, Edward H. "Why do I—a trumpeter—play the horn?" *International Trumpet Guild Newsletter* 3, no. 2 (1977): 6.

4408   Tenaglia, R. "Trumpet transposition." *The Instrumentalist* 14 (Nov. 1959): 26+.

4409   Tenaglia, R. "What grip are you using lately?" *The Instrumentalist* 21 (May 1967): 34+.

4410   Testa, Robert Francis. "The effect of jaw-thrust instruction on four selected aspects of trumpet performance and overjet of young players." *Dissertation Abstracts* 33 (Dec. 1972): 2972A.

4411   Testa, Robert Francis. "The effect of jaw-thrust instruction on four selected aspects of trumpet performance and overjet of young players." Ph.D. diss., University of Miami, 1972.

4412   Testa, Robert Francis. "Effect of jaw-thrust instruction on trumpet performance and overjet of young players." *Journal of Research in Music Education* 22, no. 3 (1974): 184–197.

4413   Tetzlaff, Daniel B. "The secret's out! [development of high register]." *The Instrumentalist* 23 (Mar. 1969): 53.

4414   Tetzlaff, Daniel B. "The transparent man (film: Videoflourographic presentation of the physiological phenomena influencing trumpet performance)." *The Instrumentalist* 23 (Mar. 1969): 81–82.

Tetzlaff, Daniel B. "Trombone and trumpet low register." *The International Musician* 56 (Oct. 1958): 26–27.

Tetzlaff, Daniel B. "Trombone and/or trumpet low register." *The International Musician* 56 (Aug. 1958): 28–29.

4415   Tetzlaff, Daniel B. "Trumpet forum." *Southwestern Brass Journal* 1 (Fall 1957): 6–10.

4416   Theurer, Britton. "Vincent Cichowicz trumpet seminar." *International Trumpet Guild Newsletter* 7, no. 1 (1980): 5.

Theurer, Britton. "An interpretive discussion of the solo passages most frequently requested at orchestral trumpet auditions." *International Trumpet Guild Newsletter* 7, no. 3 (1981): 9–21.

4417   Thomas, William W. "An approach to teaching trumpet from an educational standpoint." Master's thesis, State College of Washington, 1942.

4418   Toering, R. "Performing Hindemith's Sonata for Trumpet and Piano." *International Trumpet Guild Newsletter* 4, no. 2 (1978): 13–19.

Trumpet and bugle sounds for the army, with instructions for the training of trumpeters and buglers. London: Eyre & Spottiswoode, [1903].

4419   Tull, Mickey. "The controversial trumpet embouchure." *Southwestern Brass Journal* 1 (Fall 1957): 11–14.

4420   Tully. *Tutor for the Kent bugle*. London: R. Cocks, [ca. 1838].

Tuozzolo, James M. "Trumpet techniques in selected works of four contemporary American composers: Gunther Schuller, Meyer Kupferman, William Sydeman, and William Frabizio." *Dissertation Abstracts* 33 (Dec. 1972): 2972A-2973A.

4421   Tuozzolo, James M. "Trumpet techniques in selected works of four contemporary American composers: Gunther Schuller, Meyer Kupferman, William Sydeman, and William Frabizio." D.M.A. diss., University of Miami, 1972.

Turrentine, Edgar M. "The trumpet's day." *The Instrumentalist* 19 (Mar. 1965): 72–73.

4422   U.S. War Department. *Field manual*. Technical manual 20, no. 250. Washington: GPO, 1940.

4423   Van Ness, R. "A guide for the teaching of the cornet and trumpet." Master's thesis, University of Michigan, 1960.

4424   Vanasek, Ben. "New hints on trumpet playing." *Etude* 45 (1927): 578.

4425   Vandercook, H. A. "The modern method of cornet playing." *Metronome* (Sept. 1, 1927–Aug. 1928). A series of 20 lessons which appeared quite regularly. Also published separately.

4426   Vax, Mike. "Endurance—the key to better playing." *Crescendo International* 18 (Oct. 1979): 34.

4427   Vax, Mike. "The high note syndrome." *The Instrumentalist* 39 (Mar. 1985): 31–34+.

4428   Vax, Mike. "Questions frequently heard at clinics." *The Instrumentalist* 32 (Oct. 1977): 93–95; (Nov. 1977): 74–77.

4429   Vax, Mike. "Trumpet warm-ups." *Crescendo International* 17 (Aug. 1978): 30.

4430   Veselak, Richard D. "Effects of pre-lip resonance on cornet tone: an experimental investigation." Master's thesis, Illinois State Normal University, 1956.

4431   Wagner, W. W. "Should a trumpet for the beginner be any different from a professional model?" *The Instrumentalist* 12 (Oct. 1957): 47.

Wakser, David. "A study of the implications of history and tradition as a contributing factor to the style of orchestral trumpet performance." Master's thesis, Ohio State University, 1947.

4432   Walker, B. H. "The cornet or the trumpet." *The School Musician* 23 (Dec. 1951): 30–32.

4433   Weber, Friedrich Johannes. "Neue Verbesserungsvorschläge für den Trompeter." *Deutsche Militär-Musiker Zeitung* 59, no. 49 (1937): 5–6.

Webster, John C. *Measurable differences among trumpet players*. Proceedings [1949] of the Music Teachers National Association. 43rd series. 73rd year. Pittsburgh, 1951.

4434   Weeks, D. G. "The effectiveness of using computer-assisted instruction with beginning trumpet students." *Dissertation Abstracts* 48 (Oct. 1987): 865A.

4435   Weigmann, W. D. "Vibrato an der Trompete." *Das Musikleben* (June 1932): 7.

4436   Wheeler, J. "A curiosity in Schubert's trumpet writing." *The Galpin Society Journal* 21 (Mar. 1968): 185–186.

4437   White, E. R., and J. V. Basmajian. "Electromyographic analysis of embouchure muscle function in trumpet playing." *Journal of Research in Music Education* 22, no. 4 (1974): 292–304.

4438   White, E. R. "Electromyographic potentials of selected facial muscles and labial mouthpiece pressure measurements in the embouchure of trumpet players." *Dissertation Abstracts* 33 (Feb. 1973): 3977A-3978A.

4439   Wiehe, Douglas Dean. "A study of the use of a tape recorder in the teaching of solo trumpet literature to secondary school students." D.Mus.Ed. diss., University of Oklahoma, 1971.

4440   Wiehe, Douglas Dean. "A study of the use of a tape recorder in the teaching of solo trumpet literature to secondary school students." *Dissertation Abstracts* 32 (Jan. 1972): 4055A.

4441   Willener, A. "Conseils d'un maitre clinicien en cuivres: M. Robert Pichaureau, trompette, Paris." *Brass Bulletin—International Brass Chronicle*, no. 18 (1977): 19–25. Also in English and German.

4442   Zorn, Jay D. "Exploring the trumpet's upper register." *The Instrumentalist* 29 (June 1975): 70–74.

Zschoch, Frieder. "Zur Aufführungspraxis der Trompetenpartien in Werken Bachs, Händels und Telemanns." *Zu Fragen der Aufführungspraxis und Interpretation von Instrumentalmusik in der ersten Hälfte des 18. Jahrhunderts* (RILM76 2263): 29–34.

Trombone

4443   Ackerman, Bernard E. "Conversion method from B-flat tenor trombone to the trombone with an F attachment." Master's thesis, State College of Washington, 1957.

4444   Adams, S. R. "Trombones in the orchestra [learning the orchestral music repertoire]." *The School Musician* 47 (Mar. 1976): 8 + .

4445   Aharoni, E. "Locked triggers—a most helpful option for practicing and performing." *Newsletter of the International Trombone Association* 5, no. 3 (1978): 33.

4446   Aharoni, E. "New approach to teaching of the modern bass trombone." *Journal of the International Trombone Association* 4 (1976): 29–33. Excerpt from *New method for the modern bass trombone*.

4447   Aharoni, E. *New method for the modern bass trombone*. North Easton, MA: Robert King Music Company; Jerusalem: Noga, 1975.

4448   Alexander, A. "The double trombone [superbone]." *The Instrumentalist* 35 (Feb. 1981): 25–27.

Amstutz, A. Keith. "Guidelines for selection of tenor trombone mouthpieces." *NACWPI Journal* 23, no. 3 (1975): 38–39.

4449   Appert, D. L. "The alto-trombone—its uses, problems, and solutions."

Journal of the International Trombone Association 8 (1980): 13–14.

4450 Appert, D. L. "John Coffey's approach to teaching the trombone." *Journal of the International Trombone Association* 14, no. 3 (1986): 46–47.

4451 Appert, D. L. "Developing high register on trombone." *Journal of the International Trombone Association* 9 (1981): 9.

4452 Appert, D. L. "A progressive study of multiphonics on the trombone." *Newsletter of the International Trombone Association* 6, no. 3 (1979): 34.

4453 Armstrong, J., and J. Coombes. "A two-star discussion of trombone troubles." *Melody Maker* 26 (June 17, 1950): 8.

4454 Bachelder, Daniel Fred. "An investigation of trombone 'tone center.' " Ph.D. diss., Brigham Young University, 1976.

Bachelder, Daniel Fred. "An investigation of trombone 'tone center.' " *Dissertation Abstracts* 37 (Feb. 1977): 4681A.

4455 Back, J. "From our readers: The 'now' trombone." *The Instrumentalist* 25 (Dec. 1970): 8.

Bahr, Edward R. "Idiomatic similarities and differences of the trombone and euphonium in history and performance." *Journal of the International Trombone Association* 6 (1978): 31–36.

4456 Baker, Buddy. "It's time for the ol' trombone demonstration!" *Journal of the International Trombone Association* 14, no. 1 (Winter 1986): 12–13.

4457 Baker, Buddy. "Performing with mutes on the trombone." *International Trombone Association Newsletter* 7, no. 2 (1980): 23–24.

4458 Baker, Buddy. "Trombone demonstration [for elementary school children]." *Journal of the International Trombone Association* 14, no. 1 (1986): 12–13.

4459 Baker, Buddy. "Trombone talk." *Educator* [various issues].

4460 Baker, David. *Contemporary techniques for the trombone; a revolutionary approach to dealing with the problems of music in the 20th century.* New York: Charles Colin, 1974.

4461 Banschbach, D. L. "Alternate slide positions." *The Instrumentalist* 38 (Feb. 1984): 55–56 + .

4462 Banschbach, D. L. "Reducing pressure in the trombone embouchure." *The Instrumentalist* 33 (Oct. 1978): 54 + .

4463 Banschbach, D. L. "The trombonist's arm gestures in original and alternate movement patterns." *NACWPI Journal* 33, no. 2 (1985): 4–8.

4464 "The bass trombone for young beginners." *The Instrumentalist* 6 (Sept. 1951): 46.

4465 Bauer, Paul Donald. "Bass trombone pedagogy as practiced by selected bass trombonists in major American symphony orchestras: techniques and their origins." D.M. diss., Northwestern University, 1986.

4466 Bauer, Paul Donald. "Bass trombone pedagogy as practiced by selected bass trombonists in major American symphony orchestras: techniques and their origins." *Dissertation Abstracts* 47 (Jan. 1987): 2357A.

4467 Baxter, L. E. "The use of selected vocal materials from the classical and romantic periods as a method of teaching musical style characteristic to trombone students." *Dissertation Abstracts* 34 (June 1974): 7569A.

4468   Berendt, J. "Jazz in Germany." *Jazz Journal International* 32 (Aug. 1979): 7.

Beversdorf, Thomas. "Problems influencing trombone intonation." *The Instrumentalist* 7 (Oct. 1952): 24–25 +.

4469   Bowles, R. W. "Multiphonics on low brass instruments." *The Instrumentalist* 34 (Oct. 1979): 52 +.

Brandon, S. "Muting the low brass." *Woodwind, Brass and Percussion* 20, no. 4 (1981): 4–5 +.

4470   Brandon, S. "Teaching trombone intonation." *Woodwind World—Brass and Percussion* 15, no. 4 (1976): 32 +.

Brevig, Per Andreas. "Avant-garde techniques in solo trombone music; problems of notation and execution." Ph.D. diss., Juilliard School, 1971.

4471   Brick, J. S. "The effects of a self-instructional program utilizing the Pitch Master on pitch discrimination and pitch accuracy in performance of junior high school trombonists." *Dissertation Abstracts* 44 (Dec. 1983): 1719A.

4472   Brightwell, James R. "The development of a standard for crediting the study of trombone at college level." Master's thesis, Ohio State University, 1947.

4473   Brown, L. "Study literature for the F attachment and bass trombone [includes list of study literature]." *The Instrumentalist* 23 (June 1969): 71–75.

Brown, Leon F. "Favorite studies and solos for trombone." *Journal of the International Trombone Association* 12, no. 1 (1984): 28–31.

Brown, M. "Trombone solos performed in college student recitals." *Journal of the International Trombone Association* 5 (1977): 22–23.

4474   Buchtel, Forrest L. "Trombone problems in playing legato and slurring." *Educational Music Magazine* 19 (1939–40): 43.

4475   Bugli, D. "Low brass master class at Peabody Conservatory [includes repertoire lists for auditions]." *Journal of the International Trombone Association* 11, no. 2 (1983): 25–27.

4476   Cailliet, L. "The third trombone in the band." *Symphony* 6 (Sept. 1952): 13.

4477   Campbell, Larry D. "Why double on trombone and euphonium?" *T.U.B.A. Journal* 10, no. 4 (Spring 1983): 7–9.

4478   Cecil, Herbert M. "A treatise on the trombone." Master's thesis, Eastman School of Music, 1947.

4479   Christie, J. "New low brass studies." *The Instrumentalist* 24 (Apr. 1970): 26.

4480   Christie, J. M. "Teaching the bass trombone." *The Instrumentalist* 15 (Mar. 1961): 39–43.

4481   Cimera, Jaroslav. "Teaching the trombone." *The Instrumentalist* 3 (Sept. 1948): 11–14 +.

4482   Cimera, Jaroslav. "Trombone materials." *The Instrumentalist* 3 (Sept. 1948): 34.

4483   Clarke, E. "Hints for trombone players." *Metronome* 40 (Mar. 1924): 66 +.

4484   Clarke, Ernest. "From a trombonist's viewpoint." *Tempo* 1 (Feb. 1934): 21 +.

4485   Clarke, Ernest. "Two perfect wind instruments—the voice and the trombone." *Jacobs' Band Monthly* 18 (Dec. 1933): 5.

4486   Coffey, John. "The bass trombone." *Symphony* 2 (Sept. 1949): 5.

Colnot, C., and B. Dobroski. "Bill Watrous [interview]." *Accent* 1, no. 1 (1976): 11–13.

Conger, Robert Brian. "J. S. Bach's *Six Suites for Solo Violoncello,* BWV 1007–1021; their history and problems of transcription and performance for the trombone, a lecture recital, together with three recitals of selected works by Paul Hindemith, Georg Christoph Wagenseil, Richard Monaco, Darius Milhaud, Nino Rota, and others. D.M.A. diss., North Texas State University, 1983.

4487   "A conversation with Robert Harper." *Journal of the International Trombone Association* 12, no. 3 (1984): 15–16 + .

4488   Cornette, Victor. *Méthode de trombone ordinaire ou à coulisse, contenant les principes de cet instrument.* Paris: Richault, [ca. 1831?]. Part 2. Mainz: Schott, [1838].

4489   Cramer, William F. "Trombone techniques." *Brass Bulletin—International Brass Chronicle,* no. 49 (1985): 61–71. Also in French and German.

4490   Crimmins, R. "Strictly instrumental: Jazz is a warm trombone [breath technique]." *Jazz Journal International* 37 (May 1984): 14–15.

4491   Crump, Harold C. "Orchestral studies for trombone." Master's thesis, University of Michigan, 1954.

4492   Dalkert, C. "Improved holding position—better sound." *The Instrumentalist* 28 (Feb. 1974): 48–49.

4493   Dalkert, C. "Some aids to tone production." *Journal of the International Trombone Association* 8 (1980): 18.

4494   Dalkert, C. "Some thoughts on trombone tuning." *Journal of the International Trombone Association* 6 (1978): 19.

4495   De Young, Derald Dwight. "A videofluorographic analysis of the pharyngeal opening during performance of selected exercises for trombone." Ph.D. diss., University of Minnesota, 1975.

4496   De Young, Derald Dwight. "A videofluorographic analysis of the pharyngeal opening during performance of selected exercises for trombone." *Dissertation Abstracts* 37 (July 1976): 22A.

Dempster, Stuart. *The modern trombone: a definition of its idioms.* The New Instrumentation, no. 3. Berkeley: University of California Press, 1979.

4497   Dieppo, A. G. *Méthode complète pour le trombone.* Paris: Troupenas, [ca. 1840].

4498   Doms, J. "24 leichte bis mittelschwere Etüden für Bass-Posaune." *Brass Bulletin—International Brass Chronicle,* no. 34 (1981): 69.

4499   Douay, J. *L'A.B.C. du jeune tromboniste.* Paris: Billaudot, 1975.

4500   Driscoll, A. "The art of trombone playing: a conversation with Raymond Premru and Ralph Sauer." *The Instrumentalist* 40 (May 1986): 18–24.

4501   Duker, Guy M. "A method for the trombone based upon the unit approach to the reading of rhythms, scales and chords." Master's thesis, University of Illinois, 1942.

Dunn, F. Earl. "The brass instrument class—a workbook-text for the teacher or student of the cornet, French horn and trombone." Master's thesis, Iowa State Teachers College, 1954.

4502 Durflinger, L. "Slur and legato exercises for trombone." *The Instrumentalist* 34 (Feb. 1980): 52+.

4503 Easter, Stanley Eugene. "A study guide for the performance of twentieth century music from selected ballet repertoires for trombones and tuba." Ed.D. diss., Columbia University, 1969.

4504 Easter, Stanley Eugene. "A study guide for the performance of twentieth century music from selected ballet repertoires for trombones and tuba." *Dissertation Abstracts* 31 (Dec. 1970): 2953A-2954A.

4505 Elias, J., and L. Jones. "Extending the trombonist's range." *The Instrumentalist* 39 (Feb. 1985): 36+.

4506 Elias, J., and L. Jones. "The art of trombone section playing." *The Instrumentalist* 38 (Sept. 1983): 90+.

4507 Ellenrieder, M. *Unterricht für die Bass-, Tenor- und Alt-Posaune, nebst Uebungen.* Regensburg: Reitmayr, [by 1832].

4508 English, J. "Some solo works for the trombonist [contemporary]." *International Trombone Association Newsletter* 7, no. 1 (1979): 12–13.

4509 Ervin, T. "Precollegiate trombone workshops—a successful idea." *Journal of the International Trombone Association* 13, no. 4 (1985): 40.

4510 Ervin, T. "Precollegiate trombone workshops—a successful idea." *NACWPI Journal* 34, no. 1 (1985): 11.

4511 Ervin, T. "Stuff to practice when you run out of stuff to practice." *International Trombone Association Newsletter* 7, no. 1 (1979): 12.

4512 Everett, T. "Basic literature for bass trombone study." *The Instrumentalist* 33 (Dec. 1978): 62–66.

4513 Everett, T. "The International Trombone Association." *The Instrumentalist* 28 (Feb. 1974): 42–43.

4514 Everett, T. "A survey of orchestral bass trombonists." *Journal of the International Trombone Association* 8 (1980): 23–24.

4515 Everett, T., comp. "A survey of orchestral bass trombonists." *Journal of the International Trombone Association* 9 (1981): 28–30.

Everett, Tom. "A conversation with Frank Rehak." *Journal of the International Trombone Association* 15, no. 2 (Spring 1987): 36–45.

4516 Everett, Tom. "J. J. Johnson—on the road again [interview]." *Journal of the International Trombone Association* 16, no. 3 (Summer 1988): 22–29.

4517 "Excerpt from 'More Fun than Earth People' by Richard Coolidge [personality]." *Journal of the International Trombone Association* 6, no. 1 (1978): 5. Repr. Southwestern Musician, Mar. 78.

4518 Faulkner, Maurice. "Developing facility in auxiliary positions." *The Instrumentalist* 23 (Nov. 1968): 61–62.

4519 Feather, Leonard. "La coulisse, le swing, et l'embouchure." *Jazz Magazine* 8 (Oct. 1962): 20–25.

4520   Fetter, D. "The electronic tuner—a new practice tool for trombonists." *Journal of the International Trombone Association* 15, no. 1 (1987): 49.

4521   Fetter, D. "Slide exercises." *Journal of the International Trombone Association* 12, no. 4 (1984): 36–37.

4522   Fillmore, Henry. . . . *Jazz trombonist for slide trombone, bass clef . . . A unique treatise showing how to play practical jazzes and how and where to insert them in plain trombone parts.* Cincinnati: Fillmore Music House, 1919.

4523   "Fingering the bass trombone and 4-valve euphonium." *The Instrumentalist* 8 (Oct. 1953): 30–31.

4524   Fink, Reginald H. "The 'F' attachment tenor trombone." *The Instrumentalist* 12 (Mar. 1958): 52–54.

4525   Fink, Reginald H. "From tenor to bass trombone." *The Instrumentalist* 16, no. 5 (Jan. 1962): 50–51.

4526   Fink, Reginald H. "The sound of a bass trombone." *The Instrumentalist* 16, no. 10 (June 1962): 66–67.

4527   Fink, Reginald H. *The trombonist's handbook: a complete guide to playing and teaching the trombone.* Athens, Ohio: Accura, 1977.

4528   Flor, G. J. "Alternate positions on the trombone." *Woodwind World—Brass and Percussion* 18, no. 3 (1979): 18–19.

4529   Flor, G. J. "The alto trombone as a beginner's instrument." *Woodwind, Brass and Percussion* 22, no. 5 (1983): 13.

4530   Flor, G. J., ed. "Brass workshop: the pit orchestra trombonist." *The School Musician* 50 (Mar. 1979): 8 + .
        Flor, G. J. "The F attachment tenor trombone in the elementary school music program." *The School Musician* 47 (Nov. 1975): 12 + .
        Flor, G. J. "The F attachment tenor trombone in the the elementary school music programs [includes comparison chart of models]." *The School Musician* 47 (Jan. 1976): 16–18.

4531   Flouer, J. "Introducing the F attachment." *The Instrumentalist* 35 (Mar. 1981): 56 + .

4532   Fonseque, R. "La justesse d'intonation pour le trombone." *Brass Bulletin— International Brass Chronicle*, no. 52 (1985): 47–52. Also in English and German.

4533   Fortenberry, Robert E. "An evaluation of selected group methods for the trombone." Master's thesis, Mississippi Southern College, 1957.

4534   Fote, R. "Principles of trombone legato." *The Instrumentalist* 28 (Feb. 1974): 47–48.

4535   Fowler, B. "Thoughts of a mother (a creative approach to trombone playing)." *Journal of the International Trombone Association* 4 (1976): 4–6.

4536   Fowler, W. L. "How to bone up on slip-horn changes." *Down Beat* 41 (Dec. 5, 1974): 28 + .

4537   Froelich, J. P. "Mouthpiece forces during trombone performance." *Dissertation Abstracts* 48 (Dec. 1987): 1410A.

4538   Frohrip, Kenton Ronald. "A videofluorographic analysis of certain physiological factors involved in performance of selected exercises for trombone." Ph.D. diss., University of Minnesota, 1972.

4539　Frohrip, Kenton Ronald. "A videofluorographic analysis of certain physiological factors involved in performance of selected exercises for trombone." *Dissertation Abstracts* 33 (Apr. 1973): 5763A.

4540　Fulkerson, J. "Developpement du registre extreme-grave du trombone." *Brass Bulletin—International Brass Chronicle*, no. 13 (1976): 35–43. Also in English and German.

4541　Fulkerson, J. "Indeterminate instrumentation: a way of extending instrumental techniques." *Journal of the International Trombone Association* 4 (1977): 3–4.

4542　Galloway, D. "A new L.R.S.M. trombone performers' diploma." *South African Music Teacher*, no. 107 (1985): 23.

　　　Giddins, G. "Weatherbird: The trombone's connected to the. . . . " *Village Voice* 25 (Sept. 3, 1980): 56–57.

4543　Glasmire, David. "Trombone forum." *Southwestern Brass Journal* 1 (Fall 1957): 32–37.

4544　Gordon, Claude. *Physical approach to elementary brass playing in bass clef.* New York: Carl Fischer, 1979.

4545　Gorovoy, S. G. "Science and technology in trombone teaching." *Brass Bulletin—International Brass Chronicle*, no. 41 (1983): 37–38. Also in French and German.

4546　Gould, James F. "The proposed use of string music as study etudes for the trombone: With selected examples." Master's thesis, University of Southern California, 1952.

4547　Graham, J. "Developing your bass trombonists." *The Instrumentalist* 21 (June 1967): 49–52.

4548　Graham, J. "The legato style of the trombone." *The Instrumentalist* 19 (May 1965): 79–80 + .

　　　Gregory, Robin. *The trombone: the instrument and its music.* New York: Praeger; London: Faber & Faber, 1973.

　　　Grey, Al, and M. Grey. "Plunger techniques; the Al Grey plunger method for trombone and trumpet." Introduction by I. Gitler. New York: Second Floor Music, 1987.

　　　Guion, David M. "The seven positions: Joseph Froehlich's New Trombone Method." *Journal of the International Trombone Association* 14, no. 2 (1986): 50–53.

4549　Haskett, W. R. "Trombone performance at the collegiate level: an assessment process evaluation." *Dissertation Abstracts* 40 (Oct. 1979): 1740A.

4550　Heath, Fred. "Coping with problems in transferring to low brass from trumpet." *T.U.B.A. Journal* 7, no. 2 (Fall 1979): 16–17.

4551　Hey, Dean Edgar, Jr. "Etudes for trombone using avant-garde techniques." D.M.A. diss., University of Miami, 1973.

4552　Hey, Dean Edgar, Jr. "Etudes for trombone using avant-garde techniques." *Dissertation Abstracts* 34 (Feb. 1974): 5229A.

　　　Hildebrandt, Donald Jay. "The bass trombone in the twentieth-century orchestra: its use in twenty-seven representative scores." D.Mus. diss., Indiana University, 1976

4553 Himes, A. C. "Artistic trombone performance practices: vibrato." *Journal of the International Trombone Association* 13, no. 4 (1985): 30–32.

4554 Himes, A. C. "Get into position for trombone intonation." *The Instrumentalist* 36 (Feb. 1982): 58+.

4555 Hofacre, Marta Jean. "Getting into shape on trombone." *The Instrumentalist* 40 (Nov. 1985): 93–95.

Huber, H. "Die Posaunenzüge im Wandel der Zeit." *Brass Bulletin—International Brass Chronicle*, no. 11 (1975): 83–94. Also in English and French.

4556 Hughes, J. E. "An annotated listing of studies for the bass trombone." *The Instrumentalist* 36 (Aug. 1981): 54–57.

Humfeld, Neill H. "Bordogni 'Vocalise': exercise, etude or solo?" *Journal of the International Trombone Association* 12, no. 1 (1984): 25–26.

4557 Humfeld, Neill H. "How long is B-flat?" *Journal of the International Trombone Association* 11, no. 2 (1983): 24–25.

4558 Humfeld, Neill H. "The third T of trombone technique." *The Instrumentalist* 28 (June 1974): 47–48.

4559 Hummel, Donald A. "Continuity and fluctuation: advanced concepts of slide technique." *NACWPI Journal* 25, no. 4 (1977): 41–47.

4560 Hylander, Martha A. "A selective list of graded trombone methods and solos." Master's thesis, Eastman School of Music, 1948.

4561 "It's important to listen to what you're playing." *Melody Maker* 42 (Nov. 11, 1967): 15.

4562 Jacobs, A. "Der Posaunist als Liederbläser." *Deutsche Militär-Musiker Zeitung* 62 (1940): 147.

4563 Jaeger, Jürgen. "Zur Grundfragen des Blechbläseransatzes am Beispiel der Posaune." *Beiträge zur Musikwissenschaft* 13, no. 1 (1971): 56–73.

Jameson, Philip, comp. "Guide to orchestral excerpts." *Journal of the International Trombone Association* 13, no. 4 (1985): 29–30.

4564 Jameson, Philip, comp. "Guide to orchestral excerpts: table of contents to the Stoneberg Collection compiled." *Journal of the International Trombone Association* 14, no. 1 (Winter 1986): 30.

4565 Jameson, R. Philip. "The effect of timbre conditions on the prompted and simultaneous pitch matching of three ability groups of trombone performers." *Dissertation Abstracts* 41 (July 1980): 151A.

4566 Jameson, R. Philip. "The effect of timbre conditions on the prompted and simultaneous pitch matching of three ability groups of trombone performers." Ed.D. diss., Columbia University Teachers College, 1980.

4567 Jolly, T., and S. VanderArk. "Mouthpiece buzzing for low brass." *The Instrumentalist* 38 (May 1984): 36.

4568 Josel, Rudolf. *Posaunen-Schule, III.* Vienna: Ludwig Krenn, 1972.

Kagarice, Vern, and others. *Solos for the student trombonist: an annotated bibliography.* Nashville: Brass Press, 1979.

4569   Kagarice, Vern. "Slide technique—some basic concepts." *Journal of the International Trombone Association* 12, no. 2 (1984): 21–23.

Kaplan, Allan Richard. "A performance analysis of five major recital works: concerti for solo trombone and orchestra." Ph.D. diss., New York University, 1978.

Kaplan, Allan Richard. "A performance analysis of five major recital works: concerti for solo trombone and orchestra." *Dissertation Abstracts* 39 (Feb. 1979): 4582A.

4570   Kastner, J. -G. *Méthode élémentaire de trombone.* Paris: Troupenas, [ca. 1845].

4571   Kehrberg, R. "Trombone orchestral excerpts: a guide to published works." *Journal of the International Trombone Association* 14, no. 3 (1986): 20–22.

Kehrberg, Robert Wayne. "Nine original trombone solos incorporating twentieth century compositional techniques graded for the first ten years of playing." *Dissertation Abstracts* 44 (Nov. 1983): 1236A.

4572   Kehrberg, Robert Wayne. "Nine original trombone solos incorporating twentieth century compositional techniques graded for the first ten years of playing." D.A. diss., University of Northern Colorado, 1983.

4573   Kelly, M. "Selecting and teaching the bass trombone player." *The School Musician* 48 (May 1977): 58.

4574   Kempton, J. "Alternate positions on tenor trombone." *The Instrumentalist* 34 (Feb. 1980): 51–52.

4575   Kidd, R. L. "The construction and validation of a scale of trombone performance skills." *Dissertation Abstracts* 36 (Mar. 1976): 5905A.

4576   Kidd, R. L. "Critique: The construction and validation of a scale of trombone performance skills (Ed.D. diss., Univ. of Illinois, 1975)." *Council for Research in Music Education Bulletin,* no. 65 (Winter 1981): 80–83. Reviewed by H. Abeles.

4577   Kinney, G. "The wrist-arm leverage compromise." *The Instrumentalist* 36 (Dec. 1981): 100–101.

4578   Kleinhammer, Edward. *The art of trombone playing.* Evanston, Ill.: Summy-Birchard, 1963.

4579   Kneller, G. F. "The young trombonist." *Music Teacher and Piano Student* 41 (1962): 359+, 393+.

4580   Knepper, Jimmy. "My approach to the trombone." *Crescendo International* 19 (Apr. 1981): 23–24.

4581   Kosakoff, G. "Playing trombone in tune." *The Instrumentalist* 14 (Oct. 1959): 92–94.

Kuhlo, Johannes. *Posaunen-Fragen beantwortet.* Gütersloh: C. Bertelsmann, 1933.

Kuhlo, Johannes. *Posaunen-Fragen, beantwortet.* 3. Auss. Bethel bei Bielefeld: Buchh. de Anstalt Bethel, 1909.

4582   Kuzmich, J. "A basic jazz solo repertory [transcribed solos]." *The Instrumentalist* 29 (May 1975): 67–71.

4583   Kuzmich, J. "Update: A Basic Jazz Solo Repertory [transcribed solos]." *The Instrumentalist* 32 (Jan. 1978): 75–77.

4584 Lammers, M. E. "An electromyographic examination of selected muscles in the right arm during trombone performance." *Dissertation Abstracts* 44 (May 1984): 3315A+.

4585 Laudenslager, Samuel H. "Teaching the trombone." Master's thesis, University of Michigan, 1946.

4586 Law, G. C. "The development of trombone techniques through the study of orchestral excerpts." Ed.D. diss., Columbia, 1959.

Lemke, Jeffrey J. "French tenor trombone solo literature and pedagogy since 1836." *Dissertation Abstracts* 44 (Sept. 1983): 698A.

Lemke, Jeffrey J. "French tenor trombone solo literature and pedagogy since 1836." A.Mus.D. diss., University of Arizona, 1983.

4587 Leno, Harold Lloyd. "Lip vibration characteristics of selected trombone performers." A.Mus.D. diss., University of Arizona, 1970.

4588 Leno, Harold Lloyd. "Lip vibration characteristics of selected trombone performers." *Dissertation Abstracts* 31 (Mar. 1971): 4820A.

4589 Leno, L. "Lip vibration characteristics of the trombone embouchure in performance." *The Instrumentalist* 25 (Apr. 1971): 56–62.

4590 Leno, L. "Lip vibration characteristics of the trombone embouchure in performance." *Brass Bulletin—International Brass Chronicle*, no. 7 (1974): 7–36. Also in French and German. Reprinted from *The Instrumentalist* 25 (Apr. 1971).

4591 Lewis, Sam. "Tracking down the trombone." *Metronome* 48 (May 1932): 14+.

Lupica, Benedict. *The magnificent bone: a comprehensive study of the slide trombone.* New York: Vantage, 1974.

4592 Lusher, D., and T. Aitken. "Playing the trombone." *Brass International* 10, no. 3 (1982): 4–6.

4593 Lusher, D. "My way." *Sounding Brass & the Conductor* 3, no. 4 (1974–1975): 106–107.

4594 Lyon, E. E. "Workshop notes on trombone." *Journal of the International Trombone Association* 4 (1976): 16–20.

4595 Lyon, Ernest. "Improving slide technique." *The Instrumentalist* 5 (Jan.-Feb. 1951): 18+.

4596 Lyon, Ernest. "Outline study of how to play the trombone." *The School Musician* 21 (Feb. 1950): 10–11.

McCann, William J. "Trumpet and horn: correcting problems early." *The School Musician* 49 (May 1978): 6+. Reprinted from *The School Musician* 45 (Aug.–Sept. 1973): 20+.

4597 McCarty, F. L. "An interview with Stuart Dempster." *The Instrumentalist* 28 (May 1974): 36–38.

4598 McDunn, Mark R., and C. P. Barnes. *Trombone artistry.* Kenosha, WI: Leblanc, 1965.

4599 McDunn, Mark R. "51 + 2 = intonation." *The Instrumentalist* 20 (Jan. 1966): 7.

4600 McTerry, H. J. "Sliding into trombone intonation." *Music Journal* 26 (Jan. 1968): 38+.

4601 Malterer, Edward Lee. "The employment of ornamentation in present day trombone performance of transcriptions of Baroque literature." D.A. diss., Ball State University, 1979.

Malterer, Edward Lee. "The employment of ornamentation in present day trombone performance of transcriptions of Baroque literature." *Dissertation Abstracts* 41 (Jan. 1981): 2823A.

4602 Marcellus, John. "The joy of trombone: everything you ever wanted to know and probably won't ask again." *Journal of the International Trombone Association* 12, no. 2 (1984): 24+.

4603 "Marschmusik und Posaunenregister." *Schweizerische Instrumentalmusik* (1937): 561–563.

4604 Martz, Brian. "Some reflections on intonation." *Journal of the International Trombone Association* 13, no. 2 (1985): 39–40.

4605 Masson, Gabriel. "Le trombone." *Musique & Radio* 46 (1956): 467+, 471. English and French text.

4606 Matchett, R. K. "Improving the trombone section." *Woodwind World—Brass and Percussion* 18, no. 1 (1979): 16–17+.

4607 Matchett, R. K. "Improving the trombone section." *Woodwind World—Brass and Percussion* 18, no. 2 (1979): 34–35+.

4608 Matchett, R. K. "Solving problems in the trombone section." *The School Musician* 43 (Jan. 1972): 28+.

4609 Mathews, M. K. "Teaching legato tonguing to the trombone student." *The Instrumentalist* 32 (May 1978): 69–70.

4610 Mathie, D. "Teaching legato to young trombonists." *The Instrumentalist* 40 (Sept. 1985): 70+.

Maxted, George. *Talking about the trombone.* London: John Baker, 1970.

4611 Mays, R. "Bass trombone sound concept." *The Instrumentalist* 35 (Nov. 1980): 54+.

Mitchell, Arthur B. "The trombone: A short historical background with suggested methods and materials for its instruction in public schools." Master's thesis, University of Wichita, 1954.

Modell, Ron. "The ITL draft." *The Instrumentalist* 30 (Jan. 1976): 24–25.

4612 Mole, M. "Thoughts about trombone technique (1940)." *Journal of the International Trombone Association* 6 (1978): 15–16.

Mudge, Susan. "Conversations in Los Angeles with Charlie Loper, Dick Nash, Bill Booth, Roy Main, and Morris Repass." *Journal of the International Trombone Association* 11, no. 1 (1983): 21–24; no. 3 (1983): 32–35.

4613 Muller. *Méthode de trombone à trois pistons.* Paris: J. Meissonnier, [1845].

4614 "Musician extraordinary [Jaroslav Cimera]." *The Instrumentalist* 8 (Dec. 1953): 35.

4615 Nash, D. "Self-expression in ballad playing." *Journal of the International Trombone Association* 13, no. 4 (1985): 38–39.

4616 Nemetz, A. *Neueste Posaunenschule.* Vienna: Diabelli, 1828.

4617   "New angle on the trombone." *Symphony* 4 (Oct. 1950): 14.

4618   Oneglia, M. F. "Changing trumpet embouchure placement." *The Instrumentalist* 35 (Aug. 1980): 44+.

4619   Oram, P. "My way." *Sounding Brass & the Conductor* 9, no. 2 (1980): 23.

4620   "Orchestral audition list." *Journal of the International Trombone Association* 6, no. 2 (1978): 8–9.

4621   Ostrander, A. "From tenor to bass trombone." *Music Journal* 20, no. 2 (Feb. 1962): 75.

4622   Ostrander, A., and others. "A discussion on slide technique." *Journal of the International Trombone Association* 12, no. 3 (1984): 25–27.

4623   Ostrander, A. "Warming up." *Music Journal* 20, no. 4 (Apr. 1962): 49.

4624   Owen, Herbert E. "Trombone problems." *The Instrumentalist* 4 (Sept. 1949): 16–17+.

4625   Peer, R., and R. Bissell. "Advice to would-be professional trombonists [outline and transcript]." *International Trombone Association Newsletter* 7, no. 1 (1979): 6–12.

4626   Peightel, J. W. "The development and comparison of two recorded programed techniques in teaching the beginning trombone student." *Dissertation Abstracts* 32 (Nov. 1971): 2555A.

4627   Phillips, June C. "The trombone slur." *The Instrumentalist* 5 (May-June 1951): 20+.

4628   Poolos, J. G. "Trombone articulation—legato style." *The Instrumentalist* 27 (Mar. 1973): 74–75.

4629   Popiel, Peter. "A direct approach to legato on the low brass instruments." *T.U.B.A. Journal* 10, no. 3 (Winter 1983): 8–10.

4630   Powell, R. E. "The tape recording: gateway to the college studio teaching position." *Journal of the International Trombone Association* 14, no. 3 (1986): 11.

4631   Pryor, S. "Bass trombone jazz styles." *The Instrumentalist* 31 (June 1977): 63+.

4632   Pulis, Gordon. "On trombone technique." *Symphony* 2 (Dec. 1948).

4633   Pulis, Gordon. "On trombone technique." *Symphony* 8 (June 1954): 13–14.

4634   Purcell, R. "Playing trombone in the stage band." *The Instrumentalist* 31 (June 1977): 60–63.

4635   Quick, Jeffrey. "Which pitch? [sackbut intonation]." *Journal of the International Trombone Association* 14, no. 1 (Winter 1986): 10–11.

4636   Ramin, Fritz. "Weg zu den Blechblasinstrumenten [Posaune]." In *Hohe Schule der Musik*, vol. 4, 156–178. Potsdam: n.p., 1936–37.

4637   Raymond, William F. *The trombone and its player*. Cincinnati: Fillmore Music House, 1937.

4638   Reifsnyder, Robert. "Career patterns of professional trombonists." *Journal of the International Trombone Association* 13, no. 1 (1985): 33–39.

Reifsnyder, Robert. "A closer look at recent recital programs." *Journal of the International Trombone Association* 11, no. 1 (1983): 25–27.

4639   Reifsnyder, Robert. "Differing slide movement in legato and staccato articulation." *Journal of the International Trombone Association* 12, no. 1 (1984): 23–25.

Reifsnyder, Robert. "The Paris Conservatory solos, 1897–1945." *Journal of the International Trombone Association* 14, no. 2 (Spring 1986): 44–47.

4640   Reynolds, G. E. "Thoughts for the young trombonist." *The School Musician* 37 (Oct. 1965): 42 + .

Richardson, W. "Annual review of solos and studies: Trombone and euphonium." *The Instrumentalist* 39 (Feb. 1985): 77–79.

Richardson, W. "Annual review of solos and studies: Trombone/Euphonium." *The Instrumentalist* 37 (Jan. 1983): 52–55.

Richardson, W. "Trombone [annual review of solos and studies]." *The Instrumentalist* 35 (Dec. 1980): 34–36.

Richardson, W. "Trombone and baritone solo and study materials." *The Instrumentalist* 32 (Feb. 1978): 60–61.

Richardson, William Wells. "Lecture-recital—new directions in trombone literature and the techniques needed for its performance." Ph.D. diss., Catholic University of America, 1970.

4641   Riddle, P. H. "Legato technique for the trombone." *The School Musician* 43 (May 1972): 12 + .

4642   Roberts, J. E. "A comprehensive performance project in trombone literature with an essay consisting of an annotated guide to orchestral excerpts for trombone." *Dissertation Abstracts* 38 (Jan. 1978): 4010A.

Robertson, J. "Low brass embouchure control." *The Instrumentalist* 23 (Dec. 1968): 65–67.

4643   Rockwell, A. A. "Assuring accuracy in trombone positions." *The Instrumentalist* 21 (Oct. 1966): 30 + .

4644   Rohner, Traugott. "Introducing the F-alto trombone." *The Instrumentalist* 4 (Nov. 1949): 18–19.

4645   Rosenberg, M. "Alternate trombone positions—first year of study." *The Instrumentalist* 26 (May 1972): 52–53.

4646   Ross, S. L. "The effectiveness of mental practice in improving the performance of college trombonists." *Dissertation Abstracts* 46 (Oct. 1985): 921A.

4647   Ross, S. L. "The effectiveness of mental practice in improving the performance of college trombonists." *Journal of Research in Music Education* 33, no. 4 (1985): 221–230.

4648   Ross, S. L. "An interview with Frank Crisafulli." *The Instrumentalist* 32 (Oct. 1977): 78–82.

4649   Ross, S. L. "Teaching trombone legato." *The Instrumentalist* 30 (Feb. 1976): 56–57.

Roznoy, R. T. "Thoughts on contest performances: music for trombone/euphonium." *The Instrumentalist* 37 (Feb. 1983): 73–77.

4650   Roznoy, R. T. "Thoughts on contest performances: tone and embouchure building for the trombone." *The Instrumentalist* 37 (Mar. 1983): 41–42 + .

4651   Russell, J. "How I achieved a range of four and a half octaves on the trombone." *Etude* 48 (1930): 173 + .

4652 Russell, Joseph. "King trombone." *Etude* 52 (1934): 21 + .

4653 Russell, Joseph. "Putting heart into the tone." *Etude* 50 (1932): 100 + .

4654 Russell, Joseph. "Starting right on the trombone." *Metronome* 49 (Feb. 1933): 13 + .

4655 Russell, Joseph. "Trombone secrets." *Etude* 54 (1936): 81 + .

4656 Sandifer, Perry A. "A course of study for trombone at the college level." Master's thesis, Texas Christian University, 1952.

4657 Sauer, Ralph. "Trombone basics." *Journal of the International Trombone Association* 5 (1977): 3–5.

4658 Schoales, H. "Sniff breathing technique; diaphragm impulse playing as applied to the low brasses." *Brass and Percussion* 2, no. 4 (1974): 20–21.

4659 Schooley, J. "A practice sheet for trombone students." *Journal of the International Trombone Association* 10, no. 4 (1982): 13.

4660 Schreiber, E. A. "Quarter-tone scale, twenty-four note octave." *Journal of the International Trombone Association* 9 (1981): 10.

4661 Schrodt, James W. "Vibrato of the trombone soloist." Master's thesis, University of Illinois, 1947.

4662 Seale, Tommy Fred. "Advanced method for the slide trombone." Master's thesis, North Texas State College, 1941.

4663 Seidel, J. "The attack—some fundamentals." *Journal of the International Trombone Association* 12, no. 4 (1984): 36.

4664 Shaw, Gary Richard. "A comprehensive musicianship approach to applied trombone through selected music literature." D.M.A. diss., University of Wisconsin (Madison), 1984.

4665 Shaw, Gary Richard. "A comprehensive musicianship approach to applied trombone through selected music literature." *Dissertation Abstracts* 46 (July 1985): 16A–17A.

4666 Shepherd, W. "Beginning legato tonguing on trombone." *Woodwind World—Brass and Percussion* 16, no. 6 (1977): 13.

4667 Sherburne, Earl Larson. "An analysis of the blowing pressure used for trombone and euphonium tone production." Ph.D. diss., University of Minnesota, 1981.

4668 Sherburne, Earl Larson. "An analysis of the blowing pressure used for trombone and euphonium tone production." *Dissertation Abstracts* 42 (Apr. 1982): 4197A.

Shoemaker, J. R. "The sackbut in the school." *The Instrumentalist* 26 (Sept. 1971): 40–42.

4669 Silber, John J. "A critique of elementary trombone methods, and a suggested elementary trombone method." Master's thesis, Eastman School of Music, 1947.

4670 Sloan, Gerry. "The talking trombone in jazz." *Journal of the International Trombone Association* 6 (1978): 12–15.

4671 Sluchin, B. "Trombone workshops [their value and agendas]." *Brass Bulletin—International Brass Chronicle*, no. 52 (1985): 67–69. Also in French and German.

Smith, David Bruce. "Trombone technique in the early seventeenth century." *Dissertation Abstracts* 42 (May 1982): 4642A.

Smith, David Bruce. "Trombone technique in the early seventeenth century." D.M.A. diss., Stanford University, 1982.

4672 Smith, G. P. "Errata for Bordogni-Rochut's 'Melodious Etudes for Trombone,' Book I." *Journal of the International Trombone Association* 5 (1977): 5–9.

4673 Smith, G. P. "Match your skills with Pryor's." *Journal of the International Trombone Association* 12, no. 4 (1984): 41–43.

4674 Smith, J. *Alternate positions*. Fort Worth, TX: Harris Music Publishers, 1971.

4675 Smith, R. D. "Studies in legato." *Woodwind World—Brass and Percussion* 16, no. 3 (1977): 36 + .

4676 Sordillo, Fortunato. *Art of jazzing for the trombone; a complete treatise upon the possibilities of the slide*. Boston: G. Ditson, 1920.

4677 Sordillo, Fortunato. "More possibilities on the trombone and other brass instruments." *Metronome* 41 (Jan. 15, 1925).

4678 Sordillo, Fortunato. "Playing slurs on the slide trombone." *Metronome* 41 (Aug. 15, 1925): 70–71.

4679 Sordillo, Fortunato. "What the trombone player wants to know." *Metronome* 41 (May 15, 1925): 54–55.

4680 Stacy, C., and Frank Holton. "Some essentials of trombone playing." *Journal of the International Trombone Association* 4 (1976): 41. Reprinted from *Holton's Harmony Hints*, 1906.

Stevens, Milton. "150 difficult excerpts for the orchestral trombonist." *Newsletter of the International Trombone Association* 8, no. 1 (1980): 30–31.

4681 Stevens, Milton. "Vocalization—an introduction to avant-garde trombone techniques." *The Instrumentalist* 28 (Feb. 1974): 44–46.

4682 Stevens, Milton. "Winning an orchestral trombone audition." *Journal of the International Trombone Association* 15, no. 1 (1987): 30–35.

4683 Stevens, Milton Lewis, Jr. "New techniques required to perform recent music for the trombone." *Dissertation Abstracts* 36 (Mar. 1976): 5632A.

4684 Stevens, Milton Lewis, Jr. "New techniques required to perform recent music for the trombone." Mus.A.D. diss., Boston University School for the Arts, 1976.

4685 Stewart, M. Dee. "Material selected to assist a bass trombonist in developing playing facility utilizing the valve range." Master's thesis, Northwestern University, 1962.

4686 Stewart, M. Dee. "Material selected to assist a bass trombonist in developing playing facility utilizing the valve range." *Journal of the International Trombone Association* 7 (1979): 11–12.

4687 Stewart, M. Dee. "Material selected to assist a bass trombonist in developing playing facility utilizing the valve range; a development sequence of bass trombone valve techniques." *Journal of the International Trombone Association* 8 (1980): 15–18.

4688 Stiman, G. "Problems in trombone tone production." *The School Musician*

41 (Apr. 1970): 22+.

4689 Stiman, G. "Slurs or smears?" *The School Musician* 39 (Apr. 1968): 20+.

4690 Stiman, G. "Trombone left hand technique." *The School Musician* 38 (Apr. 1967): 30+.

4691 Stoutamire, A. "Altered positions on the trombone." *The Instrumentalist* 21 (Mar. 1967): 76–77+.

4692 Stoutamire, A. L. "Playing in first position." *The Instrumentalist* 20 (Apr. 1966): 74+.

4693 Stroetz, Robert W. "The slide technique." *The Instrumentalist* 6 (Oct. 1951): 35+.

Sweatt, M., and G. Magnuson. "Mouthpieces and wrists—two tips for trombonists." *The Instrumentalist* 28 (Oct. 1973): 54–55.

Tanner, James Cornwell, Jr. "Technical and musical uses of the trombone in selected original repertoire for the twentieth-century concert band." *Dissertation Abstracts* 44 (Nov. 1983): 1239A.

4694 Tanner, P. "About trombone teaching: a national consensus." *The Instrumentalist* 24 (Mar. 1970): 45–51; 24 (June 1970): 54–58; 25 (Sept. 1970): 75–78.

4695 Tanner, P. "Contemporary concepts of trombone playing." *The Instrumentalist* 20 (Dec. 1965): 63–65.

4696 Tanner, P. "A versatile trombone ensemble." *Music Journal* 13 (Apr.–May 1959): 36+.

4697 Taylor, S., and Vern Kagarice. "Feedback—slide movement." *Journal of the International Trombone Association* 13, no. 1 (1985): 32.

4698 Tetzlaff, Daniel B. "Trombone and trumpet low register." *The International Musician* 56 (Oct. 1958): 26–27.

4699 Tetzlaff, Daniel B. "Trombone and/or trumpet low register." *The International Musician* 56 (Aug. 1958): 28–29.

4700 Tomkins, L. "Trombone topics: Kai Winding [interview]." *Crescendo International* 19 (Nov. 1980): 23–24.

4701 "Trombonist Roy Williams offers a few tips to beginners." *Jazz Journal International* 34 (Mar. 1981): 21.

4702 Venglovsky, V. "Trombone school of the Petersburg-Petrograd-Leningrad Conservatory." *Journal of the International Trombone Association* 12, no. 2 (1984): 26–28.

4703 Vivona, Peter M. "Mouth pressure in trombone players." *Journal of the International Trombone Association* 15, no. 4 (1987): 28–31.

Vivona, Peter M. "Theater techniques in recent music for the trombone [includes bibliography of theater]." *Journal of the International Trombone Association* 10, no. 2 (1982): 20–25.

4704 Wagenknecht, R. E. "Index to orchestral excerpts for trombone." *Journal of the International Trombone Association* 6 (1978): 22–31.

4705 Wagner, I. L. "International news: trombone activities in China [formation of Chinese Trombone Association]." *Journal of the International Trombone Association* 13, no. 4 (1985): 41–42.

Weiner, H. "The trombone: changing times, changing slide positions." *Brass Bulletin—International Brass Chronicle*, no. 36 (1981): 52–63.

4706 Weiss, Robert. "State support." *Journal of the International Trombone Association* 15, no. 3 (Summer 1987): 38.

Westrup, J. A. "The misuse of the trombone." *The Musical Times* 66 (1925): 524–525.

4707 Wick, Dennis. "My way [practice routine]." *Sounding Brass & the Conductor* 5, no. 1 (1976): 8–9.

4708 Wick, Dennis. "Performer's platform: the trombone." *Composer [London]*, no. 50 (Winter 1976–1977): 36–39.

4709 Wick, Dennis. *Trombone technique*. London: Oxford University Press, 1971.

4710 Williams, A. L. "Locating positions on slide trombones." *Music Journal* 27 (Feb. 1969): 52+.

4711 Williams, J. "The trombonist as music educator." *Journal of the International Trombone Association* 13, no. 2 (1985): 41–42.

4712 Williams, M. "Thoughts on jazz trombone." *Down Beat* 29 (Jan. 18, 1962): 23–27.

4713 Winkel, Hans. "Ventilposaunen in der Volksschule." *Junge Musik* (1957): 70–71.

4714 Winking, C. "Lower brass literature." *The School Musician* 48 (Apr. 1977): 48–49.

4715 Wittekind, D. H. "A guide to some aspects of trombone performance." *Woodwind, Brass and Percussion* 23, no. 6 (1984): 20–23.

4716 Wittekind, D. H. "On trombone vibrato." *The Instrumentalist* 41 (Mar. 1987): 46+.

Yeo, Douglas. "Bass trombone equipment survey [equipment the leading American symphony bass trombonists are using]." *Journal of the International Trombone Association* 11, no. 4 (1983): 22–23.

4717 Yeo, Douglas. "A conversation with Kauko Kahila." *Journal of the International Trombone Association* 15, no. 3 (Summer 1987): 18–22.

4718 Young, Jerry A. "Duties of low brass instructors." *T.U.B.A. Journal* 9, no. 4 (Spring 1982): 13–16.

4719 Young, P. "Legato style and the student trombonist." *Woodwind World—Brass and Percussion* 16, no. 4 (1977): 26–27.

Baritone/Euphonium

4720 Bahr, Edward R. "Considerations toward purchasing a euphonium." *T.U.B.A. Journal* 9, no. 3 (Winter 1982): 7–9.

Bahr, Edward R. "Idiomatic similarities and differences of the trombone and euphonium in history and performance." *Journal of the International*

Trombone Association 6 (1978): 31–36.

4721 Blatter, Alfred. "Eunique." *T.U.B.A. Newsletter* 3, no. 2 (Winter 1976): 9.

Bowles, R. W. "Multiphonics on low brass instruments." *The Instrumentalist* 34 (Oct. 1979): 52+.

4722 Bowman, Brian. "Euphonium-tuba opportunities in service bands." *T.U.B.A. Newsletter* 1, no. 2 (Winter 1974): 8.

4723 Brasch, Harold T., Paul D. Droste, Leonard Falcone, Arthur Lehman, Earle L. Louder, Henry C. Smith, and Raymond G. Young. "Vibrato and the euphonium." *T.U.B.A. Journal* 5, no. 2 (Winter 1978): 12–20. Compiled and edited by Brian L. Bowman.

4724 Brasch, Harold T. "How to play the hose." *T.U.B.A. Journal* 9, no. 4 (Spring 1982): 6–7.

4725 Brasch, Harold T. "When is a baritone a euphonium?" *The Instrumentalist* 3 (Mar. 1949): 36–37.

4726 Bryant, William. "Research for tuba and euphonium." *T.U.B.A. Journal* 13, no. 1 (Aug. 1985): 25.

Bugli, D. "Low brass master class at Peabody Conservatory [includes repertoire lists for auditions]." *Journal of the International Trombone Association* 11, no. 2 (1983): 25–27.

Campbell, Larry D. "Why double on trombone and euphonium?" *T.U.B.A. Journal* 10, no. 4 (Spring 1983): 7–9.

4727 Conrey, George. "Baritone forum." *Southwestern Brass Journal* 1 (Spring 1957): 8–11.

4728 Corwell, Neal. "Using lieder as euphonium literature." *T.U.B.A. Journal* 9, no. 2 (Fall 1981): 20–22.

4729 Etzkorn, Cleon. "Why not take the time to develop a full baritone tone." *The School Musician* 29 (Apr. 1958): 20+.

4730 Falcone, Leonard. "An appeal for solos for baritone horn." *Music Educators Journal* 26 (Dec. 1939): 38.

4731 Falcone, Leonard. "The euphonium—cello of the band." *The Instrumentalist* 6 (Nov.-Dec. 1951): 22+.

4732 Falcone, Leonard. "How to produce a beautiful tone on the baritone." *The School Musician* 34, no. 3 (Nov. 1962): 52–53.

"Fingering the bass trombone and 4-valve euphonium." *The Instrumentalist* 8 (Oct. 1953): 30–31.

4733 Fink, Reginald H. *From treble clef to bass clef baritone.* n.p.: Accura Music, 1972.

4734 Flor, G. J. "Where to put that left hand—while playing the baritone horn." *The School Musician* 52 (Feb. 1981): 36–37.

Floyd, J. R. "The baritone horn versus the euphonium." *Woodwind World— Brass and Percussion* 20, no. 3 (1981): 8–9.

Gordon, Claude. *Physical approach to elementary brass playing in bass clef.* New York: Carl Fischer, 1979.

Heath, Fred. "Coping with problems in transferring to low brass from trumpet." *T.U.B.A. Journal* 7, no. 2 (Fall 1979): 16–17.

Heinkel, Peggy. "Analysis for interpretation: Samuel Adler's *Dialogues for Euphonium and Marimba.*" *T.U.B.A. Journal* 13, no. 3 (Feb. 1986): 10–16.

4735   Heinkel, Peggy. "Sensei [Toru Miura, euphonium teacher]." *T.U.B.A. Journal* 14, no. 4 (May 1987): 23.

Hinterbichler, Karl G. "A future for the euphonium?" *The Instrumentalist* 33 (Jan. 1979): 11.

Jolly, T., and S. VanderArk. "Mouthpiece buzzing for low brass." *The Instrumentalist* 38 (May 1984): 36.

4736   Jones, Charleen. "The euphonium and euphonium playing." Master's thesis, University of Michigan, 1951.

Louder, Earle L. "Euphonium future bright." *The Instrumentalist* 33 (Jan. 1979): 11.

Louder, Earle L. "Euphonium literature; original solo literature and study books for euphonium." *The Instrumentalist* 35 (May 1981): 29–30.

4737   Louder, Earle L. "My fellow euphoniumists." *T.U.B.A. Newsletter* 3, no. 2 (Winter 1976): 7.

4738   Lumpkin, R. "Intonation problems of the euphonium." *The Instrumentalist* 35 (May 1981): 18–22.

Maldonado, Luis. "Solo music literature for junior high and high school euphonium and tuba performers." *T.U.B.A. Journal* 14, no. 4 (May 1987): 39–41.

4739   Miles, David. "Euphonium study materials." *T.U.B.A. Journal* 13, no. 4 (May 1986): 27–29.

4740   Miura, Toru. "The euphonium and tuba in Japan." *T.U.B.A. Journal* 8, no. 3 (Winter 1981): 10–12.

4741   McMillen, Hugh. "The Baritone comes of age." *The Instrumentalist* 6 (May-June 1952): 24.

4742   Nash, E. W. "The euphonium: its history, literature and use in American Schools." Master's thesis, University of Southern California, 1962.

Nelson, Mark A. "Developing the beginning tuba/euphonium ensemble." *T.U.B.A. Journal* 9, no. 3 (Winter 1982): 14–16.

4743   Paulson, D. H. "Improving the low register on the baritone/euphonium." *Woodwind World—Brass and Percussion* 16, no. 6 (1977): 17+.

4744   Perrins, B. "Some thoughts on the euphonium and euphonium technique." *Brass Bulletin—International Brass Chronicle*, no. 22 (1978): 9+. Also in French and German.

Popiel, Peter. "A direct approach to legato on the low brass instruments." *T.U.B.A. Journal* 10, no. 3 (Winter 1983): 8–10.

4745   Reynolds, G. E. "Baritone—euphonium." *The School Musician* 34, no. 2 (Oct. 1962): 10+.

Richardson, W. "Annual review of solos and studies: Trombone and euphonium." *The Instrumentalist* 39 (Feb. 1985): 77–79.

Richardson, W. "Annual review of solos and studies: Trombone/Euphonium." *The Instrumentalist* 37 (Jan. 1983): 52–55.

Richardson, W. "Trombone and baritone solo and study materials." *The*

Instrumentalist 32 (Feb. 1978): 60–61.

4746   Robbins, E. J. "So you play the euphonium?" *The Instrumentalist* 21 (Oct. 1966): 63–66.

Robertson, J. "Low brass embouchure control." *The Instrumentalist* 23 (Dec. 1968): 65–67.

Roznoy, R. T. "Thoughts on contest performances: music for trombone/ euphonium." *The Instrumentalist* 37 (Feb. 1983): 73–77.

Schoales, H. "Sniff breathing technique; diaphragm impulse playing as applied to the low brasses." *Brass and Percussion* 2, no. 4 (1974): 20–21.

Sherburne, Earl Larson. "An analysis of the blowing pressure used for trombone and euphonium tone production." Ph.D. diss., University of Minnesota, 1981.

Sherburne, Earl Larson. "An analysis of the blowing pressure used for trombone and euphonium tone production." *Dissertation Abstracts* 42 (Apr. 1982): 4197A.

4747   Shoop, Stephen. "Tax deductions available to tuba and euphonium players and teachers." *T.U.B.A. Journal* 13, no. 3 (Feb. 1986): 19.

4748   "Some baritone solos." *The School Musician* 21 (June 1950): 26–28.

4749   Spiros, Lucas. "The band director's approach to the euphonium." *T.U.B.A. Journal* 11, no. 1 (Summer 1983): 16–17.

Steinberger, Karl Thomas. "A performance analysis of five recital works for euphonium." *Dissertation Abstracts* 42 (Aug. 1981): 448A.

Steinberger, Karl Thomas. "A performance analysis of five recital works for euphonium." Ph.D. diss., New York University, 1981.

4750   Stephenson, Robert. "Baritone forum." *Southwestern Brass Journal* 1 (Fall 1957): 37–40.

4751   Stewart, M. Dee. "Euphonium encumbrances and encouragements." *T.U.B.A. Journal* 9, no. 4 (Spring 1982): 10–12.

4752   Stewart, M. Dee. "Some thoughts on posture and holding the euphonium." *T.U.B.A. Journal* 8, no. 3 (Winter 1981): 13–14.

4753   Stewart, M. Dee. "The tenor tuba trauma." *The School Musician* 57 (May 1986): 25–26.

4754   Tilbury, Jack. "A conversation with Brian Bowman." *The Instrumentalist* 35 (May 1981): 12–15.

4755   Torchinsky, Abe, and Roger Oyster. "Utilizing the euphonium." *T.U.B.A. Journal* 10, no. 1 (Summer 1982): 4.

4756   Watson, Scott. "Three exercises for correct air flow on the tuba-euphonium." *T.U.B.A. Journal* 10, no. 2 (Fall 1982): 8–9.

Werden, David R. "A euphonium by any other name is not a baritone." *The Instrumentalist* 38 (Apr. 1984): 52–53.

Young, Jerry A. "Duties of low brass instructors." *T.U.B.A. Journal* 9, no. 4 (Spring 1982): 13–16.

Young, R. G. "Euphonium—well sounding." *The Instrumentalist* 18 (Mar. 1964): 72–73.

Young, Raymond. "Euphoniums—what's happening!" *T.U.B.A. Newsletter* 1, no. 3 (Spring 1974): 10.

Tuba

4757   Aitken, T. "Tuba Britannica: John Fletcher [interview]." *Brass Bulletin— International Brass Chronicle*, no. 47 (1984): 19–24.

4758   Bartles, Alfred H. "T.U.B.A. Canon." *T.U.B.A. Newsletter* 2, no. 3 (Spring 1975): 5.

4759   [Beaugeois]. *Nouvelle méthode de plainchant, de musique et de serpent*. Amiens: Caron-Vitet, 1827.

4760   Beauregard, Cherry. "Clarity in tuba playing." *T.U.B.A. Journal* 7, no. 4 (Spring 1980): 2–3.

4761   Beauregard, Cherry. "Learning to play lip slurs." *T.U.B.A. Journal* 7, no. 2 (Fall 1979): 6.

4762   Beauregard, Cherry. "Trills." *T.U.B.A. Journal* 7, no. 3 (Winter 1980): 7–8.

4763   Bell, William. *A handbook of information on intonation*. Elkhorn, WI: Getzen, 1968.

4764   Bell, William. "The tuba triumphs!" *The International Musician* 58 (Sept. 1959): 16+.

4765   Berman, Eric M. "Performance tasks encountered in selected twentieth-century band excerpts for tuba: their identification, categorization, and analysis." Ph.D. diss., New York University, 1981.

4766   Bishop, Ronald T. "Fundamentals of tuba playing." *T.U.B.A. Journal* 5, no. 2 (Winter 1978): 9–11.

        Bishop, Ronald T. "Arnold Jacobs on record: its influence on me." *T.U.B.A. Journal* 15, no. 4 (May 1988): 27–29.

4767   Bobo, Roger. "To the 94." *T.U.B.A. Journal* 6, no. 3 (Spring 1979): 8.

4768   Bobo, Roger. "Tuba humor." *T.U.B.A. Journal* 7, no. 2 (Fall 1979): 34.

4769   Bobo, Roger. "The tuba player versus the limitations of the tuba." *T.U.B.A. Newsletter* 2, no. 3 (Spring 1975): 1.

        Bowles, R. W. "Multiphonics on low brass instruments." *The Instrumentalist* 34 (Oct. 1979): 52+.

        Bowman, Brian. "Euphonium-tuba opportunities in service bands." *T.U.B.A. Newsletter* 1, no. 2 (Winter 1974): 8.

        Brandon, S. "Muting the low brass." *Woodwind, Brass and Percussion* 20, no. 4 (1981): 4–5+.

4770   Brandon, S. P. "Correcting faulty tuba intonation." *Woodwind World—Brass and Percussion* 17, no. 3 (1978): 28–29+.

4771   Brandon, S. P. "Improving the band's tuba section." *The Instrumentalist* 39

(Dec. 1984): 55–60.

4772 Brandon, S. P. "Improving the low register of the tuba." *Woodwind World—Brass and Percussion* 15, no. 2 (1976): 50–51.

4773 Brandon, S. P. "Tackling the tuba." *Woodwind World—Brass and Percussion* 16, no. 1 (1977): 34–35.

Bryant, William. "Research for tuba and euphonium." *T.U.B.A. Journal* 13, no. 1 (Aug. 1985): 25.

Bugli, D. "Low brass master class at Peabody Conservatory [includes repertoire lists for auditions]." *Journal of the International Trombone Association* 11, no. 2 (1983): 25–27.

4774 Butler, John. "Tuba in Australia." *T.U.B.A. Journal* 4, no. 1 (Fall 1976): 8.

4775 Catelinet, Philip. "The tuba in England." *T.U.B.A. Journal* 15, no. 2 (Nov. 1987): 29–31.

4776 Caussinus, V. *Solfège-Méthode pour l'ophicléide-basse.* Paris: Meissonnier, [ca. 1840].

4777 Chieffi, Brady. "Infectious tubitis: is there a cure?" *T.U.B.A. Journal* 10, no. 3 (Winter 1983): 13–14.

4778 Chiemingo, Rich. "Playing tuba with Guy Lombardo's Royal Canadians." *T.U.B.A. Journal* 7, no. 2 (Fall 1979): 8–10.

Christie, J. "New low brass studies." *The Instrumentalist* 24 (Apr. 1970): 26.

4779 Clements, T. "Why buy a tuba with four (or five) valves?" *Woodwind, Brass and Percussion* 23, no. 1 (1984): 20.

4780 "Conn and Phillips remake calendar with 'Octubafest.' " *The Music Trades* 127 (Jan. 1979): 110.

4781 Conner, Rex A. "Discussing the tuba." *The Instrumentalist* 19 (Dec. 1964): 80–83.

4782 Conner, Rex A. "Employing the tuba as a solo instrument." *The Instrumentalist* 8 (Feb. 1954): 26–27 +.

4783 Conner, Rex A. "Fingering the four and five valve tubas." *The Instrumentalist* 24 (Apr. 1970): 59–62.

4784 Conner, Rex A. "Fingering tricks that work." *T.U.B.A. Journal* 6, no. 3 (Spring 1979): 10–11.

4785 Conner, Rex A. "The tongue and the tuba." *The Instrumentalist* 12 (May 1958): 55–57.

4786 Conner, Rex A. "Tuba diphthongs." *T.U.B.A. Journal* 4, no. 3 (Spring/Summer 1977): 11.

4787 Conner, Rex A. "Tuba talk." *The Instrumentalist* 16 (Oct. 1961): 49–50.

4788 Cornette, Victor. *Méthode d'ophicléide alto et basse.* Paris: Richault, [ca. 1835?].

4789 Cross, Steven B. "A practical program to make your next Octubafest a complete success." *T.U.B.A. Journal* 10, no. 4 (Spring 1983): 28–29.

4790 Cummings, Barton. "A brief summary of new techniques for tuba." *Numus-West*, no. 5 (1974): 62–63.

4791 Cummings, Barton. "Choosing a tuba mouthpiece." *Woodwind World—Brass and Percussion* 17, no. 2 (1978): 24.

Cummings, Barton. "The E-flat tuba revisited." *Woodwind, Brass and Per-*

cussion 23, no. 8 (1984): 21–22.

4792   Cummings, Barton. "The early years." *T.U.B.A. Journal* 4, no. 3 (Spring/ Summer 1977): 8–10.

Cummings, Barton. "Further thoughts on the tuba in F." *Woodwind, Brass and Percussion* 22, no. 5 (1983): 8–9.

4793   Cummings, Barton. "The future of the E-flat tuba." *Woodwind World—Brass and Percussion* 18, no. 2 (1979): 38–39.

4794   Cummings, Barton. "Multiphonics and the tuba." *T.U.B.A. Newsletter* 3, no. 3 (Spring/Summer 1976): 1–3.

4795   Cummings, Barton. "The Musical Evergreen." *T.U.B.A. Journal* 4, no. 2 (Winter 1977): 18.

Cummings, Barton. "New techniques for tuba." *The Composer* 6, no. 15 (1974–1975): 28–32.

4796   Cummings, Barton. "The tuba." *Woodwind, Brass and Percussion* 24, no. 4 (1985): 22.

Cummings, Barton. "The tuba and/or sousaphone." *Woodwind, Brass and Percussion* 23, no. 2 (1984): 13–15.

4797   Cummings, Barton. "Tuba technique." *Woodwind, Brass and Percussion* 22, no. 8 (1983): 8–11+.

4798   Cummings, Barton. "What tuba is best BBb, CC, Eb or F?" *The School Musician* 57 (Oct. 1985): 26–27.

Cummings, Barton. "Why the fourth and fifth valves? [tuba]." *Woodwind, Brass and Percussion* 24, no. 3 (1985): 17–19.

Cummings, Barton. "You need four valves." *Woodwind World—Brass and Percussion* 16, no. 2 (1977): 36–37.

4799   Dutton, Brent. "Interchanges." *T.U.B.A. Journal* 7, no. 3 (Winter 1980): 5–6.

4800   Dutton, Brent. "Interchanges." *T.U.B.A. Journal* 7, no. 4 (Spring 1980): 19–21.

4801   Dutton, Brent. "Interchanges." *T.U.B.A. Journal* 8, no. 2 (Fall 1980): 8–9.

4802   Dutton, Brent. "Interchanges." *T.U.B.A. Journal* 8, no. 4 (Spring 1981): 10–12.

4803   Dutton, Brent. "Interchanges—Merle Hogg." *T.U.B.A. Journal* 10, no. 2 (Fall 1982): 10–12.

Eastep, Michael. "Authentic performance of Verdi." *T.U.B.A. Journal* 4, no. 2 (Winter 1977): 18.

Easter, Stanley Eugene. "A study guide for the performance of twentieth century music from selected ballet repertoires for trombones and tuba." Ed.D. diss., Columbia University, 1969.

Easter, Stanley Eugene. "A study guide for the performance of twentieth century music from selected ballet repertoires for trombones and tuba." *Dissertation Abstracts* 31 (Dec. 1970): 2953A–2954A.

4804   Edney, J. "Beginners' page." *Sounding Brass & the Conductor* 4, no. 2 (1975): 64.

4805   Engels, Hieronymus. "Tuba pedagogy in Germany." *T.U.B.A. Journal* 4, no. 1 (Fall 1976): 5–7.

4806 Fitzgerald, Bernard. "The tuba—foundation of the band." *The Instrumentalist* 7 (Mar.–Apr. 1953): 40–41 + .

Fletcher, John. "Even more tuba talk." *Sounding Brass & the Conductor* 2, no. 4 (1973–1974): 110–112 + .

Fletcher, John. "More tuba talk." *Sounding Brass & the Conductor* 2, no. 3 (1973): 78–79 + .

4807 Fletcher, John. "My way [warm-up routine]." *Sounding Brass & the Conductor* 4, no. 1 (1975): 10–11.

Fletcher, John. "The tuba in Britain." *T.U.B.A. Journal* 5, no. 2 (Winter 1978): 22–23.

Fletcher, John. "Tuba talk." *Sounding Brass & the Conductor* 2, no. 2 (1973): 59–61.

Fletcher, John. "Yet further tuba talk." *Sounding Brass & the Conductor* 3, no. 4 (1974–1975): 116–117.

4808 Flor, G. J. "Brass workshop: sousaphone or convertible tuba?" *The School Musician* 57 (Aug.–Sept. 1985): 22–23 + .

4809 Freeman, E. L. "The C tuba? Si, si!" *Woodwind World—Brass and Percussion* 19, no. 3 (1980): 24.

4810 Funderburk, Jeffrey L. "Proper breath." *T.U.B.A. Journal* 14, no. 2 (Nov. 1986): 17.

4811 Garnier. *Méthode élémentaire et facile d'ophicléide à pistons ou à cylindres.* Paris: Schonenberger [ca. 1845–1850].

4812 Gay, Leslie C., Jr. "B. L. Lacerta—new directions in tuba improvisation." *T.U.B.A. Journal* 7, no. 3 (Winter 1980): 23–25.

Gordon, Claude. *Physical approach to elementary brass playing in bass clef.* New York: Carl Fischer, 1979.

Halfpenny, Eric. "Playing the serpent." *Symphony* (Apr. 1952): 9.

Hammond, Ivan. "A choice of one or two or both." *T.U.B.A. Newsletter* 1, no. 3 (Spring 1974): 1.

4813 Harstine, E. L. "Are you satisfied with the bass section in your band?" *The School Musician* 31 (Feb. 1960): 35 + .

4814 Havlicek, Byron A. "Teaching the tuba in public schools with an analysis of its literature." Master's thesis, University of Wichita, 1956.

Heath, Fred. "Coping with problems in transferring to low brass from trumpet." *T.U.B.A. Journal* 7, no. 2 (Fall 1979): 16–17.

4815 Heinkel, Peggy, and Dan Vinson. "The obvious solution." *T.U.B.A. Journal* 10, no. 2 (Fall 1982): 4–7.

4816 Hepola, Ralph. "Roger Bobo talks tuba [interview]." *The Instrumentalist* 32 (Nov. 1977): 60–65.

4817 Hermenge, M. G. *Méthode élémentaire pour le serpent-forveille.* Paris: Forveille, [ca. 1833].

Holmes, William Dewey. "Style and technique in selected works for tuba and electronic prepared tape: a lecture recital, together with three recitals of selected works of V. Persichetti, A. Capuzzi, E. Gregson, W. Ross,

N. K. Brown, and others." D.M.A. diss., North Texas State University, 1985.

4818   Hovey, H. "Low sounds at an early age; or, How do you get the young students to play tuba." *Brass and Percussion* 2, no. 3 (1974): 13+.

4819   Ingalls, David M. "More tuba literature." *The Instrumentalist* 8 (Mar. 1954): 8+.

4820   Johnson, C. E. "Use that fourth valve." *The Instrumentalist* 14 (Apr. 1960): 56–58.

4821   Johnson, T. "A guide to commercial tuba playing in the Los Angeles area." *Brass Bulletin—International Brass Chronicle*, no. 25 (1979): 58–59.

Jolly, T., and S. VanderArk. "Mouthpiece buzzing for low brass." *The Instrumentalist* 38 (May 1984): 36.

4822   Kaenzig, Fritz. "Improving tone in the high register." *T.U.B.A. Journal* 13, no. 2 (Nov. 1985): 20–21.

4823   Kaenzig, Fritz, ed. "Tuba pedagogy: building a successful low register." *T.U.B.A. Journal* 13, no. 1 (Aug. 1985): 23–24.

4824   Kaenzig, Fritz. "Tuba pedagogy: the brief practice session." *T.U.B.A. Journal* 11, no. 4 (Spring 1984): 11–12.

4825   Kastner, J. -G. *Méthode élémentaire pour l'ophicléide*. Paris: Troupenas, [ca. 1845].

Keathley, Sandy. "Everyman's guide to the tuba mouthpiece." *T.U.B.A. Journal* 5, no. 3 (Spring/Summer 1978): 10–11.

4826   Kirk, Paul Judson, Jr. "The orchestral tuba player: the demands of his literature compared and contrasted with tuba training materials." *Dissertation Abstracts* 37 (Oct. 1976): 1865A.

4827   Kirk, Paul Judson, Jr. "The orchestral tuba player: the demands of his literature compared and contrasted with tuba training materials." Ph.D. diss., University of Colorado at Boulder, 1976.

Klee, J. H. "Tuba talk with Howard Johnson." *Down Beat* 39 (Feb. 3, 1972): 16+.

4828   Kleinsteuber, Carl. "An interview with Howard Johnson." *T.U.B.A. Journal* 11, no. 1 (Summer 1983): 6–11.

4829   Kridel, C. "One step for intonation; one giant step for the serpent." *Brass Bulletin—International Brass Chronicle*, no. 58 (1987): 36–39. Also in French and German.

4830   Kuehn, David L. "Helpful hints for tuba players." *The Instrumentalist* 16, no. 9 (May 1962): 70–71.

4831   Kuehn, David L. "A selected list of tuba literature." *The Instrumentalist* 17, no. 4 (Dec. 1962): 48–49.

4832   Kuehn, David L. "Toward better tuba players." *The Instrumentalist* 21 (Sept. 1966): 66–69.

4833   Kuehn, David L. "Tuba symposium-workshops." *T.U.B.A. Newsletter* 3, no. 3 (Spring/Summer 1976): 8.

Kunitz, Hans. *Die Instrumentation, Teil 9: Tuba*. Leipzig: Breitkopf & Härtel, 1968.

4834   Lhuillier, Alain. "A newsletter from France." *T.U.B.A. Journal* 10, no. 1 (Summer 1982): 15–16.

4835   Lind, Michael. "The tuba in Scandinavia." *T.U.B.A. Journal* 4, no. 2 (Winter 1977): 13–16.

4836   Litman, Ross. "The Alaskan tubist." *T.U.B.A. Journal* 7, no. 4 (Spring 1980): 4–5.

4837   Little, Don. "An Arnold Jacobs clinic." *T.U.B.A. Journal* 15, no. 4 (May 1988): 21–26.

4838   Little, Donald C. "A young tubist's guide to the breath." *T.U.B.A. Journal* 8, no. 3 (Winter 1981): 2–7.

4839   Lycan, Scott. "The back row at Disneyland." *T.U.B.A. Newsletter* 3, no. 3 (Spring/Summer 1976): 8.

4840   McAdams, Charles A. "Let it happen." *T.U.B.A. Journal* 12, no. 4 (May 1985): 9.

4841   Maldonado, Luis. "Checking up on your intonation: Part one." *T.U.B.A. Journal* 15, no. 3 (Feb. 1988): 31.

4842   Maldonado, Luis. "Checking up on your intonation: Part two." *T.U.B.A. Journal* 15, no. 4 (May 1988): 39.

4843   Maldonado, Luis. "Long tones, lip slurs, and scales—do we really need them?" *T.U.B.A. Journal* 14, no. 2 (Nov. 1986): 35.

4844   Maldonado, Luis. "Response problems. What can I do?" *T.U.B.A. Journal* 15, no. 1 (Aug. 1987): 18.

        Maldonado, Luis. "Solo music literature for junior high and high school euphonium and tuba performers." *T.U.B.A. Journal* 14, no. 4 (May 1987): 39–41.

4845   Mathez, Jean-Pierre. "Interview with John Fletcher." *Brass Bulletin—International Brass Chronicle*, no. 27 (1979): 41–44.

4846   Mathez, Jean-Pierre. "Les petites histoires de la vie des cuivres: le tuba en poudre [fiction]." *Brass Bulletin—International Brass Chronicle*, no. 52 (1985): 81–82. Also in English and German.

4847   Mazzaferro, T. "Master classes: tuba [interview with Donald Little]." *Accent* 7, no. 1 (1981): 25–27.

4848   Mead, Steven. "The great fourth valve mystery." *T.U.B.A. Journal* 15, no. 3 (Feb. 1988): 22–24.

4849   Meyer, G. C. "The tuba section." *The Instrumentalist* 15 (Dec. 1960): 57–59.

        Miura, Toru. "The euphonium and tuba in Japan." *T.U.B.A. Journal* 8, no. 3 (Winter 1981): 10–12.

4850   Moore, A. G. "Playing the serpent." *Early Music* 3, no. 1 (1975): 21–24.

4851   Morris, R. Winston. "A basic repertoire and studies for the serious tubist." *The Instrumentalist* 27 (Feb. 1973): 33–34.

        Morris, R. Winston. "New solos and studies for tuba." *The Instrumentalist* 32 (Feb. 1978): 61.

        Morris, R. Winston. "The Tennessee Technological University Tuba Ensemble." *Woodwind World—Brass and Percussion* 14, no. 1 (1975): 32 + .

4852   Morris, R. Winston. "A tuba clinic with Harvey Phillips." *The Instrumentalist* 29 (Jan. 1975): 51–55.

4853   Morris, R. Winston. "Tuba recordings might make the difference." *The Instrumentalist* 25 (Feb. 1971): 45–46.

Morris, R. Winston. "Tuba solos and studies." *The Instrumentalist* 33 (Jan. 1979): 80.

4854   Mueller, Frederick A. "Two tubas for symphony orchestra and chamber music." *T.U.B.A. Newsletter* 1, no. 3 (Spring 1974): 8.

4855   Muller. *Chromatic scale for the bass-horn.* London: n.p., [ca. 1830–1840].

Nelson, Mark A. "Developing the beginning tuba/euphonium ensemble." *T.U.B.A. Journal* 9, no. 3 (Winter 1982): 14–16.

4856   Nutaitis, Raymond. "The daily routine—do I need it?" *T.U.B.A. Journal* 8, no. 4 (Spring 1981): 2–3.

4857   Pallansch, Robert. "How to spot a PONKT." *T.U.B.A. Journal* 8, no. 1 (Summer 1980): 15.

4858   Perantoni, Daniel. "Contemporary systems and trends for the tuba." *The Instrumentalist* 27 (Feb. 1973): 24–27.

4859   Perantoni, Daniel. "Tuba talk: Performance tips." *The Instrumentalist* 38 (Jan. 1984): 40+.

4860   "Performance tasks encountered in selected twentieth-century band excerpts for tuba: their identification, categorization, and analysis." *Dissertation Abstracts* 42 (1981): 441A.

4861   Peruzzini, Andrew. "Auditioning as a hobby, an opinion." *T.U.B.A. Journal* 9, no. 1 (Summer 1980): 2.

4862   Pfaff, Fred E. "Nobody knows the tuba." *Metronome* 48 (Apr. 1932): 23–24.

4863   Pfaff, Fred E. "Nobody knows the tuba." *T.U.B.A. Journal* 10, no. 3 (Winter 1983): 2–5.

4864   Phillips, Harvey. "Letter to the membership." *T.U.B.A. Journal* 6, no. 1 (Fall 1978): 34.

Phillips, Harvey. "Tribute to friends." *T.U.B.A. Journal* 9, no. 4 (Spring 1982): 19–22.

4865   "Pilafian tames titanic tuba." *The Instrumentalist* 34 (Jan. 1980): 90.

4866   Pitts, L. P. "Using the first valve slide to adjust tuba intonation." *The Instrumentalist* 29 (Apr. 1975): 52.

4867   Pokorny, Gene. "The tuba and brass pedagogy in Israel." *T.U.B.A. Journal* 8, no. 2 (Fall 1980): 11–14.

4868   Poore, Melvyn. "A newsletter from England." *T.U.B.A. Journal* 6, no. 2 (Winter 1979): 3–8.

4869   Popiel, P. "The tuba: concepts in low-register tone production." *The Instrumentalist* 33 (Jan. 1979): 44+.

4870   Popiel, P. J. "The tuba and transposition." *The School Musician* 38 (Aug.-Sept. 1966): 88–89.

Popiel, Peter. "A direct approach to legato on the low brass instruments." *T.U.B.A. Journal* 10, no. 3 (Winter 1983): 8–10.

4871 "Potpourri [Tubists Universal Brotherhood Association]." *The Instrumentalist* 23 (Nov. 1968): 10.

4872 Pröpper, K. "Tuba-Kurs in Tirol." *Das Orchester* 35 (Oct. 1987): 1064.

4873 Randolph, David M. "Avant-garde effects for tuba—music or noise?" *T.U.B.A. Journal* 8, no. 3 (Winter 1981): 19–23.

4874 Randolph, David M. "Some thoughts on recital programming." *T.U.B.A. Journal* 6, no. 3 (Spring 1979): 9.

4875 Randolph, David M. "Toward effective performance of multiphonics." *T.U.B.A. Journal* 8, no. 2 (Fall 1980): 2–4.

4876 Randolph, David M. "The tuba in Korea, Taiwan, Hong Kong, and China: a report on the state of the art." *T.U.B.A. Journal* 15, no. 3 (Feb. 1988): 17–19.

Randolph, David M. "A tubist's introduction to the avant-garde." *NACWPI Journal* 28, no. 2 (1980–81): 4–11.

4877 Randolph, David Mark. "New techniques in the avant-garde repertoire for solo tuba." *Dissertation Abstracts* 39 (July 1978): 18A–19A.

4878 Randolph, David Mark. "New techniques in the avant-garde repertoire for solo tuba." D.M.A. diss., University of Rochester, Eastman School of Music, 1978.

4879 Rasmussen, Mary. "Building a repertoire for the tuba student." *The Instrumentalist* 8 (Jan. 1954): 36–37.

4880 Reed, David F. "A primer on the breathing process." *T.U.B.A. Journal* 9, no. 1 (Summer 1981): 8–10.

4881 Reynolds, G. E. "Tubas, recording basses and sousaphones." *The School Musician* 33, no. 7 (Mar. 1962): 22 + .

4882 Richardson, Jack. "The double B-flat bass." *T.U.B.A. Journal* 14, no. 4 (May 1987): 24–25. Reprint of *New York News Tribune* article (Oct. 1917).

Rideout, Jeffrey J. "Annual report of the T.U.B.A. Resource Library—1980." *T.U.B.A. Journal* 8, no. 4 (Spring 1981): 15–22.

4883 Roberts, Chester. "Coping with the extension register." *T.U.B.A. Newsletter* 1, no. 2 (Winter 1974): 1–2.

Robertson, J. "Low brass embouchure control." *The Instrumentalist* 23 (Dec. 1968): 65–67.

4884 Root, Rebecca. "So you want to be a pro?" *The Horn Call* 9, no. 2 (Apr. 1979): 89–92.

4885 Rowe, Barton A., and Jerry A. Young. "The tubist and the banker, or You want a loan for WHAT?!!" *T.U.B.A. Journal* 10, no. 2 (Fall 1982): 2–3.

4886 Saverino, L. "Breathe into your tuba." *The School Musician* 23 (Feb. 1952): 12 + .

Schoales, H. "Sniff breathing technique; diaphragm impulse playing as applied to the low brasses." *Brass and Percussion* 2, no. 4 (1974): 20–21.

Self, James M. "Reclaiming our heritage." *T.U.B.A. Journal* 5, no. 3 (Spring/ Summer 1978): 12–14.

Shoop, Stephen. "The dixieland band: a meaningful avenue of performance for the tuba player." *T.U.B.A. Journal* 13, no. 1 (Aug. 1985): 13–14.

4887   Shoop, Stephen. "Employment opportunities available to tuba and euphonium players at America's amusement-theme parks." *T.U.B.A. Journal* 15, no. 3 (Feb. 1988): 20–21.

Shoop, Stephen. "Tax deductions available to tuba and euphonium players and teachers." *T.U.B.A. Journal* 13, no. 3 (Feb. 1986): 19.

4888   Siener, M. "Thoughts about the tuba." *The School Musician* 38 (Feb. 1967): 44–46+.

4889   Siener, M. "Tuba notes." *The School Musician* 41 (Feb. 1970): 8+.

4890   Siener, M. "Why not be a professional tubaist?" *The School Musician* 40 (Feb. 1969): 12+.

4891   Sinder, Phillip. "Thoughts on tuba vibrato." *T.U.B.A. Journal* 10, no. 2 (Fall 1982): 15–16.

4892   Smith, Claude B. "1936 Bill Bell interview." *T.U.B.A. Newsletter* 1, no. 3 (Spring 1974): 9.

4893   Smith, Glenn P. "Tuba forum." *Southwestern Brass Journal* 1 (Fall 1957): 44–47.

4894   Sorenson, Richard Allen. "Tuba pedagogy: a study of selected method books, 1840–1911." Ph.D. diss., University of Colorado at Boulder, 1972.

4895   Sorenson, Richard Allen. "Tuba pedagogy: a study of selected method books, 1840–1911." *Dissertation Abstracts* 33 (Feb. 1973): 4462A-4463A.

4896   Stancil, D. D. "Use of a spectral model in developing concepts of tuba timbre." *Brass Bulletin—International Brass Chronicle*, no. 19 (1977): 33+. Also in French and German.

4897   Stanley, D. "Legato technique for tuba." *The Instrumentalist* 24 (Dec. 1969): 59–61.

4898   Stanley, D. "Teaching concepts for tuba." *The Instrumentalist* 21 (Feb. 1967): 66–69.

4899   Stevens, John. "Don't neglect alternate fingerings." *T.U.B.A. Journal* 15, no. 1 (Aug. 1987): 17.

Stevens, John. "Practice for performance." *T.U.B.A. Journal* 10, no. 1 (Summer 1982): 8–9.

4900   Stewart, Bob. "New roles and dimensions for the contemporary jazz tubist." *T.U.B.A. Journal* 13, no. 2 (Nov. 1985): 24.

"Student makes serpent." *The Instrumentalist* 29 (Apr. 1975): 108.

Tilbury, Jack. "Annual review of solos and studies: Tuba." *The Instrumentalist* 39 (Feb. 1985): 79–80+.

Troiano, William. "The New York State School Music Association contest list for tuba solos and tuba ensembles." *T.U.B.A. Journal* 14, no. 2 (Nov. 1986): 20–24.

4901   "The truth about the tones the tuba can't toot." *Jacobs' Band Monthly* 10 (Dec. 1925): 16–17.

4902   "Tuba player hits wrong note for mom." *T.U.B.A. Newsletter* 1, no. 2 (Winter 1974): 5.

4903   "Tuba talent." *The Instrumentalist* 30 (Dec. 1975): 103.

Tucci, Robert. "The tuba in Europe." *T.U.B.A. Journal* 4, no. 3 (Spring/Summer 1977): 2–3.

4904 "Two tons of tubas." *T.U.B.A. Newsletter* 1, no. 2 (Winter 1974): 5.

4905 Varner, Lesley. "T.U.B.A. Resource Library." *T.U.B.A. Newsletter* 2, no. 3 (Spring 1975): 5.

4906 Vesely, Stanley J., Jr. "Bibliography of methods, albums and solos related to the bass tuba." Master's thesis, Northwestern University, 1962.

4907 Vesely, Stanley J., Jr. "Tuba forum." *Southwestern Brass Journal* 1 (Spring 1957): 33–36.

Wald, A. H. "Sumner Erickson, tuba prodigy." *The Instrumentalist* 37 (May 1983): 36 + .

4908 Waldeck, L. "Symphonic tuba playing." *Brass Bulletin—International Brass Chronicle*, no. 23 (1978): 45–46. Also in French and German.

Watson, Scott. "Three exercises for correct air flow on the tuba-euphonium." *T.U.B.A. Journal* 10, no. 2 (Fall 1982): 8–9.

4909 Weldon, Constance J. "Problems in adapting advance etude and solo literature for the high school tuba student." Master's thesis, University of Miami (Fla.), 1953.

Werden, David R. "The Blaikley compensating system: a player's perspective." *T.U.B.A. Journal* 13, no. 1 (Aug. 1985): 17.

4910 Whaley, Robert. "Notes on the John Butler session." *T.U.B.A. Journal* 4, no. 1 (Fall 1976): 9.

Whitfield, Edward J. "Remembrances and recollections of Arnold M. Jacobs." *T.U.B.A. Journal* 12, no. 4 (May 1985): 7.

4911 Wick, S. "My way." *Sounding Brass & the Conductor* 9, no. 1 (1980): 27.

4912 Wooten, R. *Supplemental studies for electric bass, string bass, and tuba.* Hollywood, CA: Try, 1976.

4913 Yeo, Douglas. "Everything you always wanted to know about tuba auditions, but didn't know who to ask." *T.U.B.A. Journal* 11, no. 3 (Winter, 1984): 2–6.

4914 Yingst, G. L. "A history of the bass and contrabass tuba with an analytical survey of six selected beginning bass and contrabass instruction books." Master's thesis, Northwestern University, 1960.

Young, Jerry A. "Duties of low brass instructors." *T.U.B.A. Journal* 9, no. 4 (Spring 1982): 13–16.

4915 Zonn, Paul. "Red wiggler." *T.U.B.A. Newsletter* 2, no. 1 (Fall 1974): 3.

Ensembles

4916 Banks, E. "How to cope with contests—and win! [brass bands]." *Brass International* 10, no. 1 (1982): 20–21.

4917 Banks, T. "The Empire Brass Quintet Summer Symposium—a personal perspective." *Journal of the International Trombone Association* 12, no. 2 (1984): 17–18.

4918 Barrett, C. "Does a band play to educate or entertain?" *Sounding Brass & the Conductor* 2, no. 3 (1973): 86.

4919 Borland, John E. "Brass bands for elementary schools." *The Musical Times* 76 (1935): 822–823; 909–911; 993–996.

4920 Brain, Havergal. "The National [brass] band festival [Sept. 1923]." *Monthly Musical Record* 53 (1923): 325–326.

4921 Brand, G. "The role of the professional in amateur music making." *The Australian Journal of Music Education*, no. 25 (Oct. 1979): 15–16.

Bright, C. "The school brass band in high pitch [lowering pitch to 440]." *Music in Education* 30, no. 317 (1966): 30–31.

4922 Broadwell, R. B. "A selected list of woodwind, brass, and string ensemble literature: its use in high school music." Master's thesis, University of Southern California, 1959.

Brooks, Arthur. "Horn playing in the brass quintet context." *The Horn Call* 16, no. 2 (Apr. 1986): 99–100.

4923 Caisley, L. G. "The N.S.B.B.A. Festival." *Music Teacher and Piano Student* 54 (Aug. 1975): 18.

4924 Decker, C. "Beginning a brass quintet." *The Instrumentalist* 32 (Mar. 1978): 92–95.

4925 Decker, C. "Young audience programming for brass quintet." *NACWPI Journal* 27, no. 1 (1978): 46–49.

4926 Decker, Charles Frank. "Selected original and transcribed works for brass ensemble as a means of integrating aspects of music history, theory, and performance practice for the college brass major." D.M.A. diss., University of Texas (Austin), 1986.

4927 Decker, Charles Frank. "Selected original and transcribed works for brass ensemble as a means of integrating aspects of music history, theory, and performance practice for the college brass major." *Dissertation Abstracts* 47 (Mar. 1987): 3229A+.

4928 Droste, Paul. "Let's start a brass band." *The School Musician* 58 (Oct. 1986): 18–19.

Dutton, Brent. "British brass band championships." *T.U.B.A. Journal* 7, no. 4 (Spring 1980): 11–14.

4929 Faulkner, Maurice. "The brass choir—an asset to your program." *The Instrumentalist* 39 (Aug. 1984): 69–70.

4930 Fleming, D. "The brass choir in the high school curriculum." *Woodwind World—Brass and Percussion* 14, no. 2 (1975): 35.

4931 Fromme, Arnold. "Chamber brass: neglected in education." *Music Journal* 27 (Dec. 1969): 32–33.

4932 Glover, Ernest N. "Brass choirs have educational values." *The Instrumentalist* 7 (Oct. 1952): 18+.

4933 Gray, Skip. "North American Brass Band Association Championship III: an overview." *T.U.B.A. Journal* 13, no. 1 (Aug. 1985): 15–16.

4934 Haddad, Alex. "Bugle and drum corps judging." *The School Musician* 25 (Nov. 1953): 20–21.

4935 Hind, Harold C. "The brass band in schools." In *Brass Today*. Edited by Frank Wright, 75–79. London: Besson, 1957.

4936 Hind, Harold C. *The school brass band*. London: E. J. Arnold, 1951.

Hofacre, Marta Jean. "The use of tenor trombone in twentieth-century brass quintet music; a brief historical overview with comprehensive listing of original, published twentieth-century quintets and a discussion of tenor trombone excerpts from selected compositions." D.M.A. diss., University of Oklahoma, 1986.

Hofacre, Marta Jean. "The use of tenor trombone in twentieth-century brass quintet music; a brief historical overview with comprehensive listing of original, published twentieth-century quintets and a discussion of tenor trombone excerpts from selected compositions." *Dissertation Abstracts* 47 (Jan. 1987): 2362A–2363A.

4937 Holz, Ronald Walker. "Tuning your [brass] band." *Sounding Brass & the Conductor* 9, no. 1 (1980): 34–35.

Horwood, W. "Musical musings [National Brass Band Championships of Great Britain]." *Crescendo International* 21 (Dec. 1982): 8+.

4938 Jones, Edwin W. "Polishing the brass ensemble." *Music Journal* 13 (Mar. 1959): 30+.

Kappy, David. "The woodwind quintet: challenges and rewards for the horn player." *The Horn Call* 14, no. 1 (Oct. 1983): 83–84.

4939 Kinney, G. "The brass quintet is an educator's horn of plenty." *Music Educators Journal* 67 (Dec. 1980): 39–41.

Kiser, Daniel Wayne. "A musical and pedagogical classification of selected brass quintet literature." D.M.A. diss., University of Illinois, 1987.

4940 Lentczner, B. "The small college brass quintet." *Woodwind World—Brass and Percussion* 14, no. 5 (1975): 38–39.

4941 Lindner, R. "The junior high school brass choir [includes list of music]." *The Instrumentalist* 23 (Sept. 1968): 85–87.

4942 "Master class: The Canadian Brass; ensemble playing." *The Instrumentalist* 39 (Apr. 1985): 36+.

4943 Medjeski, John. "A survey and classification of brass ensemble music for grades 6–12." Master's thesis, Jordan College of Music of Butler University, 1955.

4944 Megules, K. I. "The high school tuba ensemble." *Woodwind World—Brass and Percussion* 15, no. 5 (1976): 32–33+.

4945 Metcalf, Owen Wells. "The New York Brass Quintet; its history and influence on brass literature and pedagogy." D.Mus. diss., Indiana University, 1978.

4946 Müller, A. "Schule für Posaunenchöre." *Bausteine* 54 (1922): 29.

Nagel, Robert. "Better sound for trumpet ensembles." *The Instrumentalist* 30 (Apr. 1976): 20.

4947 Peterson, Dennis H. "The brass ensemble: a medium in music education."

Master's thesis, University of Wichita, 1951.

Phillips, V. "Chamber music for brass workshop (Brass Chamber Music Workshop, Humboldt State University, Arcata, California, July 7–12, 1974)." *Brass and Percussion* 2, no. 5 (1974): 16.

"Der Posaunenchor als pädagogisch-psychologische Aufgabe." *Gottesdienst und Kirchenmusik*, no. 4–5 (July–Oct. 1975): 120–124.

Posten, R. "A view from below [two trombone brass quintets]." *Journal of the International Trombone Association* 5 (1977): 43–44.

4948　Rankin, J. "The student brass quintet." *The School Musician* 46 (May 1975): 26–27+.

Raph, A. "Brass ensemble programming." *The Instrumentalist* 19 (Feb. 1965): 66–67.

4949　Rhodes, S. "Brass band tuning." In *Brass Today*. Edited by Frank Wright, 83–86. London: Besson, 1957.

Rose, A. S. *Talks with bandsmen; A Popular handbook for brass instrumentalists.* London: W. Rider, [1895].

4950　Rowe, Clement E. "Good mistakes—Some practical suggestions to the brass choir." *Etude* 52 (1934): 713.

4951　Sandor, Edward. "An Asian tour with the Georgia Brass Quintet." *Journal of the International Trumpet Guild* 12, no. 3 (Feb. 1988): 4–9+.

Schaffer, W. A. "The brass choir in the band." *The Instrumentalist* 20 (Sept. 1965): 52–53.

Schlee, Martin. "Das Blasinstrument in der Jugendarbeit." *Gottesdienst und Kirchenmusik* (1957): 201.

4952　"Special hongrie: Barcs 1984; brass ensemble seminar." *Brass Bulletin—International Brass Chronicle*, no. 48 (1984): 28–29. Also in French and German.

4953　Steinbach, Eugene A. "An analytical survey of materials for development of the brass ensemble." Master's thesis, Catholic University of America, 1955.

Stivers, Davison L. "The brass choir: its instruments, history, literature and value to school instrumental music." Master's thesis, University of Southern California, 1954.

4954　"Summit Brass and the Keystone Brass Institute." *Journal of the International Trumpet Guild* 10, no. 2 (1985): 3–4.

"Summit Brass: national brass ensemble formed." *The School Musician* 57 (Oct. 1985): 9.

4955　Sweby, C. "Music through the band [transition from school bands to adult bands]." *Music Teacher and Piano Student* 52 (Feb. 1973): 17.

4956　Sweby, E. C. "Brass bands in school: the NSBBA." *Music in Education* 34, no. 345 (1970): 264–265; no. 346 (1970): 326–327.

4957　Taylor, L. "Training the young woodwind quintet." *The Instrumentalist* 18 (Jan. 1964): 71–73.

4958　Thompson, K. *Wind bands and brass bands in school and music centre.* Cambridge: Cambridge University Press, 1985.

4959   Tilbury, Jack, and Dennis Edelbrock. "When five is company; ensemble techniques of the U.S. Army Brass Quintet." *The Instrumentalist* 35 (Jan. 1981): 24–27.

4960   Treiber, F. "Erstmals: Mitarbeiterseminar 'Die Arbeit mit jungen Bläsern.' " *Gottesdienst und Kirchenmusik*, no. 1 (Jan.–Feb. 1977): 17–18.

        Troiano, William. "The New York State School Music Association contest list for tuba solos and tuba ensembles." *T.U.B.A. Journal* 14, no. 2 (Nov. 1986): 20–24.

        Turner, J. "Should brass bands play to entertain or educate?" *Sounding Brass & the Conductor* 7, no. 2 (1978): 76.

        Turrentine, Edgar M. "A study of 12 tower sonatas by Johann Pezel for public school brass ensemble." 2 vols. Master's thesis, Oberlin College, 1952.

4961   Ueberwasser, A. B. . . . *Orientierungsbuch und Schule für Posaunen- oder Bläser-Chöre.* Markneukirchen: B. Ueberwasser, 1913.

        Upchurch, John David. "A manual for college brass quintet performance and its application to selected works of Nicola Vincentino." D.Mus. diss., Indiana University, 1970.

        Wallace, Oliver C. "Problems involved in selecting and transcribing sixteenth century Italian madrigals for brass ensemble use in the high school." Master's thesis, University of Miami (Fla.), 1953.

4962   Watson, J. P. "Festival of brass band workshops." *The School Musician* 58 (Oct. 1986): 20.

4963   Willener, A. "Philip Jones Brass Ensemble: 3rd summer school for quintets." *Brass Bulletin—International Brass Chronicle*, no. 27 (1979): 13. Also in French and German.

4964   Wilson, York B., Jr. "The small brass ensemble: its use in the high school." Master's thesis, University of Southern California, 1957.

        Wright, Frank. "Who wants to be an adjudicator?" In *Brass Today*. Edited by Frank Wright, 15–19. London: Besson, 1957.

Jazz/Popular Styles

        Agrell, Jeffrey. "Jazz and the horn: workshop getting started." *Brass Bulletin—International Brass Chronicle*, no. 42 (1983): 36–40 + . Also in French and German.

        Agrell, Jeffrey. "Jazz clinic." *The Horn Call* 16, no. 2 (Apr. 1986): 25–27.

        Aitken, Allan Eugene. "A self-instructional audio-imitation method designed to teach trumpet students jazz improvisation in the major mode." *Dissertation Abstracts* 37 (July 1976): 18A.

4965   Birch, M. "Strictly instrumental: Brass tacks [analysis of complex chordal sequences via modes]." *Jazz Journal International* 37 (June 1984): 18–19.

4966   Birch, M. "Strictly instrumental: Brass tacks [chords derived from the minor scales]." *Jazz Journal International* 37 (Apr. 1984): 16–17.

4967   Birch, M. "Strictly instrumental: Brass tacks [jazz chords and blues chord sequences]." *Jazz Journal International* 37 (Jan. 1984): 18.

4968   Brofsky, Howard. "Miles Davis and *My Funny Valentine*: the evolution of a solo." *Black Music Research Journal* 3 (1983): 23–45.

Bryant, B. "Some parts a studio first trumpet player might be required to play and the reasons why they are difficult." *Down Beat* 41 (Aug. 15, 1974): 40.

Byrd, D. "Talks to young trumpeters." *Down Beat* 28 (Jan. 19, 1961): 18 + .

4969   Colombe, G. "How do they age so well? Lawrence, Dicky and Vic." *Jazz Journal* 29 (Aug. 1976): 4–6 + .

Crimmins, R. "Strictly instrumental: Jazz is a warm trombone [breath technique]." *Jazz Journal International* 37 (May 1984): 14–15.

4970   Deaton, G. "The brass section in the jazz ensemble." *The Instrumentalist* 26 (May 1972): 58 + .

Feather, Leonard. "La coulisse, le swing, et l'embouchure." *Jazz Magazine* 8 (Oct. 1962): 20–25.

Feather, Leonard. "Le piston, le swing et l'embouchure." *Jazz Magazine* 9 (Apr. 1963): 20–25.

Fillmore, Henry. . . . *Jazz trombonist for slide trombone, bass clef. . . . A unique treatise showing how to play practical jazzes and how and where to insert them in plain trombone parts.* Cincinnati: Fillmore Music House, 1919.

Fowler, W., and Dominic Spera. "How to polish your brass [playing techniques]." *Down Beat* 41 (Feb. 14, 1974): 32.

Gay, Leslie C., Jr. "B. L. Lacerta—new directions in tuba improvisation." *T.U.B.A. Journal* 7, no. 3 (Winter 1980): 23–25.

Grey, Al, and M. Grey. "Plunger techniques; the Al Grey plunger method for trombone and trumpet." Introduction by I. Gitler. New York: Second Floor Music, 1987.

Harding, J. "The lead trumpet player: a survey of training, practice, and equipment." *Brass Bulletin—International Brass Chronicle*, no. 4 (1973): 29–51. Also in French and German.

Hitt, George Lynn. "The lead trumpet in jazz (1924–1970)." D.Mus. diss., Indiana University, 1976.

Hollander, A. "Higher and louder [effect of difficult jazz charts on young players]." *The School Musician* 46 (Nov. 1974): 47.

Kase, R. "The trumpet section of a jazz ensemble." *The School Musician* 48 (Apr. 1977): 38–39 + .

Klee, J. H. "Tuba talk with Howard Johnson." *Down Beat* 39 (Feb. 3, 1972): 16 + .

Kuzmich, J. "A basic jazz solo repertory [transcribed solos]." *The Instrumentalist* 29 (May 1975): 67–71.

Kuzmich, J. "Update: A Basic Jazz Solo Repertory [transcribed solos]." *The*

Instrumentalist 32 (Jan. 1978): 75–77.

Kynaston, T. "Pro session: Randy Brecker's solo on *I Can't Get Started*, a trumpet transcription." *Down Beat* 51 (May 1984): 64–65.

4971   La Porta, J. "Improvisational techniques for woodwinds, brass and percussion." *Woodwind World—Brass and Percussion* 16, no. 2 (1977): 43–44 + .

La Place, Michel. "La trompette et le cornet dans le jazz et la musique populaire: la respiration." *Brass Bulletin—International Brass Chronicle*, no. 46 (1984): 23–30. Also in English and German.

Laplace, Michel. "La trompette et le cornet dans le jazz et la musique populaire: techniques particulieres de jazz." *Brass Bulletin—International Brass Chronicle*, no. 47 (1984): 39–45. Also in English and German.

Luty, B. "Concert jazz embellishments." *The Instrumentalist* 36 (Nov. 1981): 98 + .

McCauley, John Willys. "Jazz improvisation for the B-flat soprano trumpet: an introductory text for teaching basic theoretical and performance principles." Ph.D. diss., Louisiana State University and Agricultural and Mechanical College, 1973.

McCauley, John Willys. "Jazz improvisation for the B-flat soprano trumpet: an introductory text for teaching basic theoretical and performance principles." *Dissertation Abstracts* 35 (Aug. 1974): 1145A.

Morgenstern, D. "Armstrong at 85: The big band years." *Village Voice* 30 (Aug. 27, 1985): 70 + .

Nash, D. "Self-expression in ballad playing." *Journal of the International Trombone Association* 13, no. 4 (1985): 38–39.

Novy, D. "A new acoustical formula for better brass range, intonation, and response [paper presented at eighth annual NAJE convention]." *NAJE Research* 1 (1981): 65–68.

Pryor, S. "Bass trombone jazz styles." *The Instrumentalist* 31 (June 1977): 63 + .

Purcell, R. "Playing trombone in the stage band." *The Instrumentalist* 31 (June 1977): 60–63.

Radau, W. "Trompetenkurse mit Jerome Callet." *Jazz Podium* 24 (Mar. 1975): 20.

Reyman, Randall. "Chromatic embellishment in jazz trumpet improvisation." *Journal of the International Trumpet Guild* 12, no. 2 (Dec. 1987): 14–16.

Shew, Bobby. "Big band lead trumpet playing." *Crescendo International* 18 (Feb. 1980): 31.

Shew, Bobby. "Big band lead trumpet playing." *Crescendo International* 18 (Mar. 1980): 31.

Shew, Bobby. "Developing the trumpet section." *Crescendo International* 18 (Apr. 1980): 31.

Shew, Bobby. "Developing the trumpet section." *Crescendo International* 18 (May 1980): 31.

Shew, Bobby. "General information on mutes." *Crescendo International* 19 (Oct. 1980): 32.

Shew, Bobby. "Practising for the jazz player." *Crescendo International* 19 (Sept. 1980): 31.

Sloan, Gerry. "The talking trombone in jazz." *Journal of the International Trombone Association* 6 (1978): 12–15.

Sordillo, Fortunato. *Art of jazzing for the trombone; a complete treatise upon the possibilities of the slide*. Boston: G. Ditson, 1920.

4972   Stevens, A. "Who'd be a lead trumpet! [health problems incurred from playing]." *Crescendo International* 14 (July 1976): 16.

Stewart, Bob. "New roles and dimensions for the contemporary jazz tubist." *T.U.B.A. Journal* 13, no. 2 (Nov. 1985): 24.

Stuart, G. "How to make it as a lead trumpet player." *The Instrumentalist* 31 (Apr. 1977): 58–59.

Stuart, G. "To be 'lead trumpet' in a jazz orchestra." *Brass Bulletin—International Brass Chronicle*, no. 10 (1975): 43–47. Also in French and German.

Sudhalter, Richard M., Philip R. Evans, and William Dean-Myatt. *Bix; man and legend*. London: Quartet, 1974.

4973   Voce, S. "It don't mean a thing." *Jazz Journal* 28 (Apr. 1975): 20–21.

Williams, M. "Thoughts on jazz trombone." *Down Beat* 29 (Jan. 18, 1962): 23–27.

Medicine/Dentistry/Physiology

4974   Agrell, Jeffrey. "Overlays and bonding: new dental aids for brass players." *Brass Bulletin—International Brass Chronicle*, no. 49 (1985): 80–86. Also in French and German.

4975   Amstutz, A. Keith, and B. H. Kinnie. "Orthodontics and the trumpeter's embouchure—a practical solution." *Journal of the International Trumpet Guild* 7, no. 4 (1983): 18–20.

Amstutz, A. Keith. "A videofluorographic study of the teeth aperture, instrument pivot and tongue arch and their influence on trumpet performance." *Dissertation Abstracts* 31 (Dec. 1970): 2953A.

Amstutz, A. Keith. "A videofluorographic study of the teeth aperture, instrument pivot and tongue arch and their influence on trumpet performance." D.Mus.Ed. diss., University of Oklahoma, 1970.

Amstutz, A. Keith. "A videofluorographic study of the teeth aperture, instrument pivot and tongue arch and their influence on trumpet performance." *Journal of the International Trumpet Guild* 2 (1977): 25–26.

Amstutz, A. Keith. "A videofluorographic study of the teeth aperture, instrument, pivot, and tongue arch and their influence on trumpet performance." *Journal of Band Research* 11, no. 2 (1975): 28–39.

Aurand, Wayne O. *Physical factors in brass instrument playing*. Master's thesis, University of Michigan, 1949.

Bate, Philip. "Instruments for the disabled." *The Galpin Society Journal* 29 (May 1976): 127–128.

Belfrage, B. *Uebungsmethodik für Blechbläser auf der Basis von physiologischen Faktoren*. Frankfurt am Main: Hansen, 1984.

Berger, K., and M. S. Hoshiko. "Respiratory muscle action of trumpet players." *The Instrumentalist* 19 (Oct. 1964): 91–94.

Bjurstrom, N. "Orthodontic treatment as a factor in the selection and performance of brass musical instruments." *Missouri Journal of Research in Music Education* 3, no. 2 (1973): 31–57.

Bjurstrom, Neil Albert. "An exploratory investigation of orthodontic treatment as a factor in the selection and performance of brass musical instruments." *Dissertation Abstracts* 32 (June 1972): 7026A.

Bjurstrom, Neil Albert. "An exploratory investigation of orthodontic treatment as a factor in the selection and performance of brass musical instruments." Ph.D. diss., University of Iowa, 1972.

Briggs, G. V. "Electrophysiological examination of labial function in college-age trumpet performers." *Dissertation Abstracts* 29 (Feb. 1969): 2735A.

Briggs, Guy Vinton. "Electrophysiological examination of labial function in college-age trumpet performers." D.Mus.Ed. diss., University of Oklahoma, 1968.

Broucek, Jack W. "The relationship of orthodontics to selection of wind instruments for children." Master's thesis, University of Michigan, 1942.

4976   "Calif. Univ. medicos claim horn playing makes coronaries." *The Music Trades* 120 (Mar. 1972): 20+.

4977   Carlucci, T. "Brass: dentistry and the brass player." *Canadian Musician* 8, no. 3 (1986): 67.

Carter, W. "The role of the glottis in brass playing." *The Instrumentalist* 21 (Dec. 1966): 75–79.

Cheney, Edward A. "Adaptation to embouchure as a function of dento-facial complex." *American Journal of Orthodontics* 35 (June 1949): 440–443.

Cheney, Edward A., and Byron O. Hughes. "Dento-facial irregularity— How it influences wind instrument embouchure." *Etude* 64 (1946): 379+, 439–440, 499–500.

"The denture venture." *International Musician* 56 (July 1957): 28–29.

DeYoung, Derald. "The videofluorographic technique applied to brass players." *NACWPI Journal* 26, no. 1 (1977): 40–42.

De Young, Derald Dwight. "A videofluorographic analysis of the pharyngeal opening during performance of selected exercises for trombone." Ph.D. diss., University of Minnesota, 1975.

De Young, Derald Dwight. "A videofluorographic analysis of the pharyn-

geal opening during performance of selected exercises for trombone."
Dissertation Abstracts 37 (July 1976): 22A.

Dibbell, D. G. "Can surgery improve trumpet playing?" *NACWPI Journal*
27, no. 1 (1978): 24–25.

Dibbell, D. G. "The incompetent palate: a trumpeting disaster." *Journal of
the International Trumpet Guild* 2 (1977): 37–38.

Dunn, Richard. "Physical stress in horn playing." *The Horn Call* 4, no. 2
(Spring 1974): 26–28.

"Fainting trumpeter." *Scientific American* 200 (June 1959): 86.

4978   Farkas, Philip. "Medical problems of wind players: a musician's perspective." *The Horn Call* 17, no. 2 (Apr. 1987): 64–68.

Faulkner, Maurice. "Physical fitness for brass players." *The Instrumentalist*
22 (Sept. 1967): 46+.

Faulkner, Maurice, and E. P. Sharpey-Schafer. "Circulatory effects of trumpet playing." *International Trumpet Guild Newsletter* 8, no. 2 (1982): 22–
23+.

4979   Fensterer, M. "Therapeutische Lymphdrainage für Blechbläser." *Das Orchester* 26 (May 1978): 389–390.

Frohrip, Kenton Ronald. "A videofluorographic analysis of certain physiological factors involved in performance of selected exercises for trombone." Ph.D. diss., University of Minnesota, 1972.

Frohrip, Kenton Ronald. "A videofluorographic analysis of certian physiological factors involved in performance of selected exercises for trombone." *Dissertation Abstracts* 33 (Apr. 1973): 5763A.

4980   Frucht, A. -H. "Physiologie des Blasinstrumentenspiels." *Pflügers Archiv
für d. gesamte Physiologie der Menschen und der Tiere* 239 (193?): 419–429.

Giangiulio, R. C. "The role of orthodontics in correcting selected embouchure problems." *Journal of the International Trumpet Guild* 4 (1979): 20–
21.

Gibson, R. "Tension in brass performance: creative or destructive?" *The
Instrumentalist* 31 (Feb. 1977): 65–66.

4981   Hall, Jody C. "Effect of the oral and pharyngeal cavities on trumpet tone
quality." *Journal of the Acoustical Society of America* 27 (1955): 996.

4982   Hall, Jody C. "A radiographic, spectrographic, and photographic study of
the non-labial physical changes which occur in the transition from the
middle to low and middle to high registers during trumpet performance." *Dissertation Abstracts* 14 (Nov. 1954): 2086–2087.

Hall, Jody C. "A radiographic, spectrographic, and photographic study of
the non-labial physical changes which occur in the transition from middle
to low and middle to high registers during trumpet performance." Ph.D.
diss., Indiana University, 1954.

Henderson, W. A. "EMG potentials of the sternocleid-mastoid muscle
during trumpet performance." *Journal of the International Trumpet Guild*
4 (1979): 30–35+.

Hills, Ernie M., Jr. "Medicine and dentistry for brass players: a selected survey of recent research in the journal literature." *Journal of the International Trombone Association* 15, no. 4 (Fall 1987): 32–37.

Holdsworth, E. I. "Neuromuscular activity and covert musical psychomotor behavior: an electromyographic study." *Dissertation Abstracts* 36 (July 1975): 167A.

Horvath, S. M., and Maurice Faulkner. "Physiological observations on French horn players." *The Instrumentalist* 35 (Oct. 1980): 72+.

Hruby, A., and H. E. Kessler. "Dentistry and the musical wind instrument problem." *Dental Radiography & Photography* 32, no. 1 (1959).

Hunt, Norman J. "The cup mouthpiece with special reference to dentofacial irregularities." *The School Musician* 21 (Jan. 1950): 18+; (Feb. 1950): 23–24; (Mar. 1950): 10–11+.

Hunt, Norman J. "A study of the cup mouthpiece with special reference to dento-facial irregularity." Master's thesis, Brigham Young University, 1948.

Huttlin, Edward John. "A study of lung capacities in wind instrumentalists and vocalists." Ph.D. diss., Michigan State University, 1982.

Irving, David. "Instrumental wind playing and speech production." *The Horn Call* 8, no. 2 (1978): 19–27.

Isley, C. L. "A theory of brasswind embouchure based upon facial anatomy, electromyographic kinesiology, and brasswind embouchure pedagogy." *Dissertation Abstracts* 33 (Feb. 1973): 3956A–3957A.

Jarcho, Saul. "Two kinds of trumpet." *Bulletin of the New York Academy of Medicine* 47, no. 4 (Apr. 1971): 428–430.

4983   Johnson, D. "Brass: Dental habits & labial herpes." *Canadian Musician* 1, no. 5 (1979): 52.

Kessler, Howard E. "Dental factors concerned with instrument playing." *The Instrumentalist* 11 (June 1957): 33–34.

4984   Kilpinen, Eero. "Condition of teeth and periodontium in male wind instrument players in the city of Helsinki." *The Horn Call* 8, no. 2 (1978): 17–18.

"King makes a special instrument for a very special person [designed for handicapped boy]." *The School Musician* 45 (Jan. 1974): 41.

"King makes a special trombone for a very special person [artificial arms]." *The Music Trades* 122 (Jan. 1974): 84.

4985   Kopczyk, R. A. "Dental considerations for the brass player." *International Trumpet Guild Newsletter* 8, no. 3 (1982): 12–13.

Kurth, R. H. "Portrait of a unique instrumentalist [handicapped horn player]." *Medical Problems of Performing Artists* 2, no. 1 (1987): 29–30.

Kwalwasser, Jacob. "Lips of professional wind-instrument players—a photographic study." *Music Publishers Journal* 1 (May–June 1943): 14–15+.

Lammers, M. E. "An electromyographic examination of selected muscles in the right arm during trombone performance." *Dissertation Abstracts* 44 (May 1984): 3315A+.

4986   Lamp, Charles J., and Frances W. Epley. "Relation of tooth evenness to performance on the brass and woodwind instruments." *Journal of the American Dental Association* 22 (1935): 1232–1236.

Lieberman, W. B., and R. C. Jones. "Dental appliances as an aid to brass playing." *The Instrumentalist* 26 (Oct. 1971): 52 + .

Ligotti, A. F., and E. D. Voth. "An orthodontic aid for young trumpeters." *The Instrumentalist* 29 (Sept. 1974): 51–52.

Mayer, Abby, and Lloyd, M.D Mayer. "Better breathing." *The Horn Call* 2, no. 1 (Nov. 1971): 69–72.

Meek, Harold. "Micro-photographic studies of brass." *Symphony* 2 (Sept. 1949): 4.

Meidt, Joseph Alexis. "A cinefluorographic investigation of oral adjustments for various aspects of brass instrument performance." *Dissertation Abstracts* 28 (Aug. 1967): 710A–711A.

Meidt, Joseph Alexis. "A cinefluorographic investigation of oral adjustments for various aspects of brass instrument performance." Ph.D. diss., University of Iowa, 1967.

Mellon, Edward K. "The diaphragm and its auxiliaries as related to the embouchure." *The Instrumentalist* 5 (Sept. 1950): 22 + .

4987   Merten, Reinhold. *Die saurefesten, tuberkelbazillenähnlichen Bazillen in Blasinstrumenten.* Reprinted from *Zentralblatt für Bakteriologie, Parisitenkunde und Infektionskrankheiten,* vol 2. Jena: n.p., 1933.

4988   Mette, A. "Zahnerkrankungen der Blechbläser." *Deutsche Musiker-Zeitung* 63 (Aug. 6, 1932): 375.

4989   Morehead, T. "Dentures, braces, overlays, and brass." *The Instrumentalist* 36 (Mar. 1982): 38.

Nettaw, J. "Wind instruments and the physical development of children." *The Instrumentalist* 16, no. 1 (Aug. 1962): 25–26.

4990   Parolari, E. "Medizinische Untersuchungen an Bläsem (erstmals durchgeführt 1961 in Basel)." *Schweizerische Musikzeitung* 103, no. 6 (1963): 362–363.

4991   Porter, M. M. "Dental aspects of orchestral wind instrument playing with special reference to the 'embouchure.' " *British Dental Journal* 93 (1952): 66–73.

4992   Porter, Maurice M. "Dental problems in wind instrument playing." *British Dental Journal* 123 (Oct. 1967; Apr. 1968): series of 12 articles.

4993   Porter, Maurice M. *Dental problems in wind instrument playing.* London: British Dental Association, 1968.

Savits, M. F. "Muscle training techniques applicable to methods incorporating myological principles in elementary brass embouchure training curricula." *Dissertation Abstracts* 43 (June 1983): 3838A.

4994   Schlenger, Kurt. "Pneumographische Studien zur Atmung der Blasinstrumentalisten." *Psychotechnische Zeitschrift* (1935).

4995   Schneider, G. "Experimentelle Beiträge zur Physiologie des Blasinstrumentenspiels." *Wissenschaftliche Zeitschrift der Karl Marx Universität Leipzig* 5 (1955–56): 375–380.

Schneider, G. A. "Kieferorthopädische Hilfe bei Blasinstrumentalisten." *Fortschritte der Kieferorthopädie* 22 (1962): 483–488.

4996   Shellman, Dwight K., DDS. "The prognathic dental bite as related to playing brass instruments." *T.U.B.A. Journal* 12, no. 3 (Feb. 1985): 6–7.

"A special trombone [adapted for player with artificial arms]." *The Instrumentalist* 28 (Feb. 1974): 86.

Stevens, A. "Who'd be a lead trumpet! [health problems incurred from playing]." *Crescendo International* 14 (July 1976): 16.

Tetzlaff, Daniel B. "The transparent man (film: Videofluorographic presentation of the physiological phenomena influencing trumpet performance)." *The Instrumentalist* 23 (Mar. 1969): 81–82.

4997   Tucker, A., and others. "Electrocardiography and lung function in brass instrument players." *Journal of the International Trumpet Guild* 5 (1980): 46–52.

Turrentine, Edgar M. "The physiological aspect of brasswind performance technique: a bibliographic essay." *NACWPI Journal* 26, no. 2 (Nov. 1977): 3–5.

White, E. R., and J. V. Basmajian. "Electromyographic analysis of embouchure muscle function in trumpet playing." *Journal of Research in Music Education* 22, no. 4 (1974): 292–304.

White, E. R. "Electromyographic potentials of selected facial muscles and labial mouthpiece pressure measurements in the embouchure of trumpet players." *Dissertation Abstracts* 33 (Feb. 1973): 3977A–3978A.

4998   Whitsell, Leon J. "Why a medical column: a prospectus." *International Trumpet Guild Newsletter* 6, no. 3 (1980): 12.

Wiesner, Glenn R., Daniel R. Balbach, and Merrill A. Wilson. *Orthodontics and wind instrument performance.* Washington, D.C.: Music Educators National Conference, 1973.

4999   Winter, James H. "Pills and other medicaments: caution!" *The Horn Call* 8, no. 1 (Nov. 1977): 86–87.

Psychology/Performance Anxiety

Agrell, Jeffrey. "Zen and the art of horn playing." *Brass Bulletin—International Brass Chronicle*, no. 22; 23 (1978): 33–36; 69–72. Also in French and German.

Agrell, Jeffrey. "Zen and the art of horn playing." *Brass Bulletin—International Brass Chronicle*, no. 29 (1980): 35+. Also in French and German.

Beauregard, Cherry. "Psychology in pedagogy." *T.U.B.A. Journal* 9, no. 3 (Winter 1982): 18.

5000   Davies, J. "Brass and strings: a note on personality types among musicians [in the U.K.]." *Brass Bulletin—International Brass Chronicle*, no. 33 (1981): 33–37+. Also in French and German.

Davies, J. B., and others. "A psychological investigation of the role of mouthpiece force in trumpet performance." *Council for Research in Music Education Bulletin*, no. 91 (Spring 1987): 23–30.

5001   Farkas, Philip. "Conquering nervousness or stage fright." *The Horn Call* 8, no. 1 (Nov. 1977): 74–78.

Hill, Douglas. "Emphasizing the positive." *The Instrumentalist* 42 (Jan. 1988): 16–19.

5002   McAdams, Charles. "Performance attitude: a psychological approach." *T.U.B.A. Journal* 13, no. 3 (Feb. 1986): 17–18.

5003   Maldonado, Luis. "Nervousness: what it does and what we can do about it." *T.U.B.A. Journal* 13, no. 4 (May 1986): 39.

"Der Posaunenchor als pädagogisch-psychologische Aufgabe." *Gottesdienst und Kirchenmusik*, no. 4–5 (July–Oct. 1975): 120–124.

Robinson, William C. "Control your nerves by improving your playing." *The Instrumentalist* 30 (Jan. 1976): 53–56.

5004   Root, Rebecca. "The psychology of brass playing." *The Horn Call* 7, no. 1 (Nov. 1976): 11–17.

Ross, S. L. "The effectiveness of mental practice in improving the performance of college trombonists." *Dissertation Abstracts* 46 (Oct. 1985): 921A.

Ross, S. L. "The effectiveness of mental practice in improving the performance of college trombonists." *Journal of Research in Music Education* 33, no. 4 (1985): 221–230.

Severson, Paul, and Mark McDunn. *Brass wind artistry: master your mind, master your instrument.* Athens, OH: Accura, 1983.

5005   Stollsteimer, G. K. "Brass players: Think like a winning athlete." *The School Musician* 45 (Feb. 1974): 52–53.

Winter, James H. "Pills and other medicaments: caution!" *The Horn Call* 8, no. 1 (Nov. 1977): 86–87.

Selecting and Purchasing Equipment

Amstutz, A. Keith. "Guidelines for selection of tenor trombone mouthpieces." *NACWPI Journal* 23, no. 3 (1975): 38–39.

Bach, Vincent. *Embouchure and mouthpiece manual.* Mt. Vernon, N.Y.: V. Bach Corp., 1954.

Bach, Vincent. "How to choose a brass instrument mouthpiece." *The Instrumentalist* 26 (Jan. 1972): 32–34.

Bahr, Edward R. "Considerations toward purchasing a euphonium." *T.U.B.A. Journal* 9, no. 3 (Winter 1982): 7–9.

Baker, K. "Choosing a trumpet." *Melody Maker* 25 (Sept. 17, 1949): 9.

Benade, Arthur H. "How to test a good trumpet." *The Instrumentalist* 31 (Apr. 1977): 57–58.

"Brass mouthpieces—Standardization of measurements—Materials—Selections—Variations. A symposium." *The Instrumentalist* 7 (Nov.–Dec. 1952): 28–41. Contributors include Renold O. Schilke, Traugott Rohner, Ted Evans, and Vincent Bach. Also published separately.

Butterworth, J. "Horns of dilemma [French horn buying tips]." *Sounding Brass & the Conductor* 6, no. 1 (1977): 26 + .

Clements, T. "Why buy a tuba with four (or five) valves?" *Woodwind, Brass and Percussion* 23, no. 1 (1984): 20.

Cole, Ward K. "A study concerning the selection and use of mouthpieces for brass instruments." Diss., Columbia Teachers College, 1955.

Cummings, Barton. "Choosing a tuba mouthpiece." *Woodwind World— Brass and Percussion* 17, no. 2 (1978): 24.

Fitzgerald, Bernard. "How to select new instruments." *The Instrumentalist* 6 (Sept. 1951): 18 + .

5006   Fitzgerald, Bernard. "Selecting a mouthpiece." *The Instrumentalist* 2 (Sept. 1947): 20.

Gay, B. "Trumpets galore [how to choose]." *Sounding Brass & the Conductor* 6, no. 4 (1978): 134.

Haynie, John J. "On selecting the proper mouthpiece." *Southwestern Brass Journal* 1 (Fall 1957): 17–27.

5007   Lewis, Frederic James. "The care, repair, and selection of musical instruments for the instrumental music teacher." Master's thesis, University of Southern California, 1956.

McGavin, E., comp. *A guide to the purchase and care of woodwind and brass instruments*. Bromley, England: Schools Music Association, 1966.

Malek, Vincent F. "What is a good cornet or trumpet mouthpiece?" *The Instrumentalist* 8 (May 1954): 22–23 + .

Montagu, Jeremy. "Choosing brass instruments [includes list of brass instrument makers and dealers]." *Early Music* 4, no. 1 (1976): 35–38.

Morgan, M. "Selecting proper brass mouthpieces for beginners." *The Instrumentalist* 21 (Oct. 1966): 28.

Pottag, Max. "Selecting the right French horn." *The Instrumentalist* 1 (Nov. 1946): 30.

5008   Revelli, William D. "Choice of instrument a scientific problem." *The Instrumentalist* 6 (Mar.–Apr. 1952): 20 + .

Rosenberg, M. "Selecting brass mouthpieces." *The Instrumentalist* 23 (Aug. 1968): 30 + .

Rowe, Barton A., and Jerry A. Young. "The tubist and the banker, or You want a loan for WHAT?!!" *T.U.B.A. Journal* 10, no. 2 (Fall 1982): 2–3.

Scharnberg, William. "What type of horn should I buy?" *The Horn Call* 18, no. 1 (Oct. 1987): 39–40.

Schilke, R. "How to select a brass mouthpiece." *The Instrumentalist* 21 (Dec. 1966): 50–51.

Schooley, J. "Convertible brasses, sousaphones, or tubas: which to choose." *Woodwind, Brass and Percussion* 24, no. 1 (1985): 12–13.

Shore, M. "Pawnshop horns: bargains & busts off the beaten track." *Musician*, no. 48 (Oct. 1982): 82+.

Snell, H. "Deflated trumpets [survey of manufacturers, consumer hints]." *Sounding Brass & the Conductor* 6, no. 2 (1977): 60–61+.

5009 "Tariff Commission splits 3–3 on brasswind imports." *The Music Trades* 121 (Feb. 1973): 37.

5010 White, Edna. "Purchasing a brass instrument." *Musical Observer* 30 (Aug. 1931): 44+.

5011 Winter, James H. "On buying a used horn." *Woodwind World* 4, no. 11 (1963): 10; 5, no. 11 (1963): 8–9.

5012 "World news: the P5800 trumpet [piccolo trumpet used in recording of *Penny Lane* sold]." *Brass Bulletin—International Brass Chronicle*, no. 60 (News Suppl. 1987): 1. Also in French and German.

Zazra, H. D. "Purchasing brass instruments." *The Instrumentalist* 27 (Aug. 1972): 18.

Careers/Career Development

Aitken, T. " 'What's your proper job?' A social portrait of the British brass player [interview with Maurice Murphy, John Pigneguy, Bill Geldard and James Gourlay]." *Brass Bulletin—International Brass Chronicle*, no. 51 (1985): 14–24. Also in French and German.

Amstutz, A. Keith. "Sibelius #2 blues; or, Is specialization a dead art?" *NACWPI Journal* 25, no. 3 (1977): 57–59.

Bach, Vincent. "The cornetist's road to success." *Jacobs' Band Monthly* 13 (Mar. 1928): 56–57.

Baker, James. "Horn player's guide to work in Mexico City and Toluca." *The Horn Call* 15, no. 1 (Oct. 1984): 90–91.

Bowman, Brian. "Euphonium-tuba opportunities in service bands." *T.U.B.A. Newsletter* 1, no. 2 (Winter 1974): 8.

Bush, I. "Tell it the way it is: a viewpoint of professional trumpet playing in the United States." *Brass Bulletin—International Brass Chronicle*, no. 22 (1978): 45+. Also in French and German.

Carlucci, T. "Brass: flexibility is the key for freelance trumpet player." *Canadian Musician* 7, no. 6 (1985): 60+.

Chenoweth, Richard. "Report from Santa Fe: The twenty-eighth season of the Santa Fe Opera." *The Horn Call* 15, no. 2 (Apr. 1985): 19–27.

Chiemingo, Rich. "Playing tuba with Guy Lombardo's Royal Canadians." *T.U.B.A. Journal* 7, no. 2 (Fall 1979): 8–10.

Clarke, Herbert L. "Responsibilities of the cornet soloist." *Etude* 57 (1939): 375–376+.

Decker, James C. "Double or nothing: how tight money in Hollywood is popularizing Deskants and Tuben." *The Horn Call* 2, no. 2 (May 1972): 37–40.

Decker, Richard. "Thoughts on auditioning." *The Horn Call* 15, no. 2 (Apr. 1985): 31–32.

Evans, Eliot D. "All you ever wanted to know about the Washington D. C. military bands." *T.U.B.A. Journal* 8, no. 1 (Summer 1980): 2–12.

Flor, G. J., ed. "Brass workshop: the pit orchestra trombonist." *The School Musician* 50 (Mar. 1979): 8+.

Hickman, David R. "The classical trumpet soloist." *Woodwind World—Brass and Percussion* 16, no. 2 (1977): 32+.

Hill, Douglas. "Self development and the performance of music." *The Horn Call* 18, no. 2 (Apr. 1988): 45.

Johnson, D. "The art of positive teaching." *Canadian Musician* 1, no. 1 (1979): 40+.

5013   Johnson, D. "Brass: A professional career." *Canadian Musician* 5, no. 2 (1983): 58.

Johnson, T. "A guide to commercial tuba playing in the Los Angeles area." *Brass Bulletin—International Brass Chronicle*, no. 25 (1979): 58–59.

Jones, M. "Travel notes of a horn player." *Woodwind World* 2 (Sept. 1958): 5–6.

Kemp, Stephen. "How Vincent Bach started in the business." *Metronome* 44 (Nov. 1928): 25+.

Kemp, Stephen. "There were many obstacles in Vincent Bach's path to success." *Metronome* 44 (Mar. 1928): 29+.

Litman, Ross. "The Alaskan tubist." *T.U.B.A. Journal* 7, no. 4 (Spring 1980): 4–5.

Lycan, Scott. "The back row at Disneyland." *T.U.B.A. Newsletter* 3, no. 3 (Spring/Summer 1976): 8.

Matsubara, Chiyo. "Horn situation in Japan." *The Horn Call* 6, no. 1 (Nov. 1975): 51–56.

Mayer, Abby. "Summer horn teaching." *The Horn Call* 1, no. 1 (Feb. 1971): 23–27.

Merker, Ethyl. "The case for women in brass." *Musart* 28, no. 2 (1975): 30–32. Reprinted from *Leblanc World of Music* (Fall 1975).

Mishori, Yaacov. "Horn playing in Israel." *The Horn Call* 13, no. 2 (Apr. 1983): 40–44.

Peer, R., and R. Bissell. "Advice to would-be professional trombonists [outline and transcript]." *International Trombone Association Newsletter* 7, no. 1 (1979): 6–12.

Pennell, Harriet B. "Making a career as a cornetist. An interview with

Herbert L. Clarke." *Etude* 50 (1932): 332 + .

Peruzzini, Andrew. "Auditioning as a hobby, an opinion." *T.U.B.A. Journal* 9, no. 1 (Summer 1980): 2.

Powell, R. E. "The tape recording: gateway to the college studio teaching position." *Journal of the International Trombone Association* 14, no. 3 (1986): 11.

Pulling, J. "Les femmes et les cuivres: temoignages." *Brass Bulletin—International Brass Chronicle*, no. 28 (1979): 51–55. Also in English and German.

"Race track trumpeters." *International Musician* 48 (Mar. 1950): 14 + .

Reifsnyder, Robert. "Career patterns of professional trombonists." *Journal of the International Trombone Association* 13, no. 1 (1985): 33–39.

Richter, J. "The perils of a free lance horn player." *Woodwind World—Brass and Percussion* 15, no. 3 (1976): 40.

Riggio, Suzanne. "You say you married a horn player?" *Woodwind World* 13, no. 2 (1974): 10–11.

Riggio, Suzanne. "You say you married a horn player?" *The Horn Call* 5, no. 2 (Spring 1975): 36–38.

Root, Rebecca. "So you want to be a pro?" *The Horn Call* 9, no. 2 (Apr. 1979): 89–92.

Schweikert, Norman. "Playing assistant first horn." *The Horn Call* 5, no. 1 (Autumn 1974): 43–50.

5014   Shoop, Stephen. "The dixieland band: a meaningful avenue of performance for the tuba player." *T.U.B.A. Journal* 13, no. 1 (Aug. 1985): 13–14.

Shoop, Stephen. "Tax deductions available to tuba and euphonium players and teachers." *T.U.B.A. Journal* 13, no. 3 (Feb. 1986): 19.

Stuart, G. "How to make it as a lead trumpet player." *The Instrumentalist* 31 (Apr. 1977): 58–59.

Stuart, G. "To be 'lead trumpet' in a jazz orchestra." *Brass Bulletin—International Brass Chronicle*, no. 10 (1975): 43–47. Also in French and German.

Tetzlaff, Daniel B. "Four steps toward the professional sound." *The Instrumentalist* 9 (Nov. 1954): 36–39.

Thomas, Brian, and Seth Orgel. "Auditioning for a horn position in the United States." *The Horn Call* 13, no. 2 (Apr. 1983): 56–60.

Tritle, Thomas. "On playing horn in Brazil." *The Horn Call* 11, no. 2 (1981): 50–53.

Waldeck, L. "Symphonic tuba playing." *Brass Bulletin—International Brass Chronicle*, no. 23 (1978): 45–46. Also in French and German.

Wekre, Froydis Ree. "Being a woman brass player—so what?" *Brass Bulletin—International Brass Chronicle*, no. 26 (1979): 51–54. Also in French and German.

Yeo, Douglas. "Everything you always wanted to know about tuba auditions, but didn't know who to ask." *T.U.B.A. Journal* 11, no. 3 (Winter, 1984): 2–6.

Young, Jerry A. "Duties of low brass instructors." *T.U.B.A. Journal* 9, no. 4 (Spring 1982): 13–16.

Clinics/Conferences/Festivals

5015   Adams, S. "Report from Nashville." *Newsletter of the International Trombone Association* 6, no. 1 (1978): 7–11.

5016   "Agenda." *Brass Bulletin—International Brass Chronicle*, no. 19 (1977): 10–12. Also in French and German.

5017   Agrell, Jeffrey. "The First European Horn Symposium." *Brass Bulletin—International Brass Chronicle*, no. 33 (1981): 13–16. Also in French and German.

Agrell, Jeffrey. "Jazz and the horn: workshop getting started." *Brass Bulletin—International Brass Chronicle*, no. 42 (1983): 36–40 + . Also in French and German.

5018   Alexander, David. "Auburn University hosts first Southeast Trumpet Workshop." *Journal of the International Trumpet Guild* 12, no. 1 (1987): 57–59.

5019   Alexander, David, and Britton Theurer. "The 1988 ITG Conference: a synopsis." *Journal of the International Trumpet Guild* 13, no. 1 (Sept. 1988): 40–61.

5020   Amstutz, A. Keith. "The 1976 National Trumpet Symposium, a synopsis." *Journal of the International Trumpet Guild* 1 (1976): 20–22 + .

"Annual brass band contest at the Zoological Gardens, Bellevue, Manchester." *Musical World* 50 (1872): 607–608.

5021   Ashburn, W. L. "The 1984 Midwestern Trombone Workshop." *Journal of the International Trombone Association* 12, no. 2 (1984): 30–32.

5022   Baker, Buddy. "President's podium [International Trombone Workshop at Nashville]." *Newsletter of the International Trombone Association* 5, no. 1 (1977): 3.

5023   Baker, J. "[London] British Horn Festival." *Sounding Brass & the Conductor* 9, no. 2 (1980): 9–10.

Banks, T. "The Empire Brass Quintet Summer Symposium—a personal perspective." *Journal of the International Trombone Association* 12, no. 2 (1984): 17–18.

5024   Baroutcheva, E., and A. Selianin. "Union Sovietique: First Leningrad Horn Seminar." *Brass Bulletin—International Brass Chronicle*, no. 28 (1979): 59 + . Also in French and German.

5025   Barrow, Gary. "International brass fete [Second International Brass Congress]." *Woodwind, Brass and Percussion* 23, no. 7 (1984): 4–5.

"Barry Tuckwell at Ithaca College." *Woodwind World—Brass and Percussion* 18, no. 1 (1980): 24–25.

5026 Baumann, Hella. "Second International Competition for Hand Horn, Bad Harzburg, West Germany, June 17–20, 1987." *The Horn Call* 18, no. 1 (Oct. 1987): 19–20.

5027 Bloch, C. "The 1986 I.T.G. Conference: a personal view." *Brass Bulletin— International Brass Chronicle*, no. 56 (1986): 34–38. Also in French and German.

5028 Bobo, Roger. "Comments on the First International Brass Congress." *Brass Bulletin—International Brass Chronicle*, no. 15 (1976): 55+. Also in French and German.

5029 Bobo, Roger. "Symposium 78: looking back [tuba-euphonium]." *Brass Bulletin—International Brass Chronicle*, no. 25 (1979): 19+. Also in French and German.

5030 Bowell, Jeff. "The 1985 Eastern Trombone Workshop." *Journal of the International Trombone Association* 14, no. 2 (Spring 1986): 40–42.

5031 "Brass Conference warms New York." *Down Beat* 44 (Mar. 10, 1977): 12.

5032 Braun, Elaine. "Hooked on . . . [IHS Workshop, Provo]." *The Horn Call* 18, no. 1 (Oct. 1987): 91–97.

5033 Braun, Elaine. "Horns—and all that brass [IBC2]." *The Horn Call* 15, no. 1 (Oct. 1984): 63–65.

5034 Braun, Elaine. "International hornists [One Hundredth Jahre International Horn Symposium, Vienna]." *Woodwind, Brass and Percussion* 23, no. 4 (1984): 7+.

5035 Braun, Elaine. "Lucky no. 13." *The Horn Call* 12, no. 1 (Oct. 1981): 48–55.

5036 Braun, Elaine. "Workshop review: 17 and counting." *The Horn Call* 16, no. 1 (Oct. 1985): 51–52.

5037 Braun, Elaine. "The XIVth Annual Horn Workshop." *The Horn Call* 13, no. 1 (Oct. 1982): 38–42.

5038 "Brefs commentaires 12–24.7.1976—Weimar (DDR)." *Brass Bulletin—International Brass Chronicle*, no. 15 (1976): 9–10. Also in German and English.

5039 "British Horn Trust Festival." *The Horn Call* 11, no. 1 (Oct. 1980): 17–19. Adapted from *Orchestra World* (May 1980).

5040 Broussard, George L., comp. "The fifteenth International Trombone Workshop Nashville—'86." *Journal of the International Trombone Association* 14, no. 4 (Fall 1986): 22–41.

5041 Broussard, George L. "The seventeenth International Trombone Workshop." *Journal of the International Trombone Association* 15, no. 4 (Fall 1987): 16–25.

Bugli, D. "Low brass master class at Peabody Conservatory [includes repertoire lists for auditions]." *Journal of the International Trombone Association* 11, no. 2 (1983): 25–27.

5042 Burdett, Keith. "B.H.S.—Ripon 1100, 29th June, 1986." *The Horn Call* 17, no. 1 (Oct. 1986): 35–37.

5043   Burns, L. "National Trumpet Symposium 1972." *Brass Bulletin—International Brass Chronicle*, no. 4 (1973): 78–82. Also in French and German.

5044   Busancic, Dusan. "First seminar of horn players in Yugoslavia." *The Horn Call* 9, no. 1 (Oct. 1978): 50–51.

5045   Busancic, Dusan. "Jugoslawien: 27.3–3.4.1978—Beograd [horn clinic]." *Brass Bulletin—International Brass Chronicle*, no. 25 (1979): 23.

5046   "Buyanovskiy and Dokshidser in Kajaani [Kainuu Music Institute]." *Brass Bulletin—International Brass Chronicle*, no. 53 (1986): 3 News Suppl.

Caisley, L. G. "The N.S.B.B.A. Festival." *Music Teacher and Piano Student* 54 (Aug. 1975): 18.

5047   Caldicott, Stephen. "The first European Horn Symposium." *The Horn Call* 11, no. 2 (1981): 80–83. Reprinted from *The Blue Band* (Dec. 1980).

5048   Cania, L. M. "Horn heaven [13th Annual International Horn Workshop]." *Woodwind, Brass and Percussion* 20, no. 6 (1981): 4–7.

5049   Carter, Stewart. "Natural trumpets flourish at Third Early Brass Festival." *Journal of the International Trumpet Guild* 12, no. 3 (Feb. 1988): 18–19.

"Caught [third annual Sackbut week]." *Down Beat* 42 (Aug. 14, 1975): 34–35.

5050   "The Central New York Brass Festival." *Newsletter of the International Trombone Association* 3, no. 2 (1976): 10.

5051   "Central New York Brass Festival great success." *The School Musician* 47 (June-July 1976): 11.

5052   Champion, Anthony. "The British Horn Society visits York, 27th June, 1982." *The Horn Call* 13, no. 1 (Oct. 1982): 54–55.

5053   Champion, Anthony. "The first northern horn seminar of the British Horn Society, 4th July, 1981." *The Horn Call* 12, no. 1 (Oct. 1981): 69–70.

5054   Chenoweth, Richard. "The Barry Tuckwell symposium for brass." *The Horn Call* 12, no. 1 (Oct. 1981): 16–19.

5055   Chesebro, Gayle, and Philip Paul. "The International Horn Society Archive—a resource for regional workshops." *The Horn Call* 16, (June 1986): 58–59.

5056   Clendenin, W. R. "1977 ITG conference notes." *Brass Bulletin—International Brass Chronicle*, no. 19 (1977): 15–17. Also in French and German.

"Conn and Phillips remake calendar with 'Octubafest.' " *The Music Trades* 127 (Jan. 1979): 110.

5057   "Courses & seminars ['International Wind-Players Week' in Neuhofen a. d. Krems]." *Brass Bulletin—International Brass Chronicle*, no. 40 (1982): 5–7 News Suppl. Also in French and German.

5058   "Courses & seminars [Leningrad Conservatoire, February]." *Brass Bulletin—International Brass Chronicle*, no. 40 (1982): 7 News Suppl. Also in French and German.

5059   "Courses & seminars [second Stuttgart trumpeters' symposium]." *Brass Bulletin—International Brass Chronicle*, no. 40 (1982): 3–4 News Suppl. Also in French and German.

5060   "Courses & seminars [Thierry Caen's 'International Music Academy' in Dijon]." *Brass Bulletin—International Brass Chronicle*, no. 40 (1982): 4–5 News Suppl. Also in French and German.

5061   Cramer, William F. "The Eastern Trombone Workshop." *Newsletter of the International Trombone Association* 4, no. 3 (1977): 5.

5062   Cramer, William F. "Eastern Trombone Workshop 1982." *Journal of the International Trombone Association* 10, no. 2 (1982): 31–32.

5063   Cramer, William F. "Trombone competition at Toulon." *Brass Bulletin—International Brass Chronicle*, no. 19 (1977): 14–15. Also in French and German.

      Cross, Steven B. "A practical program to make your next Octubafest a complete success." *T.U.B.A. Journal* 10, no. 4 (Spring 1983): 28–29.

      Crown, T. "Chicago: Brass Seminar—The Trumpet." *Brass Bulletin—International Brass Chronicle*, no. 4 (1973): 67–76. Also in French and German.

5064   Dalkert, C. "1979 International Trombone Workshop." *International Trombone Association Newsletter* 6, no. 4 (1979): 14–20.

5065   Day, Joel. "International Tuba Day." *T.U.B.A. Journal* 11, no. 1 (Summer 1983): 14–15.

5066   "Deutsche Demokratische Republik: 13–23.7.1978 Weimar [horn clinic]." *Brass Bulletin—International Brass Chronicle*, no. 25 (1979): 14.

5067   Dorsam, Paul J. "Correspondence [1977 ITG Conference]." *International Trumpet Guild Newsletter* 4, no. 1 (1977): 8–9.

5068   Dowling, T. "The Second Australian National Trombone Seminar 1984." *Journal of the International Trombone Association* 12, no. 3 (1984): 22–24.

5069   "East and west [rebuilding of brass instruments and use in historical musical performance]." *Brass Bulletin—International Brass Chronicle*, no. 57 (1987): News Suppl. 6. Also in French and German.

5070   "Edward Tarr master class at Indiana." *International Trumpet Guild Newsletter* 4, no. 1 (1977): 5–6.

5071   "Edward Tarr trumpet seminar and concert." *International Trumpet Guild Newsletter* 3, no. 2 (1977): 4.

5072   "England: International Congress for Brass Musicians: 1978." *Brass Bulletin—International Brass Chronicle*, no. 25 (1979): 14–15.

5073   England, W. L. "Northampton Cornetto Weekend." *Recorder and Music* 5, no. 11 (1977): 363.

      Ervin, T. "Precollegiate trombone workshops—a successful idea." *Journal of the International Trombone Association* 13, no. 4 (1985): 40.

      Ervin, T. "Precollegiate trombone workshops—a successful idea." *NACWPI Journal* 34, no. 1 (1985): 11.

5074   Everett, T. "Charles Colin's Brass Conference for Scholarships." *Newsletter of the International Trombone Association* 3, no. 2 (1976): 9–10.

5075   Evers, G. "First Australian National Trombone Seminar." *International Trombone Association Newsletter* 6, no. 4 (1979): 12–13.

5076   "Fifth annual Horn Workshop [program]." *The Horn Call* 4, no. 1 (Autumn 1973): 58–61.

5077   "First Annual Berry College Trombone Symposium." *Newsletter of the International Trombone Association* 3, no. 2 (1976): 9.

5078   "The first major international competition for horn held at Saint-Hubert, Belgium." *Brass Bulletin—International Brass Chronicle*, no. 19 (1977): 12–14.

5079   "The First Soviet Brass Congress, Leningrad, Feb. 1–5, 1985." *Journal of the International Trumpet Guild* 10, no. 2 (1985): 21–23. Photo essay.

5080   Frigerio, G. "Brass symposium held in Sweden (Göteborg)." *International Trumpet Guild Newsletter* 7, no. 2 (1981): 3–4.

5081   Frigerio, G. "Pierre Thibaud at Brass Center Workshop (Gothenburg, Sweden)." *International Trumpet Guild Newsletter* 8, no. 2 (1982): 24.

5082   Fromme, Arnold. "The resurrection of historical brass [Windham College Summer Collegium in Early Music]." *Music Journal* 25 (Jan. 1967): 36–38+.

       "Der 15. bayerische Landesposaunentag." *Gottesdienst und Kirchenmusik* (1957): 135–138.

5083   Gaska, Leslie. "The XI Annual Horn Workshop: a retrospective." *The Horn Call* 10, no. 1 (Oct. 1979): 31–33.

5084   Gelfand, M. H. "Tuba players decide now is time to blow their own horns [Tuba Symposium at Indiana University]." *The Wall Street Journal* 181 (May 23, 1973): 1+.

5085   George, S. "Two-Carolina Low Brass Festival." *Newsletter of the International Trombone Association* 3, no. 2 (1976): 10.

       Gray, Skip. "North American Brass Band Association Championship III: an overview." *T.U.B.A. Journal* 13, no. 1 (Aug. 1985): 15–16.

5086   Gross, Steve. "A competition comes of age [American Horn Competition]." *The Horn Call* 18, no. 2 (Apr. 1988): 25–30.

5087   Groves, John. "Keystone Brass Institute: a hornist's impressions." *The Horn Call* 17, no. 1 (Oct. 1986): 55–56.

5088   "Hamar trumpet seminar held." *International Trumpet Guild Newsletter* 4, no. 3 (1978): 5.

       Henderson, Malcolm C. "Musical 'Middletown' revisited." *The Horn Call* 5, no. 2 (Spring 1975): 12–16.

5089   Henderson, Malcolm C. "Random impressions: Bloomington & Claremont." *The Horn Call* 3, no. 1 (Nov. 1972): 62–65.

5090   Herrick, Dennis. "The Japan Trumpeters' Association and The Fourth Annual Trumpet Festival." *Journal of the International Trumpet Guild* 12, no. 2 (Dec. 1987): 34–36+.

       Hill, Douglas. "The IHS and its progress." *The Horn Call* 9, no. 1 (Oct. 1978): 58–60. Also in French and German.

5091   Himes, A. C. "A trombone master class with Dean Werner." *Journal of the International Trombone Association* 10, no. 4 (1982): 15–16.

5092   Himes, A. C. "A trombone master class with Keig E. Garvin." *Journal of the International Trombone Association* 12, no. 1 (1984): 26–28.

5093 Hodgkinson, M. "News from the world: Sweden—trumpets in Växjö." *Brass Bulletin—International Brass Chronicle*, no. 34 (1981): 1–2. Also in French and German.

5094 Höltzel, Michael. "300 Jahre Horn in Böhmen (Sept. 1981, Brno)." *Brass Bulletin—International Brass Chronicle*, no. 38 (1982): 2–3 News Suppl. Also in French and English.

5095 Hogue, D. "Summer of '73 [International Trombone Association Workshop]." *The Instrumentalist* 28 (Nov. 1973): 46–47.

5096 Hogue, D. "Summer of '73 [Tuba Symposium at Indiana University]." *The Instrumentalist* 28 (Nov. 1973): 46–47.

Hopkins, John. "Visit to Melbourne by Hermann Baumann." *The Horn Call* 9, no. 1 (Oct. 1978): 18–19.

5097 "Horn workshop at Indiana U." *Woodwind World* 11, no. 3 (1972): 23.

"Horst-Dieter Bolz." *Brass Bulletin—International Brass Chronicle*, no. 45 (1984): 3 News Suppl. Also in French and German.

5098 Humfeld, Neill H. "Fifteenth ITW preview." *Journal of the International Trombone Association* 14, no. 2 (Spring 1986): 16–26.

5099 Humfeld, Neill H. "Seventeenth ITW preview." *Journal of the International Trombone Association* 16, no. 2 (Spring 1988): 28–29.

5100 Humfeld, Neill H. "Sixteenth ITW preview." *Journal of the International Trombone Association* 15, no. 2 (Spring 1987): 30–31.

5101 Hunt, P., comp. "The Fourteenth International Trombone Workshop—Nashville '85." *Journal of the International Trombone Association* 13, no. 4 (1985): 12–22 +.

5102 Hunt, P. B. "The Second International Brass Congress." *Journal of the International Trombone Association* 12, no. 4 (1984): 6–21.

5103 "Indiana University host to B.R.A.S.S., 1985." *Journal of the International Trumpet Guild* 10, no. 2 (1985): 3.

"International Brass Chamber Music Camp, Competition, and Symposium." *Journal of the International Trombone Association* 13, no. 1 (1985): 48–49.

5104 "International Brass Congress held in Montreux." *International Trumpet Guild Newsletter* 3, no. 1 (1976): 1.

5105 "International Trombone Workshop." *High Fidelity/Musical America* 28 (Oct. 1978): MA39–40.

5106 "IRCAM in action (Georges Pompidou Centre, 1985)." *Brass Bulletin—International Brass Chronicle*, no. 53 (1986): 5 News Suppl. Also in French and German.

5107 "I.T.A. Copenhagen." *Brass Bulletin—International Brass Chronicle*, no. 49 (News Suppl. 1985): 2.

Jacobs, A. "Music in London [National Brass Band Festival Concert]." *The Musical Times* 113 (Dec. 1972): 1214.

5108 Jones, George W., ed. "The Second International Brass Congress."

T.U.B.A. Journal 12, no. 1 (Aug. 1984): 10–24.

5109 Jones, S. G. "The 1981 ITG Conference: a synopsis." *Journal of the International Trumpet Guild* 6: (1981): 34–50.

5110 Kagarice, Vern. "Eastern Trombone Workshop." *Newsletter of the International Trombone Association* 8, no. 3 (1981): 30–32.

5111 Kagarice, Vern. "ITW Thirteen—end of an era [International Trombone Workshop]." *Journal of the International Trombone Association* 11, no. 3 (1983): 9–20.

5112 Kagarice, Vern. "North Texas State Trombone Symposium." *Newsletter of the International Trombone Association* 6, no. 3 (1979): 8–9.

5113 Kampen, Paul A. "Trans-Pennine horns." *The Horn Call* 14, no. 1 (Oct. 1983): 57–59.

5114 Keys, Stephen. "The University of Kentucky Regional Tuba-Euphonium Conference Review." *T.U.B.A. Journal* 15, no. 2 (Nov. 1987): 20–21.

5115 "Keystone Brass Institute." *Journal of the International Trumpet Guild* 11, no. 2 (1986): 5–6.

5116 Kierman, Sean. "Horn workshop in South Africa." *The Horn Call* 12, no. 1 (Oct. 1981): 45–46.

Krumpfer, Hans-Joachim. "III. Internationales Kammermusikseminar in Ungarn." *Brass Bulletin—International Brass Chronicle*, no. 37 (1982): 6–7 News Suppl.

Kuehn, David L. "Tuba symposium-workshops." *T.U.B.A. Newsletter* 3, no. 3 (Spring/Summer 1976): 8.

Lange, Hans Jürgen. "Zweiter Deutscher Evangelischer Posaunentag in Dortmund vom 5.-7. Oktober 1956." *Musik und Kirche* 27 (1957): 147–150.

5117 Lee, A. "Brass players shine in New York City 'blow' [5th annual New York Brass Conference for Scholarships]." *The Christian Science Monitor* 69 (Mar. 14, 1977): 28.

5118 Lewis, H. M. "The 1977 ITG Conference." *Journal of the International Trumpet Guild* 2 (1977): 28–36.

5119 Lewis, Michael. "The Eastern Trombone Workshop." *Journal of the International Trombone Association* 15, no. 2 (1987): 32–34.

5120 Lind, Michael. "Agenda [first Swedish tuba-euphonium workshop 1977]." *Brass Bulletin—International Brass Chronicle*, no. 23 (1978): 11 + . Also in French and German.

5121 Lindahl, B., and A. Millat. "To the mountain tops and back: the First Annual Keystone Brass Institute." *Journal of the International Trombone Association* 15, no. 1 (1987): 26–28.

5122 Lindahl, Robert. "The second annual Keystone Brass Institute: looking ahead." *Journal of the International Trombone Association* 16, no. 2 (Spring 1988): 24–26.

5123 Loebl, Cindy Carr. "Two important European horn competitions of 1987 [Prague Spring International Horn Competition, Scandinavian Horn

Seminar]." *The Horn Call* 18, no. 2 (Apr. 1988): 72–79.

5124 "Lyon (France) trumpet seminar features Dallas Symphony trumpet section." *International Trumpet Guild Newsletter* 8, no. 1 (1981): 9.

5125 Magliocco, H., comp. "Report on the ITW—1980." *Newsletter of the International Trombone Association* 8, no. 1 (1980): 7–16.

5126 Magliocco, H. "Report on the Midwest Trombone Workshop." *International Trombone Association Newsletter* 6, no. 4 (1979): 13–14.

5127 Maldonado, Luis. "The 1986 Japan Wind and Percussion Competition." *T.U.B.A. Journal* 14, no. 4 (May 1987): 21–22.

5128 Mansur, Paul. "Czechoslovakia's three hundredth anniversary horn symposium." *The Horn Call* 12, no. 2 (Apr. 1982): 50–59.

5129 Mansur, Paul. "The Detmold Workshop." *The Horn Call* 17, no. 2 (Apr. 1987): 16–29.

5130 Mansur, Paul. "The first European horn symposium." *The Horn Call* 11, no. 1 (Oct. 1980): 24–32.

5131 Mansur, Paul. "International Brass Congress I." *The Horn Call* 7, no. 1 (Nov. 1976): 32–34.

5132 Mansur, Paul. "International Horn Symposium Wien." *The Horn Call* 14, no. 2 (Apr. 1984): 27–40.

"Master class: The Canadian Brass; ensemble playing." *The Instrumentalist* 39 (Apr. 1985): 36+.

5133 Mathez, Jean-Pierre. "Editorial: Special Finland [Lieska Brass Week]." *Brass Bulletin—International Brass Chronicle*, no. 53 (1986): 29–37. Also in French and German.

5134 Mathez, Jean-Pierre. "Musikmesse Frankfurt [exhibition]." *Brass Bulletin—International Brass Chronicle*, no. 58 (News Suppl. 1987): 7–11. Also in English and French.

5135 Mathez, Jean-Pierre. "The second International Brass Congress (IBC2) [includes schedule]." *Brass Bulletin—International Brass Chronicle*, no. 46 (1984): 9–11. Also in French and German.

5136 Mathez, Jean-Pierre. "Special Francfort 1979." *Brass Bulletin—International Brass Chronicle*, no. 26 (1979): 17+. Also in English and German.

5137 Mayes, Martin. "International competition for horn and tuba, Markneukirchen, German Democratic Republic 11–18 May, 1984." *T.U.B.A. Journal* 12, no. 3 (Feb. 1985): 4–5.

5138 Mayes, Martin. "International competition for horn and tuba, Markneukirchen, German Democratic Republic, 11–18 May." *The Horn Call* 15, no. 1 (Oct. 1984): 44–46.

5139 Meck, R. "Ein schöner Gickser ist keine Schande; Beobachtungen beim ersten Europäischen Horn-Symposium in Trossingen." *Neue Musikzeitung*, no. 5 (Oct.–Nov. 1980): 16.

5140 Meckies, U. "Zum fünften Mal: Stapelfelder Horntage." *Das Orchester* 35 (Nov. 1987): 1195.

5141 "Mid-South Euphonium/Tuba Symposium." *T.U.B.A. Newsletter* 3, no. 3 (Spring/Summer 1976): 8.

5142 "Midwest Regional Tuba-Euphonium Symposium—a report." *T.U.B.A. Newsletter* 3, no. 2 (Winter 1976): 7.

5143 "Midwest Trumpet Guild Workshop." *International Trumpet Guild Newsletter* 3 (1977): 2.

5144 "Millikin's horn symposium features Barry Tuckwell." *The School Musician* 49 (Apr. 1978): 26.

Montagu, Jeremy. "Nuremburg conference on restoration." *Early Music* 2, no. 4 (1974): 265 + .

"Montreux (Switzerland) International Brass Symposium." *Brass Bulletin— International Brass Chronicle*, no. 9 (1974): 35–37. Also in French and German.

Morris, E. Vaughan. "The National Brass Band Festival." In *Brass Today.* Edited by Frank Wright, 31–36. London: Besson, 1957.

5145 Morris, R. Winston. " 'Harvey Phillips Day.' " *T.U.B.A. Journal* 4, no. 1 (Fall 1976): 16.

Morris, R. Winston. "A tuba clinic with Harvey Phillips." *The Instrumentalist* 29 (Jan. 1975): 51–55.

5146 Naredi-Rainer, E. "Fachtagung zur Erforschung des Blasmusikwesens 'Alta Musica' in Graz (25.-29. November 1974)." *Die Musikforschung* 28, no. 1 (1975): 59–60.

"The National Youth Brass Band of Switzerland." *Brass Bulletin—International Brass Chronicle*, no. 32 (1980): 16–17. Also in French and German.

5147 "News of the world: Hongrie—Second National Trombone and Tuba Workshop." *Brass Bulletin—International Brass Chronicle*, no. 34 (1981): 2–3. Also in French and German.

5148 "1986 International Tuba-Euphonium Conference session reviews." *T.U.B.A. Journal* 14, no. 1 (Aug. 1986): 11–34.

5149 "1975 National T.U.B.A. Symposium-Workshop." *T.U.B.A. Newsletter* 1, no. 2 (Winter 1974): 12.

5150 "1977 Boston Sackbut Week." *Newsletter of the International Trombone Association* 5, no. 1 (1977): 5.

5151 "N.T.S.U.T.U.B.A." *T.U.B.A. Newsletter* 1, no. 2 (Winter 1974): 12.

5152 "Octubafests 1975." *T.U.B.A. Newsletter* 3, no. 2 (Winter 1976): 4–5.

5153 "One giant step for the serpent [Amherst Workshop]." *The Instrumentalist* 41 (Jan. 1987): 69.

5154 "Orchestral trumpet workshop held [Dallas]." *International Trumpet Guild Newsletter* 8, no. 1 (1981): 8.

5155 Orval, Francis. "Conference du IXe Colloque S.I.C." *The Horn Call* 8, no. 1 (Nov. 1977): 32–35.

5156 "Ottoni di Verona [Verona International Brass Festival]." *Brass Bulletin— International Brass Chronicle*, no. 59 (1987): 40–41 + . In English, French and German.

5157 Owens, J. "1977 International Trombone Workshop." *Newsletter of the International Trombone Association* 5, no. 1 (1977): 6–10.

5158 Page, Malcolm. "Scandinavian Horn Workshop." *The Horn Call* 6, no. 1

(Nov. 1975): 32–41.

5159 Pedersen, Thor Johan. "International music seminar—Weimar." *The Horn Call* 13, no. 2 (Apr. 1983): 37–39.

5160 Phillips, Harvey. "The First International Brass Congress—an on-the-scene report." *T.U.B.A. Journal* 13, no. 3 (Feb. 1986): 21.

5161 Phillips, Harvey, and Bill Lake. "Octubafest." *T.U.B.A. Newsletter* 1, no. 2 (Winter 1974): 12.

5162 Phillips, Harvey. "Reflections on the Second International Brass Congress." *T.U.B.A. Journal* 12, no. 1 (Aug. 1984): 9.

5163 Phillips, V. "Chamber music for brass workshop (Brass Chamber Music Workshop, Humboldt State University, Arcata, California, July 7–12, 1974)." *Brass and Percussion* 2, no. 5 (1974): 16.

5164 "Photographic highlights of the First International Brass Congress, Montreux—June 1976." *Journal of the International Trumpet Guild* 1 (1976): 48.

5165 Plotz, Donna. "The ITG Conference: a student's view." *Journal of the International Trumpet Guild* 13, no. 1 (Sept. 1988): 78.

Pröpper, K. "Tuba-Kurs in Tirol." *Das Orchester* 35 (Oct. 1987): 1064.

5166 "Programs from International Brass Congress." *T.U.B.A. Journal* 4, no. 1 (Fall 1976): 14–15.

5167 "Report from the ITG Workshop in Växsjö, Sweden—November, 1980." *International Trumpet Guild Newsletter* 7, no. 3 (1981): 2–3.

5168 Reyman, Randall G. "Vermont, you put me in a jazzy state." *Journal of the International Trumpet Guild* 13, no. 2 (Dec. 1988): 22–23.

Riggio, Suzanne. "An American in Switzerland." *The Horn Call* 7, no. 1 (Nov. 1976): 18–19.

5169 Riggio, Suzanne. "Horn Workshop [Sixth Annual Horn Workshop at Ball State University]." *Woodwind World—Brass and Percussion* 14, no. 2 (1975): 32–33.

Riggio, Suzanne. "How to put on a horn clinic and concert." *Woodwind World* 11, no. 1 (1972): 10–12 + .

Riggio, Suzanne. "Insights in F." *The Horn Call* 8, no. 1 (Nov. 1977): 22–31.

5170 Riggio, Suzanne. "Workshop VII." *The Horn Call* 6, no. 1 (Nov. 1975): 42–45.

5171 Robertson, J. "The Western Trombone Conference." *Newsletter of the International Trombone Association* 5, no. 2 (1977): 9.

5172 Robinson, William C., and Joseph A. White. "First Annual French Horn Workshop at Florida State University featured 194 hornists from 32 states." *The School Musician* 41 (Nov. 1969): 74–75.

5173 "Rocky Mountain Trombone Workshop." *Newsletter of the International Trombone Association* 6, no. 1 (1978): 5.

5174 Romersa, Henry J. "National Trombone Workshop [Nashville, Tenn.]." *Brass Bulletin—International Brass Chronicle*, no. 2 (1972): 16–24. Also in French and German.

5175 Roth. "Early Brass Festival II." *The Horn Call* 17, no. 2 (Apr. 1987): 45–47.

Roth, Erich. "Mit Jubelklang, mit Instrumenten schön, in Chören ohne Zahl. . . . Dankbare und kritische Erinnerung. Der zweite Deutsche Evangelische Posaunentag." *Der Kirchenmusiker* 8 (1957): 46–48.

Sawhill, Clarence. "A famous brass band festival." *Music Journal* 13 (1959): 16+.

Schlee, Martin. "2. Deutscher Evangelischer Posaunentag." *Gottesdienst und Kirchenmusik* 7 (1956): 184–186.

5176   Schönfelder, G. "Peking: Bläsernachwuchs gab Debüt." *Musik und Gesellschaft* 11 (1962): 760–761.

5177   Schroeder, J. "I. Internationaler Naturhorn-Wettbewerb in Bad Harzburg." *Das Orchester* 32 (Nov. 1984): 975–976.

5178   Schwarzl, Siegfried. "Internationales Horn-Symposium Wien 1983." *Oesterreichische Musikzeitung* 38 (Sept. 1983): 464–465.

5179   Schwarzl, Siegfried. "The Wiener Waldhornverein at the International Symposium for Brass Instrument Players' Chamber Music in Hungary (Barcs—Brass)." *The Horn Call* 16, no. 1 (Oct. 1985): 79–84.

5180   Secon, Morris. "Who's sitting in that empty chair? [IBC2]." *The Horn Call* 15, no. 1 (Oct. 1984): 37–40.

5181   "2nd International Brass Colloquium." *Brass Bulletin—International Brass Chronicle*, no. 45 (1984): 5–6 News Suppl. Also in French and German.

5182   "Second National Tuba-Euphonium Symposium-Workshop." *T.U.B.A. Journal* 7, no. 3 (Winter 1980): 16–22.

5183   Seiffert, Elaine. "Reminiscences and a message—Workshop XI." *The Horn Call* 10, no. 1 (Oct. 1979): 34–38.

5184   Seiffert, Elaine. "The tenth dream." *The Horn Call* 9, no. 1 (Oct. 1978): 52. Also in French and German.

5185   Seiffert, Elaine. "Twelfth Night revisited: Workshop XII, June 16–21, Indiana University." *The Horn Call* 11, no. 1 (Oct. 1980): 20–23.

5186   Seiffert, Elaine. "What I would like to tell my friends about Workshop X." *The Horn Call* 9, no. 1 (Oct. 1978): 20–25. Also in French and German.

5187   Self, James M. "Third International Tuba-Euphonium Symposium-Workshop—an update." *T.U.B.A. Journal* 5, no. 3 (Spring/Summer 1978): 20.

5188   Selyanin, A. "Saratov brass seminar." *Brass Bulletin—International Brass Chronicle*, no. 30 (1980): 16–18. Also in French and German.

5189   "The Seventeenth International Trombone Workshop." *Journal of the International Trombone Association* 15, no. 4 (1987): 16–25.

5190   Siebert, Alan. "Summit Brass International Brass Ensemble Competition." *Journal of the International Trumpet Guild* 13, no. 2 (Dec. 1988): 28–30.

5191   "Sixth Annual International Horn Workshop [program]." *The Horn Call* 5, no. 1 (Autumn 1974): 20–27.

5192   Sluchin, B. "11e Congres International d'Acoustique." *Brass Bulletin—International Brass Chronicle*, no. 44 (1983): 13–15. Also in English and German.

Sluchin, B. "Trombone workshops [their value and agendas]." *Brass Bul-*

letin—International Brass Chronicle, no. 52 (1985): 67–69. Also in French and German.

5193 "Soviet Brass Congress." *Brass Bulletin—International Brass Chronicle*, no. 50 (News Suppl. 1985): 4.

"Special hongrie: Barcs 1984; brass ensemble seminar." *Brass Bulletin—International Brass Chronicle*, no. 48 (1984): 28–29. Also in French and German.

5194 Spilka, Bill. "11th annual Brass Conference for scholarships." *Journal of the International Trombone Association* 11, no. 3 (1983): 35–37.

5195 Spilka, Bill. "14th New York Brass Conference for Scholarships." *Journal of the International Trombone Association* 14, no. 3 (1986): 40–44.

5196 Spilka, Bill. "15th annual New York Brass Conference for Scholarships." *Journal of the International Trombone Association* 15, no. 3 (1987): 10–12.

5197 Spilka, Bill. "Bones bonanza at brass conference! [1984 New York Brass Conference for Scholarships]." *Journal of the International Trombone Association* 12, no. 3 (1984): 32–36.

5198 Spilka, Bill. "The Eastern Trombone Workshop." *Newsletter of the International Trombone Association* 6, no. 1 (1978): 11–15.

5199 Spilka, Bill. "The Eastern Trombone Workshop." *Newsletter of the International Trombone Association* 6, no. 3 (1979): 10–13.

5200 Spilka, Bill. "Eastern Trombone Workshop." *International Trombone Association Newsletter* 7, no. 2 (1980): 17–20.

5201 Spilka, Bill. "Fifteenth annual New York Brass Conference for Scholarships." *Journal of the International Trombone Association* 15, no. 3 (Summer 1987): 10–12.

5202 Spilka, Bill. "Highlights of the Tenth Annual New York Brass Conference." *International Trumpet Guild Newsletter* 8, no. 3 (1982): 10–11.

5203 Spilka, Bill. "Slush and slushpumps at Snowbird." *Journal of the International Trombone Association* 6, no. 2 (1978): 11–15.

5204 Spilka, Bill. "The spit valve [1978 New York Brass Conference]." *Journal of the International Trombone Association* 5, no. 3 (1978): 18–21.

5205 Spilka, Bill. "The spit valve [Fifth Annual Brass Conference]." *Newsletter of the International Trombone Association* 5, no. 1 (1977): 31–33.

5206 Spilka, Bill. "The spit valve [Fourth Annual Brass Conference for Scholarships]." *Newsletter of the International Trombone Association* 3, no. 2 (1976): 12–14.

5207 Spilka, Bill. "The Tenth Annual New York Brass Conference." *Journal of the International Trombone Association* 10, no. 3 (1982): 31–34.

5208 Spilka, Bill. "Trumpet highlights of the Fifth Annual New York Brass Conference for Scholarships." *International Trumpet Guild Newsletter* 4, no. 1 (1977): 12–13.

5209 Stanley, Donald. "The regional symposium; where it all begins." *T.U.B.A. Journal* 14, no. 3 (Feb. 1987): 18–19.

5210 Staples, J. "The Don Lusher seminar." *Crescendo International* 20 (Jan. 1982): 2.

5211 Streeter, Thomas W. "The Fourth Annual Mid-West Trombone Fest." *Newsletter of the International Trombone Association* 3, no. 2 (1976): 10–11.

Strevens, Patrick. "A dream come true [London Horn Reunion]." *The Horn Call* 5, no. 2 (Spring 1975): 17–25.

5212 Sumerkin, V. "Trombone seminar in Finland." *Brass Bulletin—International Brass Chronicle*, no. 36 (1981): 6–7. News Suppl.

5213 "Summer Brass Academy in Dijon." *Journal of the International Trumpet Guild* 7, no. 2 (1982): 3.

"Summit Brass and the Keystone Brass Institute." *Journal of the International Trumpet Guild* 10, no. 2 (1985): 3–4.

5214 "Summit Brass: moving musical mountains [Doc Severinsen, Harvey Phillips, David Hickman and Carl Topilow discuss a new Colorado music festival]." *The Instrumentalist* 41 (Sept. 1986): 17–24 + .

"Summit Brass: national brass ensemble formed." *The School Musician* 57 (Oct. 1985): 9.

Theurer, Britton. "Vincent Cichowicz trumpet seminar." *International Trumpet Guild Newsletter* 7, no. 1 (1980): 5.

5215 Theurer, Britton. "The Second International Brass Congress: a synopsis." *Journal of the International Trumpet Guild* 9, no. 1 (1984): 12–35.

5216 "3rd Annual Eastern Trombone Workshop." *Newsletter of the International Trombone Association* 3, no. 2 (1976): 11–12.

5217 "Third International Tuba-Euphonium Symposium-Workshop." *T.U.B.A. Journal* 6, no. 1 (Fall 1978): 18–25.

5218 "Third International Tuba-Euphonium Symposium-Workshop." *T.U.B.A. Journal* 5, no. 2 (Winter 1978): 33.

5219 "Thirteenth Annual Trumpet Workshop." *International Trumpet Guild Newsletter* 3, no. 1 (1976): 1.

"The (thirty-first) National Brass Band Festival." *The Musical Times* 77 (1936): 936–937.

5220 Torchinsky, Abe. "Aspen Music Festival." *T.U.B.A. Newsletter* 3, no. 2 (Winter 1976): 12.

5221 "Trombone workshop at Central College." *Newsletter of the International Trombone Association* 5, no. 1 (1977): 5.

5222 "Trombone workshop in Brazil." *Newsletter of the International Trombone Association* 8, no. 3 (1981): 17–18.

5223 "Trombones featured at NCMEA (North Carolina Music Educators Association)." *Newsletter of the International Trombone Association* 5, no. 3 (1978): 2–3.

5224 "Trompeten-Symposium in der Bundesakademie in Trossingen." *Das Orchester* 28 (July-Aug. 1980): 617–618.

5225 "Trompeten-Symposium in Trossingen." *Das Orchester* 28 (Mar. 1980): 218–219.

5226 "T.U.B.A. at Mid-West Band and Orchestra Convention." *T.U.B.A. Newsletter* 2, no. 1 (Fall 1974): 2.

5227 "Tuba ist in: Bericht über das Tuba-Symposium in der Bundesakademie

Trossingen." *Das Orchester* 27 (Sept. 1979): 661–662.

5228   "Tuba tuba in Walla Walla." *T.U.B.A. Newsletter* 1, no. 2 (Winter 1974): 12.

5229   "Tubas galore." *Brass Bulletin—International Brass Chronicle,* no. 52 (1985): 6 News Suppl. Also in French and German.

5230   Tuckwell, Barry. "Horn players by the gross [annual horn workshops]." *Music Journal* 33 (Apr. 1975): 10+.

5231   Tuckwell, Barry. "The horn week at Pomona College." *The Horn Call* 2, no. 1 (Nov. 1971): 54–55.

Tuckwell, Barry. "Teaching horn players by the gross." *Music in Education* 38, no. 369 (1974): 218–220.

5232   "Un cours d'ete Philip Jones Brass Ensemble (Horncastle, fin juillet 1976, Grande-Bretagne)." *Brass Bulletin—International Brass Chronicle,* no. 15 (1976): 11–13. Also in German and English.

5233   Vinson, Dan. "New England Artists Recital of the New England Tuba-Euphonium Symposium/Workshop—a review." *T.U.B.A. Journal* 15, no. 4 (May 1987): 13.

5234   Wahlström, Ake. "Impressions from the Scandinavian Horn Workshop." *The Horn Call* 6, no. 1 (Nov. 1975): 30–31.

Walmsley, P. "An Australian's impressions of a day at the National." *Sounding Brass & the Conductor* 6, no. 4 (1978): 128–129.

Watson, Catherine. "Archive celebration." *The Horn Call* 16, (June 1986): 42–55.

5235   Watson, Catherine. "Brass Valhalla—IBC2." *The Horn Call* 15, no. 1 (Oct. 1984): 21–23.

5236   Watson, Catherine. "Fabulous fifteen, the XVth Annual International Horn Workshop." *The Horn Call* 14, no. 1 (Oct. 1983): 17–23.

5237   Watson, Catherine. "Spectacular seventeen [International Horn Workshop XVII]." *The Horn Call* 16, no. 1 (Oct. 1985): 45–49.

5238   Watson, Catherine. "What they thought of the workshop." *The Horn Call* 16, no. 1 (Oct. 1985): 53–56.

Watson, J. P. "Festival of brass band workshops." *The School Musician* 58 (Oct. 1986): 20.

5239   Wekre, Froydis Ree. "Moudon: 3rd special course for brass players." *Brass Bulletin—International Brass Chronicle,* no. 27 (1979): 20–22. Also in French and German.

5240   Whaley, Robert. "The First International Brass Congress." *T.U.B.A. Journal* 4, no. 1 (Fall 1976): 2–4.

5241   Whaley, Robert. "The First International Brass Congress." *T.U.B.A. Journal* 4, no. 2 (Winter 1977): 11–12.

Whaley, Robert. "Notes on the John Butler session." *T.U.B.A. Journal* 4, no. 1 (Fall 1976): 9.

5242   Wick, Dennis. "Brass Congress (Montreux, Switzerland)." *Sounding Brass & the Conductor* 5, no. 3 (1976): 86+.

Willener, A. "Philip Jones Brass Ensemble: 3rd summer school for quintets." *Brass Bulletin—International Brass Chronicle*, no. 27 (1979): 13. Also in French and German.

5243 Willener, A. "Montreux 1976 [First International Brass Congress]." *Brass Bulletin—International Brass Chronicle*, no. 15 (1976): 41–51 + . Also in German and English.

5244 Winick, Steven. "The 1980 ITG Conference: a synopsis." *Journal of the International Trumpet Guild* 5 (1980): 29–38.

5245 Winter, James H. "Claremont: Workshop V." *The Horn Call* 4, no. 1 (Autumn 1973): 55–57.

5246 Winter, James H. "Erewhemos and Erewhemos Revisited." *The Horn Call* 3, no. 1 (Nov. 1972): 24–52.

5247 Winter, James H. "Workshop VI." *The Horn Call* 5, no. 1 (Autumn 1974): 18–19.

5248 Winter, James H. "Workshop VII." *The Horn Call* 5, no. 1 (Autumn 1974): 51–53.

5249 Witham, T. "A student's perspective of the Western Trombone Conference." *Journal of the International Trombone Association* 6, no. 2 (1978): 5.

5250 Wollitz, K. "Serpents assemble in Amherst." *American Recorder* 27, no. 4 (1986): 152–153.

5251 "Works for solo trombone and mixed ensembles performed during the 1975 National Trombone Festival." *Newsletter of the International Trombone Association* 3, no. 2 (1976): 25 + .

5252 "World news: away from it all [3rd Cluny Music Meeting, France]." *Brass Bulletin—International Brass Chronicle*, no. 59 (News Suppl. 1987): 4–5. Also in French and German.

5253 "World news: breakthrough [Lieksa Brass Week, Finland. Instrument of the year: tuba]." *Brass Bulletin—International Brass Chronicle*, no. 60 (News Suppl. 1987): 3.

5254 "World news: France." *Brass Bulletin—International Brass Chronicle*, no. 28 (1979): 10–11.

5255 "World news: Musica Riva [Italy]." *Brass Bulletin—International Brass Chronicle*, no. 60 (News Suppl. 1987): 1.

5256 Worsan, Patrick, and Koen Cools. "Horn summer course in Belgium." *The Horn Call* 13, no. 1 (Oct. 1982): 48–49.

5257 Zellner, R., and others. "Premier Congres International des Cuivres." *Brass Bulletin—International Brass Chronicle*, no. 13 (1976): 65–84. Also in English and German.

PART IV

ACOUSTICS AND CONSTRUCTION

General

8. Tonmeistertagung 19.-22 November 1969 Hamburg. Durchgeführt vom Verband deutscher Tonmeister und Toningenieure e.V. Köln: Westdeutscher Rundfunk, 1969.

5258   Ahrens, A. W. "Characteristic limitations of the internal tuning of selected wind instruments as played by amateurs." *Journal of Experimental Education* 15 (1947): 268–290.

5259   Alexander, A. "Die Stimmungsdifferenzen bei 3-ventiligen Blechblasinstrumenten und ihre Ursachen." *Zeitschrift für Instrumentenbau* 23 (1902/03): 997–998.

5260   Altenburg, Wilhelm. "Ein kleines Nachtrag zu dem Artikel über das System Mahillon-Pupeschi in Nr. 18." *Zeitschrift für Instrumentenbau* 13 (1892/93): 649–650.

5261   Altenburg, Wilhelm. "Material und Klang bei den Blasinstrumenten; das sogenannte 'Einblasen' und 'Verblasen.' " *Zeitschrift für Instrumentenbau* 31 (1910/11): 458–461, 491–494.

5262   Altenburg, Wilhelm. "Nahtlose konische Röhren für Metall-Blasinstrumente." *Zeitschrift für Instrumentenbau* 28 (1907/08): 906–907.

5263   Altenburg, Wilhelm. "Reinklingende Blechblasinstrumente und deren Herstellung durch W. Heckel in Biebrick." *Zeitschrift für Instrumentenbau* 23 (1902/03): 4.

5264   Altenburg, Wilhelm. "Die Umgestaltung des Metall-Blasinstrumentenbaues durch F. V. Cerveny." *Zeitschrift für Instrumentenbau* 11, nos. 4, 5 (1890–91).

5265   Altenburg, Wilhelm. "Die Vervollkommnung des Blechinstrumentenbaues durch die Firma C. Mahillon." *Zeitschrift für Instrumentenbau* 14 (1893/94): 127–128.

5266   Altenburg, Wilhelm. "Zur Kenntnis des 'Sudrophone.' " *Zeitschrift für Instrumentenbau* 27 (1906/07): 517–518.

5267   Bach, Vincent. "Blasinstrumente und ihre Stimmung. Nochmals: Können Blasinstrumente verblasen werden?" *Das Musikinstrument und Phono* 7 (1958): 74+.

5268   Bach, Vincent. "Brass intonation. Can brass instruments be blown out of tune?" *The Instrumentalist* 12 (Jan. 1958): 53–54+.

5269   Bach, Vincent. "Do you know your brasses?" *The Instrumentalist* 4 (Jan. 1950): 20–21; (Mar. 1950): 50–51.

5270   Bach, Vincent. "Know your brasses." *The Instrumentalist* 5 (Nov. 1950): 27+.

5271   Bach, Vincent. "Problems in intonation of brass instruments." *Symphony* 4 (Sept. 1950): 9–10.

Bach, Vincent. "The proper care of a brass instrument." *Metronome* 45 (July 1929): 20; (Aug. 1929): 23+.

5272   Bahnert, H., and others. *Metallblasinstrumente*. Wilhelmshaven: Hein-
        richshofen: 1986.

5273   Bahr, Edward R. "Some notes on the early valve." *The Galpin Society Journal*
        33 (Mar. 1980): 111–124.

        Baines, Anthony. *Brass instruments: their history and development*. London:
        Faber & Faber, 1976.

        Baines, Anthony. "Brass instruments: their history and development."
        International Trumpet Guild Newsletter 5, no. 3 (1979): 19–21.

        Baines, Anthony. "James Talbot's manuscript." *The Galpin Society Journal*
        1 (1948): 9–26.

5274   Beauchamp, James W. "Brass tone synthesis by spectrum evolution match-
        ing with non-linear functions." *Computer Music Journal* 3, no. 2 (1979):
        35–43.

5275   Beihoff, N., and F. Reis. "Bore of Brass Instruments." *The School Musician*
        23 (Dec. 1951): 37.

5276   "Beitrag zur Normung der Blechblasinstrumente." *Instrumentenbau-Zeit-
        schrift* 4 (1949–50): 154.

5277   Benade, Arthur H. *Acoustics of musical wind instruments*. Abstract in *Research
        at Case*. Cleveland: Case Institute of Technology, 1961.

5278   Benade, Arthur H. "Les cuivres." In *Sons et musique*, 62–73. 1979.

5279   Berger, E. "Zur Konstruktion der Blechblasinstrumente." *Zeitschrift für In-
        strumentenbau* 63 (1943): 6.

5280   "Beweglicher Verschluss von Tonlöchern." *Instrumentenbau-Zeitschrift* 25
        (May 1971): 348+.

5281   Blaikley, D. F. "On quality of tone in wind instruments." *Proceedings of the
        Musical Association* 6 (1879/80): 79–90.

5282   Blaikley, D. F. "On the velocity of sound in air." *Proceedings of the Musical
        Association* 9 (1882/83): 147–157.

5283   Blaikley, D. J. "Communication respecting a point in the theory of brass
        instruments." *Proceedings of the Musical Association* 4 (1877/78): 56–67.

5284   Blaikley, D. J. "How a trumpet is made." *The Musical Times* 51 (1910): 14–
        16, 82–84, 154–157, 223–225, erratum 332.

5285   Blandford, W. F. H. "The intonation of brass instruments." *The Musical
        Times* 77 (1936): 19–21, 118–121.

5286   "Blasinstrumente aus Holz und Metall." *Instrumentenbau-Zeitschrift* 8 (1953–
        54): 142–143.

5287   "Blasinstrumente ohne Ventile." *Deutsche Militär-Musiker Zeitung* 30 (1908):
        590. [Invention of J. Löw].

5288   "Blechbläser, mal herhören. Reinigen und Desinfizieren von Metallblas-
        instrumenten." *Deutsche Militär-Musiker-Zeitung* 64 (1942).

5289   Blume, N. W. "First aid for ailing brass." *Etude* 67 (Nov. 1949): 12.

        Boeringer, J., ed. "Instruments like those of the Twenty-Sixth Regimental
        Band: a catalogue of the Mark Allen Elrod Collection." *The Moravian
        Music Foundation Bulletin* 26, no. 3 (1981): 55–57.

5290   Borst, A. "Die Entwicklung des Blasinstrumentenbaues." *Das Musikin-*

strument und Phono 7 (1958): 76.

5291　Bouasse, Henri. *Instruments à vent. Vol. I: Anches metalliques et membraneuses. Tuyaux à anche et à bouche. Orgue. Instruments à embouchure de cor.* Paris: n.p., 1929.

5292　Bouasse, Henri. *Instruments à vent. Vol. II: Instruments à piston, à anche, à embouchure de flute.* Collaboration with M. Fouché. Paris: n.p., 1930.

5293　Bouasse, Henri. *Tuyaux et résonateurs; introduction à l'étude des instruments à vent.* Avec la collaboration experimentale par M. Fouché. Paris: Librarie Delagrave, 1929.

5294　Bowsher, J. M., and P. S. Watkinson. "Manufacturers' opinions about brass instruments [catalog excerpts]." *Brass Bulletin—International Brass Chronicle,* no. 38 (1982): 25–30. Also in French and German.

5295　"Boys and brass." *Music in Education* 31, no. 327 (1967): 579.

5296　Brand, Erick D. *Selmer band instrument repairing manual.* Elkhart, Ind.: H. & A. Selmer, 1959.

　　　Brass band tuning. Reprinted from the *Brass Band News.* Liverpool: Wright & Round, 1933.

　　　"Brass instruments—their improvement during the last century." *Musician* 27 (Feb. 1922): 19.

5297　"Brass vs. plastic [piston valve guides in brass instruments]." *The Instrumentalist* 35 (Sept. 1980): 115.

5298　"British Music Fair: woodwind reeds and brass." *Melody Maker* 55 (Aug. 16, 1980): 33.

　　　"Broadcasting brass [viewpoints from producers and musicians]." *Brass International* 10, no. 2 (1982): 4–7+.

5299　Burns, J. M. "Dissertation reviews: Some acoustical principles affecting the intonation of brass instruments." *Journal of the International Trumpet Guild* 10, no. 3 (1986): 23–24.

5300　"Can a brass wind instrument be blown permanently out of tune?" *Musician* 26 (Aug. 1921): 22.

5301　Cerveny, V. F. *Notice sur les progrès réalisés dans la fabrication des instruments de cuivre par la maison V. F. Cerveny.* Paris: n.p., 1889.

　　　Clappé, Arthur A. *The wind-band and its instruments; their history, construction, acoustics, technique and combination.* New York: H. Holt and Co., 1911.

　　　Clappé, Arthur A. *The wind-band and its instruments: their history, construction, acoustics, technique, and combination.* Reprint of the 1911 edition (New York: H. Holt). Portland, Me.: Longwood, 1976.

5302　"Computer errechnet Stimmung der Metallblasinstrumente." *Instrumentenbau-Zeitschrift* 27, no. 11 (1973): 702+.

5303　"Conn builds models of sound waves in search for ideal cornet design." *Musicana* 29 (May-June 1955): 16–17.

5304　"Conn photographs sound." *Music Dealer* 9 (Mar. 1955): 19–20.

　　　Conner, Rex A. "Valve clatter: its prevention and cure." *T.U.B.A. Newsletter* 2, no. 3 (Spring 1975): 3.

Cuthbert, Frank. "Take care of your instrument." In *Brass Today*. Edited by Frank Wright, 117–119. London: Besson, 1957.

5305 Dahlqvist, Rene. "Some notes on the early valve." *The Galpin Society Journal* 33 (1980): 111–124.

5306 "Darauf dommt es bei unseren Blasinstrumenten an." *Instrumentenbau Musik International* 33 (July 1979): 523–524.

De Lagueronniere, C. "Some instruments to be included in jazz exhibit [photo essay]." *The Second Line* 35 (Winter 1983): 22–23.

5307 Dekan, Karel. "Auswertung von musikalischen Dynamikbereichen bei verschiedenen Blechblas-Instrumentenspielern und die Klangfarbeänderungen bei Piano, Mezzo-forte and Forte." *IMS Report* 1972 (RILM76 179): 351–355.

5308 Diamond, R. M. "Instrument repair—the programed independent learning approach." *The Instrumentalist* (Sept. 1970): 46–47.

Draper, F. C. "The development of brass wind instruments." In *Brass Today*. Edited by Frank Wright, 90–99. London: Besson, 1957.

5309 Draper, F. C. *Notes on the Boosey & Hawkes system of automatic compensation of valved brass wind instruments*. London: Boosey & Hawkes, 1953.

5310 Drechsel, F. A. "Akustik der Blasinstrumente." *Zeitschrift für Instrumentenbau* 47 (1926–1927): 278–280; 319–322; 363–365; 406–408; 462–464.

5311 Drechsel, F. A. *Zur Akustik der Blasinstrumente*. Leipzig: P. de Wit, 1927.

5312 Dullat, G. "Reminiszenzen an modifizierte Drehventile: Patentierte Kuriositäten oder verpasste Chancen?" *Brass Bulletin—International Brass Chronicle*, no. 58 (1987): 18–27. Also in English and French.

5313 Dumont, A. "La fabrication des instruments de musique en cuivre." *Musique & Instruments* 20 (1929): 1205+.

5314 Dundas, R. J. *Twentieth century brass musical instruments in the United States*. Cincinnati, OH: Queen City Brass Publications, 1986.

5315 Dunstan, Ralph D. "Some acoustical properties of wind instruments." *Proceedings of the Musical Association* 44 (1917/18): 53–70.

5316 Durant, Felicien. "Instruments en cuivre omnitoniques à 6 pistons dependants." In *Report of the Fourth Congress of the International Musical Society, London . . . 1911*. London: Novello, 1912.

"East and west [rebuilding of brass instruments and use in historical musical performance]." *Brass Bulletin—International Brass Chronicle*, no. 57 (1987): News Suppl. 6. Also in French and German.

5317 Ecker, K. "Making and testing brass instruments." *The Instrumentalist* 15 (Oct. 1960): 64–65+.

5318 Edney, J. "Beginners' page." *Sounding Brass & the Conductor* 4, no. 3 (1975): 96.

5319 Effner, R. "Der störungsfreie Verlauf des Luftganges im Körpersystem der gebogenen Blechblasinstrumente." *Deutsche Instrumentenbau Zeitschrift* 42 (1941): 104.

Ehmann, Wilhelm. "Formen und Reformen des Blasens." *Neue Zeitschrift für Musik* 118 (1957): 522–524.

5320   Eichborn, Hermann Ludwig. "Der angebliche Erfinder des Ausgiessens mit Blei im Blechblasinstrumentenbau." *Zeitschrift für Instrumentenbau* 16 (1895/96): 577–579, 606.

5321   Eichborn, Hermann Ludwig. "Schlusswort in der Discussion mit Herrn Mahillon über Lippenblasinstrumente mit nur schallverstärkend, nicht tonbildend wirkendem Rohr." *Zeitschrift für Instrumentenbau* 16 (1895/96): 742–743.

5322   Eichborn, Hermann Ludwig. *Ueber das Octavierungs-princip bei Blechinstrumenten insbesondere bei Waldhörnern.* Leipzig: P. de Wit, 1889.

5323   Eickmann, Paul E., and Nancy L. Hamilton. *Basic acoustics for beginning brass.* Syracuse: Center for Instructional Development, Syracuse University, 1976.

       Eliason, Robert E. "Brass instrument key and valve mechanisms made in America before 1875 with special reference to the D. S. Pillsbury collection in Greenfield Village, Dearborn, Michigan." *Dissertation Abstracts* 29 (May 1969): 4036A–4037A.

       Eliason, Robert E. "Brass instrument key and valve mechanisms made in America before 1875, with special reference to the D. S. Pillsbury Collection in Greenfield Village, Dearborn, Michigan." D.M.A. diss., University of Missouri (Kansas City), 1969.

5324   Eliason, Robert E. "Brasses with both keys and valves." *Journal of the American Musical Instrument Society* 2 (1976): 69–85.

5325   Eliason, Robert E. "Dissertation: Brass instrument key and valve mechanisms made in America before 1875, with special reference to the D. S. Pillsbury Collection in Greenfield Village, Dearborn, Michigan [abstract]." *Monthly Journal of Research in Music Education* 2, no. 3 (1969): 81–82.

       Eliason, Robert E. *Early American brass makers.* Brass Research Series. Nashville: Brass Press, 1979.

       Eliason, Robert E. "Early American brass makers." *Music Educators Journal* 66 (Sept. 1979): 89.

       Eliason, Robert E. "Early American valves for brass instruments." *The Galpin Society Journal* 23 (Aug. 1970): 86–96.

5326   Eliason, Robert E. "The Meachams, musical instrument makers of Hartford and Albany [includes list of known Meacham instruments]." *Journal of the American Musical Instrument Society* 5 (1980–81): 69–70.

5327   Elliott, C. A. "Attacks and releases as factors in instrument identification." *Journal of Research in Music Education* 23, no. 1 (1975): 35–40.

5328   Engelmann, G. "Erwiderung auf die Ueberlegungen zum Thema Blechbläser." *Das Orchester* 26 (Mar. 1978): 212.

5329   Ewers, Karl. "Zur Frage des Alts im Blasorchester. Die 'Lurette' als Beitrag zur Lösung des Problems." *Die Musik-Woche* 6 (1938): 742.

5330   "Fabrication des Instruments en cuivre." *Schweizerische Instrumentalmusik* 27 (1938): 160.

5331   Fahrbach, P. "Andeutungen in Bezug auf eine reinere Construction und

Intonation der Metallinstrumente." *Allgemeine Wiener Musikzeitung* 3 (1843): 86–87.

5332 Fahrbach, P. "Ueber die Construction der Blasinstrumente." *Allgemeine Wiener Musikzeitung* 3 (1843): 413–414, 421–422, 434–435.

5333 Farrar, Lloyd P. "Under the crown & eagle [Schreiber Cornet Manufacturing Company]." *Newsletter of the American Musical Instrument Society* 14, no. 3 (1985): 4–5.

5334 Faulkner, Maurice. "Brass tone color [analysis of major European symphony orchestras]." *The Instrumentalist* 19 (Jan. 1965): 24–27 + .

5335 Faulkner, Maurice. "False security [problems concerning embouchure]." *The Instrumentalist* 20 (Oct. 1965): 74.

5336 Faulkner, Maurice. "Problems of brass intonation." *The Instrumentalist* 20 (Nov. 1965): 69–73.

5337 Fenner, Klaus. "Forschung für oder gegen die Praxis." *Das Musikinstrument* 22, no. 9 (1973).

5338 Ferron, E. "De la sensibilite des instruments de cuivre." *Brass Bulletin— International Brass Chronicle*, no. 30 (1980): 57–60. Also in German and English.

5339 Fisher, R. "How to put brass in a band." *American Machinist* 94 (May 15, 1950): 89–93.

5340 Fladmoe, G. G. "The contributions to brass instrument manufacturing of Vincent Bach, Carl Geyer, and Renold Schilke." *Dissertation Abstracts* 36 (Mar. 1976): 5904A-5905A.

5341 Fletcher, H. "Loudness, pitch and the timbre of musical tones and their relation to the intensity, the frequency and the overtone structure." *Journal of the Acoustical Society of America* 6 (1934–35): 59–69.

5342 Fletcher, H. "Newer concepts of pitch, the loudness and timbre of musical tones." *Journal of the Franklin Institute* 220 (1935): 405–429.

5343 Flor, G. J., ed. "Brass workshop: Making emergency repairs." *The School Musician* 54 (Aug.-Sept. 1982): 30–31.

5344 Flor, G. J. "Compensating devices in brass instruments." *The School Musician* 46 (Nov. 1974): 16 + .

5345 Flor, G. J. "The 'frumpet' and other marching band oddities." *The School Musician* 51 (Aug.-Sept. 1979): 24–25.

5346 Forestier. *Monographie des instruments à six pistons et tubes independants.* Paris: n.p., 1870.

5347 "Fortschrittlicher Blechblasinstrumentenbau." *Instrumentenbau-Zeitschrift* 3 (1948–49): 97.

Garofalo, R. "Using visual aids to teach the acoustical principles of brass instruments." *The Instrumentalist* 24 (Nov. 1969): 77–79).

5348 Geringer, John W., and Clifford Madsen. "Preferences for trumpet tone quality versus intonation." *Council for Research in Music Education Bulletin* 46 (Spring 1976): 13–22.

5349 "Getzen Company celebrates its 40th anniversary in brass." *Woodwind World—Brass and Percussion* 18, no. 6 (1979): 32–33.

5350   Gihle, O. "Removing dents from brass instruments." *The Instrumentalist* 3 (Nov. 1948): 12.

5351   Gihle, O. "Removing stuck slides from brass instruments." *The Instrumentalist* 2 (May 1948): 17.

5352   Globokar, V. "Entwicklungsmöglichkeiten der Blechblasinstrumente (1967)." *Brass Bulletin—International Brass Chronicle*, no. 5–6 (1973): 15–33. Also in English and French.

5353   Goodwin, J. "Brass instrument research at Surrey University." *Brass Bulletin—International Brass Chronicle*, no. 36 (1982): 8–17. Also in French and German.

5354   Goodwin, J. "Inside story." *Sounding Brass & the Conductor* 9, no. 2 (1980): 24–25.

5355   Greer, Robert Douglas. "The effect of timbre on brass-wind intonation." Ph.D. diss., University of Michigan, 1969.

5356   Guldin, J. "Preventive maintenance, cleaning, and handling." *The Instrumentalist* 34 (July 1980): 36 + .

5357   Hachenberg, K. "Korrosionserscheinungen an Blechblasinstrumenten aus Messing." *Musik International-Instrumentenbau-Zeitschrift* 40 (May 1986): 388–389.

5358   Hachenberg, K. "Korrosionserscheinungen: Punkt- und flächenförmige Korrosionserscheinungen an Blechblasinstrumenten aus Messing." *Brass Bulletin—International Brass Chronicle*, no. 54 (1986): 99–102. Also in English and French.

5359   Hague, Bernard. "The tonal spectra of wind instruments." *Proceedings of the Royal Musical Association* 73 (1946–47): 67–83.

5360   Hales, J. A. "Pre-season maintenance for brass instruments." *Music Educators Journal* 66 (Sept. 1979): 54–55.

5361   Hall, Jody C., and E. L. Kent. "Relationships between wind instruments timbre and sound spectra." *Journal of The Acoustical Society of America* 32 (1960) 935. Abstract.

5362   Hall, Jody C., and E. L. Kent. *The effect of temperature on the tuning standards of wind instruments.* Elkhart, Ind.: C. G. Conn, 1959.

5363   Hamblen, D. "Rotary valves are American." *Music Journal* 20, no. 3 (Mar. 1962): 58.

5364   Hamilton, D. "The Wagnerian orchestra." *San Francisco Opera Magazine*, no. 10 (Fall 1981): 45–48 + .

5365   Hardin, Burton E. "Character of the French horn." *The Instrumentalist* 19 (Feb. 1965): 32 + .

        Hart, G. "Bemerkungen über ältere Blasinstrumentenmacher." *Instrumentenbau-Zeitschrift* 15 (1961): 163–166.

5366   Hayes, C. "What's playing '78: brass and woodwind [British Musical Instrument Trade Fair]." *Melody Maker* 53 (Aug. 12, 1978): 40–41.

5367   Heath, R. C. "For a better brass sound." *The Instrumentalist* 27 (Mar. 1973): 22 + .

5368   Herrick, D. R. "An investigation of the frequency modulations and intensity modulations of the vibrato on selected brass instruments." *Dissertation Abstracts* 44 (Feb. 1984): 2400A.

5369 Heyde, Herbert. "Zur Frühgeschichte der Ventile und Ventilinstrumente in Deutschland (1814–1833)." *Brass Bulletin—International Brass Chronicle*, no. 26 (1979): 83–85+. Also in English and French.

5370 Hickernell, Ross. "On the care of the cornet and other brass instruments." *Cadenza* 5, no. 11 (1914): 76–79.

5371 "Hilfsgriffe une Hilfsventile bei Blechblasinstrumenten." *Musikhandel* 17, no. 7 (1966): 328.

5372 Hindsley, Mark H. "Valve-brass intonation difficulties conquered." *The Instrumentalist* 7 (Jan.-Feb. 1953): 24–25+.

5373 "Hirsbrunner brass winds." *Music Journal* 37 (Nov.–Dec. 1979): 32.

5374 Hoffman, H.-U. "Wie entsteht ein Blechblasinstrumente? Besuch in einer Klingenthaler Instrumentenfabrik." *Zeitschrift für Instrumentenbau* 59 (1938–39): 98–100.

5375 Holland, J. "Pitch finder." *Brass Bulletin—International Brass Chronicle*, no. 46 (1984): 58–61. Also in French and German.

5376 Horvath, Helmuth. "Die physikalischen Aspekte der Blasinstrumente." *Oesterreichische Musikzeitschrift* 27, no. 12 (1972): 649–657.

5377 Hüttl, A. R. "More ease of blowing with brass wind instruments." *Instrumentenbau-Zeitschrift* 25 (June 1971): 305.

5378 "Hydraulic forming techniques applied in the manufacture of musical instruments." *Machinery* (London) 82 (1953): 1080–1099, 1194–1196.

5379 "Instrument makers in Europe: Kalison (Milan)." *Brass Bulletin—International Brass Chronicle*, no. 60 (1987): 52–55. Also in French and German.

5380 Ischer, R. "Pistons ou cylindres?" *Brass Bulletin—International Brass Chronicle*, no. 13 (1976): 55–59. Also in English and German.

5381 Ischer, R. "Service apres-vente." *Brass Bulletin—International Brass Chronicle*, no. 21 (1978): 41–43. Also in English and German.

Jäger, J. "Ansatz und Atmung bei Blechbläsern." *Das Orchester* 28 (Sept. 1980): 693–696.

5382 Jäger, J. "Grundfragen des Blechblaseransatzes am Beispiel der Posaune." *Beiträge der Musikwissenschaft* 13, no. 1 (1971): 56–73.

5383 Jansson, Erik V., and Arthur H. Benade. "On plane and spherical waves in horns with non-uniform flare: prediction and measurements of resonance frequencies and radiation losses." *Acustica* 31, no. 4 (Oct. 1974): 185–202.

5384 Jansson, Erik V. "On the acoustics of musical instruments." In *Music, room and acoustics*, 82–113. 1977.

5385 Jenkins, M. "Control zone: brass [brass and wind manufacturers and dealers at the British Music Fair]." *Brass Bulletin—International Brass Chronicle*, no. 61 (1986): 38.

Johnson, K. M. "Basic intonation for brass instruments." *NACWPI Journal* 34, no. 4 (1986): 8–10.

5386 Jung, K. "Zur Theorie der Seitenbohrungen an Blechblasinstrumenten."

Des Musikinstrument 11 (1962): 332–333.

5387   Kaden, H. *Ueber die Beseitigung unreinen Töne der Messinginstrumente, Klarinette und Flöte*. 3. Auss. Hannover: Lehne, [1898].

5388   Kalähne, A. "Schallerzeugung mit mechanischen Mitteln." In *Handbuch der Physik*, vol. VIII, edited by Geigerscheel. Berlin: n.p., 1927.

5389   Kent, Earle L. *The inside story of brass instruments*. Elkhart, Ind.: C. G. Conn, 1956.

Kent, Earle L., and R. P. Iazure. "Studies of cup-mouthpiece tone quality." *Journal of The Acoustical Society of America* 31 (1959): 130. Abstract.

5390   Kirschner, F. "Valve springs." *Musical Merchandise Review* 117 (Jan. 1958): 40.

5391   "Kolbenventil für Blechblasinstrumente." *Instrumentenbau-Zeitschrift* 25 (Dec. 1971): 562.

5392   "Korrosionsfestes Ventil für Metallblasinstrumente." *Instrumentenbau Musik International* 31, no. 10 (1977): 668.

Kramer, S. "Eine praktische Neuerung zur Reinigung und Disinfektion von Metallblasmusikinstrumenten." *Archiv für Hygiene* 125 (1939–40): 347–353.

5393   Krebs, Gustav. "Die Legierungen für Blechinstrumente." *Zeitschrift für Instrumentenbau* 46 (1925–1926): 576–577.

5394   Kroll, Oskar. "Doppeltöne auf Blasinstrumenten." *Das Orchester* 9 (1932): 66.

5395   Kroll, Oskar. "Kleine Fereinreise zu deutschen Instrumentenmachern. Werdegang eines Blechblasinstruments." *Die Musik-Woche* 4, no. 40 (1936): 9–12.

5396   Krüger, Walther. "Anforderungen an den heutigen Blasinstrumentenbau unter Berücksichtigung der Aufführungspraxis von Musik des 18. Jahrhunderts." In *Bericht über das 1. Symposium zu Fragen der Anforderungen an den Instrumentenbau: Blankenburg/Harz, 31 Mai 1980*, edited by Eitelfriedrich Thom and Renate Bormann, 10–13. Magdeburg: Rat des Bezirkes, 1980.

Kurka, Martin J. "A study of the acoustical effects of mutes on wind instruments." Master's thesis, University of South Dakota, 1958.

Kurka, Martin J. *A study of the acoustical effects of mutes on wind instruments*. F. E. Olds Music Education Library. Fullerton, Cal.: F. E. Olds, 1961.

Kusinski, J. S. "The effect of mouthpiece cup depth and backbore shape on listeners' categorizations of tone quality in recorded trumpet excerpts." *Dissertation Abstracts* 45 (Oct. 1984): 1065A.

5397   "Die Lage im Blechblasinstrumentenbau." *Instrumentenbau-Zeitschrift* 1 (1946–47): 4–5.

Langwill, Lyndesay G. *An index of musical wind-instrument makers*. Edinburgh: The Author, 1960.

Langwill, Lyndesay G. *An index of musical wind-instrument makers*. Second enlarged edition. Edinburgh: The Author, 1962.

Langwill, Lyndesay G. *An index of musical wind-instrument makers*. Edinburgh: The Author, 1972.

Langwill, Lyndesay G. "Instrument-making in Paris in 1839." *Music & Letters* 39 (1958): 135–138.

Langwill, Lyndesay G. "London wind-instrument makers of the seventeenth and eighteenth centuries." *Music Review* 7 (1946): 88–102.

Langwill, Lyndesay G. *Wood-wind and brass instrument makers.* Edinburgh: The Author, 1941.

5398   Laurent, Etienne. "La facture moderne des instruments à vent." *Musique & Radio* 42 (1952): 185–186.

Lewis, Frederic James. "The care, repair, and selection of musical instruments for the instrumental music teacher." Master's thesis, University of Southern California, 1956.

5399   Lieber, E. "Ermittlung der Naturtonlagen bei Metall-blasinstrumenten." *Hochfrequenztechnik u. Elektroakustik; Jahrbuch der drahtlosen Telegraphie und Telephonie* 69 (1960): 29–34.

5400   Limac, O. L. "Die neuen Blechblasinstrumente." *Zeitschrift für Instrumentenbau* 42 (1921/22): 334–335.

5401   Limac, O. L. "Ueber die Anwendung des 4. Ventils bei Blechblasinstrumenten." *Deutsche Militär-Musiker Zeitung* 31 (1909): 58–59.

5402   Limac, O. L. "Wann stimmt ein Blasinstrument rein?" *Deutsche Militär-Musiker Zeitung* 31 (1909): 58–59.

5403   Limmer, R. "Blechblasinstrumente aus der Musikstadt Graslitz." *Brass Bulletin—International Brass Chronicle*, no. 29 (1980): 41 + . Also in French and English.

Lindlien, Doran Royce. "The design and use of video tape in teaching students the basic care and maintenance of the primary wind instruments." D.M.A. diss., University of Oregon, 1979.

5404   Long, T. H. "On the performance of cup mouthpiece instruments." *Journal of the Acoustical Society of America* 20 (1948): 875–876.

5405   Long, T. H. "The performance of cup mouthpiece instruments." *Journal of the Acoustical Society of America* 19 (1947): 723.

5406   Long, T. H. "The performance of cup-mouthpiece instruments." *Journal of the Acoustical Society of America* 19 (1947): 892–901.

5407   Loomis, Allen, and H. W. Schwartz. "Making musical instruments." *Metronome* 45 (Nov. 1929): 32–33.

5408   Loomis, Allen, and H. W. Schwartz. "Making one length of tubing produce many notes." *Metronome* 45 (Feb. 1929): 22 + .

5409   Loomis, Allen, and H. W. Schwartz. "Resonance—or why is a horn?" *Metronome* 45 (Jan. 1929): 37 + .

5410   Loomis, Allen, and H. W. Schwartz. "Tone quality—what makes it?" *Metronome* 45 (Sept. 1929): 59 + .

5411   Lorenz, Eduard. "Beitrag zum Problem: Zylinder-Maschinen für Blechblasinstrumente." *Instrumentenbau-Zeitschrift* 6 (1952): 52–54, 89.

5412   McCready, Matthew A. "Compensating systems: a mathematical comparison." *T.U.B.A. Journal* 12, no. 3 (Feb. 1985): 11–13.

McCready, Matthew A. "Compensating systems: an historical overview." *T.U.B.A. Journal* 10, no. 4 (Spring 1983): 5–6.

5413 McGavin, E., comp. *A guide to the purchase and care of woodwind and brass instruments*. Bromley, England: Schools Music Association, 1966.

5414 McGuffey, P. "Brass pitch in depth." *The Instrumentalist* 27 (June 1968): 34+.

5415 Mahillon, Victor Charles. *Guide pour l'accord des instruments à pistons*. Brussels: C. Mahillon, [189-?].

5416 [Mahillon, Victor Charles]. "Instruments à pistons." *L'Echo musical* 5, no. 12 (18 Dec. 1873).

5417 [Mahillon, Victor Charles]. "Théorie des pistons." *L'Echo musical* 2, no. 9 (15 Sept. 1870).

5418 "The making of a horn. A visit to the plant of Brua C. Keefer." *Metronome* 39 (Sept. 1923): 137+.

5419 Mang, Walter. "Zur Tonreinheit der Blechblasinstrumente." *Instrumenten-bau-Zeitschrift* 2 (1947–48): 101–102.

5420 Mann, Julius. "Herstellung von Drückformen für den Metall-Blasinstrumentenbau im Kopierdrehverfahren." *Zeitschrift für Instrumentenbau* 50 (1929–1930): 484–485.

5421 Markle, R. "Instrument care and repair." *The Instrumentalist* 17 (Nov. 1962): 12.

5422 Martin, Daniel W. "Directivity and the acoustic spectra of brass wind instruments." *Journal of the Acoustical Society of America* 13 (1942): 309–313.

5423 Martin, Daniel W. "A mechanical playing device for brass wind instruments." *Journal of the Acoustical Society of America* 12 (1941): 467.

5424 Martin, Daniel W. "A physical investigation of the performance of brass musical wind instruments." Ph.D. diss., University of Illinois, 1941.

5425 Matzke, H. "Von den alten Luren—Betrachtungen anlässlich des Neubaus von 'Ventilluren.'" *Zeitschrift für Instrumentenbau* 56 (1935–36): 150–151.

5426 Meifred, P. -J. "Notice sur la fabrication des instruments de musique en cuivre en général et sur celle du cor en particulier." In *Annuaire de la Société des anciens élèves des ecoles nationales des arts-et-métiers* (1851).

5427 Meinel, H. "Zum 'Verblasen' der Blasinstrumente und 'Einspielen' der Streich- und Zupfinstrumente." *Das Musikinstrument und Phono* 6 (1957): 147.

5428 Melich, J. "Ich möchte gleich vorausstellen, dass ein Blechblasinstrument im Sinne des Musikers nicht verblasen werden kann." *Das Musikinstrument und Phono* 6 (1957): 147–148.

5429 Menzel, Ursula. "Die Anwendung traditioneller Techniken bei der Restaurierung historischer Blechblasinstrumente." *Musical Instrument Conservation and Technology Journal* (RILM78 157): 31–38.

5430 Menzel, Ursula. "Historische Blechblasinstrumente und Restaurierung." *Brass Bulletin—International Brass Chronicle*, no. 39 (1982): 7–12. Also in French and English.

5431 Meyer, E., and G. Buchmann. "Die Klangspektra der Musikinstrumente."

Stizungsberichte der Preussischen Akademie der Wissenschaft (1931): 735–778.

5432 Meyer, Jürgen, and Klaus Wogram. "Forschung—Praxis—Falsche Thesen." *Das Musikinstrument* 23, no. 8 (1974): 1004–1005.

5433 Michaels, A. J. "A close look at tarnish." *The Instrumentalist* 34 (Aug. 1979): 10–11.

Miles, Edgar M. "Beat elimination as a means of teaching intonation to beginning wind instrumentalists." *Journal of Research in Music Education* 20, no. 4 (Winter 1972): 496–500.

5434 Mincarelli, A. D. "The sound of brass." *Brass and Percussion* 1, no. 2 (1973) 21+.

5435 "Eine moderne Blechblasinstrumentenfabrik." *Instrumentenbau-Zeitschrift* 3 (1948–49): 122.

5436 Moffitt, R. Easton. "A study of intonation tendencies of certain instruments playing at different dynamic levels." Master's thesis, Brigham Young University, 1949.

Monke, W. "Eine Erfindung setzt sich durch: Über die 150 jährige Geschichte des Metallblasinstrumentenventils." *Musikhandel* 16, no. 3 (1965): 98–99.

5437 Montagu, Jeremy. "Choosing brass instruments [includes list of brass instrument makers and dealers]." *Early Music* 4, no. 1 (1976): 35–38.

5438 Montagu, Jeremy. "Distinctions among the aerophones." *The Galpin Society Journal* 24 (July 1971): 106–108.

5439 Montagu, Jeremy. "Nuremburg conference on restoration." *Early Music* 2, no. 4 (1974): 265+.

Moore, Ward. "Tone color in brasses." *The Instrumentalist* 6 (Sept. 1951): 40.

"Musiker diskutierten mit Herstellern." *Instrumentenbau-Zeitschrift* 24 (Aug. 1970): 468+.

"Musiker diskutierten mit Herstellern; Markneukirchener Musiktage 1970." *Instrumentenbau-Zeitschrift* 24 (Aug. 1970): 468+.

5440 "La musique et le micro." *Musique & Instruments* 20 (1934): 101+, 149+, 205+.

Nakayama, F. "Painting from the 18th century [Chinese-derived brass played at the Okinawan court]." *Brass Bulletin—International Brass Chronicle*, no. 35 (1981): 44–45. Also in French and German.

5441 Nasse, M. "Von der Trompete bis zur Riesen-Tuba." *Zeitschrift für Instrumentenbau* 55 (1934–35): 179.

5442 "Die 'neuen' Blechblasinstrumente." *Deutsche Militär-Musiker Zeitung* 48 (191?): 14.

5443 "Die neuen Marsch-Musikinstrumente der K. K. österreichischen Landwehr nach dem System von V. F. Cerveny und Söhne." *Zeitschrift für Instrumentenbau* 30 (1909/10): 668–670.

5444 "Neuerung an Blechblasinstrumenten." *Zeitschrift für Instrumentenbau* 50 (1929–1930): 682.

5445 "Neuerungen im Maschinenbau für Blechblasinstrumente." *Instrumenten-*

bau-Zeitschrift 4 (1949–50): 19–20.

5446 "Neues aus der Arbeit an Metallblasinstrumenten und Gitarren." *Instrumentenbau-Zeitschrift* 24 (Nov. 1970): 585–586.

5447 "Ein neues Tonwechselventil: Das Richter'sche Tonwechselventil von Schuster & Co. in Markneukirchen." *Zeitschrift für Instrumentenbau* 18 (1897/98): 577.

5448 "New valves [Thayer rotary]." *Brass Bulletin—International Brass Chronicle*, no. 58 (News Suppl. 1987): 5. Also in French and German.

Nickel, Ekkehart. *Der Holzblas-Instrumentenbau in der Freien Reichsstadt Nürnberg*. Munich: Katzbichler, 1971.

5449 Nödl, Carl. "Klangcharakter und Vibration der Blechblasinstrumente." *Deutsche Instrumentenbau Zeitschrift* 39 (1938): 260, 262.

5450 Nödl, Carl. "Ueber Maschinen der Blechblasinstrumente." *Deutsche Instrumentenbau Zeitschrift* 39 (1938): 260.

5451 Nödl, Carl. "Wiederaufbau des Metallblasinstrumentenbaues." *Instrumentenbau-Zeitschrift* 2 (1947–48): 73–74.

5452 Nödl, Karl. "Anregung zur Normung in Metallblasinstrumenten-Bau." *Deutsche Instrumentenbau Zeitschrift* 41 (1940): 28, 64.

5453 Nödl, Karl. "Geschichtliche Entwicklung der Blechblasinstrumentenindustrie und der Niedergang der Instrumentalindustrie in Wien." *Graslitzer Volksblatt* (1936).

5454 Nödl, Karl. *Metallblasinstrumentenbau; ein Fach- und Lehrbuch über die handwerkliche Herstellung von Metallblasinstrumenten*. n.p.: Landesinnungsverband des Bayerischen Musikinstrumentenmacher-Handwerks, 1970.

5455 Nödl, Karl. "Neues aus dem Blechblasinstrumenten-Bau." *Deutsche Instrumentenbau Zeitschrift* 42 (1941): 84.

5456 Nonnenberg, W. "Können Blasinstrumente verblasen werden?" *Das Musikinstrument und Phono* 6 (1957): 180.

5457 "Un nouveau progrès instrumental." *L'Echo musical* 18 (1886): 49–52.

5458 Novy, D. "A new acoustical formula for better brass range, intonation, and response [paper presented at eighth annual NAJE convention]." *NAJE Research* 1 (1981): 65–68.

5459 Olson, R. D. "The bore of brass instruments." *The Instrumentalist* 17 (Jan. 1963): 60–63.

Orval, Francis. "Aperçu sur la fabrication, le chaudronnage et le montage des cuivres naturels anciens et des trompes de vénerie." *Bulletin de la Societe Liégeoise Musicologique* 29 (Apr. 1980): 1–13.

5460 Pepper, J. W. *How to tune piston instruments*. Philadelphia: n.p., 1903.

5461 "Perfectionnements aux pistons d'instruments à vent." *Musique & Instruments* 21 (1935): 125.

5462 Perinelli, R., and J. L. Mouton. "Comment regier sa trompette? (ou tout autre instrument a pistons)." *Brass Bulletin—International Brass Chronicle*, no. 23 (1978): 47–54. Also in English and German.

5463 Pfann, K. "Was müssen wir von unseren instrumenten erwarten?" *Gottesdienst und Kirchenmusik*, no. 5 (Sept.–Oct. 1977): 157–165.

5464   Pratt, R. L., S. J. Elliott, and J. M. Bowsher. "The measurement of the acoustic impedance of brass instruments." *Acustica* 38 (1977): 236–246.

Pressley, E. "Musical wind instruments in the Moravian musical archives, Salem, N.C." D.M.A. diss., University of Kentucky, 1975.

5465   Pruzin, R. S. "Care and maintenance of the rotary valve." *Woodwind World—Brass and Percussion* 14, no. 1 (1975): 33–35.

5466   Pyle, Robert. "Acoustical reverberations." *The Horn Call* 18, no. 1 (Oct. 1987): 42–45.

5467   Pyle, Robert. "Audiopyle: acoustical reverberations." *The Horn Call* 18, no. 2 (Apr. 1988): 80–86.

5468   Raph, A. "Tacit." *Brass and Percussion* 2, no. 2 (1974): 7–8.

5469   Redfield, J. "Certain anomalies in the theory of air column behaviour in orchestral wind instruments." *Journal of the Acoustical Society of America* 6 (1934–35): 34–36.

5470   Redfield, J. "Minimizing discrepancies of intonation in valve instruments." *Journal of the Acoustical Society of America* 3 (1931–32): 292–296.

5471   "Restaurieren von historischen Blechblasinstrumenten." *Musik International-Instrumentenbau-Zeitschrift* 36 (Aug. 1982): 568+.

Revelli, William D. "Choice of instrument a scientific problem." *The Instrumentalist* 6 (Mar.-Apr. 1952): 20+.

5472   "Reviews: Lecture by R. O. Schilke." *Sounding Brass & the Conductor* 6, no. 4 (1978): 138.

Reynolds, G. "Brass maintenance." *The School Musician* 31 (Apr. 1960): 14+.

Reynolds, G. "Factors affecting brass tone quality." *The School Musician* 31 (Feb. 1960): 14+.

Ridley, E. A. K. *Wind instruments of European art music.* Foreword by David M. Boston. London: Inner London Educational Authority, 1974.

Riedl, Alfred. "Graslitzer Blechblasinstrumente und ihre Geschichte." *Instrumentenbau-Zeitschrift* 13 (1959): 274–280.

5473   Roberts, C. "Elements of brass intonation." *The Instrumentalist* 29 (Mar. 1975): 86–90.

5474   Robinson, Trevor. *The amateur wind instrument maker.* Amherst, Mass: University of Massachusetts, 1973.

5475   Robinson, Trevor. *The amateur wind instrument maker.* Revised. Amherst: University of Massachusetts, 1981.

5476   Rohner, Traugott. "Making a perfect valve for brass instruments." *The Instrumentalist* 8 (May 1954): 14–15.

5477   Rometsch. "Ventile an den Blechblasinstrumenten." *Schweizerische Zeitschrift für Instrumentalmusik* 21 (191?): 18.

5478   Rometsch, Alfred. "Die Ventile an den Blechblasinstrumenten." *Allgemeine Volksmusikzeitung* 9 (1959): 289–291.

5479   Rudolph. "Zur Ventilfrage." *Deutsche Musiker-Zeitung* 63 (191?): 41.

Sax, Adolphe. "Un Cartel musical—Les Instruments d'Adolphe Sax." *La Belgique musicale* 7, no. 19 (10 Sept. 1846): 4–8.

5480 Schilke, Renold O. "Leader pipe and its function." *The Instrumentalist* 12 (May 1958): 26–27.

5481 Schirm, Erik. "Ueber ein neues Ventilsystem für Metallblasinstrumente." *Zeitschrift für Instrumentenbau* 33 (1912/13): 913–915.

Schlesinger, Kathleen. "Valves." In *Encyclopaedia Britannica*. 11th ed. New York, 1910–11.

Schulenburg, Robert. "The care of band instruments." *Music Educators Journal* 27 (Sept. 1940): 29–30+.

5482 Schuster, H. M. "Erwiderung auf die Ausführung des Herrn W. Altenburg." *Zeitschrift für Instrumentenbau* 14 (1893/94): 287–288.

Sebby, R. W. "Balancing the brass section of the American concert band." *Woodwind World—Brass and Percussion* 14, no. 2 (1975): 42–43.

5483 [Seifert, R]. "Ein vergessener Erfinder auf dem Gebiete des Blechblasinstrumentenbaues." *Zeitschrift für Instrumentenbau* 16 (1895–96): 497–498.

5484 Sirker, Udo. "Strukturelle Gesetzmässigkeiten in den Spektren von Blasinstrumentenklängen." *Acustica* 30, no. 1 (Jan. 1974): 49–59.

5485 Sirker, Udo. *Timbre in music and its significance in musical hearing*. New York: Audio Engineering Society, 1973.

5486 Sivian, L. J., H. K. Dunn, and S. D. White. "Absolute amplitude and spectra of certain musical instruments and orchestras." *Journal of the Acoustical Society of America* 2 (1930–31): 330–371.

Sluchin, B. "11e Congres International d'Acoustique." *Brass Bulletin—International Brass Chronicle*, no. 44 (1983): 13–15. Also in English and German.

5487 Sluchin, B. "Playing and singing simultaneously on brass instruments: acoustical explanation." *Brass Bulletin—International Brass Chronicle*, no. 37 (1982): 20–28. Also in French and German.

5488 "Ein sonderbarer Angriff auf die Blasinstrumente mit Zylinder-Maschinen." *Zeitschrift für Instrumentenbau* 24 (1903/04): 149–151.

Sordillo, Fortunato. "Peculiarities and inaccuracies of brass instruments." *Metronome* 42 (July 15, 1926): 42.

5489 "Special DDR: VEB Blechblas- und Signalinstrumentenfabrik [tour of the factory in pictures]." *Brass Bulletin—International Brass Chronicle*, no. 60 (1987): 28–32.

5490 "Spezialwerkzeuge für Blasinstrumente." *Instrumentenbau Musik International* 31, no. 6 (1977): 454.

5491 " 'Spitballs' to clean the horn." *Instrumentenbau-Zeitung* 29, no. 1 (1975): 48.

5492 Squires, M. "Sticky valves, stuck slides and other pitfalls." *Music Journal* 33 (Jan. 1975): 33–36.

5493 Stauffer, Donald W. "Intonation deficiencies of wind instruments in ensemble." Ph.D. thesis, Catholic University of America, 1954. Published. Birmingham, AL: Stauffer Press, 1988.

5494 Stauffer, Donald W. *Intonation deficiencies of wind instruments in ensemble*. Washington: Catholic University of America Press, 1954.

5495   Stauffer, Donald W. "Popular misconceptions about instrumental theory and technique." *The Instrumentalist* 15 (May 1961): 39.

5496   Stork, Karl. "Zu einer Blechinstrumentenmacher-Werkstätte. Bei Meister Max Enders in Mainz." *Die Musik-Woche* 6 (1938): 137.

5497   Strevens, P. "Bargain brass." *Making Music*, no. 72 (Spring 1970): 6–8.

5498   Strevens, P. "Warm lacquering." *Making Music*, no. 73 (Summer 1970): 12.

5499   Strong, William, and Melville Clark. "Synthesis of wind-instrument tones." *Journal of the Acoustical Society of America* 41, no. 1 (1967): 39–52.

5500   Struve, K. "Akustik der Blasinstrumente." *Technical Physics of the USSR* 3 (1936): 1045–55. In German.

5501   Suchy, Paul. "Die neue Blechblasinstrumente." *Zeitschrift für Instrumentenbau* 42 (1921/22): 268–269.

5502   Suter, S. "Instrumentenbau in USA [visits to makers]." *Brass Bulletin— International Brass Chronicle*, no. 50 (1985): 18–19+. Also in English and French.

5503   Suter, S. "Instrumentenbau in USA: C. G. Conn Ltd. Abilene, Texas." *Brass Bulletin—International Brass Chronicle*, no. 51 (1985): 54–58. Also in English and French.

5504   Suter, S. "Instrumentenbau in USA: E. K. Blessing Co., Inc., Elkhart, Indiana." *Brass Bulletin—International Brass Chronicle*, no. 56 (1986): 105–107. Also in English and French.

5505   Suter, S. "Instrumentenbau in USA: Getzen Company Inc." *Brass Bulletin—International Brass Chronicle*, no. 54 (1986): 75–78. Also in English and French.

5506   Suter, S. "Instrumentenbau in USA: Holton—G. Leblanc Corporation." *Brass Bulletin—International Brass Chronicle*, no. 53 (1986): 109–112. Also in English and French.

5507   Suter, S. "Instrumentenbau in USA: Lawson Brass Instruments, Boonsboro." *Brass Bulletin—International Brass Chronicle*, no. 52 (1985): 15–19. Also in English and French.

5508   Suter, S. "Instrumentenbau in USA: Martin—G. Leblanc Corporation." *Brass Bulletin—International Brass Chronicle*, no. 53 (1986): 113–115. Also in English and French.

5509   Suter, S. "Instrumentenbau in USA: S. W. Lewis Orchestral Horns, Chicago." *Brass Bulletin—International Brass Chronicle*, no. 52 (1985): 90–94. Also in English and French.

5510   Suter, S. "Instrumentenbau in USA: Schilke Music Products, Inc., Chicago." *Brass Bulletin—International Brass Chronicle*, no. 51 (1985): 48–53. Also in English and French.

5511   Suter, S. "Instrumentenbau in USA: Yamaha Music Products." *Brass Bulletin—International Brass Chronicle*, no. 55 (1986): 81–84. Also in English and French.

         Swett, J. P. "Brass tone quality." *The Instrumentalist* 23 (Sept. 1968): 14.

5512   Swor, William Francis. "The fusion of wind instrument sounds." D.M.A. diss., University of Texas (Austin), 1978.

5513 Tarr, Edward H. "Das gewundene Jagdinstrument von J. W. Haas." *Brass Bulletin—International Brass Chronicle*, no. 54 (1986): 8–22. Also in English and German.

"Technical drawings of historical instruments in the Metropolitan Museum of Art." *American Recorder* 16, no. 3 (1975): 101.

5514 "Teleskopisch ausziehbarer Abstimmschieber für Metallblasinstrumente." *Instrumentenbau-Zeitschrift* 26 (Mar. 1972): 280.

5515 "Die teleskopischen Blechblas-Instrumente der Firma A. K. Hüttel, Graslitz." *Deutsche Instrumentenbau Zeitschrift* 32 (1931): 70.

5516 Tepper, William F. "The intonation problem in relation to the building of brass wind instruments." Master's thesis, University of Michigan, 1955.

5517 Thayer, O. E. "The axial flow valve update." *Journal of the International Trombone Association* 10, no. 2 (1982): 34–35.

5518 "Tonal and structural characteristics of brass instruments." *American Musician* 28, no. 3 (1912): 10–11.

5519 "Tonwechselvorrichtung für Metallblasinstrumente ohne Zylinder und ohne Pumpenventile." *Deutsche Militär-Musiker Zeitung* 27 (1905): 350–351.

Utgaard, Merton. "Intonation problems of valve instruments." *The Instrumentalist* 11 (June 1957): 32 + .

5520 "Ventilmechanik für Blechblasinstrumente." *Instrumentenbau-Zeitschrift* 24 (Feb. 1970): 191.

5521 Vogel, M. "Anregendes Griechentum." *Die Musikforschung* 15 (1962): 1–11.

5522 Vogel, M. *Die Intonation der Blechbläser; Neue Wege im Metallblas-Instrumentenbau.* Orpheus—Schriftenreihe zu Grundfragen der Musik. Vol. 1. Düsseldorf: Gesellschaft zur Förderung der systematischen Musikwissenschaft, 1961.

5523 Vogel, M. "Das Problem der Ventilkombination im Metallblasinstrumentenbau." *Das Orchester* 10 (1962): 113–116.

5524 Vogel, Martin. "Blechblasinstrumente mit Umstimmhebel." *Instrumentenbau-Zeitschrift* 14 (1959): 4–5.

5525 "Von der Herstellung unserer Blechblasinstrumente." *Zeitschrift für Instrumentenbau* 56 (1935–36): 88.

5526 von Schafhäutl. "V. F. Cerveny in Königgrätz und sein Reich von Blechblasinstrumenten." *Allgemeine Musik Zeitung* 17 (1882): 841–879.

5527 von Schafhäutl. "Ist die Lehre von dem Einfluss des Materials, aus dem ein Blasinstrument verfertigt ist, auf den Ton desselben eine Fabel? Eine experimentale Untersuchung." *Allgemeine musikalische Zeitung* 14 (1879): 593–599, 609–616, 625–635.

Vorreiter, Leopold. "Die Musikinstrumente Europas im Altertum—welche Erkenntnisse vermitteln sie der Gegenwart." *Archiv für Musikorganologie* 1, no. 1 (Dec. 1976): 34–48.

5528 "Wahrscheinlich die beste Anblasvorrichtung; Dr. Meyer berichtete der Forschungsgemeinschaft bei der Jahresversammlung." *Instrumentenbau-*

Zeitschrift 25 (Nov. 1971): 503–504.

5529　Ward, Chuck, and E. Chesko. "Plastic on brass instruments." *Newsletter of the International Trombone Association* 8, no. 3 (1981): 30.

5530　Warschauer, Heinz. "Neue Wege des Blech-Blas-Instrumentenbaues." *Deutsche Musiker-Zeitung* 62 (Feb. 7, 1931): 83.

5531　Watkinson, P. S., R. Shepherd, and J. M. Bowsher. "Acoustic energy losses in brass instruments." *Acustica* 51, no. 4 (1982): 213–221.

　　　Weber, Friedrich Johannes. "Dämpfer für Blasinstrumente." *Deutsche Militär-Musiker Zeitung* 61 (1939): 29–30.

　　　Weber, Friedrich Johannes. "Die Dämpferfrage bei Blasinstrumente." *Die Musik-Woche* 7 (1939): 68–69.

　　　Weber, R. "Some researches into pitch in the 16th century with particular reference to the instruments in the Accademia Filarmonica of Verona." *The Galpin Society Journal* 28 (Apr. 1975): 7–10.

5532　Webster, John C. "An electrical method of measuring the intonation of cup-mouthpiece instruments." *Journal of the Acoustical Society of America* 19 (1947): 902–906.

5533　Welch, C. "Brass reeds [includes price guide]." *Melody Maker* 50 (Nov. 8, 1975): 38–39.

5534　Welch, C., and A. Jones. "Brass and reeds." *Melody Maker* 51 (Sept. 25, 1976): 32–33.

　　　Wenke, Wolfgang. "Die Holz- und Metallblasinstrumente der ersten Hälfte des 18. Jahrhunderts im deutschen Sprachgebiet." In *Die Blasinstrumente und ihre Verwendung. . .* , edited by Eitelfriedrich Thom, 17–21. Magdeburg: Rat des Bezirkes; Leipzig: Zentralhaus für Kulturarbeit, 1977.

　　　Werden, David R. "The Blaikley compensating system: a player's perspective." *T.U.B.A. Journal* 13, no. 1 (Aug. 1985): 17.

　　　White, Edna. "Purchasing a brass instrument." *Musical Observer* 30 (Aug. 1931): 44+.

5535　Wick, Dennis. "Instrumental exactitude." *Sounding Brass & the Conductor* 4, no. 2 (1975): 43–44.

5536　Williams, A. L. "Improving intonation on brass instruments." *Music Journal* (1965): 72+.

5537　Wimmer, J. "Noch etwas über die Intonation der Metallinstrumente." *Allgemeine Wiener Musikzeitung* 3 (1843): 137.

5538　Wimmer, J. "Ueber die Stimmung der Blechinstrumente." *Allgemeine Wiener Musikzeitung* 3 (1843): 75.

5539　Winter, James H. "Brass." *Music Educators Journal* 62 (Oct. 1975): 34–37.

5540　Winternitz, Emanuel. "Strange musical instruments in the Madrid notebooks of Leonardo da Vinci." *Metropolitan Museum Journal* 2 (1969): 115–126.

5541　Wogram, Klaus. "The acoustical properties of brass instruments." *The Horn Call* 13, no. 2 (Apr. 1983): 19–31.

5542　Wogram, Klaus. "Die Beeinflussung von Klang und Ansprache durch das

'Summenprinzip' bei Blechblasinstrumenten." *IMS Report* 1972 (RILM76 179): 715–720.

5543　Wogram, Klaus, and I. Bork. "Von Druckkennlinien und Auslingzeiten: gemessene Effekte aus der 'technischen' Musikinstrumentenforschung." *Neue Musikzeitung* 35 (Feb.-Mar. 1986): 49.

5544　Wogram, Klaus. "Diskrepanz in der Beurteilung von Blechblasinstrumenten zwischen Spieler und Zuhörer." *Das Orchester* 35 (June 1987): 639–642.

5545　Wogram, Klaus, and Jürgen Meyer. "Objektive Prüfung der Stimmung von Blechblasinstrumenten." *Das Musikinstrument* 22, no. 9 (1973): 1136–1140.

5546　Young, Frederick J. "The natural frequencies of musical horns." *Acustica* 10 (1960): 91–97.

5547　Young, Frederick J. "The optimal design and fair comparison of valve systems for brass instruments: Part II." *T.U.B.A. Journal* 14, no. 1 (Aug. 1986): 35–39.

5548　Young, Frederick J. "The optimal design and fair comparison of valve systems for brass instruments: Part III." *T.U.B.A. Journal* 14, no. 2 (Nov. 1986): 36–39.

5549　Young, Frederick J. "The optimal design and fair comparison of valve systems for brass instruments: Part IV." *T.U.B.A. Journal* 14, no. 3 (Feb. 1987): 74–77.

5550　Young, P. T. "Inventory of instruments: J. H. Eichentopf, Pörschman, Sattler, A. and H. Grenser, Grundmann." *The Galpin Society Journal* 31 (May 1978): 100–134.

5551　Young, Robert W. "Dependence of tuning of wind instruments on temperature." *Journal of the Acoustical Society of America* 17 (1946): 187–191.

5552　Young, Robert W. "On the performance of cup mouthpiece instruments." *Journal of the Acoustical Society of America* 20 (1948): 345–346.

5553　Young, Robert W. "Some characteristics of the tuning of valved wind instruments." *Journal of the Acoustical Society of America* 13 (1942): 333.

5554　Zschoch, Frieder. "Bericht über die Diskussion der Arbeitsgruppe Blasinstrumente." In *Bericht über das 1. Symposium zu Fragen der Anforderungen an den Instrumentenbau: Blankenburg/Harz—31 Mai 1980*, edited by Eitelfriedrich Thom and Renate Bormann, 22. Magdeburg: Rat des Bezirkes, 1980.

5555　"Zur Tonbildung bei Blechblasinstrumenten." *Instrumentenbau-Zeitschrift* 8 (1953–54): 110–111.

5556　"Zur Tonreinheit der Blechblasmusiker." *Instrumentenbau-Zeitschrift* 3 (1948–49): 45, 71.

Mouthpieces

5557 "Advancing mouthpiece design through modern technology." *Music Trades* 134 (Sept. 1986): 72 + .

5558 Amstutz, A. Keith. "Guidelines for selection of tenor trombone mouthpieces." *NACWPI Journal* 23, no. 3 (1975): 38–39.

5559 Bach, Vincent. *Embouchure and mouthpiece manual*. Mt. Vernon, N.Y.: V. Bach Corp., 1954.

5560 Bach, Vincent. "How to choose a brass instrument mouthpiece." *The Instrumentalist* 26 (Jan. 1972): 32–34.

5561 "Baroque trumpet mouthpieces." *International Trumpet Guild Newsletter* 4, no. 1 (1977): 5.

5562 Blackburn, C. "Trumpet modifications and repair." *International Trumpet Guild Newsletter* 4, no. 2 (1978): 10–11.

5563 "Bläser brauchen ihre persönlichen Mundstücke." *Instrumentenbau-Zeitung* 28, no. 9 (1974): 638.

5564 "Blechbläser und ihre Mundstücke, das 'beste Stück' des Spielers." *Musik International-Instrumentenbau-Zeitschrift* 35 (Oct. 1981): 682 + .

5565 Blok, N. "Inventors' corner." *Brass Bulletin—International Brass Chronicle*, no. 48 (1984): 99–100. Also in French and German.

5566 "Brass mouthpieces—Standardization of measurements—Materials—Selections—Variations. A symposium." *The Instrumentalist* 7 (Nov.-Dec. 1952): 28–41. Contributors include Renold O. Schilke, Traugott Rohner, Ted Evans, and Vincent Bach. Also published separately.

5567 Campbell, Robert. "A study of the effect of selected interior contours of the trombone mouthpiece upon the tone quality of the trombone." Master's thesis, University of Texas, 1954.

5568 Cole, Ward K. "A study concerning the selection and use of mouthpieces for brass instruments." Diss., Columbia Teachers College, 1955.

5569 Conner, Rex A. "Ben Gossick—musician/engineer." *The Instrumentalist* 27 (May 1973): 42–43.

Cummings, Barton. "Choosing a tuba mouthpiece." *Woodwind World— Brass and Percussion* 17, no. 2 (1978): 24.

5570 Deutsch, Maury. "Dimensional characteristics of trumpet/cornet mouthpieces." *Down Beat* 47 (Apr. 1980): 68–69.

5571 Dixon, Jean. "Dear Doctor Mouthpiece [resistance and the brass player]." *Brass Bulletin—International Brass Chronicle*, no. 60 (1987): 113 + . Also in French and German.

5572 "150 Mundstück-Varianten." *Instrumentenbau-Zeitschrift* 24 (Nov. 1970): 600 + .

5573 Faulkner, Maurice. "Brass mouthpieces." *The Instrumentalist* 21 (Mar. 1967): 16.

Feltz, J. "Cornet in concert band and its mouthpiece." *The School Musician*

57 (Apr. 1986): 30–31.

5574 Fitzgerald, Bernard. "Problems involved in standardizing brass mouthpieces." *The Instrumentalist* 7 (May–June 1953): 24–26.

Fitzgerald, Bernard. "Selecting a mouthpiece." *The Instrumentalist* 2 (Sept. 1947): 20.

5575 "Flesh meets metal: the rim, Part I: Inner diameter." *Brass Bulletin—International Brass Chronicle*, no. 59 (1987): 23–25. Also in French and German.

5576 "Flesh meets metal: the rim, Part II [width and contour]." *Brass Bulletin—International Brass Chronicle*, no. 60 (1987): 47 + . Also in French and German.

Froelich, J. P. "Mouthpiece forces during trombone performance." *Dissertation Abstracts* 48 (Dec. 1987): 1410A.

Gerstenberger, Richard. "A teflon-rim mouthpiece." *The Horn Call* 1, no. 2 (May 1971): 14–18.

5577 Giardinelli, Robert. "The 'ideal' mouthpiece." *The Instrumentalist* 26 (Jan. 1972): 68.

5578 Govier, S. "The French horn mouthpiece." *The School Musician* 46 (Jan., Mar. 1975): 14–17, 28–30.

5579 Haack, P. A. "Mouthpieces and tone quality: a research review." *Journal of Band Research* 15, no. 2 (1980): 50–52.

5580 Halfpenny, Eric. "British trumpet mouthpieces: addendum to 'Early British trumpet mouthpieces.' " *The Galpin Society Journal* 21 (Mar. 1968): 185.

Halfpenny, Eric. "Early British trumpet mouthpieces." *The Galpin Society Journal* 20 (Mar. 1967): 76–88.

5581 Hallquist, Robert Eugene. "A comparative study of the effect of various mouthpieces on the harmonic content of trumpet tones." Ph.D. diss., University of Minnesota, 1979.

5582 Hallquist, Robert Eugene. "A comparative study of the effect of various mouthpieces on the harmonic content of trumpet tones." *Dissertation Abstracts* 40 (Aug. 1979): 731A.

5583 Hallquist, Robert Eugene. "Critique: A comparative study of the effect of various mouthpieces on the harmonic content of trumpet tones (Ph.D. diss., Univ. of Minnesota, 1979)." *Council for Research in Music Education Bulletin*, no. 64 (Fall 1980): 59–66. Reviewed by R. E. Radocy.

5584 Haynie, John J. "On selecting the proper mouthpiece." *Southwestern Brass Journal* 1 (Fall 1957): 17–27.

5585 Hickman, David R. "Culprit: the cornet mouthpiece." *The Instrumentalist* 33 (Dec. 1978): 112.

5586 Himes, A. C. "A guide to trombone mouthpiece comparisons." *Journal of the International Trombone Association* 10, no. 2 (1982): 26–27.

5587 Hoffman, Richard J. "The classification, standardization, and analyzation of brass mouthpieces other than trumpet-cornet." Master's thesis, Northwestern University, 1955.

5588 Hunt, Norman J. "The cup mouthpiece with special reference to dentofacial irregularities." *The School Musician* 21 (Jan. 1950): 18 + ; (Feb. 1950): 23–

24; (Mar. 1950): 10–11+.

5589   Hunt, Norman J. "A study of the cup mouthpiece with special reference to dento-facial irregularity." Master's thesis, Brigham Young University, 1948.

5590   Iveson, John. "Student's page." *Sounding Brass & the Conductor* 6, no. 2 (1977): 72.

5591   Jacobs, Marion L. "Let's talk about the cup mouthpiece." *Etude* 64 (1946): 682+.

5592   Jacobs, Marion L. "Should cup mouthpieces be constructed and fitted especially for each individual?" Master's thesis, Western State College of Colorado, 1939.

5593   Jacobs, Marion L. "Uses and abuses of cup mouthpieces." *Etude* 65 (1947): 19+.

Jenkins, H. "Three important concepts." *The Instrumentalist* 24 (May 1970): 69–73.

5594   Keathley, Sandy. "Everyman's guide to the tuba mouthpiece." *T.U.B.A. Journal* 5, no. 3 (Spring/Summer 1978): 10–11.

5595   Kenny, P., and J. B. Davies. "The measurement of mouthpiece pressure." *Brass Bulletin—International Brass Chronicle*, no. 37 (1982): 50–54. Also in French and German.

5596   Kent, Earle L., and R. P. Lazure. "Studies of cup-mouthpiece tone quality." *Journal of The Acoustical Society of America* 31 (1959): 130. Abstract.

5597   Kober, Raymond P. "Effects of mouthpieces on trumpet tone quality; an experimental investigation." Master's thesis, Illinois State Normal University, 1957.

5598   Kusinski, J. S. "The effect of mouthpiece cup depth and backbore shape on listeners' categorizations of tone quality in recorded trumpet excerpts." *Dissertation Abstracts* 45 (Oct. 1984): 1065A.

5599   Malek, Vincent F. "A study of embouchure and trumpet-cornet mouthpiece measurements." Ph.D. diss., Northwestern University, 1953.

5600   Malek, Vincent F. "What is a good cornet or trumpet mouthpiece?" *The Instrumentalist* 8 (May 1954): 22–23+.

5601   Mathez, Jean-Pierre. "L'embouchure miracle: un conte de noel pour musiciens de cuivre." *Brass Bulletin—International Brass Chronicle*, no. 60 (1987): 11+. Also in English and German.

5602   Monke, W. "Mundstücke für Metallblasinstrumente." *Musikhandel* 15 (Feb. 1964): 41.

5603   Morgan, M. "Selecting proper brass mouthpieces for beginners." *The Instrumentalist* 21 (Oct. 1966): 28.

5604   Mühle, C. "Einfluss des Mundstückes auf den Klang und die Stimmung von Blechblasinstrumenten." *Gottesdienst und Kirchenmusik*, no. 1 (Jan.-Feb. 1978): 7–14.

5605   "Mundstück mit konischer Tingfläche." *Instrumentenbau Musik International* 30, no. 10 (1976): 668.

5606   "Mundstück mit Scheibenelementen." *Instrumentenbau-Zeitschrift* 25 (Sept. 1971): 418.

5607   "Mundstücke für Blechblasinstrumente, ihre Funktion und Geschichte." *Musik International-Instrumentenbau-Zeitschrift* 35 (Oct. 1981): 678 +.

5608   Myers, Frederick C. "The effect of different mouthpieces upon the tone and response of the trumpet." Master's thesis, Ohio State University, 1948.

        Neff, Carolyn Hope. "Embouchure development and the brass mouthpiece." *NACWPI Journal* 36, no. 2 (1987–88): 27–31.

5609   Nödl, Carl. "Das Mundstück des Metallblasinstrumentes." *Deutsche Instrumentenbau Zeitschrift* 39 (1938): 168.

5610   Nödl, Carl. "Wissenswertes über das Mundstück des Metallblasinstrumentes." *Deutsche Instrumentenbau Zeitschrift* (1938): 148–149, 183–184.

        Pruzin, R. S. "Review of a teaching aid." *Woodwind World—Brass and Percussion* 14, no. 4 (1975): 45 +.

5611   "Resistance and the brass player." *Brass Bulletin—International Brass Chronicle*, no. 57 (1987): 7 +. Also in French and German.

5612   Robinson, Kenneth H. "The variability of measurement of trumpet and cornet mouthpieces." Master's thesis, Northwestern University, 1954.

5613   Rohner, Traugott. "Effective new sterilizer." *The Instrumentalist* 5 (Mar.–Apr. 1951): 20.

5614   Rohner, Traugott. "How to measure a brass mouthpiece." *The Instrumentalist* 7 (Jan.-Feb. 1953): 31–34.

5615   Rose, W. H. "The birth of a new mouthpiece." *The Instrumentalist* 26 (Jan. 1972): 69–70.

5616   Rosenberg, M. "Selecting brass mouthpieces." *The Instrumentalist* 23 (Aug. 1968): 30 +.

5617   Rosenberg, M. "A visit to the Jet-Tone factory." *The Instrumentalist* 26 (Jan. 1972): 70.

5618   Schaudy, R. "Polymerholzmundstücke für Blechblasinstrumente." *Instrumentenbau Musik International* 32 (Jan. 1978): 4–5.

5619   Schilke, R. "How to select a brass mouthpiece." *The Instrumentalist* 21 (Dec. 1966): 50–51.

        Schmidt. "Neues Trompeten-Mundstück." *Evangelische Musikzeitung* 20 (191?): 2.

5620   Schmidt, W. C. "Fünf Generationen Mundstück-Spezialisten." *Brass Bulletin—International Brass Chronicle*, no. 29 (1980): 27–29 +. Also in French and English.

5621   Schuhmacher, Franz. "Mundstückfragen der Blechblaser." *Die Volksmusik—Ausg. A* (1938): 35–37.

5622   Siener, M. "Mouthpiece? Proceed with caution!!" *The School Musician* 39 (Feb. 1968): 12 +.

5623   "Something new for horns." *Philadelphia Orchestra Program Notes* (Jan. 29, 1954): 452.

5624   Starr, N. "Switching brass mouthpieces." *The Instrumentalist* 39 (Nov. 1984): 9.

Stevens, Thomas. "The trumpet in the U.S.: gadgets [backbores]." *Brass Bulletin—International Brass Chronicle*, no. 33 (1981): 41. Also in French and German.

Stiman, H. E. "Some uses of the mouthpiece rim." *The School Musician* 42 (Feb. 1971): 10+.

5625   Stockhausen, M. "Letters [mouthpieces turned on computer-controlled lathes]." *Brass Bulletin—International Brass Chronicle*, no. 57 (1987): 111. Also in French and German.

5626   Stork, J., and P. Stork. "Trumpet modifications and repair: basic guidelines for mouthpiece selection." *Journal of the International Trumpet Guild* 11, no. 2 (1986): 34–37.

5627   Stork, J. N. "Understanding the mouthpiece." *Brass Bulletin—International Brass Chronicle*, no. 55 (1986): 64–68. Also in French and German.

5628   Sweatt, M., and G. Magnuson. "Mouthpieces and wrists—two tips for trombonists." *The Instrumentalist* 28 (Oct. 1973): 54–55.

5629   Tetzlaff, Daniel B. "[Mouthpiece] Bore details are not boring." *The International Musician* 58 (Feb. 1960): 26–27.

5630   "Variables Mundstück für Blechblasinstrumente." *Instrumentenbau-Zeitschrift* 25 (Dec. 1971): 562.

5631   "Variables Mundstück für Blechblasinstrumente." *Instrumentenbau-Zeitschrift* 28, no. 5 (1974): 440.

Werden, David R. "Euphonium mouthpieces—a teacher's guide." *The Instrumentalist* 35 (May 1981): 23–26.

5632   Wick, Dennis. "Mouthpiece mystique." *Sounding Brass & the Conductor* 4, no. 1 (1975): 20+.

5633   Wilcox, Francis F. "Materials for mouthpieces." *The Instrumentalist* 12 (Nov. 1957): 67–69.

5634   Winter, James H. "The French horn mouthpiece." *Woodwind World* 6, no. 1 (1964): 3–4.

Yancich, Milan. "Carl Geyer—the mouthpiece man." *NACWPI Bulletin* 10, no. 3 (Mar. 1962): 16–19.

Mutes/Accessories

5635   Adams, S. "A good solution to a vexing problem [Velcro strips on mutes for quick adjustments]." *The School Musician* 48 (Mar. 1977): 10+.

Albrecht, C. L. "Playing trumpet with the Albrecht device [pushing valves with two trap set foot pedals]." *The Instrumentalist* 35 (Nov. 1980): 76.

5636   Ancell, J. E. "Sound pressure spectra of a muted cornet." *Journal of the*

Acoustical Society of America 27 (1955): 996.

5637   Ancell, J. E. "Sound pressure spectra of a muted cornet." *Journal of the Acoustical Society of America* 32 (1960): 1101–1104.

5638   Apperson, Ron. "Mutes or 'What are we putting down our bells?' " *T.U.B.A. Journal* 6, no. 3 (Spring 1979): 12–13.

Barrow, Gary. "Con sordino: some thoughts on trumpet muting." *Woodwind, Brass and Percussion* 24, no. 4 (1985): 20–21.

5639   Billert, Carl. "Die patentirte Wernick'sche Dämpfung bei Blechblasinstrumenten." *Musikalisches Wochenblatt* 1 (1870): 552–555.

5640   Brandon, S. "Muting the low brass." *Woodwind, Brass and Percussion* 20, no. 4 (1981): 4–5+.

Brandon, S. P. "The tuba mute." *Woodwind, Brass and Percussion* 20, no. 7 (1981): 20–21.

Brownlow, A. "The mute in contemporary trumpet performance." *The Instrumentalist* 33 (May 1979): 52+.

5641   Capper, William. "Mutes—fabricate your own." *T.U.B.A. Journal* 7, no. 3 (Winter 1980): 26–27.

5642   Colbert, P. "Musicians world: all that brass [stands and cases]." *Melody Maker* 56 (Dec. 19, 1981): 56.

Conner, Rex A. "Ben Gossick—musician/engineer." *The Instrumentalist* 27 (May 1973): 42–43.

5643   Crown, T. "Mostly Mozart's mutes." *Journal of the International Trumpet Guild* 8, no. 3 (1984): 8–13.

5644   Cryder, R. "Accessories." *Journal of the International Trombone Association* 6, no. 2 (1978): 21.

5645   Deutsch, Maury. "Pro session: the how and why of mutes." *Down Beat* 52 (Jan. 1985): 56+.

Earnest, Christopher. "The horn: stopped, muted, and open." *The Horn Call* 7, no. 2 (May 1977): 34–48.

Eichborn, Hermann Ludwig. *Die dämpfung beim horn; oder, Die musikalische natur des horns. Eine akustisch-praktische studie.* Leipzig: Brietkopf & Härtel, 1897.

Erdmann, Alfred. "Die Bedeutung der gestopften und gedämpften Waldhörner. Ein neuer Waldhorndämpfer." *Die Musik-Woche* 3, no. 10 (1935): 3–6.

Erdmann, Alfred. "Die Klangeffekte des Waldhorns. Unfug mit gedämpften und gestopften Tönen." *Deutsche Militär-Musiker Zeitung* 58, no. 41 (1936): 7–9.

Erdmann, Alfred. "Die Klangeffekte des Waldhorns. Unfug mit gedämpften und gestopften Tönen." *Die Musik-Woche* 4, no. 38 (1936): 6–8.

5646   Flor, G. J., ed. "Brass workshop: The mute outdoors." *The School Musician* 55 (May 1984): 24.

5647   Flor, G. J. "Brass workshop: The trombone mute [includes history]." *The School Musician* 51 (Jan. 1980): 34–36.

5648   Griffith, T. "Confessions of a mutemaker." *Newsletter of the International*

Trombone Association 3, no. 2 (1976): 20+.

Halfpenny, Eric. "Cotgrave and the 'sourdine.' " *The Galpin Society Journal* 23 (Aug. 1970): 116–117.

5649 Hall, Jody C., and C. E. Lockwood, Jr. "Effects of mutes on cornet tone quality." *Journal of The Acoustical Society of America* 31 (1959): 130. Abstract.

"Heavy duty case project." *International Trombone Association Newsletter* 6, no. 4 (1979): 8.

Holland, J. "Pitch finder." *Brass Bulletin—International Brass Chronicle*, no. 46 (1984): 58–61. Also in French and German.

Jensen, R. "Horn technique—muting and stopping." *The Instrumentalist* 22 (Aug. 1967): 30+.

Johnson, K. M. "The horn—mutes and muting." *The School Musician* 52 (Aug.-Sept. 1980): 32–33+.

Johnson, M. B. "Muting the French horn." *The Instrumentalist* 19 (Jan. 1965): 51–54.

5650 Jones, George W. "A study of mutes for tuba." M.M. thesis, North Texas State University, 1973.

5651 Kurka, Martin J. "A study of the acoustical effects of mutes on wind instruments." Master's thesis, University of South Dakota, 1958.

5652 Kurka, Martin J. *A study of the acoustical effects of mutes on wind instruments.* F. E. Olds Music Education Library. Fullerton, Cal.: F. E. Olds, 1961.

Leuba, Christopher. "Inserts in the horn." *The Horn Call* 6, no. 1 (Nov. 1975): 12–14.

McNerney Famera, Karen. "Mutes, flutters, and trills: a guide to composers for the horn." M.M. thesis, Yale University, 1967.

Mansur, Paul. "Hullabaloo in a horn bell OR the dilemmas of a horn [mutes/stopping]." *The Horn Call* 5, no. 2 (Spring 1975): 39–44.

5653 Mays, R. "The impossible dream [case for airplane travel]." *Newsletter of the International Trombone Association* 3, no. 2 (1976): 19–20.

"Musicians' world: sorry—I can't hear you [Le Scaffy trumpet mute]." *Melody Maker* 56 (May 16, 1981): 39.

Nichols, K. "Muted brass." *Storyville*, no. 30 (Aug.–Sept. 1970): 203–206.

5654 Pruzin, R. S. "Gestopft! Gesundheit!: a discussion of hand-muting for the French horn." *Woodwind, Brass and Percussion* 23, no. 3 (1984): 14–16.

5655 Schaefer, August H. "Varied uses of mute in tone and volume." *The Instrumentalist* 8 (Dec. 1953): 26–27+.

5656 Shew, Bobby. "General information on mutes." *Crescendo International* 19 (Nov. 1980): 33.

5657 Sluchin, B., and R. Causse. "Sourdines des cuivres." *Brass Bulletin—International Brass Chronicle*, no. 57 (1987): 20–39. Also in English and German.

5658 Smith, Nicholas Edward. "The horn mute: an acoustical and historical study." *Dissertation Abstracts* 41 (Oct. 1980): 1278A.

5659 Smith, Nicholas Edward. "The horn mute: an acoustical and historical study." D.M.A. diss., University of Rochester, Eastman School of Music, 1980.

5660 Stevens, Thomas. "The trumpet in the USA." *Brass Bulletin—International Brass Chronicle*, no. 29 (1980): 17–18. Also in French and German.

5661 Stockhausen, M. "Der Dämpfergürtel." *Brass Bulletin—International Brass Chronicle*, no. 54 (1986): 38–45. Also in English and French.

5662 Weber, Friedrich Johannes. "Dämpfer für Blasinstrumente." *Deutsche Militär-Musiker Zeitung* 61 (1939): 29–30.

5663 Weber, Friedrich Johannes. "Die Dämpferfrage bei Blasinstrumente." *Die Musik-Woche* 7 (1939): 68–69.

Winter, James H. "More on horn muting." *Woodwind World* 3 (Dec. 1, 1959): 12–13.

Winter, James H. "Muting the horn." *Woodwind World* 3 (Sept. 15, 1959): 11.

Horn

5664 Aebi, Willi. "Die innere Akustik des Waldhornes." *Brass Bulletin—International Brass Chronicle*, no. 3 (1972): 22–38. Also in English and French.

Aebi, Willi. "Stopped horn." *The Horn Call* 4, no. 2 (Spr. 1974): 40–57.

5665 Aebi, Willi. "Stopped horn." *The Horn Call* 6, no. 2 (1976): 47–50.

5666 Aebi, Willi. "Das Waldhorn und seine innere Akustik." *Schweizerische Bauzeitung* 38 (Sept. 1969): 738–745.

Agrell, Jeffrey. "Dreams and wishes: things I would like to see happen concerning the horn and horn playing." *Brass Bulletin—International Brass Chronicle*, no. 25 (1979): 29 + .

5667 Agrell, Jeffrey. "Steve Lewis, hornmaker: old world craftsmanship plus new world technology." *Brass Bulletin—International Brass Chronicle*, no. 49 (1985): 36–39. Also in French and German.

5668 Allen, Edmund. "An 8-D ascending horn: procedure and kit for converting an 8-D to an ascending third valve system without cutting or mutilating horn in any way." *The Horn Call* 11, no. 2 (1981): 38.

Baumann, Hermann. "Welches Horn für welche Musik?" *Brass Bulletin—International Brass Chronicle*, no. 3 (1972): 13–21. Also in English and French.

Beach, Robert F. "A search for better intonation." *The Horn Call* 8, no. 2 (1978): 28–37.

5669 Blandford, W. F. H. "Some observations on 'horn chords': an acoustical problem." *The Musical Times* 67 (1926): 128–131.

5670 Boegner. "Akustisch-praktische Daten zum Waldhorn." *Gravesaner Blätter* 4, no. 15/16 (1960): 59–97.

5671   Boegner. "Practical acoustic data on the French horn." *Gravesaner Blätter* 4, nos. 15–16 (1960): 98–117.

5672   Butterworth, J. "Horns of dilemma [French horn buying tips]." *Sounding Brass & the Conductor* 6, no. 1 (1977): 26+.

5673   "Ein chromatisches Signalhorn." *Zeitschrift für Instrumentenbau* 14, no. 28 (1893/94).

5674   "Le Cor." *L'Echo musical* 21 (1891): 242–245.

5675   Cresswell, T. "Come, blow your horn." *Sounding Brass & the Conductor* 2, no. 1 (1973): 17–18+.

5676   D. "Ein neues Doppelhorn." *Zeitschrift für Instrumentenbau* 27 (1906/07): 124.

       Dalrymple, Glenn V. "The stuffy horn syndrome: one cause and its cure." *The Horn Call* 2, no. 2 (May 1972): 66–70.

5677   Damm, Peter. "300 Jahre Waldhorn." *Brass Bulletin—International Brass Chronicle*, no. 31 (1980): 19–20+. Also in English and French.

5678   Damm, Peter. "300 Jahre Waldhorn." *Brass Bulletin—International Brass Chronicle*, no. 32 (1980): 19+. Also in English and French.

5679   Damm, Peter. "New piccolo horn in F/high Bb by Friedbert Syhre, Leipzig." *Brass Bulletin—International Brass Chronicle*, no. 31 (1980): 15–16. Also in French and German.

       Dutlenhoefer, Marie. "Gebr. Alexander, Mainz 1782–1982." *The Horn Call* 13, no. 1 (Oct. 1982): 28–35.

       Earnest, Christopher. "The horn: stopped, muted, and open." *The Horn Call* 7, no. 2 (May 1977): 34–48.

5680   Eichborn, Hermann Ludwig. *Die dämpfung beim horn; oder, Die musikalische natur des horns. Eine akustisch-praktische studie.* Leipzig: Breitkopf & Härtel, 1897.

5681   Eichborn, Hermann Ludwig. "Ein neues Doppelhorn." *Zeitschrift für Instrumentenbau* 20 (1899/1900): 63–65, 97–99.

       Eichborn, Hermann Ludwig. *Ueber das Octavierungs-princip bei Blechinstrumenten, insbesondere bei Waldhörnern.* Leipzig: P. de Wit, 1889.

5682   Eichborn, Hermann Ludwig. *Ueber das Oktavierungs-princip bei Blechinstrumente, insbesondere bei Waldhörnern.* Leipzig: Breitkopf & Härtel, 1889.

       Erdmann, Alfred. "Die Bedeutung der gestopften und gedämpften Waldhörner. Ein neuer Waldhorndämpfer." *Die Musik-Woche* 3, no. 10 (1935): 3–6.

5683   Erdmann, Alfred. "Die Klangeffekte des Waldhorns. Unfug mit gedämpften und gestopften Tönen." *Deutsche Militär-Musiker Zeitung* 58, no. 41 (1936): 7–9.

5684   Erdmann, Alfred. "Die Klangeffekte des Waldhorns. Unfug mit gedämpften und gestopften Tönen." *Die Musik-Woche* 4, no. 38 (1936): 6–8.

5685   Erlenbach, Julius. "French horn maintenance." *The Instrumentalist* 29 (May 1975): 51–55.

5686   Farrar, Lloyd P. "Under the crown & eagle [Schreiber bass horn]." *Newsletter of the American Musical Instrument Society* 14, no. 3 (1985): 4–5.

5687   Finke, Helmut. "Horns made by hand?" *The Horn Call* 9, no. 2 (Apr. 1979): 47–50. In English and German.

        Fitzpatrick, Horace. "Notes on the Vienna horn." *The Galpin Society Journal* 14 (Mar. 1961): 49–51.

5688   "French horn directory." *Sounding Brass & the Conductor* 6, no. 1 (1977): 28–29.

5689   "The French horn with cylinders, pistons or valves." *Metronome* 20, nos. 8–9 (1904).

5690   "Fürst-Pless-Horn." *Instrumentenbau Musik International* 30, no. 1 (1976): 30.

5691   Gardner, Gary. "The Selmer double horn, No. 77." *The Horn Call* 9, no. 1 (Oct. 1978): 68–70.

5692   Gay, B. "Horn call." *Sounding Brass & the Conductor* 5, no. 1 (1976): 11–12 + .

5693   Gerstenberger, Richard. "A teflon-rim mouthpiece." *The Horn Call* 1, no. 2 (May 1971): 14–18.

5694   Goldman, Erica Hillary. "The effect of original and electronically altered oboe, clarinet, and French horn timbres on absolute pitch judgments." D.M.A. diss., University of Oregon, 1984.

        Gregory, Robin. *The horn; a comprehensive guide to the modern instrument and its music.* 2d ed. London: Faber and Faber, 1969.

        Gregory, Robin. *The horn; a guide to the modern instrument.* London: Faber and Faber, 1961.

        Halfpenny, Eric. "Smith, London." *The Galpin Society Journal* 21 (Mar. 1968): 105–107.

        Hancock, John M. "The horns of the Stearns Collection." *The Horn Call* 14, no. 2 (Apr. 1984): 60–71.

5695   Hardin, Burton E. "Valve port dimensions effect on playing qualities of horns." *The Horn Call* 16, no. 1 (Oct. 1985): 88–89.

5696   Henderson, Malcolm C. "The 1971 horn tests at Pomona: further results." *The Horn Call* 3, no. 1 (Nov. 1972): 59–61.

5697   Henderson, Malcolm C. "The horn tests at Pomona: some results." *The Horn Call* 2, no. 1 (Nov. 1971): 55–57.

        Henderson, Malcolm C. "Thinking about stopping: new thoughts on a horny subject." *The Horn Call* 4, no. 1 (Autumn 1973): 25–29.

        Hoeltzel, Michael. "Gibt es noch einen deutschen Hornton?" *Oesterreichische Musikzeitschrift* 38 (Sept. 1983): 493–494.

        Hoeltzel, Michael. "Rund um das Horn [Hamburger Jägerschaft]." *Brass Bulletin—International Brass Chronicle*, no. 44 (1983): 16–21. Also in English and French.

5698   "Hörner in Trompetenform." *Instrumentenbau Musik International* 33 (Nov. 1979): 736.

5699   "Holding device by Allan W. Mead." *The Horn Call* 1, no. 1 (Feb. 1971): 18–19.

        Holmes, John Clellom. *The horn.* New York: Random House, 1958.

5700   "Holton offers first U.S.-made descant horn." *The Music Trades* 127 (May 1979): 108+.

5701   Hoover, W. "The French horn and the alto horn." *The Instrumentalist* 23 (Dec. 1968): 23.

5702   "Horn chords." In *Seventh Music Book*, 72–74. London: Hinrichsen, 1952.

5703   "Horn improvement survey report: an I.H.S. committee report." *The Horn Call* 10, no. 1 (Oct. 1979): 52–54.

5704   Horwood, W. "The music mechanics." *Crescendo International* 9 (July 1971): 34.

        Hoss, Wendell. "Drills and devices in playing the horn." *The Horn Call* 7, no. 1 (Nov. 1976): 9–10.

5705   Hoss, Wendell. "Gadgets and gimmicks [as aids to playing the horn]." *The Horn Call* 1, no. 1 (Feb. 1971): 20–22.

        Howe, Marvin C. "Stopped horn." *The Horn Call* 4, no. 1 (Autumn 1973): 19–24.

        Janetzky, Kurt, and Bernhard Brüchle. *Das Horn. Eine kleine Chronik seines Werdens und Wirkens.* Bern and Stuttgart: Hallwag, 1977.

        Johnson, K. M. "The horn—mutes and muting." *The School Musician* 52 (Aug.–Sept. 1980): 32–33+.

        Johnson, M. B. "Muting the French horn." *The Instrumentalist* 19 (Jan. 1965): 51–54.

5706   Kimple, Wilbert Kenneth, Jr. "The Holton H-200 double descant: a diamond in the rough." *The Horn Call* 15, no. 2 (Apr. 1985): 37–41.

5707   Kimple, Wilbert Kenneth, Jr. "Results of a national survey of professional horn players." *The Horn Call* 10, no. 1 (Oct. 1979): 55–59.

5708   Kirby, Percival R. "Horn chords: an acoustical problem." *The Musical Times* 66 (1925): 811–813.

5709   Kirby, Percival R. "Horn chords: an acoustical problem." *The Horn Call* 8, no. 1 (Nov. 1977): 40–42.

5710   Kirmser, L. "General maintenance of the horn." *The Instrumentalist* 33 (Apr. 1979): 30–32.

5711   Kleucker, Malinda. "The Finke triple horn." *The Horn Call* 14, no. 2 (Apr. 1984): 49–51.

        Körner, Friedrich. "Ein Horn von Michael Nagel in Graz." *Historisches Jahrbuch der Stadt Graz* 2 (1969): 87–96.

5712   Lawson, Walter. "Choosing a horn." *The Instrumentalist* 33 (Apr. 1979): 28–29.

5713   Lawson, Walter. "The effects of screw bell alloy on the acoustic input/output characteristics of a French horn." *The Horn Call* 11, no. 1 (Oct. 1980): 53–56.

5714   "Leblanc introduces Holton marching French horn." *The Music Trades* 128 (May 1980): 126.

5715   Leipp, Emile, and Lucien Thevet. "Le cor." *Bulletin du Groupe d'acoustique musicale* 41 (May 1969): 1–23.

        Lekvold, A. D. "French horn unique in blending and tone." *The Instru-*

mentalist 8 (Nov. 1953): 44–45.

5716 Lessing, Murray. "A response to Whipple's hybrid third valve." *The Horn Call* 11, no. 2 (1981): 62–63.

5717 "A letter from Dennis Brain." *The Horn Call* 1, no. 2 (May 1971): 48–49.

5718 Leuba, Christopher. "A centered tone." *Woodwind World—Brass and Percussion* 19, no. 5 (1980): 12–14.

Leuba, Christopher. "The descant horn." *The Instrumentalist* 26 (Feb. 1972): 46–49; (Mar. 1972): 70–73.

5719 Leuba, Christopher. "Inserts in the horn." *The Horn Call* 6, no. 1 (Nov. 1975): 12–14.

5720 Leuba, Christopher. "Recording the horn in the wind quintet." *The Horn Call* 4, no. 1 (Autumn 1973): 30–33.

Leuba, Christopher. " 'Stopped' playing on the horn." *The Horn Call* 5, no. 2 (Spring 1975): 60–64.

Leuba, Julian Christopher. "Dispute over longer slides." *The Instrumentalist* 34 (May 1980): 110–111.

McCoy, M. "How to oil rotary valves." *Woodwind World* 3, no. 12 (1961): 5.

McCoy, W. M. "How to preserve lacquer." *Woodwind World* 4, no. 3 (1961): 14.

McNerney Famera, Karen. "Mutes, flutters, and trills: a guide to composers for the horn." M.M. thesis, Yale University, 1967.

Mahillon, Victor Charles. "The horn—its history, its theory, its construction." *Dominant* 16, nos. 10–11 (1908); 17, nos. 1–2, 5 (1909).

"The making of a horn. A visit to the plant of Brua C. Keefer." *Metronome* 39 (Sept. 1923): 137 + .

5721 Mansur, Paul. "Hullabaloo in a horn bell OR the dilemmas of a horn [mutes/stopping]." *The Horn Call* 5, no. 2 (Spring 1975): 39–44.

Mansur, Paul. "Thoughts and observations on Vienna and Vienna horns." *The Horn Call* 14, no. 2 (Apr. 1984): 45–47.

5722 Markle, R. "The French horn." *The Instrumentalist* 17 (Mar. 1963): 34.

5723 Markle, R. "The French horn rotors." *The Instrumentalist* 17 (Apr. 1963): 16.

5724 Meek, Harold. "Arrangement of valves." *Symphony* 3 (Oct. 1949): 4.

Meek, Harold. "Some observations prompted by Hermann Baumann's: 'Welches Horn für welche Musik.' " *Brass Bulletin—International Brass Chronicle*, no. 4 (1973): 21–27. Also in French and German.

5725 Meinl, A. "Es blies ein Jäger wohl in sein Horn. Informationen zu Funktion, Mundstückwahl und Pflege von Jagdmusikinstrumenten." *Musik International-Instrumentenbau-Zeitschrift* 39 (Oct. 1985): 630–631.

5726 Merewether, Richard. " 'Bad notes' in horns." *The Horn Call* 7, no. 1 (Nov. 1976): 26–27.

5727 Merewether, Richard. "Even more about open & stopped horns." *The Horn Call* 7, no. 1 (Nov. 1976): 28.

5728 Merewether, Richard. *The horn, the horn.* Hornplayer's Companion Series.

London: Paxman Musical Instruments Ltd., 1978.

5729   Merewether, Richard. "Larger and smaller bores in horns." *Woodwind World—Brass and Percussion* 16, no. 3 (1977): 38+.

5730   Merewether, Richard. "A little on horn design." *The Horn Call* 16, no. 2 (Apr. 1986): 43–49.

Merewether, Richard. "The question of hand-stopping." *The Horn Call* 5, no. 2 (Spring 1975): 45–59.

5731   Meyer, Jürgen. "Akustische Untersuchungen über den Klang des Hornes." *Das Musikinstrument* 16, nos. 1, 2 (Jan., Feb. 1967): 32–37, 199–203.

Moege, Gary Ray. "A catalog of the alto brass instruments in the Arne B. Larson Collection of Musical Instruments." D.M.A. diss., University of Oklahoma, 1985.

5732   Moore, Paul B. *French horn valve care.* Portland, Ore.: University of Portland Press, 1965.

Morley-Pegge, Reginald. *The French horn.* revised edition. New York: Norton, 1973.

Nallin, Walter E. "Sonorities of the upper brass." *Symphony* (Jan 1952): 12.

5733   "Neuer Hornsatz im Stile der Corni da caccia." *Musik International-Instrumentenbau-Zeitschrift* 37 (Oct. 1983): 634.

5734   "Ein neues Doppelhorn." *Deutsche Militär-Musiker Zeitung* 28 (1906): 692.

"A new double French horn." *Metronome* 23, no. 1 (1907): 12.

"New horn set in corno da caccia style." *Musik International-Instrumentenbau-Zeitschrift* 37 (Dec. 1983): 745–746.

5735   Nödl, Karl. "Zur Normung bei den Waldhorn." *Deutsche Instrumentenbau Zeitschrift* 42 (1941): 119.

5736   Orval, Francis. "Reflexions sur le cor." *Brass Bulletin—International Brass Chronicle,* no. 9 (1974): 15–18. Also in English and German.

5737   Osmun, Robert. "Maintenance of rotary valves." *The Horn Call* 17, no. 1 (Oct. 1986): 49.

5738   Payne, Ian W. "Observations on the stopped notes of the French horn." *Music and Letters* 49, no. 2 (1968): 145–154.

5739   Pease, Edward. "French horn resonance." *The Instrumentalist* 28 (May 1974): 58–59.

Pruzin, R. S. "Gestopft! Gesundheit!: a discussion of hand-muting·for the French horn." *Woodwind, Brass and Percussion* 23, no. 3 (1984): 14–16.

5740   Pruzin, R. S. "Selection of a single model French horn." *Woodwind World—Brass and Percussion* 16, no. 1 (1977): 32–33.

5741   Pyle, Robert W., Jr. "The effect of lacquer and silver plate on horn tone." *The Horn Call* 11, no. 2 (1981): 26–29.

Pyle, Robert W., Jr. "A theory of hand-stopping." *The Horn Call* 1, no. 2 (May 1971): 53.

Righini, Pietro. *Il corno.* Ancona: Bèrben, 1972.

5742   Roberts, B. Lee. "Some comments on the physics of the horn and right-hand technique." *The Horn Call* 6, no. 2 (1976): 41–46.

Rudolph. "Doppelhorn oder B-Horn mit Quint-Ventil?" *Deutsche Militär-*

Musiker Zeitung 54 (191-?): 19.

5743   Rudolph, F. "Das 'Stopferventil' am Horn." *Zeitschrift für Instrumentenbau* 52 (1932): 156.

Schmidt, L. "The E-flat horn crook is a crook." *The Instrumentalist* 11 (Jan. 1957): 31–32.

Seiffert, Stephen L. "Tuning the double horn." *The Horn Call* 4, no. 2 (Spr. 1974): 35–39.

Seiffert, Stephen L. "Tuning the double horn." *The Instrumentalist* 29 (Apr. 1975): 54–55.

Seyfried, Erhard. "Concerning the article by Richard Merewether: The Vienna-horn—and some thoughts on its past fifty years." *The Horn Call* 16, no. 1 (Oct. 1985): 34–35.

5744   Shore, M. "Pawnshop horns: bargains & busts off the beaten track." *Musician*, no. 48 (Oct. 1982): 82+.

Smith, H. Clifford. "An engraved horn now in the possession of Miss Martineau." *Proceedings of the Society of Antiquaries* 27 (1915): 138–142.

5745   Strucel, George. "Maintenance of the horn." *The Horn Call* 2, no. 1 (Nov. 1971): 49–53.

5746   Svitavsky, Leo E. "An acoustical study of the French horn." Master's thesis, Eastman School of Music, 1947.

5747   Thévet, Lucien. "Le cor fa-sib avec troisieme piston ascendant." *The Horn Call* 4, no. 1 (Autumn 1973): 36–37.

5748   Thévet, Lucien. "The F-Bb horn with ascending third valve." *The Horn Call* 4, no. 1 (Autumn 1973): 38–41.

Tuckwell, Barry. "The horn." *Music Teacher and Piano Student* 55 (Oct., Nov., Dec. 1976): 9–10, 10, 14.

Tuckwell, Barry. "The horn." *The Australian Journal of Music Education*, no. 19 (Oct. 1976): 11–12.

5749   "Waldhörner eine Oktave höher." *Instrumentenbau-Zeitschrift* 26 (Jan. 1972): 16.

5750   "Waldhorn mit drei Stimmungen." *Instrumentenbau Musik International* 33 (Oct. 1979): 696.

5751   "Waldhorn mit Ventilen." *Deutsche Militär-Musiker Zeitung* 30 (1908): 126. [Invention of Albert Pappe.]

5752   Ward, Chuck. "The work bench: rotary valves." *The Horn Call* 16, no. 1 (Oct. 1985): 57–59.

5753   "Was unterscheidet Wiener von anderen Spitzenorchestern? Horn-Blas-Maschine soll Publikumseindrücke wissenschaftlich überprüfen." *Musik International-Instrumentenbau-Zeitschrift* 35 (Oct. 1981): 668.

5754   Washburn, C. "The French horn." *Woodwind World* 4 (June 1, 1961): 10–12.

5755   Westhof, T. "Mon nouveau double-cor dechant." *Brass Bulletin—International Brass Chronicle*, no. 13 (1976): 52–55.

Whaley, David Robert. "The microtonal capability of the horn." D.M.A. diss., University of Illinois (Urbana-Champaign), 1975.

Whaley, David Robert. "The microtonal capability of the horn." *Dissertation Abstracts* 36 (Mar. 1976): 5633A.

"What are the advantages of modern double horns?" *Canon* 8 (May, 1955): 406–407.

5756   Whipple, James F. "A five-valve double horn with hybrid third valve." *The Horn Call* 11, no. 1 (Oct. 1980): 57–62.

5757   Widholm, G. "Der 'kleine Unterschied'; Betrachtung über den speziellen Wiener Orchesterklang und seine Ursachen." *Hifi-Stereophonie* 22 (Oct. 1983): 1086–1089.

5758   Widholm, G. "Untersuchungen zum Wiener Klangstil." *Oesterreichische Musikzeitschrift* 38 (Jan. 1983): 18–27.

Winter, James H. "The French horn mouthpiece." *Woodwind World* 6, no. 1 (1964): 3–4.

Winter, James H. "Variations in horn tone." *Woodwind World* 5, no. 4 (1964): 10+.

Wogram, Klaus. "The acoustical properties of brass instruments." *The Horn Call* 13, no. 2 (Apr. 1983): 19–31.

Yaw, P. H. "The single B-flat horn." *Woodwind World—Brass and Percussion* 18, no. 2 (Apr. 1979): 22–23.

Yaw, P. H. "Tuning the double French horn." *The Instrumentalist* 21 (June 1967): 22.

Trumpet/Cornet/Bugle

5759   Ahrens, A. W. "Experimental trumpet." *Journal of Experimental Education* 37 (1943).

5760   Ahrens, Christian. "Erich Honecker und Udo Lindenberg spielen darauf; vor 60 Jahren parentiert: die Martintrompete." *Musik International-Instrumentenbau-Zeitschrift* 41 (Dec. 1987): 743–745.

5761   Albrecht, C. L. "Playing trumpet with the Albrecht device [pushing valves with two trap set foot pedals]." *The Instrumentalist* 35 (Nov. 1980): 76.

Ancell, J. E. "Sound pressure spectra of a muted cornet." *Journal of the Acoustical Society of America* 27 (1955): 996.

Ancell, J. E. "Sound pressure spectra of a muted cornet." *Journal of the Acoustical Society of America* 32 (1960): 1101–1104.

Arfinengo, Carlo. *La tromba e il trombone.* Ancona; Milano: Bèrben, 1973.

5762   Ashforth, A. "The Bolden Band photo: one more time." *Annual Review of Jazz Studies* 3 (1985): 176.

Awouters, M. "X-raying musical instruments: a method in organological study." *Revue Belge de Musicologie* 36–38 (1982–1984): 203–214+.

5763   B., Ch. "Le cornet à echo." *L'Echo musical* 6, no. 7 (18 July 1874).

5764 Bach, Vincent. "Some 'inside' facts about the trumpet." *Jacobs' Band Monthly* 11 (Nov. 1929): 15–16.

5765 "Bachtrompeten—eine Forderung des Tages." *Deutsche Militär-Musiker Zeitung* 52 (1930): 11.

Baines, Anthony. "The Galpin cornett." *The Galpin Society Journal* 29 (May 1976): 125–126.

5766 Baresel, A. "Vom Posthorn zur Martin-Trompete." *Instrumentenbau Musik International* 32 (Dec. 1978): 778.

5767 Barton, E. H., and H. Mary Browning. "Sound changes analysed by records—trumpet and cornet." *Philosophical Magazine* 50 (1925): 951–967.

5768 "Bass trumpet [new Getzen]." *The Instrumentalist* 27 (Feb. 1973): 6.

5769 Bassett, Henry. "On improvements in trumpets." *Proceedings of the Musical Association* 3 (1876/77): 140–144.

5770 Bate, Philip. "Instruments for the disabled." *The Galpin Society Journal* 29 (May 1976): 127–128.

Bate, Philip. *The trumpet and trombone; an outline of their history, development and construction.* London: E. Benn; New York: W. W. Norton, 1966.

Bate, Philip. *The trumpet and trombone; an outline of their history, development, and construction.* 2d ed. London: Benn; New York: Norton, 1972.

5771 Beauchamp, James W. "Analysis and synthesis of cornet tones using nonlinear interharmonic relationships." *Journal of the Audio Engineering Society* 23, no. 10 (Oct. 1975): 778–795.

Bell, R. E. "Natural trumpets of Leningrad; a description of the natural trumpets in the Exhibition of Musical Instruments of the Leningrad Institute of Theater, Music and Cinematography, Leningrad, U.S.S.R." *Journal of the International Trumpet Guild* 7, no. 4 (1983): 10–11+.

5772 Benade, Arthur H. "How to test a good trumpet." *The Instrumentalist* 31 (Apr. 1977): 57–58.

5773 "The birth of a trumpet." *Down Beat* 27 (Jan. 7, 1960): 18–19.

Blackburn, C. "Trumpet modifications and repair." *International Trumpet Guild Newsletter* 4, no. 2 (1978): 10–11.

5774 Blackburn, C. "Trumpet modifications and repair." *International Trumpet Guild Newsletter* 5, no. 3 (1979): 12.

5775 Blackburn, C. "Trumpet modifications and repair: valve aligning." *International Trumpet Guild Newsletter* 6, no. 3 (1980): 10.

Blaikley, D. J. "How a trumpet is made." *The Musical Times* 51 (1910): 14–16, 82–84, 154–157, 223–225, erratum 332.

5776 Blaikley, D. J. "Notes on the trumpet scale." *Proceedings of the Musical Association* 20 (1893/94): 115–123.

5777 Bloch, C. "The bell-tuning trumpet." *Brass Bulletin—International Brass Chronicle*, no. 28 (1979): 35+. Also in French and German.

5778 "Boosey & Hawkes unveils first U.S.-made F. Besson trumpet." *The Music Trades* 131 (Feb. 1983): 87+.

5779 Büttner, Manfred. "Die Trompete, das schlechteste Musikinstrumente." *VDI Nachrichten* 13, no. 26 (1959): 1, 4.

5780   "B-H/Buffet to manufacture in U.S.; company plans to reintroduce ac-
       claimed French Besson trumpet line at new plant." *The Music Trades* 130
       (July 1982): 90.

5781   Byrne, M. "The Goldsmith-trumpet-makers of the British Isles." *The Galpin
       Society Journal* 19 (Apr. 1966): 71–83.

5782   "Le clarion chromatique." *L'Echo musical* 24 (1894): 109–110.

5783   Clarke, Herbert L. "The band's three brass sopranos." *Metronome* 49 (July
       1933): 27.

       "Conn builds models of sound waves in search for ideal cornet design."
       Musicana 29 (May–June 1955): 16–17.

5784   "Conn's Heritage trumpet features plasma-welded bell (80B20ML)." *Music
       Trades* 134 (May 1986): 130–131.

5785   Cooper, G. "The perils of equal temperament." *Journal of the International
       Trumpet Guild* 9, no. 4 (1985): 32–39.

       "Cornets and clarinets—in A or B-flat?—Our readers speak their minds."
       Jacobs' Band Monthly 19 (Mar. 1934): 8+; (Apr. 1934): 8; (June 1934): 31;
       (Oct. 1934): 30.

       Dahlqvist, Rene. "Some notes on the early valve." *The Galpin Society Journal*
       33 (1980): 111–124.

       Dayley, K. Newell. "Trumpet vibrato: pedagogical significance of corre-
       lations between acoustical and physical variants." D.A. diss., University
       of Northern Colorado, 1986.

       Dayley, K. Newell. "Trumpet vibrato: pedagogical significance of corre-
       lations between acoustical and physical variants." *Dissertation Abstracts*
       47 (Mar. 1987): 3229A.

       Deutsch, Maury. "Dimensional characteristics of trumpet/cornet mouth-
       pieces." *Down Beat* 47 (Apr. 1980): 68–69.

       Deutsch, Maury. "Theory of trumpet intonation." *Down Beat* 47 (June
       1980): 72–73.

5786   Dolan, R. E. "A note on electronically amplified instruments." *American
       Recorder* 9, no. 3 (1968): 75+.

       Drake, Julian. "The Christ Church cornetts, and the ivory cornett in the
       Royal College of Music, London." *The Galpin Society Journal* 34 (1981):
       44–50.

5787   "Die 23 wichtigen Trompeten-instruments." *Instrumentenbau Musik Inter-
       national* 33 (Oct. 1979): 670.

5788   Dunnick, D. Kim. "A physical comparison of the tone qualities of four
       different brands of B-flat trumpets with regard to the presence and rela-
       tive strengths of their respective partials." D.Mus. diss., Indiana Uni-
       versity, 1980.

5789   "E flat, D, and E flat/D trumpet directory [products available in England]."
       Sounding Brass & the Conductor 6, no. 2 (1977): 62.

       "E flat soprano cornet directory." *Sounding Brass & the Conductor* 6, no. 3
       (1977): 101.

5790   Eichborn, Hermann Ludwig. "Bemerkungen ueber eine neue Trompete von X. Mor. Schuster." *Zeitschrift für Instrumentenbau* 12 nos. 31, 32 (1891/ 92).

Eliason, Robert E. "The Dresden keyed bugle." *Journal of the American Musical Instrument Society* 3 (1977): 57–63.

5791   Fairweather, D. "Strictly instrumental [report on a new trumpet]. Designed by Derek Watkins." *Jazz Journal International* 31 (Nov. 1978): 15.

Farrar, Lloyd P. "Ferdinand Coeuille: maker of The Telescope Cornets and Trumpets." *Journal of the International Trumpet Guild* 13, no. 2 (Dec. 1988): 41 +.

Farrar, Lloyd P. "Ellis Pugh and his convertible trumpet." *Journal of the International Trumpet Guild* 13, no. 2 (Dec. 1988): 45 +.

5792   Faulkner, Maurice. "The rotary valve trumpet and the Vienna style." *The Instrumentalist* 26 (Jan. 1972): 28–29.

Faulkner, Maurice. "Why American orchestras need rotary-valve trumpets." *The Instrumentalist* 39 (Feb. 1985): 98.

5793   Figgs, Linda Drake. "Critique: Qualitative differences in trumpet tones as perceived by listeners and by acoustical analysis (Ed.D. diss., Univ. of Kansas, 1978)." *Council for Research in Music Education Bulletin*, no. 64 (Fall 1980): 67–72. Reviewed by L. B. Hilton.

5794   Figgs, Linda Drake. "Qualitative differences in trumpet tones as perceived by listeners and by acoustical analysis." Ed.D. diss., University of Kansas, 1978.

5795   Figgs, Linda Drake. "Qualitative differences in trumpet tones as perceived by listeners and by acoustical analysis." *Dissertation Abstracts* 39 (May 1979): 6616A.

"$500 donation from ITG helps Edison Institute acquire rare early American trumpet [made by Samuel Graves & Co.]." *International Trumpet Guild Newsletter* 7, no. 3 (1981): 7.

Flor, G. J. "Brass workshop: The bugle past and present." *The School Musician* 56 (May 1985): 30–31.

5796   "Fluegelhorn, Kornett und Trompete." *Schweizerische Instrumentalmusik* 30 (1941): 12, 39.

5797   Fontana, Eszter. "The manufacture of ivory cornetti." *The Galpin Society Journal* 36 (1983): 29–36.

5798   Gannon, R. "For trumpet players past and present." *Popular Mechanics* 113 (1960): 201–203.

Gauffriau, J. M. "Cover [engraved 1895 Couesnon]." *Brass Bulletin—International Brass Chronicle*, no. 38 (1982): 3. Also in French and German.

5799   Gay, B. "Trumpets galore [how to choose]." *Sounding Brass & the Conductor* 6, no. 4 (1978): 134.

5800   Gelly, D. "Brass improvement and refinement." *Jazz Journal International* 31 (Aug. 1978): 16.

"Geretsried (B. R. Deutschland) [Meinl and Lauber making exact copy of trumpet by Joh. Leonhard Ehe (III), 1746]." *Brass Bulletin—International Brass Chronicle*, no. 5–6 (1973): 114. Also in English and French.

5801   "Getzen adds complete line of two-piston bugles." *Music Trades* 126 (Jan. 1978): 89.

5802   "Getzen develops tuneable bell trumpet & upright baritone." *The Music Trades* 128 (May 1980): 152.

5803   "Getzen family of Wisconsin manufactures 'Dynasty' bugles." *The Music Trades* 125 (Jan. 1977): 64–65.

5804   "Getzen unveils new Eterna trumpet [Model 1200 Eterna II B-flat]." *The Music Trades* 133 (May 1985): 126.

5805   Gibson, Daryl. "Recordings of differentiations in tone color produced by vowel sounds on the trumpet." Master's thesis, University of Minnesota, 1942.

5806   Goldman, Edwin Franko. "How to test a cornet." *Metronome* 33, no. 5 (1917): 20–21.

5807   Grocock, Robert G. "Acoustical phenomena as they relate to the performance and manufacture of the modern valve trumpet." Master's thesis, Eastman School of Music, 1950.

        Halfpenny, Eric. "Four seventeenth-century trumpets." *The Galpin Society Journal* 22 (Mar. 1969): 51–57.

5808   Halfpenny, Eric. "Notes on two later British trumpets." *The Galpin Society Journal* 24 (July 1971): 79–83.

        Halfpenny, Eric. "Two Oxford trumpets." *The Galpin Society Journal* 16 (May 1963): 49–62.

        Hall, Jody C. "Effect of the oral and pharyngeal cavities on trumpet tone quality." *Journal of the Acoustical Society of America* 27 (1955): 996.

5809   Hall, Jody C. "The rotary valve trumpet—an American revival." *The Instrumentalist* 26 (Jan. 1972): 29–30.

        Hall, Jody C., and C. E. Lockwood, Jr. "Effects of mutes on cornet tone quality." *Journal of The Acoustical Society of America* 31 (1959): 130. Abstract.

        Hall, Jody C. "A radiographic, spectrographic, and photographic study of the non-labial physical changes which occur in the transition from the middle to low and middle to high registers during trumpet performance." *Dissertation Abstracts* 14 (Nov. 1954): 2086–2087.

        Hallquist, Robert Eugene. "A comparative study of the effect of various mouthpieces on the harmonic content of trumpet tones." Ph.D. diss., University of Minnesota, 1979.

        Hallquist, Robert Eugene. "A comparative study of the effect of various mouthpieces on the harmonic content of trumpet tones." *Dissertation Abstracts* 40 (Aug. 1979): 731A.

        Hallquist, Robert Eugene. "Critique: A comparative study of the effect of various mouthpieces on the harmonic content of trumpet tones (Ph.D. diss., Univ. of Minnesota, 1979)." *Council for Research in Music Education Bulletin*, no. 64 (Fall 1980): 59–66. Reviewed by R. E. Radocy.

        Henderson, Hayward W. "An experimental study of trumpet embouchure." *Journal of the Acoustical Society of America* 14 (1942): 58–64.

5810   Henderson, Hayward W. "An experimental study of trumpet embouchure." *Bulletin of the American Musicological Society* (Oct. 1945): 11–12.

5811   Henschel, A. K. "Trompetenbau und Trompetenblasen." *Die Sendung* 9 (1932): 7.

Heyde, Herbert. "Eine Geschäftskorrespondenz von Johann Wilhelm Haas aus dem Jahre 1719." In *Aufsätze und Jahresbericht 1976*, 32–38. 1977.

Heyde, Herbert. "Medieval trumpets and trumpet playing in Europe (Thesis, Leipzig, 1965)." *Brass Bulletin—International Brass Chronicle*, no. 17 (1977): 74–79.

Hickernell, Ross. "Cornet and trumpet—What's the difference?" *Musical Observer* 30 (Mar. 1931): 42 + .

Hickernell, Ross. "On the care of the cornet and other brass instruments." *Cadenza* 5, no. 11 (1914): 76–79.

5812   Hickman, David R. "Advantages of the four-valve C/D trumpet." *International Trumpet Guild Newsletter* 6, no. 2 (1980): 22–24.

5813   Hiller, A. "Die ungewöhnliche Trompete aus dem Nürnberger Verkehrsmuseum." *Brass Bulletin—International Brass Chronicle*, no. 52 (1985): 72–73. Also in English and French.

5814   "Holton unveils 'Banana Horn' for marching bands." *Music Trades* 134 (Aug. 1986): 77–78.

Humfeld, Neill H. "The history and construction of the cornett." Dissertation, University of Rochester, 1962.

5815   Igarashi, Juichi, and Masaru Koyasu. "Acoustical properties of trumpets." *Journal of the Acoustical Society of America* 25 (1953): 122–128.

5816   "Intonationszug für B-Trompeten." *Instrumentenbau-Zeitschrift* 24 (June 1970): 381.

Jarcho, Saul. "Two kinds of trumpet." *Bulletin of the New York Academy of Medicine* 47, no. 4 (Apr. 1971): 428–430.

5817   Jenkins, H. "Buying a new trumpet." *The Instrumentalist* 25 (Jan. 1971): 48–50.

5818   Jenny, Georges. "Un nouvel instrument de musique. La trompette electronique." *Musique & Radio* 42 (1952): 181 + .

5819   Jung, K. "Die Schallsonde im Flügelhornbecher. Ein Beitrag zur Akustik der Blasinstrumente und Zungenpfeifen." *Das Musikinstrument und Phono* 6 (1957): 207.

5820   Kent, Earle L., and Jody C. Hall. "Characteristics of cornet tones." *Journal of the Acoustical Society of America* 28 (1956): 768. Abstract.

5821   Kent, Earle L. "Some related subjective and objective measurements on cornet tones." *Journal of the Acoustical Society of America* 27 (1955): 209.

5822   "King creates 'The Flugabone.' " *Music Trades* 126 (June 1978): 70.

5823   "King introduces all-new trumpet and cornet line." *The School Musician* 50 (Mar. 1979): 57.

5824   Knauss, H. P., and W. J. Yeager. "Vibrations of the walls of a cornet." *Journal of the Acoustical Society of America* 13 (1941): 160–162.

5825   L., P. "Du cornet à piston et de son emploi en fanfares." *L'Echo musical* 20 (1890): 193–194.

5826   Lane, George B. "Instruments manufacturers and specifications." *Journal of the International Trombone Association* 4 (1976): 8–16.

5827   Lanshe, R. "Some acoustical considerations when comparing the trumpet and cornet." *Woodwind World—Brass and Percussion* 16, no. 5 (1977): 26–28.

5828   "Leipziger Messegold für Hoch-B-Trompete 'Piccolino.' " *Musik International-Instrumentenbau-Zeitschrift* 35 (Oct. 1981): 670.

5829   Leslie, G. "An alternative octave controller for the bionic trumpet and sax." *Revue Belge de Musicologie* 3, no. 3 (1978): 20.

5830   Leuenberger, G. "Patch of the month: solo trumpet for the DX7." *Keyboard Magazine* 11 (Dec. 1985): 95.

    Lewis, H. M. "Extra-harmonic trumpet tones in the baroque era—natural trumpet vs. tromba da tirarsi." *Journal of the International Trumpet Guild* 5 (1980): 39–45.

5831   "A little gem." *Brass Bulletin—International Brass Chronicle*, no. 39 (1982): 1 News Suppl. Also in French and German.

5832   "Maelzel in America [mechanical trumpet]." *Musical Box Society International* 18, no. 2 (1971): 96–97. Reprinted from *Scientific American* (May 27, 1876).

5833   [Mahillon, Victor Charles]. "Un progrès dans la fanfare." *L'Echo musical* 2, no. 2 (15 Feb. 1870).

    Mahillon, Victor Charles. "The trumpet—its history—its theory—its construction." *Dominant* 16, nos. 7–9 (1908).

    Mariconda, Dominick J. "The trumpet—its history, care, repertoire and method of performance." Master's thesis, Hartt College of Music, 1952.

    Markley, R. "The difference between trumpet and cornet tone." *The School Musician* 20 (May 1949): 12 + .

5834   Martin, Daniel W. "Experiments in the analysis of a mechanically produced cornet tone." *Journal of the Acoustical Society of America* 12 (1941): 476. Abstract.

5835   Martin, Daniel W. "Lip vibrations in a cornet mouthpiece." *Journal of the Acoustical Society of America* 13 (1942): 305–308.

    Menke, Werner. *History of the trumpet of Bach and Handel; a new point of view and new instruments; forming a history of the trumpet and its music, from its earliest use as an artistic instrument to the middle of the eighteenth century. Special reference given to its employment by Bach and Handel, ...* Translated by Gerald Abraham. London: W. Reeves, 1934.

5836   Meyer, Jürgen, and Klaus Wogram. "Die Richtcharakteristiken von Trompete, Posaune und Tuba." *Musikinstrument* 19, no. 2 (Feb. 1970): 171–180.

5837   Meyer, L. "Trumpet and cornet tone quality." *The Instrumentalist* 23 (Jan. 1969): 62–67.

5838   "Miniatur-B-Trompete von M. Wendler." *Zeitschrift für Instrumentenbau* 53 (1932–33): 25.

5839   Moorer, J. A., and J. Grey. "Lexicon of analyzed tones." *Computer Music*

Journal 1, no. 2 (1977): 39–45; 1, no. 3 (1977): 12–29; 2, no. 2 (1978): 23–31.

5840 Morrill, Dexter. "Trumpet algorithms for computer composition." *Computer Music Journal* 1, no. 1 (Feb. 1977): 46–52.

5841 Mühle, C. "Akustische Untersuchungen an einer D Clarine, einer D und einer B Trompete." *Gottesdienst und Kirchenmusik* nos. 4–5 (1966): 124–137.

5842 Mühle, C. "Akustische Untersuchungen an einer D-Clarine, einer D- und einer B-Trompete." *Das Orchester* 13 (Sept. 1965): 296–302.

Müller, Ulrich Robert. "Dissertationen: Untersuchungen zu den Strukturen von Klängen der Clarin- und Ventiltrompete." *Die Musikforschung* 25, no. 3 (1972): 352–353.

5843 Müller, Ulrich Robert. "Untersuchungen zu den Strukturen von Klängen der Clarin- und Ventiltrompete." Ph.D. diss., Universität Köln, 1970.

5844 Müller, Ulrich Robert. *Untersuchungen zu den Strukturen von Klängen der Clarin- und Ventiltrompete.* Regensburg: Bosse, 1971.

5845 "Musicians' world: sorry—I can't hear you [Le Scaffy trumpet mute]." *Melody Maker* 56 (May 16, 1981): 39.

Myers, Frederick C. "The effect of different mouthpieces upon the tone and response of the trumpet." Master's thesis, Ohio State University, 1948.

5846 Nallin, Walter E. "Sonorities of the upper brass." *Symphony* (Jan 1952): 12.

5847 "Eine neue Bach-Trompete." *Instrumentenbau-Zeitschrift* 4 (1949–50): 106.

5848 "Ein neues Cornett." *Musik-Instrumenten-Zeitung* 13, no. 34 (1903): 570–571.

5849 "Ein neues Kornett." *Zeitschrift für Instrumentenbau* 23, no. 13 (1903): 323–325.

5850 "New Severinsen Signature trumpet unveiled by Conn." *The Music Trades* 133 (Oct. 1985): 80.

5851 Olsen, Paul. "Trumpet player's answer man [Elden Benge]." *Etude* 68 (Dec. 1950): 24.

Overton, Friend Robert. *Der Zink. Geschichte, Bauweise und Spieltechnik eines historischen Musikinstruments.* Mainz: Schott, 1981.

5852 "Pascucci introduces $100,000 trumpet." *The School Musician* 43 (May 1972): 58.

5853 Piechler, Arthur. "Eine neue Bach-Trompete." *Neue Musikzeitschrift* 4 (1950): 198–199.

5854 Piechler, Arthur. "Die problematische hohe Bach-Trompete." *Instrumentenbau-Zeitschrift* 4 (1949–50): 131–132.

5855 Piersig, Fritz. "Die Inventionstrompete." *Zeitschrift für Instrumentenbau* 47 (1926–1927): 57–58.

5856 Pietzsch, Hermann. "Eine neue hohe D-C-Trompete." *Zeitschrift für Instrumentenbau* 31 (1910/11): 499.

Poe, Gerald D. "Basic intonation tendencies of the trumpet-cornet." *The School Musician* 49 (May 1978): 70–71.

5857   Pratt, Bill. "Dr. Hermann Moeck talks about his firm." *American Recorder* 14, no. 1 (Feb. 1973): 3–8.

5858   "R-Kay introduces new modular trumpet." *The Music Trades* 133 (June 1985): 133–134.

5859   "Record reviews: Paramount Cornet Blues Rarities—Chicago: 1924–1927." *Jazz Journal International* 30 (Sept. 1977): 47.

5860   "Recreating the renowned French Besson trumpet." *The Music Trades* 131 (May 1983): 142+.

5861   "Replica of Gottfried Reiche's instrument available." *Journal of the International Trumpet Guild* 12, no. 1 (1987): 50–51.

5862   Richter, P. E. "Eine neue hohe D-C-Trompete mit 3 Ventilen." *Zeitschrift für Instrumentenbau* 31 (1910/11): 461.

5863   "Riesen-Fanfarentrompete von Markneukirchen auf dem Turnfest in Köln." *Zeitschrift für Instrumentenbau* 48 (1927–1928): 1121.

5864   Samuels, H. "How they make a hot trumpet." *Popular Science* 171 (Oct. 1957): 108–113.

5865   Sander, Rudolf, C. W. Moritz, and F. C. Louis. " 'Ein neues Kornett' und andere Verbesserungs-Bestrebungen im Blechblas-Instrumentenbaue." *Zeitschrift für Instrumentenbau* 23 (1902/03): 469–471, 323–324, 414–415, 445, 472. The whole series reprinted in *Deutsche Militär-Musiker Zeitung* 25 (1903): 53–54, 122–123, 175–176, 189.

        Sander, Rudolf. " 'Ein neues Kornett' und andere Verbesserungs-Bestrebungen im Blechblas-Instrumentenbaue." *Zeitschrift für Instrumentenbau* 23 (1903): 489–471.

5866   Schilke, Renold O. "Practical physics for trumpeters and teachers." *The Instrumentalist* 31 (Apr. 1977): 45–48.

5867   Schmidt. "Neues Trompeten-Mundstück." *Evangelische Musikzeitung* 20 (191-?): 2.

5868   Schmidt, W. C. "Letters: Normaphon [Trumpet Museum, Bad Säckingen]." *Brass Bulletin—International Brass Chronicle*, no. 56 (1986): 108. Also in English and French.

5869   "Second generation Getzen Eterna trumpet announced." *Journal of the International Trumpet Guild* 9, no. 4 (1985): 10.

5870   Shuck, Lenel. "When does a cornet become a trumpet?" *The School Musician* 12 (Sept. 1940): 18–19+.

5871   "Slide trumpets inspired by old prototypes from Egger & Co." *Musik International-Instrumentenbau-Zeitschrift* 39 (Oct. 1985): 687.

        Smith, Norman Edward. "A study of certain expressive-acoustic equivalents in the performance styles of five trumpet players." Ph.D. diss., Florida State University, 1968.

        Smith, Norman Edward. "A study of certain expressive-acoustic equivalents in the performance styles of five trumpet players." *Dissertation Abstracts* 30 (May 1970): 5021A–5022A.

5872   Smith, R. A. "Recent developments in trumpet design." *Journal of the International Trumpet Guild* 3 (1978): 27–29.

5873   Smith, Richard A. "It's all in the bore!" *Journal of the International Trumpet Guild* 12, no. 4 (May 1988): 42–45.

Smithers, Donald L. "The baroque trumpet after 1721—some preliminary observations: science and practice." *Early Music* 5, no. 2 (1977): 177–179+.

5874   Snell, H. "Deflated trumpets [survey of manufacturers, consumer hints]." *Sounding Brass & the Conductor* 6, no. 2 (1977): 60–61+.

5875   "Spezial Instrumente des Trompetenregisters." *Schweizerische Instrumentalmusik* 31 (1942): 205.

5876   Steele-Perkins, C. "Are you free for a Brandenburg?" *Sounding Brass & the Conductor* 7, no. 2 (1978): 58–59+.

5877   Stevens, Thomas. "The trumpet in the U.S.: gadgets [backbores]." *Brass Bulletin—International Brass Chronicle*, no. 33 (1981): 41. Also in French and German.

5878   Stevens, Thomas. "The trumpet in the U.S. [leadpipe alterations]." *Brass Bulletin—International Brass Chronicle*, no. 43 (1983): 67–68. Also in French and German.

Stevens, Thomas. "The trumpet in the USA." *Brass Bulletin—International Brass Chronicle*, no. 29 (1980): 17–18. Also in French and German.

Stewart, Gary M. *Keyed brass instruments in the Arne B. Larson collection.* Shrine to Music Museum, Catalog of the Collections, vol. 1, edited by André P. Larson. Vermillion, SD: Shrine to Music Museum, 1980.

5879   Streitweiser, Franz X. "Remembering Harry Glantz [Conn C trumpet]." *Journal of the International Trumpet Guild* 12, no. 4 (May 1988): 50–52.

Stubbins, W. H., Clifford P. Lillya, and J. R. Fredrick. "Effects of blowing pressure and embouchure factors on trumpet tone production." *Journal of the Acoustical Society of America* 28 (1956): 769.

5880   Stumpf, C. "Trompete und Flöte." In *Festschrift Hermann Kretzschmar zum 70. Geburtstag.* Leipzig: C. F. Peters, 1918.

Tarr, Edward H. "Die Musik und die Instrumente der *Charamela real* in Lissabon." *Forum Musicologie* 2 (1980): 181–229.

Tarr, Edward H. *Die Trompete.* Bern; Stuttgart: Hallwag, 1977.

5881   "Trompete in Saxophonform." *Musik International-Instrumentenbau-Zeitschrift* 35 (Mar. 1981): 307.

5882   "Trompeten für Bachpartituren." *Instrumentenbau-Zeitschrift* 26 (Apr. 1972): 304.

5883   "Tunable bit for natural trumpet." *International Trumpet Guild Newsletter* 3, no. 3 (1977): 3.

5884   "Ueber neue Verbesserungsmöglichkeiten der Trompete." *Zeitschrift für Instrumentenbau* 60 (1939–40): 144. Abstract.

Urban, Darrell Eugene. "Stromenti da tirarsi in the cantatas of J. S. Bach." *Dissertation Abstracts* 38 (Oct. 1977): 1733A.

5885   U.S. War Department. *Tests of plastic trumpet, G with slide to F.* PB18413 & 20568. July 1943, July 1944.

5886   Vanasek, Ben. "Studies on harmonics." *Etude* 45 (1927): 432.

5887   "Verbesserter Trommelträger." *Instrumentenbau Musik International* 33 (Feb. 1979): 243.

5888   Vogel, M. "Eine enharmonische Trompete." *Das Orchester* 12 (Feb. 1964): 41–45.

Wallace, S. C. "A study of high school band directors' ability to discriminate between and identify modern cornet and trumpet timbres." *Dissertation Abstracts* 40 (Apr. 1980): 5359A.

5889   Weber, Friedrich Johannes. "Die Trompete." *Deutsche Instrumentenbau Zeitschrift* 38 (1937): 148.

5890   Webster, John C. "Internal differences due to players and the taper of trumpet bells." *Journal of the Acoustical Society of America* 21 (1949): 208–214.

5891   Webster, John C. "Intonation errors due to discontinuities in the valve mechanisms of trumpets." *Journal of the Acoustical Society of America* 26 (1954): 932–933.

5892   Webster, John C. *Measurable differences among trumpet players.* Proceedings [1949] of the Music Teachers National Association. 43rd series. 73rd year. Pittsburgh, 1951.

5893   Webster, John C. "Trumpet intonation differences due to bell taper." *Journal of the Acoustical Society of America* 20 (1948): 588.

5894   Wedgwood, D. "The Wedgwood cornet." *Brass International* 10, no. 1 (1982): 18–19 + .

5895   Wheeler, J. "Further notes on the classic trumpet." *The Galpin Society Journal* 18 (Mar. 1965): 14–22.

5896   White, Jack Okey. "Renold Otto Schilke: his contributions to the development of the trumpet." *Dissertation Abstracts* 41 (Aug. 1980): 458A.

White, Jack Okey. "Renold Otto Schilke: his contributions to the development of the trumpet." D.A. diss., New York University, 1980.

5897   Whitwell, D. "The trumpet player who never missed a note [mechanical trumpet]." *The Instrumentalist* 26 (Jan. 1972): 30–31.

5898   "Wieder ein viertes Trompeten-Ventil." *Zeitschrift für Instrumentenbau* 19 (1898/99): 636–637.

5899   Woodward, J. G. "Resonance characteristics of a cornet." *Journal of the Acoustical Society of America* 13 (1941): 156–159.

5900   Yeager, William. "Vibration of the walls of a cornet." Master's thesis, Ohio State University, 1941.

Zerries, Otto. "Drei alte, figürlich verzierte Holztrompeten aus Brasilien in den Museen zu Kopenhagen, Leiden und Oxford." *Ethnologische Zeitung* 1 (1977): 77–89.

Trombone

Aharoni, E. "Locked triggers—a most helpful option for practicing and performing." *Newsletter of the International Trombone Association* 5, no. 3 (1978): 33.

Alexander, A. "The double trombone [superbone]." *The Instrumentalist* 35 (Feb. 1981): 25–27.

Arfinengo, Carlo. *La tromba e il trombone*. Ancona; Milano: Bèrben, 1973.

5901   "B flat/F tenor trombone directory." *Sounding Brass & the Conductor* 5, no. 4 (1977): 127.

Bachelder, Daniel Fred. "An investigation of trombone 'tone center.' " Ph.D. diss., Brigham Young University, 1976.

5902   Bachelder, Daniel Fred. "An investigation of trombone 'tone center.' " *Dissertation Abstracts* 37 (Feb. 1977): 4681A.

5903   Baker, Buddy. "Tenor trombone: trends in design and development." *The Instrumentalist* 40 (Nov. 1985): 44 +.

Bate, Philip. *The trumpet and trombone; an outline of their history, development and construction*. London: E. Benn; New York: W. W. Norton, 1966.

Bate, Philip. *The trumpet and trombone; an outline of their history, development, and construction*. 2d ed. London: Benn; New York: Norton, 1972.

5904   Beversdorf, Thomas. "Problems influencing trombone intonation." *The Instrumentalist* 7 (Oct. 1952): 24–25 +.

5905   Bimboni, G. "La influenza della direzione dei padiglioni sulla espansione del suono nel trombone." *Atti dell' Accademia del R. Istituto musicale di Firenze* 18 (1880): 100–110.

5906   Blanchard, Henri. "M. C. Basler et M. A. -F. M. Leonard de la Tuilerie (Le Trombone et la resonnance du corps sonore)." *Revue et gazette musicale de Paris* 15 (1850): 355–356.

Brandon, S. "Muting the low brass." *Woodwind, Brass and Percussion* 20, no. 4 (1981): 4–5 +.

Campbell, Robert. "A study of the effect of selected interior contours of the trombone mouthpiece upon the tone quality of the trombone." Master's thesis, University of Texas, 1954.

5907   Caneva, Ernest O. "Trombone versus trombonium." *The School Musician* 24 (May 1953): 8 +.

Casamorata, L. F. "Del trombone e dei suoi perfezionamenti e trasformazioni in propositio della recente invenzione del bimbonifono." *Atti dell' Accademia del R. Istituto musicale di Firenze* 13 (1875): 32–53.

5908   "Cleaning the slide trombone." *The Instrumentalist* 18 (Oct. 1963): 16.

5909   Crimmins, R. "Holton TR-183 Bb/F bass trombone." *Jazz Journal International* 38 (Jan. 1985): 23.

Duerksen, George L. "The history and acoustics of the trombone." Master's thesis, University of Kansas, 1956.

5910   Everett, T. "Tunings for double bass valve trombone." *The Instrumentalist* 30 (May 1976): 47–48+.

5911   Flor, G. J. "The bass trombone: single rotor, double rotor or in-line?" *Woodwind, Brass and Percussion* 23, no. 2 (1984): 10–12.

5912   Flor, G. J., ed. "Brass workshop: In-line rotor—a new concept [bass trombone]." *The School Musician* 53 (Nov. 1981): 26–27.

       Flor, G. J. "Brass workshop: The trombone mute [includes history]." *The School Musician* 51 (Jan. 1980): 34–36.

5913   Flor, G. J. "The contrabass trombone." *Woodwind World—Brass and Percussion* 17, no. 3 (1978): 26–27+.

5914   Flor, G. J. "The F attachment tenor trombone in the elementary school music program." *The School Musician* 47 (Nov. 1975): 12+.

5915   Flor, G. J. "The F attachment tenor trombone in the elementary school music programs [includes comparison chart of models]." *The School Musician* 47 (Jan. 1976): 16–18.

5916   Franck, James A. "A comparative study of factors in trombone timbre." Master's thesis, Ohio State University, 1950.

5917   Gatwood, D. D. "Is dual in-line really better? [double-trigger bass trombone]." *Journal of the International Trombone Association* 12, no. 2 (1984): 24.

5918   Giardinelli, Robert. "Trombone care and maintenance." *The Instrumentalist* 28 (Feb. 1974): 51.

       Gregory, Robin. *The trombone: the instrument and its music.* New York: Praeger; London: Faber & Faber, 1973.

       Griffith, T. "Confessions of a mutemaker." *Newsletter of the International Trombone Association* 3, no. 2 (1976): 20+.

       Guion, David M. "The pitch of Baroque trombones." *Journal of the International Trombone Association* 8 (Mar. 1980): 24–28.

5919   Harlow, L. "We called them trombets [E-flat valve trombone]." *The Instrumentalist* 23 (Aug. 1968): 73–76.

5920   "Heavy duty case project." *International Trombone Association Newsletter* 6, no. 4 (1979): 8.

5921   "Helikon-Posaune." *Zeitschrift für Instrumentenbau* 19 (1898/99): 381.

5922   Himes, A. C. "A comparison of the acoustical properties in solo and ensemble performance of the trombone." *Dissertation Abstracts* 45 (June 1985): 3572A.

       Himes, A. C. "A guide to trombone mouthpiece comparisons." *Journal of the International Trombone Association* 10, no. 2 (1982): 26–27.

       Jäger, J. "Grundfragen des Blechblaseransatzes am Beispiel der Posaune." *Beiträge der Musikwissenschaft* 13, no. 1 (1971): 56–73.

5923   Jameson, R. Philip. "The Arthur Pryor trombone (1888–1988): a centennial tribute." *Journal of the International Trombone Association* 16, no. 3 (Summer 1988): 30–31.

       Jameson, R. Philip. "The effect of timbre conditions on the prompted and simultaneous pitch matching of three ability groups of trombone performers." Ed.D. diss., Columbia University Teachers College, 1980.

Jameson, R. Philip. "The effect of timbre conditions on the prompted and simultaneous pitch matching of three ability groups of trombone performers." *Dissertation Abstracts* 41(July 1980): 151A.

5924 Jameson, R. Philip, and A. C. Himes. "An acoustical comparison among various trombone leadpipes." *Journal of the International Trombone Association* 15, no. 1 (1987): 50–52.

5925 Kappey, J. A. "Les trombones à pistones et les trombones à coulisses." *L'Echo musical* 20 (1890): 160–161, 147–148. Reprinted from *The British Bandsman*.

5926 Karasick, S. "The alto and contrabass trombone." *Music Journal* 26 (Jan. 1968): 30 + .

"King creates 'The Flugabone.' " *Music Trades* 126 (June 1978): 70.

5927 "King Duo-Gravis Bass Trombone extends range to bottom of piano." *The Music Trades* 118 (May 1970): 62.

5928 "King makes a special instrument for a very special person [designed for handicapped boy]." *The School Musician* 45 (Jan. 1974): 41.

5929 "King makes a special trombone for a very special person [artificial arms]." *The Music Trades* 122 (Jan. 1974): 84.

Kitzel, Larry. "The trombones of the Shrine to Music Museum." *Dissertation Abstracts* 46 (Oct. 1985): 832A.

Kitzel, Larry. "The trombones of the Shrine to Music Museum." D.M.A. diss., University of Oklahoma, 1985.

5930 Lane, George B. "Instrument manufacturers and specifications." *Journal of the International Trombone Association* 4 (1976): 8–16.

5931 "Leblanc to offer radical patented 'superbone' trombone." *The Musical Trades* 124 (May 1976): 64.

5932 Leloir, E. "Le trombone à 6 pistons independants." *Brass Bulletin—International Brass Chronicle*, no. 5–6 (1973): 97–105. Also in English and German.

5933 Lewy, Rudolf. "Cimbasso." *Journal of the International Trombone Association* 6 (1978): 18.

5934 Lister, R. "The contrabass sackbut—a modern copy." *Brass Bulletin—International Brass Chronicle*, no. 31 (1980): 71 + . Also in French and German.

5935 Lister, R. "The contrabass sackbut—a modern copy." *Journal of the International Trombone Association* 9 (1981): 23.

Lupica, Benedict. *The magnificent bone: a comprehensive study of the slide trombone*. New York: Vantage, 1974.

5936 McDunn, Mark R. "A slide trombone for short arms." *Music Journal* 24 (Mar. 1966): 81 + .

5937 [Mahillon, Victor Charles]. "Nouveau modèle de trombone ténor." *L'Echo musical* 4, no. 8 (20 Aug. 1872).

5938 Manzora, B. G. "Die Posaune mit Doppelaussenzug—ein Museumstück mit Zukunft?" *Brass Bulletin—International Brass Chronicle*, no. 30 (1980):

33 +. Also in French and English.

5939 Markle, R. "Care and maintenance of the slide trombone." *The Instrumentalist* 18 (Sept. 1963): 28.

Martz, Brian. "Some reflections on intonation." *Journal of the International Trombone Association* 13, no. 2 (1985): 39–40.

5940 Masson, Gabriel. "Le trombone et ses différentes proportions." *Musique & Radio* 41 (1951): 147.

Mays, R. "The impossible dream [case for airplane travel]." *Newsletter of the International Trombone Association* 3, no. 2 (1976): 19–20.

Meyer, Jürgen, and Klaus Wogram. "Die Richtcharakteristiken von Trompete, Posaune und Tuba." *Musikinstrument* 19, no. 2 (Feb. 1970): 171–180.

5941 Nash, H. "Instruments; a Bach with some bite." *Sounding Brass & the Conductor* 1, no. 3 (1972): 96.

5942 "New double-barrelled trombone eliminates long stretch." *The Instrumentalist* 5 (May–June 1951): 26.

"New valves [Thayer rotary]." *Brass Bulletin—International Brass Chronicle*, no. 58 (1987): [News Suppl.] 5. Also in French and German.

5943 Piering, R. "Zur Richtigstellung über 'Robert Pierings Posaunen-Zug mit Führung.' " *Zeitschrift für Instrumentenbau* 19 (1898/99): 282–283.

5944 Raph, A. "The three elephants—a tragedy." *The Instrumentalist* 23 (Feb. 1969): 46–47.

5945 Reynolds, J. C. "News on the trombone front ['Moravian sized' trombones available]." *The Moravian Music Foundation Bulletin* 28, no. 4 (1983): 74–75.

Runyan, W. E. "The alto trombone and contemporary concepts of trombone timbre." *Brass Bulletin—International Brass Chronicle*, no. 28 (1979): 43–45 +. Also in French and German.

Schreiber, E. A. "Quarter-tone scale, twenty-four note octave." *Journal of the International Trombone Association* 9 (1981): 10.

5946 "Side-angle trombone eliminates 'stretch.' " *The Instrumentalist* 5 (Nov. 1950): 35.

5947 Snyder, F. "Cleaning and lubricating the trombone." *Brass and Percussion* 1, no. 5 (1973): 15 +.

5948 "A special trombone [adapted for player with artificial arms]." *The Instrumentalist* 28 (Feb. 1974): 86.

Stewart, Gary M. "The restoration of a 1608 trombone by Jacob Bauer, Nuremberg." *Journal of the American Musical Instrument Society* 8 (1982): 79–92.

5949 Tanner, P., and K. Sawhill. "The differences between the tenor and bass trombones." *The Instrumentalist* 23 (Oct. 1968): 50–53.

5950 "Thayer valve improves trombone sound." *Musik International—Instrumentenbau-Zeitschrift* 41 (June 1987): 439.

Thein, H. "Die Kontrabassposaune; Bild—Abriss unter besonderer Berücksichtigung der bautechnischen Aspekte (1973)." *Brass Bulletin—In-*

ternational Brass Chronicle, no. 23 (1978): 55–61 + . Also in English and French.

5951 Thein, M., and H. Thein. "Neues über Alt-Posaune." *Brass Bulletin—International Brass Chronicle*, no. 40 (1982): 33. Also in English and French.

5952 Tyack, R. "Trigger happy." *Sounding Brass & the Conductor* 5, no. 2 (1976): 56–57 + .

5953 Vance, S. M. "Trombone slide position equivalence tables." *Journal of the International Trombone Association* 6 (1978): 11–12.

5954 Weber, K. "Die 'deutsche' Posaune." *Das Orchester* 26 (July-Aug. 1978): 566–570.

Wick, Dennis. "Performer's platform: the trombone." *Composer [London]*, no. 50 (Winter 1976–1977): 36–39.

5955 Wogram, Klaus. "Einfluss von Material und Oberflächen aus den Klang von Blechblasinstrumenten." *Instrumentenbau Zeitschrift* 30, no. 5 (1976): 414–418.

5956 Yeo, Douglas. "Bass trombone equipment survey [equipment the leading American symphony bass trombonists are using]." *Journal of the International Trombone Association* 11, no. 4 (1983): 22–23.

Yeo, Douglas. "The bass trombone: innovations on a misunderstood instrument." *The Instrumentalist* 40 (Nov. 1985): 22–26 + .

5957 Yeo, Douglas. "In defense of the single valve bass trombone." *Journal of the International Trombone Association* 12, no. 3 (1984): 20–22.

5958 "Zugposaune und Ventilposaune." *Schweizerische Instrumentalmusik* 32 (1943): 259.

Baritone/Euphonium

5959 Beauregard, Cherry. "Diversity of sound and adaptability." *T.U.B.A. Journal* 9, no. 4 (Spring 1982): 9.

5960 Bevan, Clifford. "The E flat horn." *Sounding Brass & the Conductor* 7, no. 2 (1978): 63–64.

5961 Bevan, Clifford. "The euphonium." *Sounding Brass & the Conductor* 7, no. 4 (1978): 128–129 + .

Brasch, Harold T. "When is a baritone a euphonium?" *The Instrumentalist* 3 (Mar. 1949): 36–37.

5962 Floyd, J. R. "The baritone horn versus the euphonium." *Woodwind World—Brass and Percussion* 20, no. 3 (1981): 8–9.

5963 Fry, Robert H. "Tuning slide devices for better euphonium intonation." *T.U.B.A. Journal* 13, no. 3 (Feb. 1986): 20.

"Getzen develops tuneable bell trumpet & upright baritone." *The Music Trades* 128 (May 1980): 152.

5964   Kurath, W. "Tuba und Euphonium heute." *Brass Bulletin—International Brass Chronicle*, no. 23 (1978): 41–44. Also in English and French.

Lumpkin, R. "Intonation problems of the euphonium." *The Instrumentalist* 35 (May 1981): 18–22.

5965   Peterson, Mary. "Baritones and euphoniums of European origins." *T.U.B.A. Journal* 9, no. 1 (Summer 1981): 3–7.

5966   Peterson, Mary. "Double-bell euphoniums in the Arne B. Larson Collection." *T.U.B.A. Journal* 8, no. 4 (Spring 1981): 4–9.

5967   Smith, W. "Baritone horn versus euphonium." *Woodwind World—Brass and Percussion* 17, no. 4 (1978): 30–31 + .

Stewart, M. Dee. "Euphonium encumbrances and encouragements." *T.U.B.A. Journal* 9, no. 4 (Spring 1982): 10–12.

"Tuba und Euphonium heute—Von Willson-Band Instruments, Flums, Schweiz." *Instrumentenbau Musik International* 31, no. 4 (1977): 375.

5968   Tucci, Robert. "Instrument design coordinator's report." *T.U.B.A. Journal* 9, no. 4 (Spring 1982): 24–25.

5969   Werden, David R. "A euphonium by any other name is not a baritone." *The Instrumentalist* 38 (Apr. 1984): 52–53.

5970   Werden, David R. "A euphonium is a baritone that's played well." *T.U.B.A. Journal* 11, no. 4 (Spring 1984): 6–8.

5971   Werden, David R. "Euphonium mouthpieces—a teacher's guide." *The Instrumentalist* 35 (May 1981): 23–26.

Tuba

5972   Altenburg, Wilhelm. "Die neue Riesenbass (Subkontrabass-Tuba) der Firma Bohland & Fuchs in Graslitz." *Zeitschrift für Instrumentenbau* 32 (1911/12): 1285–1288.

Apperson, Ron. "Mutes or 'What are we putting down our bells?' " *T.U.B.A. Journal* 6, no. 3 (Spring 1979): 12–13.

5973   Bate, Philip. "A 'serpent d'eglise': notes on some structural details." *The Galpin Society Journal* 29 (May 1976): 47–50.

Bate, Philip. "Some further notes on serpent technology." *The Galpin Society Journal* 32 (May 1979): 124–129.

5974   "BBBBBB flat tuba." *T.U.B.A. Newsletter* 1, no. 2 (Winter 1974): 6.

Bell, William. *A handbook of information on intonation*. Elkhorn, WI: Getzen, 1968.

Bevan, Clifford. *The tuba family*. London: Faber; New York: Scribner's, 1978.

5975   "Big sound [world's largest tuba]." *The Instrumentalist* 28 (Nov. 1973): 35.

5976   Bingham, S. "The double C versus the double B-flat tuba: an investigation of tonal differences." *Journal of Band Research* 15, no. 2 (1980): 45–49.

5977   Bobo, Roger. "And approach the realm of making beautiful music." *Brass Bulletin—International Brass Chronicle*, no. 18 (1977): 27 + . Also in German and French.

Brandon, S. "Muting the low brass." *Woodwind, Brass and Percussion* 20, no. 4 (1981): 4–5 + .

Brandon, S. P. "The French tuba." *Woodwind World—Brass and Percussion* 15, no. 5 (1976): 38.

5978   Brandon, S. P. "The tuba mute." *Woodwind, Brass and Percussion* 20, no. 7 (1981): 20–21.

5979   Brüchle, Bernhard. "Eine Tuba der Superlative, von historischer Bedeutung. . . . " *Brass Bulletin—International Brass Chronicle*, no. 9 (1974): 41–43. Also in English and French.

5980   Brüchle, Bernhard. "Zumindest noch höhere." *Brass Bulletin—International Brass Chronicle*, no. 7 (1974): 112–113. Also in English and French.

Capper, William. "Mutes—fabricate your own." *T.U.B.A. Journal* 7, no. 3 (Winter 1980): 26–27.

5981   Cattley, Gary Thomas. "Perception of timbral differences among bass tubas." M.M. thesis, North Texas State University, 1987.

5982   Chieffi, Brady. "Curios and collectables." *T.U.B.A. Journal* 11, no. 3 (Winter, 1984): 23.

5983   "C. G. Conn offers 15J 'concertable' tuba." *The Music Trades* 128 (June 1980): 86.

5984   Conner, Rex A. "How to care for a rotary-valved tuba." *The Instrumentalist* 26 (Nov. 1971): 40 + .

5985   Conner, Rex A. "Valve clatter: its prevention and cure." *T.U.B.A. Newsletter* 2, no. 3 (Spring 1975): 3.

5986   Coss, B. "Tuba; horn with problems." *Down Beat* 29 (Feb. 1, 1962): 14.

5987   Cummings, Barton. "The E-flat tuba revisited." *Woodwind, Brass and Percussion* 23, no. 8 (1984): 21–22.

5988   Cummings, Barton. "Further thoughts on the tuba in F." *Woodwind, Brass and Percussion* 22, no. 5 (1983): 8–9.

5989   Cummings, Barton. "The tuba and/or sousaphone." *Woodwind, Brass and Percussion* 23, no. 2 (1984): 13–15.

5990   Cummings, Barton. "Tuba technique." *Woodwind, Brass and Percussion* 22, no. 7 (1983): 8–9.

Cummings, Barton. "What tuba is best BBb, CC, Eb or F?" *The School Musician* 57 (Oct. 1985): 26–27.

5991   Cummings, Barton. "Why the fourth and fifth valves? [tuba]." *Woodwind, Brass and Percussion* 24, no. 3 (1985): 17–19.

5992   Cummings, Barton. "You need four valves." *Woodwind World—Brass and Percussion* 16, no. 2 (1977): 36–37.

5993   "Czechs display world's largest tuba—8 ft. high, 176 lbs." *Music Trades* 126 (Jan. 1978): 94.

de Broekert, Gary. "The tuba; a historical and functional consideration." Master's research project, University of Oregon, 1957.

5994   DeVore, Ronald. "Repair clinic: reducing the weight of the rotor." *T.U.B.A. Newsletter* 3, no. 1 (Fall 1975): 24.

Eliason, Robert E. "Keyed serpent." *T.U.B.A. Journal* 4, no. 1 (Fall 1976): 17–18.

Ernst, Friedrich. "Die Blechblasinstrumentenbauer-Familie Moritz in Berlin [Beitrag zur Geschichte des Berliner Instrumentenbaues]." *Das Musikinstrument* 18, no. 4 (Apr. 1969): 624–626.

5995   Farrington, Frank. "Dissection of a serpent." *The Galpin Society Journal* 22 (Mar. 1969): 81–96.

Flor, G. J. "Brass workshop: sousaphone or convertible tuba?" *The School Musician* 57 (Aug.–Sept. 1985): 22–23+.

5996   "Getzen unveils 1/4-size Meinl BBb tuba." *The Music Trades* 133 (Oct. 1985): 79.

5997   Halfpenny, Eric. "Lament for *Fusedule Tecil* [serpent]." *The Galpin Society Journal* 17 (Feb. 1964): 113–114.

Hamilton, D. "The Wagnerian orchestra." *San Francisco Opera Magazine*, no. 10 (Fall 1981): 45–48+.

5998   Hammond, Ivan. "A choice of one or two or both." *T.U.B.A. Newsletter* 1, no. 3 (Spring 1974): 1.

5999   Hensel, Otto. "Die Basstuba in F mit 6 Ventilen." *Deutsche Musiker-Zeitung* 63 (1932): 285.

6000   "Here's a giant among tubas [Kraslice, Czechoslovakia]." *The School Musician* 49 (Apr. 1978): 45.

6001   Hirsbrunner, P. "Die Geschichte der grossen York-Hirsbrunner Tuba aus der Sicht des Instrumentenbauers." *Brass Bulletin—International Brass Chronicle*, no. 40 (1982): 34–39.

6002   Hovey, Arthur. "The logic of the tuba valve system." *T.U.B.A. Journal* 8, no. 1 (Summer 1980): 18–25.

6003   "Indestructable instruments: Reinforced polyester guitar and sousaphone." *Modern Plastics* 39 (Feb. 1962): 90–91+.

Jungheinrich, H. K. "Der entfesselte Posaunenbass; 'Cimbasso'—eine Erfindung, über die man spricht." *Das Orchester* 13 (Mar. 1965): 92.

Keathley, Sandy. "Everyman's guide to the tuba mouthpiece." *T.U.B.A. Journal* 5, no. 3 (Spring/Summer 1978): 10–11.

6004   Krush, Jay. "Wingbolt Double-Bell Eight-Valve CC-BB Natural Deluxe Supertuba." *T.U.B.A. Newsletter* 2, no. 1 (Fall 1974): 8.

6005   Kuehn, David L. "Care and maintenance of the tuba." *The School Musician* 40 (Apr. 1969): 72–73.

Kunitz, Hans. *Die Instrumentation, Teil 9: Tuba*. Leipzig: Breitkopf & Härtel, 1968.

Kurath, W. "Tuba und Euphonium heute." *Brass Bulletin—International Brass Chronicle*, no. 23 (1978): 41–44. Also in English and French.

Leavis, Ralph. "More light on the cimbasso." *The Galpin Society Journal* 34 (Mar. 1981): 151–152.

Lewy, Rudolf. "Cimbasso." *Journal of the International Trombone Association* 6 (1978): 18.

Meyer, Jürgen, and Klaus Wogram. "Die Richtcharakteristiken von Trompete, Posaune und Tuba." *Musikinstrument* 19, no. 2 (Feb. 1970): 171–180.

6006 "Mirafone introduces convertible tuba." *Music Trades* 134 (May 1986): 116.

6007 "Mobile serpenphone becomes serpentine pedalphone." *T.U.B.A. Newsletter* 2, no. 1 (Fall 1974): 9.

Morris, R. Winston. "The tuba family." *The Instrumentalist* 27 (Feb. 1973): 33.

Mueller, Frederick A. "Two tubas for symphony orchestra and chamber music." *T.U.B.A. Newsletter* 1, no. 3 (Spring 1974): 8.

"Overshoulder tuba." *T.U.B.A. Newsletter* 2, no. 1 (Fall 1974): 7.

6008 Pacey, Robert. "An unusual serpent." *The Galpin Society Journal* 33 (Mar. 1980): 132–133.

6009 Pallansch, Robert. "Structural and human-engineering factors in the design and manufacture of conical-bore contrabass cup-mouthpiece valve instruments or The tuba as she is built." *T.U.B.A. Newsletter* 2, no. 1 (Fall 1974): 1.

6010 Pallansch, Robert. "Tuba design—improvements are needed." *The Instrumentalist* 27 (Feb. 1973): 31–32.

6011 Pallansch, Robert. "Venting of tuba valves." *T.U.B.A. Newsletter* 1, no. 2 (Winter 1974): 4.

Perantoni, Daniel. "Contemporary systems and trends for the tuba." *The Instrumentalist* 27 (Feb. 1973): 24–27.

6012 Perantoni, Daniel. "Tuba talk: Technical information." *The Instrumentalist* 38 (Nov. 1983): 58+.

6013 "Sam Pilafian plays on world's biggest playable tuba." *Brass Bulletin—International Brass Chronicle*, no. 5–6 (1973): 106–107. Also in French and German.

Pitts, L. P. "Using the first valve slide to adjust tuba intonation." *The Instrumentalist* 29 (Apr. 1975): 52.

Reynolds, G. E. "Tubas, recording basses and sousaphones." *The School Musician* 33, no. 7 (Mar. 1962): 22+.

6014 Robert, F. Chester. "Some otherwise logic on tuba valve systems." *T.U.B.A. Journal* 10, no. 1 (Summer 1982): 6–7.

6015 Roberts, Chester. "Tenor, bass and contrabass tubas—comparisons and contrasts." *T.U.B.A. Newsletter* 1, no. 3 (Spring 1974): 3–4.

6016 Roberts, W. "New addition to brass: soprano tuba." *Music Journal* 22 (May 1964): 36+.

Rose, W. H. "The birth of a new mouthpiece." *The Instrumentalist* 26 (Jan. 1972): 69–70.

6017 Rudolph. "Eine Tuba mit 6 Ventilen." *Zeitschrift für Instrumentenbau* 53 (191?): 9.

Sander, Rudolf, C. W. Moritz, and F. C. Louis. " 'Ein neues Kornett' und andere Verbesserungs-Bestrebungen im Blechblas-Instrumentenbaue." *Zeitschrift für Instrumentenbau* 23 (1902/03): 469–471, 323–324, 414–415, 445, 472. The whole series reprinted in *Deutsche Militär-Musiker Zeitung* 25 (1903): 53–54, 122–123, 175–176, 189.

Sander, Rudolf. " 'Ein neues Kornett' und andere Verbesserungs-Bestrebungen im Blechblas-Instrumentenbaue." *Zeitschrift für Instrumentenbau* 23 (1903): 489–471.

6018   Schooley, J. "Convertible brasses, sousaphones, or tubas: which to choose." *Woodwind, Brass and Percussion* 24, no. 1 (1985): 12–13.

6019   "Schreiber tuba." *T.U.B.A. Newsletter* 2, no. 3 (Spring 1975): 7.

6020   Sellers, R. A. "Bell-up or bell-front tubas?" *The Instrumentalist* 28 (Feb. 1974): 32–33.

6021   "Soprano tuba [invented]." *Brass Bulletin—International Brass Chronicle*, no. 45 (1984): 6 News Suppl. Also in French and German.

Stewart, Gary M. "Clean that old York on a Sunday afternoon." *T.U.B.A. Journal* 14, no. 4 (May 1987): 28–30.

Stewart, Gary M. *Keyed brass instruments in the Arne B. Larson collection.* Shrine to Music Museum, Catalog of the Collections, vol. 1, edited by André P. Larson. Vermillion, SD: Shrine to Music Museum, 1980.

6022   "Stimmung und das vierte Ventil." *Musik International-Instrumentenbau-Zeitschrift* 38 (Dec. 1984): 821.

6023   "Student makes serpent." *The Instrumentalist* 29 (Apr. 1975): 108.

"The truth about the tones the tuba can't toot." *Jacobs' Band Monthly* 10 (Dec. 1925): 16–17.

6024   "A tuba and then some." *T.U.B.A. Newsletter* 1, no. 2 (Winter 1974): 6.

"Tuba und Euphonium heute—Von Willson-Band Instruments, Flums, Schweiz." *Instrumentenbau Musik International* 31, no. 4 (1977): 375.

Tucci, Robert. "Instrument design coordinator's report." *T.U.B.A. Journal* 9, no. 4 (Spring 1982): 24–25.

6025   Weller, R. Otto. "Die Basstuba in F mit 6 Ventilen." *Deutsche Musiker-Zeitung* 63 (1932): 832–833.

6026   "Wenzel Meinl: Gebrauchsmusterschutz für Tuba-Modell Triebener." *Musik International-Instrumentenbau-Zeitschrift* 40 (Aug. 1986): 514.

6027   "Wenzel Meinl: legal protection of registered design for the Triebener tuba model." *Musik International-Instrumentenbau-Zeitschrift* 40 (Oct. 1986): opp. 646.

6028   Werden, David R. "The Blaikley compensating system: a player's perspective." *T.U.B.A. Journal* 13, no. 1 (Aug. 1985): 17.

6029   Young, Frederick J. "A new sound for the tuba." *The School Musician* 29 (Apr. 1958): 16–18+.

INDEX

TO AUTHORS AND SUBJECTS